Legacy of A Mountain People
Inventory of Cultural Resources of Ladakh

Volume 1

Leh
Khaltse

Legacy of A Mountain People
Inventory of Cultural Resources of Ladakh

Volume 1

Leh
Khaltse

Published by:
Namgyal Institute for Research on Ladakhi Art and Culture (NIRLAC)
2008

Published by:

Namgyal Institute for Research on Ladakhi Art and Culture (NIRLAC)

B-25 Qutab Institutional Area, Tara Crescent Road

New Delhi 110016 India

Funded by:

The Ford Foundation, New Delhi

Design: Grafiniti, New Delhi

Printed by: Paramount Printographics, New Delhi

Legacy of A Mountain People

Inventory of Cultural Resources of Ladakh

Volume 1 Leh | Khaltse

ISBN 978-81-907442-0-1 | 6 Volume set

Contents

Leh | **Khaltse**

Index

Foreword

It is with great interest, that I accepted the invitation to write a foreword to the 'Legacy of a Mountain People - An Inventory of Cultural Resources of Ladakh'. The process followed has been a welcome addition to the heritage discourse which deviates from conventional practices adopted and led by 'heritage professionals' aiming at an end product, most frequently a book, serving little purpose.

There is a growing realization today that we need to comprehend cultural heritage without necessarily compartmentalizing it into past, present; tangible and intangible; movable, immovable and so on. This is particularly true for living heritage places like Ladakh where communities maintain a continuous relationship with their heritage, contribute to their continuous evolution and where heritage is strongly linked to contemporary life. People's pride, identity, inspiration, sense of ownership and custodianship, traditions and skills are all intertwined and become vital aspects if we are to properly understand heritage and make attempts to conserve it. This reflects a major paradigm shift from the conventional fabric based approach to defining heritage and conservation originated and propagated by the West. The new approach attempts to appreciate heritage in its broadest perspectives, as perceived by the communities themselves, by engaging them in the task of identifying their heritage and linking this with its long term conservation and management.

Inventorisation or recognition of heritage should be the beginning of a process for engaging and empowering communities. It differs from conventional cartography of recording well recognized symbols by heritage experts. This is particularly important for places like Ladakh where we need to support and promote community based approaches to the conservation and management of heritage. It is in this context that I consider the Ladakh project as an excellent example. We should appreciate the long and exhaustive process followed through the involvement of young Ladakhis including scholars, monks, school teachers, tour guides and pilgrims with the rigorous engagement of the communities who are the custodians as well as users thus reflecting a comprehensive understanding of their heritage. The project has laid the foundation for engaging communities in the long term care for their own heritage. Undoubtedly the project would have enabled the different communities to highlight their own heritage and their values and to make connections where links have been lost or disappeared. This is one of the most important first stages of a process of engaging communities in the long term care of their heritage.

We also need to appreciate how the inventory has avoided any form of divisions within the notion of heritage. They have not limited the list to recognize 'old' and 'symbolic' structures but have instead included everything which people feel is part of their heritage. They have not limited recognition of heritage based on predominant religious or cultural groups but have extended it to all communities of Ladakh thereby ensuring that it is truly representative of the region. Extending the discussion to traditions, myths and beliefs has helped strengthen our understanding of the community's perspectives of their heritage.

The survey lays the foundation for the development of a long term strategy to preserve Ladakh's heritage entrenched in traditional community frameworks and one in which the community are the key players.

Gamini Wijesuriya
Project Manager (Sites Unit)
ICCROM
Rome, Italy

Foreword

The Namgyal Institute For Research On Ladakhi Art and Culture (NIRLAC) is a trust established in 1985 for the conservation and preservation of Ladakh's rich cultural heritage through a variety of programmes. The present inventory of cultural resources lays the foundation for developing a comprehensive and long-term programme for the conservation of Ladakh's tangible heritage, in the form of its buildings, as well as for its intangible heritage including the beliefs and practices associated with both man-made and natural heritage.

Ladakh has a vibrant living heritage, where heritage is a part of contemporary life and is not seen in isolation from the community's present way of life. Our cultural traditions have assimilated many influences from different cultures both in the region and beyond. Himalayan cultures have a long history of interactions which are bound together by the unique geographical setting in which we find ourselves. Our heritage conveys our values and beliefs to the rest of the world. This is our true wealth, benefitting others and ourselves in the long term.

The present publication "Legacy of a Mountain People - Inventory of Cultural Resources of Ladakh" shares this heritage with a larger audience. It is based on a 4-year programme that was initiated by NIRLAC to document Ladakh's immovable heritage. The project has been generously funded by the Ford Foundation for which we are deeply grateful. Our project team comprising of Ms. Tara Sharma (Project Director), Dr. Sonam Wangchuk (Programme Coordinator, Leh), Mr. Khadim Hussain (Programme Coordinator, Kargil), Mr. Stanzin Dorjay, Mr. Jamyang Phunstog, Mr.Karma Yeshi, Mr. Konchok Thinles, Mr. Jigmat Lundup, Ms. Deldan Angmo Khangsar, Ms. Jassu Singh and Mr. Mubashir-Ul-Malik have worked together with the community in identifying this heritage. I thank the community for sharing their knowledge and experience.

I hope that this publication promotes a better understanding of Ladakh's mountain culture.

Raja Jigmed Wangchuk Namgyal
Secretary
Namgyal Institute For Research On Ladakhi Art and Culture (NIRLAC)

Acknowledgements

The project, since its inception in 2003, has received support from various organizations, individuals and institutions without which it would not have succeeded. Drawing on the knowledge of the owners, custodians and traditional community leaders has been the biggest strengths of the present inventory. For this, we express our deep gratitude to all the village *goba*, custodians of religious properties, and the village people who shared their knowledge with us. This publication is dedicated to them.

The Ladakh Autonomous Hill Development Councils in Leh and Kargil have been most encouraging and supportive of this project and we hope that the inventory can help guide future development programmes in the region such that they enhance and conserve Ladakh's heritage.

In addition we acknowledge the support of the Ladakh Buddhist Association, Anjuman Imamia (Leh), Anjuman Moin-Ul-Islam (Leh), the Indian Army and the Information department (Leh) for their institutional support. In Kargil, we were fortunate to have an excellent partner in Kacho Mumtaz and his organization ACAPOH which provided much needed institutional and logistical support. His support is acknowledged with deep gratitude.

The workshops conducted with village leaders as a part of the programme gained invaluably from the presence of several eminent people. Most Ven. Changtse Chosje Sras Rinpoche, and most Ven. Togldan Rinpoche graced the workshops in Nubra and Tangtse respectively. Shri Tsewang Rigzin, (Ex) Executive Councilor for Art and Culture (LAHDC, Leh) presided over the workshops in Khaltse and Leh and has been a strong champion for preserving Ladakh's heritage. Shri Nasir Hussain Munshi, Executive Councillor, PWD of the LAHDC (Kargil) extended all support for a successful workshop in Kargil.

Many individuals contributed by sharing their knowledge of the region with us. Of them, we would like to thank Zainul-Aabedin-Aabedi, Urgyan Rigzin (Onpo, Nyungsted), Phuntsog Tundup (Rongdo, Nubra), Gelong Sonam Angchuk (Lonpo, Zanskar), Shri Tashi Rigzin (Shachukul), Gelong Gyaltsen (Tharuk), Abdul Hakeem Afridi (Leh), Gelong Thupstan Angdu (Samkar *Gonpa*).

Other institutions such as the Kharzong Odsal *Tsogspa* and the Yarma Gonbo *Tsogspa* demonstrated how this listing can be effectively used at the village level by organizing training workshops to upgrade dying building craft skills needed to preserve endangered buildings. The Youth Association of Nubra organized the Deskit workshop for us and the Youth Association for Conservation and Development, Markha valley provided us with information about the cultural resources in the valley.

The programme would not have been possible without the generous funding provided by the Ford Foundation. We would like to express our gratitude to Ms Sumathi Ramaswamy, former Program Officer, Higher Education, Arts and Culture at the Ford Foundation, New Delhi for helping us develop the project. Her successor, Dr Ravina Aggarwal provided valuable guidance based on her long association with Ladakh and deep knowledge of the region. To her, we owe special thanks. The project received an initial grant in 2003 from the Department of Culture, Government of India under the scheme "Preservation of the Himalayas" which enabled the first stage of listing to be undertaken in Khaltse. We are grateful to Mrs C.T. Misra, then Joint Secretary, Ministry of Culture for this.

The listing team began work in 2003 with a group of five youngsters from Leh who spent their summer holidays in Leh undertaking the first pilot inventory. We thank them and hope that their interest in their heritage is sustained in the future. Other young people who were involved for a brief period in the inventory include Toldan, Norboo, Angchuk and Yarphel. In 2004, the listing of Khaltse was undertaken by Deldan Angmo and Jassu Singh and a year later, Mubashir ulislam Malik revised some of the earlier listing of Leh block. A special thanks to all of them. Divay Gupta, Conservation Architect, provided technical support to the project which is much appreciated.

For the actual publication of this vast quantum of documentation, we are grateful to the designer-printer duo of Brijender S Dua (Grafiniti) and Atul Naahar (Paramount Printographics). Vandana Mohindra provided valuable and timely inputs in editing the text for the introductory sections of the first and second volumes.

Lobzang Gyaltsen (Khardong Chotukpa) will always be remembered by the team as a wonderful driver whose humour and encouragement proved to be an important contribution to the project. Part of our team were two inanimate members - Sonam Wangchok's Maruti 800 (PB -11T 8153) and Lobzang Gyaltsen's Armada and later Innova (JK-10 4617) which transported us through mighty passes and across barren mountain landscapes creating paths where none seemed to exist. Without them we could not have reached many villages.

Finally, we would like to thank our families for bearing with our long absence from home in search of Ladakh's hidden treasures.

Poject Team

Preface

Mountain cultures throughout the world have for centuries preserved a unique relationship with their natural setting. Moulded out of the often austere landscape in which they have developed, these cultures demonstrate a remarkable resilience and continue to evolve, holding relevance for contemporary generations as they have for past ancestors.

The unique relation that mountain communities enjoy with their heritage holds the key to its survival. Yet, it is this that is often ignored in conservation discourses for the region. The present inventory seeks to address this. To understand Ladakh's heritage in its larger context, it is critical that we understand the spirit of place, moving beyond the tangible to understand the many layers of intangible beliefs, functions and traditions that are associated with a site. This is best articulated by the recently formulated ICOMOS Quebec Declaration on the Preservation of the Spirit of Place (2008) *"Spirit of place is defined as the tangible (buildings, sites, landscapes, routes, objects) and the intangible elements (memories, narratives, written documents, rituals, festivals, traditional knowledge, values, textures, colours, odors, etc.), that is to say the physical and the spiritual elements that give meaning, value, emotion and mystery to place."* Thus, rather than separating the spirit from place, the tangible from the intangible and considering as well as evaluating them in isolation from each other it is important that we understand the many ways in which the two interact and mutually construct each other.

The dichotomy that arises when we separate these two facets was clearly outlined in a discussion held a few years ago with a Rinpoche in Ladakh. We had gone to seek the Rinpoche's support and blessing for the restoration of a ruined temple with exquisite wall paintings. The Rinpoche was puzzled as to why we wanted to restore an abandoned temple. He felt that what was in more urgent need of restoration was the spiritual base which had led to the creation of this temple. With the decline in the number of monks in recent years, it was difficult to depute monks to such temples to carry out the daily *pujas*. Without this function what was the need to preserve the temple? Therefore, to understand the temple simply as a building without its spiritual function presented only half the picture.

When NIRLAC launched its programme to promote and preserve Ladakh's cultural heritage, one of the key activities it recognized was the identification of cultural resources through the creation of an inventory. The inventory would serve as a dynamic tool not just to understand Ladakh's heritage but also to work with traditional and contemporary custodians of this heritage to develop long term strategies for their conservation, development and continued maintenance. Viewing this heritage as a product of a dynamic culture meant that cultural practices and beliefs associated with this heritage would need to form the basis for the inventory. *Why* a cultural resource was important to the people thus became equally important as to *what* the cultural resource was.

The present inventory of cultural resources is an attempt to understand the spirit of place and in this context differs from previous inventories carried out in the region. While prior efforts have focussed on understanding heritage within an architectural paradigm, the present process has sought to understand heritage in its local, socio cultural context i.e. as understood by the community who are its custodians and its creators. The emphasis was to understand Ladakh's heritage from the micro level i.e. from the village level up and not from a larger regional or national level down. Through a series of interactions with community leaders, religious heads, Ladakhi scholars and researchers as well as traditional knowledge holders in the community (astrologers (*onpo*), master craftsmen, *geshe* or Buddhist religious scholars, etc., which begun in 2003 and continued till 2006, the criterion for listing was drawn up. In order to ensure that the listing was representative of this mountain culture, it was decided to focus on all elements of the manmade and natural environment which had an impact on a community's culture. From small *lhato* (altars of protector deities) to large monastic complexes, and religious edifices, from *changrah* (community meeting grounds) to pastures and nomadic camping areas, from colossal rock carvings to ancient petroglyphs, from sacred trees to sacred mountains – all were included in the inventory. Due to constraints of time as well as the management of the large quantum of data, the first phase of the programme focussed primarily on the immovable heritage.

The criterion for listing was constantly revised over the course of the project to ensure that it represented all elements of Ladakh's culture. Contemporary structures which reflected the continuation of a tradition[1] were added to the listing. In addition, elements of the landscape such as sacred mountains and rock formations, which continue to be 'discovered' even today as mountain deities flee from neighbouring regions to seek refuge in Ladakh, were included as they reflect a continuity in tradition and reinforce the link between man and his environment.

"Recognizing that spirit of place is transmitted essentially by people, and that transmission is an important part of its conservation, we declare that it is through interactive communication and the participation of the concerned communities that the spirit of place is most efficiently safeguarded, used and enhanced."

ICOMOS Quebec Declaration on the Preservation of the Spirit of Place (2008)

vi

1. For example, renovated or rebuilt structures such as mosques in Kargil district have been included in the present list as the site itself continues to be used in worship over the centuries and has an intangible value that moves beyond the material form.

The inventory was conducted by a group of dedicated young Ladakhis from different walks of life and included scholars, monks, teachers and tourist guides. Through their interactions with village elders, members of *tsogspa, goba, nambardar,* custodians and owners of heritage properties the list was prepared. The principal source of information for the inventory, therefore, were the community themselves and their understanding of the value of their heritage. In most cases of preparing inventories, defining of what constitutes a regions' heritage is determined by our understanding of its value. Understanding the value of a heritage site/property is critical to answering the question of why and what are we preserving.

"Whether and how the cultural heritage is valued determines whether and how it is safeguarded and preserved (or neglected and destroyed). ...Cultural sites depend for their value on the recognition that society, or sections of society, affords them. Appropriate management for a place ...requires a detailed knowledge of the cultural values assigned to it by society, if these values are to be preserved..."[2]

Special emphasis was thus given in understanding why a listed cultural resource was important for the community. The function, or use, of a heritage site was recorded along with associated legends, folklore and historical anecdotes which were related to specific sites as well as to the founding of the village. Village names, many of which have been corrupted over the years, were traced to the original where knowledge still existed. Original village names had specific meanings related to the geographical setting or the founding of the settlement.

In addition to the field survey, workshops were organized at the block level with the *goba* and sometimes with members of the *tsogspa*. The aim of these workshops was to understand the community's concerns in conserving their heritage as well as to serve as a platform to discuss important heritage conservation issues on a broader scale. Village leaders shared their concerns and, in some cases, ways to address them were outlined. For example, at the workshop in Nubra, village leaders expressed concern on the dearth of skilled masons to repair *chorten*. A training workshop was subsequently organized wherein an elder *chorten* expert from Leh trained young masons on the renewal of *chorten*. This included the range of ritual practices of de-consecration and consecration, which were carried out by monks. The masons were also made aware of the fact that the early period *chorten* which do not conform to the later 8 forms of the Tibetan *chorten* were unique and therefore, unless there is an adequate understanding of the original form these can only be consolidated and not recreated.

Team members interact with village elders in Zanskar during the field survey

His Holiness Togdan Rinpoche addresses a gathering of village gobas at the workshop in Tangtse

The workshops also provided an opportunity for community leaders to speak about the need to preserve Ladakh's heritage. At the workshop held in Tangtse, His Holiness Togdan Rinpoche drew attention to the need to preserve Ladakh's heritage and focused specifically on the sacred landscape which His Holiness himself continues to identify.

In recent years, several factors have contributed to a more rapid pace of change in the Ladakhi way of life. Increased road building activities, for example, to link hitherto remote villages with the district and block centres, increasing tourist inflows following the large-scale promotion of Ladakh as one of India's top tourist destinations, and alarming changes in climatic patterns over the past few years have all had an impact on Ladakh's heritage as well.

2. NDORO, Webber, 2005, "The Preservation of Great Zimbabwe: Your Monument Our Shrine" ICCROM Conservation Studies 4, ICCROM, ROME

"Given that local communities are generally in the best position to comprehend the spirit of place, especially in the case of traditional cultural groups, we maintain that they are also best equipped to safeguard it and should be intimately associated in all endeavours to preserve and transmit the spirit of place"

ICOMOS Quebec Declaration on the Preservation of the Spirit of Place (2008)

viii

The listing, thus, becomes an important tool to monitor heritage in the long term. Several petroglyphs, for example, which were recorded in the listing have been subsequently destroyed in road building activities. In some cases, the floods of 2005 destroyed entire villages in Nubra and damaged many of the traditional adobe buildings. The need to develop strategies to safeguard these vulnerable sites has been raised with the local administration during the course of the workshops held with the *goba*. Developing regulations to protect this heritage, a natural outcome of the listing, was also dwelt on at length. Given that each village has a traditional system for the management of its heritage and that heritage preservation is one of the principal aims of the *tsogspa,* the creation of local or village level regulations/guidelines to preserve each village's heritage needs to be considered. In addition, broader guidelines need to be framed and adopted by the local administration to ensure that development and tourism activities promoted by the State ensures the preservation of heritage sites and is not detrimental to their long term survival. Different tiers, therefore, of regulations need to be evolved taking into account the unique geographical and cultural situation where the responsibility of safeguarding heritage rests equally with the traditional custodians as with the Government. A village, block and district level system of regulations and guidelines will need to be formulated. Unless this is done, monitoring heritage especially in remote and distant villages will become well nigh impossible and any actions to preserve endangered heritage would perhaps come too late. Training programmes with the village *goba* and tsogspa to create such regulations as an expansion of their traditional functions would need to be considered.

The present inventory covers around 400 villages and hamlets in the two districts of Leh and Kargil. Over 4250 sites have been listed. This list is by no means final and it is hoped that it is further expanded over the coming years to include sites that have not been covered in the present list. Each village will receive 'their' list of cultural resources which will be useful in prioritizing conservation efforts. Sites have not been graded in the present exercise and it is proposed that the grading is carried out through a consultative process with the community, heritage experts and researchers.

The inventory should prove a valuable tool for both researchers as well as conservators, planners and administrators with an interest in the region. It will prove invaluable in monitoring this heritage in the future.

It has been our great privilege to interact with the people of Ladakh in preparing this list which is now shared in these six volumes. The process followed has been an enriching and rewarding experience for all involved. With this six volume series, we hope to share the knowledge gained with you.

Tara Sharma
Project Director

Understanding the Listing Format

Administratively, Ladakh is divided into two large districts – Leh and Kargil – each comprising several blocks. Each block is further composed of a number of villages and it is the village that has been taken as the basic unit for this listing. Villages are often made up of numerous hamlets, which in turn are usually under the purview of a single headman. In most cases, the listing has been recorded for a village in its entirety, although in some cases, it lists individual hamlets separately.

The inventory is published in 6 volumes according to both the district and block sub-divisions.

VOLUME 1 – LEH District – Khaltse block

VOLUME 2 – LEH District – Leh and Kharu blocks

VOLUME 3 – LEH District – Nyoma and Durbuk blocks

VOLUME 4 – LEH District – Nubra block

VOLUME 5 – KARGIL District – Sankoo, Taisuru, Shergol, Chigtan, Kargil and Drass

VOLUME 6 – KARGIL District – Zanskar

Listing Format

The listing format that was adopted for the present inventory was developed on the basis of the format presently used by INTACH (Indian National Trust for Art and Cultural Heritage) with several modifications. A greater emphasis was placed on the significance of the cultural resource listed, so as to try and understand why a particular resource was important to the community. In addition, the categories of resources listed were expanded to include a broader range of sites/ structures. In general, two formats were used for the inventory – the first was to list manmade heritage, while the second was for natural/sacred landscapes and associated manmade heritage.

ix

The following illustration and explanations will help you to better understand the format of the list:

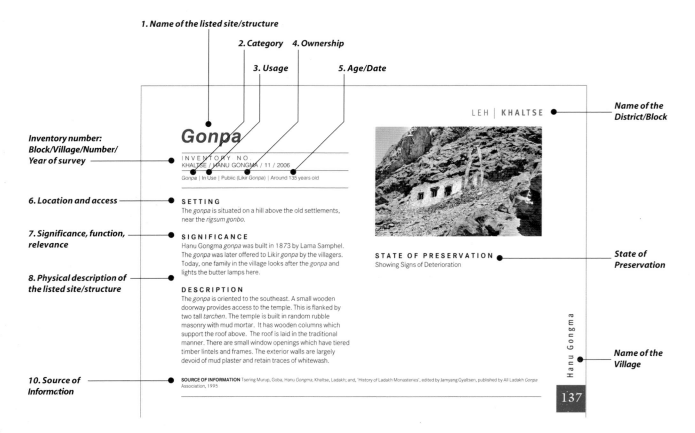

1. Name of the listed site/structure
2. Category
3. Usage
4. Ownership
5. Age/Date

Inventory number: Block/Village/Number/Year of survey

6. Location and access
7. Significance, function, relevance
8. Physical description of the listed site/structure
10. Source of Information

LEH | KHALTSE — Name of the District/Block

Gonpa

INVENTORY NO
KHALTSE / HANU GONGMA / 11 / 2006

Gonpa | In Use | Public (Likir Gonpa) | Around 135 years old

SETTING
The gonpa is situated on a hill above the old settlements, near the rigsum gonbo.

SIGNIFICANCE
Hanu Gongma gonpa was built in 1873 by Lama Samphel. The gonpa was later offered to Likir gonpa by the villagers. Today, one family in the village looks after the gonpa and lights the butter lamps here.

DESCRIPTION
The gonpa is oriented to the southeast. A small wooden doorway provides access to the temple. This is flanked by two tall tarchen. The temple is built in random rubble masonry with mud mortar. It has wooden columns which support the roof above. The roof is laid in the traditional manner. There are small window openings which have tiered timber lintels and frames. The exterior walls are largely devoid of mud plaster and retain traces of whitewash.

SOURCE OF INFORMATION Tsering Murup, Goba, Hanu Gongma, Khaltse, Ladakh; and, 'History of Ladakh Monasteries', edited by Jamyang Gyaltsen, published by All Ladakh Gonpa Association, 1995

STATE OF PRESERVATION — State of Preservation
Showing Signs of Deterioration

Hanu Gongma — Name of the Village

137

1. NAME
The principal name of the structure along with any other names by which it is known.

2. TYPOLOGIES
The criterion for the inventory has evolved through discussions with the community. It has broadly focused on manmade and natural elements of the landscape that impact the cultural life of a village.

The four general typologies recognised in the inventory are religious structures, archaeological sites, residential or civic buildings and cultural or sacred landscapes. Within these, several categories of structures/sites have been identified for the inventory. The following table provides an overview of these categories.

	TYPOLOGIES			
	RELIGIOUS STRUCTURES	ARCHAEOLOGICAL SITES	RESIDENTIAL/CIVIC BUILDINGS/SITES	CULTURAL/SACRED LANDSCAPES
CATEGORIES	Monasteries	Forts/Palaces	Vernacular Buildings (Houses, labrang, tashag)	Caves
	Temples	Petroglyphs		Water Bodies (hot springs, lakes)
	Mosques		Cemeteries, Spurkhang, Tombs, kabristan	Mountain Passes
	Imambara			Sacred Mountains
	Idgah			Sacred Rock Formations
	Chorten			Pastures
	Mane Wall			Nomadic Camping Areas
	Lhato			Sacred Trees/Groves
	Rigsum Gonbo			Community Spaces
	Rock Carving			
	Tsadkhang			
	Lubang			
	Tsamskhang			
	Tsamphuk			
	Khankah			

2.1 RELIGIOUS STRUCTURES

The vast majority of inventories relate to religious sites which are seen to be of primary importance in the village. These include a variety of categories:

Monasteries and Temples: The Buddhist monastery or *gonpa* is the most well represented image of the region. The *gonpa* is a derivative of the Buddhist *vihara* or hermitage, which was originally a place of retreat abounding in Bodhi trees. The *gonpa* is ideally located at least a thousand yards away from a village or town. Later, as settlements arose around the monasteries, these became large establishments and many settlements (especially in the central Ladakh heartland) have evolved around the original monastery. The monasteries of Ladakh fall under the four major Buddhist orders – Gelug, Sakya, Kagyud and Nyingma. In addition to the monasteries are the temples located in villages, which fall under the purview of a head monastery from where a monk is deputed to lead prayers and perform rituals for the villagers. Today, monks are stationed at a village temple for a year after which they sometimes return to the head monastery or move to another village. These temples are often maintained or supported by the village community who sponsor activities here. These activities include special prayers such as the ritual fasting of the Nyenas and Nyungas, which is accompanied by the recitation of mantras or the reading of the Bum (*Bum skhor*).

Scholars generally categorize Ladakh's monasteries as falling under two broad periods. Monasteries dating from the first period – the 10th to about the 13th or 14th centuries – are commonly known as 'early period temples'. Generally built on flat land, early period temples were usually distinguished by their wall paintings and colossal stucco configurations, both of which displayed strong Kashmiri influences. These temples were also often referred to as 'Lotsava period temples', after Lotsava Rinchen Zangpo, who founded several of them. The artists responsible for embellishing these temples returned with the Lotsava to Kashmir, which was a major Buddhist centre at the time. Recent research has revealed several interim phases and it is now known that numerous temples that were originally ascribed to the Lotsava were actually built by his followers in the centuries following his death. The temples constructed from the 13th - 14th century onwards gradually began to show a more marked Tibetan influence. Former single, or in some instances, double-storeyed temples were gradually replaced by massive structures, often perched on hilltops to fend off invasions by marauding armies. The fortified appearance of the monasteries also helped in protecting their growing wealth, seen in priceless collections of manuscripts, paintings and statues. In addition to serving as centres of Buddhist learning and monastic education, monasteries now came to perform administrative functions as well. Large allocations of land granted by the ruling kings to support their functions came with numerous administrative

responsibilities and administrative quarters were also housed within the monastic complex. Monks' residences were built all around the central gonpa, spilling down the slopes of the hill atop which the main temples were erected.

***Imambara*, Mosques, *Khankah* and *Idgah*:** Islam was introduced to Ladakh in the 15th century from Kashmir and Baltistan and gained a firm foothold in the Kargil area and in parts of Leh. Of the original 15th-century mosques, few examples survive today as most have been replaced with modern concrete structures that draw architectural inspiration from the Turco-Iranian style. The original mosques were generally built in the Ladakhi style using locally available materials such as stone and mud bricks set in mud mortar. A few mosques had timber domes that were usually built over a timber frame.

***Chorten* and *Mane* Wall:** The most prolific building types in the region are the ubiquitous *chorten* and *mane* walls that are found in every Buddhist village in the region. Generally located along a path leading to the temple/monastery, at a junction, along a village path or at the village entrance, *chorten* and *mane* walls are circumambulated in a clockwise direction as an act of merit, which is seen as the first step towards enlightenment.

Chorten are the equivalent of the Buddhist *stupa*, the earliest extant example of which is seen in Sanchi. Traditionally seen as funerary structures containing the relics or ashes of enlightened lamas, *chorten* were also commissioned as acts of merit or as commemorative structures built to remember a special event or simply for the well being of the builder and all sentient beings and sometimes even as atonement for sins committed. For example, during the reign of King Deldan Namgyal, a large number of *chorten* were constructed in Shey on the orders of the King as punishment for wrongdoings. In some rare cases, special *chorten* were also built to trap evil forces like epidemics, invasions etc. (eg: Tisseru *stupa* was built to trap an evil force – possibly an epidemic – which was troubling the residents of the area).

The most significant element in the *chorten* is its contents or *Zungs,* which are placed inside it with prescribed rituals and prayers. There are four different types of relics, namely Chos-sku'i Ring-srel (*mantras*), Ril-bu'i Ring-srel (grain), sku-gDung Ring-srel (bones or ashes) and sku-bal Ring-srel (hair and clothes).

The earliest extant *chorten* in Ladakh are believed to date back to the period of the pre-Tibetan, Indo-Iranian settlers, commonly referred to as the Mons. They can be found in areas such as Gya, Miru, Rumtse and so on. During the time of Lotsava Rinchen Zangpo in the 10th-11th century, several *chorten* were constructed near the temples built by him and his later disciples. Some of these are elaborately painted in a style similar to that adopted in the early period temples. The structure of these chorten differ from those of the post 13th–14th centuries, which followed a defined formula of proportions and iconometry (see box).

Lhato: The *lhato* are small altars that are dedicated to the protector deities of the village or a particular family or phaspun. They are usually located high up in the mountains in a pure and unpolluted environment. Many *lhato* have legends associated with them that throw light on the deity taking residence in a particular village. These have been documented in the inventory. The deities themselves are believed to reside up in the mountains and the *lhato* marks their residence. It contains ritual offerings usually in the form of a bundle of branches (often juniper) or grass that is tied with *khadag*. Prayers to the protective deity are offered by the villagers, sometimes every month, when the protection of the *lha* is sought. In some villages, a person known as the *luyar* is possessed by the *lha* which manifests at the time of renewal to make prophecies for the village. The contents of the *lhato* are renewed every year, and in some villages this responsibility rests with a particular family or person known as the *lhadag*. The renewal of the *lhato* is a cultural practice that has helped to preserve several ancient *lhato* as part of a living tradition.

Rigsum Gonbo: The *rigsum gonbo* are usually located along the slopes of a mountain on the outskirts of the village or sometimes within the village itself and are built as acts of merit and to protect the village from harm. Often found at the site of floods or landslides, they also mark the occurrence of previous natural calamities that struck the village in the past. *Rigsum gonbo* are also built over the entrance doors of houses to protect the inhabitants and their property from any harm. In some cases, they were even built to protect a family or village from the 'evil' influence of a mountain that was seen to be causing harm. They are often built on the advice of a lama.

Lubang: The *lubang* are small cubical shaped structures with a rounded roof on top, which contain a *kalash* with ritual offerings placed inside by a lama at the time of construction. The *lubang* are built to placate the *lu* or the serpent deities of the underworld, who when angered

are believed to cause harm. They are the guardians of the great treasure of the underworld and reside in a palace deep underwater. The *lubang* thus mark the residence of the *lu*. Usually found near water sources, they are built on the ground floor of the house or sometimes even outside the house. When the resident of a house suffers from a skin disease, special prayers are held to placate the *lu*. Special prayers, known as the *lu thebs,* are also held prior to the start of the agricultural season in spring in order to placate them. Monks lead these prayers and offerings made at the *lubang* are then immersed in water to ensure a good supply of water for the fields. The construction of a *lubang* follows certain rituals. A lama performs *pujas* to placate the *lu* and places a *kalash* or *bum pa* with offerings inside it. The *bum-pa* vase is filled with precious objects, mantras and grains. There are two types of *bum-pa* called *nor-bum* (for prosperity) and *lu-bum* (for abundant water).

Tsadkhang: The *tsadkhang* are small receptacles built to house *tsa-tsa*. The *tsa-tsa* are of two kinds – the first is a small clay mould shaped in the form of a *chorten* that is placed as a ritual offering inside the *tsadkhang*. The second type is made of the ashes of the deceased. *Tsadkhang* containing the latter type of *tsa-tsa* are not usually circumambulated while the former are given as ritual offerings and are circumambulated as an act of merit.

The *chorten, mane, rigsum gonbo, lubang* and *tsadkhang* are all built according to established codes with special prayers being performed to consecrate the structures.

Tsamskhang and ***Tsamphuk:*** These are meditation centres or retreats usually located slightly apart from the main settlement which are important elements in the meditative practice followed by the monks. The *tsamskhang* are buildings while the *tsamphuk* are meditation caves.

2.2 ARCHAEOLOGICAL SITES

Ladakh's earliest evidence of human habitation is to be found in a large number of petroglyph sites that are scattered across the region. Largely found along the major river networks, these sites provide valuable information on Ladakh's early history. Today, several of

A group of chorten

Mane wall

Lhato

Rigsum gonbo

these sites are threatened with the building of roads and rapid construction activity in the region for which stones are required as building material. While several of these sites have been listed in the present inventory, it is possible that there are many more that need to be identified and carefully preserved.

The second category of archaeological sites is the ruined forts that dot the landscape. Located on hilltops, these forts include former citadels that served as the capitals of various ruling dynasties in Leh and Kargil. People believe that villages were formerly located inside the forts to protect them from attacks by bandits who roamed the countryside as well as from enemy invasions. Most of the forts that survive today were heavily damaged during the Dogra wars while some were damaged during the Balti invasions during the reign of King Jamyang Namgyal. Most of the forts listed here are seen to be in danger of disappearance. The fort walls have massive foundations of rubble masonry. The walls are largely battered, tapering towards the top and their upper sections are sometimes made of rammed earth.

2.3 RESIDENTIAL/CIVIC STRUCTURES

The third typology of sites includes vernacular buildings and community properties such as the *spurkhang*, *kabristan* and cemeteries. Ladakh's vernacular buildings testify to a high degree of skill in understanding local climatic conditions and the use of locally available materials.

The Ladakhi house has evolved over the centuries to the form in which it is seen today. The introduction of cement in recent years, as well as glass rooms over the past 30-40 years has changed the layout and appearance of many traditional dwellings. In some remote villages, however, the ancient systems can still be seen.

Prior to the introduction of glass, houses had very small window openings, which protected the inhabitants from the bitter north winds. Houses were largely oriented to the east and were generally only single storeyed in height. The houses of the nobility or influential families, however, were like small palaces and were generally multi storeyed.

The central room in the house was the *chantsa*, which was the living room-cum-kitchen where the traditional clay stove burned through the day. It had a single opening in the roof for ventilation and no window openings. The *chantsa* was surrounded by a passage or *srol* around which the other rooms were arranged. There were animal pens around the *chantsa* – *tangra* for cows and sheep and *stara* for horses. The heat generated by the animals helped retain warmth in the mud walls of the *chantsa*. In summer, the animals were kept in an open pen outside the house known as the *yarlas*.

TRADITIONAL VERNACULAR DWELLINGS OF LADAKH – BELIEFS AND PRACTICES
(An interview with Gelong Dadul, Tagthog Gonpa)

The construction of the house follows certain norms. A site is first selected for the house. For this, a test pit is dug and the soil removed. The soil is then refilled into the pit. If it fills the pit completely, then the earth is sound for building a house. If it overfills or under fills the pit, then it is not considered a good area. After selection of the site, an auspicious day is selected by consulting the *onpo* (astrologer). The lama is then called to conduct the sabchog or ceremony to bless the land. The *puja* includes prayers to remove any malevolent spirits residing in the area as well as to placate the *lu* or the underworld serpent deities. Popular belief recommends that the first ground breaking is done by a person born in the Year of the Pig (*phag*) so as to dispel any serpent deities residing in the land. Serpents being pure creatures cannot abide filth, which the Pig denotes. Depending on the financial capacity of the family, rituals can also be carried out at the time of the laying of the roof or the erection of the columns.

The selection of the site for the building of houses follows certain beliefs. A house, for example, will not be built at the foot of a mountain that projects out on a ridge. This is considered an inauspicious site. Equally, a house cannot be built in front of a mountain which has a second mountain hidden behind it. This is because the hidden mountain, known as *riwo* (mountain) *phag* (hidden) *te* (seen), could be a malevolent mountain and cause harm to the inhabitants.

The orientation of the house also followed age old beliefs and practices. Doors were never oriented to the north but mostly to the south or east. Similarly, windows were much smaller in earlier times and were also oriented to the south or east. Today, with the introduction of glass rooms and larger windows as well as heating options, this has changed and people are not as conscious of this.

The family temple and the *lhato* dedicated to the family protector deity are always located on the top most floors, as the air is cleaner and purer here. The direction of the chapel is never towards the south. In particular, the temple should not fall under the path of the six-star constellation, *minduk* (possibly Pleiades), which crosses the night sky in the months of Oct-Nov, as this is considered inauspicious. The temple is usually built in the north or west, while the south and east are generally left open for the terrace. Environmentally, this also helps to retain heat generated from the east and south through the roof of the house.

xiii

Near the *chantsa* was the *changkhang,* where the traditional barley beer was fermented and stored in large jars. The *dzod* was used for storing grain while the *baang* stored vegetables. In a corner of the house on the ground floor was the *silkhang* or cold room, where dairy products such as milk and butter were stored. Water channels were cut in the corner of the room and covered by stones and these helped to keep the room cool during the summer. All family activity was centred around the *chantsa.* It was the place where food was cooked and where the family would sit around the stove during the day and sleep at night. Today, houses are double or even triple storeyed. People reside on the ground floor during winter and on the first floor in summer. In many instances, the ground floor is used for stabling animals or for storing fuel and fodder for the long winter.

The close link between the pastoral community and their land is also reflected in the agricultural practices followed here. At the time of the harvest (*srublha*), the first cut of grain is hung on the central column of the *chantsa.* The household deity known as the *khim lha* is also manifest in the house and depictions of the deity are made in dough and placed on the central *kaju* (capital) of the room or on the shelves on which the vessels are placed (*lang ska*).

In addition to the houses belonging to the lay community are the houses for monks, known as *tashag* and *labrang* owned by the monastery. Both follow building styles that are similar to that of village residences with some modifications. The *labrang,* for example, contains large bins located beneath the floor, where grain is stored. The grain is distributed in spring prior to the sowing season and collected at the time of harvest. The monk deputed by the monastery to administer the monastery's lands in the village (that are leased out to villagers), resides in the *labrang* at these times. Most monasteries have *labrang* in villages where they own lands.

The *tashag,* or monks' residences, are most commonly located along the slopes of the hill atop which the *gonpa's* main temples and assembly halls are situated. Sometimes, they are also situated in villages.

2.4 SACRED/CULTURAL LANDSCAPES

The impact of the natural landscape on Ladakh's culture is seen in several beliefs and practices that highlight the close connections communities have formed with their environment. Sacred mountains or rock formations, for example, are found in most villages with a predominant Buddhist population. Rock formations are generally believed to depict protector deities, impressions (body, hand or foot) of renowned Buddhist sages such as Guru Padmasambhava, or even legendary figures such as those from the epic Gesar Saga. Pilgrim routes have evolved around these sacred natural elements, and in Nubra, entire valleys have been connected through these routes. In some cases, rock

formations have also influenced the sites chosen for the establishment of monasteries and entire villages, which derive their names from them.

Ladakh is a largely arid, cold desert and the scarcity of trees, particularly in the Leh district, has given rise to myths and beliefs that have helped to preserve many ancient trees. Some trees, known as *lhachang,* are believed to be the abodes of deities and are never harmed in any way. Wood is not cut from these trees and khadag are often tied to the branches. *Lhato* dedicated to the deities may be located at the foot of the tree where rituals are carried out to enlist their protection. Ancient trees such as the juniper (*shugpa*) also have special meaning as the branches of juniper trees are used as offerings in *lhato* as well as for carrying out purification rites where the branches are burned and carried through the house. Today, juniper is an endangered species in Ladakh as few juniper trees survive here. Hemis Shukpachan has an entire grove of juniper trees, which are considered sacred by the community.

Water bodies such as springs, lakes and waterfalls also have sacred as well as secular relevance for Ladakh's communities. Myths related to the creation of lakes have been documented wherever possible. In addition, a large number of hot springs have been listed that are closely associated with Ladakh's traditional practice of medicine or *amchi* practice.

In ancient times, caves were used as dwellings as well as meditation retreats (*tsamphuk*). In Lamayuru and Gesar, a honeycomb of caves has been carved into the clay and pebble agglomerate that constitutes the mountains. Walls are sometimes erected at the entrance to the caves as well as within them to create smaller chambers. The caves at Lamayuru were used as dwellings while the ancient caves at Yokma Kharbu are believed to still contain bone fragments of the Soudh army who were smoked to death inside the caves. At many sites today, ancient caves are no longer in use and access to them has deteriorated. Some caves, however, such as those at Nyoma are being used to store winter fodder for livestock.

Secular community spaces also form an important part of the cultural landscape. The *changra* or community space is found in almost every village in Kargil. These are used to host village assemblies convened by the village leaders to discuss various issues. The *shagaran* or polo ground is now rarely found, but was once an important community space where polo was played regularly. Polo was introduced to the region from Baltistan and became an important sport in the region. In addition to polo, archery grounds are also found in many villages and several of these have been listed. Another natural feature found in most villages is the pastures where animals such as the dzo, yak, sheep, goats and demo are taken for grazing during the summer months. In Changthang, rearing livestock is the primary economic activity and is closely linked to the nomadic lifestyle followed by the region's communities. In some villages, temporary settlements arise during the summer months (*dok*), when villagers move up the valley with their livestock in search of grasslands.

3. USAGE

Sites/structures with a continued function and usage by the communities have been listed as 'In Use'. Sites that are no longer in use are listed as 'Abandoned'. In some cases, houses that still have a limited use for storage but are otherwise vacant are also listed as abandoned. Similarly, deserted temples where ritual artifacts have been shifted to newer temples but where butter lamps may still be lit are listed as abandoned, as they are no longer maintained.

4. OWNERSHIP

Ownership has been listed in two categories – Public and Private. The 'Public' category covers community ownership, ownership by religious bodies such as *gonpa* or ownership by the state. 'Private' ownership defines ownership by individual families. In many cases, ownership lines are blurred. Village temples are sometimes claimed as community property whereas monasteries also claim ownership of these temples to which they depute their monks to carry out rituals. Alternately, for structures such as *chorten* and *mane* walls, the land on which the structure is built may belong to an individual but the structure itself may belong to the community or vice versa.

Information on ownership that is included in this listing has been derived solely from oral interviews with villagers and published works and cannot therefore have any legal implication.

5. AGE/DATE

The age of sites has been largely recorded based on interviews with villagers and custodians of heritage properties. Age has been calculated in an interesting manner by using the 'number of generations' as an estimate. The span of a generation has been set at an average of 50 years per generation. In some cases, the date of a site has been calculated based on its association with a religious leader or historic figure. However, it has also been noted that many of the early period temples, especially *chorten,* were generically tagged as belonging to the period of Lotsava Rinchen Zangpo, when in fact, the period includes those of his followers and extends well beyond his lifetime up to almost the 14th century. Interestingly, the historicity or age of a structure alone does not appear to determine its importance. In other words, just because a site/ structure is ancient does not automatically make it significant for the community. Rather, its significance emerges through its association and continued relevance in the community's life. In some instances, dates have been recorded based on inscriptions or recorded histories. The dates of the reigns of different

rulers are based on Dr. Luciano Petech's interpretation of the Ladakh chronicles, while for the Kargil area, dates have followed the seminal works of Kacho Sikander Khan and Wazir Hashmatullah Khan.

6. SETTING

The general location and setting of the site/structure and its access. Access to the village is provided in the introduction at the beginning of each village inventory.

7. SIGNIFICANCE

The listing's principal emphasis has been on the significance of the listed site/structure for the community and on gaining an understanding of Ladakh's historic past. The significance of various sites has been documented under several heads that include cultural, historical, ecological, archaeological, architectural/art historical, ritual/religious etc. In general, emphasis has been placed on understanding why a specific site/structure is important to the village, the function it performs and its relevance today. Associated festivals and special prayers held in monasteries and mosques have been also noted. In the case of landscape elements, an additional category that has been included is of cultural practices and linkages with other sites, where information on specific cultural practices associated with the site has been documented.

8. DESCRIPTION

The physical description of the listed site, which includes materials of construction and general layout. In addition, descriptions of sacred objects and images in the *gonpa* and temples have also been included.

9. STATE OF PRESERVATION

The state of preservation is based on a visual assessment of the listed site/structure. The various stages of preservation include – *Good, Fair, Showing Signs of Deterioration, Advanced State of Decay* and *Danger of Disappearance.* In places where the original construction has been completely replaced or renovated with new materials, the site/structure has been characterised as *New Construction.* Based on this, prioritisation of conservation works can be carried out.

10. SOURCE OF INFORMATION

The information collated in this listing is based largely on interviews with village leaders, elders, owners and custodians. The names of these resource people have been noted in this section and all ownership of this knowledge rests with them. In some cases, references have been cited from published works. Details of these publications can be found in the bibliography (Volume 6).

XV

Glossary

Aga	Islamic religious leaders who are believed to be the descendents of the Prophet Mohammad
Akhon	Islamic religious head
Alam	An Islamic religious flag
Arga	Traditional plaster-floor made of pulverized pebbles, special clay and oil
Arhat	Literally means 'a worthy one'. A Buddhist saint who in life has fully realised selfless reality, and who leads others towards enlightenment - similar to a Bodhisattva. In Tibetan Buddhism there are sixteen *arhats* commonly portrayed in paintings and *thangkas*.
Ashura	The 10th day of the Islamic month of Moharram which marks the martyrdom of Imam Hussain
Bawo	Cave used for meditation and also used by travellers in ancient times as halts for the nights
Bodhisattva	An enlightened being who is dedicated to leading other beings to enlightenment
Chagdor or **Chagna Dorjey (Vajrapani)**	The Bodhisattva Vajrapani is the holder of the *vajra* (thunderbolt) who is seen as the concentrated power of the Buddha and the entire Vajrayana system. Portrayed in a variety of forms.
Chagmen	A protector deity
Chagzod	Manager of a *gonpa*
Chanrazig (Avalokitesvara)	The Bodhisattva of Compassion
Chantsa	Living room for winter usually in the ground/first floor surrounded by *changkhang* (beer room), *dZod* (store room) and animal sheds
Chorten	Literally means 'receptacle of offerings', but is the common term for a *chaitya*. In Tibet, this takes the shape of small and tall masonry monuments of settled form crowned with the emblem of the sun and moon and generally having some cavity inside for the ashes of a saint or other relics. In Tibetan Buddhism,

xvi

	eight forms of chorten came to be recognised each of which symbolizes specific events in the life of the Buddha *(see below)*.
Chosgyal	Dharma Raja or Defender of the Faith
Choskyong	The protector or defender of Buddhism
Chug-Shig-Zal	1000 armed and eyed Avalokitesvara
Chumig	Spring water
Deshag Gyad	The eight types of Tibetan chorten
Dhyani Buddhas	The five transcendental Buddhas – Vairochana, Ratnasambhava, Amoghasiddhi, Amitabha and Akshobhya
Dok	Summer pastures or the upper valley
Doljang	Green Tara
Dolma (Tara)	The female Bodhisattva Dolma (Tara) who saves human beings from trans-migratory existence. She is one of the most popular deities in Tibetan Buddhism and of whom there are supposed to be many branch emanations. Some exhibit twenty-one different manifestations of the goddess.
Dorje Chang (Vajradhara)	The Yeshes Sempa or Dhyani Bodhisattvas evolved from the second Dhyani Buddha, Akshobhya. He has been chosen as the ruling deity in the tantric system under the appellation of Chagdor (Vajrapani)
Dorje Sempa (Vajrasattva)	An Adi Buddha of the Nyingma school and a tantric form of Akshobhaya, the second Dhyani Buddha, who was introduced by Padmasambhava as the president of the eastern heaven where he sits on a white lotus
Dosku	A statue on stone or a rock carving.
Dukhang	Literally 'the hall of congregation for members in a monastery', but is a term that is today loosely assigned and is applied even to the ordinary ante-chamber of a temple
dZambala	the Tibetan Pluto or god of riches

EIGHT FORMS OF CHORTEN

The eight forms of Tibetan *chorten* derived from Indian counterparts which are believed to have been built during the Buddha's lifetime to commemorate significant events in his life.

Chorten drawings by **Han Li**

NIRLAC

Padspung Chorten

Symbolises the Buddha's birth at Lumbini

dZong	Fortress or castle	**Gyalpo**	King
Gelong	A Buddhist monk who has been ordained into the highest order. He has to observe 253 vows	**Id**	Muslim festivals like Id ul Bakr and Id ul Fitr
Gelugpa	One of the four Buddhist sects in Vajrayana Buddhism which was founded by Tsongkhapa	*Imambara*	Where Shia Muslim get together to mourn the martyrdom of Imam Hussain in the events of Karbala
Gesar	A powerful king ruling in Shanxi in China, who on account of his martial valour was deified and raised to the position of the God of war. There are various accounts of him. The people of Kham in Tibet own him for their national war-god, while the Mongolians say that Gesar was a king of Mongolia. According to some authors, he lived in the 7th century A.D. According to the collection of heroic songs called the Gyal-drung, King Gesar lived in the 8th century A.D. His origin is, however, lost in myth.	**Jigched**	Yamantaka or the God of death
		Jo Rinpoche	Crowned Buddha
		Kagan *Chorten*	Gateway stupas at the entrance of the villages so that all the people entering or leaving the village can pass through the gateway and accrue merits. This merit is considered to be the first step to enlightenment.
Goba	Village headman	**Kagyud**	The principal school of tantric Lamaism originating from Naro Pan-chen of Magadha and alleged by Milarepa to have been introduced by Marpa Lotsava in Tibet in the beginning of the 11th century A.D. Its different sub sects or branches are the following: *Karm Kagyud, Geldan Kagyud, Dagspo Kagyud, Drigung Kagyud, Dugpa Kagyud* and *Shangspa Kagyud*.
Gogpo	Ruined/abandoned		
Gonbo (Mahakala)	The tutelary deity of Tibet who is the wrathful manifestation of Avalokitesvara		
Gongma	Upper part of a village or a valley		
Gonkhang	A shrine dedicated to Mahakala and other protector deities		
Gonpa	A *vihara*, monastery or hermitage so called on account of its original situation in earlier times in isolated places abounding in Bodhi trees. A *gonpa* should be situated at least a thousand yards distant from a village or town. Monasteries in later times assumed the size of small settlements and included dwelling houses for the monks.	**Kangyur**	The instructions and precepts of Buddha which literally means 'that which has become a command'. It is the title of the great collection of Buddhist writings (mostly, but not all, translated from Sanskrit into Tibetan). The Kangyur is divided into seven series of Books containing several hundred treatises, and consists properly of 108 volumes, though editions in 100, 102, and 104 volumes are also current.
Guru Rinpoche (Padmasambhava)	An 8th century tantric teacher and the founder of Nyingma School of Tibetan Buddhism	*Khadag*	White scarf presented to persons for their acceptance. These scarves are of various descriptions. The longest and best ones are presented to the great lamas, high officials, and to other personages. They carry respect according to their quality, colour and length.
Guru Tsangyad	The eight manifestations of the great teacher; also the eight names of Padmasambhava		
Gyalmo	Queen	*Khangbu*	The 'little house' where parents move to after handing over the property and all legal ownership to the eldest son once he is married and has an heir

xvii

Changchub Chorten

Symbolises the Buddha's enlightenment under a Bodhi tree in Gaya

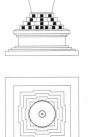

Tashi Gomang Chorten

Symbolises the first sermon expounded to the five ascetics (*bikkhus*) at Sarnath

Khangpa	Family house or residence
Khankah	A small mosque where *namaz* is performed was called *khanka* in past
Khar	Citadel, fort or castle
Labrang	Literally means 'a *lama's* residence'. Most of the major monasteries in Ladakh have *labrang* in the villages where they have land and animals. Earlier a monk was deputed from the monastery to live in the labrang to administer the land and property of the monastery. He would distribute grain at the start of the season to the tenants and would collect grain after the harvest which would be stored in the *labrang*.
Lama	A learned monk or teacher
Lha	Deity
Lhachang	A tree or grove dedicated to a protector deity. These trees are untouched by villagers and instead they make offerings
Lhadag	A family/person in charge of a *lhato* who is assigned to make offerings and renew the contents of the *lhato* dedicated to the protector of a group of households/ village protector
Lhakhang	Literally *lha* means 'god' and *khang* means 'residence'. A term used to describe a temple
Lhato	An altar that marks the residence of a protector mountain deity. It is erected in an open area higher than the settlement, usually along the slopes of a mountain.
Losar	New Year which Ladakh used to celebrate with Tibet but from the reign of King Jamyang Namgyal they have been celebrating two months earlier than Tibet i.e. in 11th month
Lu	*Lu* are the serpent deities of the underworld who are guardians of great treasure. They are able to cause rain and certain maladies especially skin diseases and become dangerous when angry. People offer prayers and worship the Naga on the days of *Lu theb*.
Lu theb	The coming forth of the *lu* in summer from their retreats. This time is fixed in Tibetan almanacs for worshiping them

Lubang or **Lu khang**	The residence of the *lu* or serpent gods. An imaginary palace supposed to exist at the bottom of the sea or of some lake where the Naga reside. A symbolic structure that is built to mark the residence of the *lu*. Prayers and offerings are made at the lubang at the *Lu thebs* by the monks to placate the *lu*. The prayers are often to seek good supply of water before the cultivation of fields in spring and offerings made to the *lu* are then immersed in water.
Luyar	Literally it means 'borrowed body' and is used to describe a person in whose body the deity enters
Mahasiddha	Literally 'great perfected beings' which refers to the 84 Indian tantric teachers or yogis
Mandala	A *mandala* is represented as a geometric or symmetrical arrangement with a deity at the centre. It can be portrayed in single dimension paintings as well as more complex two or three dimensional architectural forms.
Mane Lhagskor	*Mane* is the mystic six syllable of Tibetan Buddhism i.e. 'Om Mani Padme Hung'. *Lhagskor* is a prayer wheel that can be rotated by hand. It contains *mantras* within and rotating the wheel is considered equivalent of reciting the *mantra*.
Mane Wall	Consecrated stone wall on which mane stones are placed which contain the *mantra 'Om Mane Padme Hung'*
Markala	A fine ochre earth used as ground-colour in staining houses with whitewash
Marpa	Marpa (1012-1096 A.D) was a Buddhist monk who studied in India and forms part of the lineage of the Kagyud lineage. His disciple was Milarepa.
Marsiya	Poem which eulogizes and laments the martyrdom of Imam Hussain and his followers in the Battle of Karbala
Masjid	Mosque where ritual prayers practiced by Muslims in supplication to Allah are offered five time a day
Mihrab	It indicates the direction of Karbala, in Mecca, towards which the Muslims offer prayer or *namaz*

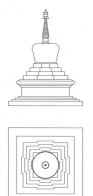

Chotul Chorten

Symbolises the Buddha's miracle showed to the six heretical teachers at Sravasti

Lhabab Chorten

Symbolises the Buddha's return from heaven at Vaishali

Milarepa Milarepa (1040–1143 A.D.) was a disciple of Marpa and the most famous of the Tibetan yogis. He was an ascetic and poet who worked miracles and delivered instruction to his votaries in verses composed for each occasion. He passed on his teachings to his disciple Gampopa.

Minar A tall structure on the roof of the mosques from where the call to prayer is made

Minbar The seat in the *masjid/imambara* for the ulema or imam from he preaches

Moharram The first month of the Islamic calendar. It marks the martyrdom of Imam Hussain, grandson of Prophet Mohammad, in the battle of Karbala which occurred on the 10th day of Moharram, known as the Ashura. This day is marked as a day of mourning by the Shias and ritual processions are taken out.

Namaz Ritual prayers practiced by Muslims in supplication to Allah which are offered five times a day

Nam-bar-nang-dzad (Vairocana) The chief of the five Dhyani Buddha who presides over the uppermost paradise situated in the zenith of the terrestrial skies

Namgyalma A goddess who is generally presented as possessed of 3 faces and 8 arms. In one of her right hands she holds an image of the Dhyani Buddha Amitabha, and from the left hand hang golden cords to which is attached the mystical syllable *Hri* wrought in silver.

Namsras /Namthosras (Vaishravana) The king of the Noijin or mountain deities who guards the northern quarters. He is also in a way, amalgamated with Kubera or Vaishravana, the god and guardian of wealth, with whom he is sometimes identical with and sometimes differentiated from.

Naropa Naropa (1016–1100 A.D.) was a Buddhist mystic and monk who was the teacher of Marpa. He forms a part of the Kagyud lineage having received his teachings from Tilopa.

Nastan Chutuk The 16 highest disciples of the Buddha

Noha Urdu, Arabic or Persian prose that portrays the martyrdom of Imam Hussain which is recited on the Ashura by the Shia Muslims to mourn the martyrdom of Imam Hussain in the Battle of Karbala

Nyenas Ritual fasting observed by Buddhists

Nyingma The oldest sect of Tibetan Buddhism founded by Padma Sambhava

Nyungnas To observe fasting and abstain from talking as religious duty

Odpakmed (Amitabha) The fourth Dhyani Buddha who resides in the heaven of Dewachan

Paldan Lhamo A fierce goddess who is the most revered of the Tibetan goddesses. She is especially revered in the Gelugpa order for she is the protector of the Dalai Lama. In all large Tibetan temples Paldan Lhamo is to be found presiding over the wrathful deities.

Pungpa Bottle-shaped ornaments in architecture, e.g., on the *chorten* and also vessel used during rituals

Pungtser A small structure to keep *pungpa*

Rabsal A small balcony or gallery, frequently seen in Ladakhi houses

Rangjon Self-evolved or self manifested

Rigsum Gonbo The three Bodhisattvas (Avalokitesvara, Manjushri and Vajrapani) who protect the three classes of beings that is the gods, humans, serpents or demi god races are called Rigsum Gonbo. The three Bodhisattvas are: Jamyang (Manjushri) – Bodhisattva of wisdom, Chanrazig (Avalokitesvara) - Bodhisattva of compassion, and Chagdor (Vajrapani) – Bodhisattva of strength.

Rinpoche The honorary titles of the Tibetan Buddhist high-priests

Saskya One of the four major schools in Tibetan Buddhism. The name of the school derived from the colour of the place (grey earth) where the first monastery was built. The school was founded by Khon Konchog Gyalpo.

Shaikh Islamic religious scholars other than a Sayeed or *Aga*

xix

Indoom Chorten

Symbolises the reconciliation of the Sangha after the discord created by Devadatta at Rajagriha

Namgyal Chorten

Symbolises the first sermon expounded to the five ascetics (*bikkhus*) at Sarnath

Shugpa	Identified as juniper, the plant is considered sacred and is most often used for purification rituals and ceremonies
Skudung	Funeral *chorten* containing relics
Skyoba Jigsten Gonbo	The founder of Drigung Kagyud School in Tibet
Spurkhang	Literally 'a house for keeping dead bodies', *spurkhang* is used to describe a structure that is used to cremate the dead
Srog-shing	Literally means 'the tree of life'. The central pole in a *chorten* is also referred to as *srog-shing*
Srub lha	Ceremony that marks the commencement of harvesting
Standin (Hayagriva)	A deity with a man's body but having the head of a horse which neighs fearfully to frighten beings who are mischievous to Buddhism
Tabaruk	Food/sweet distributed among people as a token of blessing during Moharram
Tabut	A replication coffin of Imam Hussain
Tangyur	A miscellaneous collection of Buddhist literary works, both sacred and general consisting of 225 volumes. Very few of the Tangyur treatises belong to Tibetan authorship. They are mostly translation into Tibetan from Chinese and Sanskrit texts.
Tarchen	Tall poles with prayer flags tied to them which are usually posted in courtyards of gonpa or outside the main entrance of residences
Tashag	Residence of monks
Thangka	A painting or representation of a deity on cloth or paper
Tilopa	Tilopa (988–1069 A.D.) is regarded as the founder of the Kagyud lineage
Tungshak	Depiction of the 35 Buddhas
Tsa-Tsa	Miniature conical figures moulded of clay and used as ritual offerings. *Tsa-tsa* are sometimes made of human ashes. The latter are not worshipped.

Tsadkhang	A structure built to house *tsa-tsa*
Tsamkhang	Meditation cells
Tsamphuk	Solitary cavern in a rock or steep mountains used by the meditative *lamas*
Tsan	A species of demon, inhabiting a given locality and sometimes entering into a person visiting the place for a brief period and causing serious illness
Tsokhang	Assembly hall
Tsongkhapa	Tsongkhapa (1357–1419 A.D.) was the founder of the Gelugpa sect. He was born in a district in Amdo, Tibet. Tsongkhapa literally means 'a native of Tsong-kha', but the term now signifies the great reformer himself whose real name was Lobzang Dagspa. He laid the foundations of the Gelugpa sect.
Tsuglakhang	Temple
Yarkhang	Summer living room mostly situated on top floor
Yokma	Lower part primarily of a village or a valley
Zhabjes	Literally means 'foot print'. Foot prints of high *lamas* on stones, rocks and mountain surfaces that are found throughout Ladakh
Zimchung	A residence in a monastery for a Rinpoche or head *lama*

Nyangdas Chorten

Symbolises Buddha's attainment of *parinirvana* at Kushinagar

XX

Leh | **Khaltse**

Achinathang

The name of the village derives from the Dard language and is a combination of two words – *achi* meaning mountain and *na* meaning big. The earlier name of the village was Achina Lungpa since the village is located near a big mountain. According to legend, during the reign of King Tsewang Namgyal (1760 – 1800 A.D.), war broke out with the neighbouring Balti principality at Shigar which was under Jo Hussein Khan. The Ladakhi army was led by Ayu Kalon Tsewang Palbar. Impressed with the skill and bravery of Tsewang Palbar, the king awarded him a large tract of uninhabited land. In 1778 A.D., Ayu Khan brought in people from Chigtan and Skyurbuchan to settle in these lands. Many of these families were followers of Islam which their descendents continue to follow to this day. Ayu Khan named the village 'Achinathang' (plains near the big mountain). In 1812, some of the villagers became followers of Gang Ngon (Phiyang) Gonpa. In 1853, a meditating lama named Duwang Konchok Wangpo came to the village and built about 15 *chorten*, a *rigsum gonbo*, *mane* walls and a temple in the village. In 1915, Kharbupa Hassan Khan from Chigtan founded Thang yokma.

From the main Leh - Srinagar highway, a path diverts just before Khaltse towards Dha. Midway along this path, a footpath branches off and leads through the fields towards the village of Achinathang. Today, there are 80 families in the village with a population of 537 people.

{*Source: Sonam Phuntsog*}

Listed by: Deldan Angmo, Jassu Singh, Dr Sonam Wangchok, Karma Yeshi and Stanzin Dorjay
Year: 2004, 2007

Rock Inscription

INVENTORY NO.
KHALTSE / ACHINATHANG / 01 / 2004

Rock Inscription | In Use | Around 70 years old

SETTING
The rock inscription is oriented to the south and is located along the pedestrian pathway which leads to the village of Achinathang. The rock is situated a little above the residential settlement of Abdal Pa, which lies to its southwest. It is surrounded by the village pathway to the west and by agricultural fields on the other sides.

SIGNIFICANCE
The rock inscription marks the entrance to the village and contains the sacred Buddhist mantra *"Om Mani Padme Hung"*.

DESCRIPTION
The inscription is on a large rock which marks the entrance to the village. The letters have been pecked onto the rock surface and are in the Tibetan script. New text has been recently painted on the rock in blue and yellow paint which mars the inscription in some places.

STATE OF PRESERVATION
Advanced State of Decay

SOURCE OF INFORMATION Tashi Dorjey, Achinathang Gongma, Khaltse, Ladakh

Group of *Chorten*

INVENTORY NO.
KHALTSE / ACHINATHANG / 02 / 2004

Chorten | In Use | Public (Community) | Around 180 years old

SETTING
Oriented to the southeast, the group of *chorten* are located on the right hand side of the path which leads to the village. It is surrounded by apricot trees and agricultural fields to the south and by the residential settlement of Dongborogpa to the east.

SIGNIFICANCE
The *chorten* are both Changchub *chorten* symbolizing the Buddha's enlightenment. Located along the path which leads to the village, the *chorten* are circumambulated by villagers as they travel along this path in order to gather merit.

DESCRIPTION
The site comprises of two Changchub *chorten* of different sizes. The larger *chorten* is built on a stone masonry square base. The smaller *chorten* is built on a smaller square base. The *chorten* are built in stone masonry with mud mortar

and are mud plastered and whitewashed externally. There is a *srog-shing* embedded in the domes of both *chorten*.

STATE OF PRESERVATION
Advanced State of Decay

SOURCE OF INFORMATION Yangskit Dolma, Achinathang Gongma, Khaltse, Ladakh

Achinathang

6

Kholepe House and *Chorten*

INVENTORY NO.
KHALTSE / ACHINATHANG / 03 / 2004

Vernacular Building / *Chorten* | In Use | Private (Individual) | Around 100 years old

SETTING
The Kholepe house is oriented to the northeast and is located at the entrance to the village. It is surrounded by two *chorten* on the northeast and another *chorten* on the east. There are other village houses to the south and west of the Kholepe House.

SIGNIFICANCE
The Kholepe house is the ancestral home of the Kholepe family and is a good example of traditional architecture in the village. The house has a *rigsum gonbo* over the doorway as a protection against evil forces.

DESCRIPTION
The Kholepe house is a three storeyed building constructed in stone and mud brick masonry with mud mortar. A flight of stairs leads to the entrance located on the first floor.

There is a *rigsum gonbo* over the entrance door. The family's living areas are located on the upper floors while the ground floor is used primarily for storage. The third floor has large openings in timber which overlook the *chorten* below. The house has a traditional roof made of timber beams, joists, dried grass, *taalu* and compacted mud supported on timber columns and brackets. The *chorten* located near the house have been cement plastered and white washed over.

STATE OF PRESERVATION
Showing Signs of Decay

SOURCE OF INFORMATION Yangskit Dolma, Achinathang Gongma, Khaltse, Ladakh

Group of *Chorten* and *Mane* Walls

INVENTORY NO.
KHALTSE / ACHINATHANG / 04 / 2004

Chorten / *Mane* Wall | In Use | Public (Community) | Around 225 years old

SETTING
The group of *chorten* and *mane* walls is oriented to the south and is built on an open space surrounded by newly constructed houses.

SIGNIFICANCE
The *chorten* and *mane* wall are built on an open space near village houses and are circumambulated by villagers as acts of merit. The *chorten* are primarily Changchub *chorten*, symbolizing the Buddha's enlightenment.

DESCRIPTION
The site consists of a series of *mane* walls and *chorten* constructed in two clusters. The first cluster comprises of five *chorten* and four *mane* walls. The *chorten* are of the same size and are built in stone and mud brick masonry with mud mortar and have an external layer of mud plaster and whitewash. There are two circular and two linear *mane* walls in this group all built in stone and whitewashed externally. The second group comprises of a linear *mane* wall, three circular *mane* walls, a *tarchen* and a *chorten* adjacent to the linear *mane* wall. The *mane* walls are all built in dry stone masonry while the *chorten* is built in stone and mud brick masonry with mud mortar.

STATE OF PRESERVATION
Advanced State of Decay

SOURCE OF INFORMATION Dechan Angmo, Achinathang Gongma, Khaltse, Ladakh

Achinathang

7

Thangpa House, *Chorten* and *Mane*

INVENTORY NO.
KHALTSE / ACHINATHANG / 05 / 2004

Vernacular Building / *Chorten* / *Mane* Wall | In Use | Private (Individual) | Around 100 years old

STATE OF PRESERVATION
Advanced State of Decay

SETTING
The Thangpa house is oriented to the southeast and is located along a path which leads the village. A *chorten* and *mane* are located to the southwest while the Kholepe house and *chorten* lie beyond. The Khaldagpa house is located to the northwest of the house.

SIGNIFICANCE
The house is built in the traditional style and was constructed by the grandfather of the present owner. The family continues to reside in the house. It forms part of a cluster of vernacular dwellings in the village. The *chorten* and *mane* wall located near the house form part of the complex and are circumambulated by family members as an act of merit.

DESCRIPTION
The site consists of a two storeyed house with a *chorten* and *mane* wall nearby. The Thangpa house has an entrance doorway along the southeast facade. The lower floor is constructed in stone masonry and the upper floor is built in mud brick masonry with mud mortar. Externally, the house is mud plastered and whitewashed. The ground floor is used as a cattle shed while the upper levels are used by the family as their living quarters. The house has a flat traditional roof made of timber beams, joists, *taalu*, dried grass and a layer of compacted mud. There is a *rigsum gonbo* above the entrance doorway and a timber framed *rabsal* against the living room on the first floor. There is a Changchub *chorten* to the southwest of the house which is built in stone masonry and has some traces of external mud plaster and whitewash. To the north, there is a *mane* wall built in dry stone masonry with inscribed *mane* stones placed on the top horizontal surface.

Group of *Mane* Walls and *Chorten*

INVENTORY NO
KHALTSE / ACHINATHANG / 06 / 2004

Chorten / *Mane* Wall | In Use | Public (Community)

SETTING
The group of *chorten* and *mane* walls is oriented to the south and is located along the village road which lies to the north while the village stream flows to the south of the site. There are apricot trees to the south west.

SIGNIFICANCE
The group of *mane* walls and *chorten* are located along the village road and are circumambulated by villagers, as they travel along this path, in order to accumulate merit. The *chorten* are Changchub *chorten* which symbolize the Buddha's enlightenment.

DESCRIPTION
The site comprises of a group of four *mane* walls and two *chorten* built alongside each other. The first in the group is a linear *mane* wall which is followed by a *chorten*. This is followed by another linear *mane* wall and *chorten* and at

the end are two circular *mane* walls. The *mane* walls are all built in dry stone masonry while the Changchub *chorten* have been repaired in cement and painted over. The *chorten* have tall *chugsum khorlo* over the dome.

STATE OF PRESERVATION
Showing Signs of Deterioration

SOURCE OF INFORMATION Dechan Angmo, Achinathang Gongma,Khaltse, Ladakh

Achinathang

9

Mane Walls

INVENTORY NO.
KHALTSE / ACHINATHANG / 07 / 2004

Mane Wall | In Use | Public (Community) | Around 125 years old

SETTING
The *mane* walls are oriented to the south and are located along the road leading to the settlement. The site is surrounded by a road on the east and the River Indus along the west.

SIGNIFICANCE
The *mane* walls are circumambulated by passers-by as an act of merit while travelling along this path.

DESCRIPTION
The site comprises of two *mane* walls - one cubical and the second circular in shape. Both of them are built in dry stone masonry and are whitewashed externally. Inscribed *mane* stones are placed on the flat horizontal surface. The cubical shaped *mane* wall is larger in size.

STATE OF PRESERVATION
Advanced State of Decay

SOURCE OF INFORMATION Tashi Dorjey, Achinathang Gongma, Khaltse, Ladakh

Kagan *Chorten*

INVENTORY NO.
KHALTSE / ACHINATHANG / 08 / 2004

Chorten | In Use | Private (Individual)

SETTING
The *chorten* is oriented to the south and is located along the road leading to the settlement. It stands a short distance away from the Saperthang army post.

SIGNIFICANCE
The Kagan *chorten* is a gateway *chorten* and merit is believed to accrue to believers who pass through the passage of the *chorten*.

DESCRIPTION
The Kagan *chorten* consists of a large Changchub *chorten* built over two parallel walls with a passage beneath. The walls are about three feet in thickness and are built in stone masonry with mud mortar. Over the roof, the *chorten* is built in stone masonry with mud mortar and is mud plastered and whitewashed on the exterior. It is surmounted by a traditional *chugsum khorlo* over which rests a metal crown and crescent.

SOURCE OF INFORMATION Dechan Angmo, Achinathang Gongma, Khaltse, Ladakh

STATE OF PRESERVATION
Showing Signs of Deterioration

Achinathang

10

Mane Wall

INVENTORY NO.
KHALTSE / ACHINATHANG / 09 / 2004

Mane Wall | In Use | Public (Community)

SETTING
The *mane* wall is oriented to the east and is approached from the main Leh - Srinagar highway, 9 kms ahead of Skyurbuchan. The road runs to the north of the *mane* while the River Indus flows to its south.

SIGNIFICANCE
The *mane* wall is located near the road and is circumambulated by villagers as an act of merit.

DESCRIPTION
The *mane* wall is circular in shape. It is built in stone masonry with mud mortar over a square base made of larger stones. There is a small rectangular opening towards the east which houses a small prayer wheel within. The *mane* wall is mud plastered and whitewashed externally.

STATE OF PRESERVATION
Showing Signs of Deterioration

SOURCE OF INFORMATION Tashi Dorjey, Achinathang Gongma, Khaltse, Ladakh

Group of *Mane* Wall and *Chorten*

INVENTORY NO.
KHALTSE / ACHINATHANG / 10 / 2004

Chorten / *Mane* Wall | In Use | Public (Community) | Around 120 years old

SETTING
The group of *chorten* and *mane* walls are oriented to the east and are located at the base of a hill 6 kms from Skyurbuchan, towards the village. The main Leh - Srinagar highway lies to the north and there are some willow trees near the *chorten*, located at one end of the *mane* wall.

SIGNIFICANCE
The long *mane* wall and *chorten* are located before the village of Achinathang Gongma and are circumambulated by villagers as an act of merit. The *chorten* is a Changchub *chorten* which symbolizes the Buddha's enlightenment.

DESCRIPTION
The *mane* wall is about 250 feet long and is built over a stone masonry base. At the end of the *mane* wall is a *chorten* built in stone and mud brick masonry with mud mortar which is mud plastered and white washed externally.

SOURCE OF INFORMATION Dechan Angmo, Achinathang Gongma, Khaltse, Ladakh

STATE OF PRESERVATION
Advanced State of Decay

House of Mohamad Isaq

INVENTORY NO.
KHALTSE / ACHINATHANG / 11 / 2004

Vernacular Building | In Use | Private (Individual) | Around 100 years old

SETTING
The house is located beyond the agricultural fields abutting the main village road in Achinathang Yokma.

SIGNIFICANCE
The house was built by the grandfather of the present owner named Mohamad Hussain about 100 years ago and his descendents continue to reside here. It is one of the oldest houses in the village. The house is built in the traditional style and is a good example of vernacular architecture in the village.

DESCRIPTION
The house is a large, three storeyed building built in random rubble masonry. The ground floor is used to house sheep and the first and second floors comprise the family's living quarters. The living room on the first floor has a

large wooden column in the centre supporting the traditional roof above. The living rooms have a traditional wooden flooring. The house has small window openings on the second floor. The roof is laid in the traditional manner with timber beams, joists, willow twigs, grass and compacted mud. The house is mud plastered and whitewashed on the exterior.

STATE OF PRESERVATION
Showing Signs of Deterioration

SOURCE OF INFORMATION Mohamad Isaq, Achinathang Yokma, Khaltse, Ladakh

Chan *Masjid*

INVENTORY NO.
KHALTSE / ACHINATHANG / 12 / 2007

Mosque | In Use | Public (Individual) | Around 100 years old

SETTING
The mosque is located beyond the agricultural fields abutting the main village road of Achinathang Yokma. It lies close to the house of Mohamad Isaq and the village school.

SIGNIFICANCE
The mosque was built during the time of Nambardar Ruse Ali and Hajji Bakr of Yokmapa about 100 years ago. The mosque was renovated by the villagers around 15 - 20 years ago. The mosque is the principal place of worship for the village. Villagers gather here for daily *namaz,* the weekly *Jumma* and the annual *roza.*

DESCRIPTION
The masjid is a single storeyed building, constructed on a hill. It is built in stone masonry with mud mortar. The entrance door leads directly onto the main prayer hall. Two large wooden columns inside support a traditional roof above. There is a *mihrab* at the northwest end of the hall.

Prayer mats are laid out in front of the *mihrab*. There is a small wooden shelf against the north eastern wall on which is placed the Koran. The building has large windows on the side walls with timber frames. Externally, the building has been cement plastered.

STATE OF PRESERVATION
Fair

SOURCE OF INFORMATION Abdul Aziz Tsudpa, Achinathang Yokma, Khaltse, Ladakh

Kabristan / Spurkhang

INVENTORY NO.
KHALTSE / ACHINATHANG / 13 / 2007

Burial Ground | In Use | Public (Community) | Around 100 years old

SETTING
The *kabristan* is located beyond the agricultural fields abutting the main village road of Achinathang Yokma. It lies behind the village school.

SIGNIFICANCE
The burial ground is a large area in the village which is used by the both Muslims and Buddhists for burying/cremating the dead. Half of the land is used by the Muslims as a *kabristan* while the other half is used by the Buddhists as a *spurkhang.*

STATE OF PRESERVATION
Fair

DESCRIPTION
The site comprises of a large area of barren land with a low boundary wall running along the edge in some areas. There are graves scattered across the site.

SOURCE OF INFORMATION Abdul Aziz Tsudpa, Achinathang Yokma, Khaltse, Ladakh

Achinathang

12

Hajji Mousa House

INVENTORY NO.
KHALTSE / ACHINATHANG / 14 / 2007

Vernacular Building | In Use | Private (Individual) | Around 100 years old

SETTING
The house is located beyond the agricultural fields abutting the main village road in Achinathang Yokma. It lies close to the mosque.

SIGNIFICANCE
The house was built by an ancestor of the family named Apo Hussain around 100 years ago. The family continues to reside in the house which is one of the oldest in the village.

DESCRIPTION
The house is a double storeyed house in random rubble masonry with mud mortar. The ground floor is used for housing cattle while the family's living rooms are on the first floor. The first floor has three rooms, two of which are used as living room while the third is used for storage. The living rooms have a wooden floor and a wooden column in the centre supporting the traditional roof above. There are no window openings on the ground floor while the first floor has small windows. The exterior walls are largely devoid of mud plaster and whitewash.

STATE OF PRESERVATION
Showing Signs of Deterioration

SOURCE OF INFORMATION Abdul Aziz Tsudpa, Achinathang Yokma, Khaltse, Ladakh

Achinathang

13

Imambara

INVENTORY NO.
KHALTSE / ACHINATHANG / 15 / 2007

Imambara | In Use | Public (Community) | Around 100 years old

SETTING
The *imambara* is located near the main road and is surrounded by Yoktsopa House on one side and fields on the other sides.

SIGNIFICANCE
The *imambara* was built by Bakr Ali Khan and villagers around 40 years go. Villagers gather on the occasion of Moharram every year.

DESCRIPTION
The *imambara* is a large building constructed on a rectangular plan. There are three entrance doors leading into the main prayer hall which separate the congregational areas for men and women. Finely carved wooden partitions separate the women's areas inside the hall. There is a timber *minbar* at one end of the hall and carpets laid out in front on the floor. Timber columns inside the hall support the roof above. The roof is a sloping roof covered with tin sheets. The mosque is built in stone masonry with mud mortar.

STATE OF PRESERVATION
Fair

SOURCE OF INFORMATION Abdul Aziz Tsud pa, Achinathang Yokma, Khaltse, Ladakh,

Rigsum Gonbo

INVENTORY NO.
KHALTSE / ACHINATHANG / 16 / 2007

Rigsum Gonbo | In Use | Public (Community) | Around 150 - 200 years old

SETTING
The *rigsum gonbo* is situated on top of a hill on the right side of the stream in Achinathang Lungba hamlet.

SIGNIFICANCE
The *rigsum gonbo* is believed to have been built around 3 - 4 generations ago by the villagers to protect the village from natural calamities and evil forces.

DESCRIPTION
The *rigsum gonbo* consists of a high platform built in stone masonry with two side walls. The front and rear is open and inside, on the top of the platform, are three *chorten* built which are mud plastered and painted in the traditional colours of blue, white and yellow. There are timber columns to the front and rear of the *chorten* which support the overhead roof. The structure is mud plastered and white washed.

STATE OF PRESERVATION
Fair

SOURCE OF INFORMATION Lawang Rigzin, Achinathang, Khaltse, Ladakh

Petroglyphs

INVENTORY NO.
KHALTSE / ACHINATHANG / 17 / 2007

Rock Carving | Abandoned | Public (State)

SETTING
The petroglyphs are located along the main road which leads from Khaltse to Kargil near the village of Achinathang. It is located alongside the road amid some wild vegetation.

SIGNIFICANCE
The petroglyphs, like several others in Ladakh, date back to the earliest period of human habitation in Ladakh.

DESCRIPTION
The petroglyphs are pecked onto a large boulder and depict animal as well as human figures. There is a small boulder nearby which also contains petroglyphs. The large boulder has been defaced with graffiti.

STATE OF PRESERVATION
Showing Signs of Deterioration

Rigsum Gonbo

INVENTORY NO.
KHALTSE / ACHINATHANG / 18 / 2007

Rigsum Gonbo | In Use | Public (Community) | Around 200 - 250 years old

SETTING
The *rigsum gonbo* is located along a footpath that leads to the *gonpa*. It lies at the foot of a mountain, left of the path.

SIGNIFICANCE
The *rigsum gonbo* was built around 4 - 5 generations ago to protect the village from natural calamities and evil forces.

DESCRIPTION
The *rigsum gonbo* is built on a rectangular plan and comprises of a dry stone masonry platform over which rest three *chorten*. The *chorten* are mud plastered and painted in the traditional colours of blue, white and red. The mountain side abuts the structure to the rear and there is a small wall on one side. The other three sides are open. Four timber columns in front support the overhead roof. The roof is made of timber joists and beams and there are flat stones and grass placed on the top.

STATE OF PRESERVATION
Showing Signs of Deterioration

SOURCE OF INFORMATION Thinlas Dorjay, Achinathang, Khaltse, Ladakh

Gonpa

INVENTORY NO.
KHALTSE / ACHINATHANG / 19 / 2007

Gonpa | In Use | Public (Community) | Around 700 - 800 years old

SETTING
The *gonpa* is situated in Achinathang Lungba on a the slope of a hill, just above the settlement. A footpath leads from the village into the narrow valley and is a three-hour walk from the village. The *gonpa* is located in the upper part of the valley and there are many juniper trees in this part of the village.

SIGNIFICANCE
The *gonpa* was originally built around 800 years ago and was renovated around 15 years ago by the villagers. It is a branch of the Lamayuru *Gonpa* and a monk is deputed here to look after the temple. Villagers offer butter lamps here every day and the Kangyur and Bum are read in the 5th month of the Tibetan calendar as a special prayer.

DESCRIPTION
The *gonpa* is a double storeyed building constructed in stone and mud brick masonry with mud mortar. Externally, it is mud plastered and whitewashed. The main entrance is from the south east. The main chapel is located on the ground floor. It has two timber columns supporting the roof. The central image is that of Chanrazig which is surrounded by smaller images of Guru Rinpoche, Jamyang and other deities. These are all housed within an elaborate timber cabinet which is brightly painted and has glass shutters. Volumes of the Bum and Kangyur are also placed here. There is a kitchen and some other rooms to the left of the *dukhang*. The upper floor houses the *Zimchung* which is known as the Bakula Rangdol Nyima Rinpochay *Zimchung*. There is a natural spring and a pair of juniper trees in front of the *gonpa*.

STATE OF PRESERVATION
Fair

SOURCE OF INFORMATION Lawang Rigzin, Achinathang, Khaltse,Ladakh

Achinathang

15

Chorten and *Mane* Wall

INVENTORY NO.
KHALTSE / ACHINATHANG / 20 / 2007

Chorten / Mane Wall | In Use | Public (Community) | Around 150 – 200 years old

SETTING
The *chorten* and *mane* wall are built on a hill, to the left of the *gonpa*. The site lies above the village.

SIGNIFICANCE
The *chorten* and *mane* wall are believed to have been built many years after the temple. The structures were built as an act of merit. The *chorten* is a Changchub *chorten* which symbolizes the Buddha's enlightenment.

DESCRIPTION
The site consists of a *chorten* and a *mane* wall located a short distance apart. The *chorten* is built on a stone masonry base and is constructed in stone and mud brick masonry. It has been recently mud plastered and white washed. There is a tall *chugsum khorlo* over the dome. The *mane* wall is built on a square plan and is constructed in stone masonry with mud mortar. There is a small parapet

running around the edge of the roof which is painted in red. The wall has an infill of mud over which the *mane* stones are arranged.

STATE OF PRESERVATION
Fair

SOURCE OF INFORMATION Lawang Rigzin, Achinathang, Khaltse, Ladakh

---

Group of *Chorten*

INVENTORY NO.
KHALTSE / ACHINATHANG / 21 / 2007

Chorten | In Use | Public (Community) | Around 150 – 200 years old

SETTING
The *chorten* are located in a field and are surrounded by trees. They lie on the right side of the path leading to the *gonpa*.

SIGNIFICANCE
The *chorten* are said to have been built around 3 - 4 generations ago by a village ancestor for the well being of all sentient beings. Today, since the *chorten* lie in a grove of trees, people rarely circumambulate them. The *chorten* appear to be Changchub *chorten*.

DESCRIPTION
The site comprises of a group of two *chorten* located in a grove of trees. The *chorten* are of similar size and are built over individual bases of stone masonry. They are constructed in stone masonry and are largely devoid of the external layer of mud plaster and whitewash. The *chorten* have eroded over time and lost their original form making them difficult to identify.

STATE OF PRESERVATION
Fair

SOURCE OF INFORMATION Lawang Rigzin, Achinathang, Khaltse, Ladakh

Gonpa

INVENTORY NO.
KHALTSE / ACHINATHANG / 22 / 2007

Gonpa | In Use | Public (Community) | Under Construction

SETTING

The *gonpa* is situated on the left side of the link road to Achinathang. It is located near the Government school and is surrounded by village houses.

SIGNIFICANCE

The *gonpa* is currently under construction and is being built as a place of worship for the Buddhist community.

STATE OF PRESERVATION
Fair

DESCRIPTION

The *gonpa* is a double storeyed building built in stone masonry with cement mortar and is cement plastered on the exterior. The ground floor is used as a community hall while the chapel is on the first floor. The main image in the temple is that of Chanrazig which is surrounded by smaller images of Guru Rinpoche as well as volumes of the Bum and Kangyur. These are all kept inside a timber and glass cabinet which is painted and embellished with floral motifs. The chamber has a wooden floor and pillars which support the overhead roof.

SOURCE OF INFORMATION Thinlas Dorjay, Achinathang, Khaltse, Ladakh

Chorten

INVENTORY NO.
KHALTSE / ACHINATHANG / 23 / 2007

Chorten | In Use | Public (Community) | Around 150 – 200 years old

SETTING

The *chorten* are located in the middle of the village fields, to the right of the footpath leading to the *gonpa*. There is a large tree nearby.

STATE OF PRESERVATION
Showing Signs of Deterioration

SIGNIFICANCE

The *chorten* were built around 3 - 4 generations ago by village ancestors for the well being of all sentient beings. The structures are still circumambulated by villagers as an act of merit when travelling along this path.

DESCRIPTION

The site comprises of two *chorten* built a short distance apart. Each of them stands on a square base made of random rubble masonry in mud mortar. The *chorten* are built in stone masonry with mud mortar and have traces of external mud plaster and white wash. One *chorten* has a tall *chugsum khorlo* over the dome. Both structures have eroded over time and the external layer of mud plaster is no longer evident over the domes.

SOURCE OF INFORMATION Lawang Rigzin, Achinathang, Khaltse, Ladakh

Alchi

According to popular belief, in ancient times Alchi was not connected with villages across the River Indus. People from the other side had, thus, to shout across the river to pass messages to the residents. Often, the message would not be received by the residents given the wide span of the river. The village, therefore, came to be known as *Ha-Ichi* or people with hearing impairment. This was later corrupted to Alchi. The settlement today consists of four small hamlets – Yulkhor, Shangrong, Gonpa and Choskor. There are 128 households in Alchi.

Listed by: Deldan Angmo and Jassu Singh
Year: 2004

Atitse

Atitse is situated along an unmetalled road that diverts from the main Leh – Srinagar highway after Lamayuru.

Listed by: Deldan Angmo and Jassu Singh
Year: 2004

Mane Walls

INVENTORY NO.
KHALTSE / ALCHI / 01 / 2004

Mane Wall | In Use | Public (Community) | Around 1000 years old

SETTING
The *mane* walls are located on an elevated stretch of land along the main road leading to Alchi. The site is about two kms from the main village of Alchi. There is a house located near the *mane.*

SIGNIFICANCE
The *mane* walls were built in the past as an act of merit and are still circumambulated by villagers to gather merit.

DESCRIPTION
The site comprises of two *mane* walls. One is circular in plan while the other *mane* is rectangular in plan. Both are built in dry stone masonry and have inscribed *mane* stones placed on the top.

STATE OF PRESERVATION
Showing Signs of Deterioration

SOURCE OF INFORMATION Tsering Yangskit Sergar, Alchi, Khaltse, Ladakh

Group of *Chorten*

INVENTORY NO.
KHALTSE / ALCHI / 02 / 2004

Chorten | In Use | Public (Community)

SETTING
The *chorten* are located long the slope of a barren hill abutting the main vehicular road which leads to Alchi. Approaching Alchi from Leh, the *chorten* are located on the left of the road some two kms before the village.

SIGNIFICANCE
The *chorten* are both Changchub *chorten* and symbolize the Buddha's enlightenment. The *chorten* are located along the path leading to the village and are circumambulated by villagers, as they travel along this path, as an act of merit.

DESCRIPTION
The site comprises two *chorten* of similar size built on a common rectangular platform. The *chorten* are built in stone masonry with mud mortar. The external layer of mud plaster appears to have eroded completely. The *chorten* are whitewashed.

STATE OF PRESERVATION
Advanced State of Decay

SOURCE OF INFORMATION Tsering Yangskit Serger, Alchi, Khaltse, Ladakh

Mane Wall and *Tarchen*

INVENTORY NO.
KHALTSE / ALCHI / 03 / 2004

Mane Wall / *Tarchen* | In Use | Public (Community)

SETTING
The *mane* wall is located along the main vehicular road approximately 500 metres before the village. There are two *tarchen* nearby and barren mountains beyond.

SIGNIFICANCE
The *mane* wall is located along the main access road leading to the village and is circumambulated by villagers, as they travel along this route, to gather merit. The two *tarchen* mark the entrance to the village.

DESCRIPTION
The site comprises of a *mane* wall and two *tarchen*. The *mane* wall is a long rectangular shaped dry stone masonry wall. Inscribed *mane* stones are placed on its horizontal surface. The *tarchen* comprise of wooden poles embedded in a square stone base and a prayer flag tied to the poles.

SOURCE OF INFORMATION Tsering Yangskit Serger, Alchi, Khaltse, Ladakh

STATE OF PRESERVATION
Showing Signs of Decay

Alchi

21

Group of *Chorten* and *Mane* Walls

INVENTORY NO.
KHALTSE / ALCHI / 04 / 2004

Chorten / *Mane* Walls | In Use | Public (Community)

SETTING
The group of *chorten* and *mane* walls are located along the vehicular road which leads to the village. The mountainside forms the backdrop to the site.

SIGNIFICANCE
Located before the entrance to the village, this group of *chorten* and *mane* walls is circumambulated by villagers as they travel along this road, as an act of merit. The *chorten* appear to be largely Changchub *chorten*, and symbolize the Buddha's enlightenment.

DESCRIPTION
The site comprises of a group of *chorten* of different sizes with *mane* walls interspersed in between. Many of the *chorten* have collapsed and it is difficult to ascertain the original form. The *chorten* are built in stone as well as mud brick masonry with mud mortar. These are mud plastered

and whitewashed on the exterior. The outer layer of mud plaster and whitewash has eroded in most cases. The *mane* walls are built in dry stone masonry and are linear in plan. The horizontal surfaces of the *mane* walls are covered with inscribed *mane* stones.

STATE OF PRESERVATION
Advanced State of Decay

SOURCE OF INFORMATION Tsering Yangskit Serger, Alchi, Khaltse, Ladakh

Group of *Chorten*

INVENTORY NO.
KHALTSE / ALCHI / 05 / 2004

Chorten | In Use | Public (Community)

SETTING
The *chorten* are oriented to the south. A pathway diverts from the main vehicular road and after passing via some houses and fields leads to the site. The mountainside borders the site towards the southwest and the River Indus flows to the north of the site. Agricultural fields lie to the west of the precinct.

SIGNIFICANCE
The site comprises of several *chorten* of different styles. The most significant of these is an early period (possibly 12th century) *chorten*. This *chorten* is distinct from the traditional 8 forms of *chorten* more commonly found in the region. Most of the *chorten* have collapsed and it is difficult to discern their original form. The structures are circumambulated by villagers as an act of merit.

DESCRIPTION
The site comprises of a group of over a dozen *chorten* in different sizes. Most significant among them is a large

chorten that resembles an early period chorten. It stands on a large square base built in stone and mud brick masonry with mud mortar. Further south is a rectilinear platform with seven *chorten* built on the top. Most of the *chorten* are Changchub *chorten*, many of which are in complete ruin. The *chorten* are built in stone and mud brick masonry and have traces of mud plaster and whitewash on the exterior surface. Some of the *chorten* have *srog-shing* projecting from the top.

STATE OF PRESERVATION
Danger of Disappearance

SOURCE OF INFORMATION Tsering Yangskit Serger Alchi, Khaltse, Ladakh

Alchi

22

Tsa-Tsa Puri *Gonpa*

INVENTORY NO.
KHALTSE / ALCHI / 06 / 2004

Gonpa | In Use | Public (Ridzong *Gonpa*) | Around 11th – 12th century

SETTING
The *gonpa* forms part of a larger complex that includes the Thug-Je Chenmo and is located at the end of the Alchi link road. The Thug-Je Chenmo temple is situated to the south east and the Tongspon house is located to the south west.

SIGNIFICANCE
The *gonpa* is believed by villagers to have been built during the same period as the Alchi *Choskhor*. The *chorten* inside the temple as well as the wall paintings appear to date back to the early period of Buddhist art in the region. On the 4th month of the Tibetan calendar, monks from Ridzong Gonpa visit the *gonpa* and perform prayers here for several days.

DESCRIPTION
The Tsa-Tsa Puri *gonpa* is a square shaped building which is approached through a low height wooden doorway on the south western side. A flight of stone steps leads up to the doorway which opens onto a courtyard. The *gonpa* is a

single storeyed structure with a clear height of around four metres. Inside the temple, four wooden columns support a traditional roof above. There is a *chorten* at the centre of the room above which there is an open skylight. The walls are covered with paintings of *mandala* and thousand Buddha images. The panels below the skylight also have wall paintings. The only source of light and ventilation to the *gonpa* is the open skylight and the low height doorway. The *gonpa* is built in stone and mud brick masonry with mud mortar and is mud plastered and whitewashed on the exterior. There is a parapet painted in red, running along the edge of the roof.

STATE OF PRESERVATION
Advanced State of Decay

Thug-Je Chenmo
Gonpa

INVENTORY NO.
KHALTSE / ALCHI / 07 / 2004

Gonpa | In Use | Public (Ridzong *Gonpa*) | 11th – 12th century

SETTING
The *gonpa* forms part of a larger complex that includes the Tsa-Tsa Puri *gonpa* and is located at the end of the Alchi link road. The Tsa-Tsa Puri *gonpa* is situated to the north east and the Tongspon house is located to the southwest.

SIGNIFICANCE
The temple falls under the purview of Ridzong *gonpa*. In the 4th month of the Tibetan calendar, monks from Ridzong visited the *gonpa* and perform prayers for several days. It is believed to have been built during the same period as the Alchi *Choskhor* (1000 years ago).

DESCRIPTION
Thug-Je Chenmo is part of the *gonpa* complex and accessed through the same courtyard as the Tsa-Tsa Puri *gonpa*. It is a double storeyed structure and is accessed through a doorway on the southeast of the courtyard. Inside the temple, four decorated columns and brackets support the traditional roof above. The central portion of the chamber has an opening on the ceiling through which are visible two more levels above. The walls of the upper levels have elaborate paintings of Buddhist deities. The walls of the main shrine are covered with paintings of *mandala*. The rear wall of the chamber has paintings of the thousand Buddhas in front of which is a large statue of Chanrazig placed on a pedestal. The rear wall appears to have been recently repaired and the paintings have been repainted. There are small images of ducks on the side panel of the corner beams. *Thangka* are hung from the central wooden columns. The *gonpa* is built in stone and mud brick masonry with mud mortar and the exterior walls of the temple are mud plastered and white washed. There is a large window opening above the entrance doorway. To the north east of the *gonpa* is a Tan Tong Shrung Ma chapel that houses the guardian deity of the Tongspon family.

STATE OF PRESERVATION
Advanced State of Decay

Alchi

23

Group of *Chorten*

INVENTORY NO.
KHALTSE / ALCHI / 08 / 2004

Chorten | In Use | Public (Community)

SETTING
The *chorten* are located at the end of the village settlement near the market square. They are built along the Tsa-Tsa Puri *gonpa* complex wall.

SIGNIFICANCE
The *chorten* are believed to have been built at the same time as the Tsa-Tsa Puri *gonpa* and Thug-Je Chenmo although they appear to be a later period construction. Located near the *gonpa* complex, the *chorten* are circumambulated by villagers as an act of merit. They appear to be Changchub *chorten* and symbolize the Buddha's enlightenment.

DESCRIPTION
The site comprises of a group of three *chorten* in different sizes. The central one is the largest. Each of the *chorten* stands on a large square base of random rubble masonry and is built in stone and mud brick masonry with mud mortar. Externally, the *chorten* are mud plastered and whitewashed. The top section of the *chorten* has lost its form due to extensive erosion of the outer layers.

STATE OF PRESERVATION
Advanced State of Decay

SOURCE OF INFORMATION Tsering Yangskit, Serger Alchi, Khaltse, Ladakh

Alchi

24

Chorten and *Lubang*

INVENTORY NO.
KHALTSE / ALCHI / 09 / 2004

Chorten / Lubang | In Use | Public (Community)

SETTING
The *chorten* and *lubang* are oriented to the northeast and are located near the Garbapa and Dagopa houses. The site is surrounded by the Garbapa house to the northwest and the Dagopa house to the southeast. The village pathway, which leads to the Gonpa, runs to the north of the site. The *lubang* is located to the south of the *chorten* and is built along the slope of a hill next to the Garbapa house.

SIGNIFICANCE
The village path bifurcates near the *chorten* to form a circumambulatory path which is used by villagers to circumambulate the *chorten* as an act of merit. The *chorten* is a Changchub *chorten* and symbolizes the Buddha's enlightenment. The *lubang* is located near the *chorten* and marks the residence of the *lu* or serpent deities of the underworld.

DESCRIPTION
The site comprise of a *chorten* and a *lubang*. The *chorten* stands on a square base made of stone masonry in mud mortar. The main body of the *chorten* is built in stone and mud brick masonry and is mud plastered and whitewashed on the exterior. The *lubang* is a small cubical structure built in stone and mud brick masonry with mud mortar. It has a small opening on one side and is topped with a roof made of *taalu*, compacted mud and stone.

STATE OF PRESERVATION
Advanced State of Decay

SOURCE OF INFORMATION Tsering Yangskit, Serger Alchi, Khaltse, Ladakh

Lotsava Tree

INVENTORY NO.
KHALTSE / ALCHI / 10 / 2004

Landscape (Sacred Tree) | In Use | Community | 11th century

SETTING
The Lotsava tree can be reached from a narrow pathway which branches off from the main village path near the market square. It is located southeast of the Alchi *Choskhor*. The tree is surrounded by houses to the north and east and by agricultural fields on the southeast.

SIGNIFICANCE / ASSOCIATED BELIEFS
According to popular belief, after building the temple complex in Alchi, Lotsava Rinchen Zangpo planted his walking stick next to the *gonpa* which took root as the Lotsava tree.

DESCRIPTION
There are three trees today at the site, with the central one being considered being the original tree which sprouted from the walking stick planted by the Lotsava.

CULTURAL LINKAGES / CULTURAL PRACTICES
The tree is located on the way to the Alchi *Choskhor* which, along with Mangyu and Sumda Chun, forms one of the principal pilgrim circuits in Ladakh. The tree is considered sacred and is visited by pilgrims who come to the *gonpa*.

STATE OF PRESERVATION
Fair

Alchi

25

SOURCE OF INFORMATION Ishey Thamphel Ragopa, Alchi, Khaltse, Ladakh

Group of *Chorten* and *Mane* Wall

INVENTORY NO.
KHALTSE / ALCHI / 11 / 2004

Chorten / *Mane* Wall | In Use | Public (Community) | Around 1000 years old

SETTING
The *chorten* and *mane* wall are located along the southwest and northwestern boundary walls of the *gonpa* complex. They lie along a narrow pedestrian pathway which bifurcates from the main village path leading from the main square to the *gonpa*. Village houses lie to the rear of the site.

SIGNIFICANCE
The cluster of *chorten* and *mane* walls lie near the *gonpa* complex and are circumambulated by villagers and pilgrims as an act of merit. The *chorten* include Changchub and Namgyal *chorten*. The Changchub *chorten* symbolizes the Buddha's enlightenment while the Namgyal *chorten* symbolizes the Buddha's victory over illness.

DESCRIPTION
The site comprises of a group of six *chorten* of different sizes and forms and a long *mane* wall alongside a *tarchen*. The

largest of this group of *chorten* comprises of two Changchub *chorten* placed on a rectilinear platform. The *chorten* stand on a large square base built in stone masonry with mud mortar. The *chorten* are plastered with mud and white washed. Next to the group of *chorten*, is a rectangular structure similar to a *rigsum gonbo*, which houses a group of three Namgyal *chorten*. The *chorten* rest on an elevated platform within an enclosed building which is open on one side. The interiors are painted in bands of blue, red and green. The structure is covered with a traditional roof. Adjacent to this, is a *tarchen* comprising of a stone masonry base on which rests a prayer flag. Near the *tarchen* is a linear mane wall built in dry stone masonry.

STATE OF PRESERVATION
Showing Signs of Deterioration

SOURCE OF INFORMATION Gen. Lobzang Toldon, Alchi, Khaltse, Ladakh

Alchi

26

Gomang *Chorten*

INVENTORY NO.
KHALTSE / ALCHI / 12 / 2004

Chorten | In Use | Public (Likir *Gonpa*) | 12th century

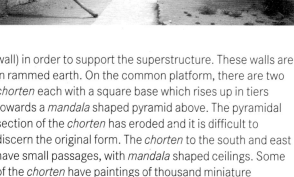

SETTING
The Gomang *chorten* are located within the Alchi *Choskhor* near the Sumsteg *lhakhang*. A narrow pathway leads from the main village square towards the complex.

SIGNIFICANCE
Alchi *Choskhor* along with other early period sites such as Mangyu and Sumdha Chun forms part of a pilgrim circuit which pilgrims undertake over one day. The Gomang *chorten* are believed to have been built during the same period as the temples i.e. 12th – 13th centuries and are some of the earliest extant structures dating to the early period of Buddhism in the region. There is a circumambulatory path around the *chorten* which are used by pilgrims visiting the site.

DESCRIPTION
The site comprises of a group of six *chorten*, which further occur in pairs. Each pair share a common rectangular base against which rests a large tapering wall (like a retaining

wall) in order to support the superstructure. These walls are in rammed earth. On the common platform, there are two *chorten* each with a square base which rises up in tiers towards a *mandala* shaped pyramid above. The pyramidal section of the *chorten* has eroded and it is difficult to discern the original form. The *chorten* to the south and east have small passages, with *mandala* shaped ceilings. Some of the *chorten* have paintings of thousand miniature Buddhas and various Bodhisattvas. There is a large prayer flag in the courtyard right in front. The exterior of the *chorten* are plastered and whitewashed.

STATE OF PRESERVATION
Advanced State of Decay

SOURCE OF INFORMATION Gelong Lobzang Toldan, Likir *Gonpa*, Alchi, Khaltse, Ladakh

Gonga *Chorten*

INVENTORY NO.
KHALTSE / ALCHI / 13 / 2004

Chorten | In Use | Public (Likir *Gonpa*) | 12th - 13th century

SETTING
The Gonga *chorten* is located within the Alchi *Choskhor* at the entrance to the complex. The site is accessed from a pathway which leads from the main square to the *gonpa*. There are several apricot trees located nearby.

SIGNIFICANCE
The Gonga *chorten* dates back to the 12th century and is contemporary to other buildings within the complex such as the Sumsteg *dukhang* and Lotsava *lhakhang*. This group of structures represent some of the earliest extant examples of early Buddhist art in the region.

DESCRIPTION
The Gonga *chorten* stands on a large square base with a tiered plinth tapering towards the wall of the *chorten*. It looks like a retaining wall provided to support the thick mud walls of the *chorten*. A larger square *chorten* stands on the top of the plinth with four smaller *chorten* at each corner. All these *chorten* have square bases with tapering tiers rising towards the dome. The dome in most cases has eroded over time and has lost its original form. There is an opening on the eastern wall of the main *chorten* that leads to the interior. Inside there is a hollow space below the large central *chorten*. The walls of the interior panels are adorned with paintings including the thousand Buddha images. The ceiling of this chamber has a *mandala* painting with depictions of various Buddhist deities and intricate floral motifs. The space inside the *chorten* contains a smaller *chorten* which has decorative stucco relief on the exterior surfaces. The interior panels of the *chorten* have images of various head lamas including Lotsawa Rinchen Zangpo himself, and the ceiling is also painted. The exterior is mud plastered and whitewashed. There is a small circular *mane* wall right in front of the Gonga *chorten* and a larger circular *mane* wall, at a distance of about 8 metres, under the apricot trees.

STATE OF PRESERVATION
Showing Signs of Deterioration

SOURCE OF INFORMATION Gen. Lobzang Toldan, Alchi, Khaltse, Ladakh

Kangyur *Lhakhang*

INVENTORY NO.
KHALTSE / ALCHI / 14 / 2004

Temple | In Use | Public (Community) | Around 600 years old

SETTING
The Kangyur *lhakhang* is oriented towards the south and is located near the entrance to the *choskhor* north of the pathway. The *choskhor* is approached along a narrow pathway that winds down from the main village square.

SIGNIFICANCE
The Kangyur *lhakhang* is believed to have been built by the village community around 600 years ago. The temple is used in worship and is maintained by the villagers.

DESCRIPTION
The Kangyur *lhakhang* is a double storeyed structure. A flight of stairs leads to the entrance on the first floor. The door leads onto an open court which is also the porch to the small *lhakhang*. A small wooden doorway leads into the lhakhang. The *lhakhang* is a small chamber with two wooden columns supporting the traditional roof above. There is a skylight above the central portion of the room. There is a shelf on the rear wall of the *lhakhang* on which

are placed images of a naturally formed Tsongkhapa, 21 Dolma and Paldan Lhamo. The *lhakhang* also houses two Changchub *chorten*, one in gold and silver and the second in wood painted over in silver. The *lhakhang* has timber flooring and the walls are covered with paintings. There are several *thangka* hanging against the wall surface, most noteworthy of which is a large *thangka* depicting the Potala complex in Tibet. There are two side rooms which are used as guest rooms. The rooms on the ground floor are used for storage. The building is built largely in stone and mud masonry with some repairs carried out in cement. Externally, the building is mud plastered and whitewashed.

STATE OF PRESERVATION
Showing Signs of Deterioration

SOURCE OF INFORMATION Ishey Thamphel Ragopa, Alchi, Khaltse, Ladakh

Lhakhang Soma

INVENTORY NO.
KHALTSE / ALCHI / 15 / 2004

Temple | In Use | Public (Likir *Gonpa*)

SETTING
The *Lhakhang* Soma is oriented towards the south and is located within the Alchi *Choskhor*. A narrow footpath near the Kangyur *lhakhang* leads to the *Lhakhang* Soma. A pathway from the main village square leads to the complex.

SIGNIFICANCE
The *Lhakhang* Soma or new temple forms part of the complex of the Alchi *Choskhor*. It is under the purview of Likir *gonpa* and monk from Likir performs daily pujas and ritual here.

DESCRIPTION
The *Lhakhang* Soma is a single storeyed structure with an entrance doorway from the southern side of the building. It is built in rammed earth and the exterior walls are mud plastered and white washed. The doorway and the parapet wall are painted in red. The temple is at present empty without any images. However, the interior walls are covered with wall paintings including images of

Shakyamuni Buddha on the rear wall and images of the thousand Buddha's on the side walls. The *lhakhang* has a wooden ceiling with a traditional roof above. There are no window openings and the small doorway is the only source of light and ventilation. To the east of the *lhakhang*, there are some Changchub *chorten* and a *mane* wall. The *chorten* are built in stone and mud brick masonry while the *mane* wall is built in stone.

STATE OF PRESERVATION
Showing Signs of Deterioration

SOURCE OF INFORMATION Ven. Lobzang Toldan, Alchi, Khaltse, Ladakh

Nangbar Nang Dzad *Dukhang* (Vairochana Temple)

INVENTORY NO.
KHALTSE / ALCHI / 16 / 2004

Temple | In Use | Public (Likir *Gonpa*) | 11th - 12th centuries

SETTING

The Nangbar Nang Dzad *dukhang* is oriented to the south and is located within the Alchi *Choskhor*. It is the third temple in the complex. It is also the largest of the temples and is located between the Sumsteg and the Lotsava *lhakhang*. A narrow footpath leads from the main parking area to the *choskhor*.

SIGNIFICANCE

The Nangbar Nang Dzad (Vairochana) temple is the main *dukhang* of the Alchi Choskhor complex and one of the principal buildings within the complex associated with the great translator Lotsava Rinchen Zangpo. An inscription within the *dukhang* indicates that it was founded by the monk Galden-sherab who was educated at Nyarma. The paintings and sculpture within the *dukhang* are believed to have been executed by artists brought in by the Lotsava from Kashmir and display a distinct North Indian influence stylistically. The temple is of significance for the community because of its close links with the legendary Lotsava . Alchi, along with Mangyu and Sumda Chun, forms a pilgrim circuit which is undertaken by pilgrims over one day. The complex was taken over in the 15th century by the Gelugpa sect and is under the Likir *gonpa* today.

DESCRIPTION

Nangbar Nang Mzad (Vairocana) temple is the third temple within the complex. It is entered through a courtyard, which has galleries on either side of the entrance doorway. The roof of the gallery is supported on wooden columns and beams. The walls of the gallery are painted with the images of the thousand Buddhas. The entrance door of the *dukhang* is of timber and is elaborately carved and painted. The lintel of the wooden door has carvings of the five Thathagatas. The porch of the entrance door has small chambers on either sides housing images of Chanrazig and Chamba. The doorway leads into a large chamber which has four wooden columns supporting the traditional roof above. The walls are covered with paintings depicting various *mandalas* dedicated to Vairocana. To the rear of the chamber, there is a large niche which houses a large configuration of stucco images representing Vairocana (central figure) seated on a throne with other deities around. This niche is today enclosed behind an elaborate wooden and glass frame. The wooden ceiling of the *dukhang* is painted with floral motifs while the floor is in timber.

STATE OF PRESERVATION
Showing Signs of Deterioration

SOURCE OF INFORMATION Ven. Lobzang Toldon, Alchi , Khaltse, Ladakh

Alchi

29

Lotsava *Lhakhang*

INVENTORY NO.
KHALTSE / ALCHI / 17 / 2004

Temple | In Use | Public (Likir *Gonpa*) | Around 11th - 12th century

SETTING
The Lotsava temple is oriented to the south and is located near within the Alchi *Choskhor*. The *lhakhang* is the fourth temple from the entrance to the complex and is adjacent to the Manjushri *lhakhang*.

SIGNIFICANCE
The *lhakhang* is dedicated to its founder Lotsava Rinchen Zangpo and it forms part of the complex of temples in Alchi.

DESCRIPTION
The Lotsava temple is a single storeyed building built on a rectangular plan. It has a front porch supported on two wooden columns with carved brackets. The door has been finely carved. It opens on to a small shrine housing stucco images of Shakyamuni Buddha and Lotsava Rinchen Zangpo. The walls have paintings of thousand miniature Buddhas and the rear wall has a large image of the Lotsava and Shakyamuni Buddha. The flooring is in timber and the

ceiling is painted with floral motifs. The door is the only opening in the building. The walls are made of rammed earth and are mud plastered and white washed. The entrance door as well as the parapet are painted in red.

STATE OF PRESERVATION
Showing Signs of Deterioration

SOURCE OF INFORMATION Ven. Lobzang Toldan, Likir *Gonpa*, Alchi, Khaltse, Ladakh

Alchi

30

Manjushri *Lhakhang*

INVENTORY NO.
KHALTSE / ALCHI / 18 / 2004

Temple | In Use | Public (Likir *Gonpa*) | Around 1000 years old

SETTING
The Manjushri *lhakhang* is also located near the entrance to the Alchi complex. The *gonpa* is located at the end of the village settlement, near market square. A narrow pathway from the market square leads us to Alchi *gonpa*.

SIGNIFICANCE
The *lhakhang* is dedicated to the Bodhisattva Jamyang (Manjushri) and forms a part of the Alchi *choskhor* complex dating back to the 11th century built by Lotsava Rinchen Zangpo.

DESCRIPTION
The Manjushri *lhakhang* is adjacent to the Lotsava temple with which it shares a common wall. It is a small modest mud structure similar to the Lotsava *lhakhang*. It has a front porch supported on two wooden columns with carved brackets. The door has been finely carved. It opens on to a

small shrine with a pedestal right in the centre. The pedestal has four images of Bodhisattvas – Jamyang (Manjushri) in their four different manifestations facing the four directions. The statues are intricately decorated with ornamentation and jewellery. The walls and the ceilings are covered with wall paintings. The flooring is of timber. There is a circumambulatory pathway around the images. The only source of ventilation and access to the temple is through the doorway.

STATE OF PRESERVATION
Showing Signs of Deterioration

SOURCE OF INFORMATION Ven. Lobzang Toldan, Likir *Gonpa*, Alchi, Khaltse, Ladakh

Sumsteg *Lhakhang*

INVENTORY NO.
KHALTSE / ALCHI / 19 / 2004

Temple | In Use | Public (Likir *Gonpa*) | Around 11th – 12th century

SETTING

The Sumtseg *lhakhang* is oriented to the south and is located within the Alchi *Choskhor* complex. It is the second building along the pathway. It is after the Kangyur *lhakhang*. There is a group of *chorten* opposite the temple. A pathway from the main village square leads to the complex.

SIGNIFICANCE

The Sumtseg *lhakhang* is the most famous of the group of temples within the *Choskhor* and indeed in the entire Western Himalayan region. The temple is associated with the great translator Lotsava Rinchen Zangpo and represents some of the earliest extant Buddhist art in the region. The colossal stucco images within the temple as well as the intricate paintings are believed to have been executed by Kashmiri artists and are stylistically distinct from later paintings in Ladakh. Alchi, along with Mangyu and Sumda Chhun which have contemporary temples again associated with the Lotsava, form part of a pilgrim circuit in Ladakh. Sumsteg, along with other temples within the complex, are under the purview of the Gelugpa sect in the 15th century and are today managed by Likir *Gonpa*.

DESCRIPTION

The Sumtseg is a three tiered temple with an entrance from the south. Preceding the entrance is a small porch which has ornamented timber columns and beams. These beams support another set of beams over which the second floor level rests. The ends of the floor beams are carved in the form of lion heads. The recess in between the two levels of beams is embellished with wood carvings depicting Buddhist deities framed within triangular frames and trifoliate arches. The Sumtseg is roughly square in plan with three alcoves each of which houses large stucco images of standing Bodhisattvas. The central niche contains the largest image which is that of the Chamba, the left hand side niche contains a large image of Chanrazig while the third niche contains an image of Jamyang. The *dhotis* of all three Bodhisattvas are richly painted with various themes. The walls of this temple are also painted with some of the most beautiful wall paintings in Ladakh depicting both religious and secular subjects. The upper floor is accessed through a stairway outside the temple made of a single log with grooves cut into it. The Sumtseg has a traditional wooden floor and ceiling. The ceiling is also decorated with painted motifs.

STATE OF PRESERVATION
Showing Signs of Deterioration

Alchi

31

SOURCE OF INFORMATION Ven. Lobzang Toldan, Likir *Gonpa*, Alchi, Khaltse, Ladakh

Alchi *Lonpo* House

INVENTORY NO.
KHALTSE / ALCHI / 20 / 2004

Vernacular Building | In Use | Private (Individual) | Around 300 - 400 years

SETTING
The Alchi *Lonpo* house is oriented to the east and is located along the village pathway which leads to the *Choskhor*. It is surrounded by several apricot trees.

SIGNIFICANCE
The *Lonpo* were traditionally the King's ministers and in the past resided in the large palace located on a hill in the village. The family abandoned the old palace and moved into this house some centuries ago. The family is one of the oldest in the village.

DESCRIPTION
The Alchi *Lonpo* house is a three storeyed structure which has been built in phases. The oldest section of the house is to the rear and has an elaborate wooden framed verandah facing west. The ground floor is used for storage and stabling animals. The entrance to the house is from the first floor through a flight of steps that opens onto a corridor. On either side of this corridor are the family's living rooms. To the left is the traditional family kitchen with the old stove and layout. To the right are other rooms including living rooms and guest rooms / store rooms. A wooden staircase leads onto an open court yard on the second floor. Rooms have been recently added at this level and have large window openings on the eastern facade. The third floor houses the family's chapel with an elaborately carved wooden doorway and two window openings on either side. There is an elaborate *rabsal* on the northern facade facing the footpath.

STATE OF PRESERVATION
Showing Signs of Deterioration

SOURCE OF INFORMATION Sonam Kunzom Dildispa, Alchi, Khaltse, Ladakh

Alchi

32

Group of *Chorten*

INVENTORY NO.
KHALTSE / ALCHI / 21 / 2004

Chorten | In Use | Public (Community)

SETTING
The *chorten* are located along the slope of a hill in the village. These *chorten* are above the Alchi Yul with village houses nearby.

SIGNIFICANCE
The group comprises of four *chorten*, three of which are grouped together in a line while the fourth is located slightly apart. All four are Changchub *chorten* which symbolize the Buddha's enlightenment.

DESCRIPTION
The site comprises of four *chorten* of which the first three are located side by side while the fourth is located in front of this group and stand apart. The *chorten* are of similar size and are built in stone masonry with mud mortar. The exterior surface is mud plastered and whitewashed.

STATE OF PRESERVATION
Advanced State of Decay

SOURCE OF INFORMATION Sonam Kunzom Dildispa, Alchi, Khaltse, Ladakh

Skumbum *Chorten*

INVENTORY NO.
KHALTSE / ALCHI / 22 / 2004

Chorten | In Use | Public (Community) | Around 12th century

SETTING
The Skumbum *chorten* is oriented to the south and is located beyond the agricultural fields on a stretch of land in Alchi village. From the main village square, a narrow path diverts and passes through narrow village paths and houses and across agricultural fields to the site.

SIGNIFICANCE
The *chorten* is believed to date back to the same period as the temples in Alchi *Choskhor*. It is built over what appears to be a *mandala* plan seen in other early period *chorten* in the region. It is believed that the *chorten* once housed images of deities which no longer survive.

DESCRIPTION
The Skumbum *chorten* is a large structure built over a *mandala* shaped plan with many right angled corners and tiers. It is built in random rubble masonry. Most of the *chorten* has collapsed and its exact form is no longer discernible. Debris from the *chorten* lies scattered around it. There are two completely ruined structures located towards the east of the *chorten*. These are rectangular structures of which only the walls survive upto the level of the plinth.

STATE OF PRESERVATION
Danger of Disappearance

SOURCE OF INFORMATION Sonam Kunzom Dildispa Alchi, Khaltse, Ladakh

Group of *Chorten* and *Lhakhang*

INVENTORY NO.
KHALTSE / ALCHI / 23 / 2004

Temple / *Chorten* | In Use | Public (Community) | 13th century

SETTING
The *lhakhang* and *chorten* are located on a small rocky mound amid agricultural fields in the Shangrong area of Alchi village. A narrow pathway from the market square leads to the site. The Marpopa's house lies to the north of the site.

SIGNIFICANCE
The temple and *chorten* are believed to date back to the same period as the temples within the Alchi *Choskhor*.

DESCRIPTION
The site consists of a cluster of a *lhakhang*, two large *chorten* and around a dozen smaller *chorten*. All are placed on a small hillock and are all lined up in a row. The *lhakhang* is a square structure without any window openings. The walls are mud plastered and whitewashed and taper towards the top. A small door on the eastern facade leads into the structure. It is a square space which houses various stucco images of deities. The walls are covered with early period paintings. There are a number of chorten of different sizes located near the *lhakhang*. The *chorten* have a square base and a square plinth with tiers tapering towards the top. There is a *srog-shing* projecting from the centre. The exterior of the structure is whitewashed.

STATE OF PRESERVATION
Advanced State of Decay

SOURCE OF INFORMATION Sonam Kunzom Dildispa, Alchi, Khaltse, Ladakh

Alchi

33

Chorten Marpo

INVENTORY NO.
KHALTSE / ALCHI / 24 / 2004

Chorten | In Use | Public (Community) | Around 600 - 700 years old

SETTING
The *Chorten* Marpo is located on a small rocky mound amid agricultural fields in the Shangrong area of Alchi village. A narrow pathway diverts from the market square (Alchi square) and leads to the site. The Marpopa house lies to the east of the *chorten* and there are apricot trees and agricultural fields nearby.

SIGNIFICANCE
The *Chorten* Marpo were built a little later than the *chorten* of Alchi *Choskhor*. They are circumambulated by villagers as an act of merit. The *chorten* are both Changchub *chorten* which symbolize the Buddha's enlightenment.

DESCRIPTION
The site comprises of two *chorten* both built on a square plan. The *chorten* are built in stone and mud brick masonry with mud mortar and are mud plastered and whitewashed externally. One of the *chorten* is built on a high platform of random rubble masonry. The base panels of both *chorten*

are embellished with motifs in stucco. One of them has human figures which are painted in red. The four panels beneath the dome of the *chorten* are also decorated with animal figures in stucco relief again painted in red. To the northwest of this *chorten* is a small *lubang*. The *lubang* is mud plastered and whitewashed on the exterior and has red markings near the top.

STATE OF PRESERVATION
Showing Signs of Deterioration

SOURCE OF INFORMATION Sonam Kunzom Dildispa, Alchi, Khaltse, Ladakh

---

Chotarpa *Lhato*

INVENTORY NO.
KHALTSE / ALCHI / 25 / 2004

Lhato | In Use | Public (Community) | Around 200 years old

SETTING
The Chotarpa *lhato* is oriented to the northeast and is built on a rocky mound in the Shangrong area of Alchi village. The *lhato* is located next to the Chotarpa house and has agricultural fields to the northeast.

SIGNIFICANCE
The Chotarpa *lhato* is dedicated to Chotar, the protector deity of the the hamlet. The contents of the *lhato* are renewed on the Tibetan new year by the villagers every year.

DESCRIPTION
The Chotarpa *lhato* is built on a square plan and rises up as a tall structure with ritual offerings placed on the top. It is built in stone masonry with mud mortar and is mud plastered on the exterior. The exterior is whitewashed has red marking on it. There is a small *lubang* with a large *tarchen* along the eastern side of the *lhato*.

STATE OF PRESERVATION
Fair

SOURCE OF INFORMATION Phuntsog Dolma, Choterpa, Alchi, Khaltse, Ladakh

Alchi

34

Skudung *Chorten* and *Mane* Wall

INVENTORY NO.
KHALTSE / ALCHI / 26 / 2004

Chorten / *Mane* Wall / *Tarchen* | In Use | Public (Community) | Around 100 - 125 years old

SETTING

The group of *chorten*, *mane* wall and *tarchen* are built along the slope of a hill near the Druggyasling *gonpa*. From the market square, a steep pathway diverts through fields and houses to the Shangrong area. The *chorten* and *mane* wall are located at the entrance to the Druggyasling *gonpa*. The main *gonpa* building lies to the southwest and a house lies to the south of the site.

SIGNIFICANCE

The *mane* wall, *chorten* and *tarchen* are located near the entrance to the *gonpa* and are circumambulated by villagers as they visit the *gonpa*. The *chorten* is a Changchub *chorten* which symbolizes the Buddha's enlightenment.

DESCRIPTION

The site comprises of a group of sacred elements – *mane* wall, *chorten* and a *tarchen*. The *mane* wall is circular in plan and continues further down to form a linear wall. It is built in dry stone masonry wall and has inscribed *mane* stones placed on the top. Next to the *mane* wall is a stone masonry platform over which stands a *chorten*. The *chorten* is built in stone and mud brick masonry and is mud plastered and whitewashed on the exterior. Each of the four panels at the base has animal and other motifs depicted in stucco relief which are painted in red. The *chorten* is surmounted by a tall *chugsum khorlo* over the dome. To the south of the *chorten* is a *tarchen* which consists of a square base over which is posted a long wooden pole with a prayer flag tied to it.

STATE OF PRESERVATION
Showing Signs of Deterioration

Alchi

35

SOURCE OF INFORMATION Sonam Kunzom-Dildispa and Tundup Spenba – Unglungapa, Alchi ,Khaltse, Ladakh

Druggyasling *Gonpa*

INVENTORY NO.
KHALTSE / ALCHI / 27 / 2004

Gonpa | In Use | Public (Chemday *Gonpa*) | Around 100 - 125 years old

SETTING
The Druggyasling *gonpa* is oriented to the west and is located on a hill in the Shangrong area of Alchi. From the market square, a steep pathway diverts through fields and houses and leads to the Shangrong area. The Druggyasling *gonpa* is surrounded by the Unglungapa house to the east and the village to the west.

SIGNIFICANCE
The Druggyasling *gonpa* falls under the purview of Chemday *gonpa* and monks from Chemday are deputed here to take care of the *gonpa* and carry out prayers and rituals. The *gonpa* is dedicated to Guru Rinpoche.

DESCRIPTION
The Druggyasling *gonpa* is a double storeyed structure built on a rectangular plan in stone and mud brick masonry. The exterior walls of the *gonpa* are mud plastered and whitewashed. An external flight of stairs leads to the first floor. Below this staircase is the main entrance to the ground floor. The *gonpa* has two *dukhang* housing images of Guru Rinpoche, Sendongma and Guru Takpo. The walls are adorned with paintings of various guardian deities. The first floor has large windows with wooden shutters and glass panes. The doors and windows are framed with black borders and have decorated tiered wooden lintels. Galvanized iron sheets are placed over the traditional roof and the parapets are built over the sheets. The parapets are whitewashed in red and prayer flags are posted on the roof top. The right side of the building has two *dukhang* and the left side has the living quarters of the caretaker monks. The corridor has a skylight and the walls are covered with paintings of the four guardian deities.

STATE OF PRESERVATION
Fair

Alchi

36

Labrang

INVENTORY NO.
KHALTSE / ALCHI / 28 / 2004

Vernacular Building | In Use | Public (Chemday *Gonpa*)

SETTING
The *labrang* is oriented to the south and is in the Shangrong area of Alchi. From the main market square, a steep pathway diverts through fields and houses to the Shangrong area. The *labrang* is surrounded by agricultural fields and the village stream flows behind it. There are apricot trees on either side of the building.

SIGNIFICANCE
The *labrang* was traditionally used by monks from Chemday *gonpa* who were deputed to the village to administer lands owned by the *gonpa* in Alchi. It is built in the traditional style and is an example of vernacular architecture in the village.

DESCRIPTION
The *labrang* is a double storeyed building with a terrace in the centre of the second floor. The building is entered from a porch on the ground floor. To the left of the entrance is the kitchen. The ground floor is built in stone masonry and has small openings. The first floor is built in mud brick masonry and has larger windows. This level also houses the monks' rooms. To the rear of the building is a prayer room which has a small skylight. The building has a traditional roof on which are placed are prayer flags.

STATE OF PRESERVATION
Showing Signs of Deterioration

SOURCE OF INFORMATION Sonam Kunzom-Dildispa and Tundup Spenba – Unglungapa, Alchi ,Khaltse, Ladakh

Alchi

37

Bongrapa House

INVENTORY NO.
KHALTSE / ALCHI / 29 / 2004

Vernacular Building | In Use | Private (Individual) | Around 80 years old

SETTING
The Bongrapa house is oriented to the east and is located in the Shangrong area of Alchi. It is surrounded by agricultural fields in the front while the village street runs to the rear of the house.

SIGNIFICANCE
The Bongrapa house was built by the grandfather of the present owner. It is built using traditional materials and techniques and is a good example of vernacular architecture in the village.

DESCRIPTION
The Bongrapa house is a three storeyed house with a terrace abutting a room on the second floor. The house is entered at the level of the first floor through a flight of steps. A wooden doorway leads to a corridor which is flanked by the family kitchen and living rooms. The second floor comprises of a single room which is the family temple. The ground floor is used for stabling animals and for storage. These rooms are of a low height with small window openings. The first and second floor windows are larger and have timber frames and lintels. There is a large tarchen in front of the house. The ground floor is built in stone masonry while the upper two floors are built in mud brick masonry. The walls are mud plastered and whitewashed.

STATE OF PRESERVATION
Showing Signs of Deterioration

SOURCE OF INFORMATION Tundup Wangchuk – Bongrapa, Alchi, Khaltse, Ladakh

Chorten and Old *Lhakhang*

INVENTORY NO.
KHALTSE / ALCHI / 30 / 2004

Chorten / Temple | Abandoned | Public (Community)

SETTING
The *chorten* and the old *lhakhang* are located in the Shangrong area of Alchi. The *chorten* is built on a hill just above the Yul Alchi.

SIGNIFICANCE
The *lhakhang* is believed to be as old as the temples in the Alchi *Choskhor* (11th - 12th century). However, there is no evidence of this and it appears to be a later period construction.

DESCRIPTION
The site comprises of a large square *chorten*, one ruined *chorten* and the ruins of a square *lhakhang*. The large *chorten* is built in stone and mud brick masonry and is mud plastered and whitewashed externally. The smaller *chorten* is in complete ruins and it is difficult to discern its form. The *lhakhang* too is in ruins and only some walls survive.

These are built in stone masonry at the lower level and in mud brick masonry at the upper levels. There are traces of the external mud plaster and whitewash on the walls.

STATE OF PRESERVATION
Danger of Disappearance

SOURCE OF INFORMATION Tsewang Dolma, Alchi, Khaltse, Ladakh

Alchi

38

Orkorpa *Chorten*

INVENTORY NO.
KHALTSE / ALCHI / 31 / 2004

Chorten | In Use | Private (Individual) | Around 100 - 110 years old

SETTING
The *chorten* are located in the Shangrong area of Alchi village. The *chorten* are located near the Orkorpa house – one near the entrance door while the second is located in the front of the house in the garden compound.

SIGNIFICANCE
The *chorten* were built by the ancestors of the Orkorpa family a century ago. One *chorten* is a Namgyal *chorten* which symbolizes the Buddha's victory over illness. The other *chorten* is a Changchub *chorten* which symbolizes the Buddha's enlightenment. Located at the entrance to the house, the *chorten* are circumambulated to gather merit in this lifetime.

DESCRIPTION
There are two *chorten* at the entrance to the house. The first is oriented to the west and is in complete ruins. All that survives is a small wall near the *chorten*. The second *chorten* is a Namgyal *chorten* and is in a better condition. It shares a common platform. The other *chorten* is built in the compound in front of the house and is a Changchub *chorten* built on a large square plinth. The *chorten* is built in stone and mud brick masonry and is mud plastered and whitewashed on the exterior.

STATE OF PRESERVATION
Advanced State of Decay

SOURCE OF INFORMATION Tsewang Dolma- Orkorpa, Alchi, Khaltse, Ladakh

Chorten and *Lubang* (Skubar *Chorten*)

INVENTORY NO.
KHALTSE / ALCHI / 32 / 2004

Chorten / Lubang | In Use | Community | Around 250 - 300 years old

SETTING
The *chorten* and *lubang* are located in the Shangrong area of Alchi village. They are built on a rocky outcrop above the Dorjepa and Kharmadpa houses. To the east, lies the village road.

SIGNIFICANCE
The *chorten* and *lubang* were built about five generations ago. The *chorten* is a Changchub *chorten* which symbolizes the Buddha's enlightenment. The *lubang* is dedicated to the *lu*, or serpent deities of the underworld.

DESCRIPTION
The site comprises of a small *chorten* and a *lubang* built on a rocky outcrop. The *chorten* is built in stone and mud brick

masonry. The *lubang* is a small cubical structure built in stone masonry. Both structures are mud plastered and whitewashed on the exterior.

STATE OF PRESERVATION
Showing Signs of Deterioration

SOURCE OF INFORMATION Morup Dorjey, Alchi, Khaltse, Ladakh

Alchi

39

Group of *Chorten*

INVENTORY NO.
KHALTSE / ALCHI / 33 / 2004

Chorten | In Use | Public (Community)

SETTING
The *chorten* are located on a rocky mound in the Shangrong area of Alchi village. The site is above the settlement and is surrounded by barren rocky land.

SIGNIFICANCE
The *chorten* were built in the past for the well being of all sentient beings. These are Changchub *chorten* which symbolize the Buddha's enlightenment. These are circumambulated by the villagers as an act of merit.

DESCRIPTION
The site comprises of a group of six *chorten* of similar size. The first two are placed on a common stone plinth while three other *chorten* are located some distance away on another common plinth. The last one is in ruins. The *chorten* are all built in stone and mud brick masonry and are mud plastered and whitewashed externally.

STATE OF PRESERVATION
Advanced State of Decay

SOURCE OF INFORMATION Morup Dorjey, Alchi, Khaltse, Ladakh

Chorten and Lubang

INVENTORY NO.
KHALTSE / ALCHI / 34 / 2004

Chorten / Lubang | In Use | Public (Community)

SETTING
The *chorten* and *lubang* are located in the Yul area of Alchi village. They are built on the left side of the link road in front of Zopa Khangbu.

SIGNIFICANCE
The *chorten* was built in the past for the well being of all sentient beings. Located along the link road, it is circumambulated by villagers as an act of merit. The *chorten* is a Changchub *chorten* which symbolizes the Buddha's enlightenment. The *lubang* marks the residence of the *lu,* or serpent deities of the underworld.

DESCRIPTION
The site comprises of a *chorten* and a *lubang*. The *chorten* is built on an elevated plinth in stone and mud brick masonry and is mud plastered and whitewashed externally. There is a banner on the top of the *chorten*. The panels at

the base of the *chorten* are decorated in stucco relief. The *lubang*, located near the *chorten*, is built in stone and mud brick masonry and is mud plastered and whitewashed externally. There is a small niche on the eastern facade of the *lubang*.

STATE OF PRESERVATION
Advanced State of Decay

SOURCE OF INFORMATION Sonam Dorjey Spon, Alchi, Khaltse, Ladakh

Rigsum Gonbo (Zimskhang) and Lhato

INVENTORY NO.
KHALTSE / ALCHI / 35 / 2004

Rigsum Gonbo / Lhato | In Use | Private (Individual) | Around 300 - 400 years old

SETTING
The *rigsum gonbo* and *lhato* are oriented to the east and are located behind the Zimskhang palace. After entering the village, a footpath diverts from the left of the road and leads to the Zimskhang. The structures are located on a rocky outcrop between the village and the River Indus.

SIGNIFICANCE
The *rigsum gonbo* is part of the Zimskhang complex - the earliest palace of the Lonpo family. It was built by one of the ancestors of the Lonpo family in order to protect the family and the village from evil. The *lhato* was built as an altar for the protector deity of the Zimskhang.

DESCRIPTION
The site consists of a *rigsum gonbo* with a *lhato*. The *lhato*

has an opening in the front through which ritual offerings are placed inside. It is built in mud brick masonry and has a traditional roof of willow twigs, grass and mud plaster. The *rigsum gonbo* is a rectangular structure with a platform within on which are placed three chorten. The base has been built in stone masonry while the walls are in mud brick masonry. It is covered by the traditional roof comprising of willow twigs, grass and mud. The walls and roof of the *rigsum gonbo* have collapsed in some sections.

STATE OF PRESERVATION
Danger of Disappearance

SOURCE OF INFORMATION Sonam Kunzom Dildispa, Alchi, Khaltse, Ladakh

Banka *Chorten* Area

INVENTORY NO.
KHALTSE / ALCHI / 36 / 2004

Chorten / Rock Carving / Precinct | In Use | Public (Community) | Around 700 - 800 years old

SETTING
The Banka area is located near the Zimskhang and the Sponpa house. After entering the village, a footpath turns left from the road and leads towards the Zimskhang.

SIGNIFICANCE
The Banka area has served as the community's gathering space for several centuries. The grounds contain a *chorten*, a prayer wheel and a *dosku*. The *chorten* appears to be a Changchub *chorten* which symbolizes the Buddha's enlightenment. Villagers circumambulate the *chorten* as an act of merit. The prayer wheel is similarly rotated by villagers as they circumambulate the *chorten* as an act of merit.

DESCRIPTION
The Banka area is a large open space with a *chorten*, a prayer wheel and a *dosku*. The *chorten* is built in stone masonry and is mud plastered and whitewashed on the exterior. There is a small niche on the eastern side of the dome which may have housed the image of a deity that no longer exists. In front of the *chorten,* there is a small structure with an opening within which is a prayer wheel. On the right, there is a large stone with an engraving of a deity that is now obliterated and can no longer be identified.

STATE OF PRESERVATION
Advanced State of Decay

Alchi

41

SOURCE OF INFORMATION Sonam Dorjey Spon, Alchi, Khaltse, Ladakh

Tseblhamo *Lhato* and *Lubang*

INVENTORY NO.
KHALTSE / ALCHI / 37 / 2004

Lhato / Lubang | In Use | Public (Community) | Around 400 years old

SETTING
The Tseblhamo *lhato* and *lubang* are oriented to the east and are located on a rocky outcrop south of the Zimskhang palace and above the old Kharmadpa house. From the Banka area, a path leads to the Kharmadpa house from where a steep climb leads to the site.

SIGNIFICANCE
The *lhato* is dedicated to the protector deity Tseb Lha Gyalmo and is believed to be around 400 years old. It is maintained by the Thangpa and Tongspon families. The contents of the *lhato* are renewed during the Ladakhi New Year on the 1st day of the 1st month of the Tibetan calendar. The lubang are dedicated to the *lu* - the serpent deities of the underworld. Monks from Ridzong *gonpa* perform ritual prayers at this site.

DESCRIPTION
The site consists of a group of five *lubang* and a *lhato*. The *lhato* is a tall structure with an opening on one side which is built in stone and mud brick masonry and whitewashed on the exterior. The *lhato* contain ritual offerings of juniper branches, *khadag* and animal horns. To the east of the *lhato* are a group of five *lubang* which are built in stone masonry and are whitewashed externally.

STATE OF PRESERVATION
Advanced State of Decay

SOURCE OF INFORMATION Sonam Dorjey - Spon, Alchi, Khaltse, Ladakh

---

Kharmadpa Old House

INVENTORY NO.
KHALTSE / ALCHI / 38 / 2004

Vernacular Building | Abandoned | Private (Individual) | Around 300 years old

SETTING
The Kharmadpa house is oriented to the south and is located along the slope of a mountain near the Zimskhang complex. From the village road, a footpath diverts to the left which leads onto the Zimskhang and the Banka area. The Kharmadpa house is located along this path. To the north of the house are the Tseblamo *lhato* and *lubang* while other old houses are located to the south.

SIGNIFICANCE
The Kharmadpa house is one of the oldest houses in the village and is believed to have been built some 300 years ago by the ancestors of the present owners. The house is built in the traditional style and is a good example of vernacular architecture in the village.

DESCRIPTION
The Kharmadpa house is a four storeyed structure with an entrance through a small wooden opening on the first floor. This is due to the topography of the site. A steep wooden staircase leads to the second floor which was the living areas of the family and included the kitchen and living room. The third floor is in ruins. The remains of the family temple can still be seen and there are traces of wall paintings on the walls of the temples. There is a small terrace outside the temple room on the second floor, with a rammed earth parapet. Most of the timber members in the house have been removed and used in the construction of the family's new house nearby.

STATE OF PRESERVATION
Advanced State of Decay

SOURCE OF INFORMATION Sonam Dorjey Spon, Alchi, Khaltse, Ladakh

Alchi Lonpo Zimskhang

INVENTORY NO.
KHALTSE / ALCHI / 39 / 2004

Vernacular Building | In Use | Private (Individual) | Around 300 - 400 years old

SETTING
The Alchi Lonpo Zimskhang house is oriented to the west and faces the main village road. From the main road, a path diverts to the left and leads to the Zimskhang. There is a *lhato* and *lubang* to the east and another *lhato* and *rigsum gonbo* to the north.

SIGNIFICANCE
The Alchi Lonpo was the minister to the King and the family of the lonpo is one of the oldest in the village. The house is believed to have been built 3 or 4 centuries ago but was later abandoned with the family moving into a new house in the village. The house is an impressive structure built in the traditional style and a good example of traditional architecture of the village.

DESCRIPTION
The Alchi Lonpo Zimskhang house is a large four storeyed house built along the slope of a mountain. The house is built in stone masonry at the lower level and in mud brick masonry at the upper levels. The ground and first floor were used for storage and for housing animals. These levels have narrow windows for ventilation. The second floor housed the family's living quarters and has a large *rabsal*. The uppermost levels have open terraces and partially covered verandahs. The family temple is on the topmost floor and consists of two chambers. One of these houses images of Tsongkhupa, Chanrazig, Chamba, Shakyamuni and Chagdor. A number of *thangka* hang from the walls and the ceiling.

STATE OF PRESERVATION
Advanced State of Decay

Alchi

43

SOURCE OF INFORMATION Sonam Dorjey Spon, Alchi, Khaltse, Ladakh

Group of *Chorten* and *Mane* Walls

INVENTORY NO.
KHALTSE / ALCHI / 40 / 2004

Chorten / Mane Wall | In Use | Public (Community) | Around 800 years old

SETTING
The *chorten* and *mane* walls are located near the Zopapa house on the left side of the road leading to Alchi.

SIGNIFICANCE
The *chorten* and *mane* walls are located along the road leading to the village and are circumambulated by villagers as an act of merit. The chorten are largely Changchub *chorten* which symbolize the Buddha's enlightenment.

DESCRIPTION
The site comprises of almost two dozen *chorten* and three *mane* walls in a single row parallel to the main village road. Most of the *chorten* have lost their original form though some Changchub *chorten* can be identified. The *chorten* are all built in stone and mud brick masonry and are mud plastered and whitewashed on the exterior. The *chorten* near the school has been recently repaired and it has

colorful decorative motifs on the side panels of the base and near the dome. This *chorten* is also surmounted by a tall *chugsum khorlo* painted in red and topped with a metal crescent. The *mane* walls are located between the *chorten* and are both circular and linear walls built in stone masonry.

STATE OF PRESERVATION
Advanced State of Decay

SOURCE OF INFORMATION Sonam Dorjey -Spon, Alchi, Khaltse, Ladakh

---

Spurkhang

INVENTORY NO.
KHALTSE / ALCHI / 41 / 2004

Cremation Ground | In Use | Public (Community) | Around 300 years old

SETTING
The *spurkhang* is located before the village on the road from Saspol to Alchi on a rocky mountainside. The village school and road lie to the south of the site.

SIGNIFICANCE
The ground contains *spurkhang* traditionally used by each family for cremating the dead. Each family has one unit which is repaired and reused on the death of a family member.

STATE OF PRESERVATION
Advanced State of Decay

DESCRIPTION
The area comprises of a number of *spurkhang* and one *chorten*. The *spurkhang* are small cubical structures built in stone and mud brick masonry and covered with willow twigs. The older units are whitewashed on the exterior while newer units have some decorative motifs painted around them. The *chorten* is a Changchub *chorten* and is built in stone and mud brick masonry. The exterior surface of the *chorten* is mud plastered and whitewashed.

SOURCE OF INFORMATION Sonam Dorjey -Spon, Alchi, Khaltse, Ladakh

Alchi

44

Group of Chorten and *Mane* Walls

INVENTORY NO.
KHALTSE / ALCHI / 42 / 2004

Chorten / Mane Wall / *Rigsum Gonbo* | In Use | Public (Community) |
Around 300 years old

SETTING
The *chorten* and *mane* wall are located along the road leading to the village near the Government Middle School.

SIGNIFICANCE
The *chorten* and *mane* wall are believed to have been built 300 years ago at the same time as the Zimskhang palace. Located along the road leading to the village, the structures are circumambulated by villagers as an act of merit. A *rigsum gonbo* is built to protect the village from evil forces.

DESCRIPTION
The site comprises of a number of *chorten* and *mane* walls. The smaller *chorten* are arranged in groups each placed on a common stone plinth. Most of these have lost their original form and cannot be identified. The *chorten* all appear to be built in stone and mud brick masonry and are mud plastered and whitewashed externally. The *mane* walls are linear stone walls with *mane* stones placed on the horizontal surface. There are two Kagan *chorten* on either end of the group. These are built in stone and mud brick masonry and are mud plastered and whitewashed externally. The timber ceilings over the passages of the Kagan *chorten* are built in the shape of a *mandala*. Near the Kagan *chorten*, there is a *rigsum gonbo*. This is a rectangular shaped building with walls on three sides while the fourth side is open. Within this enclosure are three small *chorten*, painted in orange, white and blue, built over a high platform. The enclosure is built in stone and mud brick masonry and is mud plastered and whitewashed externally. Timber columns and brackets within the enclosure support the roof above.

STATE OF PRESERVATION
Advance State of Decay

Alchi

45

SOURCE OF INFORMATION Sonam Dorjey -Spon, Alchi, Khaltse, Ladakh

Thangpa Khangbu
Chorten

INVENTORY NO.
KHALTSE / ALCHI / 43 / 2004

Chorten | In Use | Public (Community)

SETTING
The Thangpa Khangbu *chorten* is located before the settlement of Alchi village. Before reaching the village, a steep pathway descends from the main road towards the *chorten*. There are agricultural fields near the *chorten* which is located in front of the Thangpa Khangbu house.

SIGNIFICANCE
The Thangpa Khangbu *chorten* was built by a village ancestor for the well being of all sentient beings. It is a Changchub *chorten* which symbolizes the Buddha's enlightenment. The *chorten* is circumambulated by villagers as an act of merit.

DESCRIPTION
The Thangpa Khangbu *chorten* is a built on a square base of random rubble masonry. The *chorten* is built in stone and

mud brick masonry with mud mortar and is mud plastered and whitewashed externally.

STATE OF PRESERVATION
Showing Signs of Deterioration

SOURCE OF INFORMATION Sonam Dorjey -Spon, Alchi, Khaltse, Ladakh

Chorten

INVENTORY NO.
KHALTSE / ALCHI / 44 / 2004

Chorten | In Use | Public (Community) | Around 400 years old

SETTING
The *chorten* is built on a small rocky outcrop on the left of the vehicular road which leads to Alchi. It is surrounded by barren mountains on all sides.

SIGNIFICANCE
The *chorten* was built in the past act of merit. It is a Changchub *chorten* which symbolizes the Buddha's enlightenment. It is circumambulated by villagers as an act of merit.

STATE OF PRESERVATION
Showing Signs of Deterioration

DESCRIPTION
The *chorten* is built on a high random rubble masonry platform. It is constructed in stone and mud brick masonry. The exterior surface is mud plastered and whitewashed. There is a small niche on the southwestern panel.

SOURCE OF INFORMATION Sonam Dorjey -Spon, Alchi, Khaltse, Ladakh

Group of *Chorten* and *Mane* Walls

INVENTORY NO.
KHALTSE / ALCHI / 45 / 2004

Chorten / *Mane* Wall | In Use | Community | Around 300 - 350 years old

SETTING
The *chorten* and *mane* wall are located along the road leading to Alchi village. These lie along the road with the mountainside beyond.

SIGNIFICANCE
The *chorten* and *mane* walls are located before the entrance to the village and can therefore be circumambulated by villagers as an act of merit. The *chorten* are predominantly Changchub *chorten* symbolizing the Buddha's enlightenment.

DESCRIPTION
The site comprises of a group of *chorten* and *mane* walls arranged alternately in a single row. Some of the *chorten* have lost their original form and are difficult to identify. However, some can be identified as Changchub *chorten*, built in stone and mud brick masonry. The exterior surfaces

of the *chorten* are mud plastered and whitewashed. The *mane* walls are linear stone walls with *mane* stones placed on the horizontal surface.

STATE OF PRESERVATION
Danger of Disappearance

SOURCE OF INFORMATION Sonam Dorjey -Spon, Alchi, Khaltse, Ladakh

Alchi

47

Petroglyphs

INVENTORY NO.
KHALTSE / ALCHI / 46 / 2006

Rock Carvings | Abandoned | Public (State)

SETTING
The petroglyphs are located along a barren stretch of land along the main vehicular road leading to Alchi.

SIGNIFICANCE
The petroglyphs are some of the earliest evidence of human habitation in Ladakh. These depict early representations of animal and human figures as well as later depictions of *chorten* and other symbols.

DESCRIPTION
The petroglyphs are scattered over a wide area of barren land all along the road leading to Alchi. They are pecked onto boulders and depict both animal and human figures, symbols such as the inverted swastika as well as later depictions of *chorten*.

STATE OF PRESERVATION
Danger of Disappearance

SOURCE OF INFORMATION Sonam Dorjey -Spon, Alchi, Khaltse, Ladakh

Chorten and *Mane* Wall

INVENTORY NO.
KHALTSE / ATITSE / 01 / 2004

Chorten / Mane Wall */ Lubang* | In Use | Public (Community) | Around 220 years old

SETTING
The group of *chorten*, *mane* wall and *lubang* are located on a small mound near the agricultural fields. The village *gonpa* lies to the north of the site.

SIGNIFICANCE
The group of structures are located near the agricultural fields and were built in the past for the well being and prosperity of the village. The site is still circumambulated by villagers as an act of merit. The *chorten* is a Changchub *chorten*, symbolizing the Buddha's enlightenment. The *lubang* marks the residence of the *lu,* or the serpent gods. Prayers and offerings are made at the *lubang* on a fixed date in spring, known as *Lu thebs*, by the monks to placate the *lu*. The prayers are offered to seek good supply of water before the cultivation of fields in spring and offerings made to the *lu* are then immersed in water.

DESCRIPTION
The site comprises of a Changchub *chorten*, a *lubang* and a *mane* wall. The *chorten* is housed in an enclosure with an opening on the east. The enclosure has thick walls and a traditional roof above made of *taalu*, grass and compacted mud. Inside the enclosure, the *chorten* is built in stone and mud brick masonry with mud mortar and is mud plastered on the exterior. A small *lubang* is located against the east wall of the enclosure. The *lubang* is built in mud brick masonry and is mud plastered and whitewashed on the exterior. There is a small opening on the northern face of the *lubang*. The *mane* wall is a large stone wall built on a rectangular plan without the use of any mortar. Flat *mane* stones are placed on the horizontal surface of the wall.

STATE OF PRESERVATION
Advanced State of Decay

Atitse

48

Gonpa

INVENTORY NO.
KHALTSE / ATITSE / 02 / 2004

Gonpa | In Use | Public (Lamayuru *Gonpa*)

SETTING
The *gonpa* is oriented to the south and is located on a small mound near agricultural fields. There are groves of trees nearby.

SIGNIFICANCE
The *gonpa* is believed to have been built before the Yungdrug Tharpaling *gonpa* in Lamayuru. According to legend, during the Dogra war in the 19th century, an old woman prayed to the image of Chagdor who spoke and told her to take the image to Atitse and place it in the *gonpa*. This image can still be seen inside the *gonpa*. The *gonpa*, today, belongs to the Drigung pa sect and monks from Lamayuru reside here and conduct prayers and rituals for the village.

DESCRIPTION
The *gonpa* is a large two storeyed structure with an entrance through a flight of stairs on the southern facade. The stairs lead onto a courtyard from where a doorway provides access to the old *dukhang*. The *dukhang* has images of a thousand Dolma. From the courtyard, another doorway leads onto a smaller courtyard around which are two temples. The walls of the courtyard have elaborate wall paintings depicting religious symbols and motifs. The temple houses a large image of Gyalwa Chamba. The window openings and shutters are also finely painted. The second temple houses images of several Bodhisattvas as well as an image of the protector deity which is the central image. Dark narrow steps lead down into a single room shrine housing an unusual standing image of a bearded Naropa with elaborate ornamentations indicating the influence of a Kashmiri art tradition. The *gonpa* is built in stone and mud brick masonry with mud mortar. The exterior walls are mud plastered and whitewashed. The building has a traditional roof with a red bordered parapet running along the edge. The windows have timber frames.

STATE OF PRESERVATION
Showing Signs of Deterioration

Atitse

49

Chorten and *Mane* Wall

Chorten / Mane Wall | In Use | Public (Community) | Around 300 years old

SETTING
The *chorten* and *mane* wall are located on a mound near the agricultural fields. Some willow trees grow nearby.

SIGNIFICANCE
The *chorten* and *mane* wall were built around 300 years ago for the well being of the village and are circumambulated by villagers as an act of merit. The *chorten* is Changchub *chorten* that symbolizes the Buddha's enlightenment.

DESCRIPTION
The *chorten* is built over a square plan in stone and mud brick masonry with mud mortar. It has an external layer of mud plaster and whitewash. There is a tall *chugsum khorlo* over the dome. There are large flat inscribed stones placed against the tiers of the *chorten*. The *mane* wall located near the *chorten*, is built in dry stone masonry and is rectangular in shape with *mane* stones placed on the horizontal surface. There is a small circumambulatory path around the structures.

STATE OF PRESERVATION
Advanced State of Decay

Atitse

50

Baima

The village of Baima is situated at a distance of about 180 kms from Leh on the right bank of the Indus river. From the Khaltse bridge, a diversion to the right leads on to Baima. The village is one of the few Dard villages in Ladakh. The inhabitants of Baima are a distinct ethnic group who are believed to have migrated from the Gilgit area many centuries ago. Baima actually means the '*land of sand*', as the village is situated in a sandy area. There are about 60 households living in this village.

Listed by: Deldan Angmo and Jassu Singh
Year: 2004, 2007

Baldesh

The village of Baldesh is situated at a distance of about 180 kms from Leh on the left bank of the Indus river. There is a hanging bridge made of rope which was used to cross the river. The name of the village derives from the Dard word for '*difficult*' as it was difficult to reach the village in the old days. Baldesh is a Dard village and its inhabitants are believed to have migrated many centuries ago from the Gilgit area. Today, there are about 30-35 households in the village.

Listed by: Deldan Angmo and Jassu Singh
Year: 2004

Chamakpa House

INVENTORY NO.
KHALTSE / BAIMA / 01 / 2004

Vernacular Building | Abandoned | Private (Individual) | About 100 years old

SETTING
The Chamakpa house is oriented to the south and is surrounded by agricultural fields. An old willow tree grows near the house and a stream runs in front. The new Chamakpa house is located nearby.

SIGNIFICANCE
The house is a good example of traditional vernacular architecture. It was built by the grandfather of the present owner around 100 years ago. The family has moved into a new house built nearby and this house is now used for storing fodder etc.

DESCRIPTION
The structure is located right above the new Chamakpa house. The building is built along a slope. The ground floor has living rooms which were used during winter while the rooms of the upper floors were used during the summer months. The ground floor does not have of any openings and is accessed through a wooden door towards the west. Entry to the upper level is through a separate door on the upper level. There are many rooms adjacent to the main one and accessed from different doorways. These rooms are built at various levels and reached by stone steps. The upper floors have small openings. The house is built in the traditional materials of stone masonry in the lower levels and mud brick masonry with mud mortar on the upper levels. It has a traditional roof consisting of wooden joists, willow twigs (*taalu*), local grass and a layer of compacted mud.

STATE OF PRESERVATION
Advanced State of Decay

SOURCE OF INFORMATION Nima Tsering, Chamakpa, Baima, Khaltse, Ladakh

Malchang Tree

INVENTORY NO.
KHALTSE / BAIMA / 02 / 2004

Landscape (Sacred Tree) | In Use | Public (Community)

SETTING
The Malchang tree is located near the entrance to the village. It is approached through terraced agricultural fields and is surrounded by village houses, the nearest being the Chamakpa house. A stream flows nearby.

SIGNIFICANCE / ASSOCIATED BELIEFS
It is one of the oldest trees in the village and the area around it is used by the villagers as a gathering space.

DESCRIPTION
The tree is a large willow tree believed to be about 250 years old. It has a large trunk with a diameter of about 13 feet near the ground.

CULTURAL LINKAGES / CULTURAL PRACTICES
The space near the Malchang tree is used as a community gathering space.

STATE OF PRESERVATION
Good

SOURCE OF INFORMATION Nima Tsering, Baima, Khaltse, Ladakh

Sharstepa

INVENTORY NO.
KHALTSE / BAIMA / 03 / 2004

Vernacular Building | In Use | Private (Individual) | Around 200 years old

SETTING
Sharstepa, or fodder storage structure, is oriented to the south and can be approached through a steep walk of about 500 metres up from the village. It is surrounded by village houses and agricultural fields.

SIGNIFICANCE
The building has been used as a storage shed for almost a century. Cattle fodder is stored within.

DESCRIPTION
The storage sheds are a series of single storeyed structures lining a steep pathway which leads further up to the village. Built in random rubble with no mud mortar or plaster, the sheds have traditional roofs above.

STATE OF PRESERVATION
Advanced State of Decay

SOURCE OF INFORMATION Norzom Dolma, Baima, Khaltse, Ladakh

Baima

55

Logbupa House

INVENTORY NO.
KHALTSE / BAIMA / 04 / 2004

Vernacular Building | In Use | Private (Individual) | Around 100 years old

SETTING
The house is oriented to the south and is located along the slope of a hill near the Miksukpa house. It is surrounded by agricultural fields and a stream flows towards the south.

STATE OF PRESERVATION
Advanced State of Decay

SIGNIFICANCE
The house was part of the old settlement and was built when the village was first settled about 100 years ago.

DESCRIPTION
The Logbupa house is a large structure built on a random plan. The residential area is spread over two floors. There are no window openings on the ground floor. The first floor has some windows. There are small, low height doorways on the first floor. The section towards the east is used for housing animals and is built in three levels each of which is of low height. The house is built in random rubble masonry and has a traditional roof which is still extant in some sections.

SOURCE OF INFORMATION Padma Tsomo, Migsugpa, Baima, Khaltse, Ladakh

Migsugpa House

INVENTORY NO.
KHALTSE / BAIMA / 05 / 2004

Vernacular Building | In Use | Private (Individual) | 100 years old

SETTING
The Migsugpa house is oriented to the south. A steep climb from the village leads to the house. It is surrounded by other residences and there are walnut orchards and agricultural fields to the south.

SIGNIFICANCE
The Migsugpa house is one of the older residences of the village and an example of vernacular architecture. It was built by Gang Tsering, an ancestor of the Migsugpa family about a century ago.

DESCRIPTION
The Migsugpa house is a large three storeyed structure. The main entrance is on the middle floor. The openings of the house on the ground floor are small with undecorated timber frames while the upper floors have larger openings. The ground floor is made in random rubble masonry and the upper floors are built in mud brick masonry. The structure is covered with a flat traditional roof comprising of *taalu*, dried grass and a layer of mud. The external mud plaster has largely eroded.

STATE OF PRESERVATION
Advanced State of Decay

SOURCE OF INFORMATION Padma Tsomo, Migsugpa, Baima, Khaltse, Ladakh

Baima

56

Mane Wall

INVENTORY NO.
KHALTSE / BAIMA / 06 / 2004

Mane Wall | In Use | Public (Community) | Around 400 years old

SETTING
The *mane* wall is oriented to the south and is located along the route leading from Baima to Hanu, about three kms from Hanu. It is built along the slope of a mountain, north of the road and is surrounded by boulders.

SIGNIFICANCE
The *mane* wall is located along the path leading from Baima to Hanu and is circumambulated by passers-by to gain merit. This *mane* wall is believed to have been built during the same period as the *gonpa* at Dha which is about 400 years old.

STATE OF PRESERVATION
Danger of Disappearance

DESCRIPTION
The *mane* wall is a long linear structure and is built along the slope of a mountain. It is built in dry stone masonry and has inscribed *mane* stones placed on the top. These stones are scattered all over the site and the *mane* wall itself is difficult to identify from the road below.

SOURCE OF INFORMATION Phuntsog Dorjey, Serkyangpa, Baima, Khaltse, Ladakh

Phrogpa House

INVENTORY NO.
KHALTSE / BAIMA / 07 / 2004

Vernacular Building | Abandoned | Private (Individual) | Around 120 years old

SETTING
The Phrogpa house is oriented to the south and is surrounded by other residences and an open community space in front.

SIGNIFICANCE
The Phrogpa house is an example of traditional vernacular architecture and is among the oldest houses in the village. It is around 120 years old. The family has moved to a new house and this house is now being used for storing fodder and housing animals.

DESCRIPTION
The Phrogpa house is a double storeyed structure built completely in stone masonry. The entrance was originally from the lower level. The house lies in ruins today as the family has moved out of the house. Large sections of the house have caved in. Openings in the form of small doors with timber frames still exist. Remains of a traditional roof can still be seen.

SOURCE OF INFORMATION Tsering Gangzom, Phrogpa, Baima, Khaltse, Ladakh

STATE OF PRESERVATION
Danger of Disappearance

Street (Next to Serkyangpa)

INVENTORY NO.
KHALTSE / BAIMA / 08 / 2004

Precinct | In Use | Public (Community)

SETTING
The street is located amidst agricultural fields and orchards and is flanked by village houses and old trees. A stream flows alongside the street.

SIGNIFICANCE
It is one of the oldest streets in the village and many old residences line the street. It, thus, presents a good example of vernacular architecture.

DESCRIPTION
The street is a rammed earth and stone cobbled pedestrian pathway about two to three metres wide. It widens in front of the houses forming their spill-over areas. The Serkyangpa house marks the end of the street.

STATE OF PRESERVATION
Good

SOURCE OF INFORMATION Tsamsthan Dolma, Baima, Khaltse, Ladakh

Baima

57

Community Space

INVENTORY NO.
KHALTSE / BAIMA / 09 / 2004

Community Space | In Use | Public (Community)

SETTING
The space is located amidst agricultural fields and orchards on the south and southeast, while village houses lie on the other sides.

SIGNIFICANCE
The community space is used to hold village functions and forms one of the oldest areas in the village. Villagers gather here for community functions.

DESCRIPTION
The community space is a terraced area of hillside with various levels dropping down towards the village houses. The levels have been edged by stone retaining walls.

STATE OF PRESERVATION
Good

SOURCE OF INFORMATION Samsthan Dolma, Baima, Khaltse, Ladakh

Gesar's Drum (Gesar-re-Daman)

INVENTORY NO.
KHALTSE / BAIMA / 10 / 2004

Landscape (Rock Formation) | In Use | Public (Community)

SETTING
The rock formation is located across the River Indus, opposite the highway leading to Hanuthang. It is surrounded by other rocks and stone boulders.

SIGNIFICANCE / ASSOCIATED BELIEFS
The rock formation is believed to be the drum of the famous epic warrior king Gesar.

DESCRIPTION
The rock formation is in the shape of a cylindrical drum located within the recess of a larger rock.

CULTURAL LINKAGE / CULTURAL PRACTICES
It is generally linked with Gesar's ear (namchog) located one kilometre away.

STATE OF PRESERVATION
Fair

Gesar's Ear
(Gesar *Namchog*)

INVENTORY NO.
KHALTSE / BAIMA / 11 / 2004

Landscape (Rock Formation) | In Use | Public (Community)

SETTING
The rock formation is located along the River Indus, opposite the highway leading to Hanuthang. It is surrounded by other rocks and stone boulders and the river. It is located about one km from the Gesar's drum.

SIGNIFICANCE / ASSOCIATED BELIEFS
The rock formation is believed to represent the ear of the famous warrior king Gesar.

DESCRIPTION
The rock formation is believed to be in the form of a ear and is located along the banks of the River Indus.

CULTURAL LINKAGES / CULTURAL PRACTICES
The rock formation is located on the highway leading from Baima to Hanuthang. It is generally linked with the Gesar's drum rock formation which is located one kilometre away.

STATE OF PRESERVATION
Fair

SOURCE OF INFORMATION Nimma Tsering, Chamakpa, Baima, Khaltse, Ladakh

Petroglyphs

INVENTORY NO.
KHALTSE / BAIMA / 12 / 2007

Rock Carvings | Abandoned | Public (State)

SETTING
The petroglyphs are located along the main road leading from Khaltse to Dha, before the village of Baima. It is located along the slope of a hill adjacent to the road and the River Indus flows on the opposite side of the road.

SIGNIFICANCE
The petroglyphs date back to the earliest period of human habitation in the region. The entire belt from Khaltse towards Dha appears to have had petroglyphs, many of which have disappeared over the years with the road construction.

DESCRIPTION
The petroglyphs are pecked onto a large boulder located above the road. It is a large boulder with a large number of depictions including animal and human figures and symbols.

STATE OF PRESERVATION
Showing Signs of Deterioration

Baima

59

Mane Wall

INVENTORY NO.
KHALTSE / BALDESH / 01 / 2004

Mane Wall | In Use | Public (Community)

SETTING
The *mane* wall is oriented towards the south and is located along the vehicular road leading from Khaltse to Dha.

SIGNIFICANCE
The *mane* wall is circumambulated by passers-by to gain merit as they travel along this route.

DESCRIPTION
The *mane* wall is built in three parts. The first section consists of a linear stone placed on a rectangular dry stone masonry base. This is followed by a six feet long rectangular dry stone masonry base. The last section is a cylindrical *mane* wall of around five feet diameter. The base of the *mane* wall is whitewashed. The horizontal surface of the *mane* wall is covered with flat *mane* stones inscribed with sacred *mantras* in Tibetan.

STATE OF PRESERVATION
Advanced State of Decay

SOURCE OF INFORMATION Tashi Yangskit, Gyalchukpa, Baldesh, Khaltse, Ladakh

Mane Wall

INVENTORY NO.
KHALTSE / BALDESH / 02 / 2004

Mane Wall | In Use | Public (Community) | Around 250 years old

SETTING
The *mane* wall is oriented towards the south and is located at the beginning of a wooden bridge that leads to the village. It is surrounded by a road to the north and the river to its south.

SIGNIFICANCE
The *mane* wall is built on the route leading to the village and is circumambulated by passers-by to gain merit.

STATE OF PRESERVATION
Advanced State of Decay

DESCRIPTION
The *mane* wall is a small structure with its base built in dry stone masonry. The whitewash has been applied directly on the stones. The horizontal surface of the *mane* wall is covered with *mane* stones inscribed with sacred *mantras* in Tibetan.

SOURCE OF INFORMATION Tashi Yangskit, Gyalchukpa, Baldesh, Khaltse, Ladakh

Rigsum Gonbo

INVENTORY NO.
KHALTSE / BALDESH / 03 / 2004

Rigsum Gonbo | In Use | Public (Community) | Around 150 years old

SETTING
The *rigsum gonbo* is oriented towards the north and is located along the face of a mountain above the Khashpa house.

SIGNIFICANCE
The *rigsum gonbo*, it is believed, was built by an old couple from the village who wished to have a child. It is thought to be about 150 years old.

DESCRIPTION
The *rigsum gonbo* is built inside a niche in the mountain face. It consists of a stone plinth with three Changchub *chorten*. The *chorten* are painted in two colors - white and red and are similar in shape and size. They have a square base which rises up in tiers to a dome.

STATE OF PRESERVATION
Advanced State of Decay

SOURCE OF INFORMATION Tashi Palmo, Baldesh, Khaltse, Ladakh

Changra

INVENTORY NO.
KHALTSE / BALDESH / 04 / 2004

Landscape (Community Space) | In Use | Public (Community)

SETTING
The area is located in the middle of the village with the Gyalchukpa house to the north and an open area to the south. The village footpath lies to the west.

SIGNIFICANCE
The space is a large open area which is used for village gatherings such as *panchayat* meetings as well as by the Gyalchukpa family.

DESCRIPTION
The site is a large expanse of rammed earth with walnut trees. It is a multilevel space flanked with stone edging.

STATE OF PRESERVATION
Fair

SOURCE OF INFORMATION Tashi Palmo, Baima, Khaltse, Ladakh

Rigsum Gonbo

INVENTORY NO.
KHALTSE / BALDESH / 05 / 2004

Rigsum Gonbo | In Use | Private (Individual) | Around 65 years old

SETTING
The *rigsum gonbo* is oriented towards the east and is located at one end of the village. It is built near the pathway leading to the village from the river. There are village houses to the east and west.

SIGNIFICANCE
The *rigsum gonbo* was built about 65 years ago in order to protect the village from natural calamities and other misfortune. It was repaired around three years back by the residents of Dogapa house.

DESCRIPTION
The *rigsum gonbo* is built against a mountainside with a large opening towards the east. It contains three Changchub *chorten* painted in orange, blue and white. It is built in stone masonry with mud mortar and has a traditional roof of timber beams, joists, *taalu*, and a layer of mud. The *chorten* are similar in size and have a *chugsum khorlo* over the dome.

STATE OF PRESERVATION
Fair

SOURCE OF INFORMATION Tashi Palmo, Baldesh, Khaltse, Ladakh

Mane Wall

INVENTORY NO.
KHALTSE / BALDESH / 06 / 2004

Mane Wall | In Use | Public (Community) | Around 250 years old

SETTING
The *mane* wall is oriented to the south and is located on the way to the Dogapa house. It is surrounded by other village houses.

SIGNIFICANCE
The *mane* wall is believed to have been built around 250 years ago for the well being of the village and is still circumambulated by villagers as an act of merit.

DESCRIPTION
The mane wall is a small structure with its base built in stone masonry with mud mortar. The horizontal surface of the *mane* wall is covered with about 17 inscribed *mane* stones.

STATE OF PRESERVATION
Showing Signs of Deterioration

SOURCE OF INFORMATION Tsering Phel, Tsangyapa, Baldesh, Khaltse, Ladakh

Tsangyapa House

INVENTORY NO.
KHALTSE / BALDESH / 07 / 2004

Vernacular Building | In Use | Private (Individual) | Around 200 years old

SETTING
The house is oriented towards the north east and is located on the way to Dogapa house. It is surrounded by agricultural fields on the southwest.

SIGNIFICANCE
The Tsangyapa house is a good example of vernacular architecture. It was built about 200 years ago by a great grandfather of the present owner. The family continues to reside in the house.

DESCRIPTION
The Tsangyapa house is a double storeyed structure built in the traditional style. The ground floor is built in stone masonry with mud mortar while the first floor is built in mud brick masonry. The house has a flat traditional roof comprising of timber joists, *taalu*, grass and a layer of compacted mud on top. The house is accessed from the village footpath which descends down a small doorway opening onto a corridor. A flight of stairs leads up to the first floor. The first floor houses the kitchen and a family temple housing antique images of Chagdor, Jamyang and Gonbo. The kitchen has an elaborate wooden framed *rabsal* with shutters. The house has a total of ten rooms. The ground floor is used during the winters while the upper floor is used during the summer months.

STATE OF PRESERVATION
Advanced State of Decay

Baldesh

63

SOURCE OF INFORMATION Tsering Phel, Tsangyapa, Baldesh, Khaltse, Ladakh

Bhuk-Bhuktse

A small village of seven households, Bhuk-Bhuktse is located near Wanla, about 115 kms from Leh. It falls under the village head of Wanla.

Listed by: Deldan Angmo and Jassu Singh
Year: 2004

Dha

Dha is located about 185 kms from Leh. The village is home to the Brogpas who are said to have migrated many centuries ago from Gilgit. Dha literally means an '*arrow*'. According to legend, in ancient times the people of Dha lived in the upper valley. One day, a man shot an arrow from the upper valley, saying that the village would settle wherever the arrow would fall. The arrow fell on land where the present village is located. To this day, the mark of the arrow can be seen and water for the village is taken from this point. Today, there are about 35 households in the village.

{*Source: Tsetan Gurmet (Shartsing pa)*}

Listed by: Deldan Angmo, Jassu Singh and Dr. Sonam Wangchok
Year: 2004, 2006, 2007

Mane Wall

INVENTORY NO.
KHALTSE / BHUK-BHUKTSE / 01 / 2004

Mane Wall | In Use | Public (Community)

SETTING
The *mane* wall is located along the right side of the road leading to Bhuk-Bhuktse. There are agricultural fields towards the southwest.

SIGNIFICANCE
The *mane* wall is located along the road leading to the village and is circumambulated by villagers as an act of merit.

DESCRIPTION
The *mane* wall is rectangular in plan and is built in dry stone masonry. *Mane* stones are placed on its flat horizontal surface. There is a prayer flag embedded in one side of the *mane* wall. A circumambulatory path surrounds the site.

STATE OF PRESERVATION
Showing Signs of Deterioration

SOURCE OF INFORMATION Tsewang Dolma, Khibzungpa, Bhuk-Bhuktse, Khaltse, Ladakh

Rigsum Gonbo

INVENTORY NO.
KHALTSE / BHUK-BHUKTSE / 02 / 2004

Rigsum Gonbo | In Use | Public (Community)

SETTING
The *rigsum gonbo* is located along the slope of a mountain near the road leading to the village of Bhuk-Bhuktse. The village school and agricultural fields are located further south of the site.

SIGNIFICANCE
The *rigsum gonbo* was built to protect the village from natural calamities such as floods, landslides, etc. and other misfortune.

DESCRIPTION
The *rigsum gonbo* comprises of three Changchub *chorten* built over a high stone platform. The *chorten* are built in stone and mud brick masonry with mud mortar. These are mud plastered and painted externally in the three colours of blue, white and red.

STATE OF PRESERVATION
Showing Signs of Deterioration

SOURCE OF INFORMATION Tsewang Dolma, Khibzungpa, Bhuk-Bhuktse, Khaltse, Ladakh

Bhuk-Bhuktse

66

Mane Wall

INVENTORY NO.
KHALTSE / BHUK-BHUKTSE / 03 / 2004

Mane Wall | In Use | Public (Community)

SETTING
The *mane* wall is located along the road leading to the village, just below the village school. There are agricultural fields beyond the site.

SIGNIFICANCE
The *mane* walls are located along the road leading to the village and are circumambulated by villagers as an act of merit. These were built in the past by a village ancestor for the well being of the village.

DESCRIPTION
The *mane* wall is a long L-shaped dry stone masonry wall. The base is wider at one end and tapers slightly towards the opposite end. There is a large prayer flag adjacent to the *mane* wall.

STATE OF PRESERVATION
Showing Signs of Deterioration

Bhuk-Bhuktse

67

Michungpa House

INVENTORY NO.
KHALTSE / DHA / 01 / 2004

Vernacular Building | In Use | Private (Individual) | Around 200 years old

SETTING
The Michungpa house is oriented towards the south and is located south of the agricultural fields and has apricot orchids nearby. The Dogapa house lies to the west and other village houses are located nearby.

SIGNIFICANCE
The house was built by an ancestor of the present owner and is a good example of vernacular architecture in the village of Dha. The family continues to reside in the house.

DESCRIPTION
The Michungpa house is a large three storeyed house. It has a large corridor opening at the ground floor level which leads to the entrance of the house. The ground floor is built in stone masonry with mud mortar and is used primarily for keeping animals and storing fodder. The first and the second floors, built in mud brick masonry with mud mortar, house the living areas for the family. The ground floor has small openings while the two upper floors have larger window openings. The house has an elaborate *rabsal* with wooden segmental arches and wooden lattice shutters. There are small windows on the eastern wall of the structure. These also have segmental arch openings. The house is covered with a flat traditional roof on which prayer flags are posted. The roof is supported on timber beams and columns flanked with wooden brackets.

STATE OF PRESERVATION
Advanced State of Decay

SOURCE OF INFORMATION Lobzang Gyaltsan-Dogapa, Dha, Khaltse, Ladakh

Lagskor

INVENTORY NO.
KHALTSE / DHA / 02 / 2004

Prayer Wheel | In Use | Public (Community) | Around 400 - 500 years old

SETTING
The prayer wheel is located in front of the cluster of village houses including the Michungpa and Dogapa houses.

SIGNIFICANCE
The prayer wheel was built during the reign of one of the kings of this area. This was earlier located in the forecourt of the palace complex and was later brought down by the villagers when the palace started falling apart. It is believed to be around 400 - 500 years old. Villagers rotate the prayer wheel as an act of merit.

DESCRIPTION
The *lagskor* is a drum-like structure mounted on two wooden joists and supported by wooden logs. The wheel is painted in red and the wooden members are painted in green. It is supported with stones against the nearby Michungpa house.

STATE OF PRESERVATION
Advanced State of Decay

SOURCE OF INFORMATION Lobzang Gyaltsan, Dogapa, Dha, Khaltse, Ladakh

Dha *Gonpa*

INVENTORY NO.
KHALTSE / DHA / 03 / 2004

Gonpa | In Use | Public (Community) | Around 300 years old

SETTING

The *gonpa* is oriented towards the east and forms part of a complex near the *tashag*. Beyond this lies the village square or *changra*.

SIGNIFICANCE

The *gonpa* is the principal place of worship in the village. The main images inside the temple are of Chamba and Chanrazig. A monk of the Drigung Kagyud sect is deputed here to carry out prayers and rituals within the temple.

DESCRIPTION

The *gonpa* is entered through a forecourt on which stand two *tarchen*. The building is a double storeyed structure with a central porch. There is a small side room used for storage. Access to the main shrine is from a porch which leads to a small wooden entrance doorway. It comprises of two chambers, the front one contains several images of guardian deities as well as the founder Lamas of the *gonpa*. There are two ornamental wooden columns supporting the roof and the other two floors with a skylight. The wall panels of the skylight at the second floor have paintings on them. The walls on the east, north and southern sides are adorned with images of the Buddha. A small opening towards the western wall leads to the second shrine housing a large image of Chamba, and Chanrazig and Guru Rinpoche. They are all placed on a pedestal. There is a skylight above the Chamba. The walls are adorned with paintings of various guardian deities. The wall partition between the two shrines has two openings at both levels. The upper level has an elaborate wooden frame with intricate wooden lattice shutters. The ground floor of the *gonpa* is built in stone masonry while the upper floors are in mud brick masonry with mud mortar. The exterior walls of the *gonpa* and mud plastered and whitewashed.

STATE OF PRESERVATION
Advanced State of Decay

Dha

69

Mane Wall

INVENTORY NO.
KHALTSE / DHA / 04 / 2004

Mane Wall | In Use | Public (Community) | Around 150 years old

SETTING
The *mane* wall is oriented to the east and forms part of the *gonpa* complex. It is surrounded by trees and stone boulders and a stream flows nearby.

SIGNIFICANCE
The *mane* wall forms a part of the *gonpa* complex and is circumambulated by villagers as an act of merit when they visit the temple.

DESCRIPTION
The site consists of a circular *mane* wall built over a large boulder. The *mane* wall is built in dry stone masonry with mud mortar and is mud plastered and whitewashed on the exterior. *Mane* stones are placed on the top and there is a prayer flag posted on the top.

STATE OF PRESERVATION
Showing Signs of Deterioration

SOURCE OF INFORMATION Tsering Kushkit, Dha, Khaltse, Ladakh

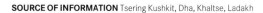

Chorten

INVENTORY NO.
KHALTSE / DHA / 05 / 2004

Chorten | In Use | Public (Community) | Around 150 years old

SETTING
The *chorten* is located in the *gonpa* complex towards the end of the village. It is surrounded by apricot trees, large stone boulders and an inscribed rock.

SIGNIFICANCE
The *chorten* is a Namgyal *chorten* and symbolizes the Buddha's victory over illness.

DESCRIPTION
The *chorten* is built on a high stone masonry base and is constructed in stone and mud brick masonry with mud mortar. It is mud plastered and whitewashed on the exterior.

STATE OF PRESERVATION
Showing Signs of Deterioration

SOURCE OF INFORMATION Tsering Kushkit, Dha, Khaltse, Ladakh

Dha

70

Mane Wall

INVENTORY NO.
KHALTSE / DHA / 06 / 2004

Mane Wall | In Use | Public (Community)

SETTING
The *mane* wall is oriented to the south and is located along a narrow pathway in the old quarter of the village in front of the Skyabapa house. This pathway goes on towards the newer settlement. A walnut tree grows nearby. The *mane* wall is surrounded by old stone houses which are now used as cattle sheds.

SIGNIFICANCE
The *mane* wall is located along a pathway in the older quarters of the village and is circumambulated by villagers as an act of merit while travelling along this path.

DESCRIPTION
The *mane* wall is a circular wall built in stone masonry with mud mortar. Its exterior surface is mud plastered and whitewashed and there is a prayer flag posted on the top.

STATE OF PRESERVATION
Showing Signs of Deterioration

SOURCE OF INFORMATION Rigzen Dolma, Dha, Khaltse, Ladakh

Dha

71

Skyabapa House

INVENTORY NO.
KHALTSE / DHA / 07 / 2004

Vernacular Building | In Use | Private (Individual) | Around 100 years old

SETTING
The house is oriented towards the south and is located in the old settlement with other old houses located nearby.

SIGNIFICANCE
The Skyabapa house is one of several old houses in the village belonging for generations to the Skyabapa family. It forms part of a cluster of traditional vernacular dwellings in the old quarter of the village.

DESCRIPTION
The Skyabapa house is a double storeyed building with the ground floor constructed in stone masonry. The first floor is built in mud brick masonry. The rear half of the house is of a lower height than the front. The ground floor is used for as animal stables and for storing fodder. The first floor houses the family's living area with larger window openings than the ground floor. The house has a traditional roof which is supported on timber beams and columns flanked with wooden brackets. Externally, the first floor of the house is mud plastered and whitewashed.

STATE OF PRESERVATION
Advanced State of Decay

SOURCE OF INFORMATION Rigzen Dolma, Dha, Khaltse, Ladakh

Dipling

The village of Dipling is a 7-hour trek from Lingshed. Originally the village was known as Duling which means '*the land of grain*' as it was very fertile. There are 14 households in the village.

Listed by: Deldan Angmo and Jassu Singh
Year: 2006

Gonchung

INVENTORY NO.
KHALTSE / DIPLING / 01 / 2006

Gonpa | In Use | Private (Individual) | Around 700 years old

SETTING
The *gonchung* located on the northeast of the village near the Dipling *gonpa*.

SIGNIFICANCE
According to legend, a monk used to mediate in this *gonpa* a long time ago. However, a conflict arose between him and the villagers and he was murdered. His spirit, it is believed, began to harm the village. The villagers abandoned this *gonpa* and built a new one which continues to be used in worship today.

DESCRIPTION
The *gonchung* is in complete ruins today and only some of the walls still survive. These are constructed in stone masonry. The roof of the building no longer exists and it is possible that the timber from the roof was reused in the new *gonpa*.

STATE OF PRESERVATION
Danger of Disappearance

Dipling

80

Phuntsog Lingpa House

INVENTORY NO.
KHALTSE / DIPLING / 02 / 2006

Vernacular Building | In Use | Private (Individual) | Around 700 years old

SETTING
The house is located in the middle of the village.

SIGNIFICANCE
The Phuntsog Lingpa house was built by the ancestors of the Phuntsog Lingpa family. It is one of the largest and oldest houses in the village. It is built in the traditional style and is a good example of vernacular architecture in the village.

DESCRIPTION
The Phuntsog Lingpa house is a three storeyed building. The ground floor is built in stone masonry and has small window openings. It is used primarily for storage and for housing animals. The first floor is built in mud brick masonry with mud mortar and has larger window openings with timber lintels and frames painted in red. The windows have a black border around them. This level is the family's living area. The second floor comprises of the family temple and a terrace. The roof of the house is a built of timber joists, *taalu*, grass and compacted mud. There is a small parapet running along the edge of the temple roof which is painted in red.

STATE OF PRESERVATION
Fair

Mane Ringmo

INVENTORY NO.
KHALTSE / DIPLING / 03 / 2006

Chorten / *Mane* Wall | In Use | Public (Community) | Around 300 - 400
years old

SETTING
The group of *chorten* and *mane* walls is located in the
village in the middle of agricultural fields.

SIGNIFICANCE
The *chorten* and *mane* wall were built around 3 to 4
centuries ago as an act of merit and are still
circumambulated by the villagers. The *chorten* is a
Changchub *chorten* and symbolizes the Buddha's
enlightenment.

DESCRIPTION
The *chorten* is built over a square plan and rests on a stone
masonry plinth. The *chorten* is built in stone and mud brick
masonry with mud mortar and is mud plastered and
whitewashed on the exterior. The base panels of the
chorten have red marking painted on them. The *chorten*
has a *srog-shing* embedded in the dome. The *mane* wall is
built in dry stone masonry and has mane stones inscribed
on the top.

STATE OF PRESERVATION
Showing Signs of Deterioration

Doktha *Yokma*

INVENTORY NO.
KHALTSE / DIPLING / 04 / 2006

Vernacular Building | Abandoned | Private (Individual) | Around 325 years
old

SETTING
The house is situated towards the end of the Dipling village.
It is surrounded by a footpath and agricultural fields beyond.

SIGNIFICANCE
The Doktha *Yokma* was built by the ancestors of the family
about 325 year ago. It is one of the oldest houses in the
village and is built in the traditional style.

STATE OF PRESERVATION
Danger of Disappearance

DESCRIPTION
The Doktha *Yokma* house is a double storeyed house built
over a slope of a hill. Additions to the house appear to have
been made over time. The ground floor of the house is built
in stone masonry with mud mortar while the first floor is in
mud brick masonry. The house has a traditional roof that
has collapsed in several areas. There is a large hole in the
rear wall of the house. There are few window openings in
the house. As with most traditional houses, the ground floor
was used for storage and for housing animals while the
family resided in the first floor.

Dipling

81

Doktha *Gongma*

INVENTORY NO.
KHALTSE / DIPLING / 05 / 2006

Vernacular Building | In Use | Private (Individual) | Around 250 years old

SETTING
The house is situated on the northeast of the village near the Dipling *gonpa*. There are agricultural fields near the house.

SIGNIFICANCE
The Doktha *Gongma* was built by the ancestors of the family about 250 year ago and the family still resides here. It is one of the oldest houses in the village.

DESCRIPTION
The Doktha *Gongma* house is a double storeyed house built along the slope of a hill. The ground floor of the house is built in random rubble masonry while the first floor is in mud brick masonry with mud mortar. The house has a traditional roof. There is a terrace on the first floor which is also the roof of the ground floor. The family's living rooms are built along the edge of the terrace. The exterior walls of the house are mud plastered and whitewashed and have red markings along the corners to ward off evil.

STATE OF PRESERVATION
Showing Signs of Deterioration

82

Dipling

Khyunge *Lhato*

INVENTORY NO.
KHALTSE / DIPLING / 06 / 2006

Lhato | In Use | Public (Community) | Around 400 years old

SETTING
The *lhato* is located along the slope of a mountain on a small rocky outcrop towards the north of the village.

SIGNIFICANCE
The *lhato* is dedicated to the protector deity of the village who is believed to have come from Tibet and settled in the village. The *luyar* is Tsering Phuntsog. The *lhato* is renewed every year amid elaborate rituals when the contents are replaced.

DESCRIPTION
The *lhato* consists of small cubical structures built in stone and mud brick masonry with a traditional roof. Ritual offerings of *khadag*, animal horns and juniper are placed on the roof of the *lhato*.

STATE OF PRESERVATION
Fair

Phuntsog Tundup pa House

INVENTORY NO.
KHALTSE / DIPLING / 07 / 2006

Vernacular Building | In Use | Private (Individual) | Around 700 years old

SETTING
The house is situated in the middle of the village and is surrounded by other houses. A footpath runs along the edge of the house.

SIGNIFICANCE
The Phuntsog Tundup pa house was built by the ancestors of the family many generations ago and the family still resides here. It is one of the oldest houses in the village.

DESCRIPTION
The Phuntsog Tundup pa house is a double storeyed house built along the slope of a hill. Additions to the house have been made over a period of time. The ground floor of the house is built in random rubble masonry while the first floor is in mud brick masonry with mud mortar. Entrance to the house is through a small entrance doorway in front of which is a small compound. Passing through the doorway, there is

a small courtyard around which several rooms are built. The first floor houses the family's living areas. The house has a traditional roof over which fodder is stacked.

STATE OF PRESERVATION
Showing Signs of Deterioration

Yokmapa House

INVENTORY NO.
KHALTSE / DIPLING / 08 / 2006

Vernacular Building | In Use | Private (Individual) | Around 700 years old

SETTING
The house is situated in the middle of the village and is surrounded by agricultural fields.

SIGNIFICANCE
The Yokmapa house was built by the ancestors of the family over seven hundred years ago and the family still resides here. It is one of the oldest houses in the village.

DESCRIPTION
The Yokmapa house is a large double storeyed structure built in stages with additions being made to the main house over a period of time. The oldest part of the house appears to be in the rear of the house. The house is entered at the level of the first floor through a flight of stairs leading from a small compound. The ground floor is built in random rubble masonry and is used primarily for storage and for housing animals. This level has small window openings for ventilation and light. The first floor houses the family's living quarters and is built in mud brick masonry with mud

mortar. The exterior walls of the house are mud plastered and whitewashed. The house has a traditional roof on which fodder is stacked.

STATE OF PRESERVATION
Showing Signs of Deterioration

Dipling

83

Tseringpa House

INVENTORY NO.
KHALTSE / DIPLING / 09 / 2006

Vernacular Building | In Use | Private (Individual) | Around 1000 years old

SETTING
The house is situated in the middle of the village and is surrounded by other houses. There is a footpath running along the edge of the house.

SIGNIFICANCE
The Tseringpa house was built by the ancestors of the family a thousand years ago and the family still resides here. It is one of the oldest houses in the village and is built in the traditional style.

DESCRIPTION
The Tseringpa house is a large double storeyed structure built in stages with additions being made to the main house over a period of time. The oldest part of the house appears to be to the rear of the house, on the extreme right of the main entrance doorway. The house is entered through a small doorway which is in the corner of the building and leads from the right to the main house. The ground floor is built in random rubble masonry and is used primarily for storage and for housing animals. This level has small window openings for ventilation and light. The first floor houses the family's living quarters and is built in mud brick masonry. The exterior walls of the house are mud plastered and whitewashed. The house has a traditional roof on which fodder is stacked. The roof has a red parapet running along its edge. The family's temple is built above the first floor.

STATE OF PRESERVATION
Showing Signs of Deterioration

Lungse Zhung *Chorten*

INVENTORY NO.
KHALTSE / DIPLING / 10 / 2006

Chorten / *Mane* Wall | In Use | Public (Community) | Around 450 years old

SETTING
The *chorten* is located in the middle of agricultural fields in the village. A small stream flows nearby.

SIGNIFICANCE
The *chorten* and *mane* wall were built by the Dipling community about 450 years ago in the middle of the agricultural fields and is therefore known as Lungse Zhung *chorten*. The *chorten* and *mane* wall are circumambulated by villagers as an act of merit. The *chorten* is a Changchub *chorten* that symbolizes the Buddha's enlightenment.

DESCRIPTION
The *chorten* is built over a square plan and rests on a tiered random rubble masonry plinth. It is built in stone and mud brick masonry with mud mortar and is mud plastered and whitewashed on the exterior. The *chorten* is surmounted by a *srog-shing*. There is a *mane* wall near the chorten which is built over a rectangular plan in dry stone masonry and contains *mane* stones on the horizontal surface.

STATE OF PRESERVATION
Showing Signs of Deterioration

Tashi Gangpa House

INVENTORY NO.
KHALTSE / DIPLING / 11 / 2006

Vernacular Building | In Use | Private (Individual) | Around 700 years old

SETTING
The house is situated in the middle of the village and is surrounded by other village houses. There is a broad footpath running along the edge of the house.

SIGNIFICANCE
The Tashi Gangpa house was built by the ancestors of the family about 700 years ago and the family still resides here. It is one of the oldest houses in the village and is built in the traditional style.

DESCRIPTION
The Tashi Gangpa house is a large double storeyed structure built in stages with additions being made to the main house over a period of time. The oldest part of the house appears to be to the rear of the house. The ground floor is built in random rubble masonry and is used primarily for storage and for housing animals. This level has small window openings for ventilation and light. The first floor houses the family's living quarters and is built in mud brick masonry. The first floor has larger window openings with timber lintels. The exterior walls of the house are mud plastered and whitewashed. The house has a traditional roof on which fodder is stacked. The roof has a parapet running along its edge.

STATE OF PRESERVATION
Showing Signs of Deterioration

Dipling

85

Lingshed *Labrang*

INVENTORY NO.
KHALTSE / DIPLING / 12 / 2006

Vernacular Building | In Use | Public (Lingshed *Gonpa*) | Around 350 years old

SETTING
The *labrang* is located along a footpath with village houses and agricultural fields in its vicinity.

SIGNIFICANCE
The *labrang* was built by Lingshed *gonpa* about 350 years ago to house the resident monk deputed by the *gonpa* to administer the lands and livestock owned by the *gonpa* in the village.

DESCRIPTION
The Lingshed *labrang* is a double storeyed structure with few window openings. It is built in stone masonry with mud mortar and is mud plastered on the exterior. The building could not be accessed at the time of the listing.

STATE OF PRESERVATION
Showing Signs of Deterioration

Srangzhung

INVENTORY NO.
KHALTSE / DIPLING / 13 / 2006

Landscape (Community Space) | In Use | Public (Community)

SETTING
The Srangzhung is located in the middle of the village and is surrounded by village houses and agricultural lands.

SIGNIFICANCE
The Srangzhung is the principal meeting place for the village where the traditional village body meets to discuss village issues.

DESCRIPTION
The Srangzhung is a large open area surrounded by village houses and agricultural fields.

STATE OF PRESERVATION
Fair

Group of *Chorten* and *Mane* Wall

INVENTORY NO.
KHALTSE / DIPLING / 14 / 2006

Chorten / *Mane* Wall | In Use | Public (Community) | Around 400 years old

SETTING
The group of *chorten* and *mane* walls is built on the top of a hill to the north of the village.

SIGNIFICANCE
The *chorten* are believed to be around 400 years old and have been maintained by the villagers. The *chorten* are largely Changchub *chorten* which symbolize the Buddha's enlightenment. The *chorten* are circumambulated by the villagers to accrue merit.

DESCRIPTION
The site comprises of a group of four *chorten* which appear to be Changchub *chorten*. One of the *chorten* has collapsed completely and its form is no longer discernible. The *chorten* are built in stone masonry and the exterior surface is mud plastered and whitewashed. The *chorten* have red markings on the lower base panels and one of the *chorten*

is topped with a red tapering *chugsum khorlo*. The *mane* wall is built near the *chorten* and is constructed in dry stone masonry. Inscribed *mane* stones are placed on the top.

STATE OF PRESERVATION
Advanced State of Decay

Dipling *Gonpa*

INVENTORY NO.
KHALTSE / DIPLING / 15 / 2006

Gonpa | In Use | Public (Lingshed *Gonpa*) | Around 700 years old

SETTING
The *gonpa* is built along the slope of a mountain to the east of the village and overlooks the village.

SIGNIFICANCE
Dipling *gonpa* is believed to be around 700 years old. It is a branch of Lingshed *gonpa* and one monk from Lingshed *gonpa* resides here to take care of the *gonpa*. It is the principal place of worship for the villagers. Several major prayers are performed here each year. Monks from Lingshed come to the *gonpa* and perform prayers which are sponsored by the villagers. On the 15th day of the 1st month of the Tibetan calendar both the monastic and lay communities observe *Nyenas* and *Nyungnas* (fasting) for three days. In the 5th month of the Tibetan calendar, they read religious texts and whitewash all the *chorten* in the village.

DESCRIPTION
Dipling *gonpa* is a two storeyed building which is constructed on a rectangular plan. It houses of a *dukhang*, a *zimchung*, kitchen and monks' quarters. The entrance is from the east. This leads to the *dukhang* which is a large hall with four timber columns supporting the overhead roof. There is a skylight in the centre through which light enters the room. The floor is laid in mud. There are statues of the Buddha, Gonkar, Guru Rinpoche, Tsongkhapa, Chanrazig, Dukar, Tsepakmed, Chamba houses within the *dukhang* along with volumes of the Bum which are said to have been brought here from Tibet. The *zimchung* and kitchen are located on the first floor. There is a smaller temple to the east of the main building. This houses statues of the Buddha, Dolma, Chagdor, Tsongkhapa and Tsepakmed. The *gonpa* has large window openings at both levels. The doors and windows have wooden lintels and frames and are bordered in black. The roof is laid in the traditional manner with timber beams, joists, willow twigs, grass and compacted mud. A low parapet bordered in black runs along the edge. The *gonpa* is built in stone and mud brick masonry with mud mortar. It is mud plastered and whitewashed on the exterior.

STATE OF PRESERVATION
Showing Signs of Deterioration

Dipling

87

Zhukthipa House

INVENTORY NO.
KHALTSE / DIPLING / 16 / 2006

Vernacular Building | In Use | Private (Individual) | Around 400 years old

SETTING
The Zhukthipa house is located near the Dipling *gonpa* to the east of the village. It is surrounded by open land and the Phuntsog Lingpa Khangbu house.

SIGNIFICANCE
The Zhukthipa house was built by the ancestors of the family about 400 years ago and the family still resides here. It is one of the older houses in the village and is built in the traditional style.

DESCRIPTION
The Zhukthipa house is a large double storeyed structure built in stages with additions being made to the main house over a period of time. The house is built in stone and mud brick masonry with mud mortar. The ground floor is used primarily for storage and for housing animals and has small window openings for ventilation and light. The first floor houses the family's living quarters and has larger window openings with timber lintels. The window frames are painted in red and the windows have a red border around them. The house has a traditional roof with a red parapet running along the edges. The exterior walls of the house are mud plastered and whitewashed. There are red markings along the edges of the house to ward off evil.

STATE OF PRESERVATION
Showing Signs of Deterioration

Phuntsog Ling *Khangbu*

INVENTORY NO.
KHALTSE / DIPLING / 17 / 2006

Vernacular Building | In Use | Private (Individual) | Around 700 years old

SETTING
The house is located a little below the Dipling *gonpa* and is near the Zhukthipa house.

SIGNIFICANCE
The Phuntsog Ling house was built by the ancestors of the Phuntsog Ling family. It is built in the traditional style and is a good example of vernacular architecture in the village.

DESCRIPTION
The Phuntsog Lingpa house is a double storeyed building with an entrance passageway which divides the house into two unequal sections. The house is built in random rubble masonry and the exterior is mud plastered and whitewashed. The ground floor is used primarily for storage and the family's living quarters are on the first floor. The ground floor has small openings for ventilation and light while the first floor has a large window. The house has a traditional roof with a red parapet running along its edge.

STATE OF PRESERVATION
Showing Signs of Deterioration

Barmela

INVENTORY NO.
KHALTSE / DIPLING / 18 / 2006

Landscape (Pass) | In Use | Public (Community)

STATE OF PRESERVATION
Showing Signs of Deterioration

SETTING
The pass is about 4 - 5 kms from Lingshed and connects Dipling to Lingshed.

SIGNIFICANCE / ASSOCIATED BELIEFS
The pass connects Dipling and Lingshed and is crossed by villagers as they move out of the village. There is a *chorten* and *mane* wall built on the pass with prayer flags tied to them. People circumambulate these as they cross this pass. Villagers tie prayer flags here and pray to the gods for a safe journey by shouting "*Kye Kye Soso Lha Gyalo*" which means 'may gods be victorious'.

DESCRIPTION
The pass is located at an altitude of about 4850 metres and is part of the Zanskar range of mountains. There is a *chorten* and *mane* wall built here by the villagers on which prayer flags are tied. The *chorten* is built on a stone masonry platform and is built in stone masonry with mud mortar. The exterior surface has a few traces of external mud plaster and whitewash. The *mane* wall is a small cubical-shaped dry stone masonry wall with *mane* stones placed on its horizontal surface. Prayer flags are tied across the *chorten* and *mane* wall.

Domkhar

Domkhar is situated in the Sham area of Khaltse block about 112 kms from Leh. According to legend, an old man from Rubshu Kharnag (Changthang) planted seven grains in the soil while going up to the pastures with his animals. When he returned a few weeks later, he found that the grain had taken root and ripened. Seeing that the soil was fertile, he decided to settle here and start cultivating the land. Today, there are about 110 families spread over the three hamlets of Domkhar Gongma (Upper Domkhar), Domkhar Barma (Middle Domkhar) and Domkhar Dho (Lower Domkhar).

{*Source: Phuntsog Tundup*}

Listed by: Deldan Angmo and Jassu Singh
Year: 2004, 2006

Kagan *Chorten*

INVENTORY NO.
KHALTSE / DOMKHAR BARMA / 01 / 2004

Chorten | In Use | Public (Community)

SETTING
The *chorten* is oriented to the east and is located along the vehicular road leading to the settlement. It is surrounded by trees and agricultural fields.

SIGNIFICANCE
The *chorten* marks the entrance to the village. Villagers pass through the passage of the *chorten* and circumambulate it as an act of merit.

DESCRIPTION
The Kagan *chorten* has two thick parallel stone masonry walls over which rest a Changchub *chorten*. The passage beneath is about two metres in height. The *chorten* is built in mud brick masonry with mud mortar and the entire structure is mud plastered and whitewashed on the exterior. The Changchub *chorten* has decorative stucco relief motifs (*pa-tra*) on its base panels and is surmounted by a red *chugsum khorlo* with a metal crown. The ceiling over the passage is built in timber and is in the shape of a

mandala. Elaborate paintings of Buddhist deities, executed on cloth, have been pasted onto the timber members. An engraved stone is placed near the surface of the plinth.

STATE OF PRESERVATION
Advanced State of Decay

SOURCE OF INFORMATION Tsetan Dolma, Domkhar Barma, Khaltse, Ladakh

Domkhar Barma

92

Group of *Chorten*

INVENTORY NO.
KHALTSE / DOMKHAR BARMA / 02 / 2004

Chorten | In Use | Public (Community) | Around 200 Years old

SETTING
The *chorten* are oriented to the west and are located along the vehicular road leading to the village. The *chorten* are surrounded by trees and agricultural fields with the village stream flowing nearby. Across the road is the Gongma Khangpa.

SIGNIFICANCE
The *chorten* and *mane* wall are located along the road leading to the village and are circumambulated by villagers as they travel along this road. The *chorten* are all Changchub *chorten* and symbolize the Buddha's enlightenment.

DESCRIPTION
The site consists of three Changchub *chorten* and a *mane* wall. The *mane* wall is a dry stone masonry wall built on a rectangular plan with flat *mane* stones placed on its horizontal surface. There are two small *chorten* and one larger *chorten*. The *chorten* are all built in stone and mud

brick masonry with mud mortar. These are mud plastered and whitewashed on the exterior. The smaller *chorten* have eroded considerably and the domes have collapsed. The external plaster of the larger *chorten* is also eroded.

STATE OF PRESERVATION
Advanced State of Decay

SOURCE OF INFORMATION Tsetan Dolma, Domkhar Barma, Khaltse, Ladakh

Onpunpa House

INVENTORY NO.
KHALTSE / DOMKHAR BARMA / 03 / 2004

Vernacular Building | Abandoned | Private (Individual) | Around 150 years old

SETTING

The Onpunpa house is oriented to the southeast and is located along a cobbled pathway which leads to the *gonpa*. There are agricultural fields and apricot trees nearby.

SIGNIFICANCE

The house was built by the ancestors of the Onpunpa family about 150 years ago. The house is built in the traditional style and is part of the vernacular architecture of the village.

DESCRIPTION

The Onpunpa house is a three storeyed building. The ground and first floors are constructed in stone masonry with mud mortar, while the second floor is constructed in mud brick masonry with mud mortar. The ground floor is used for storage and for keeping animals. There are no window openings at this level. The upper levels house the family's living quarters. There is a *rabsal* on the front facade facing southeast. The house has a traditional roof made of timber joists, *taalu*, grass and compacted mud. The house is mud plastered and white washed on the exterior.

STATE OF PRESERVATION
Showing Signs of Deterioration

SOURCE OF INFORMATION Padma Dolma, Domkhar Barma, Khaltse, Ladakh

Mane Wall

INVENTORY NO.
KHALTSE / DOMKHAR BARMA / 04 / 2004

Mane Wall | In Use | Public (Community)

SETTING

The *mane* wall is oriented to the west and is located long the vehicular road leading to the village with the river beyond. The site is surrounded by trees and agricultural fields. There is a newly constructed storage house nearby.

SIGNIFICANCE

The *mane* wall is built along the road leading to the village and is circumambulated by villagers while travelling along this path as an act of merit.

DESCRIPTION

The *mane* wall is a cubical stone masonry structure built on a square plan. It is mud plastered and whitewashed on the exterior. Inscribed *mane* stones are placed on the horizontal surface of the wall.

STATE OF PRESERVATION
Showing Signs of Deterioration

SOURCE OF INFORMATION Padma Dolma, Domkhar Barma, Khaltse, Ladakh

Old *Gonpa*

INVENTORY NO.
KHALTSE / DOMKHAR BARMA / 05 / 2004

Gonpa | Abandoned | Public (Hemis *Gonpa*) | Around 150 years old

SETTING
The *gonpa* is oriented to the south and is located on a hill along a steep zigzag path. The village lies further south of the site.

SIGNIFICANCE
The *gonpa* is believed to have been built around 150 years ago and was the principal place of worship for the village. The temple was abandoned and the images shifted to the new temple.

DESCRIPTION
The *gonpa* is a double storeyed block with a *rabsal* on the first floor. The *rabsal* overlooks the village below. The entry to the *gonpa* is from the west. A staircase leads to the main hall on the first floor. The ground floor walls are constructed in stone masonry and the upper storey is in mud bricks. The structure has a traditional roof comprising of timber joists, dried grass and mud. The internal walls are decorated with paintings and the chamber houses images of Guru Rinpoche. The parapet and the openings are decorated with bands of red and black. The openings have elaborative decorated timber lintels. The structure is plastered and whitewashed.

STATE OF PRESERVATION
Showing Signs of Deterioration

Domkhar Barma

94

Village Street

INVENTORY NO.
KHALTSE / DOMKHAR DHO / 01 / 2004

Precinct | In Use | Public (Community) | Around 150 - 200 years old

SETTING
The street is located in the interior of the village. There are old village houses to the north. There is a prayer wheel at the junction where the street joins the village road.

SIGNIFICANCE
The street is one of the oldest quarters in the village. There are traditional village houses along its edge with agricultural fields on the opposite side. The houses are about 150 – 200 years old and are built in the traditional style and contribute to the vernacular architecture of the village. The street serves as a hub of activity through the course of the day as all the houses face the street.

DESCRIPTION
The street is a footpath paved in stone with old residences along its side. It is approximately two metres wide. The houses are all built in the traditional style. The lower levels are constructed in random rubble masonry while the upper

levels are made of mud brick or stone masonry in mud mortar. All the openings are made of timber. The houses are mud plastered and whitewashed on the exterior.

STATE OF PRESERVATION
Fair

SOURCE OF INFORMATION Ishey Dolma - Pugapa, Domkhar Dho, Khaltse, Ladakh

Domkhar Dho

95

Pugapa's House

INVENTORY NO.
KHALTSE / DOMKHAR DHO / 02 / 2004

Vernacular Building | In Use | Private (Individual) | Around 150 years old

SETTING
The house is oriented to the south and is located in the interiors of the village. It is surrounded by other village dwellings to the east and west and by agricultural fields and apricot groves to the south.

SIGNIFICANCE
The house was built by an ancestor of the Pugapa family about 150 year ago and the family has been in residence here ever since. It is built in the traditional style and is a good example of vernacular architecture in the village.

DESCRIPTION
The Pugapa House is a large three storeyed structure. The ground floor is constructed in stone masonry without any openings and is used for housing animals and storing fodder. The first floor is built in stone masonry while the second floor is constructed in mud brick masonry and is used mainly for summer habitation. The entire building is whitewashed externally. The central room on the second

floor has an elaborate window opening facing south. This has a decorative tiered lintel and wooden frames with lattice work on the wooden members. There is an open verandah on the second floor towards the centre. The first floor has relatively bigger windows with tiered lintels. The second floor has large windows with decorative wooden frames and lintels. The house has a flat traditional roof made of timber beams, joists, *taalu*, grass and a layer of compacted mud.

STATE OF PRESERVATION
Fair

SOURCE OF INFORMATION Ishey Dolma - Pugapa, Domkhar Dho, Khaltse, Ladakh

Standup pa House

INVENTORY NO.
KHALTSE / DOMKHAR DHO / 03 / 2004

Vernacular Building | In Use | Private (Individual) | Around 150 years old

SETTING
The Standup pa house is oriented to the south and is located along the pathway which leads to Domkhar Barma. The house is located to the north of the village street, west of Pugapa's house. To the south, lie agricultural fields and apricot orchards.

SIGNIFICANCE
The house was built by ancestors of the Standup pa family 150 years ago and has been the family residence ever since. It is built in the traditional style and contributes to the vernacular architecture of the village.

DESCRIPTION
The Standup pa house is a three storeyed structure with an entrance directly from the street. The ground floor is constructed in random rubble masonry and mud mortar with narrow openings for ventilation. The first floor is built in stone masonry where as the second floor is built in mud brick masonry and used mostly for summer habitation. The

first floor has narrow window openings with decorated timber lintels. The second floor has a large *rabsal* facing the south which has a decorated tiered lintel and wooden frames. The house has a traditional roof made of timber beams, joists, *taalu*, grass, and compacted mud.

STATE OF PRESERVATION
Fair

SOURCE OF INFORMATION Ishey Dolma - Pugapa, Domkhar Dho, Khaltse, Ladakh

Standup pa House

INVENTORY NO.
KHALTSE / DOMKHAR DHO / 04 / 2004

Vernacular Building | Abandoned | Private (Individual) | Around 150 years old

SETTING
The house is oriented to the south and is located along the pathway which leads to Domkhar Barma. The house is located right below the *gonpa* complex, north of the village street.

SIGNIFICANCE
The house was built by the ancestors of the Standup pa family and was used as a *tashag* before it was abandoned. The house is built in the traditional style and is an example of the vernacular architecture of the village.

DESCRIPTION
The Standup pa house is a double storeyed building built along the slope of a hillside just below the *gonpa* complex. The entrance is through a wooden doorway on the south which leads to the ground floor. The ground floor has narrow openings for ventilation and is built in random

rubble masonry. There is a large elaborate *rabsal* on the first floor which has having decorated wooden frames and lintels. The house has a flat traditional roof.

STATE OF PRESERVATION
Showing Signs of Deterioration

SOURCE OF INFORMATION Ishey Dolma - Pugapa, Domkhar Dho, Khaltse, Ladakh

Balupa *Khangpa*

INVENTORY NO.
KHALTSE / DOMKHAR DHO / 05 / 2004

Vernacular Building | In Use | Private (Individual) | Around 150 years old

SETTING
The Balupa *khangpa* is oriented to the south and is located along the pathway which leads to Domkhar Barma. The house is located to the north of the village street and is adjacent to the Dagshospa's house which has been recently repaired. There are agricultural fields and apricot orchards to the south.

SIGNIFICANCE
The house was built by the ancestors of the Balupa family about 150 years ago and has served as the family's residence since then. It is built in the traditional style and contributes to the vernacular architecture of the village.

DESCRIPTION
The Balupa *khangpa* is a triple storeyed building facing the village street. There is a small wooden doorway on the ground level which opens onto a corridor. The ground floor is built in stone masonry with mud mortar and is used for housing animals and storing fodder. The first floor is built in

stone masonry while the second floor is built in mud brick masonry with mud mortar. The first floor is used for storage purposes while the second houses the family's living quarters. The second floor has an elaborate window opening which has a decorative timber frame and lintel. The rooms like kitchen and guest room have timber flooring while the rest of the rooms have a mud flooring. The house has a traditional roof of timber joists, grass and compacted mud.

STATE OF PRESERVATION
Fair

SOURCE OF INFORMATION Ishey Dolma, Pugapa, Domkhar Dho, Khaltse, Ladakh

Chorten

INVENTORY NO.
KHALTSE / DOMKHAR DHO / 06 / 2004

Chorten | In Use | Public (Community) | Around 150 years old

SETTING
The *chorten* is oriented to the south and is located along the pathway which leads to the village. It is surrounded by village houses and there is a *rigsum gonbo* further up.

SIGNIFICANCE
The *chorten* is believed to have been built about 150 years ago. It is located along the village path and is circumambulated by villagers as an act of merit while crossing this path. It is a Changchub *chorten* and symbolizes the Buddha's enlightenment.

DESCRIPTION
The *chorten* is built over a square plan on a random rubble masonry platform. The *chorten* is built in stone masonry and is mud plastered and whitewashed externally. There is a *srog-shing* embedded on the dome of the *chorten*. The *chorten* has eroded over time and the external form is largely lost.

STATE OF PRESERVATION
Advanced State of Decay

SOURCE OF INFORMATION Ishey Dolma, Domkhar Dho, Khaltse, Ladakh

Rigsum Gonbo

INVENTORY NO.
KHALTSE / DOMKHAR DHO / 07 / 2004

Rigsum Gonbo | In Use | Public (Community) | Around 200 years old

SETTING
The *rigsum gonbo* is oriented to the south and is located on the way to the *gonpa*. There are several village houses nearby.

SIGNIFICANCE
The *rigsum gonbo* was built to protect the village against natural calamities and other evil forces.

STATE OF PRESERVATION
Advanced State of Decay

DESCRIPTION
The *rigsum gonbo* comprises of three small *chorten* built over a common plinth. The plinth is approximately two metres high and is built in random rubble masonry. The *chorten* are built in stone and mud brick masonry and are mud plastered and painted on the exterior. The *chorten* are painted in red, white and blue. The *chorten* have eroded considerably and the external plaster over the domes is lost.

SOURCE OF INFORMATION Ishey Dolma, Domkhar Dho, Khaltse, Ladakh

---

Tashag

INVENTORY NO.
KHALTSE / DOMKHAR DHO / 08 / 2004

Vernacular Building | Abandoned | Public (Hemis *Gonpa*)

SETTING
The *tashag* is oriented to the south and is located next to the *gonpa*. It is surrounded by the *gonpa* complex to the south and a hill to the north.

SIGNIFICANCE
The *tashag* served as the dwelling for the resident monks who were deputed to the village from Hemis *Gonpa* to oversee the religious activities in the neighbouring *gonpa*. It is built in the traditional style and contributes to the vernacular architecture of the village.

DESCRIPTION
The *tashag* is a double storeyed building with a ground floor constructed in random rubble masonry. This level has narrow ventilation openings. The first floor is built in mud brick masonry and was traditionally used for summer habitation. There is a large timber framed *rabsal* on the first floor. The interior walls of the chamber have wall paintings. There was another level over this floor which no longer exists except for some sections of the walls. The roof over the first floor is a traditional one composed of timber, grass, willow twigs and compacted mud. The rear section of the building has collapsed and the wall paintings on the first floor are damaged due to water infiltration.

STATE OF PRESERVATION
Advanced State of Decay

SOURCE OF INFORMATION Ishey Dolma – Pugapa, Domkhar Dho, Khaltse, Ladakh

Domkhar Dho

NIRLAC

Gonpa

INVENTORY NO.
KHALTSE / DOMKHAR DHO / 09 / 2004

Gonpa / Chorten / Mane Wall | In Use | Public (Hemis *Gonpa*)

STATE OF PRESERVATION
Advanced State of Decay

SETTING
The *gonpa* is oriented to the south and is located on a hill. There is a pathway on the south and a monk's ruined cell to the north. There are hills to the northeast and east of the complex.

SIGNIFICANCE
The *gonpa* is the principal place of worship in the village and comes under the Dugpa Kagyud sect. Monks are deputed to the village from Hemis *Gonpa* to perform pujas inside the temples. Villagers perform fasting in the Chanrazig lhakhang during the 1st month of the Tibetan calendar. The *chorten* and *mane* walls located within the complex as well as outside are circumambulated by villagers as an act of merit.

DESCRIPTION
The *gonpa* is accessed from the south through a doorway which leads into a courtyard surrounded by a colonnaded gallery. The walls of the courtyard are painted with images of the four guardian deities and the wheel of life. A wooden door in one corner opens into the main *dukhang* which is a square room with eight decorated wooden columns. There is an image of Chanrazig in the centre and images of Guru Rinpoche and Chamba encased in a wooden ornamental frame. To the right of these images, there are shelves on which are placed the Kangyur. There is a square clerestory in the centre of the chamber. The roof is supported by eight wooden columns. The walls of the clerestory as well as those of the *dukhang* are adorned with wall paintings depicting deities from the Buddhist pantheon. There is a small space to the left which is used for burning butter lamps. From the courtyard, another door leads to the Chanrazig *lhakhang*. It houses an image of Chanrazig which is single storey high. On either side of this image are images of other deities. The chamber has four decorative wooden columns which support the roof above. The parapet is painted in red on all sides and the door, window openings are framed within a black border. There are several *chorten* and *mane* walls within the complex. Principal among them is a Deshag Gyad which has a rectangular base over which rest the eight traditional forms of *chorten*. There is a large Changchub *chorten* to the southeast and two more *chorten* in front of the Deshag Gyad. In between these two *chorten*, there is a circular *mane* wall.

SOURCE OF INFORMATION Ishey Stanzin-Phyrdezug, Domkhar Dho, Khaltse, Ladakh

Domkhar Dho

99

Chorten

INVENTORY NO.
KHALTSE / DOMKHAR DHO / 10 / 2004

Chorten | In Use | Public (Community) | Around 180 years old

SETTING
The *chorten* is oriented to the east and is located along the slope of a mountain near a pathway which leads to the village.

SIGNIFICANCE
The *chorten* is believed to have been built around 180 years ago. It is a Changchub *chorten*, and symbolizes the Buddha's enlightenment. Located along the path which leads to the village, the *chorten* is circumambulated by villagers as an act of merit.

DESCRIPTION
The *chorten* is built on a random rubble masonry base. It is built in stone and mud brick masonry above. Externally, the surface is mud plastered and whitewashed. The *chorten* has a tall *chugsum khorlo* over the dome which is made of baked tiles and is surmounted by a crescent shaped crown made of mud.

STATE OF PRESERVATION
Advance State of Decay

SOURCE OF INFORMATION Ishey Dolma, Domkhar Dho, Khaltse, Ladakh

Group of *Mane* Wall and Deshag Gyad

INVENTORY NO.
KHALTSE / DOMKHAR DHO / 11 / 2004

Chorten / Mane Wall | In Use | Public (Community)

SETTING
The structures are oriented to the south and are located to the left of the vehicular road which leads to the village. The site is surrounded by agricultural fields and trees with the road lying to the northeast of the site.

SIGNIFICANCE
The Deshag Gyad contains all the eight forms of *chorten* i.e. Padspung, Tashi Gomang, Chotul, Changchub, Lhabab, Indoom, Namgyal and Nyangdas. Each of these symbolizes events in the life of the Buddha. The *chorten* and *mane* wall are located along the vehicular road and are circumambulated by villagers to earn merit as they travel along this route.

DESCRIPTION
The site consists of a Deshag Gyad and a *mane* wall. The Deshag Gyad has a random rubble masonry platform over

which are built eight *chorten* of different forms. The *chorten* are mud plastered and whitewashed externally. The external surface of the *chorten* has eroded leading to a loss of the original form. The *mane* wall is a cubical random rubble masonry wall over which are placed inscribed *mane* stones.

STATE OF PRESERVATION
Advanced State of Decay

SOURCE OF INFORMATION Tashi Stanbar, Domkhar Dho, Khaltse, Ladakh

Domkhar Dho

100

Group of *Chorten* and *Mane* Walls

INVENTORY NO.
KHALTSE / DOMKHAR DHO / 12 / 2004

Chorten | In Use | Public (Community) | Around 300 years old

SETTING
The structures are oriented to the east and are located along the pathway which leads to the village of Domkhar Dho. The site is surrounded by agricultural fields and apricot orchards to the west. The main road lies to the east and beyond this flows the river.

SIGNIFICANCE
The *chorten* and *mane* walls are believed to be about 300 years old. These are located along the path leading to the village and are circumambulated by villagers as an act of merit while travelling to and from the village.

DESCRIPTION
The site consists of a cluster of *mane* walls and *chorten*. At the start, there is a stone *mane* wall which is followed by a group of eight *chorten* built on a raised rectangular and rubble masonry platform. The *chorten* are all built in stone

masonry and are whitewashed and mud plastered. This cluster is followed by another *mane* wall and a platform on which rest a group of four *chorten*. These *chorten* are of the same size and are whitewashed externally. Following these is a larger *chorten* built in stone masonry. At the end of the group is a long *mane* wall built in dry stone masonry. The structures are all eroded and most of the *chorten* have lost their original form making them difficult to identify.

STATE OF PRESERVATION
Advanced State of Decay

SOURCE OF INFORMATION Tsewang Dorjey, Domkhar Dho, Khaltse, Ladakh

Domkhar Dho

101

Group of *Chorten* and *Mane* Walls

INVENTORY NO.
KHALTSE / DOMKHAR DHO / 13 / 2004

Chorten / Mane Wall | In Use | Public (Community)

SETTING
The structures are oriented to the east and are located along the pathway which leads to the village. The site is surrounded by agricultural fields. There is a river flowing to the southwest while the main road lies to the north east of the site.

SIGNIFICANCE
The *chorten* and *mane* walls were built in the past to accumulate merit and are still circumambulated by villagers as they travel along this path as an act of merit. The *chorten* are Changchub *chorten*, and symbolize the Buddha's enlightenment.

DESCRIPTION
The site comprises of a group of nine *chorten* of different and two *mane* walls. The *mane* walls are built in dry stone masonry and are circular as well as linear in shape. The

horizontal surface of the *mane* walls has inscribed *mane* stones. The *chorten* are built in stone and mud brick masonry and are mud plastered and whitewashed externally. The largest *chorten* has a tapering *chugsum khorlo* over the dome made of baked tiles.

STATE OF PRESERVATION
Showing Signs of Deterioration

SOURCE OF INFORMATION Tsewang Dorjey, Domkhar Dho, Khaltse, Ladakh

Group of *Chorten*

INVENTORY NO.
KHALTSE / DOMKHAR DHO / 14 / 2004

Chorten | In Use | Public (Community)

SETTING

The *chorten* are oriented to the northeast and are located along the path that leads onto the village of Domkhar Dho. The site is surrounded by agricultural fields to the southwest and apricot groves and the river to the south.

SIGNIFICANCE

The *chorten* are located along the path leading to the village and are circumambulated by villagers as an act of merit while travelling on this path. All the *chorten* are Changchub *chorten*, and symbolize the Buddha's enlightenment.

DESCRIPTION

The site comprises of a group of seven *chorten* of different sizes. The *chorten* are built in random rubble masonry and are mud plastered and whitewashed externally. The external surfaces of all the *chorten* are eroded and most have lost their original form.

STATE OF PRESERVATION
Advanced State of Decay

SOURCE OF INFORMATION Tsewang Dorjey, Domkhar Dho, Khaltse, Ladakh

Domkhar Dho

Group of *Chorten* and *Mane* Wall

INVENTORY NO.
KHALTSE / DOMKHAR DHO / 15 / 2004

Chorten / *Mane* Wall | In Use | Public (Community)

SETTING

The *chorten* and *mane* wall are oriented to the south and are located in the interior of the village. The site is surrounded by a vehicular pathway to the south and village houses to the north. Beyond the road, there is a grove of apricot trees.

SIGNIFICANCE

The *chorten* and *mane* wall were built by villagers in the past to accumulate merit. They are all Changchub *chorten* which symbolize the Buddha's enlightenment.

DESCRIPTION

The site comprises of a group of three *chorten* of similar size and a circular *mane* wall. The *chorten* are all built in random rubble and are mud plastered and whitewashed externally. The *chorten* have lost their original form due to erosion of the external mud plaster. The *mane* wall is a circular structure built in dry stone masonry and contains numerous *mane* stones on its horizontal surface. The base of the *mane* wall has collapsed.

STATE OF PRESERVATION
Danger of Disappearance

SOURCE OF INFORMATION Tsewang Dorjey, Domkhar Dho, Khaltse, Ladakh

Group of *Chorten*

INVENTORY NO.
KHALTSE / DOMKHAR DHO / 16 / 2004

Chorten | In Use | Public (Community) | Around 300 years old

SETTING
The *chorten* are oriented to the north and are located to the left of the main road which leads to the village. The *chorten* are surrounded by village houses to the south and east while the main vehicular road lies to the north.

SIGNIFICANCE
The *chorten* are built along the road leading to the village and are circumambulated by villagers as an act of merit. The *chorten* are all Changchub *chorten* that symbolize the Buddha's enlightenment.

DESCRIPTION
The site comprises of a group of three *chorten* of different sizes. The *chorten* are built in random rubble masonry and the exterior surface is mud plastered and whitewashed. The external layer of mud plaster has partially eroded in all the *chorten*.

STATE OF PRESERVATION
Danger of Disappearance

SOURCE OF INFORMATION Tashi Stanbar, Domkhar Dho, Khaltse, Ladakh

Group of *Chorten* and *Mane* Walls

INVENTORY NO.
KHALTSE / DOMKHAR DHO / 17 / 2004

Chorten / *Mane* Wall | In Use | Public (Community)

SETTING
The *chorten* and *mane* wall are oriented to the south and are built on a rocky outcrop along a mountainside.

SIGNIFICANCE
The *chorten* and *mane* wall are circumambulated by villagers to accumulate merit. The *chorten* are all Changchub *chorten* and symbolize the Buddha's enlightenment.

DESCRIPTION
The site comprises of a group of fifteen *chorten* of similar size and four *mane* walls. The chorten are built over a random rubble base and are built in stone masonry with an external layer of mud plaster and whitewash. The *mane* walls are built in dry stone masonry and contain *mane* stones on the horizontal surface.

STATE OF PRESERVATION
Advanced State of Decay

SOURCE OF INFORMATION Tashi Stanbar, Domkhar Dho, Khaltse, Ladakh

Domkhar Dho

103

Group of *Chorten* and *Mane* Wall

INVENTORY NO.
KHALTSE / DOMKHAR GONGMA / 01 / 2006

Chorten / Mane Wall | In Use | Public (Community) | Around 100 - 150 years old

SETTING
The *chorten* and *mane* wall are oriented to the east and are located along the path leading to the village. The site is built at the foot of a hill.

SIGNIFICANCE
The *chorten* and *mane* wall are located along the path leading to the village and were circumambulated in the past as an act of merit.

DESCRIPTION
The group of *chorten* and *mane* wall is built along the path that leads to the village. The *chorten* is almost in ruins. It is constructed in random rubble masonry and is devoid of any external plaster. The *mane* wall is circular in shape and is built in random rubble masonry. It is around 4 feet in diameter and 3 feet in height. There are inscribed *mane* stones placed on the horizontal surface.

STATE OF PRESERVATION
Danger of Disappearance

Zurkhang pa House

INVENTORY NO.
KHALTSE / DOMKHAR GONGMA / 02 / 2006

Vernacular Building | In Use | Private (Individual) | Around 150 - 200 years old

SETTING
The house is located along the village footpath. It is built along the slope of a hill.

SIGNIFICANCE
The house was built around 3 - 4 generations ago by an ancestor of the Zurkhang pa family and the family has continued to reside here. The house is built in the traditional style and is an example of vernacular architecture in the village.

DESCRIPTION
The Zurkhang pa house is a large double storeyed building built along the slope of a hill. The house is in two sections – the older section was built around 150 – 300 years ago while the new section was added some fifteen years ago. The entrance to the house is from the older section and a flight of stairs leads directly up to the first floor. The ground floor is built in random rubble masonry with mud mortar and is used for storage. It has a *chang khang* (room for storing *chang*). The first floor contains the family's living areas. There is a large *rabsal* in the centre of the first floor which has wooden lattice worked shutters and frames. The house has about sixteen rooms and includes a traditional kitchen. The window openings in the ground floor are narrow openings while those of the first floor are larger and have timber lintels. The first floor is built in both random rubble as well as mud brick masonry with mud mortar. The exterior walls of the old section are devoid of any mud plaster and whitewash.

STATE OF PRESERVATION
Showing Signs of Deterioration

SOURCE OF INFORMATION Tsering Phuntsog Zurkhang pa, Domkhar Gongma, Khaltse, Ladakh

Lubang

INVENTORY NO.
KHALTSE / DOMKHAR GONGMA / 03 / 2006

Lubang | In Use | Public(Community) | Around 150 - 200 years old

SETTING
The *lubang* is located in the middle of the pasture lands and there are some streams of water nearby.

SIGNIFICANCE
The *lubang* marks the residence of the *lu,* or the serpent gods. Prayers and offerings are made at the *lubang* on a fixed date in spring known as *Lu thebs* by the monks to placate the *lu*. The prayers are made to seek a good supply of water before the cultivation of fields begin in spring and offerings made to the *lu* are then immersed in water.

DESCRIPTION
The *lubang* is a small cubical structure built in random rubble masonry which is mud plastered and whitewashed on the exterior. It has a rounded dome-like roof and is approximately two feet in height.

STATE OF PRESERVATION
Fair

SOURCE OF INFORMATION Tsering Phuntsog Zurkhang pa, Domkhar Gongma, Khaltse, Ladakh

Domkhar Gongma

105

Group of *Chorten*

INVENTORY NO.
KHALTSE / DOMKHAR GONGMA / 04 / 2006

Chorten | In Use | Public (Community) | Around 150 - 200 years old

SETTING
The group of *chorten* is located on a stretch of rocky land along the slope of a hill. There are fields beyond.

SIGNIFICANCE
The *chorten* were built along a path, around 3 - 4 generations ago by a village ancestor. These are circumambulated by villagers as act of merit.

DESCRIPTION
The site consists of four *chorten*, three of which are arranged in a single row while the fourth is located a little higher up the slope. The *chorten* are built in random rubble masonry with mud mortar and have lost all trace of the external mud plaster and whitewash.

STATE OF PRESERVATION
Advanced State of Decay

Group of *Chorten*

INVENTORY NO.
KHALTSE / DOMKHAR GONGMA / 05 / 2006

Chorten | In Use | Public (Community) | Around 150 - 200 years old

SETTING
The group of *chorten* is located on a stretch of rocky land along the slope of a hill. The village *lhato* is located nearby.

SIGNIFICANCE
The *chorten* were built in the past as an act of merit. These are circumambulated by villagers as an act of merit.

DESCRIPTION
The site consists of two *chorten* built on a common random rubble masonry platform. The *chorten* are also built in random rubble masonry with mud mortar and have traces of external mud plaster and whitewash. The *chorten* have eroded over time and have lost their original form.

STATE OF PRESERVATION
Advanced State of Decay

Mane Wall

INVENTORY NO.
KHALTSE / DOMKHAR GONGMA / 06 / 2006

Mane Wall | In Use | Public(Community) | Around 150 - 200 years old

SETTING
The *mane* wall is oriented to the north and is located along the village path near the Zurkhang pa house. It is surrounded by agricultural fields.

SIGNIFICANCE
The *mane* wall was built in the past as an act of merit and is still circumambulated by villagers to accumulate merit.

DESCRIPTION
The *mane* wall is a circular wall built in random rubble masonry. Inscribed *mane* stones are placed on the top.

Photograph Not Available

STATE OF PRESERVATION
Advanced State of Decay

Domkhar Gongma

106

Group of *Chorten*

INVENTORY NO.
KHALTSE / DOMKHAR GONGMA / 07 / 2006

Chorten | Abandoned | Public (Community) | Around 300 years old

SETTING
The *chorten* are located behind the Beldisupa house and are surrounded by fields.

SIGNIFICANCE
The *chorten* were built around 300 years ago by the earliest settlers in the village for the peace and prosperity of the village.

DESCRIPTION
The *chorten* are built in stone masonry with mud mortar. They have deteriorated over time and parts of the *chorten* have collapsed.

Photograph Not Available

STATE OF PRESERVATION
Danger of Disappearance

SOURCE OF INFORMATION Tsering Domla, Domkhar Gongma, Khaltse, Ladakh

Lhakhang Nyingpa

INVENTORY NO.
KHALTSE / DOMKHAR GONGMA / 08 / 2006

Temple | Abandoned | Public (Community) | Around 200 - 250 years old

SETTING
The *Lhakhang* Nyingpa is oriented towards the west and is built to the east of the old settlement. It is surrounded by village houses and trees.

SIGNIFICANCE
The *lhakhang* is believed to have been built around 200 – 250 years ago and was earlier the principal place of worship in the village. The temple has now been abandoned and the images shifted to the new temple built to the west of the old settlement.

DESCRIPTION
The *lhakhang* is a single storeyed building constructed in stone masonry. There are traces of mud plaster on the exterior walls. The temple within has timber columns and beams supporting a traditional roof above. The roof has collapsed in places and water seepage has resulted in extensive damage to the wall paintings inside the temple.

The walls of the *lhakhang* are painted with images of the Buddha, Dorje Sempa, Guru Rinpoche, Tsepakmed and other deities and teachers.

STATE OF PRESERVATION
Advanced State of Decay

SOURCE OF INFORMATION Tashi Norboo, Domkhar Gongma, Khaltse, Ladakh

Group of *Chorten*

INVENTORY NO.
KHALTSE / DOMKHAR GONGMA / 09 / 2006

Chorten | Abandoned | Public (Community) | Around 200 - 250 years old

SETTING
The group of *chorten* are located northwest of the *Lhakhang* Nyingpa. They are oriented to the southeast and surrounded by some trees. There are village houses beyond.

SIGNIFICANCE
The *chorten* formed part of the *lhakhang* complex and were circumambulated by villagers as an act of merit when they visited the temple.

DESCRIPTION
The site consists of three *chorten*. Of these, the ones on the southern edge are in complete ruins and only the base survives. The third and larger *chorten* still survives. The *chorten* are all built in random rubble masonry and were originally mud plastered and whitewashed externally. There is a *srog-shing* embedded in the centre of the *chorten*.

STATE OF PRESERVATION
Danger of Disappearance

SOURCE OF INFORMATION Tashi Norboo, Domkhar Gongma, Khaltse, Ladakh

Domkhar *Gonpa*

INVENTORY NO.
KHALTSE / DOMKHAR GONGMA / 10 / 2006

Gonpa | In Use | Public (Hemis *Gonpa*)

SETTING
Domkhar *Gonpa* is oriented to the southeast and is situated below a rocky mountain, on the left side of the vehicle road, to the west of the village.

SIGNIFICANCE
The *gonpa* is under the purview of Hemis monastery and a monk from Hemis is deputed here to carry out prayers and rituals for the village.

DESCRIPTION
The *gonpa* is a large structure built on a rectangular plan. There are structures to the left of the main shrine which are in ruins now and no longer in use. The main *dukhang* was closed at the time of the visit and could not be accessed. The *gonpa* is built in random rubble and mud brick masonry with mud mortar and is mud plastered and whitewashed on the exterior. There are a row of *chorten* in a walled enclosure adjacent to the *gonpa*.

STATE OF PRESERVATION
Advanced State of Decay

Lhakhang

INVENTORY NO.
KHALTSE / DOMKHAR GONGMA / 11 / 2006

Temple | In Use | Public (Hemis *Gonpa*)

SETTING
The *lhakhang* is oriented to the north and is situated near the fields to the left of the vehicle road. There are village houses around the building.

SIGNIFICANCE
The *lhakhang* houses images which were shifted from Nyingpa and is today one of the principal temples in the village used in worship by the community.

DESCRIPTION
The *lhakhang* is a single storeyed building with a skylight in the centre. It is built in random rubble masonry and is mud plastered and whitewashed on the exterior. It houses statues brought from the old *lhakhang*. The roof is a traditional one made of timber joists, *taalu*, grass and compacted mud and is supported on timber columns and brackets beneath. The *lhakhang* was closed at the time of the visit and could not be accessed.

STATE OF PRESERVATION
Fair

SOURCE OF INFORMATION Tashi Norboo, Domkhar Gongma, Khaltse, Ladakh

109

Group of *Chorten* and *Mane* Wall

INVENTORY NO.
KHALTSE / DOMKHAR GONGMA / 12 / 2006

Chorten / *Mane* Wall | In Use | Public (Community) | Around 200 - 250 years old

SETTING
The *chorten* and *mane* wall are located to the right of the main vehicular road near the fields. They are located before the old settlement.

SIGNIFICANCE
The *chorten* and *mane* wall were built in the past as an act of merit along the village path and are still circumambulated by villagers.

DESCRIPTION
The *chorten* and *mane* wall are almost in ruins and only half the *chorten* still survive. The *chorten* are all built in random rubble masonry and have traces of external mud plaster and whitewash. The *mane* wall is built in random rubble masonry and has collapsed.

STATE OF PRESERVATION
Advanced State of Decay

SOURCE OF INFORMATION Tashi Nurboo, Domkhar Gongma, Khaltse, Ladakh

Domkhar Gongma

Group of *Chorten*

INVENTORY NO.
KHALTSE / DOMKHAR GONGMA / 13 / 2006

Chorten | In Use | Public (Community) | Around 250 - 300 years old

SETTING
The group of *chorten* is located at the beginning of the village, near the fields. It lies a little below the main vehicular road towards the right.

SIGNIFICANCE
The *chorten* were built in the past as an act of merit and mark the entrance to the village. They are circumambulated by villagers as they travel along this route in order to accumulate merit.

DESCRIPTION
The site consist of a Kagan *chorten* and a Changchub *chorten*. The Kagan *chorten* has two thick parallel walls over which rests a Changchub *chorten*. The walls are made of stone and mud brick masonry as is the *chorten* above. The exterior surface is mud plastered and whitewashed and there is a *chugsum khorlo* over the dome of the *chorten* made of baked clay tiles. The ceiling of the passage beneath the *chorten* is devoid of any paintings and is made

of timber. The Changchub *chorten* is located a short distance away from the Kagan *chorten* and is also made of stone masonry. The external layer of mud plaster and whitewash has largely eroded.

STATE OF PRESERVATION
Showing Signs of Deterioration

SOURCE OF INFORMATION Tashi Nurboo, Domkhar Gongma, Khaltse, Ladakh

Chorten

INVENTORY NO.
KHALTSE / DOMKHAR GONGMA / 14 / 2006

Chorten | In Use | Public (Community) | Around 250 - 300 years ago

SETTING
The *chorten* are located at the edge of a field to the east of the Kagan *chorten*.

SIGNIFICANCE
The *chorten* was built in the past as an act of merit. It lies along the village footpath and is circumambulated by villagers. The *chorten* is a Changchub *chorten* that symbolizes the Buddha's enlightenment.

DESCRIPTION
The *chorten* is built in random rubble masonry and has traces of external mud plaster and whitewash. Most of the outer surface has, however, eroded.

STATE OF PRESERVATION
Advanced State of Decay

SOURCE OF INFORMATION Tashi Nurboo, Domkhar Gongma, Khaltse, Ladakh

Group of *Chorten*

INVENTORY NO.
KHALTSE / DOMKHAR GONGMA / 15 / 2006

Chorten | In Use | Public (Community) | Around 200 years old

SETTING
The *chorten* are located a little below the new *gonpa* which lies to the north where the vehicular road ends.

SIGNIFICANCE
The *chorten* were built around 200 years ago by the villagers as an act of merit. The *chorten* are Changchub *chorten* and symbolize the Buddha's enlightenment.

DESCRIPTION
The site consist of two *chorten* built on a common random rubble masonry platform. The *chorten* are built in stone masonry and have traces of external mud plaster and whitewash. One of the *chorten* is larger than the other. Both the *chorten* have eroded over time and have lost their original form.

STATE OF PRESERVATION
Advanced State of Decay

SOURCE OF INFORMATION Tashi Nurboo, Domkhar Gongma, Khaltse, Ladakh

Domkhar Gongma

111

Sharchog Spundun *Lhato*

INVENTORY NO.
KHALTSE / DOMKHAR GONGMA / 16 / 2006

Lhato | In Use | Public (Community) | Around 250 - 300 years ago

SETTING
The *lhato* is located at Thongros, about three kms before Domkhar Gongma. It is built on a huge rock on the right side of the road.

SIGNIFICANCE
The *lhato* is dedicated to the protector deity called 'Sharchog Spundun'. Villagers worship the protectors and offer special prayers in the 4th and 5th month of the Tibetan calendar at which time the juniper branches and *khadag* are renewed.

DESCRIPTION
The *lhato* is a cubical shaped structure built on a large boulder. It is built in stone masonry and has offering of juniper branches and *khadag* placed on the top.

STATE OF PRESERVATION
Showing Signs of Deterioration

SOURCE OF INFORMATION Tashi Nurboo, Domkhar Gongma, Khaltse, Ladakh

Stambu Lharten
Lhato

INVENTORY NO.
KHALTSE / DOMKHAR GONGMA / 17 / 2006

Lhato | In Use | Public (Community) | Around 250 - 300 years old

SETTING
The *lhato* is located in Thongros about three kms before Domkhar Gongma on the left side of the road. It is built along a mountain side on rocky stretch of land.

SIGNIFICANCE
The *lhato* is dedicated to the protector deity called 'Stambu Lharten'. People worship the deity and offer special prayers during Losar when the juniper offerings are renewed.

DESCRIPTION
The *lhato* is a small cubical structure built in dry stone masonry. It has ritual offerings of juniper placed on the top.

STATE OF PRESERVATION
Showing Signs of Deterioration

Domkhar Gongma

112

Gongma

Gongma lies on a three-day trek from Phanjilla. From the Leh - Srinagar highway, a road diverts between Khaltse and Lamayuru towards Shilla. Phanjilla lies on this road. The village is called Gongma meaning 'upper village' as it is situated at a higher altitude than other villages. There are about eight households in Gongma.

Listed by: Gelong Tsewang Jorgyes
Year: 2006

Gyera

The village of Gyera is situated at the edge of the Mangyu valley, about 70 kms from Leh. Originally, the village was known as Skyid-gra meaning a 'place of happiness'. The Gongmapa family were the first family to settle in the village. Today, there are 8 households in the village.

{*Source: Murup Tashi (Thangmatpa)*}

Listed by: Deldan Angmo and Jassu Singh
Year: 2004

Chorten

INVENTORY NO.
KHALTSE / GONGMA / 01 / 2006

Chorten | In Use | Private (Individual) | Around 45 years old

SETTING
The *chorten* is located near the Gongmapa house and is surrounded by a meadow and the house.

SIGNIFICANCE
The *chorten* was built about 45 years ago by the Gongmapa family as an act of merit. It is a Changchub *chorten*, and symbolizes the Buddha's enlightenment.

DESCRIPTION
The *chorten* is built in stone and mud brick masonry and is mud plastered and whitewashed on the exterior. There is a red tapering *chugsum khorlo* over the dome of the *chorten*. Near the base of the *chorten* there is a small *mane* wall and several stones inscribed with sacred *mantras* and texts are placed both on the *chorten* as well as on the *mane* wall. The *mane* wall is built in dry stone masonry and is of an irregular shape.

STATE OF PRESERVATION
Showing Signs of Deterioration

Lingshed *Labrang* *Gongma* (Thango)

INVENTORY NO.
KHALTSE / GONGMA / 02 / 2006

Vernacular Building | In Use | Public (Lingshed *Gonpa*) | Around 700 years old

SETTING
The *labrang* is located at the beginning of the village and is surrounded by meadows and mountains.

SIGNIFICANCE
The *labrang* has belonged to the Lingshed *gonpa* since the 15th century and served as the residence for the monks from Lingshed. Presently, it is leased to a family who stays there and cultivates the land owned by the *gonpa*. The building is built in the traditional style and is part of the vernacular architecture in the village.

DESCRIPTION
The Lingshed *labrang* is a large double storeyed building. It is built in random rubble masonry at the lower levels and in mud brick masonry in the upper levels. The ground floor is used for storage while the upper level houses the family's living quarters. The exterior walls of the *labrang* are mud plastered and whitewashed. It has a traditional roof above.

STATE OF PRESERVATION
Showing Sign of Deterioration

Lhakhang Gogpo

INVENTORY NO.
KHALTSE / GONGMA / 03 / 2006

Temple | Abandoned | Public (Lingshed *Gonpa*) | Around 850 years old

SETTING
The *lhakhang* is located at the beginning of the village on the northwest edge of the village.

SIGNIFICANCE
The *lhakhang* once served as a place of worship for the village and belonged to Lingshed *gonpa*. It was abandoned long ago and has been reduced to ruins over the past 200 years.

DESCRIPTION
The *lhakhang* is in complete ruins today and only remnants of the walls survive. The walls are built in random rubble masonry.

STATE OF PRESERVATION
Danger of Disappearance

Chorten

INVENTORY NO.
KHALTSE / GONGMA / 04 / 2006

Chorten | In Use | Public (Community) | Around 90 years old

SETTING
The *chorten* is located on a barren hill at the beginning of the village, beyond the *Lhakhang* Gogpo. It is surrounded by mountains and the village lies beyond.

SIGNIFICANCE
The *chorten* was built about 90 years ago by the villagers to fulfill a prophecy about two *chorten* being built at the beginning and at the end of the village.

DESCRIPTION
The *chorten* is built on a barren stretch of land. It is built over a random rubble masonry platform in stone and mud brick masonry with mud mortar and is mud plastered and whitewashed on the exterior. The *chorten* is surmounted by a red *chugsum khorlo* with a metal crown on top. There is a *tarchen* posted near the *chorten*.

STATE OF PRESERVATION
Advanced State of Decay

Gongma

117

Tsamphuk
(Joshila Kangshan)

INVENTORY NO.
KHALTSE / GONGMA / 05 / 2006

Cave | Abandoned | Public (Community) | Around 11th century

SETTING
The *tsamphuk* is situated to the north of the village between two small waterfalls.

SIGNIFICANCE
According to legend, Lotsawa Rinchen Zangpo lived in these caves and made paper on which he transcribed sacred texts. Thereafter, two rooms were built here for meditation and many monks meditated here. These caves were abandoned around 300 years ago.

DESCRIPTION
The caves are located in the mountains and were used till 300 years ago. Two rooms were built near the caves to serve as meditation cells but these have been abandoned now. The walls of the caves are bare and without any paintings.

STATE OF PRESERVATION
Showing Signs of Deterioration

Thangopa House

INVENTORY NO.
KHALTSE / GONGMA / 06 / 2006

Vernacular Building | In Use | Private (Individual) | Around 160 years old

SETTING
The house is located in the middle of the village and is surrounded by mountains and open area.

SIGNIFICANCE
The Thangopa house was built by the ancestors of the Thangopa family about 160 years ago. It is built in the traditional style and is an example of vernacular architecture in the village.

DESCRIPTION
The Thangopa house is built on a random plan. The ground floor is constructed in random rubble masonry while the first floor is built in mud brick masonry. The house has very few openings. The roof is laid in the traditional manner and rests on timber columns, beams and joists below. The exterior walls of the first floor are mud plastered and white washed.

STATE OF PRESERVATION
Showing Signs of Deterioration

Gongma

118

Rigsum Gonbo

INVENTORY NO.
KHALTSE / GONGMA / 07 / 2006

Rigsum Gonbo | In Use | Private (Individual) | Around 300 years old

SETTING
The *rigsum gonbo* is located in the middle of agricultural fields and meadows in the village.

SIGNIFICANCE
The *rigsum gonbo* was built 300 years ago by ancestors of the Gongma family to protect them from evil and misfortune.

DESCRIPTION
The *rigsum gonbo* is built on a rectangular plan with walls on three sides while the fourth side is open. Within this enclosure is a plinth on which are built three *chorten* painted in orange, blue and white symbolizing the deities Jamyang, Chagdor and Chanrazig. The *chorten* are built in stone and mud brick masonry and are mud plastered on the exterior. The walls of the *rigsum gonbo* are built in random rubble and mud brick masonry and are mud plastered and

whitewashed on the exterior. The structure has a traditional roof above which is supported on wooden columns below.

STATE OF PRESERVATION
Showing Signs of Deterioration

Srangyokpa House

INVENTORY NO.
KHALTSE / GONGMA / 08 / 2006

Vernacular Building | In Use | Private (Individual) | Around 190 years old

SETTING
The Srangyokpa house is located in the middle of the village near the Gongmapa house.

SIGNIFICANCE
The Srangyokpa house was built by Meme Dukgyas, an ancestor of the family, about 190 years ago. The house is built in the traditional style and is an example of vernacular architecture in the village.

DESCRIPTION
The Srangyokpa house is a double storeyed house built in random rubble masonry at the ground floor and in mud brick masonry on the first floor. The exterior walls of the house are mud plastered and some areas are whitewashed. There are red markings on the corners of the house as well as around the doors and windows to ward off evil. Some sections of the house appear to have collapsed. The house has few window openings which are small in size. The

ground floor is used largely for storage while the family's living quarters are on the first floor. The house has a traditional roof on which is fodder is stored.

STATE OF PRESERVATION
Advanced State of Decay

Gongma

11

Gongmapa House

INVENTORY NO.
KHALTSE / GONGMA / 09 / 2006

Vernacular Building | In Use | Private (Individual) | Around 11th century

SETTING
The Gongmapa house is located along a footpath in the middle of the village.

SIGNIFICANCE
The Gongmapa is the oldest family in the village and one of the earliest settlers in the village. The family is one of the most influential in the village and has over the past built several *chorten*, *mane* walls etc. in the village. The family chapel in the house contains a unique image of the Lotsawa (about 12 inches long) which is brought out and taken to the fields whenever crops are threatened by insect attacks or other natural calamities.

DESCRIPTION
The Gongmapa house is a double storeyed house built along the slope of a hill with an entrance from the footpath which runs along the house. The house has several later additions. The ground floor is built largely in random rubble masonry while the first floor is built in mud brick masonry.

The house is mud plastered and whitewashed on the exterior. There is a red parapet running along the edge of the roof which is a traditional roof built of timber joists, *taalu*, grass and compacted mud. The window openings on the first floor have timber lintels and there is a large timber framed *rabsal* on the first floor.

STATE OF PRESERVATION
Showing Signs of Deterioration

Chorten

INVENTORY NO.
KHALTSE / GONGMA / 10 / 2006

Chorten | In Use | Public (Community) | Around 90 years old

SETTING
The *chorten* is located at the end of the village on a bare patch of land. It is surrounded by the mountains and the village lies behind it.

SIGNIFICANCE
The *chorten* was built about 90 years ago by the villagers to fulfill a prophecy about two *chorten* being built at the beginning and at the end of the village. The *chorten* is a Changchub *chorten* and symbolizes the Buddha's enlightenment.

DESCRIPTION
The *chorten* is built on a barren stretch of land. It is built over a random rubble masonry platform. The *chorten* is also built in random rubble masonry and is mud plastered and whitewashed on the exterior. It has a *srog-shing* projecting through the centre of the dome on which rests a metal crown. There is a *tarchen* posted near the *chorten* with *mane* stones placed at its base.

STATE OF PRESERVATION
Showing Signs of Deterioration

Gongma

20

Gongmapa *Chorten*

INVENTORY NO.
KHALTSE / GYERA / 01 / 2004

Chorten | In Use | Private (Individual) | Around 250 years old

SETTING
The Gongmapa *chorten* are oriented to the northeast and are located southeast of the Gongmapa house and northwest of the primary school building. There is a stream flowing nearby.

SIGNIFICANCE
The *chorten* fall on the old footpath which leads from Gyera to Mangyu and were circumambulated by villagers to accumulate merit as they travelled on this route. The *chorten* were built by the ancestors of the Gongmapa family and are still maintained by them. The *chorten* are all Changchub *chorten* and symbolize the Buddha's enlightenment.

DESCRIPTION
The site comprises of a group of three *chorten* of different sizes placed in a row. The central *chorten* is the largest followed by the one adjacent to the school building and the one on the opposite side is the smallest in size. The *chorten*

are all built on a random rubble masonry base in stone and mud brick masonry with mud mortar. The exterior surface of the *chorten* is mud plastered and whitewashed. The base of the *chorten* have stucco relief motifs (*pa-tra*) of animal and floral designs with some portions painted in red. The domes of the *chorten* have small niches facing the northeast with wooden frames.

STATE OF PRESERVATION
Showing Signs of Deterioration

SOURCE OF INFORMATION Yeshi Namgyal Dagchanpa, Gyera, Khaltse, Ladakh

Gyera

121

Gongampa House

INVENTORY NO.
KHALTSE / GYERA / 02 / 2004

Vernacular Building | In Use | Private (Individual) | Around 250 - 300 years old

SETTING
The Gongmapa house is oriented to the southwest and is located behind the Dagchanpa house, near Gongmapa *mane* and a group of *chorten*.

SIGNIFICANCE
The house was built by ancestors of the Gongma family 5 - 6 generations ago. The Gongma family was one of the five families that first settled in this village. The house has its own *lhato* dedicated to the protector deity of the family. The house is built in the traditional style and is a good example of vernacular architecture in the village.

DESCRIPTION
The Gongmapa house is a large three storeyed house. A new wing has been added to the old house on the southwest side. The ground floor is built in stone masonry with mud mortar and has narrow openings for ventilation. This level is used primarily by the family for housing animals. The first and the second floors are built in mud

brick masonry and have larger window openings with tiered lintels. These levels form the family's living quarters. The roof top has a flag post at each corner and fodder is stored along the parapet line. It is a traditional roof comprising of timber, dried grass and a layer of compacted mud. The exterior walls of the house are mud plastered and whitewashed. There is a *lhato* on the southern corner of the roof which is dedicated to the guardian deity of the family. It is a cubical structure containing juniper branches and *khadag*.

STATE OF PRESERVATION
Showing Signs of Deterioration

SOURCE OF INFORMATION Yeshi Namgyal Dagchanpa, Gyera, Khaltse, Ladakh

Gongmapa *Mane* Wall and *Chorten*

INVENTORY NO.
KHALTSE / GYERA / 03 / 2004

Chorten / *Mane* Wall | In Use | Private (Individual) | Around 200 years old

SETTING
The *chorten* and *mane* wall are oriented to the west and are located along a stream, southeast of the Gongmapa house. The primary school building stands opposite.

SIGNIFICANCE
The *chorten* and *mane* wall were built by ancestors of the Gongma family about 200 years ago to accumulate merit. The family is one of the five families who first settled here. The structures are circumambulated by villagers as an act of merit. The *chorten* is a Changchub *chorten* that symbolizes the Buddha's enlightenment.

DESCRIPTION
The site comprises of a large Changchub *chorten* and a *mane* wall. The *chorten* is built over a low random rubble masonry plinth in stone masonry with mud mortar. The exterior surface is mud plastered and whitewashed. The base panels of the chorten are decorated with stucco motifs (*pa-tra*) and the corners are painted in red. The dome has a tall *chugsum khorlo* made of baked tiles with a crescent shaped crown on the top. The *mane* wall, located next to the *chorten*, is cylindrical in shape and is built in stone masonry. The horizontal surface contains *mane* stones. There is a small niche to the southwest which is bordered in red. The *mane* wall is also mud plastered and whitewashed externally.

STATE OF PRESERVATION
Showing Signs of Deterioration

SOURCE OF INFORMATION Yeshi Namgyal Dagchanpa, Gyera, Khaltse, Ladakh

Gyera

122

Group of *Chorten*

INVENTORY NO.
KHALTSE / GYERA / 04 / 2004

Chorten | In Use | Private (Individual) | Around 200 years old

SETTING
The *chorten* are oriented to the east structures are located south of the Gongmapa house and east of the primary school building.

SIGNIFICANCE
The *chorten* were built by ancestors of the Gongmapa family about 200 years ago. The Gongmapa family was one of the five families who first settled in this village.

DESCRIPTION
The site consists of a group of 6 - 7 *chorten*, four of which are in ruins. The first three *chorten* are Changchub *chorten* in a relatively good condition and share a common platform. The other four *chorten* placed on a separate base, have collapsed and debris is lying all over the site. The *chorten* are built in stone masonry and are mud plastered and whitewashed externally.

STATE OF PRESERVATION
Danger of Disappearance

SOURCE OF INFORMATION Yeshi Namgyal Dagchanpa, Gyera, Khaltse, Ladakh

Chotar *Lhato*

INVENTORY NO.
KHALTSE / GYERA / 05 / 2004

Lhato | In Use | Public (Community)

SETTING
The *lhato* is oriented to the northeast and is located on a large boulder along the slopes of a hill, northwest of the Gongmapa house and *chorten*.

SIGNIFICANCE
The *lhato* is dedicated to the protector guardian deity of the village and is believed to have been built when the village was first settled. The juniper plants, *khadag* etc. are renewed and the *lhato* whitewashed every year on the 1st day of the 1st month of the Tibetan calendar amidst ritual and prayers.

DESCRIPTION
The *lhato* is a small cubical structure built over a large stone boulder. It is built in stone masonry and faces the settlement. It contains a bunch of juniper twigs and animal horns with *khadag* tied around it. The exterior is mud

plastered and whitewashed. The corners of the structure are painted in red and there is a crescent drawn on the surface wall in red.

STATE OF PRESERVATION
Fair

SOURCE OF INFORMATION Yeshi Namgyal Dagchanpa, Gyera, Khaltse, Ladakh

123

Gyera

Spurkhang

INVENTORY NO.
KHALTSE / GYERA / 06 / 2004

Cemetery / Cremation Ground / Tomb | In Use | Public (Community) | Around 350 years old

SETTING
The *spurkhang* is oriented to the east and is surrounded by agricultural fields, the village stream and apricot orchards to the east and mountains to the west.

SIGNIFICANCE
The area has been used as a cremation ground by the villagers for many centuries. Each family has its own *spurkhang* which is reused on the death of a family member.

DESCRIPTION
The area comprises of a group of 4 – 5 *spurkhang* scattered over a large area. Each is a small square structure with sides of about one metre each. The newer *spurkhang* are decorated with floral motifs and paintings while the older ones are disintegrating.

STATE OF PRESERVATION
Showing Signs of Deterioration

SOURCE OF INFORMATION Yeshi Namgyal Dagchanpa, Gyera, Khaltse, Ladakh

Khang gyab-pe *Chorten*

INVENTORY NO.
KHALTSE / GYERA / 07 / 2004

Chorten | In Use | Public (Community) | Around 200 years old

SETTING
The *chorten* are oriented to the north and are located south of the agricultural fields and the village stream. Some ruined structures used for storing fodder are located to the west of the site.

SIGNIFICANCE
The *chorten* are circumambulated by villagers as an act of merit. These are Changchub *chorten* and symbolize the Buddha's enlightenment. The *tsadkhang* contains numerous *tsa-tsa*.

DESCRIPTION
The site comprises of two Changchub *chorten* and a *tsadkhang* placed in a singe row along the village stream. One of the *chorten* is larger than the other. Both *chorten* are built in stone masonry and stand on a random rubble masonry plinth. The exterior surface of the *chorten* is mud

plastered and whitewashed. The *tsadkhang* is a small square structure housing a number of *tsa-tsa* with a small timber framed opening facing east. It is covered by a traditional roof comprising of wooden joists, willow twigs and a layer of compacted mud on top.

STATE OF PRESERVATION
Showing Signs of Deterioration

SOURCE OF INFORMATION Yeshi Namgyal Dagchanpa, Gyera, Khaltse, Ladakh

Gyera

Chorten Chan

INVENTORY NO.
KHALTSE / GYERA / 08 / 2004

Chorten | In Use | Public (Community) | Around 900 - 1000 yearrs old

SETTING
The *chorten* are oriented to the south and are surrounded by agricultural fields and some ruined structures. It is located in close proximity of the Thangmaranpa house.

SIGNIFICANCE
The *chorten* are believed to have been built at the time of Lotsava Rinchen Zangpo (11th century). The *chorten* lie on the old path which led to Mangyu and was used by the villagers before the vehicular road was laid. The *chorten* would have been circumambulated by the villagers as they travelled along this path.

STATE OF PRESERVATION
Advanced State of Decay

DESCRIPTION
The site comprises of three *chorten* - one large and two small, and a smaller square structure which is in ruins. The *chorten* are built in stone masonry with mud mortar and are mud plastered and whitewashed externally. The external layer of plaster has largely eroded over time and it is difficult to discern the original form of these *chorten*.

SOURCE OF INFORMATION Yeshi Namgyal Dagchanpa, Gyera, Khaltse, Ladakh

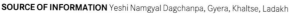

Chorten Gogpo

INVENTORY NO.
KHALTSE / GYERA / 09 / 2004

Chorten | In Use | Public (Community)

SETTING
The *chorten* is oriented to the east and is surrounded by agricultural fields, village stream and several willow trees to the east.

SIGNIFICANCE
The *chorten* is circumambulated by villagers to accumulate merit. The *chorten* is a Changchub *chorten*, symbolizing the Buddha's enlightenment.

DESCRIPTION
The site consists of a Changchub *chorten* built over a random rubble masonry platform in stone masonry and mud mortar. It is mud plastered and whitewashed on the exterior. The second structure is in complete ruins and appears to have been another *chorten* though its form cannot be identified.

STATE OF PRESERVATION
Advanced State of Decay

SOURCE OF INFORMATION Yeshi Namgyal Dagchanpa, Gyera, Khaltse, Ladakh

Gyera *Lhakhang*

INVENTORY NO.
KHALTSE / GYERA / 10 / 2004

Temple | In Use | Public (Community) | Around 200 years old

SETTING
The *lhakhang* is oriented to the south and is built along the slope of a mountain above the village. The Chotar *lhato* lies further south of the *lhakhang* on top of a hillock above the settlement. A narrow footpath from the foothills leads up to the temple.

SIGNIFICANCE
The *lhakhang* is believed to be about 200 years old. Although the building has been recently repaired, it still contains the old images and ritual artifacts. It is the principal place of worship in the village and villagers perform prayers and rituals here.

DESCRIPTION
The *lhakhang* is a small single storeyed building built along the slope of a mountain. A tall prayer flag is located south at the entrance. The *lhakhang* is a single room temple with images of various guardian deities. The building itself is new with large window openings and wooden frames painted in red.

STATE OF PRESERVATION
Fair

SOURCE OF INFORMATION Yeshi Namgyal Dagchanpa, Gyera, Khaltse, Ladakh

Gyera

125

Dagchanpa's *Rigsum Gonbo*

INVENTORY NO.
KHALTSE / GYERA / 11 / 2004

Rigsum Gonbo | In Use | Private (Individual) | Around 200 years old

STATE OF PRESERVATION
Showing Signs of Deterioration

SETTING
The *rigsum gonbo* is oriented to the east and is located north of the Dagchanpa house, over the entrance staircase of the house.

SIGNIFICANCE
The *rigsum gonbo* is believed to have been built around 200 years old by the ancestors of the Dagchanpa family in order to protect the family from evil forces and diseases.

DESCRIPTION
The *rigsum gonbo* is rectilinear in plan built in front of Dagchanpa house. It has a high plinth and there is a small niche within the plinth housing several small prayer wheels made out of old tin cans. The upper level has an elaborate decorated wooden frame. It has three openings, each with a segmental arch above. It has a wooden parapet and above the arches are the decorated wooden tiers painted in colorful floral colors. The interior walls are painted with images of three guardian deities' representing Jamyang, Chanrazig and Chagdor. The structure houses small *chorten* - Namgyal *chorten*, Changchub *chorten* and Indoom *chorten*. All the *chorten* are decorated with *pa-tra* and painted over. Stones inscribed with sacred *mantras* are placed inside the *rigsum gonbo*. In addition, there are small *tsa-tsa* also placed inside. To the north of the *rigsum gonbo* is a small square structure which has prayer wheels placed one on top of another.

Gyera

126

Tongspon (Gyerapa) House and *Rigsum Gonbo*

INVENTORY NO.
KHALTSE / GYERA / 12 / 2004

Vernacular Building / *Rigsum Gonbo* | In Use | Private (Individual) | Around 200 years old

SETTING

The Gyerapa house is oriented to the southwest and is the first house on entering the village. It is located 50 meters from Dagchanpa house which lies to the north. It is surrounded by apricot orchards and willow trees.

SIGNIFICANCE

The Gyerapa house is one of the earliest houses in the village and was built by the ancestors of the Gyerapa family about 200 years ago. The family continues to reside in the house. The house is built in the traditional style and is a good example of vernacular architecture in the village. The *rigsum gonbo* was built by the forefathers of the Gyerapa family to protect the family from evil forces.

DESCRIPTION

The Gyerapa house is a large three storeyed structure built along the village street. The house has been repaired and new sections added over time. The southwest side of the house is the oldest section and has small openings on the front facade. There is an open verandah with wooden columns and brackets on the first floor. The ground floor is built in stone masonry while the upper levels are built in mud brick masonry. The windows have carved timber lintels. The exterior walls of the house are mud plastered and whitewashed. The main entrance door has a *rigsum gonbo* above it. It is a linear structure with a large wooden opening in front. The wooden frame has decorated segmental arches and wooden tiers above. There are three small *chorten* with decorated motifs and painted surfaces within. The interior walls have been painted with bands in different colours and designs including the eight Tibetan auspicious signs. Externally, the structure is mud plastered and whitewashed and has a parapet on the roof top.

STATE OF PRESERVATION
Showing Signs of Deterioration

Gyera

127

SOURCE OF INFORMATION Ishay Namgyal Dagchanpa, Gyera, Khaltse, Ladakh

Tongspon (Kagan *Chorten*)

INVENTORY NO.
KHALTSE / GYERA / 13 / 2004

Chorten | In Use | Private (Individual) | Around 200 years old

SETTING
The *chorten* is oriented to the south and is located south of the Tongspon house at the entrance to the village.

SIGNIFICANCE
The Kagan *chorten* was built by the ancestors of the Tongspon family about 200 years ago to protect the village from evils and diseases. Merit is believed to accrue to believers who pass under the passage of the *chorten*.

DESCRIPTION
The Kagan *chorten* consists of two thick parallel walls of stone masonry over which rests a Changchub *chorten*. The ceiling of the passage beneath is in the shape of *mandala* with paintings of various Buddhist deities and sages and a central *mandala*. Panels of religious texts are painted along the side. The Changchub *chorten* is built in stone masonry with mud mortar and is mud plastered and whitewashed externally. The base panels of the chorten have *pa-tra*. There is a *chugsum khorlo* over the dome of the *chorten* over which rests a crescent shaped metal crown.

STATE OF PRESERVATION
Showing Signs of Deterioration

Gyera

SOURCE OF INFORMATION Yeshi Namgyal Dagchanpa, Gyera, Khaltse, Ladakh

NIRLAC

Mane Wall and Rock Inscription

INVENTORY NO.
KHALTSE / GYERA / 14 / 2004

Mane Wall | In Use | Public (Community)

SETTING
The *mane* wall is oriented to the south and is located along the village road south of the River Indus.

SIGNIFICANCE
The *mane* wall is located along the road and is circumambulated by villagers to accumulate merit.

DESCRIPTION
The *mane* wall is a linear wall built in dry stone masonry and has numerous *mane* stone placed on its horizontal surface. There is a large flat stone with an inscription placed on the *mane* wall which is painted in deep red.

STATE OF PRESERVATION
Fair

SOURCE OF INFORMATION Yeshi Namgyal Dagchanpa, Gyera, Khaltse, Ladakh

Gyera

129

Chorten and *Mane* Wall

INVENTORY NO.
KHALTSE / GYERA / 15 / 2004

Chorten / *Mane* Wall | In Use | Public (Community)

SETTING
The *chorten* and *mane* wall are oriented to the south and are located along the village road, south of the River Indus.

SIGNIFICANCE
The *chorten* and *mane* wall are located along the road leading to the village and are circumambulated by villagers to accumulate merit. The *chorten* are both Changchub *chorten* and symbolize the Buddha's enlightenment.

DESCRIPTION
The site comprises of two *chorten* and a *mane* wall. The *chorten* are located to the west of the *mane* wall and are both Changchub *chorten*. The *chorten* are built in stone masonry with mud mortar and have traces of external mud plaster and whitewash. However, most of the external surfaces have eroded and the *chorten* have lost their original form. The *mane* wall is a linear wall built in dry

stone masonry with a wide horizontal surface on which are placed inscribed *mane* stones. There is a square structure towards the east of the *mane* wall.

STATE OF PRESERVATION
Showing Signs of Deterioration

SOURCE OF INFORMATION Yeshi Namgyal Dagchanpa, Gyera, Khaltse, Ladakh

Hanu

Hanu is situated in a valley about 190 kms from Leh. It lies on the old Leh - Skardu road which passes through the Hanu Pass. Hanu literally means *'ancient people with high cheeks'*. The village is divided into two hamlets - Hanu *Gongma* (upper Hanu) and Hanu *Yokma* (lower Hanu). Hanu is one of the several Dard villages in Khaltse. The Dards, are an ethnically distinct race who are believed to have migrated to the valley from the Gilgit region many centuries ago. There are about 85 families in Hanu *Gongma* and 100 families in Hanu *Yokma* today.

{*Source: Tsering Murup*}

Listed by: Deldan Angmo, Jassu Singh and Dr. Sonam Wangchok
Year: 2004, 2006

Kagan *Chorten* (Pharka)

INVENTORY NO.
KHALTSE / HANU GONGMA / 01 / 2004

Chorten | In Use | Public (Community) | Around 100 years old

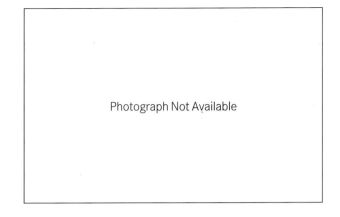

Photograph Not Available

SETTING

The *chorten* is oriented to the south and is located in the middle of fields in the village of Hanu *Gongma*. It is surrounded by agricultural fields and there is a river along the southwest.

SIGNIFICANCE

The *chorten* is believed to have been built around 100 years ago. It is a gateway *chorten* and merit is believed to accrue to believers who pass through the passage of the *chorten* and circumambulate it.

DESCRIPTION

The site consists of a Kagan *chorten* with two thick random rubble masonry walls supporting a Changchub *chorten* above. The *chorten* is built in stone and mud brick masonry and is mud plastered and whitewashed on the exterior. It has *pa-tra* motifs on the base panels and a tall *chugsum*

khorlo over the dome. The passage beneath the *chorten* has a ceiling made of timber and is in the shape of a *mandala* but devoid of any paintings. There is a pathway around the *chorten* for circumambulation.

STATE OF PRESERVATION
Advanced State of Decay

SOURCE OF INFORMATION Nawang Dorjey - Sarpanch, Hanu *Gongma*, Khaltse, Ladakh

Kagan *Chorten*

INVENTORY NO.
KHALTSE / HANU GONGMA / 02 / 2004

Chorten | In Use | Public (Community) | Around 250 years old

Photograph Not Available

SETTING

The *chorten* is oriented to the east and is located near the *gonpa* complex in the village of Hanu *Gongma*.

SIGNIFICANCE

The *chorten* is believed to be around 250 years old and is a gateway *chorten*. Merit is believed to accrue to believers who pass through the passage of the *chorten* and circumambulate it.

DESCRIPTION

The Kagan *chorten* has two thick random rubble masonry walls supporting a Changchub *chorten* above. The *chorten* is built in stone and mud brick masonry and is mud plastered and whitewashed on the exterior. It has *pa-tra* motifs on the base panels and a tall *chugsum khorlo* over the dome. The passage beneath the *chorten* has a timber ceiling built in the shape of a *mandala* with traces of paintings. There is a circumambulatory path around the *chorten*.

STATE OF PRESERVATION
Advanced State of Decay

SOURCE OF INFORMATION Nawang Dorjey – Sarpanch, Hanu *Gongma*, Khaltse, Ladakh

Mane Wall

INVENTORY NO.
KHALTSE / HANU GONGMA / 03 / 2004

Mane Wall | In Use | Public (Community)

SETTING
The *mane* wall is oriented to the west and is located along the pathway leading from Hanu *Yokma* to Hanu *Gongma*.

SIGNIFICANCE
The *mane* wall is located along the path leading from Hanu *Yokma* to Hanu *Gongma* and is circumambulated by villagers as they travel along this route.

DESCRIPTION
The site consists of a *mane* wall and a *tarchen.* The *mane* wall is a roughly rectangular structure built in dry stone masonry with numerous inscribed stones, containing religious texts and *mantras,* placed on the top. To the right of the *mane* wall, there is a *tarchen.*

STATE OF PRESERVATION
Danger of Disappearance

SOURCE OF INFORMATION Nawang Dorjey - Sarpanch, Hanu *Gongma*, Khaltse, Ladakh

Nas Mal *Mane*

INVENTORY NO.
KHALTSE / HANU GONGMA / 04 / 2006

Landscape (Community Space) | In Use | Public (Community) | Around 300 years old

SETTING
The *mane* is located in the middle of the old settlement and is surrounded by village houses.

SIGNIFICANCE
The area has been used as a community space for more than 300 years. It is used on the occasion of village festivals, marriages and other ceremonies. Village meetings are also held here.

DESCRIPTION
The site forms a sort of square and there is a row of stones which are used for seating during functions. In the middle, there is a *mane* wall which is constructed in stone masonry and has *mane* stones placed on the top.

STATE OF PRESERVATION
Showing Signs of Deterioration

SOURCE OF INFORMATION Tsering Murup, Goba Hanu, Hanu *Gongma*, Khaltse, Ladakh

Hanu Gongma

133

Gangapa House

INVENTORY NO.
KHALTSE / HANU GONGMA / 05 / 2006

Vernacular Building | In Use | Private (Individual) | Around 250 years old

SETTING
The house is situated near the Nas mal. It is surrounded by other village houses and is in the middle of the old settlement.

SIGNIFICANCE
The house was built more than 250 years ago by an ancestor of the Gangapa family. Successive generations have continued to reside here. The house is built in the traditional style and is an example of vernacular architecture in the village.

DESCRIPTION
Oriented towards the Nas mal, the Gangapa residence is a double storeyed structure with the entrance from the village street. It is constructed in random rubble and mud brick masonry with a wooden frame on the top floor. The kitchen and living spaces are on the first floor. The house has a mud floor and a timber roof supported by columns and the brackets.

SOURCE OF INFORMATION Stanzin Dorje, Hanu *Gongma*, Khaltse, Ladakh

STATE OF PRESERVATION
Showing Signs of Deterioration

Hanu Gongma

134

Skyi Sonampa House

INVENTORY NO.
KHALTSE / HANU GONGMA / 06 / 2006

Vernacular Building | In Use | Private (Individual) | Around 250 years old

SETTING
The house is located near the Nas mal next to the Gangapa house. The site is surrounded by other village houses and is in the middle of the old settlement.

SIGNIFICANCE
The house is more than 250 years old and was built by an ancestor of the Skyi Sonampa family. The family has continued to reside here. The house is built in the traditional style and is an example of vernacular architecture in the village.

DESCRIPTION
Oriented towards the Nas mal *mane*, the Skyi Sonampa residence is a double storeyed structure with the entrance from the village street. The house is built in random rubble and mud brick masonry and has a mud floor and a traditional roof.

STATE OF PRESERVATION
Showing Signs of Deterioration

SOURCE OF INFORMATION Stanzin Dorje, Hanu *Gongma*, Khaltse, Ladakh

Gangu Lhundup pa *Khangchen*

INVENTORY NO.
KHALTSE / HANU GONGMA / 07 / 2006

Vernacular Building | In Use | Private (Individual) | Around 300 years old

SETTING
The house is located a little below the Nas mal. The site is surrounded by other village houses in the old settlement.

SIGNIFICANCE
It is one of the oldest structures in Hanu *Gongma* built by an ancestor of the Gangu Lhundup pa family about 300 years ago. The house is built in the traditional style and is a good example of vernacular architecture in the village.

DESCRIPTION
The Gangu Lhundup pa Khangchen residence is a double storeyed structure with the entrance from the east. The structure has been constructed in the random rubble and mud brick masonry. Part of the wall on the first floor is built in mud brick masonry. Some parts of the first floor were built on a passage which leads to the village street. It has some windows with timber frames facing the northwest.

STATE OF PRESERVATION
Showing Signs of Deterioration

SOURCE OF INFORMATION Tsering Murup, Goba Hanu, Hanu *Gongma*, Khaltse, Ladakh

Gonpa Gogpo

INVENTORY NO.
KHALTSE / HANU GONGMA / 08 / 2006

Gonpa | In Use | Public (Likir *Gonpa*) | Around 135 years old

SETTING
The *Gonpa Gogpo* is oriented towards the west and is located near the Sponpa house, to the left of the village street while walking down. The site is surrounded by village houses in the old settlement.

SIGNIFICANCE
The *gonpa* was built in 1873 by Lama Samphel and was later offered by the villagers to Likir *gonpa*. There is only one family in the village who make offerings at the *gonpa* and there are no festival or special prayers held here.

DESCRIPTION
The *gonpa* is a large double storeyed building constructed in random rubble and mud brick masonry. Some parts of the first floor have collapsed and there is a large crack in the corner of the northwestern side of the external wall. There is a *tarchen* on the first floor level courtyard. The

openings are framed in timber. The *gonpa* has a traditional roof above made of timber beams, joists, willow twigs, grass and compacted mud.

STATE OF PRESERVATION
Advanced State of Decay

SOURCE OF INFORMATION Tsering Murup, Goba Hanu, Hanu *Gongma*, Khaltse, Ladakh; and, 'History of Ladakh Monasteries', edited by Jamyang Gyaltsen, published by All Ladakh *Gonpa* Association, 1995

Chorten

INVENTORY NO.
KHALTSE / HANU GONGMA / 09 / 2006

Chorten | In Use | Public (Community) | Around 200 years old

SETTING
The *chorten* is built on a hill a little above the old settlement.

SIGNIFICANCE
The *chorten* was built around 200 years ago and is still worshipped by people who circumambulate the *chorten* to accrue merit. It is a Changchub *chorten* which symbolizes the Buddha's enlightenment.

DESCRIPTION
The *chorten* is built on a rocky stretch of land and is constructed in random rubble masonry. It has traces of external mud plaster and whitewash and there is a *srog-shing* embedded the dome of the *chorten*.

STATE OF PRESERVATION
Showing Signs of Deterioration

SOURCE OF INFORMATION Tsering Murup, Goba Hanu, Hanu *Gongma*, Khaltse, Ladakh

Rigsum Gonbo

INVENTORY NO.
KHALTSE / HANU GONGMA / 10 / 2006

Rigsum Gonbo | In Use | Public (Community) | Around 200 years old

SETTING
The *rigsum gonbo* is located on a hill a little above the old settlement. It lies near the Changchub *chorten*.

SIGNIFICANCE
The *rigsum gonbo* is believed to have been built around 200 years ago to protect the village from evil forces.

DESCRIPTION
The *rigsum gonbo* consists of a walled enclosure which is open in the front. It has a high plinth over which rest three *chorten* painted in red, white and what was originally blue but has now faded. Each *chorten* has a *chugsum khorlo* over the dome. The enclosure is built in random rubble and mud brick masonry and is mud plastered and whitewashed on the exterior. The structure has a roof made of willow twigs, timber beams and joists.

STATE OF PRESERVATION
Advanced State of Decay

SOURCE OF INFORMATION Tsering Murup, Goba Hanu, Hanu *Gongma*, Khaltse, Ladakh

Gonpa

INVENTORY NO.
KHALTSE / HANU GONGMA / 11 / 2006

Gonpa | In Use | Public (Likir *Gonpa*) | Around 135 years old

SETTING
The *gonpa* is situated on a hill above the old settlements, near the *rigsum gonbo*.

SIGNIFICANCE
Hanu Gongma *gonpa* was built in 1873 by Lama Samphel. The *gonpa* was later offered to Likir *gonpa* by the villagers. Today, one family in the village looks after the *gonpa* and lights the butter lamps here.

STATE OF PRESERVATION
Showing Signs of Deterioration

DESCRIPTION
The *gonpa* is oriented to the southeast. A small wooden doorway provides access to the temple. This is flanked by two tall *tarchen*. The temple is built in random rubble masonry with mud mortar. It has wooden columns which support the roof above. The roof is laid in the traditional manner. There are small window openings which have tiered timber lintels and frames. The exterior walls are largely devoid of mud plaster and retain traces of whitewash.

SOURCE OF INFORMATION Tsering Murup, Goba, Hanu *Gongma*, Khaltse, Ladakh; and, 'History of Ladakh Monasteries', edited by Jamyang Gyaltsen, published by All Ladakh *Gonpa* Association, 1995

Garwapa House

INVENTORY NO.
KHALTSE / HANU GONGMA / 12 / 2006

Vernacular Building | In Use | Private (Individual) | Around 250 years old

SETTING
The house is located at the lowest part of the village near the field. It is surrounded by willow trees.

SIGNIFICANCE
The house was built by an ancestor of the Garwapa family about 250 - 300 years ago and since then the family has been residing here. It is built in the traditional style and is an example of vernacular architecture in the village.

DESCRIPTION
The Garwapa residence is a double storeyed structure with an entrance from the west. The house is built in random rubble masonry with some sections in mud brick masonry. Timber bracings are inserted in between the stone masonry. The ground floor has very few openings while the first floor has larger openings with tiered timber lintels and frames. The ground floor is used primarily for storage. The family resides on the first floor. The house has a traditional roof above made of timber beams, joists, willow twigs, grass and compacted mud. The exterior walls are devoid of any mud plaster or whitewash.

STATE OF PRESERVATION
Showing Signs of Deterioration

SOURCE OF INFORMATION Tsering Murup, Goba Hanu, Hanu *Gongma*, Khaltse, Ladakh

Ganchungpa House

INVENTORY NO.
KHALTSE / HANU GONGMA / 13 / 2006

Vernacular Building | In Use | Private (Individual) | Around 250 years old

SETTING
The house is situated in the lowest part of the settlement next to the Garwapa house. It is near the fields.

SIGNIFICANCE
The Ganchungpa house was built by an ancestor of the Ganchungpa family about 250 - 300 years ago. The family has continued to reside in the house. The house is built in the traditional style and is an example of vernacular architecture in the village.

DESCRIPTION
The Ganchungpa house is a large double storeyed building built on a rectangular plan. The entrance is from the west. It is built largely in random rubble masonry with a portion of the first floor being constructed in mud brick masonry. The upper level has large window openings while the ground floor has very small openings for ventilation. The family's living areas are located on the first floor and the ground floor is used primarily for storage. There is a *tarchen* located near the entrance.

STATE OF PRESERVATION
Showing Signs of Deterioration

Hanu Gongma

138

Doangpa *Khangpa*

INVENTORY NO.
KHALTSE / HANU YOKMA / 01 / 2004

Vernacular Building | In Use | Private (Individual) | Around 200 years old

SETTING
The Doangpa house is oriented towards the south and is located on a hill in the village. It is surrounded by other houses and a *mane* wall to the southwest.

SIGNIFICANCE
The Doangpa house was built by the ancestors of the Doangpa family about 200 years ago. It is built in the traditional style and is a good example of vernacular architecture in the village.

DESCRIPTION
The Doangpa house is a three storeyed stone masonry structure. The ground floor has no openings and is used for storage as well as a cattle shed. The first floor has small rectangular openings and is used by the family as a living space during the winters. The second floor has large timber framed openings and is used during the summer months by the family. This floor also houses the family temple and living room. The house has a traditional timber roof

SOURCE OF INFORMATION Tsering Chorol, Hanu *Yokma*, Khaltse, Ladakh

comprising of wooden joists, dried grass and a layer of mud. The house has mud floors and the internal walls are plastered.

STATE OF PRESERVATION
Advanced State of Decay

Hanu Yokma

139

Mane Wall

INVENTORY NO.
KHALTSE / HANU YOKMA / 02 / 2004

Mane Wall | In Use | Public (Community) | Around 150 years old

SETTING
The *mane* wall is oriented to the south and is located near the new *gonpa* and is surrounded by village houses on all sides. The Doangpa house is to its northeast side.

SIGNIFICANCE
The *mane* wall is located in the village square and is circumambulated by villagers as an act of merit. It was built by village ancestors around three generations ago.

DESCRIPTION
The *mane* wall is circular in plan and is built in dry stone masonry. It has inscribed *mane* stones placed on the top.

STATE OF PRESERVATION
Showing Signs of Deterioration

SOURCE OF INFORMATION Tsering Chorol, Hanu *Yokma*, Khaltse, Ladakh

Nas Mal *Mane*

INVENTORY NO.
KHALTSE / HANU YOKMA / 03 / 2004

Community Space / *Mane* Wall | In Use | Community | Around 150 years old

SETTING
The Nas mal *mane* is oriented towards the south and is surrounded by residential structures to the north and northeast. There is a vast open space to its south and a willow tree nearby.

SIGNIFICANCE
The area is used as a village gathering place to celebrate festivals and other community gatherings. The *mane* wall is circumambulated by passers-by in order to gain merit.

DESCRIPTION
The area is a large open space with a *mane* wall on one side. The *mane* wall is a cubical structure constructed in dry stone masonry. Inscribed *mane* stones are placed on the top. There is a path for circumambulation around the structure.

STATE OF PRESERVATION
Showing Signs of Deterioration

SOURCE OF INFORMATION Tsering Chorol, Hanu *Yokma*, Khaltse, Ladakh

Hanu Yokma

140

Dompa House

INVENTORY NO.
KHALTSE / HANU YOKMA / 04 / 2004

Vernacular Building | In Use | Private (Individual) | Around 150 years old

SETTING
The Dompa house is oriented towards the south and is located along a narrow path which leads upto the village from the main road. The La-dopa house is located in front of the Dompa house.

SIGNIFICANCE
The Dompa house was built by the ancestors of the Dompa family and is one of the oldest houses in the village. Built in the traditional style, it is a good example of vernacular architecture in the village.

DESCRIPTION
The Dompa house is a two storeyed structure constructed in stone masonry. It is rectangular in plan and the hillside forms its northern wall. The entrance is from the south and the first floor is used for living purposes. The house has small rectangular timber framed openings with undecorated timber lintels. The structure has a traditional roof comprising of timber joists, dried grass and mud which is supported on timber beams and columns with timber brackets. The house has traditional mud flooring. The family temple is located at the south west corner of the upper level and is constructed entirely in timber. The house today lies in ruins.

STATE OF PRESERVATION
Advanced State of Decay

SOURCE OF INFORMATION Tsering Chorol, Hanu *Yokma*, Khaltse, Ladakh

Sotopa House

INVENTORY NO.
KHALTSE / HANU YOKMA / 05 / 2004

Vernacular Building | In Use | Private (Individual) | Around 200 years old

Photograph Not Available

SETTING
Sotopa house is oriented to the south. A narrow pathway leads up from the main road and the house is located along this path which leads upto the old *gonpa*. The old *gonpa* is located further north of the house while other residential structures are located to the southwest and west. The village lies to the southeast.

SIGNIFICANCE
The Sotopa house was built by the ancestors of the Sotopa family about 200 years ago. Built in the traditional style, it is a good example of the local vernacular architecture.

DESCRIPTION
The Sotopa residence is a double storeyed structure built on a rectangular plan with the lower levels built in stone masonry and the upper levels are built in unbaked mud brick masonry. Externally, the house is mud plastered and whitewashed. The house is entered from the village street towards the south. The lower floor is devoid of any other openings except the entrance door and a small ventilator. This level is used by the family as a cattle shed and for storage purposes. A timber staircase leads up to the first floor. This level has a large kitchen and living space to the southwest. There is a large timber framed *rabsal* to the southwest and another *rabsal* to the east. There are small window openings on this floor. The house has a mud floor and a traditional roof supported by timber columns and brackets. There is a low height parapet above this floor.

STATE OF PRESERVATION
Advanced State of Decay

SOURCE OF INFORMATION Tsering Chorol, Hanu *Yokma*, Khaltse, Ladakh

Hanu Yokma

Khachaype House

INVENTORY NO.
KHALTSE / HANU YOKMA / 06 / 2004

Vernacular Building | In Use | Private (Individual)

SETTING
The house is oriented towards the northeast and is surrounded by the Gozongpa house to the southeast and the village to the west. A steep climb from the open space below leads up to the house.

SIGNIFICANCE
The house was built by the ancestors of the Khachaype family and is constructed in the traditional style. It forms part of a larger group of vernacular dwellings in the village.

DESCRIPTION
The Khachaype house is a double storeyed structure built over a rectangular plan. Both levels are constructed in stone masonry. The external walls are devoid of mud plaster and whitewash. There are small rectangular window openings on the upper floor. The entrance is from the northwest and leads to the first floor. The lower floor has a stone floor and is used for storage and as a cattle shed. The upper floor houses the family's living area and has a

traditional mud floor. The house has a traditional roof and the internal walls are mud plastered and whitewashed. The structure is devoid of any kind of ornamentation. The timber members are also unadorned.

STATE OF PRESERVATION
Advanced State of Decay

SOURCE OF INFORMATION Tashi Palmo, Hanu *Yokma*, Khaltse, Ladakh

Lokhil Dorjey *Lhakhang* (*Lhakhang* Nyingpa)

INVENTORY NO.
KHALTSE / HANU YOKMA / 07 / 2004

Gonpa | In Use | Public (Lamayuru *Gonpa*) | Around 135 years old

SETTING
The Lokhil Dorjey *lhakhang* is oriented towards the south and is approached from a narrow path which bifurcates from the main road. The Khalogpa house is to its west while the Spormazampo house is to its east.

SIGNIFICANCE
The *gonpa* is believed to have been built around 1873 A.D. by a monk named Gelong Samphel. Today, the *gonpa* is under the purview of the Lamayuru *gonpa* and a monk is deputed here from the monastery to look after the temple and carry out prayers here and in the village.

DESCRIPTION
The old temple is built in a random roughly rectangular plan with an entrance from the south. It is constructed in

stone masonry and is mud plastered and whitewashed externally. There is a large timber framed opening to the southwest. The temple has a traditional mud floor and a timber roof comprising of timber beams, joists, dried grass, willow twigs and mud. Four timber columns support the roof inside the *lhakhang*. Towards the south, there is a clerestory with a large opening. The internal walls are mud plastered and embellished with paintings depicting the life of the Buddha.

STATE OF PRESERVATION
Advanced State of Decay

SOURCE OF INFORMATION Nawang Dorjey, Hanu *Yokma*, Khaltse, Ladakh

142

Hanu *Yokma Gonpa*

INVENTORY NO.
KHALTSE / HANU YOKMA / 08 / 2004

Gonpa | In Use | Public (Likir *Gonpa*) | Around 1873 A.D.

SETTING
The *gonpa* is oriented to the south and is accessed from narrow steep path which heads upto the *gonpa* from the road below. The village lies below to its south and southeast. There are some structures to its south and a *chorten* to its east.

SIGNIFICANCE
The *gonpa* is believed to have been built around 1873 A.D. by a monk named Gelong Samphel. Today, the *gonpa* is under the purview of the Likir *Gonpa* and a monk is deputed here from the monastery to look after the temple and carry out prayers here and in the village.

DESCRIPTION
The *gonpa* is a single storeyed structure built in stone masonry over a rectangular plan. Externally, the building is mud plastered and whitewashed. There are two large timber framed openings on the either sides of the door. The *gonpa* consists of a single hall with a traditional mud floor

and timber roof. Four undecorated timber columns inside the temple support the roof above. The temple houses images of Chanrazig, Skyoba Jigsten Gonbo, Chagdor and Tsongkhapa. The walls have been freshly repainted. To the southeast of the *gonpa* is a Changchub *chorten* built in stone and mud brick masonry. The *chorten* is whitewashed and mud plastered.

STATE OF PRESERVATION
Showing Signs of Deterioration

SOURCE OF INFORMATION Tsering Chorol, Hanu *Yokma*, Khaltse, Ladakh

Zangldan *Lhato*

INVENTORY NO.
KHALTSE / HANU YOKMA / 09 / 2004

Lhato | In Use | Public (Community) | Around 300 years old

SETTING
The *lhato* is oriented towards the east and is located en route from Hanu Gongma to Hanu Yokma.

SIGNIFICANCE
The *lhato* is dedicated to the village protector deity, Zangldan Gyapo. The contents of the *lhato* are renewed every year amid rituals.

DESCRIPTION
The *lhato* is built over a square plan of a loose pile of stones which rises to a height of about four feet. At the centre of the *lhato*, there is a tall prayer flag post with *khadag* tied around it. Around the flag post on the horizontal surface of the *lhato* are four stones containing inscriptions in Tibetan.

STATE OF PRESERVATION
Showing Signs of Deterioration

SOURCE OF INFORMATION Tsering Chorol, Hanu *Yokma*, Khaltse, Ladakh

Precinct of Old Houses

INVENTORY NO.
KHALTSE / HANU YOKMA / 10 / 2004

Precinct | In Use | Private (Individual) | Around 200 years old

SETTING
The cluster of houses is oriented to the south and is located on a hill. The houses are built close to each other. The village *gonpa* is to the southeast.

SIGNIFICANCE
The precinct forms an old quarter of the village and contains several old residences built close to each other, a feature common in the area of Dha - Hanu. The layout of the precinct is specific to this region which experiences severe winters.

DESCRIPTION
The site consists of a group of dwellings built close to each other. This enabled the houses to retain heat in the cold winters. The dwellings consist of single room units which open onto a covered street. They have mud and stone floors and a traditional roof.

STATE OF PRESERVATION
Danger of Disappearance

SOURCE OF INFORMATION Tashi Palmo, Hanu *Gongma*, Khaltse, Ladakh

Gonjongpa House

INVENTORY NO.
KHALTSE / HANU YOKMA / 11 / 2006

Vernacular Building | In Use | Private (Individual) | Around 200 years old

SETTING
The house is located towards the right and above the road which leads to Hanu *Gongma*.

SIGNIFICANCE
The house was built about 200 years back by one of the ancestors of Gonjongpa family. It is a fine example of traditional vernacular architecture.

DESCRIPTION
The Gonjongpa house is a double storeyed building which is built on a rectangular plan. The ground floor is built in stone masonry. A lot of wood work can be seen on the upper floor. There is a low height parapet on top which has been built using stone and mud brick masonry.

STATE OF PRESERVATION
Advance State of Decay

SOURCE OF INFORMATION Tsering Murup, Goba Hanu, Hanu *Yokma*, Khaltse, Ladakh

144

Kagan *Chorten*

INVENTORY NO.
KHALTSE / HANU YOKMA / 12 / 2006

Chorten | In Use | Public (Community) | Around 150 years old

SETTING
The *chorten* is located towards the left after crossing the bridge at Hanu Yokma.

SIGNIFICANCE
The *chorten* is a Kagan *chorten* built over a village path. Merit is believed to accrue to believers who pass through the passage of the *chorten*.

DESCRIPTION
The *chorten* consists of two thick walls made of stone masonry in mud mortar over which rests a *chorten*. The *chorten* is also built in stone and mud brick masonry with mud mortar. The ceiling over the passage is made of timber and is devoid of any paintings. The entire structure is mud plastered and whitewashed. There is a tapering *chugsum khorlo* over the dome.

STATE OF PRESERVATION
Showing Signs of Deterioration

SOURCE OF INFORMATION Tsering Murup, Goba Hanu, Hanu *Yokma*, Khaltse, Ladakh

Hanupatta

Hanupatta lies on a 15-km trek from Phanjilla. From the Leh - Srinagar highway, a road diverts between Khaltse and Lamayuru, towards Shilla. Phanjilla lies on this road. Hanupatta was earlier known as Lhayul meaning '*heaven*' or the '*valley of gods*' as the village is very clean and there are a lot of sacred juniper trees. Formerly, it used to be a part of Wanla but today has an independent village head (Goba). There are about 12 households in the village today.

Listed by: Deldan Angmo and Jassu Singh
Year: 2004

Hanuthang

Hanuthang is situated at the edge of the Hanu valley, about 50 kms from Khaltse.

Listed by: Deldan Angmo, Jassu Singh, Dr. Sonam Wangchok and Karma Yeshi
Year: 2004, 2007

Dungsten *Chorten*

INVENTORY NO.
KHALTSE / HANUPATTA / 01 / 2004

Chorten / Mane Wall | In Use | Public (Community) | Around 200 years old

SETTING
The Dungsten *chorten* is located along the pathway leading to Hanupatta village. It is to the north of the path which leads from Phanjilla to Hanupatta. The river flows on the southeast side while there are mountains to the north.

SIGNIFICANCE
The *chorten* and *mane* wall lie along the path leading to the village and are circumambulated by villagers as an act of merit. The *chorten* contains relics and is a Changchub *chorten,* symbolizing the Buddha's enlightenment.

DESCRIPTION
The site comprises of a Changchub *chorten* and four *mane* walls. The *chorten* is built in stone masonry with mud mortar and is mud plastered and whitewashed on the exterior. The exterior surface of the *chorten* has eroded. There is a tall *chugsum khorlo* made of baked tiles, over the dome of the *chorten* on which rests a metal crescent

crown. The *mane* walls are scattered around the site. They are all built in dry stone masonry and have inscribed *mane* stones on the horizontal surface.

STATE OF PRESERVATION
Advanced State of Decay

SOURCE OF INFORMATION Tashi Yangzes, Hanupatta, Khaltse, Ladakh

Hanupatta

148

Mane Wall

INVENTORY NO.
KHALTSE / HANUPATTA / 02 / 2004

Mane Wall | In Use | Public (Community) | Around 250 years old

SETTING
The *mane* wall is located along the pathway which leads further onto the village. It stands along the mountainside with the river flowing to its south and boulders lying to its east. There is some vegetation to the south and southeast of the site.

SIGNIFICANCE
The *mane* wall is located along the path leading to the village and is circumambulated by villagers as an act of merit.

STATE OF PRESERVATION
Advanced State of Decay

DESCRIPTION
The site comprises of a long *mane* wall built in stone. The *mane* wall has hundreds of inscribed *mane* stones placed on its horizontal surface. There is a circumambulatory pathway all around the *mane* and a huge stone boulder to its east.

SOURCE OF INFORMATION Tashi Yangzes, Hanupatta, Khaltse, Ladakh

Chorten and *Mane* Wall (Manego)

INVENTORY NO.
KHALTSE / HANUPATTA / 03 / 2004

Chorten / *Mane* Wall | In Use | Public (Community) | Around 300 years old

SETTING
The Manego *chorten* is located along the pathway which leads to the village. The *chorten* is located south of the village footpath which leads onto Photoksar.

SIGNIFICANCE
The *chorten* and the *mane* wall are located at the beginning of the village and hence the name 'Mane-go' (*mane* at the beginning). The structures are believed to have been constructed around 300 years ago as an act of merit. The villagers still circumambulate the site to accumulate merit.

DESCRIPTION
The site comprises of two *chorten*, one *mane* wall and two *tarchen*. The *tarchen* are placed on either side of the

footpath marking the beginning of the settlement. The *chorten* are built in stone masonry with mud mortar and are mud plastered and whitewashed on the exterior though most of the external layer has eroded. At the top of the dome, there is *chugsum khorlo* made of baked tiles over which rests a metal crescent crown. The *mane* wall is a cylindrical stone masonry wall with numerous *mane* stones placed on its horizontal surface. A part of the *mane* wall has collapsed. At the base of the *chorten*, there is a flat stone etched with a fine image of Shakyamuni Buddha.

STATE OF PRESERVATION
Advanced State of Decay

SOURCE OF INFORMATION Tashi Yangzes, Hanupatta, Khaltse, Ladakh

Mane Wall

INVENTORY NO.
KHALTSE / HANUPATTA / 04 / 2004

Mane Wall | In Use | Public (Community)

SETTING
The *mane* wall is located along the path which leads to the village and is surrounded by a stream and agricultural fields to the south with the mountainside to the north.

SIGNIFICANCE
The *mane* wall is located along the path which leads to the village and was built in the past as an act of merit. It is circumambulated by villagers while travelling along this path.

DESCRIPTION
The *mane* wall is a long dry stone masonry wall with bigger stone boulders near at the base and smaller stones towards the top. The horizontal face of *mane* wall has numerous *mane* stones.

STATE OF PRESERVATION
Showing Signs of Deterioration

SOURCE OF INFORMATION Tashi Yangzes, Hanupatta, Khaltse, Ladakh

Mane Walls

INVENTORY NO.
KHALTSE / HANUPATTA / 05 / 2004

Mane Wall | In Use | Public (Community) | Around 250 years old

SETTING
The *mane* walls are located on hill along the path that leads to the village from Photoksar.

SIGNIFICANCE
The *mane* walls lie along the path which links Hanupatta from Photoksar and villagers circumambulate it when travelling along this path as an act of merit.

DESCRIPTION
The site comprises of two *mane* walls - one cylindrical and the other linear in shape. The cylindrical *mane* is built in stone masonry with mud mortar and is mud plastered and whitewashed externally. The outer layer of mud plaster has however, eroded to a large extent. The linear *mane* is built in dry stone masonry. Gravel from the path has deposited on the surface of the *mane* wall. Both *mane* walls have inscribed *mane* stones placed on the horizontal surface.

STATE OF PRESERVATION
Advanced State of Decay

SOURCE OF INFORMATION Tashi Yangzes, Hanupatta, Khaltse, Ladakh

150

Hanupatta

Larten *Chorten*

INVENTORY NO.
KHALTSE / HANUPATTA / 06 / 2004

Chorten / *Mane* Wall | In Use | Public (Community)

SETTING
The Larten *chorten* is located along the path leading to the village some distance from the village itself. There is a *tarchen* to the southeast, the juniper tree and *lhato* to the northeast and agricultural fields and willow trees to the southwest.

SIGNIFICANCE
The Larten *chorten* lies along the path leading to the village and is circumambulated by villagers as an act of merit. The *chorten* is a Changchub *chorten* symbolizing the Buddha's enlightenment.

DESCRIPTION
The site comprises of a *chorten*, a *mane* wall and a smaller *chorten*. The Larten *chorten* is housed in a stone masonry enclosure with four stone masonry pillar-like structures at the corners flanked by a roof. The *chorten* is built on a square base. The *chorten* rests on a high random rubble masonry plinth and is built in stone and mud brick masonry.

The exterior surface of the *chorten* is mud plastered and whitewashed. The base panels of the *chorten* have *pa-tra* and the corners are painted in red. Near the *chorten* is a *mane* wall built in dry stone masonry with inscribed *mane* stones placed on its horizontal surface. At the end, is another *chorten* which is in compete ruins.

STATE OF PRESERVATION
Advanced State of Deterioration

SOURCE OF INFORMATION Rigzen Yangdol, Hanupatta, Khaltse, Ladakh

Lhashug and Kaju Konra *Lhato*

INVENTORY NO.
KHALTSE / HANUPATTA / 07 / 2004

Landscape (Tree) / *Lhato* | In Use | Public (Community)

SETTING
The juniper tree is located along the path that links Hanupattta with Photoksar. The tree is surrounded by mountains to the north, a *lhato* under it and a *chorten* to the southwest.

SIGNIFICANCE / ASSOCIATED BELIEFS
The juniper tree is associated with the village protector deity Kaju Konra and is considered sacred by the villagers for which reason it is protected by them. The *lhato* is dedicated to the village protector deity and is believed to have been built when the village was first inhabited.

DESCRIPTION
The juniper tree is one of the largest in the region and appears to be quite old. The *lhato* is a huge cubical structure which rises upwards, tapering to form a smaller rectangle at the top. It is constructed in stone masonry and is mud plastered and whitewashed externally. There are red markings painted at the corners as well as the front face of the *lhato*. There is a smaller square structure on the top which contains the ritual offerings of juniper branches, animal horns and white scarves (*khadag*). There is a *chorten* and *mane* wall near the site.

CULTURAL LINKAGES / CULTURAL PRACTICES
The village oracle appears here once a year on the eve of Ladakhi New Year on the occasion of Losar amid elaborate rituals. The contents of the *lhato* are also changed at this time.

STATE OF PRESERVATION
Advanced State of Decay

Hanupatta

15l

SOURCE OF INFORMATION Tashi Lamo, Yokmapa, Hanupatta, Khaltse, Ladakh

Yokmapa House

INVENTORY NO.
KHALTSE / HANUPATTA / 08 / 2004

Vernacular Building | In Use | Private (Individual) | Around 250 years old

SETTING
The Yokmapa House is oriented to the southeast and is located in the interiors of the village. It is surrounded by a prayer wheel and the Sonam Rigzin guest house.

SIGNIFICANCE
The Yokmapa house was built by ancestors of the Yokmapa family about 250 years ago and is one of the oldest houses in the village which has retained it original architecture. The family still resides in the house.

DESCRIPTION
Yokmapa House is a large double storeyed building built on a random plan. The ground floor is used primarily for storage while the family's living quarters are on the first floor. The house is built in stone and mud brick masonry with mud mortar and has a traditional roof of timber beams, joists, *taalu,* grass and compacted mud.

STATE OF PRESERVATION
Advanced State of Decay

SOURCE OF INFORMATION Tashi Lhamo - Yokmapa, Hanupatta, Khaltse, Ladakh

Hanupatta

152

Hanupatta *Gonpa*

INVENTORY NO.
KHALTSE / HANUPATTA / 09 / 2004

Gonpa | In Use | Public (Lamayuru *Gonpa*) | Around 130 years old

SETTING
Hanupatta *gonpa* is built along the slope of a hill above the village and faces the southwest.

SIGNIFICANCE
The *gonpa* is the principal place of worship in the village and villagers gather here for prayers and rituals. The temple falls under the Drigung-pa sect and a monk from Lamayuru is deputed here to carry out prayers in the temple. The old temple building was pulled down and a new one built in its place three years ago. The older *gonpa* was around 130 years old. All the images and ritual artifacts from the old *gonpa* were re-enshrined in the new *gonpa*.

DESCRIPTION
The *gonpa* is entered through a wooden doorway on the southwest which opens onto a court yard. The courtyard is flanked by a gallery to the west and monks' rooms to the east. A wooden doorway leads further into a small hall with four decorated wooden columns and beams supporting the traditional roof. There is a skylight in the centre of this chamber which has a large wooden frame with glass panes and a panelled plywood ceiling below the traditional roof. The floor is of timber. The rear wall of the room has a decorative wooden frame housing images of Chanrazig, Guru Rinpoche, Chamba as well as the Buddhist cannons. The walls are painted in yellow, blue and green bands. The side walls have large *thangka* hung from the ceiling along the length of the wall and also along the wooden columns. The temple has large window openings which have a black border painted around them. The building is whitewashed externally.

STATE OF PRESERVATION
Fair

SOURCE OF INFORMATION Tashi Yangzes, Hanupatta, Khaltse, Ladakh

Chorten Yogma

INVENTORY NO.
KHALTSE / HANUPATTA / 10 / 2004

Chorten / Mane Wall | In Use | Public (Community) | Around 300 years old

SETTING
Chorten Yogma is located at the beginning of the village along the footpath and marks the entrance to the village.

SIGNIFICANCE
The *chorten* was built about 300 years ago at the time when people started settling in the valley. The location of the *chorten* is significant as it marks the entrance to the village which is highlighted by the two *tarchen* erected here. The *chorten* and *mane* wall were built in the past as an act of merit and are still circumambulated by villagers to gather merit.

DESCRIPTION
The site comprises of two *chorten*, two *tarchen* and a long *mane* wall. The *chorten* are located along the pathway, half embedded in the ground. They are built in stone masonry with mud mortar and are mud plastered and whitewashed externally. One of the *chorten* has a tall *chugsum khorlo* made of baked tiled over which rests a metal crown. The

tarchen are on the either side of the pathway forming a gateway to the village. Near the *tarchen* is a circular *mane* wall with a number of carved mane stones on its horizontal surface. There is a *parikrama* path around the *mane* wall.

STATE OF PRESERVATION
Advanced State of Decay

SOURCE OF INFORMATION Tashi Yangzes, Hanupatta, Khaltse, Ladakh

---

Chorten Yogma

INVENTORY NO.
KHALTSE / HANUPATTA / 11 / 2004

Chorten | In Use | Public (Community) | Around 300 years old

SETTING
Chorten Yogma is located at the beginning of the village near the footpath. It is surrounded by agricultural fields and the river to the south, the footpath to the north while the village lies to the west.

SIGNIFICANCE
The *chorten* were built around 300 years ago at the time when people first began settling in the village. These lie along the main approach to the village. Both are Changchub *chorten* which symbolize the Buddha's enlightenment.

DESCRIPTION
The site comprises of two *chorten* built in stone and mud brick masonry with mud mortar. The chorten are of different sizes – the larger one is built on a random rubble masonry square plinth. There are traces of the external

layer of mud plaster and whitewash although most of this layer has eroded over time. Both the *chorten* have a *srog-shing* embedded on the dome.

STATE OF PRESERVATION
Advanced State of Decay

SOURCE OF INFORMATION Tashi Yangzes, Hanupatta, Khaltse, Ladakh

Hanupatta

153

Manego *Chorten*

INVENTORY NO.
KHALTSE / HANUPATTA / 12 / 2004

Chorten | In Use | Public (Community) | Around 300 years old

SETTING
Manego *chorten* is located at the beginning of the village along the pathway which leads from Hanupatta to Photoksar.

SIGNIFICANCE
The Manego *chorten* is located at the beginning of the village and hence the name Manego. It is believed to have been built around 300 years ago when people first settled in the valley. The *chorten* are all Changchub *chorten*, one of the eight traditional forms of chorten in Tibetan Buddhism, symbolizing the Buddha's enlightenment.

DESCRIPTION
The site comprises of three *chorten* built on a common rectangular random rubble plinth. The *chorten* are of different sizes and are built in stone and mud brick masonry with mud mortar. The external surface of the *chorten* is mud plastered and whitewashed. This outer layer has eroded over time and the *chorten* are losing their original form.

SOURCE OF INFORMATION Tashi Yangzes, Hanupatta, Khaltse, Ladakh

STATE OF PRESERVATION
Advanced State of Deterioration

Hanupatta

154

Chorten

INVENTORY NO.
KHALTSE / HANUPATTA / 13 / 2004

Chorten | Abandoned | Public (Community)

SETTING
The *chorten* is located along the pathway leading from Hanupatta to Photoksar. The river flows to the south of the site. The *chorten* lie to the north of the path while moving from Hanupatta to Photoksar.

SIGNIFICANCE
The *chorten* lie along the path leading to Photoksar and would have been circumambulated by villagers as they travelled along this path in the past, as an act of merit.

DESCRIPTION
The *chorten* are in complete ruins and are difficult to identify. Nothing much survives of the structure except the base and the square plinth with square stone tiers. The upper portion of the *chorten* has collapsed with the fragments scattered around the site place. The base panels have fragments of *pa-tra*.

STATE OF PRESERVATION
Danger of Disappearance

Mane Wall

INVENTORY NO.
KHALTSE / HANUTHANG / 01 / 2004

Mane Wall | In Use | Public (Community) | Around 150 - 175 years old

SETTING
The *mane* wall is oriented to the south and is located on an undulating stretch of land across the river. It lies above Ulekhapa house.

SIGNIFICANCE
The *mane* wall was constructed by the villagers about 150 - 175 years ago to protect the village from evil forces.

STATE OF PRESERVATION
Showing Signs of Deterioration

DESCRIPTION
The *mane* wall is a rectangular structure with a square window facing the south and north. It is quite unusual from others as it is a room-like structure with two small windows-like openings. The *mane* wall is built in stone masonry with mud plaster and whitewash on the exterior surface. There is a *tarchen* to the west of the *mane* wall. There is a prayer flag on top of the *mane* with a large number of stone boulders around it.

SOURCE OF INFORMATION Sonam Yangskit, Hanuthang, Khaltse, Ladakh

Mane Wall

INVENTORY NO.
KHALTSE / HANUTHANG / 02 / 2004

Mane Wall | In Use | Public (Community)

SETTING
The *mane* wall is located along a pathway in the village and is surrounded by village houses to the northwest and agricultural fields to the south and east. There is an apricot tree next to the *mane* wall.

SIGNIFICANCE
The *mane* wall is located along a path and is circumambulated by villagers to accumulate merit as they cross this path.

STATE OF PRESERVATION
Advanced State of Deterioration

DESCRIPTION
The site consists of a rectangular low height *mane* wall built in dry stone masonry. From a distance, it looks like a heap of stones. There are flat inscribed *mane* stones placed on the top of the mane wall.

SOURCE OF INFORMATION Sonam Yangskit, Hanuthang, Khaltse, Ladakh

Mane Wall

INVENTORY NO.
KHALTSE / HANUTHANG / 03 / 2004

Mane Wall | In Use | Public (Community) | Around 120 years old

SETTING
The *mane* wall is oriented to the south and is located along a pathway next to a village shop.

SIGNIFICANCE
The *mane* wall is located along a path which leads to the village and is circumambulated by villagers to accumulate merit.

DESCRIPTION
The *mane* wall is a rectangular wall built in dry stone masonry with *mane* stones placed on the top horizontal surface. There are two *tarchen* near the mane wall on which are tied prayer flags.

STATE OF PRESERVATION
Advanced State of Decay

SOURCE OF INFORMATION Mohammad Ismail, Hanuthang, Khaltse, Ladakh

Kabristan

INVENTORY NO.
KHALTSE / HANUTHANG / 04 / 2007

Cemetery | In Use | Public (Community) | Around 100 years old

SETTING
The cemetery is located near the newly constructed *imambara* of Hanuthang.

SIGNIFICANCE
The cemetery is the principal burial ground for the Muslim community of Hanuthang.

DESCRIPTION
The *kabristan* is located on an open stretch of land behind the *imambara*. The area is dotted with small stone masonry structures with a timber framed opening beneath which the graves are placed.

STATE OF PRESERVATION
Fair

SOURCE OF INFORMATION Abdul Aziz Tsud pa, Hanuthang, Khaltse, Ladakh

NIRLAC

Hanuthang

Jamia *Masjid*

INVENTORY NO.
KHALTSE / HANUTHANG / 05 / 2007

Mosque | In Use | Public (Community) | Around 150 years old

SETTING
The Jamia *masjid* is located near the *imambara* and is surrounded by village houses on other sides.

SIGNIFICANCE
The original mosque was built around 150 years ago and it was renovated by the Muslim community in 1994. It is the principal mosque in the village where the villagers gather for their daily *namaaz* as well as for the Friday prayers.

DESCRIPTION
The mosque is built on a square plan and is a single storeyed building. There is a small porch at the entrance which has five timber columns supporting the roof. The entrance is from the east and leads directly to the main prayer hall. This has a *mihrab* at one end and prayer mats and carpets are laid out on the floor. The roof is made of timber and is cement plastered on the top. The building is constructed in stone masonry with cement mortar and is cement plastered and whitewashed on the exterior.

SOURCE OF INFORMATION Abdul Aziz Tsud pa, Hanuthang, Khaltse, Ladakh

STATE OF PRESERVATION
New Construction

Hanuthang

157

Banpa House

INVENTORY NO.
KHALTSE / HANUTHANG / 06 / 2007

Vernacular Building | In Use | Public (Community) | Around 150 years old

SETTING
The house is located between the new *imambara* and the *masjid*.

SIGNIFICANCE
The house was built by Apo Mousa around 150 years ago and the first floor was added 48 years ago. The family continues to reside here. The house is built in the traditional style and is an example of vernacular architecture in the village.

DESCRIPTION
The house is a double storeyed building with a traditional roof. The ground floor is built in stone masonry and the first floor is constructed in mud brick masonry with mud mortar. There are five rooms in the ground floor and one large room on the first floor. Three rooms in the ground floor are used as living rooms while animals are housed in the remaining two rooms. The main living room has an old traditional cabinet and the floor is laid out in timber. The rest of the rooms have mud floors. The main entrance is from the east. The house is mud plastered and whitewashed on the exterior and has small window openings on the ground floor. The first floor has larger windows.

STATE OF PRESERVATION
Showing Signs of Deterioration

SOURCE OF INFORMATION Mohammad Hussain Banpa, Hanuthang, Khaltse, Ladakh

Ehsarpa House

INVENTORY NO.
KHALTSE / HANUTHANG / 07 / 2007

Vernacular Building | In Use | Private (Individual) | Around 150 years old

SETTING
The house is located along the foot path that leads to the *masjid*. It is surrounded by the *imambara* and other residential houses.

SIGNIFICANCE
The house was built 3 generations ago by Apo Ibrahim of the Ehsarpa family and the family has continued to reside here. The house is built in the traditional style and is an example of vernacular architecture in the village.

DESCRIPTION
The house is a double storeyed building with a traditional roof. The ground floor is built in stone masonry and the first floor is constructed in mud brick masonry with mud mortar. There are four rooms in the ground floor. Three rooms are used as living rooms while animals are housed in fourth room. The main living room has a timber floor. The rest of the rooms have mud floors. The first floor has larger window openings than the ground floor. The house is mud plastered and whitewashed on the exterior.

STATE OF PRESERVATION
Showing Signs of Deterioration

Hanuthang

158

Hemis Shukpachan

Hemis Shukpachan is located about 15 kms from Likir. A rough road
diverts from the main Leh - Srinagar highway after Likir and leads
towards the settlement. The village is known for its sacred grove of
juniper trees from which it also derives its name.

Listed by: Deldan Angmo and Jassu Singh
Year: 2004

Toropa House and *Chorten*

INVENTORY NO.
KHALTSE / HEMIS SHUKPACHAN / 01 / 2004

Vernacular Building | In Use | Private (Individual) | Around 100 years old

STATE OF PRESERVATION
Showing Signs of Deterioration

SETTING

The house is oriented to the southeast and is built on an elevated stretch of land at the foot of the hill on which the palace was earlier located. The Khangpa is located behind the house. A narrow winding pathway from the village leads to the forecourt of the house.

SIGNIFICANCE

The name of the house Toropa derives from the word '*toro*' meaning the sound of falling water as the house was built near a waterfall. The house was built by an ancestor of the Toropa family around 300 - 350 years ago and successive generations have continued to reside here. It is built in the traditional style and is a good example of vernacular architecture in the village.

DESCRIPTION

The Toropa house is a large house built on a rectangular plan along the slope of a hillock. Access is provided by a flight of stairs which leads to a corridor on the first floor. There are rooms on either side of the corridor. A door to the right leads to the main kitchen while the living rooms are on the opposite side. A flight of wooden stairs leads to the second floor and onto the terrace. The corridor and the exterior staircase have been repaired in cement while the kitchen has timber flooring. The roof is made of traditional wooden joists, *taalu*, grass and a layer of compacted mud. Many alterations have been made on the building. The exterior walls are mud plastered and whitewashed. All the window openings are on the front facade while the rear and side walls are devoid of any windows. The parapet is neatly bordered in black colour as are the door and window openings. The lower floor of the house is built in stone masonry while the upper floors are in mud brick masonry with mud mortar. There are two small Toropa *chorten* towards the southwest of the house. The *chorten* are built on a large boulder and are largely in ruins.

SOURCE OF INFORMATION T.T. Namgyal Toropa, Hemis Shukpachan, Khaltse, Ladakh

Phikarpe *Tsadkhang*

INVENTORY NO.
KHALTSE / HEMIS SHUKPACHAN / 02 / 2004

Tsadkhang | In Use | Private (Individual) | Around 250 - 300 years old

STATE OF PRESERVATION
Showing Signs of Deterioration

SETTING
The *tsadkhang* is oriented to the southeast and is located behind the Phikarpa house. It lies southwest of the Toropa house.

SIGNIFICANCE
The *tsadkhang* was built by ancestors of the Phikarpa family around 250 - 300 years ago to house *tsa-tsa*.

DESCRIPTION
The *tsadkhang* is located on a rocky outcrop on which are also placed the Toropa *chorten*. It is a tall linear structure built on a square plan in stone and mud brick masonry. There is a small opening to the southeast through which are placed the *tsa-tsa*. The exterior is whitewashed while the parapet line has some traces of red paint. There are small engraved *mane* stones places on the plinth of the structure.

SOURCE OF INFORMATION T.T. Namgyal Toropa, Hemis Shukpachan, Khaltse, Ladakh

Group of *Chorten* and *Tsadkhang*

INVENTORY NO.
KHALTSE / HEMIS SHUKPACHAN / 03 / 2004

Chorten / Tsadkhang | In Use | Public (Community) | Around 200 - 250 years old

SETTING
The *chorten* and *tsadkhang* are oriented to the north and are located above the Toropa chorten and the Phikarpe *tsadkhang*.

with mud mortar. There is a small opening on one side which contains the *tsa-tsa*. It has a mud roof on top and the walls are mud plastered and whitewashed externally.

STATE OF PRESERVATION
Showing Signs of Deterioration

SIGNIFICANCE
The *tsadkhang* houses small *tsa-tsa* while the *chorten* was built in the past as an act of merit. These were built around 4 - 5 generations ago by village ancestors for the well being of all sentient beings. The structures are circumambulated by people as act of merit.

DESCRIPTION
The site comprises of two *chorten* and three *tsadkhang*. The *chorten* are small in size and their shapes can no longer be discerned as the outer surfaces have eroded. The *tsadkhang* are square linear structures built in stone and mud bricks

SOURCE OF INFORMATION T.T. Namgyal Toropa, Hemis Shukpachan, Khaltse, Ladakh

Hemis Shukpachan

163

Phikare Kagan

INVENTORY NO.
KHALTSE / HEMIS SHUKPACHAN / 04 / 2004

Chorten | In Use | Public (Community) | Around 250 years old

SETTING

The Kagan *chorten* is oriented to the east and is located west of Toropa house and the Khangpa. It lies between the houses and the large boulder on which the *chorten* and *tsadkhang* are located.

SIGNIFICANCE

The Kagan *chorten* is a gateway *chorten* and merit is believed to accrue to believers who pass through the passage of the *chorten*.

DESCRIPTION

The Kagan *chorten* consists of two thick parallel side walls over which rests a large Changchub *chorten*. The walls of the *chorten* are built in stone and mud brick masonry with mud mortar as is the *chorten* above. The Kagan *chorten* is mud plastered and whitewashed on the exterior. The ceiling above the passage is made in timber and is in the shape of a *mandala*. The *chorten* has a tall *chugsum khorlo* on the top with a metal crown above.

STATE OF PRESERVATION
Showing Signs of Deterioration

SOURCE OF INFORMATION T.T. Namgyal Toropa, Hemis Shukpachan, Khaltse, Ladakh

Chug shig-zhal *Gonpa*

INVENTORY NO.
KHALTSE / HEMIS SHUKPACHAN / 05 / 2004

Gonpa | In Use | Public (Chemday *Gonpa*)

SETTING

The Chug shig zhal *gonpa* is oriented to the southeast and is located behind the Khangpa house and west of Padma Tsering.

SIGNIFICANCE

According to popular belief, the small temple within the *gonpa* was painted with pigments left over after completing Alchi. However, stylistically the paintings date to a much later period. It is believed that King Jamyang Namgyal stayed here when he was suffering from small pox.

DESCRIPTION

The *gonpa* has a courtyard to the east and appears to have undergone many additions and alterations over time. It is built in stone and mud brick masonry and is mud plastered and whitewashed on the exterior. The main shrine is dedicated to Chanrazig (Chug shig-zhal) and houses an

elaborate image of the deity. The parapet is bordered in red paint. There are prayer flags posted at the corners of the roof.

STATE OF PRESERVATION
Showing Signs of Deterioration

SOURCE OF INFORMATION T.T. Namgyal Toropa, Hemis Shukpachan, Khaltse, Ladakh

Phikarpa *Khangpa*

INVENTORY NO.
KHALTSE / HEMIS SHUKPACHAN / 06 / 2004

Vernacular Building | In Use | Private (Individual) | Around 300 - 350 years old

SETTING
The house is oriented to the south and is located east of Toropa House and the Chug shig-zhal *gonpa*.

SIGNIFICANCE
The Phikarpa house is one of the oldest houses in the village. The entire village was enclosed within a boundary wall and the Phikarpa house was the only house outside the enclosure and hence the name 'Phikarpa' meaning one who lives outside the boundary. The house was built around 300 - 350 years ago by an ancestor of the Phikarpa family and successive generations continue to reside here.

DESCRIPTION
The Phikarpa house is effectively three storeys high and is built along the slope of a hillock. It is built on a rectangular plan. The ground floor is constructed in stone masonry and is used for housing animals and storing fodder. The first and second floors house the family's living quarters and have few openings while the third level has a large *rabsal* with an elaborate wooden frame. The frame has lattice work and segmental arches. Most of the openings are on the second floor which houses the living areas and the family temple. The upper levels are made of mud brick masonry and the exterior of the building is mud plastered and whitewashed.

STATE OF PRESERVATION
Showing Signs of Deterioration

SOURCE OF INFORMATION Deldan Spalzes, Hemis Shukpachan, Khaltse, Ladakh

Phuntsog Ling *Chomoling*

INVENTORY NO.
KHALTSE / HEMIS-SHUKPACHAN / 07 / 2004

Gonpa | In Use | Public (Ridzong *Gonpa*) | Around 150 years old

SETTING
The *chomoling* is oriented to the southeast and is located at the foot of a hill across the village settlement.

SIGNIFICANCE
The *chomoling* was built around 150 years ago by Ridzong *gonpa* for the nuns of the village and is the first nunnery in the area.

DESCRIPTION
The *chomoling* is located along the slope of a hillock. It is effectively a three-storey high structure. The ground floor is without any openings while the upper levels have large openings. It is built in stone and mud brick masonry and is mud plastered and whitewashed externally.

STATE OF PRESERVATION
Showing Signs of Deterioration

SOURCE OF INFORMATION T.T. Namgyal Toropa, Hemis Shukpachan, Khaltse, Ladakh

Padma Tsering House

INVENTORY NO.
KHALTSE / HEMIS SHUKPACHAN / 08 / 2004

Vernacular Building | In Use | Private (Individual) | Around 200 years old

STATE OF PRESERVATION
Fair

SETTING

The Padma Tsering house lies to the east of the Chug shig-zhal *gonpa* and is surrounded by trees on all sides. It is oriented to the south east.

SIGNIFICANCE

The Padma Tsering house was built around 200 years ago by ancestors of the present owners. It is built in the traditional style and is a good example of vernacular architecture in the village. The entrance doorway has a *rigsum gonbo* above it built to protect the family from evil forces.

DESCRIPTION

The house is built along a slope of a hill on a rectangular plan. It is effectively three storeys high. The ground floor is built in stone masonry and is used for housing animals and storing fodder. It has openings for ventilation and light. The first floor has the family kitchen and living areas. This level has larger window openings. The third level houses the family temple, towards the rear, and a large court in the front. The most interesting feature of the building is the entrance doorway which has a large wooden frame above the main door housing a *rigsum gonbo*. The wooden frame is decorated with segmental arches and has a tiered lintel. The exterior is mud plastered and whitewashed and the parapet is painted in black. There is another *rigsum gonbo* adjacent to the house on the southwest. It is a rectangular structure facing the house and has an opening on one side through which are visible three small *chorten* painted in white, orange and blue symbolizing Jamyang, Chanrazig and Chagdor. The interior walls of the *rigsum gonbo* are painted with images of Jamyang, Chanrazig and Chagdor and appear to have been recently painted or renewed.

SOURCE OF INFORMATION Deldan Spalzes, Hemis Shukpachan, Khaltse, Ladakh

Tseb-Lhamo (Tseb-lha-gyal-mo) *Lhato* and *Chorten*

INVENTORY NO.
KHALTSE / HEMIS SHUKPACHAN / 09 / 2004

Lhato / Chorten / Tsadkhang | In Use | Public (Community) | Around 350 years old

STATE OF PRESERVATION
Showing Signs of Deterioration

SETTING
The *lhato* is oriented to the south and is located on top of a hill overlooking the settlement.

SIGNIFICANCE
Tseb-Lha-gyal-mo, the *yul-lha* of the village, established herself in the village to help the villagers face of the wrath of the *lu*, deities of the underworld. They had been angered due to the digging of an immense canal in the midst of their territories commissioned by King Jamyang Namgyal who wanted to bring water to a deserted plain in order to transform it into a winter garden. The Lhadagpa traditionally holds the responsibility, on behalf of he king, for the maintenance and renewal of the *lhato*. This is done annually on the occasion of Losar. The chorten was built by the grandfather of T.T. Toropa about 100 years ago and houses a relic of a precious stone which belonged to Lama Chosphel Toropa.

DESCRIPTION
The group of structures is located on a hill overlooking the village. The site comprises of a *lhato*, a *chorten* and a *tsadkhang*. The *chorten* is a Changchub *chorten* built in stone and mud brick masonry with mud mortar which is mud plastered and whitewashed on the exterior. The *lhato* is located above the *chorten* and is square in plan. The exterior is whitewashed with red markings on its sides. The *tsadkhang* is located a little lower than the other two structures. It is a cubical structure and houses a number of *tsa-tsa*.

SOURCE OF INFORMATION T.T. Namgyal Toropa, Hemis Shukpachan, Khaltse, Ladakh; and, 'No Sacred Mountains in Central Ladakh?' by P. Dollfus in 'Reflections of the Mountain', edited by Anne-Marie Blondeau & Ernst Steinkellner

Dungsten *Chorten*

INVENTORY NO.
KHALTSE / HEMIS SHUKPACHAN / 10 / 2004

Chorten / Mane Wall | In Use | Public (Community) | Around 350 - 400 years old

SETTING
The group of *chorten* is oriented to the east and is located near the agricultural fields before the village. The main road runs to the north of the site.

SIGNIFICANCE
The *chorten* dates back to the period of King Deldan Namgyal (1640 - 1675 A.D.). An inscription on the *mane* wall bears the name of the king. The *chorten* and *mane* wall are located before the entrance to the village and are circumambulated by villagers to accumulate merit. The *chorten* are largely Changchub *chorten* symbolizing the Buddha's enlightenment.

DESCRIPTION
The site comprises of a cluster of *mane* walls and *chorten* located along the village road. These structures are scattered across a large area. Long linear *mane* walls built in stone masonry run along the path. These contain inscribed *mane* stones on the horizontal surface. The

chorten are of different sizes and are interspersed between the *mane* walls. The *chorten* are built in stone and mud brick masonry and are mud plastered and whitewashed on the exterior. Between the *mane* walls and *chorten* is the Shalipe *spurkhang* while across the path there are several other *chorten*.

STATE OF PRESERVATION
Advanced State of Decay

SOURCE OF INFORMATION Tsewang Namgyal, Hemis Shukpachan, Khaltse, Ladakh

Paldan Dzomba *Lhato*

INVENTORY NO.
KHALTSE / HEMIS SHUKPACHAN / 11 / 2004

Lhato | In Use | Public (Community)

SETTING
The *lhato* is oriented to the west and is located to the east of the settlement on top of a mountain.

SIGNIFICANCE
The *lhato* is believed to be as old as the settlement and is dedicated to a protective deity of the village, Paldan Dzomba. The contents of the *lhato* are renewed every year by the villagers amid prayers and rituals.

DESCRIPTION
The *lhato* comprises of two structures built on a square plan in stone masonry. Externally, these are mud plastered and whitewashed. The ritual offerings of juniper branches, animal horns and *khadag* are placed on the top of the *lhato*. Prayer flags are also tied around the site.

STATE OF PRESERVATION
Showing Signs of Deterioration

SOURCE OF INFORMATION Tsewang Namgyal Toropa, Hemis Shukpachan, Khaltse, Ladakh

Surichana *Mane*

INVENTORY NO.
KHALTSE / HEMIS SHUKPACHAN / 12 / 2004

Mane Wall | In Use | Public (Community) | Around 250 - 300 years old

SETTING
The *mane* is oriented to the north and is located along the village road. It is surrounded by agricultural fields belonging to the Surichana family on the east.

SIGNIFICANCE
The *mane* is believed to have been built during the reign of King Deldan Namgyal (1640 – 1675 A.D.). It is located along the village road and is circumambulated by villagers as an act of merit.

STATE OF PRESERVATION
Advanced State of Decay

DESCRIPTION
The *mane* wall is a long linear stone masonry wall running along the village road. There is a pile of debris at the beginning of the *mane* wall which is possibly the remains of a *chorten*. A number of *mane* stones are placed randomly on the surface of the *mane* wall. There is a small niche to the north which houses a single *mane* stone.

SOURCE OF INFORMATION Tsewang Namgyal Toropa Khangbu, Hemis Shukpachan, Khaltse, Ladakh

SambaTsering *Chorten*

INVENTORY NO.
KHALTSE / HEMIS SHUKPACHAN / 13 / 2004

Chorten / Mane Wall | In Use | Public (Community) | Around 300 - 350 years old

SETTING
The *chorten* are oriented to the south and are located along the road and the power house is to its north.

SIGNIFICANCE
The *chorten* are believed to date back to the period of King Deldan Namgyal. The *chorten* are located at the beginning of the village along the path that was used before the road was laid. These are circumambulated by villagers to accumulate merit.

DESCRIPTION
The site comprises of a group of *chorten* and a *mane* wall located at the beginning of the settlement. These are arranged in a single row and are of various sizes built over a common plinth. The *chorten* are built in mud brick and stone masonry with mud mortar and are mud plastered and whitewashed on the exterior. The *mane* wall is built in stone masonry and has inscribed *mane* stones placed on the horizontal surface.

STATE OF PRESERVATION
Advanced State of Decay

SOURCE OF INFORMATION Tsewang Namgyal Toropa Khangbu, Hemis Shukpachan, Khaltse, Ladakh

Aba Gune *Mane*

INVENTORY NO.
KHALTSE / HEMIS SHUKPACHAN / 14 / 2004

Mane Wall / *Chorten* | In Use | Public (Community) | Around 250 - 300 years old

SETTING
The *chorten* and *mane* walls are oriented to the north and are located at the beginning of the settlement, north of the village road.

SIGNIFICANCE
The *chorten* and *mane* walls are located before the village and are circumambulated by villagers as an act of merit. The *chorten* are largely Changchub *chorten* and symbolize the Buddha's enlightenment.

DESCRIPTION
The site consists of six *chorten* and three *mane* walls scattered across a large arid stretch of land. The *chorten* are of various sizes. They are built in stone and mud brick masonry with mud mortar and have traces of external mud plaster and whitewash. The external surface has eroded considerably and the *chorten* have lost their original form. The *mane* walls are located in between the *chorten* and are linear stone masonry walls with *mane* stones placed on the horizontal surface. This group of structures is clearly visible from a great distance as one approaches the village.

STATE OF PRESERVATION
Advance State of Decay

SOURCE OF INFORMATION Tsewang Namgyal Toropa Khangbu, Hemis Shukpachan, Khaltse, Ladakh

Tsesemo dzing

INVENTORY NO.
KHALTSE / HEMIS SHUKPACHAN / 15 / 2004

Landscape (Community Space) | In Use | Public (Community)

SETTING
The field is oriented to the south and is located along the village road on an elevated stretch of land. It is surrounded by houses and fields.

SIGNIFICANCE / ASSOCIATED BELIEFS
In ancient times, Losar celebrations were held at the palace. However, an epidemic struck the village and subsequently the celebrations were shifted to the Tsesemo dzing and continue to be held here every year.

DESCRIPTION
The site consists of a large open area surrounded by village houses and boundary walls. During summer the land is used for agriculture but during the winters it is used for community gatherings.

CULTURAL LINKAGES / CULTURAL PRACTICES
The annual Losar celebrations are held here.

STATE OF PRESERVATION
Fair

SOURCE OF INFORMATION Deldan Spalzes, Hemis Shukpachan, Khaltse, Ladakh

Shalipa *Spurkhang*

INVENTORY NO.
KHALTSE / HEMIS SHUKPACHAN / 16 / 2004

Chorten / *Mane* Wall / Cremation Ground | In Use | Public / Private |
Around 300 - 350 years old

SETTING
The structures are oriented to the east and are located west of the main road. The precinct is sandwiched between the village roads to the east and west and a pathway to the north. A group of *chorten* lies to the south.

SIGNIFICANCE
The structures are believed to date back to the period of King Deldan Namgyal (1640 - 1675 A.D.). The *chorten* and *mane* walls are located along the village road and are circumambulated by villagers as an act of merit. The *spurkhang* belong to the Shalipa family and are used by them on the death of a family member.

DESCRIPTION
The site comprises of numerous *chorten* and *mane* walls. Most of the *chorten* are lying in ruins. The *chorten* are built in mud brick and stone masonry with mud mortar. The *mane* walls are rectangular in plan and built in dry stone masonry with inscribed stones placed on the horizontal

surface. There are two small *spurkhang*, belonging to the Shalipa family, located nearby. The *spurkhang* are mud plastered and whitewashed. These structures are surrounded by willow trees and wild grass.

STATE OF PRESERVATION
Advanced State of Decay

SOURCE OF INFORMATION Tsewang Namgyal Toro Khangbu, Hemis Shukpachan, Khaltse, Ladakh

---

Changpa pa House

INVENTORY NO.
KHALTSE / HEMIS SHUKPACHAN / 17 / 2004

Vernacular Building | In Use | Private (Individual) | Around 150 - 200 years old

SETTING
The Changpa pa house is oriented to the south and is located at a junction where three roads meet. It is surrounded by fields and willow trees.

SIGNIFICANCE
The house was built around 150 – 200 years ago by an ancestor of the Changpa family and the family has continued to reside here ever since, making additions and alterations over time. It is built in the traditional style and is a good example of vernacular architecture in the village.

DESCRIPTION
The house is a large structure located along the village road. A pathway from the road leads to a forecourt on the southern facade. This side also has the maximum window openings. The house is divided into two sections. The one to the east is the oldest section and is abandoned at the moment. The space is currently used to store fodder and firewood. The building adjacent to this was constructed at a

later date and is used by the family today. It is effectively three storeys high with a large open verandah on the second floor in front of the temple and the guest rooms. The kitchen and living rooms for the family are on the first floor. The ground floor is used for housing animals. The first level has been constructed in stone masonry while the upper levels are built in mud bricks with mud mortar. The window openings have wooden frames and decorated tiered lintels. The house has a traditional roof edged with a parapet which is bordered in black. Prayer flags are posted on corners of the roof.

STATE OF PRESERVATION
Fair

SOURCE OF INFORMATION Deldan Spalzes Sinipa, Hemis Shukpachan, Khaltse, Ladakh

Yurogpa *Mane* and Yurogpa *Khangpa*

INVENTORY NO.
KHALTSE / HEMIS SHUKPACHAN / 18 / 2004

Vernacular Building / *Mane* Wall / *Chorten* | Abandoned |
Private (Individual) | Around 200 - 250 years old

SETTING
The Yurogpa house and *mane* are oriented to the southeast and are located near the Changpa pa house. The site is surrounded by fields and willow trees.

SIGNIFICANCE
The Yurogpa house and *chorten* were built around 200 – 250 years ago by ancestors of the Yurogpa family. The house is built in the traditional style and is a good example of vernacular architecture in the village. The *chorten* and *mane* wall located near the house were possibly built by the family as an act of merit.

DESCRIPTION
The house is a small rectangular structure with a high plinth. It is a single storey house with few openings. The entrance door is on the southeast facade. It is built in stone masonry and mud brick masonry with mud mortar and the exterior is mud plastered and whitewashed. The structure is very simple and is probably abandoned. There are three *chorten* are located to the east of the house and are built on a large boulder in the middle of the agricultural fields. All three *chorten* have a common base and are built in stone and mud brick masonry with mud mortar. Externally, they are mud plastered and whitewashed. There is a small *mane* to the south of the house which is circular in plan and has numerous inscribed *mane* stones on its horizontal surface.

STATE OF PRESERVATION
Showing Signs of Deterioration

SOURCE OF INFORMATION Dechan Spalzes, Hemis Shukpachan, Khaltse, Ladakh

Lung Thed de *Chorten*

INVENTORY NO.
KHALTSE / HEMIS SHUKPACHAN / 19 / 2004

Chorten | In Use | Public (Community) | Around 250 - 300 years old

SETTING
The *chorten* is oriented to the southwest and is located along the edge of a hill at one end of the settlement.

SIGNIFICANCE
The *chorten* were possibly built in the past as an act of merit. The *lubang* marks the residence of the *lu,* or serpent gods. Prayers and offerings are made at the *lubang* on a fixed date in spring known as *Lu thebs* by the monks to placate the *lu*. The prayers are often to seek good supply of water before the cultivation of fields in spring and offerings made to the *lu* are then immersed in water.

DESCRIPTION
The site comprises of a cluster of *chorten* and a *lubang* built along the edge of a hill. The *chorten* are built in mud brick and stone masonry and are mud plastered and whitewashed on the exterior. The *lubang* is a small cubical structure with a rounded top. It is located towards the extreme corner. It is built in mud brick masonry and has an external layer of mud plaster and whitewash. The structures are all placed in a single row.

STATE OF PRESERVATION
Showing Signs of Deterioration

SOURCE OF INFORMATION Tundup Phuntsog, Sarpanch, Hemis Shukpachan, Khaltse, Ladakh

Stamgo Kagan

INVENTORY NO.
KHALTSE / HEMIS SHUKPACHAN / 20 / 2004

Chorten | In Use | Public (Community) | Around 45 years old

SETTING
The Kagan *chorten* is oriented to the east and is located west of the village road and southwest of the Dak bungalow.

SIGNIFICANCE
The Kagan *chorten* is a gateway *chorten* and it is believed that by passing through the passage of the *chorten* believers can accumulate merit which is seen as the first step towards enlightenment.

DESCRIPTION
The Kagan *chorten* is built over a square plan with two thick parallel side walls which support a large Changchub *chorten* above. There is a passage under the roof and the ceiling of this is in the shape of a *mandala* and is built in timber. The ceiling is painted with images of Shakyamuni Buddha and a *mandala* in the centre. The Kagan *chorten* is built in stone and mud brick masonry and is mud plastered and whitewashed externally. There is a tall *chugsum khorlo* over the dome which is surmounted by a metal crown.

STATE OF PRESERVATION
Showing Signs of Deterioration

SOURCE OF INFORMATION Tundup Phuntsog, Sarpanch, Hemis Shukpachan, Khaltse, Ladakh

Aba Gune *Chorten*

INVENTORY NO.
KHALTSE / HEMIS SHUKPACHAN / 21 / 2004

Chorten | In Use | Private (Individual) | Around 250 - 300 years old

SETTING
The Aba Gune *chorten* is oriented to the north and is located to the east of the Aba Gune house. It is surrounded by agricultural fields and trees.

SIGNIFICANCE
The *chorten* was built about 250 - 300 years ago by an ancestor of the Aba Gune family as an act of merit. The *chorten* are both Changchub *chorten* and symbolize the Buddha's enlightenment. The *tsadkhang* located nearby contains *tsa-tsa*.

DESCRIPTION
The site comprises of two Changchub *chorten* and a *tsadkhang*. The *chorten* are built in stone and mud brick masonry with mud mortar and are mud plastered and whitewashed externally. The *tsadkhang* is a tall structure built on a square plan with a small opening on the east side within which are placed the *tsa-tsa*. It is also built in stone and mud brick masonry with mud mortar and has an external layer of mud plaster and whitewash.

STATE OF PRESERVATION
Advanced State of Decay

SOURCE OF INFORMATION Tundup Phuntsog, Sarpanch, Hemis Shukpachan, Khaltse, Ladakh

Lha chang Tree

INVENTORY NO.
KHALTSE / HEMIS SHUKPACHAN / 22 / 2004

Landscape (Sacred Tree) | In Use | Public (Community)

SETTING
The tree is located to the north of the village next to a house and *mane* wall.

SIGNIFICANCE / ASSOCIATED BELIEFS
The tree is considered to be one of the oldest trees in the village. A spirit is believed to reside in the tree and, therefore, the tree is never cut or damaged by the villagers.

DESCRIPTION
The tree is surrounded by boundary walls, a small *mane* wall and the village road. It is around 20 metres high. The tree appears to be decaying as some of the branches are withering away and the trunk of the tree appears to be drying.

CULTURAL LINKAGES / CULTURAL PRACTICES
A small *mane* is built near the base of the tree and this is circumambulated by villagers.

STATE OF PRESERVATION
Showing Signs of Deterioration

SOURCE OF INFORMATION Tundup Phuntsog, Sarpanch, Hemis Shukpachan, Khaltse, Ladakh

Lagekhore *Mane*

INVENTORY NO.
KHALTSE / HEMIS SHUKPACHAN / 23 / 2004

Mane Wall | In Use | Public (Community) | Around 200 - 250 years old

SETTING
The *mane* wall is oriented to the south and is located along the village road with agricultural fields to the south.

SIGNIFICANCE
The *mane* wall is built along the village path and is circumambulated by villagers as an act of merit while travelling along this path.

DESCRIPTION
The *mane* wall is cylindrical in shape. It is built in stone masonry with mud mortar and is mud plastered and whitewashed externally. The upper edge of the *mane* is painted in a band of red. The surface is like a mound with *mane* stones placed on the surface.

STATE OF PRESERVATION
Showing Signs of Deterioration

SOURCE OF INFORMATION Tundup Phuntsog, Sarpanch, Hemis Shukpachan, Khaltse, Ladakh

Kali Kagan

INVENTORY NO.
KHALTSE / HEMIS SHUKPACHAN / 24 / 2004

Chorten / Mane Wall / Prayer Wheel | In Use | Public (Community) |
Around 45 years old

SETTING
The *chorten* is oriented to the south and is located northwest of the main village road. It is surrounded by houses, trees and agricultural fields.

SIGNIFICANCE
The Kagan *chorten* is a gateway *chorten* and merit is believed to accrue to believers who pass through its passage. The *chorten* and *mane* wall are circumambulated by villagers as an act of merit. The *chorten* are Changchub *chorten* and symbolize the Buddha's enlightenment.

DESCRIPTION
The site comprises of a Kagan *chorten*, Changchub *chorten*, a *mane* wall and a prayer wheel. The Kagan *chorten* consists of two thick parallel walls over which rests a large Changchub *chorten*. There is a passage below the roof and the ceiling of the passage is in the form of a *mandala* with paintings on them. The Kagan *chorten* is built in mud brick and stone masonry with mud mortar and is mud plastered

and whitewashed externally. The *chorten* above the roof has a tall *chugsum khorlo* symbolizing the thirteen steps towards enlightenment. A short distance away from the Kagan *chorten*, there is a Changchub *chorten* built in mud brick and stone masonry with an external layer of mud plaster and whitewash. There is a large *mane* wall built in stone masonry adjacent to the *chorten* which has numerous *mane* stones on its surface. There is a new prayer wheel nearby.

STATE OF PRESERVATION
Showing Signs of Deterioration

SOURCE OF INFORMATION Tundup Phuntsog, Sarpanch, Hemis Shukpachan, Khaltse, Ladakh

Khaltag Kangar

INVENTORY NO.
KHALTSE / HEMIS SHUKPACHAN / 25 / 2004

Chorten / Tsadkhang | In Use | Public (Community) | Around 300 - 350 years old

SETTING
The Khaltag Kangar is oriented to the south and is located near the ruined palace wall. The site is surrounded by fields and the village road to the west.

SIGNIFICANCE
It is believed to be contemporary to the palace wall. However, it has been repaired many times. The villagers gather around the chorten for festivities on the occasion of Losar. The *tsadkhang* contains small *tsa-tsa*.

DESCRIPTION
The *chorten* is a large Changchub *chorten* built along the base of a hill on which the Tseb-lha-gyal-mo *lhato* is located. It is built in mud brick and stone masonry with mud mortar and is mud plastered and whitewashed on the exterior. The *chorten* has a tall *chugsum khorlo* over the

dome which symbolizes the thirteen steps towards enlightenment. There is a small square *tsadkhang* in front which contains numerous *tsa-tsa*.

STATE OF PRESERVATION
Showing Signs of Deterioration

SOURCE OF INFORMATION T.T. Namgyal, Toropa, Hemis Shukpachan, Khaltse, Ladakh

Methog *Khar*

INVENTORY NO.
KHALTSE / HEMIS SHUKPACHAN / 26 / 2004

Fort / Palace | Abandoned | Public (Community) | Around 450 years old

SETTING
The ruins of the *khar* are located on the same hill over which the Tseb-lha-gyal-mo lhato is built. The *khar* is oriented to the south.

SIGNIFICANCE
King Jamyang Namgyal's mother Zizi Khatoon, while on her way to Kargil, built many palaces of which this is one. She discovered this large area between Hemis Shukpachan and Temisgang and wanted to settle a Balti community here. Two huge lizards appeared when the river was being dug. The lizards moved towards Tia and were killed on the way. As a result, a curse fell on the entire community and the village was hit by an epidemic. This was cured later when monks performed prayers in the village. As a reward, the king built the first Drigung *gonpa* in Phiyang. The palace was called Methog *khar* because the entire pathway leading to the palace had rose plants on either side. It is said the view from the palace window was spectacular and overlooked the entire village.

DESCRIPTION
The *khar* is largely in ruins and only a single wall remains. Almost the entire structure has collapsed which would once have enclosed the entire village settlement within its high boundary walls. The stone plinth is wide and the mud brick wall tapers towards the top. There is debris of the collapsed wall lying on one side. The wall is built in rammed earth.

STATE OF PRESERVATION
Danger of Disappearance

SOURCE OF INFORMATION T.T. Namgyal Toropa, Hemis Shukpachan, Khaltse, Ladakh

176

Tomba House

INVENTORY NO.
KHALTSE / HEMIS SHUKPACHAN / 27 / 2004

Vernacular Building | In Use | Private (Individual) | Around 150 - 200 years old

SETTING
The Tomba house is oriented to the southwest and is located north of the village road. It is surrounded by fields and other houses.

SIGNIFICANCE
The Tomba house was built by ancestors of the present owner some 150 - 200 years ago and the family has resided here ever since. It is built in the traditional style and is a good example of vernacular architecture in the village. The house has an elaborate *rigsum gonbo* over the entrance door to protect the family from evil forces.

DESCRIPTION
A narrow pathway from the village road leads to the entrance of the house. There is an elaborate *rigsum gonbo* over the entrance which houses three small *chorten*. The *rigsum gonbo* has walls on three sides and is open from the front. It has a traditional roof over it. The house is three storeys high with no openings on the ground floor, small openings on the first floor and larger openings on the second floor. There is a large open verandah on the second floors. The parapet on the upper floor is bordered in black and there are flag posts on the roof. The lower floor is built in stone masonry while the upper floors are built in mud brick masonry. The flooring is predominantly in mud and the house has a traditional roof of timber joists, *taalu* and a layer of mud.

STATE OF PRESERVATION
Showing Signs of Deterioration

SOURCE OF INFORMATION Deldan Spalzes, Hemis Shukpachan, Khaltse, Ladakh

Chorten Kurkur

INVENTORY NO.
KHALTSE / HEMIS SHUKPACHAN / 28 / 2004

Chorten | In Use | Public (Community) | Around 300 years old

SETTING
The *chorten* is oriented to the southwest and is built along the village pathway between two boundary walls, near the Tomba House.

SIGNIFICANCE
The *chorten* are believed to date back to the same period as the fort. The *chorten* is circumambulated by villagers to accumulate merit. The *lubang* is dedicated to the deities of the underworld.

DESCRIPTION
The *chorten* is a large *chorten* built in the middle of the village pathway. It has a large base built in stone masonry while the *chorten* above is built in stone and mud brick masonry with mud mortar. There are traces of mud plaster and whitewash on the external surface although much of this layer has eroded over time. A plinth adjacent to the larger base contains two smaller structures – one is a

chorten and the second is a *lubang*. The pathway runs all around the structure providing access to the villager for circumambulation.

STATE OF PRESERVATION
Advanced State of Decay

SOURCE OF INFORMATION Dechan Spalzes, Hemis Shukpachan, Khaltse, Ladakh

Hemis Shukpachan

177

Rigsum Gonbo

INVENTORY NO.
KHALTSE / HEMIS SHUKPACHAN / 29 / 2004

Rigsum Gonbo | In Use | Public (Community) | Around 300 years old

SETTING
The *rigsum gonbo* is oriented to the east and is built along the slope of a hill near the Ganjushpa house. It is surrounded by large boulders and is located at the extreme end of the village.

SIGNIFICANCE
There are several *rigsum gonbo* built along the peripheral hills of the village. The *rigsum gonbo* are built to protect the village from natural calamities and disasters.

DESCRIPTION
The *rigsum gonbo* is a rectangular structure built along the slope of a hill. It has walls on three sides and is open from the front. There are three *chorten* inside which are placed on a plinth and painted in orange, white and blue representing Jamyang, Chanrazig and Chagdor respectively. The structure is built in stone and mud brick

masonry and has a traditional roof of wooden joists, *taalu* and compacted mud. Externally, the structure is mud plastered and whitewashed.

STATE OF PRESERVATION
Fair

SOURCE OF INFORMATION T.T. Namgyal Toropa, Hemis Shukpachan, Khaltse, Ladakh

Pastures

INVENTORY NO.
KHALTSE / HEMIS SHUKPACHAN / 30 / 2004

Landscape (Pastures / Waterbody) | In Use | Public (Community)

SETTING
The pastures are located along the village road and are surrounded by houses and fields.

SIGNIFICANCE / ASSOCIATED BELIEFS
The pastures are the principal grazing areas for the village livestock. There is a fresh water stream which flows through the pastures and provides water to the village. There are ruins of an old shrine, northwest of the *chumig*, where monks used to meditate and pray.

DESCRIPTION
The pastures cover a vast area and there is a fresh water stream which flows through. There is a small shrine where monks used to reside. A small stone structure has been built over the *chumig* and there is a *chuskhor* (prayer wheel) which turns with the flow of the water built over the stream.

CULTURAL LINKAGES / CULTURAL PRACTICES
Monks from Ridzong *gonpa* perform pujas at the site in the 6th month of the Tibetan calendar.

STATE OF PRESERVATION
Showing Signs of Deterioration

SOURCE OF INFORMATION T.T. Namgyal, Hemis Shukpachan, Khaltse, Ladakh

178

Sasa Kongkar

INVENTORY NO.
KHALTSE / HEMIS SHUKPACHAN / 31 / 2004

Chorten / *Mane* Wall | In Use | Public (Community) | Around 200 years old

SETTING
The *chorten* is oriented to the south and is located in front of the *gonpa* near a large boulder.

SIGNIFICANCE
Villagers offer prayers during Losar and festivities are held around this chorten as well as at the Khaltak Kongar. The Kagan *chorten* is a gateway chorten and it is believed that by passing through the passage of the *chorten,* believers can accumulate merit seen as the first step towards enlightenment.

DESCRIPTION
The site comprises of a Kagan *chorten*, a Changchub *chorten* and a *mane* wall. The Kagan *chorten* has two parallel side walls over which rests a Changchub *chorten*. There is a passage way beneath, the ceiling of which is in the shape of a *mandala*. The plinth panels of the Changchub *chorten* above stucco relief motifs (*pa-tra*). These are painted in different colors mainly red, orange and yellow.

There is a tall *chugsum khorlo* above the *chorten* which is painted in red and is surmounted with a metal crown. There is a smaller *chorten* located next to the Kagan *chorten* and the *mane* walls. The *mane* wall is a small cylindrical stone masonry structure with numerous *mane* stones placed on its horizontal surface.

STATE OF PRESERVATION
Showing Signs of Deterioration

SOURCE OF INFORMATION T.T. Namgyal, Toropa, Hemis Shukpachan, Khaltse, Ladakh

Serpay *Lhakhang*

INVENTORY NO.
KHALTSE / HEMIS SHUKPACHAN / 32 / 2004

Gonpa | In Use | Public (Likir *Gonpa*) | Around 200 years old

SETTING
The Serpay *lhakhang* is located on the top of a hill above the Sasa Kongkar *chorten* and is surrounded by houses.

SIGNIFICANCE
The original *gonpa* is believed to have been built around 200 years ago and a new section was added 80 years ago. The *gonpa* belongs to the Gelugpa sect and is under the purview of Likir *gonpa*. A monk from Likir is deputed here to carry out prayers and rituals in the temple.

DESCRIPTION
From the narrow street, a small door leads through a corridor to the first floor where the main *dukhang* is located. The structure is three storeys high. The ground floor is not in use. There is a large open verandah and a portico in front of the *dukhang*. A wooden door on the southwest wall leads into a large colonnaded hall. At the centre of the hall, there is a skylight which is double storeyed. The wooden columns and brackets are richly decorated and painted over. The walls are covered with paintings. The main image is that of Shakyamuni Buddha and is located against the rear wall in a frame. Volumes of the Kangyur are placed on the left and images of Bodhisattvas stand to the right. There are glass rooms on the second floor which house the *zimchung*. The *gonpa* is built in stone and mud brick masonry with mud mortar and is mud plastered and whitewashed on the exterior. It has a traditional roof comprising of timber joists, *taalu* and a layer of compacted mud on top. The roof is edged with a low height parapet which is painted in red. There is prayer flags posted on the roof. The flooring of the *dukhang* is in timber.

STATE OF PRESERVATION
Showing Signs of Deterioration

SOURCE OF INFORMATION T.T. Namgyal Toropa, Hemis Shukpachan, Khaltse, Ladakh

179

Hemis Shukpachan

Shugpa Forest

INVENTORY NO.
KHALTSE / HEMIS SHUKPACHAN / 33 / 2004

Landscape (Sacred Grove) | In Use | Public (Community)

SETTING
The Shugpa forest is surrounded by hills on one side and fields on the other side.

SIGNIFICANCE / ASSOCIATED BELIEFS
The Shugpa, or juniper, is a sacred species and its branches and leaves are used for ritual purposes such as offerings in *lhatos* as well as for purification. The juniper forest is the oldest in the region and some trees are believed to be about 2000 years old.

DESCRIPTION
The site comprises of a vast green area surrounded by boundary walls. Juniper trees of various heights grow here. One of the trees is almost 20 metres high.

CULTURAL LINKAGES / CULTURAL PRACTICES
The villagers circumambulate the trees and there is a small *mane* beneath where offerings are made.

STATE OF PRESERVATION
Showing Signs of Deterioration

SOURCE OF INFORMATION Tundup Phuntsog, Sarpanch, Hemis Shukpachan, Khaltse, Ladakh

Hinju

Hinju is located on an 8-km trek from Ursi Dho. From the Leh - Srinagar highway, a road diverts between Khaltse and Lamayuru, towards Shilla. Phanjilla lies on this road and from here there is a path which leads to Ursi Dho. The village was formerly a part of Wanla but today has an independent village head (*goba*). There are about 25 households in the village.

Listed by: Deldan Angmo and Jassu Singh
Year: 2004

Kanji

Kanji lies along a new link road that diverts from the Leh - Srinagar highway near Henaksu. The link road ends after 4 kms from where an 8 kms trek along the stream and through the fields leads to Kanji. The village is called Skan bZhi as it is situated between four precipices. The name was later corrupted to Kanji. There are about 42 households in Kanji village.

Listed by: Deldan Angmo and Jassu Singh
Year: 2004

Lame *Mane*

INVENTORY NO.
KHALTSE / HINJU / 01 / 2004

Mane Wall | In Use | Public (Community) | Around 300 year old

SETTING
The *mane* wall is oriented to the southeast and is located en route from Ursi do to Hinju. It is surrounded by fields to the southwest and northeast.

SIGNIFICANCE
It is referred to as the Lame *mane* or '*mane* along the way' and is located in Hinju Wangsay, where the villages of Hinju have agricultural fields. The *mane* walls were built in the past to protect the fields and are circumambulated by villagers as an act of merit.

DESCRIPTION
The site comprises of two circular *mane* walls. The one to the northwest is a large *mane* wall consisting of a mound of earth and a peripheral stone masonry wall. Inscribed *mane* stones are placed over its horizontal surface. The second *mane* wall is built on a stone platform. It is built in dry stone masonry with inscribed *mane* stones placed on its horizontal surface.

SOURCE OF INFORMATION Tashi Yangskit, Hinju, Khaltse, Ladakh

STATE OF PRESERVATION
Advanced State of Decay

Shistipa House

INVENTORY NO.
KHALTSE / HINJU / 02 / 2004

Vernacular Building | In Use | Private (Individual) | Around 250 years old

SETTING
The Shistipa house is oriented to the south and is built over a small hill before the main village. It is surrounded by the Gompapa house to the west and Zomalpa house to the east.

SIGNIFICANCE
The Shistpa house was constructed by the great grand father of the present owner and the family has been residing in this house ever since. It is built in the traditional style and is a good example of vernacular architecture.

DESCRIPTION
The Shistipa house is a three storeyed building built along a slope. The rear section of the house has three floors while the front portion has two floors. The mountainside forms its rear wall. The lower floors are constructed in stone masonry while the upper levels are in mud brick masonry. There is a small courtyard to the west from where an entrance door leads to the house. The house has narrow timber openings and a traditional roof comprising of timber beams, joists, dried grass, willow twigs and compacted mud. The internal flooring is made of compacted mud and the walls are mud plastered. Externally, too, the walls are mud plastered and whitewashed.

STATE OF PRESERVATION
Advanced State of Decay

SOURCE OF INFORMATION Tashi Yangskit, Hinju, Khaltse, Ladakh

Lhachang Tree

INVENTORY NO.
KHALTSE / HINJU / 03 / 2004

Landscape (Sacred Tree) | In Use | Public (Community)

SETTING
The tree is located in Hinju Wangsay which lies on the way from Ursi Dho to Hinju. It is surrounded by fields and orchards.

SIGNIFICANCE / ASSOCIATED BELIEFS
The *lhachang* tree is one of the oldest trees in the village and is considered sacred by the villagers. It is protected by the villagers.

DESCRIPTION
The *lhachang* is an ancient tree with a wide trunk of almost fifteen feet diameter. There is a *chorten* built at the base of the tree.

CULTURAL LINKAGES / CULTURAL PRACTICES
Villagers offer prayers at the tree before harvesting their crops.

SOURCE OF INFORMATION Gelags Paljor, Hinju, Khaltse, Ladakh

STATE OF PRESERVATION
Fair

Tsabgyat *Mane* and *Lhato*

INVENTORY NO.
KHALTSE / HINJU / 04 / 2004

Chorten / Lhato | In Use | Public (Community) | Around 300 years old

SETTING
The *chorten* is oriented to the south and is located at the top of a bare hill on the way to Hinju from Ursi Dho. Fields lie to the south and southwest at the base of the hill.

SIGNIFICANCE
The *lhato* is dedicated to the protector deity of Hinju Wangsay which is the winter habitation settlement for the villagers of Hinju. The contents of the *lhato* are changed every year on the occasion of Losar amid rituals and prayers. The *mane* wall and *chorten* were built in the past as an act of merit.

DESCRIPTION
The site comprises of a *mane* wall, a *chorten* and a *lhato* on top of a hill and a circular *mane* wall with an opening to the south below. The *mane* wall has a large elliptical base made of dry stone masonry with *mane* stones placed on its

horizontal surface. The *chorten* is built on a random rubble masonry base. It is, however, lying in ruins and is difficult to identify. To the south of these structures is a whitewashed *lhato* built in stone and mud brick masonry. It is mud plastered and whitewashed externally. Juniper branches, *khadag* and animal horns are placed in the *lhato*.

STATE OF PRESERVATION
Advanced State of Decay

SOURCE OF INFORMATION Tashi Yangskit, Hinju, Khaltse, Ladakh

Hinju

183

Rhoungi *Mane*

INVENTORY NO.
KHALTSE / HINJU / 05 / 2004

Chorten / *Mane* Wall | In Use | Public (Community) | Around 300 years old

SETTING
The *chorten* and *mane* wall are oriented to the south and are located from Hinju Wangsay to Hinju, just before Hinju village. They are built on a bare hillside with agricultural fields to the south.

SIGNIFICANCE
The *mane* walls mark the entrance to the settlement of Hinju and are circumambulated by villagers as an act of merit. The *chorten* are all Changchub *chorten* symbolizing the Buddha's enlightenment.

DESCRIPTION
The site comprises of a line of *mane* walls and *chorten*. The first group consists of a whitewashed *chorten* and a linear *mane* wall attached to another circular *mane* wall. This is followed by a second group consisting of a *chorten* built over a square base and a rectangular *mane* wall. A little further ahead is a group of two *chorten* placed on a common stone platform and a linear *mane* wall. At the end of the path is a group of three whitewashed *chorten* placed on a common stone masonry platform forming a *rigsum gonbo*. The *mane* walls are built in dry stone masonry and have *mane* stones placed on the horizontal surface. The *chorten* are built in stone and mud brick masonry and are mud plastered and whitewashed externally.

STATE OF PRESERVATION
Advanced State of Decay

SOURCE OF INFORMATION Gelags Paljor, Hinju, Khaltse, Ladakh

Mathang *Mane*

INVENTORY NO.
KHALTSE / HINJU / 06 / 2004

Chorten / *Lhato* | In Use | Community | Around 100 years old

SETTING
The structures are oriented to the east and are built on a rocky outcrop in the middle of agricultural fields. The site lies at the entrance to the village and is surrounded by fields on all sides.

SIGNIFICANCE
The Mathang *mane* was built by the villagers to protect the village from evil forces. The *lhato* is dedicated to the protector deity while the *lubang* is built as an altar to the spirits of the underworld. All these structures serve to protect the agricultural fields from disease and natural calamities.

DESCRIPTION
The site comprises a *lhato*, seven *chorten*, a *tsadkhang* and a small whitewashed *lubang*. The *chorten* are of various sizes. The largest is to the south of the site and has a square base. There is a group of two *chorten* built on stone masonry platforms placed perpendicular to each other. The *tsadkhang* and another *chorten* are placed on a common stone masonry platform. The *tsadkhang* is a huge cubical structure built on a rectangular plan with an opening to the south. All these structures are built on a huge rock in the middle of the fields. The *lhato* is placed on another boulder. It is a cubical whitewashed structure built in stone and mud brick masonry. There is a small opening to the east. The primary construction material is stone and mud brick masonry.

STATE OF PRESERVATION
Danger of Disappearance

SOURCE OF INFORMATION Sonam Norzas, Hinju, Khaltse, Ladakh

Chorten

INVENTORY NO.
KHALTSE / HINJU / 07 / 2004

Chorten | In Use | Public (Community) | Around 400 years old

SETTING
The *chorten* are oriented to the southeast and are located on the top of a hill near the entrance to the village. The village lies to the northeast and the Mathang *mane* lies to the west.

SIGNIFICANCE
The *chorten* were built in the past by a villager as an act of merit. The *lubang* are dedicated to the spirits of the underworld. The structures are circumambulated by villagers as an act of merit.

DESCRIPTION
The site comprises of a group *chorten* and *lubang* built on the top of a hill. The *chorten* are of various sizes and are constructed in stone and mud brick masonry. They are mud plastered and whitewashed externally. The *lubang* are small whitewash cubical structures built in stone and mud brick masonry.

STATE OF PRESERVATION
Danger of Disappearance

SOURCE OF INFORMATION Sonam Norzas, Hinju, Khaltse, Ladakh

Hinju

185

Kagan *Chorten*

INVENTORY NO.
KHALTSE / HINJU / 08 / 2004

Chorten | In Use | Public (Community) | Around 80 years old

SETTING
The chorten is oriented to the east and is surrounded by Yangtopa house to the east, Cokhambo house to the west and Zomal *Khangbu* to the north.

SIGNIFICANCE
The *chorten* was built around 80 years ago by a villager Tashi Tsewang, as an act of merit. Merit is believed to accrue to believers who pass through the passage of the *chorten* and circumambulate it.

DESCRIPTION
The Kagan *chorten* consists of two parallel walls over which rests a large Changchub *chorten*. The passage is oriented from east to west. The supporting walls are constructed in stone masonry and are mud plastered and whitewashed. The structure has a timber *mandala* roof without any painting. Over the roof of this passage rests a Changchub *chorten* which is mud plastered and whitewashed externally.

STATE OF PRESERVATION
Advanced State of Decay

SOURCE OF INFORMATION Tsewang Laskit, Hinju, Khaltse, Ladakh

Lotsava *Lhakhang*

INVENTORY NO.
KHALTSE / KANJI / 01 / 2004

Temple | In Use | Private (Individual) | 11th / 13th century

SETTING

The Lotsava *lhakhang* is oriented to the south and is located on a steep elevated site in the village of Kanji. To the east of the Lotsawa *lhakhang* is a cluster of Lagchung *chorten* with the residential buildings along south.

SIGNIFICANCE

The Lotsava *lhakhang* is named after the great translator Lotsava Rinchen Zangpo in the 11th century. Believed by the community to have been built in the 11th century, it has been placed based on its iconography and style to the 13th century. The paintings and stucco images belong to an early period of Buddhist art in the region.

DESCRIPTION

Lotsava *lhakhang* is a single storeyed structure with a high parapet. A small square structure with a forecourt, it is made in rammed earth with a flat traditional roof comprising of willow twigs, dried grass and mud. Externally, the structure is mud plastered and whitewashed in red and

white. The structure is completely free from any sort of opening except the entrance doorway which is the only source of light. There is a porch in front of the doorway which is supported on a single wooden column flanked with a bracket. The walls of the porch have fragments of paintings left on it. There are some stucco decorations still visible above the wooden doorway. The room is a small structure with a wooden column supporting the roof. The rear wall towards the north has a pedestal with three large images of Shakyamuni Buddha, Chanrazig and Chamba. The walls of the *lhakhang* are adorned with *mandala* paintings dedicated to Vairocana. The temple has been recently restored.

STATE OF PRESERVATION
Advanced State of Decay

SOURCE OF INFORMATION Konchak Norbu-Khoshalpa, Kanji, Khaltse, Ladakh

Rigsum Gonbo

INVENTORY NO.
KHALTSE / KANJI / 02 / 2004

Rigsum Gonbo | In Use | Public (Community)

SETTING

The *rigsum gonbo* is oriented to the northwest and is located on a steep elevated site near the Lotsava *lhakhang*. The *rigsum gonbo* stands in the middle of agricultural fields and a stream flows nearby.

SIGNIFICANCE

The *rigsum gonbo* was built by the villagers to protect their cattle and fields from natural calamities and disease.

DESCRIPTION

The *rigsum gonbo* is a small rectangular whitewashed enclosure with parallel side walls and openings on the southeast and northwest sides. The opening to the northwest is larger and through this are seen three *chorten*, one of which has collapsed. The enclosure is built in stone masonry with mud mortar and is mud plastered and whitewashed externally though the external layer has eroded considerably. The *chorten* are built in stone

masonry and are mud plastered and painted on the exterior. There are, however, no traces of the traditional colours of orange, blue and white usually seen on these *chorten*.

STATE OF PRESERVATION
Advanced State of Decay

SOURCE OF INFORMATION Tashi Dolma Yokmapa, Kanji, Khaltse, Ladakh

Dzum-me
Rigsum Gonbo

INVENTORY NO.
KHALTSE / KANJI / 03 / 2004

Rigsum Gonbo / Chorten | In Use | Public (Community)

SETTING
The *rigsum gonbo* is located along the slope of a hill across the river and settlement. The river flows to the north and east of the site with the village on the opposite shore of the river.

SIGNIFICANCE
The *rigsum gonbo* was constructed by the villagers to protect the village from natural calamities and other evil forces. The *chorten* is a Changchub *chorten* symbolizing the Buddha's enlightenment. It was built in the past by a villager as an act of merit. The *lubang* is located near the river and is dedicated to the *lu*, deities of the underworld.

DESCRIPTION
The site comprises of a Changchub *chorten*, a *rigsum gonbo*, a *lubang* and the ruins of another *lubang*. The *chorten* is constructed on an exposed stone masonry base, on the edge of the river. The *chorten* is mud plastered and whitewashed on the exterior surface and has a tall *chugsum khorlo* over its dome on which rests a metal crown. The ruins of a *lubang* are located near the base of the *chorten*. There is a *rigsum gonbo* further up the hill side. It is a tall whitewashed structure with a large opening to the north. It is covered by a traditional roof. The structure is constructed out of stone masonry with mud mortar and is mud plastered and whitewashed. There are three *chorten* within painted in orange, white and blue. There is small whitewashed *lubang* to the west.

STATE OF PRESERVATION
Advanced State of Decay

SOURCE OF INFORMATION Tashi Dolma Yokmapa, Kanji, Khaltse, Ladakh

---

Nyerbak *Chorten*

INVENTORY NO.
KHALTSE / KANJI / 04 / 2004

Chorten | Abandoned | Public (Community) | Around 500 years old

SETTING
The Nyerbak *chorten* are located along the slope of a mountain above some village houses. The Dongstot pa house lies to the northwest.

SIGNIFICANCE
The *chorten* are believed to have been built 500 years ago as an act of merit. These are Changchub *chorten* that symbolize the Buddha's enlightenment. The *chorten* are circumambulated by the villagers as an act of merit.

DESCRIPTION
The site consists of two Changchub *chorten* built close to each other on a common stone masonry platform. The *chorten* are similar in size and are built in stone and mud brick masonry with mud mortar. The *chorten* have an external layer of mud plaster and whitewash which has eroded considerably.

STATE OF PRESERVATION
Advanced State of Decay

SOURCE OF INFORMATION Tashi Dolma Yokmapa, Kanji, Khaltse, Ladakh

Zurkhangpa House

INVENTORY NO.
KHALTSE / KANJI / 05 / 2004

Vernacular Building | In Use | Private (Individual) | Around 250 years old

SETTING
The Zurkhangpa house is oriented to the southeast and is located on the extreme northeast corner of the village. The Kakapey house lies to the southwest and a Stago-Sgoa *chorten* lies to the northeast.

SIGNIFICANCE
The Zurkhangpa house is one of the oldest in the village and was built by the ancestors of the present owner 250 years ago. Its name derives from the word *'zurkhang'* meanings cornermost house. The house is built in the traditional style and is a good example of vernacular architecture in the village.

DESCRIPTION
The Zurkhangpa house is a large three storeyed house built along the slope of a hill. It is built in stone and mud brick masonry with mud mortar. There are long dark alleys under the house connecting the courtyard through passageways. The ground floor is used for housing animals and the two

upper floors constitute the family's living quarters. There are two large *rabsal* on the southeastern and north eastern facades. The family temple is at the top on the southeastern facade. It has a cantilevered verandah around for circumambulation which has timber balusters and rails. The house has a traditional roof composed of timber beams, joists, *taalu*, grass and compacted mud. The facade towards the village has small and large window openings with the timber lintels over the larger windows. There are prayer flags on the roof top.

STATE OF PRESERVATION
Fair

SOURCE OF INFORMATION Tashi Dolma Yokmapa, Kanji, Khaltse, Ladakh

Kakapey *Khangpa*

INVENTORY NO.
KHALTSE / KANJI / 06 / 2004

Vernacular Building | In Use | Private (Individual) | Around 200 years old

SETTING
Kakapey *Khangpa* is oriented to the south east and is located southwest of the Zurkhangpa house. The Lotsava *chorten* are located near the entrance.

SIGNIFICANCE
The Kakapey family is one of the oldest in the village. An ancestor of the family, Kakapey Apo, was the first to come to the village and start this settlement. The house was built by him 200 years ago and the family continues to reside here. It is built in the traditional style and is a good example of vernacular architecture in the village.

DESCRIPTION
The Kakapey *Khangpa* is a large three storeyed house built along the slope of a mountain. The ground floor is largely the foundation of the building while the first floor is used for storage. The family's living quarters and the temple are located on the second floor. This level has elaborate timber framed window openings on the extreme right corner. The

house is built in stone masonry at the lower levels and in mud brick masonry at the upper levels. It has a traditional roof composed of timber beams, joists, *taalu*, grass and compacted mud. The exterior walls of the house are mud plastered and whitewashed.

STATE OF PRESERVATION
Fair

SOURCE OF INFORMATION Tashi Dolma Yokmapa, Kanji, Khaltse, Ladakh, 194106, J&K

Lugupey House

INVENTORY NO.
KHALTSE / KANJI / 07 / 2004

Vernacular Building | In Use | Private (Individual) | Around 250 years old

SETTING
The Lugupey house is oriented to the east and is located on an elevated area in the village north of Dongstut, south of Kakapey and west of Shalepey house.

SIGNIFICANCE
The Lugupey house was built by the ancestors of the Lugupey family about 250 years ago and the family continues to reside in this house. It is built in the traditional style and is a good example of vernacular architecture in the village.

DESCRIPTION
The Lugupey house is a large double storeyed building built on a hill over a high foundation. The ground floor is used primarily for storage and is built in stone masonry with mud mortar. It has narrow slit like openings for ventilation. The first floor has rows of timber framed windows and is built in mud brick masonry with mud mortar. This level houses the family's living quarters. The house has a traditional roof of timber beams, joists, *taalu*, grass and compacted mud. The exterior walls of the house are mud plastered and whitewashed.

STATE OF PRESERVATION
Fair

Kanji

189

SOURCE OF INFORMATION Tashi Dolma Yokmapa, Kanji, Khaltse, Ladakh

Khaltse

Khaltse is the main capital of the Sham region.
During the reign of King Naglug (1150 – 1175 A.D.),
the Danak *Khar*, or palace, was built. Since it was
one of the earliest palaces in Ladakh, the settlement
was named Kharlatse. Today, there are around 50
households with a population of 530 residents living
in Khaltse.

*{Source: Tashi Lundup (Sabipa),
and 'History of Ladakh' by Tashi Rabgyas}*

Listed by: Deldan Angmo and Jassu Singh
Year: 2004, 2007

Goche *Chorten*

INVENTORY NO.
KHALTSE / KHALTSE / 01 / 2004

Chorten | In Use | Public (Community) | Around 1000 years old

SETTING
From the main Leh - Srinagar road, a narrow path winds between the boundary walls of the forest lands and leads to the site. The River Indus flows to its south and the Khaltsipa house lies to the southeast.

SIGNIFICANCE
According to legend, the *chorten* were built by a group of fairies a thousand years ago from sheep's milk. The *chorten* are in ruins and are difficult to identify.

DESCRIPTION
The site consists of two large white *chorten* , two small *chorten* , a completely ruined *chorten* and a newly constructed *mane* wall. The *chorten* are built on a square base in mud brick and stone masonry. The *chorten* are, however, in ruins with the smaller ones having almost disappeared leaving behind a pile of debris. The external layer of mud plaster and whitewash have eroded making it difficult to identify the *chorten* .

STATE OF PRESERVATION
Danger of Disappearance

SOURCE OF INFORMATION Stanzin Namgyal (Sarpanch), Khaltse, Khaltse, Ladakh

Group of *Chorten* and *Mane* Wall

INVENTORY NO.
KHALTSE / KHALTSE / 02 / 2004

Chorten / *Mane* Wall | In Use | Public (Community) | Around 300 years old

SETTING
The group of *chorten* and *mane* wall is oriented to the south and are located to the left of the main Leh - Srinagar highway after crossing Khaltse. The vehicular road lies to the north, forest department land to the southeast and an army camp to the southwest.

SIGNIFICANCE
The group of *chorten* and *mane* wall is located along the main access road to Khaltse and is circumambulated by villagers to accumulate merit. The *chorten* are all Changchub *chorten* symbolizing the Buddha's enlightenment.

DESCRIPTION
The site comprises of a group of 28 *chorten* and two *mane* walls. The *mane* walls are built in dry stone masonry with *mane* stones placed on the horizontal surface. The *chorten* are of different sizes. The road cuts through the group dividing them into two clusters – one with only two *chorten* and the second with the remaining *chorten* and *mane* walls. Of the larger group, nine small *chorten* are built on a rectangular stone masonry base. The other 17 *chorten*, including the largest *chorten*, have another stone masonry base. The *chorten* are all built in mud brick and stone masonry and are mud plastered and whitewashed externally. Some of the *chorten* have lost their original form with the erosion of the external layer.

STATE OF PRESERVATION
Advanced State of Decay

SOURCE OF INFORMATION Stanzin Namgyal (Sarpanch), Khaltse, Khaltse, Ladakh

Ralupey *Khangpa*

INVENTORY NO.
KHALTSE / KHALTSE / 03 / 2004

Vernacular Building | In Use | Private (Individual) | Around 70 years old

SETTING
The Ralupey *khangpa* is oriented to the south and is situated off the main Leh - Srinagar highway, after crossing the town. It is located at the foot of a mountain on which the Daknak *khar* is built. It lies to the north of the Khaltse road, opposite the group of *chorten* and the *mane* wall.

SIGNIFICANCE
The Ralupey house was built by an ancestor of the Ralupey family about 70 years ago. It is built in the traditional style and is an example of vernacular architecture in the town.

DESCRIPTION
The Ralupey house is a large double storeyed building built on a rectangular plan There is a small shop on the ground floor while the family's living quarters are on the first floor. The entrance to the house is from the east. There are four windows on the first floor with decorated timber lintels. On the west facade of the house, there are windows and a

narrow window opening on the ground floor. The house is built in stone and mud brick masonry and is mud plastered and whitewashed externally.

STATE OF PRESERVATION
Fair

SOURCE OF INFORMATION Stanzin Namgyal (Sarpanch), Khaltse, Khaltse, Ladakh

Sgang Ge *Mane*

INVENTORY NO.
KHALTSE / KHALTSE / 04 / 2004

Mane Wall | In Use | Public (Community)

SETTING
The *mane* wall is oriented to the east and is located to the left of the main highway when approaching from Leh to Srinagar. It lies opposite Ralupey *khangpa* which is to its north, and to the south there are apricot trees and agricultural fields.

SIGNIFICANCE
Originally, there was a huge chorten on the site which was in complete ruins. The villagers brought debris from the ruins of a *mane* wall located in Pasta Shang and constructed the present *mane* walls on the site of the *chorten*. The *chorten* and *mane* walls were built by the villagers along the main highway so that passers-by may circumambulate the structures as an act of merit. The *chorten* are all Changchub *chorten* symbolizing the Buddha's enlightenment.

DESCRIPTION
The site has a cluster of eleven *chorten* and five *mane* walls.

They are placed in a single row along the vehicular road. There is a large *chorten* at one end built over a square base. This is followed by a long *mane* wall, followed by ten small *chorten*. All the *chorten* are mud plastered and whitewashed. There is a large square *mane* wall in the centre. It is built in random rubble masonry and is whitewashed. The horizontal surface of the *mane* contains numerous *mane* stones. At the end of the group, there is a long rectangular *mane* wall and a smaller circular *mane* wall. These *mane* walls are mud plastered and whitewashed.

STATE OF PRESERVATION
Showing Signs of Deterioration

SOURCE OF INFORMATION Stanzin Namgyal (Sarpanch), Khaltse, Khaltse, Ladakh

Khaltse *Gonpa*

INVENTORY NO.
KHALTSE / KHALTSE / 05 / 2004

Gonpa / Chorten / Mane Wall | In Use | Public (Lamayuru *Gonpa*)

SETTING

From the main Leh – Srinagar road, a path on the right leads to the *gonpa* through residential building and apricot orchards. The *gonpa* complex is surrounded by apricot orchards on its north and the northeast, *tashag* on the east, south and the west. There are fields on its southwest.

SIGNIFICANCE

The *gonpa* is believed to have evolved from a hermitage used by a great saint who came from Tibet which later evolved into the *gonpa*. It is believed to be contemporary to Lamayuru *gonpa*. The Nyenas *lhakhang* was built about 60 years ago. Monks from Lamayuru *gonpa* are deputed here to perform prayers and rituals.

DESCRIPTION

The *gonpa* complex comprises a large area surrounded by a high fenced wall. A metal gate to the south leads into the complex. There is a long *mane* wall to the west side and a *chorten* to the east. There is a throne made of mud bricks to the west of the *gonpa* building which is believed to have been constructed for the previous Karmapa. The *gonpa* building is a double storey structure built on an L-shaped plan. There is a court in the front of the structure, and a cement pedestrian path which leads to the Aapchi *dukhang*. This is the main *dukhang*. It is square in plan and has four ornamental wooden columns and brackets supporting a traditional roof above. There is a skylight above the central space. The chamber houses images of Chug-shig-zal, Chamba, Namgyalma and an image of Guru Rinpoche seated on the petal of a lotus. This is a rare image and the only other example is in Kanji. The walls are adorned with painting which are not clearly visible due to soot deposits on the surface. The original flooring is made of *arga* which has been covered by a wooden floor.

The building to the west is a double storey structure known as Nyenes *dukhang*. It houses a double storey statue of Chug-shig-zal. It is one of the largest images of Chug-shig-zal in the region, the second being in the Skyurbuchan *gonpa*. There are wooden shelves on the side which contain the Buddhist cannons, Kangyur and Bum. The *dukhang* is a rectangular space with two columns in the front and four columns to the rear supporting the roof and the skylight. The panels of the skylight and the walls are covered with recently painted images of Boddhisatvas. The head lama's quarter is above the structure on the first floor. There is a double storey structure to the west of the *dukhang* which has been recently constructed by the village committee.

STATE OF PRESERVATION

Showing Signs of Deterioration

SOURCE OF INFORMATION Gelong Konchok Chosphel, Khaltse, Khaltse, Ladakh

Khaltse

194

NIRLAC

Tashag (Khangchakpe)

INVENTORY NO.
KHALTSE / KHALTSE / 06 / 2004

Vernacular Building | Abandoned | Private (Individual) | Around 150 years old

SETTING
From the main Leh - Srinagar highway, a narrow pedestrian path leads to the *gonpa*. The *tashag* is located near the *gonpa* complex with fields towards the east. It is oriented to the south.

SIGNIFICANCE
The *tashag* was used in the past as a residence for monks but is abandoned today. The building is constructed in the traditional style and is an example of vernacular architecture of the village.

DESCRIPTION
The *tashag* is a double storeyed building with a large entrance courtyard to the south. The entrance is from the ground floor. The ground floor walls are constructed in random rubble masonry with mud mortar and this level has very small timber framed openings. The first floor is

constructed in mud brick masonry and has slightly larger window openings. There is a terrace on the first floor towards the south. Externally, the walls are mud plastered and whitewashed. The structure has a traditional roof of timber joists, *taalu*, *yagzes* and a layer of compacted mud. The roof is supported by timber beams and columns. The lower floor has a mud floor and the upper level has a timber floor.

STATE OF PRESERVATION
Advanced State of Decay

SOURCE OF INFORMATION Stanzin Namgyal (Sarpanch), Khaltse, Khaltse, Ladakh

Khaltse

195

Group of *Chorten*

INVENTORY NO.
KHALTSE / KHALTSE / 07 / 2004

Chorten | In Use | Public (Community)

SETTING
From the main Leh - Srinagar highway, a concrete pedestrian path diverts and leads to the *chorten*. It is surrounded by the Saipa house to the north, the path and vehicular road to the south. The *chorten* are oriented to the south.

SIGNIFICANCE
The *chorten* were built along a village path and are still circumambulated by villagers to accrue merit when travelling along this path.

DESCRIPTION
The site comprises of a cluster of six *chorten* lined in a row along the path. The first three *chorten* are built on a common plinth. The last one is built over a large boulder which is also whitewashed. The plinth is built in stone masonry while the *chorten* are built in stone and mud brick masonry with mud mortar and are mud plastered and

whitewashed externally. The panels at the base of the *chorten* have some stucco relief motifs (*pa-tra*) which are, however, fading away.

STATE OF PRESERVATION
Advanced State of Decay

SOURCE OF INFORMATION Stanzin Namgyal (Sarpanch), Khaltse, Khaltse, Ladakh

Group of *Chorten*

INVENTORY NO.
KHALTSE / KHALTSE / 12 / 2004

Chorten | In Use | Public (Community) | Around 100 years old

STATE OF PRESERVATION
Showing Signs of Deterioration

SETTING
From the main Leh - Srinagar highway, a concrete pathway diverts passing via the medical centre and the Moravian church to the outskirts of the village where the *chorten* are located. The *chorten* are oriented to the south and are located along the slope of a hill, north of the Amchipa house.

SIGNIFICANCE
The Kagan *chorten* was built along with the *rigsum gonbo*. It is believed that about 100 years ago no male child was being born in the village. On being approached by the villagers, a great Tibetan sage suggested that they build four *rigsum gonbo* at the four corners of the village facing the four directions and also the Kagan *chorten*. The Kagan *chorten* is a gateway *chorten* usually built on the outskirts of the village. Passing through the passage of the *chorten* is believed to accumulate merit. The remaining *chorten* are all Changchub *chorten* which symbolize the Buddha's enlightenment.

DESCRIPTION
The site comprises of a large cluster of twenty two *chorten* and one Kagan *chorten* in the centre. One *chorten* is towards the extreme west. The *chorten* are of different sizes and are built in a row. The *chorten* are built on a square base in stone and mud brick masonry and are mud plastered and white washed externally. The Kagan *chorten* consist of two thick parallel walls over which rests a Changchub *chorten*. The walls are built in stone and mud brick masonry as is the *chorten* above. The passage under the *chorten* has a wooden ceiling in the shape of a *mandala* and is devoid of any paintings. The Kagan *chorten* as well as the large *chorten* have a tall *chugsum khorlo* over the dome made of baked clay tiles.

Dakschanpa
Tashag

INVENTORY NO.
KHALTSE / KHALTSE / 13 / 2004

Vernacular Building | Abandoned | Private (Individual) | Around 100 years old

SETTING
From the main Leh - Srinagar highway, a steep climb along a gravel / cement zigzag pathway leads to the house. The *tashag* is oriented to the south and is located along the slope of a hill above the Gongmapa *khangpa*.

SIGNIFICANCE
Built by the uncle of Tundup Sonam, the house served as a *tashag* or monk's residence for monks from the Dakschanpa family. Today, the family rents it out to migrant workers. The house is built in the traditional style and is a good example of vernacular architecture in the village.

DESCRIPTION
The *tashag* is a double storeyed building built over a rectangular plan along the slope of the hill. The house has an elaborate wooden door on the southern facade that leads into the house. The ground floor is built in stone masonry and is used mainly for storage. There are no window openings at this level. The first floor comprises the living areas and has an elaborate timber framed *rabsal* above the entrance door. There are smaller windows on either side of the *rabsal*. The windows openings have decorated wooden lintels and are bordered in red. The roof is a traditional one made of timber beams, joists, *taalu*, grass and compacted mud with a parapet running along its edge which is painted in red. There are prayer flags posted at the corners of the roof.

STATE OF PRESERVATION
Showing Signs of Deterioration

SOURCE OF INFORMATION Tundup Sonam, Dakschanpa, Khaltse, Khaltse, Ladakh

Gongmapa
Khangchen House

INVENTORY NO.
KHALTSE / KHALTSE / 14 / 2004

Vernacular Building | In Use | Private (Individual) | Around 150 years old

SETTING
From the main Leh - Srinagar highway, a steep gravel path leads to the house. The house is oriented to the south and is located along the slope of a hill in front of the Dagchanpa's new house. The main road lies to the southeast.

SIGNIFICANCE
The house was built three generations ago by ancestors of the Gongmapa family who continue to reside here. It is built in the traditional style and is a good example of vernacular architecture in the village.

DESCRIPTION
The Gongmapa house is a large three storeyed building built on a rectangular plan along the slope of a hill. There is a separate entrance to the ground floor, which is used for keeping animals and storing fodder for the winter. The ground floor is built in stone masonry. A door to the east leads to the first floor which houses the family kitchen and living rooms. The family temple and the guest rooms are on the second floor. The guest room has an elaborate wooden framed window with glass panels facing south. There is an open verandah in the centre between the temple and the guest room. The first and second floors are built in mud brick masonry. The exterior of the house is mud plastered and whitewashed. The roof is a traditional one with prayer flags posted in the corners.

STATE OF PRESERVATION
Showing Signs of Deterioration

SOURCE OF INFORMATION Tashi Palkit, Gongmapa Khahupa, Khaltse, Khaltse, Ladakh

Zhabzes

INVENTORY NO.
KHALTSE / KHALTSE / 15 / 2004

Landscape (Rock Formation) | In Use | Private (Individual)

SETTING
From the main Khaltse road, a narrow pathway leads through the agricultural fields to the rock. It is oriented to the south and is located under an apricot tree with fields nearby.

SIGNIFICANCE / ASSOCIATED BELIEFS
According to legend, Guru Padmasambhava, chasing a she devil, jumped from the mountain on the opposite side and landed on the stone leaving his footprint behind. In earlier times, villagers used to gather here and perform prayers along with those of the chorten nearby.

DESCRIPTION
The imprint is on the surface of a rock which is embedded in the ground. The rock is in a deep pit with a high stone wall built around it and resembles a well.

STATE OF PRESERVATION
Advanced State of Decay

SOURCE OF INFORMATION Tundup Sonam, Khaltse, Khaltse, Ladakh

Khaltse

200

Rigsum Gonbo

INVENTORY NO.
KHALTSE / KHALTSE / 16 / 2004

Rigsum Gonbo | In Use | Private (Individual) | More than 100 years old

SETTING
From the main Khaltse market, a narrow footpath leads to the structure passing through fields and apricot orchards. It is oriented to the southeast and is located in the middle of an agricultural field, surrounded by apricot trees.

SIGNIFICANCE
The *rigsum gonbo* is built to protect the village from natural calamities and evil forces. Located in the middle of the field, the *rigsum gonbo* also protects the crops from insect attacks, disease and natural calamities.

DESCRIPTION
The *rigsum gonbo* consists of two eroded *chorten* placed on a rectangular base. The third *chorten* no longer exists. The base is made in random rubble masonry. The *chorten* are built in stone masonry and are mud plastered and whitewashed on the exterior.

STATE OF PRESERVATION
Danger of Disappearance

SOURCE OF INFORMATION Tundup Sonam, Khaltse, Khaltse, Ladakh

Mane Wall

INVENTORY NO.
KHALTSE / KHALTSE / 17 / 2004

Mane Wall | In Use | Public (Community) | Around 100 years old

SETTING
The *mane* wall is oriented to the east and is a short walk from the main Leh - Srinagar highway, after entering Khaltse. The *mane* wall is on a pedestrian path. There is a prayer wheel to its northwest and the village pond to its south. There is a huge willow tree to its west.

SIGNIFICANCE
The *mane* wall was built by villagers more than 100 years ago and is circumambulated by them to accumulate merit.

DESCRIPTION
The *mane* wall is built in dry stone masonry on a rectangular plan and has a small opening toward the east. The base is mud plastered and whitewashed. The *mane* wall has a large number of mane stones placed on the top.

STATE OF PRESERVATION
Showing Signs of Deterioration

SOURCE OF INFORMATION Sonam Morup (Sonam Phelpa), Khaltse, Khaltse, Ladakh

201

Khaltse

Zangsthar *Starga*

INVENTORY NO.
KHALTSE / KHALTSE / 18 / 2004

Landscape (Tree) | Private (Individual)

SETTING
From the main Khaltse market, a steep concrete pathway leads near the Saipa house to the pond and to the tree. Alternately, there is a dirt road which starts at the beginning of the market. It is located to the east of the pond and south of the road and Api Danak Chomo complex.

SIGNIFICANCE / ASSOCIATED BELIEFS
It is one of the oldest trees in the village and is believed to have existed before the village was settled. It is located near the village pond (*zing*).

DESCRIPTION
The tree is a large walnut tree with dense foliage. It is one of the few walnut trees that still grow in Ladakh.

STATE OF PRESERVATION
Fair

SOURCE OF INFORMATION Sonam Morup (Sonam Phelpa), Khaltse, Khaltse, Ladakh

Api Daknak Chomo *Lhato*

INVENTORY NO.
KHALTSE / KHALTSE / 19 / 2004

Lhato | In Use | Public (Community)

SETTING
From the main Leh – Srinagar highway, a trail enters the forest before the main Khaltse town. The *lhato* is oriented to the south and is built on a hillside, visible from the main road. It is surrounded by poplar trees and boulders.

SIGNIFICANCE
The *lhato* is dedicated to the village protective deity Api Daknak Chomo. On the 15th day of the 4th month of the Tibetan calendar, the villagers carrying the Buddhist cannons and offerings visit the *lhato*. With the playing of drums and performance of prayers, the protection of the deity is sought for the village. At this time, the contents of the *lhato* are also replaced.

DESCRIPTION
The *lhato* is a large linear whitewashed structure sitting on whitewashed bounders. It is built on a square plan. There is a smaller square structure on the top that contains the ritual offerings of juniper branches, *khadag* and animal horns. The *lhato* is built in stone masonry and is mud plastered and whitewashed on the exterior.

STATE OF PRESERVATION
Fair

Api-Daknak Chomo

INVENTORY NO.
KHALTSE / KHALTSE / 20 / 2004

Lhato | In Use | Public (Community) | More than 1000 years old

SETTING
The *lhato* can be accessed from the main Leh - Srinagar highway. A pathway diverts from the highway and leads to the structure. It is oriented to the south and is located between the government buildings on the top of a cliff, east of the main settlement.

SIGNIFICANCE
The *lhato* was first located on a mountain opposite this mountain. It is believed that three shepherds were fighting in the village and throwing sand at each other. The oracle, who resided in the opposite mountain, was amused by their antics and climbed down to settle in the village on this hill. Subsequently, the *lhato* was shifted to the forest where it currently stands.

DESCRIPTION
The *lhato* is a tall linear structure built over a square plan and is mud plastered and whitewashed on the exterior. The

square structure at the upper level contains juniper branches, white scarves and animal horns as offerings. The exterior walls are of stone masonry.

STATE OF PRESERVATION
Showing Signs of Deterioration

SOURCE OF INFORMATION Sonam Morup, Tashi Sabipa, Khaltse, Khaltse, Ladakh

Dannak *Khar* (Bragnag *Khar* / *Khargog*)

INVENTORY NO.
KHALTSE / KHALTSE / 21 / 2004

Fort / Palace | Abandoned | Public (State / Community) | 12th century

SETTING
From the main Leh - Srinagar highway, a steep winding gravel path leads up to the castle which is oriented to the south.

SIGNIFICANCE
The castle was built by King Naglug (1110 - 1140 A.D.), the seventh king in the lineage of the First Ladakhi dynasty in the year of the Dragon. It is believed that it was the first castle ever built in the region for defence purposes and accommodated 16 families. King Naglug also constructed the first bridge across the Indus in Khaltse where the new bridge today stands. The stone inscriptions in close vicinity to the present bridge, gives the record of the first construction of the bridge by the great minister Gar-ka.

DESCRIPTION
The fort is not noticeable from the village below if not for the colourful prayer flags fluttering on top of the ruins. Only fragments of the fort walls exists which is not quite distinguishable from the rest of the mountain. The exterior walls are of stone masonry.

STATE OF PRESERVATION
Danger of Disappearance

SOURCE OF INFORMATION 'A Study on the Chronicles of Ladakh' by Dr Luciano Petech; and, Tashi Sabipa, Khaltse, Khaltse, Ladakh

Yoto *Chorten*

INVENTORY NO.
KHALTSE / KHALTSE / 22 / 2004

Chorten / Mane Wall | In Use | Public (Community) | Around 300 years old

SETTING
The *chorten* are oriented to the south and are located along the main Leh - Srinagar road which lies to the south. There are willow and poplar trees nearby.

SIGNIFICANCE
According to the legend, Yoto *chorten* were built by the friends and maids of a princess who was getting married in the village, and, thus the name Yoto, or 'maid's *chorten*'.

DESCRIPTION
The site comprises of two *chorten* and a *mane* wall. The *mane* wall is a rectangular in plan and is built in stone masonry with mane stones placed on its horizontal surface. One of the *chorten* is a Changchub *chorten* built on a square base while the second chorten is an Indoom *chorten* built on a square base with octagonal tiers rising up towards the dome. The exterior surfaces of both *chorten* are cement plastered and whitewashed. There are *chugsum*

khorlo over the domes of both *chorten*. Two large prayer flags (*tarchen*) are located on the either side of the road and a stream of prayer flags has been tied across both.

STATE OF PRESERVATION
Fair

SOURCE OF INFORMATION Stanzin Namgal (Sarpanch), Khaltse, Khaltse, Ladakh

---

Balu *Khar*

INVENTORY NO.
KHALTSE / KHALTSE / 23 / 2004

Fort / Palace | Abandoned | Public (State) | 12th century

SETTING
The Balu *khar* is oriented to the south and can be approached from the main Leh - Srinagar road, two kms before reaching the village. It is located to the south of the road between the River Indus and the highway, and is surrounded by the army encampment.

SIGNIFICANCE
The fort was built during the reign of King Lhachen Naglug (1150 - 1175 A.D.) to collect taxes from the nearby villages.

DESCRIPTION
The Balu *khar* is located on a hilltop along the banks of the River Indus. Today, it is surrounded on all three sides by the army encampment. The structure has fragments of remaining walls along the edge of the hillock. It is a stone masonry construction with exposed stone work. There is no trace of any external plaster.

Photograph Not Available

STATE OF PRESERVATION
Danger of Disappearance

SOURCE OF INFORMATION Tashi Sabipa, Khaltse, Khaltse, Ladakh

Moravian Mission School

INVENTORY NO.
KHALTSE / KHALTSE / 24 / 2004

Historic Building | In Use | Private (Moravian Mission) | Early 20th century

STATE OF PRESERVATION
Showing Signs of Deterioration

SETTING
The Moravian Mission school is oriented to the south and can be approached from the main Leh – Srinagar road, after passing Khaltse. It is located south of the main road and is surrounded by poplar and willow trees to the north and east.

SIGNIFICANCE
The school was founded by A.H. Francke, a historian and a Christian missionary who came to Ladakh in the early 20th century. He was in Skurbuchan in 1891 and started his campaign in 1893. He spend a considerable amount of time in Khaltse translating the great epic Gesar and writing the history of great Tibet. He also introduced schools for the first time in Ladakh, in Khaltse. A hospital for the local community was also built in the same compound. He had a huge library with a large collection of books, which were destroyed during the war with Pakistan. Francke introduced new techniques in construction of traditional houses. The use of glass was first introduced at this time, along with recessed windows in rammed earth construction. The glass and metal latches used in the building were brought all the way from the Germany. A small church was also built within the same complex which was later shifted into the village in 1945.

DESCRIPTION
The main school building is double storeyed high while the front office structure, is only a single storey. A large metal gate leads into the complex and pathways leads to the office block, which is the oldest section of the building. There are ten rooms on the ground floor and ten on the first floor as well. All the rooms have timber flooring and a traditional roof over it. The windows are recessed with double sided frames. Some of the windows still have the original decorated lattice wooden frames. The doors have been designed in the modern style with glass panels and the latches brought from Germany. The rooms are used as classrooms on the ground floor while the entire first floor is used as the living quarters for the school teachers. Each room has its own inbuilt cupboards. The walls are three feet thick and built in rammed earth. There are wooden re-enforcements at intervals as a precaution against earthquake.

SOURCE OF INFORMATION Pastor and Principal of the school

Precinct of Petroglyphs

INVENTORY NO.
KHALTSE / KHALTSE / 25 / 2007

Rock Carvings | Abandoned | Public (State)

SETTING
The petroglyphs are located all along the main Khaltse – Kargil road both towards the river Indus as well as across the road.

SIGNIFICANCE
The petroglyphs are scattered all across the route leading from Khaltse towards Kargil along the River Indus as well as along the mountain side. The petroglyphs date back to an early period of human habitation in the region.

DESCRIPTION
The petroglyphs are pecked onto large boulders which have a blackened patina on which the images are pecked. They depict both animal and human figures as well as symbols and motifs. The petroglyphs are threatened today by the large scale road construction activity all across Ladakh as well as the need for stone as building material with the increased building activity.

STATE OF PRESERVATION
Danger of Disappearance

Chorten

INVENTORY NO.
KHALTSE / KHALTSE / 26 / 2007

Chorten | In Use | Public (Community)

SETTING
The *chorten* is located on a barren stretch of land along the main Leh - Srinagar highway about 11 kms from Khaltse in an area known as Nyarmo do.

SIGNIFICANCE
The *chorten* was built in the past as an act of merit and possibly lay along an old route linking Khaltse with the neighbouring villages.

DESCRIPTION
The *chorten* is built in stone masonry on a base of random rubble masonry. The outer layers of mud plaster and whitewash have eroded over time.

STATE OF PRESERVATION
Advanced State of Decay

Mane Wall

INVENTORY NO.
KHALTSE / KHALTSE / 27 / 2007

Mane Wall | In Use | Public (Community)

SETTING
The *mane* wall is located beyond the main Khaltse town along the base of a mountain. It runs parallel to the main Leh - Srinagar highway and is about 12 kms from Khaltse.

SIGNIFICANCE
The *mane* wall runs along an old route which linked Khaltse possibly with a neighboring village. It was built in the past as an act of merit.

DESCRIPTION
The *mane* wall is a long dry stone masonry wall with a *chorten* at one end. It has inscribed *mane* stones placed on the top.

STATE OF PRESERVATION
Advanced State of Decay

Lamayuru

Lamayuru is situated at a distance of about 110 kms from Leh on the Leh - Srinagar highway. The historical name of the village was Yung-Drung meaning '*swastika*' in Sanskrit. It is said that the *arhat* Nyimagung predicted that a great monastery would flourish here. At that time, there used to be a vast lake in this area. Nyimagung offered prayers here to all the guardian serpent deities and then gave ritual offerings of grain. The grain mixed with the earth and sprouted in the form of a *swastika*. This was considered an auspicious sign and the monastery was founded here with the name Yung-Drung. Today, it is commonly known as Lamayuru. The settlement arose around the main monastery and at present, there are about 82 households living here.

Listed by: Deldan Angmo and Jassu Singh
Year: 2004

Lardo

Lardo is situated about 65 kms from Leh, on the left bank of the River Indus. The upper part of the valley is called Lar and the lower part is called Do which gives the name Lardo meaning the '*lower part of the Lar valley*'. There are 11 households in the village.

Listed by: Deldan Angmo and Jassu Singh
Year: 2004

Yungdrug Tharpaling *Gonpa* (Lamayuru / Yuru *Gonpa*)

INVENTORY NO.
KHALTSE / LAMAYURU / 01 / 2004

Gonpa | In Use | Public (Lamayuru *Gonpa*) | Around 1000 years old

SETTING

Yungdrug Tharpaling *gonpa* is located on a hillock above the lower settlement comprising of village houses and shrines in the village. The *gonpa* has a large number of *chorten* to the north and a courtyard flanked by monks' cells to the east.

SIGNIFICANCE

It is believed that the site of the present *gonpa* was a vast lake in ancient times. The *arhat* Nyima Gwagpa made a prediction that a monastery would be founded here and then offered prayers to all the Naga serpent spirits, who were the guardians of the place. The grains of the corn that formed part of this offering got mixed with the earth and sprouted in the shape of a *swastika*. Later, when the monastery was founded it was named Yung Drung meaning *swastika*. In the 11th century, the Mahasiddha Naropa came here and mediated in a cave (around 1016 - 1100 A.D.). Lotsawa Rinchen Zangpo, the great translator came and built many temples and *chorten*. There after, for many years the monastery was administered by Zha-mar-pa (Red Hats) after which King Jamyamg Namgyal offered it to Chosje Danma. The rituals and observances of the Drigung-Kagyud School were also introduced. The successive reincarnations of Skyabje Togden Rinpoche act as the incumbents of the monastery. A festival 'Yungdrug Kabgyad' is observed on the 17th and 18th of the 5th Tibetan month. Presently, there are around 60 monks and 50 norces residing in the monastery.

DESCRIPTION

The *gonpa* is a large five storeyed structure built on a random plan. There are no openings on the first two levels while the upper floors have large windows with wooden frames and decorated lintels. The entrance to the main *dukhang* area is through a small door accessed from a flight of steps along the circumambulatory path. The door leads into a small courtyard, which is partially covered and flanked with a gallery all around. Opposite the entrance lies the *dukhang* with murals of the four guardian deities near the entrance door. The *dukhang* has decorated wooden columns supporting the traditional flat roof above. There is a clerestory within the chamber, the walls of which have paintings which have been retouched recently. There are two thrones opposites the entrance door, the Skabgon Chetsang and the Skabgon Chungtsang along with numerous images of deities. These include Guru Rinpoche, Choskyi Nyima,

Ratnashri Skyopa, Jowo Rinpoche, Mitugpa, Thinley Sangpo, Choskyi lotus, Sheri Mangat and the Chosje Dhanma. There are four window openings with decorated frames towards the left side and towards the right is the decorated frame housing Kangyur and Bum (Buddhist cannons). There are two rows of seating in the hall where the monks assemble every day for prayers. The panels of the clerestory are painted and number of *thangka* hang from the ceiling. To the right, is a small cave housing three images of Naropa and other saints. It is believed that the great saint Naropa meditated in this cave from 1016 - 1100 A.D. A small opening opposite the entrance door leads to a small shrine to the rear of the assembly hall. This *lhakhang* is dedicated to Apchi and houses an image of Apchi riding on a horse. Other deities in the *lhakhang* include Mahakala, Skyoba, Khorlo Dechok, Namdras and Choskyong. From the courtyard, a flight of stairs leads to an upper storey which houses the *gonkhang*. It is a small room with small relic stupas and images of a few deities. They include Guru Rinpoche, Skyoba, Jisgsten Gonbo, Rigzin Choedrak, Dorjey Chang and Milarepa. A small Dolma *lhakhang* dedicated to the goddesses Dolma lies in an adjacent room. The top most floors house the living quarters of the head lama and the guest rooms. The rooms have a combination of timber, mud and *arga* flooring and at some places the flooring has been replaced with cement finish. The roof top has a low height parapet wall with exterior is painted in black. There are cylindrical shaped drums posted at each corner of the roof representing the prayer flags. The drums are painted in black and flanked with white ribbons.

STATE OF PRESERVATION
Showing Signs of Deterioration

SOURCE OF INFORMATION Gelong. Ven. Sonam Rinchen, Lamayuru Monastery, Khaltse, Ladakh; and, 'The Guide to the Buddhist Monasteries & Royal Castles of, Ladakh' by Gelong Thupstan Paldan

Senge-Gang
Lhakhang

INVENTORY NO.
KHALTSE / LAMAYURU / 02 / 2004

Temple | In Use | Public (Lamayuru *Gonpa*) | Around 1000 years old

SETTING
The temple is oriented to the southeast and is surrounded by village houses on three sides including Lalogpa house to the east and Khangsar house to the west.

SIGNIFICANCE
The Senge-Gang is popularly believed to have been one of the many temples founded by the great Translator Rinchen Zangpo in the 11th century. Recent research, however, suggests a later date for the temple (13th - 14th centuries). The paintings as well as stucco images inside the temple are associated with an early period of Buddhist art in the region. The Senge Gang houses the main protector deity of Lamayuru 'Tamchen'.

DESCRIPTION
The Senge-Gang *lhakhang* is a single storeyed structure built on a square plan. It has a simple exterior without any window openings and a wooden doorway which leads into the chamber. There is a clerestory in the centre of the chamber. The *lhakhang* is a square room with two wooden (Juniper) columns and carved brackets. The rear wall has the stucco images of Vairocana and four other Thathagats on each of the four sides. The images are placed on a pedestal and are painted in different colors. The image of Vairocana is in the centre and is surrounded by a floral configuration with a protector deity on the top. The walls of this room are covered with paintings depicting images of various Bodhisattvas and *mandalas* dedicated to Vairocana. Towards the right of this *lhakhang* is a small doorway leading to a rectangular room housing the main protector deity of Lamayuru village, named 'Thamchen'. The other fierce deities of this room include four-armed Gombo and Paldan Lhamo. Just near the entrance to this room is a wooden carved Changchub *chorten*. The walls of this room have been repainted in the recent past. Like the previous room, the only source of light in this room is through a small clerestory above the central space. Wooden barricades are provided all along the painted walls to prevent further damages.

Lamayuru

211

STATE OF PRESERVATION
Advanced State of Decay

SOURCE OF INFORMATION Gelong. Ven. Sonam Rinchen, Lamayuru, Khaltse, Ladakh

Singe-Nang pa House

INVENTORY NO.
KHALTSE / LAMAYURU / 03 / 2004

Vernacular Building | In Use | Private (Individual) | Around 300 years old

SETTING
The house is oriented to the east and is located on a hill just below the *gonpa*. The house is surrounded by the Lalogpa house to the south, Senge-Gang to the southwest and the *gonpa* to the north.

SIGNIFICANCE
Singe-Nang pa house was built around 300 years ago by ancestors of the Singe Nang pa family and subsequent generations have continued to reside in the house. It is built in the traditional style and is a good example of vernacular architecture in the village.

DESCRIPTION
Singe-Nang pa house is a three storeyed whitewashed building. The ground floor is built in stone masonry with mud mortar and is used primarily for storage. The entrance to the house is from the western facade which leads

directly onto the first floor. The windows of the first floor are small with timber frames while those of the second floor are larger. The first and second floors are constructed in mud brick masonry and are the family's living quarters. The first floor is used for habitation during winter while the second floor is used by the family during the summer months. The lower floors have mud flooring while the upper floor has timber flooring. The house has a traditional roof comprising of timber joists, *taalu*, grass and a layer of compacted mud. The roof is supported on timber beams and columns flanked by wooden brackets. The external walls of the house are mud plastered and whitewashed.

STATE OF PRESERVATION
Showing Signs of Deterioration

SOURCE OF INFORMATION Chuzin Dolma, Lamayuru, Khaltse, Ladakh

Lalogpa House

INVENTORY NO.
KHALTSE / LAMAYURU / 04 / 2004

Vernacular Building | In Use | Private (Individual) | Around 300 years old

SETTING
The Lalogpa house is oriented to the north and is located on a hill just below the *gonpa*. The house is surrounded by the Singe-Nang pa house to the north while the *gonpa* itself lies beyond the house.

SIGNIFICANCE
The house was built by an ancestor of the Lalogpa family about 300 years ago. Since then, the subsequent generations of the family have resided here. It is built in the traditional style and is an example of the vernacular architecture of the village.

DESCRIPTION
The Lalogpa house is a three storeyed building which is mud plastered and whitewashed on the exterior. The ground floor is built in stone masonry with mud mortar and has no openings while the upper levels are built in mud brick masonry. The entrance to the house is through a low height timber framed doorway on the south. There are

small timber framed windows on the first floor while the second floor has larger window openings. The ground and first floors have mud flooring while the second floor has timber flooring. Timber beams and columns flanked with wooden brackets support the traditional roof above.

STATE OF PRESERVATION
Showing Signs of Deterioration

SOURCE OF INFORMATION Chuzin Dolma, Lamayuru, Khaltse, Ladakh

Group of *Chorten* and *Mane* Walls

INVENTORY NO.
KHALTSE / LAMAYURU / 05 / 2004

Chorten / Mane Wall | In Use | Public (Lamayuru *Gonpa*) | Around 500 years old

SETTING
The *chorten* and *mane* walls are located on top of a hill below the main *gonpa*. There are village houses to the southwest and northwest and the main *gonpa* lies to the south. The old kitchen lies to the northeast of the site.

SIGNIFICANCE
The *chorten* are believed to have been built in the 16th century when the *gonpa* was being constructed. The group of *chorten* and *mane* walls are circumambulated by pilgrims when they visit the *gonpa* as an of merit. The *chorten* are all Changchub *chorten*, symbolizing the Buddha's enlightenment.

DESCRIPTION
The site consists of a group of *chorten*, *mane* walls and prayer wheels. The *chorten* are built in stone and mud brick masonry with mud mortar and are mud plastered and

whitewashed externally. The domes of the *chorten* have a long *chugsum khorlo* on top over which rests metal crescents. Some of the *chorten* have a *srog-shing* posted on the dome. The base panels of the *chorten* are embellished with decorative stucco relief (*pa-tra*) depicting floral and animal motifs. There are small niches in the domes for images. The *mane* walls are built in stone masonry and have *mane* stones placed on the horizontal surface. There are several *tarchen* with stone masonry bases in the site.

STATE OF PRESERVATION
Showing Signs of Deterioration

SOURCE OF INFORMATION Gelong Sonam Rinchen, Lamayuru, Khaltse, Ladakh

Tsadkhang

INVENTORY NO.
KHALTSE / LAMAYURU / 06 / 2004

Tsadkhang | In Use | Public (Community) | Around 450 years old

SETTING
The *tsadkhang* is oriented to the south east and is located on top of a hill opposite the *gonpa*. It is accessed along a gravel pathway which diverts from the village road below. There are several *tashag* to the southeast of the site.

SIGNIFICANCE
The *tsadkhang* has been used by the villagers for several centuries to house *tsa-tsa*.

DESCRIPTION
The *tsadkhang* is a small cubical structure built in stone and mud brick masonry with mud mortar. It is mud plastered and whitewashed on the exterior. The structure has a traditional roof with a red border around it. There is an opening on one side through which the *tsa-tsa* are placed inside the *tsadkhang*.

STATE OF PRESERVATION
Showing Signs of Deterioration

SOURCE OF INFORMATION Gelong Sonam Rinchen, Lamayuru, Khaltse, Ladakh

213

Precinct of *Tashag*

INVENTORY NO.
KHALTSE / LAMAYURU / 07 / 2004

Precinct | In Use | Public (Lamayuru *Gonpa*) | Around 500 years old

SETTING

The *tashag* are oriented to the southeast and are located on top of a hill. The cells are built along the slope of the hill and form tiers up to the top. The site is accessed via a zigzag pathway which diverts from the village road below. The *tashag* are located to the north of the gonpa and north west of the *tsadkhang*.

SIGNIFICANCE

The *tashag* are believed to have been built in the same period as the *gonpa* i.e. 16th century and have been used as residential units for the monks ever since.

DESCRIPTION

The *tashag* are a cluster of a large number of small rectangular structures built along the slope of a hill. The units are small two or three roomed structures used as residences for the monks. They are built in stone and mud brick masonry with mud mortar and are mud plastered and whitewashed on the exterior. The cells have entrance

doorways with large windows facing the southeast. The door and window openings are bordered in red and the parapets re also painted in red. The window openings have wooden frames with tiered lintels. Each unit has square posts on the roof for tying prayer flags.

STATE OF PRESERVATION
Showing Signs of Deterioration

SOURCE OF INFORMATION Gelong Sonam Rinchen, Lamayuru, Khaltse, Ladakh

Group of *Mane* Walls and *Chorten*

INVENTORY NO.
KHALTSE / LAMAYURU / 08 / 2004

Chorten / *Mane* Wall | In Use | Public (Community) | Around 450 - 500 years old

SETTING

The *chorten* and *mane* are located on the right hand side of the road before reaching the *gonpa*. The *mane* walls are located to the west of the road leading to the village settlement and north of the *gonpa* complex.

SIGNIFICANCE

The *chorten* are believed to have been built in the 16th century at the same time as the *gonpa*. The *chorten* are both Namgyal (symbolizing the Buddha's victory) as well as Changchub (symbolizing the Buddha's enlightenment) *chorten*. The *chorten* and *mane* walls are circumambulated by villagers to accumulate merit.

DESCRIPTION

The site consists of a group of *chorten* and *mane* walls extending from the *gonpa* complex near the Niranjana Hotel to the village settlement. The *mane* walls are

interspersed with *chorten* in between. The *mane* walls are both linear and circular in shape and are built in stone masonry with inscribed mane stones placed on the horizontal surface. The *chorten* are built in stone and mud brick masonry with mud mortar and are mud plastered and whitewashed on the exterior. The *chorten* have tall *chugsum khorlo* over the domes with a crescent on the top.

STATE OF PRESERVATION
Showing Signs of Deterioration

SOURCE OF INFORMATION Gelong Sonam Rinchen, Lamayuru, Khaltse, Ladakh

Chanrazig *Lhakhang*

INVENTORY NO.
KHALTSE / LAMAYURU / 09 / 2004

Temple | In Use | Public (Lamayuru *Gonpa*) | Around 500 years old

STATE OF PRESERVATION
Showing Signs of Deterioration

SETTING
Chanrazig *lhakhang* is oriented to the south and lies to the west of the pathway that leading to the main *dukhang*. It is surrounded by *tashag* and the kitchen to the north and west respectively.

SIGNIFICANCE
The *lhakhang* was built during the reign of King Jamyang Namgyal in the 16th century. It is contemporary to the main Lamayuru *gonpa*. The temple is used in worship by the villagers and monks from the *gonpa* perform prayers and rituals here.

DESCRIPTION
The Chanrazig *lhakhang* is a simple double storeyed building, constructed in stone and mud brick masonry with mud mortar. A flight of steps leads to the porch of the shrine which has paintings of the four guardian deities on the walls and an elaborate wooden entrance doorway. The door leads into the main hall which is rectangular in plan with an antechamber to the rear that houses stucco images of Chug-Shig-Zal together with numerous stucco images of other deities. This antechamber is open to the front and has a wooden frames. A clerestory window lights the area in the antechamber. The walls of the chamber are intricately painted with small images of buildings and human figures which is perhaps unique in this region. The *lhakhang* has a timber and mud floor. The roof is a traditional one supported on timber columns and beams and made of joists, *taalu* and compacted mud. Buttresses have been built for support all around the structure. There are two small skylights with a high mud parapet on the roof top. Black cylindrical drums representing prayer flags are placed on the roof. The exterior walls of the *lhakhang* are mud plastered and whitewashed.

Lamayuru

215

SOURCE OF INFORMATION Gelong. Ven. Sonam Rinchen, Lamayuru, Khaltse, Ladakh

Rigsum Gonbo

INVENTORY NO.
KHALTSE / LAMAYURU / 10 / 2004

Rigsum Gonbo | In Use | Public (Lamayuru *Gonpa*) | Around 500 years old

SETTING
The *rigsum gonbo* is built along the slope of a mountain to the right of the road which leads on to the *gonpa*. It is surrounded by the *gonpa* complex to the northwest while the road lies to the south.

SIGNIFICANCE
The *rigsum gonbo* is believed to have been built in the 16th century at the same time as the *gonpa*. It was built to protect the village from natural calamities and evil forces.

DESCRIPTION
The *rigsum gonbo* consists of a group of three *chorten* built on a common plinth. The *chorten* have been recently repaired in cement and are whitewashed with decorative floral motifs (*pa-tra*) painted in yellow and gold on the base panels. The *chorten* have a niche in the dome facing the path within which are placed images. The domes of the *chorten* have tapering *chugsum khorlo* which are surmounted by metal crescents.

STATE OF PRESERVATION
Fair

SOURCE OF INFORMATION Gelong Sonam Rinchen, Lamayuru, Khaltse, Ladakh

---

Deshag-Gyad

INVENTORY NO.
KHALTSE / LAMAYURU / 11 / 2004

Chorten | In Use | Private (Individual) | Around 500 years old

SETTING
The Deshag-Gyad is oriented to the north and is located within the *gonpa* complex in the courtyard to the south of the gallery. The Niranjana Hotel is located to its east.

SIGNIFICANCE
The Deshag-Gyad is believed to have been built at the same time as the *gonpa* in the 16th century. It comprises of the eight traditional forms of *chorten* in Tibetan Buddhism i.e. Namgyal (symbolizing victory), Changchub (symbolizing the Buddha's enlightenment), Labab (symbolizing the Buddha's return from heaven in Vaishali), Indoom (symbolizing the reconciliation of the Sangha after the discord created by Devadatta in Rajagriha), Padspung (symbolizing the Buddha's birth in Lumbini), Chotul (symbolizing the Buddha's miracles shown to the six heretical ascetics in Sarvasti) and Nyangdas (symbolizing the Buddha's *parinirvana* in Kushinagar) and Tashi Gomang (symbolizing the first sermon expounded by the Buddha to the five ascetics at Sarnath).

DESCRIPTION
The Deshag-Gyad is an enclosure built on a high stone masonry rectangular plinth. It is almost two storeyed high with the upper level containing the eight traditional *chorten* placed in a single row. The enclosure has walls on three sides and is open to the north. The interior walls of have wall painting. The opening to the front has wooden frames with segmental arches and decorated wooden columns and brackets which support a traditional roof above. The Deshag-Gyad is built in stone and mud brick masonry and is mud plastered and whitewashed on the exterior.

STATE OF PRESERVATION
Fair

SOURCE OF INFORMATION Gelong Sonam Rinchen, Lamayuru, Khaltse, Ladakh

Chorten

INVENTORY NO.
KHALTSE / LAMAYURU / 12 / 2004

Chorten | In Use | Public (Community) | Around 300 - 350 years old

SETTING
The *chorten* is located on the right hand side of the main vehicular road. There are shops a little lower down to the southwest.

SIGNIFICANCE
The *chorten* is believed to have been built around 300 – 350 years ago. It is a Changchub *chorten* symbolizing the Buddha's enlightenment and is circumambulated by villagers to accumulate merit.

DESCRIPTION
The Changchub *chorten* is built in stone and mud brick masonry with mud mortar and is mud plastered and whitewashed on the exterior. The base of the *chorten* has been renovated in cement plaster. The dome of the *chorten* has a *srog-shing* posted in the centre. There is a low rammed earth wall around the *chorten*.

STATE OF PRESERVATION
Advanced State of Decay

SOURCE OF INFORMATION Tashi Lhamo, Lamayuru, Khaltse, Ladakh

Group of *Mane* Walls and *Chorten*

INVENTORY NO.
KHALTSE / LAMAYURU / 13 / 2004

Chorten / *Mane* Wall | In Use | Public (Community) | Around 300 - 350 years old

SETTING
The *chorten* and *mane* wall are located on a bare hill of sand along the footpath which leads to the upper area of the village. It is surrounded by agricultural fields below and by the mountain side above.

SIGNIFICANCE
The *chorten* are believed to have been built around 300 – 350 years ago. They are located along the footpath which leads to the upper settlement and are circumambulated by villagers as an act of merit. The *chorten* are largely Changchub *chorten* and symbolize the Buddha's enlightenment.

DESCRIPTION
The site consists of a group of *mane* walls alternating with sixty *chorten* of different sizes. The *mane* walls and *chorten* are placed in a row with a circumambulatory pathway around. The *chorten* are built in stone and mud brick masonry with mud mortar and are mud plastered and whitewashed on the exterior. Some *chorten* have stucco relief work (*pa-tra*) on the base panels. The main *mane* wall is a long wall built in stone masonry with mane stones placed on its horizontal surface. This group of *chorten* and *mane* walls extend over an area of approximately 500 metres with the main vehicular road cutting through the site.

STATE OF PRESERVATION
Showing Signs of Deterioration

SOURCE OF INFORMATION Tashi Lhamo, Lamayuru, Khaltse, Ladakh

Stong Shong Bawo

INVENTORY NO.
KHALTSE / LAMAYURU / 14 / 2004

Caves | Abandoned | Community | Around 600 years old

SETTING
The Stong Shong Bago cave houses are located along a steep pathway which bifurcates from the *gonpa*. They are located above the village houses inside a v-shaped mountain.

SIGNIFICANCE
The cave houses were used about 600 years ago to house the *chomo* (nuns) who served the monastery. It is believed that due to the shortage of timber at the time, the caves were seen as a cost effective option for providing housing for the nuns. When the nuns moved out, the villagers took over some of the caves and begun residing there. The spaces are large enough to be used as living purposes. Some of the caves are at a greater heights and in the past there was a network for reaching them. Today, access is almost impossible as the mountain has eroded.

DESCRIPTION
The cave structures are tucked within a small hillock and present the best example of cave dwellings in Ladakh. There are a number of rooms belonging to different families of the village. The caves have small openings facing south and a small doorway leading to the small spaces within. The rooms have mud floors and ceilings. Over a period of time, the walls have turned black due to soot deposits from the kitchen.

STATE OF PRESERVATION
Danger of Disappearance

SOURCE OF INFORMATION Sonam Dorjey, Gorongpa, Lamayuru, Khaltse, Ladakh

Serpope *Khangpa*

INVENTORY NO.
KHALTSE / LAMAYURU / 15 / 2004

Vernacular Building | In Use | Private (Individual) | Around 250 years old

SETTING
The Serpope house is oriented to the east and is located near the Senge-Gang temple. It is surrounded by other village houses on all sides and the temple to the north.

SIGNIFICANCE
The Serpope house was built by ancestors of the Serpope family 250 years ago and the family has been residing here since then. The house is built in the traditional style and is an example of vernacular architecture in the village.

DESCRIPTION
The Serpope house is a double storeyed building built along the slope of a hill. The ground floor is built in random rubble masonry and has no openings. The first floor is built in mud brick masonry with mud mortar and has a large wooden balcony with a wooden lattice frame work on the front facade of the building. The elaborate frame is painted in red. There are two smaller windows on either side of the balcony. The openings are highlighted with black bands.

The structure is covered with a flat traditional roof comprising of wooden beams, joists, *taalu*, grass and a layer of compacted mud. The roof is supported on timber beams and columns flanked with wooden brackets. The exterior walls of the house are mud plastered and whitewashed. Abutting the Khangpa is a small Changchub *chorten*.

STATE OF PRESERVATION
Showing Signs of Deterioration

SOURCE OF INFORMATION Tashi Tsomo-Yokmapa, Lamayuru, Ladakh

Group of *Chorten*

INVENTORY NO.
KHALTSE / LAMAYURU / 16 / 2004

Chorten | In Use | Public (Community) | Around 500 - 1000 years old

SETTING

The *chorten* are located at the base of the mountain over which the *gonpa* is built. The site is surrounded by village houses and there is a large open space to the west. The main vehicular road lies to the south.

SIGNIFICANCE

The group of *chorten* is believed to have been built over a period of time starting from the 11th century upto the time of the construction of the *gonpa* in the 16th century. The earliest *chorten* are ascribed to the period of Lotsawa Rinchen Zangpo and are shaped in the form of a *mandala*. Most of the *chorten* are Changchub *chorten* which symbolizes the Buddha's enlightenment. The *chorten* are circumambulated by villagers to accumulate merit.

DESCRIPTION

The site consists of a group of around fifty two *chorten*, most of which are Changchub *chorten*. The largest of them is the Lotsawa *chorten*. It has a square base and an entrance into the *chorten*. It has a timber roof in the shape of a *mandala* with elaborate paintings on the ceiling panels. The structure on top is in the form of a *mandala* with a number of panels tapering up to form a dome. There are four large Kagan *chorten* with images of the thousand Buddhas painted inside. The site also consists of another five *mandala* shaped *chorten*. The other *chorten* are all Changchub *chorten* of various sizes. The *chorten* are built in stone and mud brick masonry and are mud plastered and whitewashed on the exterior. The larger *chorten* have stucco relief motifs on the base panels. There is a circumambulatory path around the *chorten*.

STATE OF PRESERVATION
Danger of Disappearance

Lamayuru

219

Larjepe *Khangpa*

INVENTORY NO.
KHALTSE / LAMAYURU / 17 / 2004

Vernacular Building | In Use | Private (Individual) | Around 300 years old

SETTING
The house is oriented to the south and is located near the Senge-Gang *lhakhang*. The house lies to the west of the *lhakhang* and the Khangsarpa house.

SIGNIFICANCE
The Larjepe house is one of the oldest in the village and was built around 300 years ago by ancestors of the Larjepe family. It is a good example of vernacular architecture in the village.

DESCRIPTION
The Larjepe Khangpa is a large four storeyed house built on a random plan on a hill. It has a high retaining wall along the edge of the cliff which acts as the foundation. The lower levels of the house are built in random rubble masonry and are used for housing animals and storing fodder. The upper levels are used as the family's living quarters. The front facade has small window openings. Externally, the house is mud plastered and whitewashed. The roof is built in the traditional style of timber beams, joists, *taalu*, grass and a layer of compacted mud. The roof is supported on timber beams and columns flanked with wooden brackets. The first two levels have been built in random rubble masonry and the upper levels are built in mud brick masonry with mud mortar.

STATE OF PRESERVATION
Showing Signs of Deterioration

SOURCE OF INFORMATION Tashi Tsomo-Yokmapa, Lamayuru, Ladakh

Khangsarpa *Khangpa*

INVENTORY NO.
KHALTSE / LAMAYURU / 18 / 2004

Vernacular Building | Abandoned | Private (Individual) | Around 300 years old

SETTING
The Khangsarpa house is oriented to the east and is located on a hill above the village settlement and below the monastery complex. It lies between the Senge-Gang *lhakhang* and the Larjepa house.

SIGNIFICANCE
The house is one of the oldest houses in the village and was built around 300 years ago by the ancestors of the Khangsarpa family. The house has been abandoned by the family and they have moved into a new house. The house is built in the traditional style and is a good example of vernacular architecture in the village.

DESCRIPTION
The Khangsarpa house is a two storeyed building built on top of a hill. The ground floor is built in random rubble masonry and has no openings. The front facade of the house has a large wooden *rabsal* with wooden lattice frame work. The elaborate frame is painted in red. There are two smaller windows on either side of the balcony. The openings are highlighted with black bands. The structure is covered with a flat traditional roof comprising of wooden beams, joists, *taalu*, grass and a layer of compacted mud. The structure is supported on timber beams and columns flanked with wooden brackets.

STATE OF PRESERVATION
Advanced State of Decay

SOURCE OF INFORMATION Tashi Tsomo-Yokmapa, Lamayuru, Khaltse, Ladakh

Lalogpa *Khangpa*

INVENTORY NO.
KHALTSE / LAMAYURU / 19 / 2004

Vernacular Building | In Use | Private (Individual) | Around 250 - 300 years old

SETTING
The house is oriented to the south and is located on a hill above the village and below the monastery. It is built next to the Khangsarpa house below the palace.

SIGNIFICANCE
The house is one of the earliest in the village built in the close vicinity of the 11th century temple Senge-Gang and is around 250 - 300 years old. It is built in the traditional style and forms a part of the complex of vernacular dwellings in the village.

DESCRIPTION
Lalogpa Khangpa is a four storeyed house built along a slope. It is a large house with the first level forming the foundation of the building. The second and the third levels are also built in random rubble masonry with small window openings on the front facade. The uppermost level has an elaborate *rabsal* with decorated wooden panels and lintels. The window openings are framed with black borders. The

house has a flat traditional roof comprising of wooden beams, joists, *taalu*, grass and a layer of compacted mud. The roof is supported on timber beams and columns flanked with wooden brackets. The roof top has been stacked with fire wood for the winters.

STATE OF PRESERVATION
Showing Signs of Deterioration

SOURCE OF INFORMATION Sonam Dorjey-Gorongpa, Lamayuru Khaltse, Ladakh

Lamayuru

221

Chankar *Chorten*

INVENTORY NO.
KHALTSE / LAMAYURU / 20 / 2004

Chorten | In Use | Public (Community)

SETTING
The *chorten* are located across the village near the fields. The path leads to the summer habitation site. The *chorten* are surrounded by agricultural fields to the south and east with mountains to the west. The village stream flows to the north of the site.

SIGNIFICANCE
The *chorten* are among the oldest chorten in the village and lie along the route which leads to the fields. Villagers circumambulate the *chorten* to accumulate merit. The *chorten* are all Changchub *chorten* and symbolize the Buddha's enlightenment. The *lubang* marks the residence of the *lu,* or serpent gods. Prayers and offerings are made at the *lubang* on a fixed date in spring known as *Lu thebs* by the monks to placate the *lu*. The prayers are often to seek a good supply of water before the cultivation of fields in spring and offerings made to the *lu* are then immersed in water.

DESCRIPTION
The site consists of a group of three Changchub *chorten* of similar size placed on a common random rubble masonry base. The *chorten* are built in stone and mud brick masonry with mud mortar and are mud plastered and whitewashed on the exterior. There is a small rectangular *lubang* to the west.

STATE OF PRESERVATION
Advanced State of Decay

SOURCE OF INFORMATION Tashi Tsomo, Lamayuru, Khaltse, Ladakh

Rantakchanpa House

INVENTORY NO.
KHALTSE / LARDO / 01 / 2004

Vernacular Building | Abandoned | Private (Individual) | Around 100 years old

Photograph Not Available

SETTING
The Rantakchanpa house is oriented to the northwest and is located on the left side of the main road. The house is surrounded by smaller structures which are in complete ruins and the new Rantakchanpa house.

SIGNIFICANCE
The house was built about a hundred years ago by an ancestor of the Rantakchanpa family. The family no longer resides here. The house is built in the traditional style and is part of the vernacular architecture of the village.

DESCRIPTION
The house is a double storeyed building with the ground floor made in random rubble masonry. This level was used for storing fodder and has narrow openings for ventilation. There are two *lubang* near the entrance to the house. The first floor is constructed in mud brick masonry with mud

mortar and has large window openings. The house has a flat traditional roof made of wooden beams, joists, *taalu*, grass and compacted mud. The flooring at both levels is of mud. The house is deteriorating rapidly as it is no longer used by the family.

STATE OF PRESERVATION
Danger of Disappearance

SOURCE OF INFORMATION Phuntsog Angchuk, Lardo, Khaltse, Ladakh

Group of *Chorten* and *Mane* Wall

INVENTORY NO.
KHALTSE / LARDO / 02 / 2004

Chorten / *Mane* Wall | In Use | Public (Community)

SETTING
The *chorten* and *mane* wall are located on the left of the main road and are surrounded by apricot and willow trees. The vehicular road lies to the northeast.

SIGNIFICANCE
The *chorten* and *mane* wall lie along the main village road and are circumambulated by villagers as an act of merit. The *chorten* are Changchub *chorten*, which symbolize the Buddha's enlightenment.

DESCRIPTION
The site consists of two large *chorten* and a circular *mane* wall. The *chorten* are both of the same size and are built on square platforms. The platforms are built in random rubble masonry while the *chorten* are built in stone and mud brick masonry with mud mortar. Externally, the surface is mud

plastered and whitewashed. Near the *chorten* there is a circular *mane* wall built in dry stone masonry with *mane* stones placed on its horizontal surface.

STATE OF PRESERVATION
Showing Signs of Deterioration

SOURCE OF INFORMATION Phuntsog Angchuk, Lardo, Khaltse, Ladakh

Chorten

INVENTORY NO.
KHALTSE / LARDO / 03 / 2004

Chorten | In Use | Public (Community)

SETTING
The *chorten* is located on the left side of the main vehicular road and has village houses nearby.

SIGNIFICANCE
The *chorten* was built in the past as an act of merit and is still circumambulated by villagers to accumulate merit. It is a Changchub *chorten* and symbolizes the Buddha's enlightenment.

DESCRIPTION
The site consists of a Changchub *chorten* built in stone and mud brick masonry with mud mortar. The external surface of the *chorten* was originally mud plastered and whitewashed though much of this layer has eroded. There is a *srog-shing* embedded on the dome of the *chorten*.

STATE OF PRESERVATION
Showing Signs of Deterioration

SOURCE OF INFORMATION Phuntsog Angchuk, Lardo, Khaltse, Ladakh

Lardo

223

Group of *Mane* Walls

INVENTORY NO.
KHALTSE / LARDO / 04 / 2004

Mane Wall | In Use | Public (Community)

SETTING
The *mane* walls are oriented to the south and located to the right of the vehicular road. They are surrounded by rocks and some shrubs. The river runs to the north while the road lies to the south of the site.

SIGNIFICANCE
The *mane* walls are located along the road and are circumambulated by villagers to accumulate merit.

DESCRIPTION
The site consists of a cluster of three *mane* walls. Two of them are circular while the third is a linear structure. All three *mane* walls are built in dry stone masonry and have inscribed *mane* stones placed on the horizontal surface.

STATE OF PRESERVATION
Advanced State of Decay

SOURCE OF INFORMATION Phuntsog Angchuk, Lardo, Khaltse, Ladakh

Lehdo

Lehdo is situated about 135 kms from Leh, on the left bank of the River Indus. It is said that the village was earlier approached after passing three passes (Leme-la, Kuksho-la, and Urbis-la) while travelling from Leh. It is called La-mdo meaning 'lower part of the valley after the passes'. Earlier, the village was also known as Burtse Thang meaning 'a plain area with bushes'. It is said that there were only two families in the beginning. Today, there are about 50 households in the village. The village consists of four small hamlets namely Farka, Kabto, Lehdo and Singethang.

{Source: Rigzin Namgyal (Goba)}

Listed by: Dr. Sonam Wangchok, Gelong Jamyang Phuntsog and Karma Yeshi
Year: 2006

Kagan *Chorten*

INVENTORY NO.
KHALTSE / LEHDO / 01 / 2006

Chorten | In Use | Private (Individual) | Around 70 - 80 years old

SETTING
The Kagan *chorten* is oriented to the north and is located on the left side of the River Indus near the Khatotpa house.

SIGNIFICANCE
The Kagan *chorten* was built by an ancestor of the Khatotpa family, a monk named Tashi Tsewang, around 70 - 80 years ago for the well being of all living beings and for peace in the entire village.

DESCRIPTION
The Kagan *chorten* consists of two thick parallel walls made of random rubble masonry over which rests a *chorten* also made in stone masonry. The *chorten* has a tall *chugsum khorlo* on the dome made of baked clay tiles. The ceiling of the passage is made of timber and has paintings painted on canvas and glued onto the timber surface. The paintings depict *mandalas* and images of Buddhas. The side walls of the *chorten* are not plastered. However, the

chorten above the passage is mud plastered and whitewashed.

STATE OF PRESERVATION
Showing Signs of Deterioration

SOURCE OF INFORMATION Tashi Jorphel, Lehdo, Khaltse, Ladakh

Lehdo

226

Tashag

INVENTORY NO.
KHALTSE / LEHDO / 02 / 2006

Vernacular Building | Abandoned | Private (Individual) | Around 70 - 80 years old

SETTING
The *tashag* is oriented to the north and is located along the village footpath leading to the Bhemapa area. The Khatotpa house is situated nearby.

SIGNIFICANCE
The *tashag* was built by a monk named Tashi Tsewang from the Khatotpa family with the help of his family members. Tashi Tsewang became a monk when he was a child and lived in Lamayuru *Gonpa* until he completed his education. This *tashag* was built specially for him to enable him to carry out his prayers and religious activities whenever he visited the village. It is built in the traditional style and is an example of vernacular architecture in the village.

DESCRIPTION
The *tashag* is a three storeyed building built largely in random rubble masonry with some sections of the upper levels built in mud brick masonry. The ground floor is built at a lower level than the village foot path and possibly

served as a storage area. The first floor was used as the living area with a small chamber on the second floor that was probably the temple. The second floor appears to have had a large terrace in front of the chamber. This chamber has a large window with a timber frame and shutters. Sections of the house have collapsed and the external layer of mud plaster and whitewash have completely eroded.

STATE OF PRESERVATION
Danger of Disappearance

SOURCE OF INFORMATION Tashi Jorphel, Lehdo, Khaltse, Ladakh

Rigsum Gonbo

INVENTORY NO.
KHALTSE / LEHDO / 03 / 2006

Rigsum Gonbo | In Use | Private (Individual) | Around 6 years old

SETTING
The *rigsum gonbo* is oriented to the east and is located along the slope of a mountain above the Bemapa house. The River Indus flows below the mountain.

SIGNIFICANCE
The *rigsum gonbo* was built by the Bemapa family on the advice of the Togdan Rinpoche as it was believed that evil forces were harming the family from the other side of the mountain. The *rigsum gonbo* was built to protect the family from these evil forces.

DESCRIPTION
The *rigsum gonbo* consists of three *chorten* plastered in cement and painted in the traditional ochre, white and blue colours symbolizing the deities Jamyang, Chanrazig and Chagdor. The *chorten* are built on a cement concrete base and the domes have niches facing the east within which are placed images of the deities. *Khadag* are tied on the *chugsum khorlo* at the top of each dome.

SOURCE OF INFORMATION Tsering Tondup, Lehdo, Khaltse, Ladakh

STATE OF PRESERVATION
Good

Mane Lagskor

INVENTORY NO.
KHALTSE / LEHDO / 04 / 2006

Prayer Wheel | In Use | Private (Individual)

SETTING
The *mane* Lagskor is built in front of Tsering Tondup house in the Bemapa settlement.

SIGNIFICANCE
The prayer wheel was built in memory of Tsering Tondup's son who died while crossing over the Indus river on a trolley 5 - 6 years ago. It was built by the family for his liberation from suffering. Turning the prayer wheel in the clockwise direction and reciting the *mantra* of Chanrazig by the devout is seen as an act of merit for oneself as well as others.

DESCRIPTION
The *mane* wheel is enclosed within a structure which has four columns at the corners over rests a roof. There is a concrete platform on which the prayer wheel rests. The prayer wheel is made of metal and the drum of the wheel is richly embellished with gilded decorative motifs.

SOURCE OF INFORMATION Tsering Tondup, Lehdo, Khaltse, Ladakh

STATE OF PRESERVATION
Good

Tsamskhang

INVENTORY NO.
KHALTSE / LEHDO / 05 / 2006

Vernacular Building | Abandoned | Public (Lamayuru *Gonpa*) | Around 150 - 200 years old

SETTING
The *tsamskhang* are located towards the end of the village, above the River Indus. A village footpath leads via the Bemapa houses to the site.

SIGNIFICANCE
The *tsamskhang* were used by monks and nuns from Lamayuru *gonpa* for meditation. It is said that a nun from the village meditated here continuously for three years in one of the cells. Today, it is no longer in use.

DESCRIPTION
The building is built along a slight slope and is single storeyed high with some evidence of a second floor which no longer exists. It is built in stone masonry and is devoid of any external plaster or whitewash. There are three meditation cells inside the building, each with its own kitchen and retreat.

STATE OF PRESERVATION
Advanced State of Decay

SOURCE OF INFORMATION Tsering Tondup, Lehdo, Khaltse, Ladakh

Lehdo

228

Rigsum Gonbo

INVENTORY NO.
KHALTSE / LEHDO / 06 / 2006

Rigsum Gonbo | In Use | Private (Individual) | Around 5 - 6 years ago

SETTING
The *rigsum gonbo* is oriented to the east and is located above the Singethang area of the village behind the Khangsarpa house. The Government High School is located nearby.

SIGNIFICANCE
The *rigsum gonbo* was rebuilt around 5 - 6 years ago replacing an older *rigsum gonbo* built over the entrance door of the Khangsarpa family. It was shifted here to protect the family from natural calamities such as floods that had occurred some years ago.

DESCRIPTION
The *rigsum gonbo* consists of a tall platform over which stand three *chorten* painted in ochre, white and blue symbolizing the Bodhisattvas Jamyang, Chanrazig and Chagdor respectively. The platform is built in stone and is cement plastered and painted on the exterior. There are thin iron posts at the four corners of the plinth over which a roof of corrugated metal sheet has been placed.

STATE OF PRESERVATION
Good

SOURCE OF INFORMATION Tsering Tondup, Lehdo, Khaltse, Ladakh

Rigsum Gonbo

INVENTORY NO.
KHALTSE / LEHDO / 07 / 2006

Rigsum Gonbo | In Use | Private (Individual) | Around 200 years old

SETTING
The *rigsum gonbo* is oriented to the south and is located behind Lama Tsewang Gyatso's house, at the foot of a high mountain.

SIGNIFICANCE
The *rigsum gonbo* was built to protect the family and village against natural calamities and disasters.

DESCRIPTION
The *rigsum gonbo* is located within a small enclosure with walls on the three sides – to the rear and sides – and open in the front. The walls are made of stone masonry and there are some traces of external plaster and whitewash. The *chorten* are located inside the enclosure and are built in stone and mud brick masonry and are mud plastered on the exterior. One of the *chorten* is painted in red and the central *chorten* is painted in white. The third *chorten,*

originally painted in blue, has large deposits of whitewash on the surface. The *chorten* have tall *chugsum khorlo* over the dome made of baked clay tiles.

STATE OF PRESERVATION
Showing Signs of Deterioration

SOURCE OF INFORMATION Tsewang Dolma (*Chomo*), Lehdo, Khaltse, Ladakh

Group of *Chorten* and *Mane* Wall

INVENTORY NO.
KHALTSE / LEHDO / 08 / 2006

Chorten / *Mane* Wall | In Use | Private (Individual) | Around 200 years old

SETTING
The *chorten* and *mane* wall are oriented to the southeast and are located on the right of the road leading to the village. The site is reached after crossing the bridge and heading towards the village.

SIGNIFICANCE
The *chorten* and *mane* wall were built around 200 - 250 years ago and are said to have been built by the earliest settlers in the village. The structures were built along the old footpath and would have been circumambulated by villagers as an act of merit while they travelled along this path. The *chorten* are all Changchub *chorten* and symbolize the Buddha's enlightenment.

DESCRIPTION
The site consists of a large *chorten*, a group of five smaller *chorten* and a *mane* wall. The *chorten* are all built in stone

masonry and only the large *chorten* is mud plastered and whitewashed. The large *chorten* was renewed by the community three years ago. The five smaller *chorten* are all built on a common random rubble masonry base. Between the large *chorten* and the group of smaller *chorten* is a circular *mane* wall built in random rubble masonry with inscribed *mane* stones placed on the horizontal surface.

STATE OF PRESERVATION
Showing Signs of Deterioration

Lehdo

229

Precinct of Petroglyphs

INVENTORY NO.
KHALTSE / LEHDO / 09 / 2006

Petroglyphs | Abandoned | Public (State)

SETTING
The petroglyphs are located to the left side of the vehicular road after crossing the bridge and heading towards the village. The stones are scattered across a large area around the river banks.

SIGNIFICANCE
The petroglyphs date back to the earliest period of human habitation in the region. Some of the depictions of stupas in these rock carvings appear to be those of the Bon religion.

DESCRIPTION
The site consists of a large precinct of petroglyphs executed on boulders scattered across the site. The petroglyphs portray both human and animals figures as well as those of later stupas, some inscriptions and symbols. One of the major threats to the site is that stones from this area are broken and used for construction activity.

STATE OF PRESERVATION
Danger of Disappearance

Lehdo

230

Gothepey *Khangbu*

INVENTORY NO.
KHALTSE / LEHDO / 10 / 2006

Vernacular Building | In Use | Private (Individual) | Around 500 years old

SETTING
The Gothepey house is located just before the village *gonpa*, about two kms after crossing the bridge and heading towards the village.

SIGNIFICANCE
The Gothepey house was built by Meme Tsering Targyas of the Gothepey family approximately 500 years ago and successive generations have continued to reside here. It is believed to be one of oldest house in the village and is built in the traditional style contributing to the vernacular architecture of the village.

DESCRIPTION
The Gothepey house is a large three storeyed building. From the entrance doorway, a flight of stairs leads up to the first floor which is the family's winter living area. The ground floor is used primarily for storage and is built in random rubble masonry with no window openings. The upper levels are built in mud brick masonry with mud mortar and the exterior walls of the house are mud plastered and whitewashed. The second floor constitutes the family's summer living area and houses the kitchen as well as the family chapel. The kitchen has a traditional clay stove while the chapel has a ornate wooden cabinet with images of various deities within. The house has a traditional roof above made of timber beams, joists, *taalu*, *phugma*, and a layer of compacted mud above. The windows on the second floor have elaborately carved timber shutters in a lattice pattern.

STATE OF PRESERVATION
Advanced State of Decay

SOURCE OF INFORMATION Thinles Dhuntup, Gothepa, Lehdo, Khaltse, Ladakh

---

Lehdo

231

Thangthig pa House

INVENTORY NO.
KHALTSE / LEHDO / 11 / 2006

Vernacular Building | In Use | Private(Individual) | Around 400 years old

SETTING
The Thangthig pa house is located just below the village *gonpa*. After crossing the bridge, a dirt track of around two kms leads to the village from where a short walk along the village road leads to the house.

SIGNIFICANCE
The Thangthig pa house was built by Meme Sherab of the Thangthig pa family about 8 generations ago and successive generations have continued to reside here. It is believed to be one of oldest house in the village and is built in the traditional style contributing to the vernacular architecture of the village.

DESCRIPTION
The Thangthig pa house is a double storeyed building with the ground floor built in random rubble masonry while the first floor is built in mud brick masonry. The ground floor is used primarily for storage while the first floor constitutes the living areas. The family chapel and kitchen are located on the first floor. The chapel has a large window with an elaborate timber shutter intricately carved in a latticed pattern. The house has a traditional roof made of timber beams, joists, *taalu*, *phugma* and compacted mud supported by wooden columns and brackets beneath. There are prayer flags posted on the roof which has a low parapet running all around the edge. The exterior walls of the house are mud plastered and whitewashed.

STATE OF PRESERVATION
Showing Signs of Deterioration

SOURCE OF INFORMATION Thinles Dhuntup, Gothepa, Lehdo, Khaltse, Ladakh

Mane Wall

INVENTORY NO.
KHALTSE / LEHDO / 12 / 2006

Mane Wall | In Use | Private (Individual)

SETTING
The *mane* wall is oriented to the north and is located along the village footpath.

SIGNIFICANCE
The *mane* wall is built along the village footpath and is circumambulated by villagers as an act of merit. It was built in the past to accumulate merit as the building of *mane* walls and *chorten* is believed to benefit all sentient beings.

DESCRIPTION
The *mane* wall is built in dry stone masonry and is a long, linear wall. Inscribed *mane* stones and rock carvings of Buddhist deities are placed on the horizontal surface of the wall.

STATE OF PRESERVATION
Showing Signs of Deterioration

SOURCE OF INFORMATION Rigzin Namgyal, Tashispa, Lehdo, Khaltse, Ladakh

Chosangpa House

INVENTORY NO.
KHALTSE / LEHDO / 13 / 2006

Vernacular Building | In Use | Private (Individual) | Around 200 years old

SETTING
The Chosangpa house is located along the village footpath about 450 metres from where the footpath begins at the entrance to the village.

SIGNIFICANCE
The house was built by Meme Sonam Phuntsog of the Chosangpa family four generations ago and successive generations have continued to reside here. It is believed to be one of oldest house in the village and is built in the traditional style contributing to the vernacular architecture of the village.

DESCRIPTION
The Chosangpa house is a triple storeyed building built in random rubble masonry at the ground floor and mud brick masonry in the upper levels. The entrance to the house is from a flight of stairs that leads onto the first floor. The ground floor is used primarily for storage. The first floor is used for winter dwelling of the family while the second floor is used as the summer quarters. The kitchen and the family chapel are located on the first floor. It has a traditional roof made of timber beams, joists, *taalu*, grass and compacted mud supported on timber columns and brackets. There is a low height parapet around the edge of the roof. The ground floor has small windows openings for ventilation and light while the first and second floors have larger windows openings with tiered timber lintels. There is a large window with an elaborately carved timber shutter on the second floor. The exterior walls of the house are mud plastered and whitewashed.

STATE OF PRESERVATION
Showing Signs of Deterioration

SOURCE OF INFORMATION Tsewang Nurboo, Chosang pa, Lehdo, Khaltse, Ladakh

Mane Wall

INVENTORY NO.
KHALTSE / LEHDO / 14 / 2006

Mane Wall | In Use | Public (Community) | Around 200 - 300 years old

SETTING
The *mane* wall is oriented to the north and is located along the village footpath.

SIGNIFICANCE
The *mane* wall is built along the village footpath and is circumambulated by villagers as an act of merit. It was built in the past to accumulate merit as the building of *mane* walls and *chorten* is believed to benefit all sentient beings.

DESCRIPTION
The *mane* wall is a long linear dry stone masonry wall built alongside the village footpath at a lower level. It has inscribed *mane* stones placed on the top horizontal surface. Part of the *mane* wall is embedded in the footpath.

STATE OF PRESERVATION
Advanced State of Decay

SOURCE OF INFORMATION Rigzin Namgyal, Tashispa, Lehdo, Khaltse, Ladakh

Lehdo

233

Tashispa House

INVENTORY NO.
KHALTSE / LEHDO / 15 / 2006

Vernacular Building | In Use | Private (Individual) | Around 150 years old

SETTING
The Tashispa house is located along the village footpath about 400 metres from where the footpath begins at the entrance to the village.

SIGNIFICANCE
The house was built by Meme Tsetan Paljor of the Tashispa family three generations ago and successive generations have continued to reside here. It is believed to be one of oldest house in the village and is built in the traditional style contributing to the vernacular architecture of the village.

DESCRIPTION
The Tashispa house is a large triple storeyed building built in random rubble masonry base at the ground and in mud brick masonry and mud mortar at the upper levels. A flight of stairs leads to the entrance at the at the first floor level. The ground floor is used primarily for storage while the first floor is used for winter dwelling by the family. The second floor is used as the living quarters during the summer months. The kitchen and family chapel are located on the first floor. The house has a traditional roof above made of timber beams, joists, *taalu*, grass and a layer of compacted mud. The roof is supported on timber columns and brackets. A low parapet surrounds the roof. The ground floor has no window openings while the first has narrow window openings. The second floor has large windows with timber frames and tiered timber lintels, timber frames and glass panes.

STATE OF PRESERVATION
Fair

SOURCE OF INFORMATION Rigzin Namgyal, Tashis pa, Lehdo, Khaltse, Ladakh

Lobdhepa House

INVENTORY NO.
KHALTSE / LEHDO / 16 / 2006

Vernacular Building | In Use | Private (Individual) | Around 300 years old

SETTING
The Lobdhepa house is located along the village footpath about 400 metres from where the footpath begins at the entrance to the village. It is located near the village *gonpa*, opposite the Tashispa house.

SIGNIFICANCE
The Lobdhepa house was built by an ancestor of the family named Meme Tashi about six generations ago and subsequent generations have continued to reside here. It is believed to be one of oldest house in the village and is built in the traditional style contributing to the vernacular architecture of the village.

DESCRIPTION
The Lobdhepa house is a large triple storeyed building built in random rubble masonry at the ground floor and in mud brick masonry at the upper levels. A flight of stairs from the exterior leads to the entrance on the first floor. There is a *rigsum gonbo* above the entrance door. The ground floor is used primarily for storage while the first floor is used by the family for winter dwelling. The second floor is used during the summer as the family's living quarters. The family chapel is located on the second floor. The house has a traditional roof made of timber joists, *taalu*, grass and compacted mud which is supported by timber columns and brackets below. A low parapet surrounds the roof and there are prayer flags posted at the corners of the roof. There is a large window on the south facade at the second floor level which has a timber frame.

STATE OF PRESERVATION
Showing Signs of Deterioration

SOURCE OF INFORMATION Rigzin Namgyal, Tashispa, Lehdo, Khaltse, Ladakh

Lehdo

234

Mane Wall

INVENTORY NO.
KHALTSE / LEHDO / 17 / 2006

Mane Wall | In Use | Public (Community) | Around 17th century

SETTING
The *mane* wall is oriented to the north and is located along the village footpath.

SIGNIFICANCE
The *mane* wall it is believed was built by a villager on the order of King Senge Namgyal (1590 - 1640 A.D.) as a punishment to atone for his sins. The *mane* wall is built along the village footpath and is circumambulated by villagers as an act of merit.

STATE OF PRESERVATION
Advanced State of Decay

DESCRIPTION
The *mane* wall is a long linear dry stone masonry wall built alongside the village footpath. It has inscribed *mane* stones placed on the top horizontal surface as well as several inscriptions placed along the length of the wall.

SOURCE OF INFORMATION Rigzin Namgyal, Tashispa, Lehdo, Khaltse, Ladakh

Gambupa House

INVENTORY NO.
KHALTSE / LEHDO / 18 / 2006

Vernacular Building | In Use | Private (Individual) | Around 400 years old

STATE OF PRESERVATION
Showing Signs of Deterioration

SETTING
The Gambupa house is located along a village footpath.

SIGNIFICANCE
The house was built by an ancestor of the Gambupa family during the reign of King Senge Namgyal (1590 - 1640 A.D.) and successive generations have continued to reside here. It is believed that the family was one of the wealthiest in Ladakh and gave land and money to the king. In gratitude, the king commissioned the wall painting of the Life of Guru Padmasambhava in the Lehdo *gonpa* which can still be seen today. The house is built in the traditional style and is a fine example of vernacular architecture in the village. The house still retains its original *arga* floor, a technique that is no longer used in Ladakh, as well as fragments of wall paintings in the family chapel.

DESCRIPTION
The Gambupa house is a large triple storeyed building built in random rubble masonry at the ground floor and in mud brick masonry at the upper levels. The house consists of fourteen rooms including a chapel. A flight of stairs leads onto the entrance of the house at the first floor level. There is a *rigsum gonbo* above the entrance doorway. The ground floor is used primarily for storage while the first floor is used for winter dwelling by the family. The summer habitation as well as the family chapel is located on the second floor. Ruins of wall paintings depicting various Buddhas can still be seen in the chapel. The northeastern section of the house is in ruins. There is a large timber framed *rabsal* on the front facade. Externally, the walls are mud plastered and whitewashed. The house has a traditional roof made of timber beams, joists, *taalu*, grass and compacted mud supported on wooden columns and brackets. The house has an *arga* floor and in the kitchen is an old traditional stove made of clay.

Lehdo

235

SOURCE OF INFORMATION Rigzin Namgyal, Tashis pa, Lehdo, Khaltse, Ladakh

Singey Thangpa

INVENTORY NO.
KHALTSE / LEHDO / 19 / 2006

Vernacular Building | In Use | Private (Individual) | Around 17th century

SETTING
The Singey Thangpa house is located along the village footpath and is surrounded by other village houses.

SIGNIFICANCE
The house was built by an ancestor of the Singey Thangpa family during the reign of King Senge Namgyal (1590 - 1640 A.D.) and successive generations have continued to reside here. The house is built in the traditional style and is a fine example of vernacular architecture in the village.

DESCRIPTION
The Singey Thangpa house is a large triple storeyed building built in stone masonry at the ground floor and in mud brick masonry at the upper levels. The house consists of twenty rooms including a chapel. A flight of stairs leads onto the entrance of the house at the ground floor level. The ground floor is used primarily for storage while the first floor is used for winter dwelling by the family. The summer habitation as well as the family chapel is located on the second floor. The chapel has a finely carved latticed timber window. Externally, the walls are mud plastered and whitewashed. The house has a traditional roof made of timber beams, joists, *taalu*, grass and compacted mud supported on wooden columns and brackets. The house has an *arga* floor and in the kitchen is an old traditional stove made of clay.

STATE OF PRESERVATION
Showing Signs of Deterioration

SOURCE OF INFORMATION Rigzin Namgyal, Tashis pa, Lehdo, Khaltse, Ladakh

Group of *Chorten*

INVENTORY NO.
KHALTSE / LEHDO / 20 / 2006

Chorten | In Use | Public (Community)

SETTING
The *chorten* are oriented to the southeast and are located along the village road with the river flowing beyond.

SIGNIFICANCE
The *chorten* were built along the old footpath and would have been circumambulated by villagers as an act of merit while they travelled along this path. The *chorten* are all Changchub *chorten* which symbolize the Buddha's enlightenment.

DESCRIPTION
The site consists of four *chorten* built on a random rubble masonry platform. The *chorten* are built in stone masonry with an external layer of mud plaster and whitewash, most of which has eroded over time.

STATE OF PRESERVATION
Danger of Disappearance

SOURCE OF INFORMATION Rigzin Namgyal, Tashispa, Lehdo, Khaltse, Ladakh

Guntsar Thangpa

INVENTORY NO.
KHALTSE / LEHDO / 21 / 2006

Vernacular Building | Abandoned | Private (Individual) | Around 450 - 500 years old

SETTING
The Guntsar Thangpa is located along the village footpath and is surrounded by other village houses.

SIGNIFICANCE
The house was built by an ancestor of the Guntsar pa family during the reign of King Senge Namgyal (1590 - 1640 A.D.) named Meme Sonam Chosphel and successive generations have continued to reside here. The house is built in the traditional style and is a fine example of vernacular architecture in the village.

DESCRIPTION
The Guntsar Thangpa is a large triple storeyed building built in random rubble masonry at the ground floor and in mud brick masonry with mud mortar at the upper levels. The house consists of fifteen rooms including a chapel. A flight of stairs leads onto the entrance of the house at the ground floor level. The ground floor is used primarily for storage while the first floor was used for winter dwelling by the

family. The summer habitation as well as the family chapel was located on the second floor. The chapel has a finely carved timber columns and brackets. Externally the walls are mud plastered and white washed. Remnants of the old roof made of timber beams, joists, *taalu*, grass and compacted mud supported on wooden columns and brackets can still be seen. The house has been abandoned by the family and is now only used for storage. Sections of the house have collapsed and are lying in ruins

STATE OF PRESERVATION
Danger of Disappearance

SOURCE OF INFORMATION Sonam Tsering (Guntsar pa), Lehdo, Khaltse, Ladakh

Kabto *Gonpa*

INVENTORY NO.
KHALTSE / LEHDO / 22 / 2006

Gonpa | In Use | Public (Lamayuru *Gonpa*) | Around 200 years old

SETTING
The *gonpa* is located in the old settlement of Kabto about three kms from the bridge towards the south. There are willow trees to the front of the *gonpa* and a village footpath to the rear.

SIGNIFICANCE
The Kabto *gonpa* falls under the purview of the Drigung Kagyud sect and is a branch of the Lamayuru *gonpa*. One monk from Lamayuru *gonpa* is deputed here to carry out prayers and rituals in the temple. The villagers offer prayers to the protectors on the 10th day of every month. The principal image in the temple is that of Guru Rinpoche.

DESCRIPTION
The *gonpa* is a single storeyed building with two shrines. The old *dukhang* is located to the west of the new one and images have been shifted into the new *dukhang* built three years ago. A flight of stairs leads up to the front porch. There are paintings of the four guardian deities outside the

entrance wall of the old *dukhang*. Two wooden columns and brackets support a traditional roof above. The walls of the *gonpa* are built in stone and mud brick masonry with mud mortar and are mud plastered and whitewashed on the exterior. The southern wall of the old *dukhang* was reconstructed three years ago and no paintings survive on this wall. The statues are kept in a new wooden altar in the new shrine. The principal images in the *gonpa* are those of Guru Rinpoche, Chanrazig, Chamba and Buddha. There are wall paintings of Kabgyat and Tungshak in the *dukhang*. The exterior walls of the new *dukhang* are painted in red.

STATE OF PRESERVATION
Showing Signs of Deterioration

Group of *Chorten* and *Mane* Walls

INVENTORY NO.
KHALTSE / LEHDO / 23 / 2006

Chorten / *Mane* Wall | In Use | Public (Community) | Around 150 - 200 years old

SETTING
The group is located near the Phelzompa house in the old settlement of Kabto, about three kms south from the bridge.

SIGNIFICANCE
The *chorten* were built along the old footpath and are circumambulated by villagers as an act of merit when they travel along this path. The *chorten* are all Changchub *chorten* and symbolize the Buddha's enlightenment.

DESCRIPTION
The site consists of two *chorten* and *mane* walls. The *chorten* are built on a high random rubble masonry platform. The *chorten* are built in stone masonry and mud mortar with an external layer of mud plaster and whitewash, most of which has eroded over time. There is a long linear *mane* wall as well as a circular *mane* wall built

in stone masonry before the *chorten*. Inscribed *mane* stones are placed on the horizontal surface of the *mane* walls as well as on the *chorten*.

STATE OF PRESERVATION
Advanced State of Decay

SOURCE OF INFORMATION Tashi Gyurmet, Lehdo, Khaltse, Ladakh

Lehdo

238

Urbis Chomo *Lhato*

INVENTORY NO.
KHALTSE / LEHDO / 24 / 2006

Lhato | In Use | Public (Community) | Around 250 - 300 years old

SETTING
The *lhato* is oriented to the west and is located above Kabto village on top of a steep mountain about three kms south of the bridge.

SIGNIFICANCE
According to legend, the protector deity Urbis Chomo has seven sisters (*spundun*). One of them is in Tagmachig village, another in Urbis and one in Lehdo. They are all known by same name. Villagers offer prayers to the *Lha* during Losar on 3rd day of 11th month and on 15th of 4th month. The contents of the *lhato* are renewed at this time.

STATE OF PRESERVATION
Showing Signs of Deterioration

DESCRIPTION
The *lhato* is built in stone masonry and is a cubical shaped structure which has traces of mud plaster and whitewash on the exterior surface. There are juniper branches, animal horns and *khadag* placed on the top of the *lhato*.

SOURCE OF INFORMATION Tashi Gyurmet, Lehdo, Khaltse, Ladakh

Mane Wall

INVENTORY NO.
KHALTSE / LEHDO / 25 / 2006

Mane Wall | In Use | Public (Community) | Around 150-200 years old

STATE OF PRESERVATION
Showing Signs of Deterioration

SETTING
The *mane* wall is located behind the Phelzompa house in the old settlement of Kabto about three kms south of the bridge.

SIGNIFICANCE
The *mane* wall is built along the village footpath and is circumambulated by villagers as an act of merit when travelling along this path.

DESCRIPTION
The *mane* wall is a long linear dry stone masonry wall built alongside the village footpath at a lower level. It has inscribed *mane* stones placed on the top horizontal surface.

SOURCE OF INFORMATION Tashi Gyurmet, Lehdo, Khaltse, Ladakh

Lehdo

23

Chorten

INVENTORY NO.
KHALTSE / LEHDO / 26 / 2006

Chorten | In Use | Public (Community) | Around 150 years old

STATE OF PRESERVATION
Fair

SETTING
The *chorten* is situated near the Lehdo *gonpa* to the right of the village.

SIGNIFICANCE
The *chorten* was built around 150 years ago along the village footpath and is circumambulated by villagers as an act of merit when they cross this path. The *chorten* is a Changchub *chorten* which symbolizes the Buddha's enlightenment.

DESCRIPTION
The site consists of a large *chorten* built on a random rubble masonry base. The *chorten* is built in stone masonry and is mud plastered and whitewashed on the exterior. It has a tall *chugsum khorlo* on the dome topped by a metal crown symbolizing the 13 steps towards enlightenment.

SOURCE OF INFORMATION Tashi Gyurmet, Lehdo, Khaltse, Ladakh

Lehdo *Gonpa*

INVENTORY NO.
KHALTSE / LEHDO / 27 / 2006

Gonpa | In Use | Public (Lamayuru *Gonpa*) | 17th century

SETTING

The *gonpa* is situated in the middle of the village about two kms south of the bridge. It is surrounded by village houses and *tashag* to the north and trees to the south.

SIGNIFICANCE

The *gonpa* falls under the purview of the Drigung Kagyud sect and is a branch of the Lamayuru *gonpa*. Monks from Lamayuru *gonpa* are deputed here and perform several prayers in the *gonpa* sponsored by the villagers. These include the sixteen days of *nyenas* (fasting) in the 1st month, five days of prayers for protectors in the 4th month, *lamachodpa* (offerings to lamas) on 3rd day of the 11th month, three days of reading sacred texts in the 4th month, prayer for protectors on the 15th day of the 4th month and prayers for Guru Takpo on the 10th day of every month of the Ladakhi calendar. The *gonpa* has unique wall paintings depicting the life of Guru Padmasambhava said to have been copied from the collection of *thangkas* at Stok Palace.

STATE OF PRESERVATION
Showing Signs of Deterioration

DESCRIPTION

The *gonpa* is a small building with two *dukhang* attached to each other. The *gonpa* is built in random rubble and mud brick masonry with mud mortar and is mud plastered and whitewashed on the exterior. The *gonpa* has a traditional roof above made of timber joists, *taalu*, grass and compacted mud supported on timber columns and brackets beneath. The parapet is painted in red. A flight of stairs leads upto the main door of the *dukhang*. The inner *dukhang* has wall paintings of Apchi (the main protector of Drigung Kagyud), Mahakala, and other protectors on the northern wall and medicine Buddha, Odpakmed and Chanrazig on the southern wall. This chamber also houses manuscripts and statues of Dolma and Chamba. The main *dukhang* has a skylight in the centre of the chamber and four wooden columns supporting the roof above. The walls of the chamber are richly embellished with paintings of dzambala, Mitugpa, Chagdor, Buddhas, Chanrazig, Lamas, Protectors, 16 *Arhat*, Guru Takpo. On the northern wall is the exquisite painting depicting the life of Guru Padmasambhava. The principal statues in the *dukhang* are Jo Rinpoche, Skyoba Jigsten Gonbo, Guru Rinpoche, Chanrazig, Dorjechang, Mahakala and other protectors.

SOURCE OF INFORMATION Gelong Konchog Choswang, Lehdo, Khalste, Ladakh 194106 J&K

Kagan *Chorten*

INVENTORY NO.
KHALTSE / LEHDO / 28 / 2006

Chorten | In Use | Public (Community) | Around 200 Years old

SETTING
The *chorten* is oriented to the southeast and is located at the entrance to the main settlement a little before the *gonpa* to left of the village road.

SIGNIFICANCE
The Kagan *chorten* is located at the entrance to the village over the village footpath. It is a gateway *chorten* and merit is believed to believers who pass through the *chorten* as well as circumambulate the *chorten*.

DESCRIPTION
The Kagan *chorten* consists of two thick parallel walls made of stone masonry over which rests a *chorten* which is also made in stone masonry. The *chorten* has a tall *chugsum khorlo* on the dome made of baked clay tiles. The ceiling of the passage is made of timber but has no paintings. The *chorten* has been recently repaired and has been cement plastered and whitewashed.

SOURCE OF INFORMATION Sonam Angchuk, Tashispa, Lehdo, Khaltse, Ladakh

STATE OF PRESERVATION
Fair

Chomaksang *Lhato*

INVENTORY NO.
KHALTSE / LEHDO / 29 / 2006

Lhato | In Use | Public (Community)

SETTING
The *lhato* is located on a hill to the right of the main road near the entrance to the village.

SIGNIFICANCE
The *lhato* is dedicated to the village protector named Chomoksang. The protector deity was possessed in a village oracle who passed away six years ago. The villagers get together during the Ladakhi New Year on the 3rd day of the 11th month of the Tibetan calendar at which time the contents of the *lhato* are renewed. Prayers are also offered here on the 15th day of the 4th month of the Tibetan calendar.

DESCRIPTION
The *lhato* is built in random rubble masonry with mud mortar and is a cubical shaped structure which is mud plastered and whitewashed on the exterior. There are

juniper branches, animal horns and *khadag* placed on the top of the *lhato*. There is an open area in the front where the community gathers on the occasion of Losar.

STATE OF PRESERVATION
Showing Signs of Deterioration

SOURCE OF INFORMATION Sonam Angchuk, Tashispa, Lehdo, Khaltse, Ladakh

Lehdo

241

Group of *Chorten*

INVENTORY NO.
KHALTSE / LEHDO / 30 / 2006

Chorten | In Use | Public (Community) | Around 150 - 200 years old

SETTING
The *chorten* are located along the road below the *lhato* of the village protector and are surrounded by walnut trees to the east and mountains to the west.

SIGNIFICANCE
The *chorten* were built around 150 - 200 years ago along the village footpath and are circumambulated by villagers as an act of merit when they cross this path. The *chorten* are Changchub *chorten* which symbolize the Buddha's enlightenment.

DESCRIPTION
The site consists of two *chorten* built in stone and mud brick masonry with mud mortar which are mud plastered and whitewashed on the exterior. The outer surface of the *chorten* have eroded over time and the *chorten* have lost their original form. The base of the *chorten* is embedded in the path. The *chorten* have *srog-shing* embedded in the domes.

STATE OF PRESERVATION
Showing Signs of Deterioration

SOURCE OF INFORMATION Sonam Angchuk, Tashispa, Lehdo, Khaltse, Ladakh

242

Group of *Chorten* and *Mane* Wall

INVENTORY NO.
KHALTSE / LEHDO / 31 / 2006

Chorten / *Mane* Wall | In Use | Public (Community) | Around 200 years old

SETTING
The *chorten* and *mane* wall are located to the right of the main village road below the *lhato* of the village protector.

SIGNIFICANCE
The *chorten* and *mane* wall were built along the village footpath and are circumambulated by villagers as an act of merit when they travel along this path. The *chorten* are all Changchub *chorten* which symbolize the Buddha's enlightenment.

DESCRIPTION
The site consists of two *chorten* and a *mane* wall built on a high random rubble masonry platform. The *chorten* are built in stone and mud brick masonry with an external layer of mud plaster and whitewash, most of which has eroded over time. There is a long linear *mane* wall built in dry stone masonry with inscribed *mane* stones placed on the

horizontal surface. The *chorten* stand at either ends of the *mane* wall. There is a tall *tarchen* next to the *chorten*. The construction of the road has damaged the foundation of the structures and some sections at the base of the *chorten* have collapsed.

STATE OF PRESERVATION
Showing Signs of Deterioration

SOURCE OF INFORMATION Sonam Angchuk (Tashispa), Lehdo, Khaltse, Ladakh

Group of *Chorten* and *Mane* Wall

INVENTORY NO.
KHALTSE / LEHDO / 32 / 2006

Chorten / Mane Wall | In Use | Public (Community) | Around 300 years old

SETTING
The *chorten* and *mane* wall are located to the right of the road in the Singethang hamlet of the village with the village school nearby. The site is surrounded by village houses and a huge walnut tree to the east.

SIGNIFICANCE
The *chorten* and *mane* wall were built 300 years ago in the Singethang hamlet of the village and are circumambulated by villagers as an act of merit when they travel along this path. The *chorten* is a Changchub *chorten* which symbolizes the Buddha's enlightenment.

DESCRIPTION
The site consists of two *chorten* and a *mane* wall. The *chorten* are built on a tiered random rubble masonry platform in stone and mud brick masonry with mud mortar and have an external layer of mud plaster and whitewash.

SOURCE OF INFORMATION Rigzin Namgyal, Lehdo, Khaltse, Ladakh

Between the *chorten* there is a long linear mane wall built in dry stone masonry with inscribed *mane* stones placed on the horizontal surface.

STATE OF PRESERVATION
Advanced State of Decay

Group of *Chorten* and *Mane* Wall

INVENTORY NO.
KHALTSE / LEHDO / 33 / 2006

Chorten / Mane Wall | In Use | Public (Community) | Around 250 years old

SETTING
The *chorten* and *mane* wall are located on the right side of the road just before the Singethang settlement near a water reservoir.

SIGNIFICANCE
The *chorten* and *mane* wall were built along the village road around 250 years ago. Many of the *chorten* and *mane* walls in Lehdo are said to have been built on the orders of a king. The *chorten* and *mane* wall are circumambulated by villagers as an act of merit when they travel along this path. The *chorten* is a Changchub *chorten* which symbolizes the Buddha's enlightenment.

DESCRIPTION
The site consists of a *chorten* and a *mane* wall. The *chorten* is built in stone and mud brick masonry in mud mortar with an external layer of mud plaster and whitewash. The *mane*

SOURCE OF INFORMATION Rigzin Namgyal, Lehdo, Khaltse, Ladakh

wall is a rectangular dry stone masonry wall with inscribed *mane* stones placed on the horizontal surface. The *mane* wall has collapsed in some section with the building of the road nearby.

STATE OF PRESERVATION
Danger of Disappearance

Gonbopa House

INVENTORY NO.
KHALTSE / LEHDO / 34 / 2006

Vernacular Building | In Use | Private (Individual) | Around 300 years old

SETTING
The Gonbopa house is located at the beginning of the Singethang hamlet near a small water reservoir on the right side of the road. A huge walnut tree grows next to the house.

SIGNIFICANCE
The house was built by an ancestor of the Gonbopa family around 300 years ago and successive generations have continued to reside here. The house is built in traditional style and is a fine example of vernacular architecture in the village.

DESCRIPTION
The Gonbopa house is a large triple storeyed building built in random rubble masonry at the ground and first floor and in mud brick masonry at the second floor. The ground floor is used primarily for storage and for housing animals. The ground floor has no window openings while the first floor has narrow windows with tiered timber lintels. The second floor has large timber *rabsals* with glass panes. The first and second floors constitute the family's living areas. The family chapel is located on the first floor and this chamber has wall paintings as well as images of Chanrazig and a collection of Buddhist cannons (*Bum*) believed to have been brought back from Tibet. A stone staircase leads from the ground to the first floor from where a wooden staircase leads to the second floor. The second floor has a gallery all around. The gallery is supported on timber columns. The house has a traditional roof made of timber beams, joists, *taalu*, grass and compacted mud supported on wooden columns and brackets. Prayer flags are posted on the roof most of which is covered by the old walnut tree which grows near the house.

STATE OF PRESERVATION
Showing Signs of Deterioration

Lehdo

244

Lingshed

Lingshed has two different meanings - it is called Lingzhi meaning '*comprised of four hamlets*', and it is also called Lingnyed that means means '*the place of hunting*'. The village consists of five small hamlets namely - Gonpa Khor, Tau, Yos, Kartse and Tiling Berber. There are 76 households in Lingshed today.

Listed by: Deldan Angmo and Jassu Singh
Year: 2004

Group of *Chorten* and *Rigsum Gonbo* (Pagthabe *Chorten*)

INVENTORY NO.
KHALTSE / LINGSHED / 01 / 2004

Chorten / Rigsum Gonbo | In Use | Public (Community / Lingshed *Gonpa*) | Around 550 years old

SETTING

The group of *chorten* is oriented to the south and is located along the village pathway which leads to the *gonpa*. These are located on a rocky cliff and are surrounded by shrubs and boulders. The *gonpa* is located further up to the north.

SIGNIFICANCE

The *chorten* are believed to have been built around 550 years ago at the same time as the Lingshed *gonpa*. The *rigsum gonbo* was built to protect the village from natural calamities and misfortune. The *chorten* are circumambulated by villagers in order to accumulate merit as they proceed to the *gonpa*. These are largely Changchub *chorten* and symbolize the Buddha's enlightenment.

DESCRIPTION

The site comprises of a group of four Changchub *chorten*, a Kagan *chorten* and a *rigsum gonbo*. The *rigsum gonbo* is housed in a stone and mud brick masonry enclosure with a traditional timber roof and a large opening to the south. Within the enclosure are three *chorten* painted in the traditional orange/yellow, white and blue. Near the *rigsum gonbo* are four large Changchub *chorten*. The *chorten* are built on random rubble masonry bases and are constructed in stone and mud brick masonry with an external layer of mud plaster and whitewash. The domes of the *chorten* have a *chugsum khorlo* symbolizing the 13 steps towards enlightenment.

STATE OF PRESERVATION
Showing Signs of Deterioration

SOURCE OF INFORMATION Tsering Yang skit Serger, Lingshed, Khaltse, Ladakh

NIRLAC

Pagthabe *Chorten*

INVENTORY NO.
KHALTSE / LINGSHED / 02 / 2004

Chorten | In Use | Public (Lingshed *Gonpa*) | Around 200 years old

SETTING

The *chorten* is oriented to the south and is located inside the local school complex in between the Government school building and the Lingshed solar school building. There is a small bush of wild roses growing nearby. It is approached along a footpath which diverts from the main path that leads to the village.

SIGNIFICANCE

The *chorten* is a small Changchub *chorten* which was built around 200 years ago as an act of merit. It symbolizes the Buddha's enlightenment. It is still worshipped by the villagers.

DESCRIPTION

The *chorten* is built over a square random rubble masonry base. It is built in stone and mud brick masonry with mud mortar and is mud plastered and whitewashed on the

exterior. There is a tall *srog-shing* embedded in the centre of the dome to which are tied several *khadag*. It is located within a ruined enclosure which has almost disappeared.

STATE OF PRESERVATION

Showing Signs of Deterioration

SOURCE OF INFORMATION Tashi Yangskit, Lingshed, Khaltse, Ladakh

Lingshed

249

Mane Ringmo *Chorten*

INVENTORY NO.
KHALTSE / LINGSHED / 03 / 2004

Chorten / *Mane* Wall | In Use | Public (Community) | Around 300 years old

SETTING

The *chorten* is oriented to the south and is located near the *gonpa* forest land and the medical centre building. It can be approached along a footpath which diverts from the main path leading to the village. The *gonpa* forest lies to the north. There are wild rose bushes near the structures.

SIGNIFICANCE

The *chorten* and *mane* walls are believed to have been after the *gonpa* and were built as an act of merit. The *chorten* are all Changchub *chorten* and symbolize the Buddha's enlightenment. The *chorten* and *mane* walls are circumambulated by villagers to gather merit.

DESCRIPTION

The site consists of a group of seven Changchub *chorten* and three *mane* walls. The *chorten* are built in stone and mud brick masonry over a square plinth and are mud

plastered and whitewashed externally. Some of the *chorten* have a *srog-shing* posted on the dome. The *mane* walls are linear dry stone masonry walls with inscribed *mane* stones placed on the horizontal surface. The *mane* walls and *chorten* are placed in one row on an east-west axis.

STATE OF PRESERVATION

Advanced State of Decay

SOURCE OF INFORMATION Tashi Yangskit, Lingshed, Khaltse, Ladakh

Chorten Nyis-tsag

INVENTORY NO.
KHALTSE / LINGSHED / 04 / 2004

Chorten / Mane Wall | In Use | Public (Lingshed *Gonpa*) | Around 300 years old

SETTING
The *chorten* are oriented to the south and are located on the slope of a hill along the pathway which leads towards the *gonpa* from the village below. There are some rose bushes next to the *chorten*.

SIGNIFICANCE
The *chorten* are called 'Mane-Nyis- tsag' as they are built side by side near the circular shaped *mane* walls.

DESCRIPTION
The site consists of two *chorten* located between two *mane* walls. The *chorten* are small in size with square bases. The top portion of the *chorten* has collapsed making them difficult to identify. The *mane* walls are cylindrical in shape and located towards north and south of the *chorten*. They are built is stone masonry.

STATE OF PRESERVATION
Danger of Disappearance

SOURCE OF INFORMATION Lundup Norgyal, Lingshed, Khaltse, Ladakh

Lingshed

250

Bandoma *Lhato* and Bandopa House

INVENTORY NO.
KHALTSE / LINGSHED / 05 / 2004

Lhato / Vernacular Building | In Use | Private (Individual)

SETTING
The house is oriented to the south and is located at the foot of a small hill east of the *chorten* Nyis-tsag. There are agricultural fields nearby.

SIGNIFICANCE
The house was built by ancestors of the Bandopa family and the family continues to reside there. The house is built in the traditional style and is a good example of vernacular architecture in the village. The *lhato* is dedicated to the guardian deity of the Bandopa family and hence called Bandoma *lhato*. The *rigsum gonbo* was built to protect the house from natural calamities and misfortune.

DESCRIPTION
The Bandopa house is a large structure built on a random plan. The ground floor is built in random rubble masonry while the first floor is built in mud brick masonry with mud mortar. The window openings are all on the southern facade of the building. On the first floor, there is an open verandah facing the south. The *lhato* is built on a large boulder in the middle of the western facade. The boulder is integrated into the building. The *lhato* is built in mud brick masonry and is mud plastered and whitewashed on the exterior. It has juniper branches tied with *khadag* on the top. The roof is a traditional roof built of timber joists, *taalu*, grass and a layer of compacted mud. There is a *rigsum gonbo* on the hill right above the house. This comprises of three small *chorten* built over a random rubble masonry platform.

STATE OF PRESERVATION
Showing Signs of Deterioration

SOURCE OF INFORMATION Tashi Yangskit, Lingshed, Khaltse, Ladakh

Group of *Chorten* and *Mane* Walls

INVENTORY NO.
KHALTSE / LINGSHED / 06 / 2004

Chorten / *Mane* Wall | In Use | Public (Community) | Around 300 years old

SETTING
The *chorten* and *mane* walls are oriented to the south and are located along the village stream which flows below the *gonpa*. The stream flows to the north of the site and the Phagirpa house is located south of the *chorten*.

SIGNIFICANCE
The *chorten* and *mane* walls were built in the past as an act of merit and are still circumambulated by villagers to accumulate merit. The *chorten* is a Changchub *chorten* symbolizing the Buddha's enlightenment.

DESCRIPTION
The site consists of a Changchub *chorten* and two *mane* walls. The *chorten* is built in stone and mud brick masonry and is mud plastered and whitewashed on the exterior. The dome of the *chorten* has a *chugsum khorlo* of baked tiles. The *mane* walls are irregular in shape and contain a large

SOURCE OF INFORMATION Lundup Norgyal, Lingshed, Khaltse, Ladakh

number of engraved *mane* stones. The walls are made of loosely piled stones.

STATE OF PRESERVATION
Danger of Disappearance

251

Bothepa House and *Chorten*

INVENTORY NO.
KHALTSE / LINGSHED / 07 / 2004

Vernacular Building / *Chorten* | Abandoned | Private (Individual) | Around 120 years old

SETTING
The house is oriented to the northwest and is located at a higher level than the settlement on a hill. It lies southwest of the *gonpa*.

SIGNIFICANCE
The house is one of the oldest houses in the village and was built by ancestors of the Bothepa family. It is built in the traditional style and is a good example of vernacular architecture in the village. The *chorten* was built in the past as an act of merit and is a Changchub *chorten* symbolizing the Buddha's enlightenment.

DESCRIPTION
The Bothepa house is a large double storeyed building built in stone masonry. The front facade faces the northwest and has small window openings with wooden frames. Externally, the house is mud plastered and whitewashed. The entrance

SOURCE OF INFORMATION Stanzin Dolma, Lingshed, Khaltse, Ladakh

to the house is from the southeast. The ground floor was used for housing animals while the first floor housed the family's living quarters. The house has a traditional roof comprising of timber beams, joists, *taalu*, grass and a layer of compacted mud. The roof is used for storing fodder and firewood for the winter. Near the house, to the southwest, is a small Changchub *chorten* built in stone masonry which is mud plastered and whitewashed externally. However, the outer layer of mud plaster and whitewash of both the *chorten* and the house has largely eroded.

STATE OF PRESERVATION
Advanced State of Decay

Sharchog *Chorten*, *Lhato* and *Rigsum Gonbo*

INVENTORY NO.
KHALTSE / LINGSHED / 08 / 2004

Chorten / Rigsum Gonbo | In Use | Public (Lingshed *Gonpa*) | Around 550 years old

STATE OF PRESERVATION
Advanced State of Decay

SETTING

The *chorten*, *lhato* and *rigsum gonbo* are oriented to the south and are located on a hill above the settlement. The village is located some distance away.

SIGNIFICANCE

The *chorten* and the *rigsum gonbo* are believed to date back to the same period as the Lingshed *gonpa* i.e. around 550 years old. The *chorten* is a Changchub *chorten* and symbolizes the Buddha's enlightenment. The *rigsum gonbo* was built to protect the village from natural calamities and other disasters. The *lhato* is dedicated to the guardian deity of the village and its contents are renewed with ceremony every year by the villagers.

DESCRIPTION

The site comprises of a large Changchub *chorten*, a *lhato* and a *rigsum gonbo*. The *chorten* is built in stone masonry on a large square rand rubble masonry base and is mud plastered and whitewashed on the exterior. Both the *chorten* and *lhato* stand on a rocky outcrop. The *lhato* is a small cubical structure built in stone masonry and is mud plastered and whitewashed externally. There are ceremonial offerings of juniper twigs, and *khadag* placed on the top of the *lhato*. The *rigsum gonbo* consists of a small enclosure with walls on three sides and open to the front. Within the enclosure are three *chorten* on a common platform. The *rigsum gonbo* is built in stone and mud brick masonry and is mud plastered and whitewashed on the exterior. It has a traditional roof above.

SOURCE OF INFORMATION Tsering Yang skit Serger, Lingshed, Khaltse, Ladakh

Chorten

INVENTORY NO.
KHALTSE / LINGSHED / 09 / 2004

Chorten | In Use | Public (Community)

SETTING
The *chorten* is oriented to the southeast and is located below the *gonpa* en route to the village. It is surrounded by agricultural fields and willow trees.

SIGNIFICANCE
The *chorten* is located along the path leading from the *gonpa* to the village and is circumambulated by villagers as an act of merit when travelling along this path. The *chorten* is a Changchub *chorten*, and symbolizes the Buddha's enlightenment. The *chorten* is circumambulated by villagers to accumulate merit.

DESCRIPTION
The *chorten* is built over a square stone masonry base and is built in stone masonry with a thick layer of mud plaster on its exterior surface. The base panels of the *chorten* are whitewashed and have red markings along the corners.

There is a *srog-shing* embedded in the dome of the *chorten*. The *chorten* is built over a small mound near the agricultural fields.

STATE OF PRESERVATION
Showing Signs of Deterioration

SOURCE OF INFORMATION Tashi Yangskit, Lingshed, Khaltse, Ladakh

Lingshed

253

Gyapo Dungsten *Chorten*

INVENTORY NO.
KHALTSE / LINGSHED / 10 / 2004

Chorten | Abandoned | Public (Community)

SETTING
The *chorten* is oriented to the southwest and is located on a hill above the village. It lies east of the Berbera house.

SIGNIFICANCE
The *chorten* contains the relics of king according to its name. It is a Changchub *chorten*, symbolizing the Buddha's enlightenment.

DESCRIPTION
The *chorten* is built on a small mound near the Berbera house. It is built in stone masonry and is mud plastered on the exterior. The external layer of whitewash has largely eroded. There is a *srog-shing* embedded in the dome of the *chorten*.

STATE OF PRESERVATION
Advanced State of Decay

SOURCE OF INFORMATION Sonam Dolma, Lingshed, Khaltse, Ladakh

Goypa House

INVENTORY NO.
KHALTSE / LINGSHED / 11 / 2004

Vernacular Building | In Use | Private (Individual)

SETTING
The Goypa house is oriented to the east and is located near agricultural fields with other village houses nearby.

SIGNIFICANCE
The Goypa house is one of the larger houses in the village and is built in the traditional style. It is a good example of vernacular architecture in the village.

DESCRIPTION
The house is a large horizontal mass with an interesting facade. It is three storeys high and appears to rise in tiers from the front facade stepping away towards the rear of the building. There are two open chambers in the front for housing animals. There are open terraces at each level. The family's living spaces are located on the first and second floors. There are small window openings with timber frames on the ground and first floor and larger openings on the second floor. The windows and the parapet are bordered in red color. The house is built in stone and mud brick

masonry and is mud plastered and whitewashed on the exterior. There are red markings in the corners to protect the house against the *tsan*. It has a traditional roof supported on timber columns and beams.

STATE OF PRESERVATION
Fair

SOURCE OF INFORMATION Stanzin Dolma Tsewangma, Lingshed, Khaltse, Ladakh

Garbi *Mane*

INVENTORY NO.
KHALTSE / LINGSHED / 12 / 2004

Mane Wall | In Use | Public (Community)

SETTING
The Garbi *mane* is oriented to the south and is located in the lower part of the village. It is built near the agricultural fields and is along the village pathway.

SIGNIFICANCE
The *mane* wall is located along the village path and is circumambulated by villagers to accumulate merit.

DESCRIPTION
The *mane* wall is a dry masonry wall of an irregular shape located next to the village stream. It has *mane* stones placed on its horizontal surface.

STATE OF PRESERVATION
Showing Signs of Deterioration

SOURCE OF INFORMATION Stanzin Dolma, Lingshed, Khaltse, Ladakh

Pangong *Lhato* and Shalangpa House

INVENTORY NO.
KHALTSE / LINGSHED / 13 / 2004

Vernacular Building / *Lhato* | In Use | Private (Individual) | Around 500 years old

SETTING
The Shalangpa house is oriented to the south and is located south of the Goypa house. It is surrounded by agricultural fields on all the sides.

SIGNIFICANCE
The Shalangpa family was one of the first to settle in the village. According to legend, some hunters were hunting deer and came to this village. They decided to settle here and began skinning the hunted deer at this spot, and hence the name of the family 'Shalangpa'. The house was built around 500 years ago and additions have been made to the original structure over time. The Shalangpa family continues to reside in the house. There is a small *lhato* near the house dedicated to the guardian deity of the family Pangong.

DESCRIPTION
The Shalangpa house is a double storeyed building built in stone and mud brick masonry with mud mortar. The oldest section of the house is to the rear. The front portion is single storeyed while the rear section of the house is double storeyed. The old house has hardly any window openings and the doorways are small and low in height, while the new house has relatively larger window openings. The roof is built in the traditional style and comprises of wooden beams, joists, *taalu*, grass and a layer of compacted mud on the top. The roof top has huge stacks of firewood and also some prayer flags tied from one corner to the other. There is a small *lhato* is located to the east of the house. It is cubical in shape with a sloping roof above. It is built in mud brick masonry. It is mud plastered and whitewashed externally with red markings at the corners.

STATE OF PRESERVATION
Advanced State of Decay

Lingshed

255

SOURCE OF INFORMATION Stanzin Dolma Tsewangma, Lingshed, Khaltse, Ladakh

Lung Ze *Mane*

INVENTORY NO.
KHALTSE / LINGSHED / 14 / 2004

Chorten / *Mane* Wall | In Use | Public (Community)

SETTING
The Lung Ze *mane* are oriented to the south and are located in the middle of the agricultural fields towards the lower part of the village.

STATE OF PRESERVATION
Advanced State of Decay

SIGNIFICANCE
It is believed that a reincarnation of Lama Panchen Rinpoche advised the villagers to build these *chorten* in the middle of the fields as a protection against drought. The name Lung Ze means in the 'middle of the fields'. Both the *chorten* are Changchub *chorten* and symbolize the Buddha's enlightenment.

DESCRIPTION
The site consists of two *chorten* placed at a little distance from each other and a *mane* wall, located near the larger *chorten*. Both the *chorten* are built on a square base in stone masonry and are mud plastered and whitewashed externally. The *mane* wall is built in dry stone masonry and the *mane* stones are whitewashed.

SOURCE OF INFORMATION Stanzin Dolma Tsewangma, Lingshed, Khaltse, Ladakh

Chorten Chugpe *Mane*

INVENTORY NO.
KHALTSE / LINGSHED / 15 / 2004

Chorten | In Use | Public (Community)

SETTING
The *chorten* Chugpe *mane* is oriented to the south and is located southwest of the Shalangpa house. It is surrounded by fields and a narrow pathway.

STATE OF PRESERVATION
Showing Signs of Deterioration

SIGNIFICANCE
The *chorten* is a Changchub *chorten*, symbolizing the Buddha's enlightenment. It is circumambulated by villagers to accumulate merit.

DESCRIPTION
The site comprises of two *chorten,* one of which has been recently repaired by the villagers while the second lies in complete ruins. The larger *chorten* is built in stone masonry and is mud plastered externally. The base panel of this *chorten* is whitewashed. There is a *srog-shing* embedded in the dome of the *chorten*.

SOURCE OF INFORMATION Stanzin Dolma Tsewangma, Lingshed, Khaltse, Ladakh

Lingshed Palace (Ringsten *Khar* / Sumur *Khar*)

INVENTORY NO.
KHALTSE / LINGSHED / 16 / 2004

Fort / Palace | Abandoned | Public (State / Community) | Around 550 years old

SETTING
The three ruins are oriented to the southeast and are located on a rocky outcrop along the slope of a mountainside. They are located south of the *gonpa*, lower down the village.

SIGNIFICANCE
The fragments of the former fort and palace are scattered across three locations in the village and are known as Sumur *Khar*, Ringsten *Khar* and *Khargog*. They form the remains of the fort and palace which date back to the reign of King Tashi Namgyal (1500 – 1535 A.D.). Tashi Namgyal inherited the kingdom from his father Bhagan after blinding his elder brother and rightful heir to the throne Lhawang Namgyal. Subsequently, Lhawang appears to have ruled over lower Ladakh under the suzerainty of his brother with palaces at Lingshed and Temisgang.

DESCRIPTION
The fort is in complete ruins today and only some fragments survive. These include remains of walls which hint at the scale of the complex. The spaces within the walls are now filled with debris. Wide retaining walls built in stone masonry act as the foundation whereas the upper levels are built in rammed earth.

STATE OF PRESERVATION
Danger of Disappearance

SOURCE OF INFORMATION Venerable Sonam Wangdus Phupa, Lingshed, Khaltse, Ladakh, 194106, J&K

Lingshed

257

Phunis Gang *Lhato*

INVENTORY NO.
KHALTSE / LINGSHED / 17 / 2004

Lhato | In Use | Public (Community)

SETTING
The *lhato* is oriented to the south and is located some thorny bushes and bushes of wild roses. It is surrounded by fields on all sides.

SIGNIFICANCE
The Phunis Gang *lhato* is dedicated to the protector deity of the village, Phunis Gang. The offerings of juniper plants, *khadag* etc. in the *lhato* are renewed every year by the villagers amid ceremony and rituals.

DESCRIPTION
The *lhato* is a cubical structure built in mud brick masonry and mud plastered externally. The *lhato* tapers towards the top and there are ritual offering of juniper twigs and *khadag* placed on the top. The roof of the *lhato* is built of *taalu* and compacted mud over which rests a smaller cubical structure within which are placed the ritual offerings.

STATE OF PRESERVATION
Showing Signs of Deterioration

SOURCE OF INFORMATION Stanzin Dolma, Lingshed, Khaltse, Ladakh

Tashi Odbar *Gonpa* (Lingshed *Gonpa*)

INVENTORY NO.
KHALTSE / LINGSHED / 18 / 2004

Gonpa | In Use | Public (Lingshed *Gonpa*) | Around 1000 years old

SETTING

The *gonpa* is oriented to the south and is located on a hill at the beginning of the village towards the north.

SIGNIFICANCE

According to legend, the great translator Lotsawa Rinchen Zangpo, after building the *gonpa* at Wanla came to Lingshed. On his way, he spent several years in the caves near Yulchung which is named after him - Rinchen Srase *tsamphuk*. There he wrote the *kangyur* and it is believed that after he got tired writing it with his hands, he used his foot. The *kangyur* is named as Aalongma on account of the ring-like shapes that he introduced at the end of each page. When he reached Lingshed, he built the first *dukhang* which is called Tsankhang. Later, Kilkhor *dukhang* and many shrines were built around this shrine. Subsequently, Changsem Sherab Zangpo expanded the *gonpa* and established the Gelugpa order. Among the images in the *gonpa*, the principal one is the magnificent image of a tutelary deity (Berava) about one foot in height, which is said to have spoken. This can only be viewed once a year on the 15th day of the 4th month of Tibetan calendar. Prior to the foundation of the monastery, it is said that a great lama after attaining his education from Tibet went to Zanskar. On his return from Zanskar via Lingshed, he saw a fire burning up on a small rock next to the Lotsawa shrine. It was taken as an auspicious sign and later a monastery was built over it. A small Changchub *chorten* was built over the rock and named as Tashi Odbar which can be still seen in the temple. The name of the monastery derives from this rock. The successive reincarnations of Ven. Ngari Rinpoche act as incumbents of the monastery.

DESCRIPTION

The monastic complex is a large maze of buildings built over a hillock. The main monastery is entered from east and is located on top of a hill with the monks cells built along the lower slopes. The *gonpa* is approached through a narrow footpath leading past *chorten* and prayer wheels. The wooden gateway opens onto a large courtyard with galleries on three sides and a parapet wall towards the south. The walls of the galleries are painted in different bands of color and auspicious signs. The roof above the galleries is of the traditional style with decorated wooden columns, beams, joists, *taalu* and compacted mud. From the main entrance a corridor leads to the north where a flight of steps leads to the first floor. Towards the right is a half covered verandah and porch of the main *dukhang* named as Tsogkhang. Monks gather here every morning to perform prayers. The *dukhang* is a large hall with 16 decorated wooden columns and brackets supporting the roof above. It has timber flooring and to the rear of the room is an elaborate wooden frame housing images of Paldan Lhamo and Jigjed. There are a number of wooden shelves on either side of the walls on which are placed Buddhist cannons. The walls are elaborately painted.

To the left of the main corridor is a small chamber which is the Kilkhor *lhakhang*, the oldest shrine in the *gonpa*. The *lhakhang* has timber flooring and the walls are covered with wall paintings depicting images of various guardian deities and images of Buddha. It has four decorated wooden columns, brackets and beams holding the traditional roof above. The shrine houses the Changchub *chorten*, built on the Tashi Odbar rock, which is placed in a corner of the room. In the centre of the room, there is a Kilkhor, or *mandala,* in the form of a three dimensional image encased in a glass frame. The other corner has a wooden frame housing images of various Bodhisattvas including Chug-Shig-Zhal. The *chorten* has been recently mud plastered and whitewashed. The kitchen is also located on the first floor, left of the wooden staircase which leads to the second floor. The head lama's living room and guest rooms are towards the right. Towards the left is the new *dukhang* with new wall paintings and decorations. There is a large roof terrace overlooking the entire village. There is a large open courtyard in the centre of the roof of the monastery. Towards the lower section of the monastery are the small houses for the resident monks. Each structure is individual with separate entrances, kitchens, living rooms and a verandah. The structures form an interesting arrangement with a very well planned circulation system and quarters built in single rows intercepted with pathways. The window and door openings are small with wooden frames and shutters. All the openings as well as the parapet are bordered in red and black. The top most level of the monastery has large window openings with glass panes and wooden frames. Externally, the *gonpa* is mud plastered and whitewashed.

STATE OF PRESERVATION
Showing Signs of Deterioration

SOURCE OF INFORMATION Venerable Sonam Wangdus Phupa, Lingshed, Khaltse, Ladakh

Pharkapa House

INVENTORY NO.
KHALTSE / LINGSHED / 19 / 2004

Vernacular Building | In Use | Private (Individual) | Around 200 years old

SETTING
The Pharkapa house is oriented to the southwest and is located below the *gonpa* beyond the agricultural fields. There are some willow trees nearby and other village houses at some distance from the house.

SIGNIFICANCE
The Pharkapa house was built by ancestors of the Pharkapa family around 200 years ago. Since then, successive generations have resided in the house. It is built in the traditional style and is an example of vernacular architecture in the village. The house has a *rigsum gonbo* over the entrance to protect the family from misfortune and evil forces.

DESCRIPTION
The Pharkapa house is a large double storeyed building with an interesting facade. There is a *rigsum gonbo* above the entrance door on the front facade. The front facade also has a small open chamber used by the family to feed their

cattle. The ground floor is used for housing animals and storing fodder, while the first floor is used as the family's living quarters. The ground floor is built in random rubble masonry while the first floor is built in mud brick masonry with mud mortar. The first floor has an open verandah and small window openings. The rooms have mud flooring. The house has a traditional roof made of wooden beams, joists, *taalu*, grass and compacted mud. It is supported on timber beams and columns. The roof has a low parapet and firewood for the winter is stacked along the edge of the parapet.

STATE OF PRESERVATION
Advanced State of Decay

SOURCE OF INFORMATION Venerable Sonam Wangdus, Lingshed, Khaltse, Ladakh

Chorten

INVENTORY NO.
KHALTSE / LINGSHED / 20 / 2004

Chorten / Prayer Wheel | In Use | Public (Lingshed *Gonpa*) | Around 550 years old

SETTING
The *chorten* are oriented to the south and are located at the entrance to the monastery, north of the pathway. Some of the *chorten* are located behind the monastery building.

SIGNIFICANCE
The *chorten* are believed to have been built at the same time as the *gonpa* in the 15th century. The prayer wheels were added later. The *chorten* are largely Changchub *chorten* symbolizing the Buddha's enlightenment. The *chorten* and prayer wheels form a part of the sacred geography of the *gonpa* with devotees circumambulating the *chorten* and rotating the prayer wheels as they move around the complex.

DESCRIPTION
The group comprises of five Changchub *chorten*, one Kagan *chorten* and two large prayer wheels. The largest of the Changchub *chorten* is adjacent to the Kagan *chorten*. Another *chorten* is surrounded by an enclosure with a traditional roof on the top. The borders and the parapet are highlighted in red. The *chorten* are built in stone masonry and are mud plastered and whitewashed externally. They have a linear *chugsum khorlo* on the dome which symbolizes the 13 steps towards enlightenment. The Kagan *chorten* consists of two thick parallel walls built in stone and mud brick masonry over which rests a large Changchub *chorten*. The ceiling of the passage is in the shape of a *mandala*. The prayer wheels are large cylindrical shaped metal drums rotating around a central axis.

STATE OF PRESERVATION
Advanced State of Decay

SOURCE OF INFORMATION Venerable Sonam Wangdus Phupha, Lingshed, Khaltse, Ladakh

Zong-ge Bawo (*Tsamskhang*)

INVENTORY NO.
KHALTSE / LINGSHED / 21 / 2004

Landscape (Sacred Cave) | Abandoned | Public (Lingshed *Gonpa*)

SETTING
The caves are located northwest of the monastic complex at the entrance to the village.

SIGNIFICANCE / CULTURAL BELIEFS
It is believed that in the past great monks used to meditate in these caves and hence they are also called *tsamskhang*. Another view holds that early inhabitants of Lingshed used to live in these caves. As the caves were used by monks in the past, villagers consider them sacred and offer prayers here. Prayer flags are also offered once a year.

DESCRIPTION
The caves are scattered along the side of the mountains. The mountain itself is made of an agglomerate of clay and stones and has eroded considerably over time. Today, there are just five caves left and others have possibly collapsed. The walls are covered with layer of the soot deposits and are at different levels.

CULTURAL LINKAGE / CULTURAL PRACTICES
These caves are associated with similar caves in Yulchung, called Rinchen Sras se *tsamphuk* which are believed to have been used in the 11th century by Lotsava Rinchen Zangpo.

STATE OF PRESERVATION
Danger of Disappearance

Lingshed

261

Mangyu

Mangyu is situated about 75 kms from Leh. The original name of the village was Smangyu as the valley was full of medicinal herbs and hot springs. The village is divided into six small hamlets namely Lhangkhar, Gabforto, Farka, Sapta, Zum and Khantse. Today, there are about 71 households in Mangyu.

{*Source: Tsering Dorjey [Shukpan Khangbu]*}

Listed by: Deldan Angmo and Jassu Singh
Year: 2004

Tsa-Tsa Puri
Chorten

INVENTORY NO.
KHALTSE / MANGYU / 01 / 2004

Chorten | In Use | Public (Likir *Gonpa*) | 11th century

SETTING

The *chorten* is located inside the *gonpa* complex in the village of Mangyu. The *chorten* forms a part of the *gonpa* complex which is located to the southwest and is surrounded by other *chorten* and residential structures. The *chorten* is reached after passing a long line of prayer wheels.

SIGNIFICANCE

The Tsa-Tsa Puri *chorten* is believed to have been built at the same time as the Mangyu *gonpa* i.e. 11th century and is linked with the legendary Lotsava Rinchen Zangpo. The style of paintings inside the *chorten* represent an early period of Buddhist art in Ladakh. For the villagers, the *chorten* is also significant as it is believed that bringing the body of a deceased person under this *chorten* garners the same merit as that accrued from performing pujas for the deceased.

DESCRIPTION

The Tsa-Tsa Puri chorten is built in the shape of a *mandala* and is supported on wide thick mud walls. Externally, the *chorten* has traces of mud plaster and whitewash, though most of the external surface has eroded. There are a number of niches on the surface of the *chorten* and an entrance way that leads into the *chorten*. The interior of the *chorten* is hollow and the walls are painted with original images of a thousand miniatures Buddhas. Within the *chorten* is a smaller *chorten* supported on wooden beams and resting against the side walls. The panels inside the smaller chorten have paintings of Lotsava Rinchen Zangpo and other important deities. The lower portion of the *chorten* has been built in rammed earth construction with juniper beams supporting the structure on top which is built in mud bricks.

STATE OF PRESERVATION
Advanced State of Decay

Mangyu

264

Likir *Tashag*

INVENTORY NO.
KHALTSE / MANGYU / 02 / 2004

Vernacular Building | Abandoned | Public (Likir *Gonpa*) | Around 200 - 250 years old

SETTING
The Likir *tashag* is oriented towards the south east and is located adjacent to the Chemday *tashag*. Below the *tashag* are the Tsa-Tsa Puri *chorten* and the prayer wheel. To the east lies the Dugyal *gonpa*.

SIGNIFICANCE
The Likir *tashag* were built around 200 - 250 years ago as living quarters for the Likir monks who resided in the village to perform pujas and rituals for the villagers. The monks also maintain the *gonpa*. The *tashag* are today abandoned and falling into ruins.

DESCRIPTION
The Likir *tashag* consists of two blocks used earlier by the monks from Likir. From the main circumambulatory pathway, several stone steps lead through a small wooden door into the buildings. These are simple rectangular structures with small openings in the front facade and an open terrace on the first floor. Both the buildings have the

same plan, form and appearance. The ground floor is constructed in stone masonry while the first floor is built in mud brick masonry with mud mortar. The *tashag* have traditional mud floors and timber roofs. There are prayer flags posts at each corner of the roof.

STATE OF PRESERVATION
Showing Signs of Deterioration

SOURCE OF INFORMATION Tsering Rigzen-Shukpanpa, Mangyu, Khaltse, Ladakh

265

Mangyu

Mangyu *Chorten*

INVENTORY NO.
KHALTSE / MANGYU / 03 / 2004

Chorten | In Use | Public (Community) | Around 200 years old

SETTING
The *chorten* is located in front of the Likir *tashag*, along the circumambulatory pathway of the Lotsava complex. Mangyu *gonpa* lies to the northwest.

SIGNIFICANCE
The *chorten* is believed to be contemporary to the Dugyal *gonpa* located nearby. It is a Changchub *chorten* which symbolizes the Buddha's enlightenment.

DESCRIPTION
Mangyu *chorten* is a Changchub *chorten* built on a square base in stone and mud brick masonry with mud mortar and is mud plastered and whitewashed externally. The *chorten* is unusual because it is enclosed within a small square structure which is open from the front. This enclosure is built in mud brick masonry with mud mortar and is whitewashed externally. This enclosure has two roofs of timber – one built around the base of the *chorten's* dome while the other is built over the top of the dome. Both the

roofs are built in timber. The upper section of the enclosure has one wall on the rear side while the other three sides are open and supported on wooden columns. There is a *chugsum khorlo* over the dome of the chorten which passes through the roof of the enclosure.

STATE OF PRESERVATION
Showing Signs of Deterioration

SOURCE OF INFORMATION Tsering Rigzen Shukpanpa, Mangyu, Khaltse, Ladakh

Dugyal *Gonpa*

INVENTORY NO.
KHALTSE / MANGYU / 04 / 2004

Gonpa | In Use | Public (Chemday *Gonpa*) | Around 300 years old

SETTING
The Dugyal *gonpa* is oriented towards the north west and is located northwest of the Lotsava complex and west of Nagldan chorten.

SIGNIFICANCE
The *gonpa* is believed to have been built about 300 years ago and is today under Chemday *gonpa*. Monks from Chemday perform prayers and rituals within the temple for the welfare of the villagers. The *gonpa* is one of two found in the village of Mangyu, the other being the Nang-Bar-Nang Dzad.

DESCRIPTION
The Dugyal *gonpa* is a large double storeyed structure built over a rectangular plan along the slope of a hill. The *gonpa* is entered from the west and the entrance leads into a newly built courtyard. A wooden doorway leads from the courtyard into a large temple that houses an image of Guru Rinpoche along with the Kangyur (canons) and Bum. The

walls of this temple are painted with images of deities. A narrow dark corridor leads to the first floor which opens onto the roof terrace. A door towards the northwestern side opens into a large prayer hall housing images of Guru Rinpoche, Jo Rinpoche, Chanrazig and a silver *chorten* studded with precious stones. The first floor has an elaborately decorated wooden *rabsal* facing the southeast. There are small windows on the south and east which have wooden tiered lintels. The parapet painted in black.

STATE OF PRESERVATION
Showing Signs of Deterioration

SOURCE OF INFORMATION Tsering Rigzen Shukpanpa, Mangyu, Khaltse, Ladakh

Cholgog *Chorten*

INVENTORY NO.
KHALTSE / MANGYU / 05 / 2004

Chorten | Abandoned | Public (Community) | Around 300 years old

SETTING
The Cholgog *chorten* are oriented towards the south and are located towards the north of the village. The *chorten* are surrounded by barren land and to the rear are mountains.

SIGNIFICANCE
The Cholgog *chorten* are believed to be around 300 years old and are considered to be one of the oldest groups of *chorten* in the village after the Lotsava *chorten*. It is said that there was an old *lhakhang* near the *chorten*, of which only the ruined walls survive. The *lhakhang* was badly damaged during a flood which struck the village a long time ago.

DESCRIPTION
The site consists of a group of two or three *chorten* and the ruins of a square structure which is probably the *lhakhang*.

The *chorten* are built in stone and mud brick masonry with traces of mud plaster and whitewash on the external surface. The *chorten* are almost in ruins.

STATE OF PRESERVATION
Advanced State of Decay

SOURCE OF INFORMATION Tsering Rigzen Shukpanpa, Mangyu, Khaltse, Ladakh

Group of *Chorten*

INVENTORY NO.
KHALTSE / MANGYU / 06 / 2004

Chorten | In Use | Public (Community) | Around 200 years old

SETTING
The group of *chorten* is oriented to the east and are built along a slope of a hill in front of the Government Middle School. There is a newly built *rigsum gonbo* to the west.

SIGNIFICANCE
The *chorten* are all Changchub *chorten* which symbolize the Buddha's enlightenment. These are circumambulated by villagers as an act of merit.

DESCRIPTION
The site consists of a group of three *chorten* built along the slope of a hill. The *chorten* are all built on a square base and are constructed in stone and mud brick masonry with mud mortar. The exterior is mud plastered and whitewashed. There are small niches on the eastern side of the domes.

STATE OF PRESERVATION
Showing Signs of Deterioration

SOURCE OF INFORMATION Tsering Rigzen Shukpanpa, Mangyu, Khaltse, Ladakh

Chemday *Tashag*

INVENTORY NO.
KHALTSE / MANGYU / 07 / 2004

Vernacular Building | Abandoned | Public (Chemde *Gonpa*) | Around 200 - 250 years old

SETTING
The Chemday *tashag* are oriented towards the southeast and are located in front of the Tsa-Tsa Puri *chorten*, southwest of the Lotsava complex.

SIGNIFICANCE
The Chemday *tashag* were built by the Chemday monastery to house their monks who resided in the village. Of the two structures, one is abandoned while the second is used by the villagers.

DESCRIPTION
The Chemday *tashag* are located along the circumambulatory pathway of the Lotsava complex. There are two structures. The first *tashag* is built in front of the Tsa-Tsa Puri *chorten* and appears to have been recently constructed. It is double storeyed structure with large glass windows facing south. The second building is located west of the Lotsava complex and is an older building. It is a single storey structure with a small wooden doorway and a small window opening. This *tashag* has a high stone masonry plinth while the superstructure is built in mud brick masonry with mud mortar. The structure has a high parapet in mud blocks. The exterior is mud plastered and whitewashed.

STATE OF PRESERVATION
Showing Signs of Deterioration

SOURCE OF INFORMATION Tsering Rigzen Shukpanpa, Mangyu, Khaltse

Nang-Bar-Nang Dzad

INVENTORY NO.
KHALTSE / MANGYU / 08 / 2004

Gonpa | In Use | Public (Likir *Gonpa*) | 12th - 13th century

SETTING

The Nang-Bar-Nang Dzad is oriented towards the southwest and is located amidst residential structures with the Nagldan *chorten* to the southwest.

SIGNIFICANCE

The *dukhang* within the complex, along with the temples at Alchi and Sumda Chun, represent some of the earliest extant Buddhist temples in Ladakh. This group of temples represent an early phase of Buddhist art and architecture in the region, associated with the great Translator Rinchen Zangpo (958 - 1055 A.D.). The wall paintings as well as stucco imagery within these temples are unique in the region having been created, it is believed, by groups of Kashmiri artists who were brought back from Kashmir by the Lotsava to embellish the numerous temples and religious establishments he founded. The two *dukhang* within the complex can be dated to the 12th - 13th century and are dedicated to Vairocana and Shakyamuni Buddha.

DESCRIPTION

A narrow pathway passes through residential buildings and agricultural fields before leading to the *gonpa's* courtyard which has a large *tarchen* in the centre. From the courtyard, a flight of concrete steps leads to the portico of the main shrine dedicated to Nang-Bar-Nang-Dzad (a manifestation of Vairocana). The portico has two wooden decorated columns with wooden brackets supporting the wooden beams and a traditional roof above. An elaborately decorated wooden frame leads inside the shrine. The door frame has been beautifully carved with images of five Tathagatas and floral designs. The shrine is square in plan with two wooden columns and lion shaped wooden brackets. The rear wall has a large niche containing spectacular stucco images around a central image of Vairocana. The other deities in this ensemble include Akshobhya, Ratnasambhava, Amitabha and Amoghasiddhi. These are surrounded by stucco images of flying deities and floral designs painted in different colors. The ceiling contains fragments of textile paintings. The walls on either side of the niche as well as the right wall retain the original painting. The paintings are, today, obscured with soot deposit. The paintings within this *dukhang* include a number of *mandala* of which that of the Vairocana is particularly significant. The flooring is in timber. From the same porch, a small door on the right leads to another small chamber containing a colossal image of Chamba decorated with ornaments, an elaborate *dhoti* and a crown. The walls are covered with images of the thousand miniature Buddhas. There is a small window opposite the image at the level of

its eye. The roof has uneven joists and willows. The Chanrazig *lhakhang* is reached from the same court. It has a separate portico, again with two columns and a richly carved wooden framed doorway. The roof of the *lhakhang* is supported on two wooden columns over which are brackets carved in the shape of a lion. Like the other *lhakhang*, the walls are covered with large *mandala* paintings. The rear wall of the shrine has a large painting of Buddha Shakyamuni which is believed to be the largest in the region dating back to the 11th century. However, it is concealed by a large wooden frame that houses the image of Avalokitesvera and the Kangyur. The roof is built in the traditional style while the floor is a traditional timber floor. The last and the fourth chamber is a small chamber dedicated to the Chamba. It is approached from a door way that leads off the portico of the Nang bar-Nang Dzad *lhakhang*. This *lhakhang* houses a colossal stucco image of Chamba placed on a lotus petal throne. The robes of the image are richly embellished with images if human figures and buildings. The walls are covered with images of a thousand miniatures Buddhas. The buildings are all attached to one another with one clerestory and two small windows in the Chamba *lhakhang*.

STATE OF PRESERVATION

Advanced State of Decay

SOURCE OF INFORMATION 'Buddhist Sculptures in Clay' by Christian Luczanits; and, Nawang Tsering, Mangyu, Khaltse, Ladakh

Nag-Ldan *Chorten*

INVENTORY NO.
KHALTSE / MANGYU / 09 / 2004

Chorten | In Use | Public (Likir *Gonpa*) | 12th - 13th century

SETTING

The Nag-Ldan *chorten* is oriented towards the southeast and is built along the slope of a hill. It lies northeast of the Lotsava complex while the Dugyal *gonpa* is towards the east behind the Shukpanpa's House.

SIGNIFICANCE

The Nag-Ldan *chorten* is believed to have been built around the same time as the temples and date back to the early period of Buddhist art in the region. The paintings and stucco imagery within are some of the few extant examples of this period to survive in Ladakh. The *chorten* contains stucco images of Chanrazig, Jamyang, Chagdor and Tsongkhapa located within niches on four sides under the inner roof as well as original paintings depicting deities from the Buddhist pantheon.

DESCRIPTION

The *chorten* has a large square base above which the superstructure rises up over a *mandala* plan. The *chorten* is built in stone masonry and is mud plastered and whitewashed externally. It has been recently restored. To the southeast, there is a small door that leads inside the structure. It has a cubic void above the central space just below the cylindrical dome. There is a *mandala* shaped wooden ceiling with images of flying deities and floral patterns. There are also small niches on all the four sides of the walls that house images of Chanrazig, Jamyang, Chagdor and Tsongkhapa. The side walls of the niches also are painted with images of Chanrazig and other deities. It appears that the front and rear walls were once open and the *chorten* served as a Kagan *chorten* with a passage below. This was blocked at some point and an access provided through a doorway.

STATE OF PRESERVATION
Showing Signs of Deterioration

Mangyu

269

SOURCE OF INFORMATION 'Buddhist Sculptures in Clay' by Christian Luczanits; and, Nawang Tsering, Mangyu, Khaltse, Ladakh

Chorten Thugu (Cholgog)

INVENTORY NO.
KHALTSE / MANGYU / 10 / 2004

Chorten / Mane Wall | In Use | Public (Community) | Around 200 years old

SETTING
The structures are oriented towards the southeast and are located northwest of the Nag-Ldan *chorten* and east of Dugyal *gonpa*. On the northeastern side, there is a cliff.

SIGNIFICANCE
The *chorten* and *mane* walls are contemporary to the Dugyul *gonpa* and mark the pathway to the neighbouring villages beyond Mangyu. Many *chorten* collapsed during a landslide next to the cliff. A new *rigsum gonbo* was built above the village, in front of the Government Middle School to replace these *chorten* and protect the village from further natural calamities. The *chorten* are predominantly Changchub *chorten* which symbolize the Buddha's enlightenment. The *chorten,* along with the *mane* wall, are circumambulated by the villagers to gain merit.

DESCRIPTION
The site comprises of many *chorten* and *mane* walls spread over a large area. The *chorten* are of different sizes. Most of them are Changchub *chorten* built over square bases in stone and mud brick masonry with mud mortar. The external surface of the *chorten* have traces of mud plaster and whitewash, most of which has eroded altering the original form of the *chorten*. The *mane* wall is built in dry stone masonry and has inscribed *mane* stones placed on the top. Engraved stones can also be seen lying on the plinth of the *chorten*.

STATE OF PRESERVATION
Advanced State of Decay

SOURCE OF INFORMATION Tsering Rigzen, Mangyu, Khaltse, Ladakh

Mangyu

270

Lhato

INVENTORY NO.
KHALTSE / MANGYU / 11 / 2004

Lhato | In Use | Public (Community)

SETTING
The *lhato* is oriented towards the south and is located on the slope of the mountain opposite the village stream. It is located along a pathway which leads from Mangyu to Sapta village.

SIGNIFICANCE
The *lhato* is dedicated to the village protector deity. The contents of the *lhato* are renewed every year by the villagers.

DESCRIPTION
The structure is small and built on a square plan along the slope of a mountain. The climb is steep and difficult. The *lhato* contains juniper branches (*Shukpa*) and *khadag* in the centre. Externally, the structure is mud plastered and whitewashed.

STATE OF PRESERVATION
Advanced State of Decay

SOURCE OF INFORMATION Tsering Rigzen-Shukpanpa, Mangyu, Khaltse, Ladakh

Chorten and *Mane* Wall

INVENTORY NO.
KHALTSE / MANGYU / 12 / 2004

Chorten / Mane Wall | In Use | Public (Community) | Around 200 years old

SETTING
The structures are oriented towards the south and are located above the village settlement and the Thugu *chorten* precinct.

SIGNIFICANCE
The structures are circumambulated by the villagers as an act of merit.

DESCRIPTION
The site consists of a *mane* wall and *chorten*. The *mane* wall is a long linear structure with a wide low height base built of loosely piled stones. Flat stones, inscribed with sacred *mantras*, are placed on the horizontal surface of the *mane* wall. Adjacent to the *mane* wall is a Changchub *chorten*. The *chorten* is built on a random rubble masonry plinth and is constructed in stone and mud brick masonry. Externally, it is mud plastered and whitewashed.

SOURCE OF INFORMATION Tsering Rigzen Shukpanpa, Mangyu, Khaltse, Ladakh

STATE OF DETERIORATION
Advanced State of Decay

Mangyu

271

Spurkhang

INVENTORY NO.
KHALTSE / MANGYU / 13 / 2004

Cemetery / Cremation Ground / Tomb | In Use | Public (Community) | Around 700 - 800 years old

SETTING
The *spurkhang* is oriented to the southeast and is located a short climb above village along the slope of a mountain. The site located north of the Nag-Ldan *chorten* and is surrounded by several *chorten*. There is a cliff towards the east.

SIGNIFICANCE
The *spurkhang* is believed to be as old as the village itself. Each household in the village owns one unit, or *spurkhang,* which is used by them on the death of a family member.

DESCRIPTION
The *spurkhang* is a precinct spread over a large area. The graves are built amidst *chorten* and along a steep slope. The *spurkhang* are small square structures built in stone masonry at the base and mud brick masonry at the upper level. It is covered with *taalu* and a layer of mud.

STATE OF PRESERVATION
Showing Signs of Deterioration

SOURCE OF INFORMATION Tsering Rigzen Shukpanpa, Mangyu, Khaltse, Ladakh

Chorten

INVENTORY NO.
KHALTSE / MANGYU / 14 / 2004

Chorten | In Use | Public (Community) | Around 200 years old

SETTING
The *chorten* are oriented towards the south and are located amid agricultural fields. A group of willow trees are located the east.

SIGNIFICANCE
The *chorten* are all Changchub *chorten* which symbolize the Buddha's enlightenment. The *chorten* are circumambulated by villagers as an act of merit.

DESCRIPTION
The site comprises of a cluster of four *chorten* built in a row over a common plinth. The *chorten* are of different sizes and are built in random rubble masonry with mud mortar. They are mud plastered and whitewashed externally. The external layer has largely eroded and the *chorten* have lost their original form.

STATE OF PRESERVATION
Showing Signs of Deterioration

SOURCE OF INFORMATION Tsering Rigzen, Mangyu, Khaltse, Ladakh

Chorten and Spurkhang

INVENTORY NO.
KHALTSE / MANGYU / 15 / 2004

Chorten / Cremation Ground | In Use | Public (Community) | Around 200 years old

SETTING
The site is oriented towards the southwest and is located on a small mound surrounded on one side by agricultural fields and by a mountain cliff on the other side.

SIGNIFICANCE
The site consists of a number of *spurkhang*, *chorten* and a *lubang*. The *spurkhang* is the cremation unit used by the family on the death of a family member. The *chorten* were possibly built in the memory of deceased ancestors. The *lubang* is dedicated to the deities of the underworld.

DESCRIPTION
The site comprises of a group of two *chorten*, one *lubang* and some *spurkhang*. One of the *chorten* is larger in size and located on an elevated land while the second smaller *chorten* is next to the *spurkhang*. The *lubang* is located on a short distance from the *chorten*. The structures are all built in random rubble and mud brick masonry with mud mortar and are mud plastered and whitewashed externally.

STATE OF PRESERVATION
Advanced State of Decay

SOURCE OF INFORMATION Tsering Rigzen, Mangyu, Khaltse, Ladakh

Mangyu

272

Rigsum Gonbo

INVENTORY NO.
KHALTSE / MANGYU / 16 / 2004

Rigsum Gonbo | In Use | Public (Community) | Around 300 - 350 years old

SETTING
The *rigsum gonbo* is oriented towards the west and is located on top of a hillock facing the flat land on which the village is situated.

SIGNIFICANCE
The *rigsum gonbo* was built by the community to protect the village from natural calamities and other evil forces. It faces the village and is believed to guard the village.

DESCRIPTION
The *rigsum gonbo* consists of a group of three *chorten* of similar size built over a common random rubble masonry platform. The *chorten* are built in stone and mud brick masonry with mud mortar and are mud plastered externally. A single *chorten* stands apart from the *rigsum gonbo*.

STATE OF PRESERVATION
Advanced State of Decay

SOURCE OF INFORMATION Tsering Rigzen, Mangyu, Khaltse, Ladakh

Mangyu

273

Chorten

INVENTORY NO.
KHALTSE / MANGYU / 17 / 2004

Chorten | In Use | Public (Community)

SETTING
The *chorten* are oriented towards the south and is located along the slope of a hillock besides the narrow pathway leading to the settlement.

SIGNIFICANCE
The *chorten* marks the entrance to the village of Mangyu. It appears to be a *rigsum gonbo* which was possibly built to protect the village from evil.

DESCRIPTION
The site comprises of a group of three *chorten* which appears to be a *rigsum gonbo*. Two of the *chorten* have eroded considerably while the third is in ruins. The two *chorten* are embedded in the ground and cannot be identified except for a small niche facing the south. The *chorten* are built in random rubble and mud brick masonry and show traces of mud plaster and whitewash on the external surface.

STATE OF PRESERVATION
Advanced State of Decay

SOURCE OF INFORMATION Rigzen Shukpanpa, Mangyu, Khaltse, Ladakh

Rongpa *Chorten*

INVENTORY NO.
KHALTSE / MANGYU / 18 / 2004

Chorten | In Use | Public (Community)

SETTING
The *chorten* are oriented towards the southwest and are
built over a hill to the rear of the main village settlement. A
residential dwelling is located nearby.

SIGNIFICANCE
The *chorten* are believed to have been built around the
same period when the village was settled. These are all
Changchub *chorten* which represent the Buddha's
enlightenment. The *rigsum gonbo* was built to protect the
village from evil forces.

DESCRIPTION
The site comprises of a group of six *chorten* of which three
appear to form a *rigsum gonbo*. All the *chorten* are
Changchub *chorten* built in stone and mud brick masonry
with mud mortar. Externally, the *chorten* are mud plastered
and whitewashed.

STATE OF PRESERVATION
Advanced State of Decay

SOURCE OF INFORMATION Nawang Tsering, Mangyu, Khaltse, Ladakh

Meme Sku

INVENTORY NO.
KHALTSE / MANGYU / 19 / 2004

Rock Carving / Rock Inscription | In Use | Public (Community) | Around
140 years old

SETTING
The site is a short twenty-minute walk from the village. It is
oriented towards the south and is located north of the
pathway leading to the village.

SIGNIFICANCE
The rock carving is believed to have been commissioned by
the mother of the previous reincarnation of Sras Rinpoche.
The carving is of an image of Stonba or Shakyamuni
Buddha.

DESCRIPTION
The image is carved on a large boulder and depicts an
image of the Buddha. The carved image has been painted
in various colours. There is a prayer flag posted on the
boulders right above the image. Two narrow side walls and
a roof have been built in random rubble masonry encasing
the image within.

STATE OF PRESERVATION
Showing Signs of Deterioration

SOURCE OF INFORMATION Tsering Rigzen Shukpanpa, Mangyu, Khaltse, Ladakh

Mangyu

274

NIRLAC

Nyerak

Nyerak is a three-day trek from Phanjilla. From the
Leh - Srinagar highway, a road diverts between Khaltse
and Lamayuru, towards Shilla. Phanjilla lies on this
road. It was called Nyerak as the heat of sun was very
strong in the village. Nyerak is very cold in winter and
hot in summer. There are about 14 households in
Nyerak today.

Listed by: Gelong Tsewang Jorgyes
Year: 2006

Bridge

INVENTORY NO.
KHALTSE / NYERAK / 01 / 2006

Bridge | In Use | Public (Community) | Around 800 yrs old

SETTING
The bridge spans across the Zanskar river and is located at the end of Nyerak village.

SIGNIFICANCE
The bridge connects several villages such as Lamayuru, Photoksar, Yulchung, Zangla and Zanskar. It is built in the traditional style with timber, stone and mud mortar and is one of the few surviving traditional bridges in Ladakh.

DESCRIPTION
The bridge is built of timber and is a flat bridge laid across the river. It has stone masonry piers on either side.

STATE OF PRESERVATION
Showing Signs of Deterioration

Nyerak *Khar*

INVENTORY NO.
KHALTSE / NYERAK / 02 / 2006

Vernacular Building | In Use | Private (Individual) | Around 700 years old

SETTING
The *khar* is located in the middle of the village and is surrounded by other village houses.

SIGNIFICANCE
The *khar* is believed to have been built around 700 years ago and belonged originally to a noble family from Nyerak. The family has recently moved to Henaksu *khar* and the building is now owned by the Denkhangpa family. It is built in the traditional style and is a good example of traditional architecture in the village.

DESCRIPTION
The *khar* is a large building built on a rectangular plan. It is built in stone masonry at the lower level and in mud brick masonry at the upper levels. It has few window openings which are not very large and have tiered timber lintels. The building is triple storeyed. The roof has collapsed over sections of the top most floor. The mud plaster and whitewash over the exterior walls has eroded.

STATE OF PRESERVATION
Advanced State of Decay

Sharchok *Lhato*

INVENTORY NO.
KHALTSE / NYERAK / 03 / 2006

Lhato | In Use | Public (Community) | Around 600 - 700 years old

SETTING
The *lhato* is located on a hill towards the end of the village.

SIGNIFICANCE
The *lhato* is dedicated to the village protector deity Sharchok. In ancient times, villagers would sacrifice animals to placate the deity. Nowadays, prayers are performed by the monks from Nyerak *gonpa* to seek the protection of the deity. The contents of the *lhato* are renewed twice a year on the 3rd day of the 11th month and in the 4th month of the Tibetan calendar amid rituals and prayers.

STATE OF PRESERVATION
Fair

DESCRIPTION
The *lhato* consists of a high stone masonry platform over which rest three groups of ritual offerings comprising of bundles of twigs tied together with *khadag*. Near the *lhato* is a tall boulder over which rests a large bundle of animal horns.

Chorten

INVENTORY NO.
KHALTSE / NYERAK / 04 / 2006

Chorten | In Use | Public (Community) | Around 600 - 700 years old

SETTING
The *chorten* is located along a footpath on the slope of a hill towards the end of the village.

SIGNIFICANCE
The *chorten* is located along a path and is circumambulated by villagers as an act of merit. A rock inscription on a mane wall near the chorten states that the *chorten* was built by Skyurbuchan Skitchan Yokmapa.

DESCRIPTION
The *chorten* is built along a slope of a hill on a square stone masonry base. The *chorten* is built in stone masonry and has traces of the external mud plaster and whitewash. There is a *srog-shing* embedded through the centre of the dome.

STATE OF PRESERVATION
Showing Signs of Deterioration

Lhato Sharchok

INVENTORY NO.
KHALTSE / NYERAK / 05 / 2006

Lhato | In Use | Public (Community) | Around 1000 years old

SETTING
The *lhato* is located beneath an ancient juniper tree in the village.

SIGNIFICANCE
The *lhato* is dedicated to the village protector deity Sharchok. Villagers perform prayers here on the 3rd day of every month seeking the protection of the deity. On the 3rd day of the 11th month of the Tibetan calendar, the contents of the *lhato* are renewed.

DESCRIPTION
The *lhato* consists of a small cubical structure built in between the gnarled roots of the old juniper tree. The *lhato* is built in stone masonry and is mud plastered and whitewashed on the exterior. There are numerous *khadag* tied to the branches of the juniper tree.

STATE OF PRESERVATION
Fair

Phelepa House

INVENTORY NO.
KHALTSE / NYERAK / 06 / 2006

Vernacular Building | In Use | Private (Individual) | Around 400 years old

SETTING
The house is located in the middle of the village.

SIGNIFICANCE
The house was built around 400 years ago by an ancestor of the Phelepa family and successive generations continue to reside here. The house is one of the oldest houses in the village and contributes to the traditional architecture of the village.

STATE OF PRESERVATION
Advanced State of Decay

DESCRIPTION
The Phelepa house is a double storeyed building which has had several additions to the original building over the years. The ground floor is built in random rubble masonry while the first floor is built in mud brick masonry. The exterior walls of the house have traces of mud plaster and whitewash. There are red markings, as protection against the *tsan,* on the corners of the house.

Tsuksapa House

INVENTORY NO.
KHALTSE / NYERAK / 07 / 2006

Vernacular Building | In Use | Private (Individual) | Around 250 - 300 years old

SETTING
The Tsuksapa house is situated in the middle of the village and is surrounded by residential houses.

SIGNIFICANCE
The house was built by an ancestor of the Tsuksapa family around 5 - 6 generations and the family continues to reside here. It is built in the local style and is a good example of traditional architecture in the village.

DESCRIPTION
The house is built on a roughly rectangular plan and is constructed in random rubble and mud brick masonry with mud mortar. There have been several additions to the building over time. The oldest section has very small window openings while the newer section has larger windows with timber frames and lintels. The house has a traditional roof above.

STATE OF PRESERVATION
Showing Signs of Deterioration

Onpopa House

INVENTORY NO.
KHALTSE / NYERAK / 08 / 2006

Vernacular Building | In Use | Private (Individual) | Around 1000 yrs old

SETTING
The house is located near the *gonpa* in the beginning of the village.

SIGNIFICANCE
The Onpopa is the oldest house in the village. It is said that one of their ancestors visited Tibet and brought back many objects used by *onpo* (astrologers) in their rituals. These objects are still preserved by the family. One branch of the family continues to reside here.

DESCRIPTION
The Onpopa house is a large double storeyed building built in stone and mud brick masonry. The first floor of the house has large *rabsal* with timber frames and shutters. The house has a traditional roof made of timber beams, joists, *taalu*, grass and compacted mud. The exterior walls of the house have traces of mud plaster and whitewash.

STATE OF PRESERVATION
Advanced State of Decay

Nyerak

281

Onpo *Khangbu*

INVENTORY NO.
KHALTSE / NYERAK / 09 / 2006

Vernacular Building | In Use | Private (Individual) | Around 800 years old

SETTING

The house is located near the *gonpa* in the beginning of the village. It lies next to the Onpopa house.

SIGNIFICANCE

The Onpo *khangbu* is one of the four Onpo families in the village and the house lies close to the Onpopa house. The houses was built around 800 years ago by an ancestor of the Onpo family and successive generations have continued to reside here. The house is built in the traditional style and is a good example of vernacular architecture in the village.

DESCRIPTION

The Onpo *khangbu* is a large house to which several additions have been made over the centuries. The house is double storeyed with few and small window openings. It is built in stone masonry at the ground floor and in mud brick masonry on the first floor. The house has a traditional roof made of timber beams, joists, *taalu*, grass and compacted

mud. The exterior walls of the house have traces of mud plaster and whitewash. The walls have red markings at the corners as a protection against the *tsan*.

STATE OF PRESERVATION

Showing Signs of Deterioration

Tashi Samstanling (Nyerak *Gonpa*)

INVENTORY NO.
KHALTSE / NYERAK / 10 / 2006

Gonpa | In Use | Public (Lingshed *Gonpa*) | Around 500 years old

SETTING

The *gonpa* is located on a hill at the beginning of the village.

SIGNIFICANCE

The *gonpa* is believed to have been built around 500 years ago and is a branch of Lingshed *gonpa*. One monk from Lingshed lives here to take care of the *gonpa* and to perform various rituals and prayers. On the 15th day of the 1st month, the Nyenas and Nyungnas (fasting) for three days is held here. In the 3rd month of the Tibetan calendar, both monks and lay people read manuscripts. In the 4th month of the Tibetan calendar, sacred texts are read for three days at which time people also carve mane stones. This culminates with the whitewashing of the *chorten* and is followed by a festival in the village.

DESCRIPTION

The *gonpa* is built on a hill near the entrance to the village. Of the old portion, only the *dukhang* survives today. There have been a number of additions in recent years. The *gonpa* is built in stone and mud brick masonry and is mud plastered and whitewashed on the exterior. It is in roughly two sections, one of which is double storeyed in height. There is a *tarchen* at the entrance which leads to a small portico with timber columns and brackets. From here, a doorway leads to the main *gonpa*. There is a small *rigsum gonbo* beyond the *gonpa* and a *mane* wall to the rear. The *gonpa* has a traditional roof above.

STATE OF PRESERVATION

Showing Signs of Deterioration

Mane Wall and Ruila *Chorten*

INVENTORY NO.
KHALTSE / NYERAK / 11 / 2006

Mane Wall / *Chorten* | In Use | Public (Community) | Around 700 years old

SETTING
The group of *chorten* and *mane* wall is located at the beginning of the village a little before the *gonpa*.

SIGNIFICANCE
The *mane* wall and *chorten* were built around 700 years ago by the villagers when they were faced with a severe shortage of water for irrigation. The *chorten* and *mane* wall are still circumambulated by the villagers as an act of merit.

DESCRIPTION
The site consists of a large irregular shaped *mane* wall and a group of *chorten* to one side. The *mane* wall is a low height wall made of dry stone masonry with inscribed *mane* stones placed on the flat horizontal surface. The *chorten* are built in stone masonry and have traces of external mud plaster and whitewash on the external surface. Some of the *chorten* have a *srog-shing* embedded in the centre of the dome.

STATE OF PRESERVATION
Showing Signs of Deterioration

Shugtser Spundun

INVENTORY NO.
KHALTSE / NYERAK / 12 / 2006

Landscape (Grove) | In Use | Public (Community)

SETTING
The juniper grove is located above the village along the slope of a hill.

SIGNIFICANCE / ASSOCIATED BELIEFS
Juniper, or *shugpa*, is an important plant in Ladakh and its branches are used for purification rites as well as offerings in *lhato*. Within this grove, seven trees are considered sacred by the villagers and are never cut. Villagers believe that certain protectors reside in these trees. The spring which supplies water to the village originates here.

DESCRIPTION
The area is a large slope of a hill on which several small juniper trees grow. The trees are of low height.

STATE OF PRESERVATION
Showing Signs of Deterioration

Chorten Sumpo

INVENTORY NO.
KHALTSE / NYERAK / 13 / 2006

Chorten / Mane Wall | In Use | Public (Community) | Around 700 years old

SETTING
The *chorten* are located on the western side of the village.

SIGNIFICANCE
The *chorten* and *mane* walls were built around 700 years ago and are still worshipped by the community. Villagers circumambulate the chorten as an act of merit.

DESCRIPTION
The site comprises of a group of *chorten* and *mane* walls. The *chorten* are built in stone masonry and have traces of external mud plaster and whitewash. One of the *chorten* has a *chugsum khorlo* over the dome while the other *chorten* have *srog-shing* embedded in the domes. The *mane* walls are located in front of the *chorten* and are irregular shaped dry stone masonry walls with inscribed *mane* stones placed on the top horizontal surface.

STATE OF PRESERVATION
Showing Signs of Deterioration

Khumbupa House

INVENTORY NO.
KHALTSE / NYERAK / 14 / 2006

Vernacular Building | In Use | Private (Individual) | Around 230 years old

SETTING
The house is located some distance away from the main village. It is surrounded by agricultural fields to the front and mountains to the rear.

SIGNIFICANCE
The house was built about 4 - 5 generations ago by an ancestor of the Khumbupa family and the family continues to reside here. The house is built in the traditional style and is a good example of vernacular architecture in the village.

DESCRIPTION
The Khumbupa house is a large three storeyed building built on a random plan. The house has seen several additions over time. The ground floor is built in random rubble masonry and the upper floors are built in mud brick masonry. The older sections of the house have very small window openings while the newer sections have larger windows with timber frames and lintels. There is a large terrace on the second floor. The roof is a traditional one made of timber beams, joists, *taalu*, grass and compacted mud.

STATE OF PRESERVATION
Showing Signs of Deterioration

Katpe *Chorten*

INVENTORY NO.
KHALTSE / NYERAK / 15 / 2006

Chorten | In Use | Public (Community) | Around 900 years old

SETTING
The *chorten* are located on the western edge of the village on a rocky and barren stretch of land.

SIGNIFICANCE
The *chorten* were built several centuries ago in fulfillment of a prophecy and are still worshipped by the villagers.

DESCRIPTION
The *chorten* are built along a slope of a hill on a common random rubble masonry base. The *chorten* are built in random rubble masonry and have traces of the external mud plaster and whitewash. There is a *srog-shing* embedded through the centre of the domes of each of the *chorten*.

STATE OF PRESERVATION
Advanced State of Decay

Chocho Kuru la

INVENTORY NO.
KHALTSE / NYERAK / 16 / 2006

Landscape (Mountain Pass) | In Use | Public (State)

SETTING
The pass is located between Nyerak and Yulchung about five kms from the Singhela.

SIGNIFICANCE / ASSOCIATED BELIEFS
The pass is crossed while traveling between Nyerak and Yulchung and is believed to be the residence of certain deities.

DESCRIPTION
The mountain pass contains a Changchub *chorten* and a *tarchen*. The *chorten* is built in random rubble masonry and is mud plastered and whitewashed on the exterior. There is a *srog-shing* embedded through the centre of the dome and prayer flags are tied to this at one end and to the *tarchen* at the other.

CULTURAL LINKAGES / CULTURAL PRACTICES
The pass links the villages of Nyerak and Yulchung and travellers traversing this route tie prayer flags, or *khadag* and circumambulate the chorten to seek protection on their journey.

STATE OF PRESERVATION
Showing Signs of Deterioration

Katpe
Rigsum Gonbo

INVENTORY NO.
KHALTSE / NYERAK / 17 / 2006

Rigsum Gonbo | In Use | Public(Community) | Around 800 years old

SETTING
The *rigsum gonbo* is located on the western edge of the village on a rocky and barren stretch of land.

SIGNIFICANCE
The *rigsum gonbo* was built to protect the village from misfortune and disasters.

DESCRIPTION
The *rigsum gonbo* consists of a high random rubble masonry platform over which rest three *chorten* built in stone and mud brick masonry with mud mortar. The *chorten* are painted in the traditional colours of white, blue and ochre and have tall *chugsum khorlo* over the dome. There is another *chorten* located a short distance away from the *rigsum gonbo* which is built in stone and mud brick masonry and is mud plastered and whitewashed on the exterior.

STATE OF PRESERVATION
Fair

Nyerak

286

Nyurla

Nyurla is situated on the Leh - Srinagar road, about 90 km from Leh. The exact meaning of Nyurla is not known but it is believed that it was called Myur-la as it was formed in a very short time. There are about 42 households in Nyurla today. It is a prosperous village as different kind of fruit ripen here early in summer.

Listed by: Deldan Angmo and Jassu Singh
Year: 2004

Phanjilla

Phanjilla can be reached on the vehicular road that diverts from the Leh - Sriangar highway towards Shilla. The name of the village is derived from the pass Phanjilla. Earlier, the villagers had to travel through Phanjilla pass to reach their village. There are about 12 households in the village today.

Listed by: Deldan Angmo and Jassu Singh
Year: 2004

Group of *Chorten*

INVENTORY NO.
KHALTSE / NYURLA / 01 / 2004

Chorten / Mane Wall | In Use | Public (Community) | Around 75 years old

SETTING

The group of *chorten* is oriented to the east and is located at the beginning of the settlement, to the left of the vehicular road. The vehicular road lies to the north of the site. There are agricultural fields to the south and south west and a prayer wheel to the west of the site.

SIGNIFICANCE

The *chorten* are located along the road leading to the village and are circumambulated by villagers to accumulate merit as they travel along this path. The group consists of large Changchub *chorten* which symbolize the Buddha's enlightenment. The Kagan *chorten* is a gateway chorten and merit is believed to accrue to believers who pass through the passage of the *chorten*.

DESCRIPTION

The site consists of a group of twenty four *chorten*, a Kagan *chorten* and a *tarchen*. There is a linear dry stone masonry *mane* wall in the beginning which is followed by two Changchub *chorten*. Beyond the *mane* wall is a line of Changchub *chorten* built on a platform. The *chorten* are built in stone and mud brick masonry with mud mortar and are mud plastered and whitewashed externally. Some *chorten* have *pa-tra* on the base panels. There is a huge Kagan *chorten* at the end of the line of the *chorten*. The *chorten* above the Kagan *chorten* is cement plastered and whitewashed externally and has motifs painted on the base panels. The ceiling of the passage is in the shape of a *mandala* and is made of wooden planks with elaborate paintings on cloth pasted on it. There is a circumambulatory path around the group of *chorten* and *mane* wall.

STATE OF PRESERVATION
Showing Signs of Deterioration

Nyurla

290

Khargogpa House

INVENTORY NO.
KHALTSE / NYURLA / 02 / 2004

Vernacular Building | In Use | Private (Individual) | Around 250 years old

SETTING

The Khargogpa House is oriented to the southeast. It is surrounded by agricultural fields to the north and northwest. There is a large open space to the southeast side.

SIGNIFICANCE

The house was built about 250 years ago by the ancestors of the Khargogpa family. The family has been residing in the house ever since. The house is built in the traditional style and is a good example of vernacular architecture in the village.

DESCRIPTION

The Khargogpa house is built in two sections – one is the original and older section while the second has been newly constructed to the east of the original house. The old section is three storeys high with the ground floor constructed in stone masonry. This level has small timber framed openings. The first and second floors are built in

mud brick masonry. The middle floor has rectangular timber framed window openings. There is a *rabsal* on the uppermost floor with wooden lattice work shutters. The *rabsal* is flanked by two small windows which have two shutters each and segmental arches in the timber shutters. The windows have tiered lintels. The house is mud plastered and whitewashed externally. The ground floor has a mud floor and is used primarily for storage while the upper levels house the family's living quarters. The house is covered with a traditional roof consisting of timber joists, *taalu*, grass and a layer of compacted mud. The roof is supported by timber beams and columns with timber brackets.

STATE OF PRESERVATION
Fair

SOURCE OF INFORMATION Wangdus Norbu, Nyurla, Khaltse, Ladakh

Khargogpa *Chorten*

INVENTORY NO.
KHALTSE / NYURLA / 03 / 2004

Chorten | In Use | Public (Community) | Arund 250 years old

SETTING

The *chorten* is oriented to the southeast and is located at the entrance to the village, left of the vehicular road. The *chorten* is surrounded by agricultural fields to the south and west. The Khargogpa house lies to the northwest and there is a *lubang* to the southwest.

SIGNIFICANCE

The *chorten* is located at the entrance to the village and is circumambulated by villagers as an act of merit. It is a Changchub *chorten* and symbolizes the Buddha's enlightenment. The *lubang* is dedicated to the deities of the underworld.

DESCRIPTION

The site comprises of a Changchub *chorten* and a *lubang*. The *chorten* is built on a small rocky outcrop in stone

masonry and is mud plastered and whitewashed on the exterior. There is a small *lubang* near the chorten which is cubical in shape and is mud plastered on the exterior.

STATE OF PRESERVATION
Showing Signs of Deterioration

SOURCE OF INFORMATION Tsering Yangskit Khargogpa, Nyurla, Khaltse, Ladakh

Chug-Shig-Zhal *Gonpa*

INVENTORY NO.
KHALTSE / NYURLA / 04 / 2004

Gonpa | In Use | Public (Likir *Gonpa*) | Around 150 years old

SETTING
The Chug-Shig-Zhal *gonpa* is oriented to the south and is built along the slope of a hill. It is approached from a narrow footpath which diverts from the main vehicular road. There are apricot and walnut trees to the southwest.

SIGNIFICANCE
The *gonpa* is believed to have been built around 150 years ago by Meme Joldan Thangpa at the time of Zorawar Singh. The *gonpa* is the principal place of worship in the village. It is managed by monks from the Gelugpa sect who are deputed here from Likir monastery to perform prayers and rituals in the temple and in the village.

DESCRIPTION
The *gonpa* is a double storeyed building with an entrance from the east where a staircase leads up to the first floor. The ground floor is constructed in stone masonry while the first floor is in mud brick masonry. The external walls are mud plastered and whitewashed. The walls of the main dukhang have images of Guru Rinpoche and other deities of the Buddhist pantheon. The *gonpa* has huge timber framed windows with wooden shutters. There are rammed earth lintels over the windows which are painted in red and yellow. The main hall has a mud and timber floor. The rest of the rooms have a mud floor. The structure has a traditional roof comprising of timber beams, joists, *taalu*, grass and a layer of compacted mud.

STATE OF PRESERVATION
Showing Signs of Deterioration

SOURCE OF INFORMATION Wangdus Norbu, Nyurla, Khaltse, Ladakh

Kirkirope House

INVENTORY NO.
KHALTSE / NYURLA / 05 / 2004

Vernacular Building | Abandoned | Private (Individual) | Around 180 years old

SETTING
The Kirkirope house is oriented to the south and is located along a pathway which winds through fields and orchards towards the mountains beyond. There is a pathway to the southwest side of the house and a newly constructed building beyond the path.

SIGNIFICANCE
The house was built around 180 years ago by ancestors of the Kirkirope family. The family resided in the house for several generations and has now moved out into a new house. The house is built in the traditional style and is a good example of vernacular architecture in the village.

DESCRIPTION
The Kirkirope house is a double storeyed building with the lower floor constructed in random rubble masonry and the upper floor in mud brick masonry with mud mortar. The entrance is from the east along the pathway. The ground floor has two narrow rectangular openings on all sides. There is a *rabsal* on the first floor which has a wooden frame. The *rabsal* is flanked by two smaller windows with timber frames. The *rabsal* and windows have tiered timber lintels. The house is mud plastered and whitewashed on the exterior. The ground floor has a mud floor and was used primarily for storage whereas the first floor would have housed the family's living quarters. The house is covered with a flat traditional roof consisting of timber joists, *taalu*, grass and a layer of compacted mud. The roof is supported on timber beams and columns with timber brackets.

STATE OF PRESERVATION
Advanced State of Decay

SOURCE OF INFORMATION Wangdus Norbu, Nyurla, Khaltse, Ladakh

Petugpa House

INVENTORY NO.
KHALTSE / NYURLA / 06 / 2004

Vernacular Building | Abandoned | Private (Individual) | Around 180 years old

SETTING
The Petugpa house is oriented to the southeast and is located along the pathway which leads towards the mountains via fields and orchards. The house is surrounded by agricultural fields to the west, apricot trees and the new Petugpa house to the south and a Changchub *chorten* to the southeast.

SIGNIFICANCE
The Petugpa house was built by ancestors of the Petugpa family about 180 years ago. The family resided in the house for several generations before moving into a new residence built next to the old house. The old house is built in the traditional style and contributes to the vernacular architecture of the village.

DESCRIPTION
The Petugpa house is a double storeyed building with an entrance from the northeast. The ground floor is constructed in random rubble masonry and used for storage

SOURCE OF INFORMATION Wangdus Norbu, Nyurla, Khaltse, Ladakh

while the first floor is built in mud brick masonry with mud mortar and would have housed the family's living quarters. The ground floor has small rectangular openings for ventilation while the first floor has larger window openings with timber frames and lintels. The family chapel was located on the first floor and the walls of the chapel are painted with images of Buddhist deities. The house has a traditional roof comprising of timber joists, *taalu*, grass and a layer of compacted mud. The roof rests on timber beams and columns with timber brackets.

STATE OF PRESERVATION
Showing Signs of Deterioration

Nyurla

293

Thangpe *Chorten*

INVENTORY NO.
KHALTSE / NYURLA / 07 / 2004

Chorten | Abandoned | Private (Individual) | Around 200 years old

SETTING
The Thangpe *chorten* is oriented to the east and is located along a path which leads to the village. There are apricot orchards and agricultural fields to the west and a newly constructed community hall further west.

SIGNIFICANCE
The *chorten* are believed to have been built around 200 years ago as an act of merit. Both are Changchub *chorten* and symbolize the Buddha's enlightenment.

DESCRIPTION
The site comprises of two *chorten* built on a random rubble masonry rectangular platform. The *chorten* are built in stone and mud brick masonry and would have been mud plastered and whitewashed on the exterior. However, the external surfaces of the *chorten* have completely eroded. There are small rectangular openings on the dome of the *chorten* which face the east.

SOURCE OF INFORMATION Wangdus Norbu, Nyurla, Khaltse, Ladakh

STATE OF PRESERVATION
Danger of Disappearance

Spurkhang

INVENTORY NO.
KHALTSE / NYURLA / 08 / 2004

Cremation Ground | In Use | Public (Community) | Around 150 years old

SETTING
The *spurkhang* is oriented to the south and is located on an elevated area north of the village. A pathway leads from the village to the grounds. The village lies to its south and southeast.

SIGNIFICANCE
The *spurkhang* has been used by the villagers as the cremation area for over 150 years. Each family in the village has their own unit, or *spurkhang*, which is repaired and reused on the death of a family member.

DESCRIPTION
The site comprises of a group of four *spurkhang* of different sizes. These are built on a rectangular or square plan and rise up as a box. The units are built in mud brick masonry and are mud plastered and whitewashed externally.

STATE OF PRESERVATION
Advanced State of Decay

Nyurla

294

Petroglyphs

INVENTORY NO.
KHALTSE / NYURLA / 09 / 2004

Rock Carving | Abandoned | Public (State)

SETTING
The petroglyphs are located along the main Leh - Srinagar highway in a stretch of grassy lands, near the River Indus.

SIGNIFICANCE
The petroglyphs provide evidence of some of the earliest human habitation in the region and are linked to several other petroglyph sites that are to be found along the banks of the Indus and Zanskar rivers.

DESCRIPTION
The site contains a number of boulders with figures pecked onto them. The boulder have a dark patina and the figures are pecked on this. The images include human and animal figures as well as some symbols.

STATE OF PRESERVATION
Advanced State of Decay

Group of *Chorten* and *Mane* Wall

INVENTORY NO.
KHALTSE / NYURLA / 10 / 2004

Chorten / Mane Wall | In Use | Public (Community) | Around 120 years old

SETTING

The group of *chorten* and *mane* wall are oriented to the east and are located along the path which leads to the village. The vehicular road lies to the northeast and there are agricultural fields to the south and west of the site. The village lies to the southeast.

SIGNIFICANCE

The group of *chorten* and *mane* wall was built around 120 years ago along the path which led from Leh to Khaltse and marked the entry to Nyurla from Khaltse. The *chorten* and *mane* wall are circumambulated by villagers to accumulate merit. The *chorten* are largely Changchub *chorten* symbolizing the Buddha's enlightenment.

DESCRIPTION

The site comprises of a group of twenty four *chorten*, a Kagan *chorten*, a *mane* wall and a *tarchen*. The *mane* wall is linear in shape and is built in dry stone masonry with *mane* stones placed on the horizontal surface. There are two Changchub *chorten* ahead of the *mane* wall and another line of Changchub *chorten* built on platforms behind the *mane* wall. The *chorten* are of varies sizes and some of them are in complete ruins. There is a large Kagan *chorten* at the end of the line of the *chorten*. The Kagan *chorten* has two thick parallel walls over which rests a Changchub *chorten* built on a square base. The ceiling of the passage is built in the shape of a *mandala* using wooden planks over which are pasted elaborate paintings on cloth. The Kagan *chorten* was repaired two years back by the villagers and has *pa-tra* motifs on the rectangular base panels. The *chorten* has a tall *chugsum khorlo* over its dome on which rests a metal crescent. The *chorten* are constructed in stone masonry with mud mortar and are mud plastered and whitewashed. The *chorten* over the Kagan *chorten* is cement plastered. Some of the *chorten* have *pa-tra* work on the base panels.

STATE OF PRESERVATION
Showing Signs of Deterioration

SOURCE OF INFORMATION Tsering Dolma, Nyurla, Khaltse, Ladakh

Group of *Chorten* and *Mane* Walls

INVENTORY NO.
KHALTSE / PHANJILLA / 01 / 2004

Chorten / Mane Wall | In Use | Public (Community)

SETTING

The *chorten* and *mane* walls are located on a hillside across the village stream. They are located south of a Kagan *chorten* and the road runs to the southeast of the site.

SIGNIFICANCE

The *chorten* and *mane* walls are located along the path leading to the village. The site is circumambulated by villagers as an act of merit while travelling along this path. The *chorten* is a Changchub *chorten* and symbolizes the Buddha's enlightenment.

DESCRIPTION

The site consists of a *chorten* and two *mane* walls of different sizes. The larger *mane* wall shares a common base with the *chorten* while the smaller one is located a little higher up. The *mane* walls are linear dry stone masonry walls with inscribed *mane* stones placed on the horizontal

surface. The Changchub *chorten* is built in random rubble and mud brick masonry with mud mortar and is mud plastered and whitewashed externally. There is a *srog-shing* embedded in the centre of the dome.

STATE OF PRESERVATION
Advanced State of Decay

SOURCE OF INFORMATION Sonam Tsephel - Chiphzongpa, Phanjilla, Khaltse, Ladakh

Chorten

INVENTORY NO.
KHALTSE / PHANJILLA / 02 / 2004

Chorten | In Use | Public (Community)

SETTING

The *chorten* is located on a hill across the village stream. It is built on an elevated area with a *rigsum gonbo* to the northeast and Deregspa house to the south.

SIGNIFICANCE

The *chorten* was built in the past for the well being of the village. It is a Changchub *chorten* and symbolizes the Buddha's enlightenment. The *chorten* is circumambulated by villagers to accumulate merit.

DESCRIPTION

The Changchub *chorten* is housed in a structure which is formed of four pillars built in random rubble and mud brick masonry with a flat timber roof above. The *chorten* is built over a square base in stone and mud brick masonry with mud mortar and is mud plastered and whitewashed externally. There is a *chugsum khorlo* on the dome of the *chorten* made of baked tiles. This is surmounted by a metal

crescent and crown. There are some rock inscriptions placed at the base of the *chorten*.

STATE OF PRESERVATION
Advanced State of Decay

SOURCE OF INFORMATION Sonam Tsephel - Chiphzongpa, Phanjilla, Khaltse, Ladakh

Rigsum Gonbo

INVENTORY NO.
KHALTSE / PHANJILLA / 03 / 2004

Rigsum Gonbo | In Use | Public (Community)

SETTING
The *rigsum gonbo* is oriented to the west and is located along the slope of a hill to the east of the village road. There is a *chorten* to the west and Deregspa house to the southwest.

SIGNIFICANCE
The *rigsum gonbo* was built to protect the village from natural calamities and misfortune.

DESCRIPTION
The *rigsum gonbo* is a small structure built over a rectangular plan. It has walls on three sides and is open to the front. The walls are built in random rubble and mud brick masonry with mud mortar and are mud plastered and whitewashed on the exterior. There is a wooden column in front of the *chorten* supporting the roof above. The ceiling is made of timber joists and *taalu* over which rests a flat traditional roof. There are three *chorten* inside the

enclosure built on a common plinth and painted in orange (representing Jamyang), blue (representing Chagdor) and white (representing Chanrazig).

STATE OF PRESERVATION
Showing Signs of Deterioration

SOURCE OF INFORMATION Sonam Tsephel - Chiphzongpa, Phanjilla, Khaltse, Ladakh

Phanjilla

297

Group of *Chorten* and *Mane* Wall

INVENTORY NO.
KHALTSE / PHANJILLA / 04 / 2004

Chorten / *Mane* Wall | In Use | Public (Community)

SETTING
The *chorten* and *mane* wall are located along the village road and are surrounded by agricultural fields and the river to the south.

SIGNIFICANCE
The *chorten* and *mane* wall are located along the village path and are circumambulated by villagers to accumulate merit as they travel along this path. The *chorten* is a Changchub *chorten*, symbolizing the Buddha's enlightenment.

DESCRIPTION
The site comprises of a linear *mane* wall and a *chorten* located in between the *mane* wall. The *mane* wall is built in dry stone masonry and has mane stones placed on its horizontal surface. The *chorten* is built in stone and mud

brick masonry with mud mortar and is mud plastered and whitewashed externally. A circumambulatory path surrounds the site.

STATE OF PRESERVATION
Showing Signs of Deterioration

SOURCE OF INFORMATION Sonam Tsephel - Chiphzongpa, Phanjilla, Khaltse, Ladakh

Rigsum Gonbo

INVENTORY NO.
KHALTSE / PHANJILLA / 05 / 2004

Rigsum Gonbo | In Use | Public (Community)

SETTING
The *rigsum gonbo* is oriented to the southeast and is located on an undulating stretch of land northwest of the village road and above Ribzongpa house.

SIGNIFICANCE
The *rigsum gonbo* was built to protect the village from natural calamities and misfortune.

DESCRIPTION
The *rigsum gonbo* is built along the slope of a hill and consists of a walled enclosure open to the front. The walls of the structure are built in stone and mud brick masonry with mud mortar and are mud plastered and whitewashed externally. Inside are three *chorten* built in stone and mud brick masonry which are mud plastered and painted in the traditional colours of blue, orange and white. The roof is made of *taalu* and mud.

STATE OF PRESERVATION
Advanced State of Decay

SOURCE OF INFORMATION Sonam Tsephel - Chiphzongpa, Phanjilla, Khaltse, Ladakh

Monpa House

INVENTORY NO.
KHALTSE / PHANJILLA / 06 / 2004

Vernacular Building | In Use | Private (Individual) | Around 100 years old

SETTING
The Monpa house is oriented to the southeast and is located near the bridge which spans across the village stream. It is surrounded by other houses including the Kharapa house to the northeast and a *chorten* to the south.

SIGNIFICANCE
The Monpa house was built by the forefathers of the Monpa family about 100 years ago and successive generations continue to reside here. It is built in the traditional style and is a good example of vernacular architecture in the village.

DESCRIPTION
The Monpa house is built in levels with two storeys on the southeastern side and three storeys on the northeastern side. The entrance to the house is from the northwest. From the street, the entrance leads onto a courtyard. The ground floor is constructed in random rubble masonry while the upper floors are in mud brick masonry with mud mortar. The lower floors are used for winter habitation and have small timber openings. The upper floor is used for summer habitation and has larger window openings. The topmost floor has a single room which is the family's prayer room and has a large window opening. The building has a traditional roof supported on wooden columns and beams. The walls of the house are mud plastered and whitewashed externally. There is a Kagan *chorten* over the entrance to the house. It consists of two random rubble masonry walls over which rest a Changchub *chorten*. The *chorten* is built in stone and mud brick masonry with traces of mud plaster and whitewash on the external surface. It is built on a square base. There is a *srog-shing* embedded in the dome of the *chorten*.

STATE OF PRESERVATION
Advanced State of Decay

SOURCE OF INFORMATION Sonam Angchuk Khibzungpa, Phanjilla, Khaltse, Ladakh

Group of *Mane* Wall and *Chorten*

INVENTORY NO.
KHALTSE / PHANJILLA / 07 / 2004

Chorten / *Mane* Wall | In Use | Public (Community)

SETTING

The *mane* wall and *chorten* are located near the river and the road. These lie to the west of the river and the village road and there is a bridge which connects the two groups of *chorten*.

SIGNIFICANCE

The *chorten* and *mane* wall were built in the past as an act of merit and are still circumambulated by villagers to accumulate merit. The *chorten* are Changchub *chorten*, symbolizing the Buddha's enlightenment.

DESCRIPTION

The site comprises of a group of three *chorten* and a *mane* wall. The group is divided into two clusters. The first consists of two *chorten* and a *mane* wall which lie to the southwest and the second cluster consists of one *chorten* and a *tarchen* which lie to the northeast. A small bridge

connects the two. The *chorten* are built in stone and mud brick masonry with mud mortar and are mud plastered and whitewashed externally. The *mane* walls is built in dry stone masonry and has inscribed *mane* stones placed on its horizontal surface.

STATE OF PRESERVATION
Danger of Disappearance

SOURCE OF INFORMATION Tundup Tsephel - Chiphzongpa, Phanjilla, Khaltse, Ladakh

Mane Walls

INVENTORY NO.
KHALTSE / PHANJILLA / 08 / 2004

Mane Wall | In Use | Public (Community)

SETTING

The *mane* walls are located to the right of the main vehicular road and are about a half km before the village.

SIGNIFICANCE

The *mane* walls are located before the entrance to the village and are circumambulated by villagers to accumulate merit as they travel along this route.

DESCRIPTION

The site consists of two *mane* walls both of which are linear in shape and built in dry stone masonry. *Mane* stones are placed on the top of the walls.

STATE OF PRESERVATION
Showing Signs of Deterioration

SOURCE OF INFORMATION Sonam Tsephel - Chiphzongpa, Phanjilla, Khaltse, Ladakh

Phanjilla

299

Photoksar

The village of Photoksar can be reached from the vehicular
road that diverts towards Shila from the Leh - Srinagar
National Highway. From Phanjilla, a 30-kms trek leads
past Hanupatta to Photoksar. There are about 45
households in Photoksar village today.

Listed by: Deldan Angmo and Jassu Singh
Year: 2004

Shishila Pass

INVENTORY NO.
KHALTSE / PHOTOKSAR / 01 / 2004

Landscape (Pass) | In Use | Public (State)

SETTING
Shishila Pass is located on the way to Photoksar village and marks the beginning of the village. The pass is surrounded by snow capped mountains and a narrow pathway which leads to the village.

SIGNIFICANCE / ASSOCIATED BELIEFS
Shishila Pass is a mountain pass that links Hanupatta and Photoksar. There is a *lhato* here which is believed to protect travellers on their journey through the mountain passes.

DESCRIPTION
The pass is located on the path linking Hanupatta and Photoksar. The *lhato* built at the pass is made of stones and there are numerous prayer flags and *khadag* tied here as offerings by travellers.

CULTURAL LINKAGES / ASSOCIATED CULTURAL PRACTICES
The pass lies along the route linking Leh to Zanskar. The route goes on from Photoksar and Lingshed to Padum. Villagers offer prayers at the *lhato* and tie prayer flags when crossing this pass and pray for a safe journey. It forms a pilgrimage as well as trade route for people moving from Leh to Zanskar.

STATE OF PRESERVATION
Advanced State of Decay (*Lhato*)

SOURCE OF INFORMATION Deleks Paljor, Photoksar, Khaltse, Ladakh

Kagan *Chorten*

INVENTORY NO.
KHALTSE / PHOTOKSAR / 02 / 2004

Chorten / *Mane* Wall / *Lhato* | In Use | Public (Community) | Around 60 years old

SETTING
The Kagan *chorten* is oriented to the south and to the left of the pathway leading to the village. It lies before the village.

SIGNIFICANCE
The *chorten* were built around 60 years ago to protect the crops in the village fields which were being affected by the cold. On the advice of the Ven. Kushok Bakula Rinpoche, a *chorten* was built before the village to prevent cold winds from blowing into the village and affecting the crops.

DESCRIPTION
The site consists of a Kagan *chorten*, a small Changchub *chorten*, a long *mane* wall and a small *lhato* on top of a large stone boulder. The Kagan *chorten* consists of two thick parallel side walls with a *chorten* above. The walls are built in stone and mud brick masonry and are mud plastered and whitewashed with red markings along the corners. There are fragments of stucco relief still visible on the *chorten*. The *mane* wall is built in dry stone masonry and

is linear in shape with *mane* stones placed on its horizontal surface. The Changchub *chorten* is built in stone and mud brick masonry and is mud plastered and whitewashed externally. It has red markings along the edges. The *lhato* is located a short distance away and is built on a stone boulder. It is a cubical structure with juniper branches and *khadag* placed in the centre.

STATE OF PRESERVATION
Showing Signs of Deterioration

SOURCE OF INFORMATION Dorjey Angchuk – Thakshapa, Photoksar, Khaltse, Ladakh

Mane Wall

INVENTORY NO.
KHALTSE / PHOTOKSAR / 03 / 2004

Mane Wall | In Use | Public (Community)

SETTING
The *mane* wall is oriented to the east and is located before the village. A stream runs to the south of the site and there is a barren stretch of land to the north.

SIGNIFICANCE
The *mane* wall is located along the path leading to the village and is circumambulated by villagers to accumulate merit as they travel along this path. It was built in the past as an act of merit.

DESCRIPTION
The site comprises of a long *mane* built in dry stone masonry. A portion of the *mane* wall is higher than the rest of the *mane* wall. There are inscribed *mane* stones placed on the horizontal surface.

STATE OF PRESERVATION
Advanced State of Decay

SOURCE OF INFORMATION Tundup Gombo, Sarpanch, Photoksar, Khaltse, Ladakh

Group of *Chorten*

INVENTORY NO.
KHALTSE / PHOTOKSAR / 04 / 2004

Chorten | In Use | Public (Community)

SETTING
The group of *chorten* is located en route to the village over a hill. The *chorten* are surrounded by a camping ground to the south and agricultural fields to the north.

SIGNIFICANCE
The *chorten* are located along a path before the village and are circumambulated by villagers to accumulate merit. The *chorten* are all Changchub *chorten* symbolizing the Buddha's enlightenment.

DESCRIPTION
The site consists of a group of three *chorten* in different sizes. The largest one has collapsed and only its base survives. The remaining two *chorten* are of similar size. All the *chorten* are built in stone and mud brick masonry with mud mortar and are mud plastered and whitewashed externally, although much of the external layer has eroded. The *chorten* have *srog-shing* embedded in the dome and there is a circumambulatory pathway around it.

STATE OF PRESERVATION
Advanced State of Decay

SOURCE OF INFORMATION Tundup Gombo, Sarpanch, Photoksar, Khaltse, Ladakh

Konchok *Mane*

INVENTORY NO.
KHALTSE / PHOTOKSAR / 05 / 2004

Mane Wall | In Use | Public (Community) | Around 200 years old

SETTING
The *mane* wall is located at the entrance to the village and is located north of the Zurwapa house. There are agricultural fields to the north of the site.

SIGNIFICANCE
The Konchok *mane* is believed to have been built around 200 years ago by a villager named Konchok as an act of merit. His name was inscribed on one of the *mane* stones but this stone no longer exists. It is still circumambulated by villagers to accumulate merit.

DESCRIPTION
The Konchak *mane* is a linear *mane* wall with a wide base which taper slightly towards the top. It is built in dry stone masonry and has inscribed *mane* stones on its horizontal surface.

STATE OF PRESERVATION
Danger of Disappearance

SOURCE OF INFORMATION Tashi Phuntsog - Chumikpa, Photoksar, Khaltse, Ladakh

Zurwa *Khangpa*

INVENTORY NO.
KHALTSE / PHOTOKSAR / 06 / 2004

Vernacular Building | In Use | Private (Individual) | Around 200 years old

SETTING
The Zurwa *khangpa* is oriented to the south and is located at the entrance to the village, south of Konchok *mane*. It is one of the first houses of the village.

SIGNIFICANCE
The Zurwa *khangpa* is believed to have been built around 200 years ago by ancestors of the Zurwa family and successive generations have continued to reside in the house. It is one of the oldest houses of Photoksar village and also marks the beginning of the village. The house is built in the traditional style and is a good example of vernacular architecture in the village.

DESCRIPTION
The Zurwa *khangpa* is a long structure built along the village street. It is a two storeyed house with an entrance doorway on the northern facade. The front facade has very small window openings with wooden shutters and no frames. The spaces inside are small and low in height with small doors leading to various living areas and the main kitchen. The ground floor does not have any window openings. The exterior has a rough mud plastered surface and is whitewashed. The roof is a traditional roof made of timber beams, joists, *taalu*, grass and compacted mud. It is used for storing fodder and dried twigs used as firewood in winter.

STATE OF PRESERVATION
Advanced State of Decay

SOURCE OF INFORMATION Tundup Gombo, Sarpanch, Photoksar, Khaltse, Ladakh

Lagang Mane

INVENTORY NO.
KHALTSE / PHOTOKSAR / 07 / 2004

Temple / *Chorten* | In Use | Public (Community) | Around 180 years old

SETTING
The *Lagang mane* is oriented to the south east and is located in the centre of the village. *Lagang mane* is surrounded by village houses on three sides and a steep cliff on the fourth side.

SIGNIFICANCE
The *Lagang mane* is thought to have been built by Lobzang Phuntsog, an ancestor of the Chumikpa family around 200 years ago. The *Lagang* is one of the temples in the village and continues to be used in worship. The *chorten* are both Changchub *chorten* which symbolize the Buddha's enlightenment. The site is circumambulated by villagers to accumulate merit.

DESCRIPTION
The *Lagang mane* is a small complex consisting of a small shrine, a kitchen space, gallery and two *chorten*. There is a small court in front on which stands a large prayer flag (*tarchen*). The shrine has a portico with a single wooden column in the centre. Several steps from the court lead into the shrine through a wooden doorway. The shrine is a small space with a single wooden column in the centre, supporting the traditional roof of *taalu*, grass and compacted mud above. It has a small skylight which is the only source of light inside. It houses three large stucco images of Bodhisattvas which are placed on a pedestal. There are Buddhist canons on either side of the images. The *Lagang* is built in stone and mud brick masonry and is mud plastered and whitewashed on the exterior. The complex also comprises of two *chorten* to the southwest. The base of one *chorten* is completely embedded in the walls of the *Lagang* porch. The second *chorten* is opposite the first one and is located on a cliff. The *chorten* are built in stone and mud brick masonry and are mud plastered and whitewashed on the exterior. Several inscribed stones are placed around and on the *chorten* and there is a small niche in the dome. The *chorten* has a tall *chugsum khorlo* on the dome which symbolizes the 13 steps towards enlightenment. To the northeast of the *Lagang* is the kitchen which is abandoned now.

STATE OF PRESERVATION
Advanced State of Decay

Photoksar

305

SOURCE OF INFORMATION Tashi Phuntsog - Chumikpa, Photoksar, Khaltse, Ladakh

Rchachan, Tiruma, Spumsal *Lhato* (Yurla)

INVENTORY NO.
KHALTSE / PHOTOKSAR / 08 / 2004

Lhato | In Use | Public (Community)

SETTING
The *lhato* are oriented to the north and are located on a barren hill south of the village.

SIGNIFICANCE
The *lhato* are dedicated to the three protector deities of the village named Rchachan, Tiruma and Spumsal who settled in the village when the village began. An oracle appears every year on the occasion of the Ladakhi Losar and performs rituals at the site when the contents of the *lhato* are renewed.

DESCRIPTION
The site comprises of three *lhato* placed in row at a little distance from each other and dedicated to the three protector deities of the village. The *lhato* are of different sizes and are built in stone and mud brick masonry. They are mud plastered and whitewashed on the exterior and have red markings along the corners. The offerings are placed on the top of the *lhato*.

STATE OF PRESERVATION
Advanced State of Decay

SOURCE OF INFORMATION Tundup Gombo - Zurwapa, Photoksar, Khaltse, Ladakh

Yato *Chorten*

INVENTORY NO.
KHALTSE / PHOTOKSAR / 09 / 2004

Mane Wall / *Chorten* / *Tsadkhang* | In Use | Public (Hemis *Gonpa*) | More than 200 years old

SETTING
The Yato *chorten* is located on a hill next to *Gonpa Yokma*. It is surrounded by the main temple building on the southeast and with a school building to the northwest.

SIGNIFICANCE
The Yato *chorten* is believed to be more than 200 years old. It is circumambulated by villagers and prayers are carried out here especially on the 10th, 15th and 30th days of the month to accumulate merit. The *chorten* is a Changchub *chorten* which symbolizes the Buddha's enlightenment.

DESCRIPTION
The site comprises of a long *mane* wall, a large *chorten*, three smaller *chorten* and a *tsadkhang*. The *mane* wall is built in dry stone masonry and has inscribed *mane* stones placed on the horizontal surface. The large *chorten* lies to the northwest and is built on a stone masonry base in stone and mud brick masonry. The *chorten* is mud plastered and whitewashed on the exterior. There is a large niche in the dome which has a wooden frame. This is bordered in red as are the corners of the *chorten*. To the east is a group of three *chorten* and a *tsadkhang* housing *tsa-tsa*. There is a *Zhingshrak* to the southeast. The *chorten* are made in stone and mud brick masonry and are mud plastered and whitewashed on the exterior. The *tsadkhang* is built in stone masonry and has a traditional roof made of timber beams, joists, grass and compacted mud. There is an opening on one side and there are several *tsa-tsa* placed within. The *tsadkhang* also has red markings along the corners.

STATE OF PRESERVATION
Advanced State of Decay

SOURCE OF INFORMATION Tundup Gombo, Photoksar, Khaltse, Ladakh

Gonpa Gongma

INVENTORY NO.
KHALTSE / PHOTOKSAR / 10 / 2004

Gonpa | In Use | Public (Lamayuru *Gonpa*) | Around 30 - 40 years old

SETTING
Gonpa Gongma is oriented to the southwest and is located on an elevated area within the village. It is located along the slope of a hill above the village school, *Gonpa Yokma* and Yato *chorten*.

SIGNIFICANCE
Gonpa Gongma was built around 30 - 40 years ago to house the sacred images and artifacts from the old *gonpa* (Photoksar *Gonpa Gongma*) which had fallen into disuse as access to the *gonpa* was difficult particularly during the winter. The *gonpa* falls under Lamayuru *gonpa*. Monks from Lamayuru are stationed here to carry out prayers and rituals both within the temple as well as in the village.

DESCRIPTION
Gonpa Gongma is located along a hill with an entrance from the east. A small wooden doorway leads into a courtyard. There is a large prayer flag in the courtyard and a gallery to the south. The gallery has a traditional roof supported on wooden columns with openings facing the south. Steps lead from the courtyard to a small portico supported by timber columns. From the portico, an entrance door leads to the *dukhang*. The *dukhang* is single storeyed and square in plan with two wooden columns and brackets supporting the traditional roof above. There is a small skylight in the centre. The rear wall has a wooden frame housing images of Tundup Chosgyal, Shakayamuni, Guru Padmasambava and various other deities. The Buddhist cannons (*Bum*) are placed on wooden shelves along the side walls. To the west of the *dukhang*, is a kitchen (*thabsang*) and to the east are the living quarters for the resident monks. Above the *gonpa* complex, there is a *rigsum gonbo* and a *lubang*.

STATE OF PRESERVATION
Showing Signs of Deterioration

Photoksar

307

SOURCE OF INFORMATION Ven. Konchak Chotak – Resident Monk, Photoksar, Khaltse, Ladakh, 194106, J&K

Rigsum Gonbo

INVENTORY NO.
KHALTSE / PHOTOKSAR / 11 / 2004

Rigsum Gonbo | In Use | Public (Community)

SETTING
The *rigsum gonbo* is located on the top of a hill above the *Gonpa Gongma*. The *Gonpa Gongma* lies below to the southwest and there is a huge stone boulder to the southeast.

SIGNIFICANCE
The *rigsum gonbo* protects the *gonpa* and village from natural calamities and misfortune. The *lubang* marks the residence of the *lu,* or underworld deities.

DESCRIPTION
The *rigsum gonbo* consists of three Changchub *chorten* placed in a single row on a common stone masonry base. The *chorten* are built in dry stone masonry and are painted in the traditional colours of blue, white and orange symbolizing Chagdor, Chanrazig and Jamyang respectively. There is a small whitewashed *lubang* to the north of the *rigsum gonbo*.

STATE OF PRESERVATION
Advanced State of Decay

SOURCE OF INFORMATION Tundup Gombo, Photoksar, Khaltse, Ladakh

Ldal Thong Ge *Khar (Khargog)*

INVENTORY NO.
KHALTSE / PHOTOKSAR / 12 / 2004

Fort / Palace | Abandoned | Public (State / Community)

SETTING
The Ldal Thong Ge *khar* (old palace) is located on a steep mountain side south of the old *Gonpa Gongma*. A gravel path leads to the ruins from the village.

SIGNIFICANCE
The fort ruins are the oldest structures in the village although it is unclear as to when it was constructed.

DESCRIPTION
The ruins of the palace and fort are located on a mountain side above the village settlement. Only fragments of the old walls and watchtowers survive and it is difficult to identify the ruins as they merge with the surrounding landscape.

STATE OF PRESERVATION
Danger of Disappearance

SOURCE OF INFORMATION Tundup Gombo-Zurwapa, Photoksar, Khaltse, Ladakh

Photoksar
Gonpa Gongma

INVENTORY NO.
KHALTSE / PHOTOKSAR / 13 / 2004

Gonpa / *Mane* Wall / *Chorten* / *Rigsum Gonbo* | Abandoned | Public
(Lamayuru *Gonpa*)

STATE OF PRESERVATION
Advanced State of Decay

SETTING
The *Gonpa Gongma* is located on a steep hill to the northeast of the main village. An uneven path leads upto the site.

SIGNIFICANCE
The *gonpa* was built when the village was first settled and was the principal temple of the Drigung Kagyud sect in the village. The *gonpa* is difficult to access as the path has deteriorated and it was difficult for villagers to visit the temple, particularly in winter. A new *gonpa* was constructed 30 - 40 years ago and the images and ritual artifacts were transferred there. The *gonpa* presently lies abandoned. The *chorten* and *mane* wall formed part of the complex and would have been circumambulated by villagers when visiting the temple. The *rigsum gonbo* was built to protect the *gonpa* from evil forces.

DESCRIPTION
The complex comprises of a *gonpa*, a *rigsum gonbo*, four Changchub *chorten* and a *mane* wall. The *chorten* are distributed in two groups. One of them is to the north of the *gonpa*, while the other three are in front. There is a *rigsum gonbo* and a mane wall located in front of the *gonpa*. The entry to the *gonpa* is through a small doorway along the southeast. It opens into a court yard with a low wall on the southwest side having small openings. From the court, several steps lead into *dukhang*. The walls are covered with paintings. The images and artifacts have been shifted to the new *gonpa*. The ruins of a kitchen lie to the northwest of the *dukhang*. The *gonpa* is built in stone and mud brick masonry and is mud plastered and whitewashed on the exterior. There are red markings on the outer walls of the *gonpa*.

Photoksar

309

SOURCE OF INFORMATION Ven. Konchak Chotak, Photoksar, Khaltse, Ladakh

Gonpa Yokma

INVENTORY NO.
KHALTSE / PHOTOKSAR / 14 / 2004

Gonpa / Chorten / Mane Wall | In Use | Public (Hemis *Gonpa*) | Around 300 years old

SETTING

Gonpa Yokma is oriented to the south west and is located near agricultural fields with some village houses nearby. It is below the *Gonpa Yokma* and north of the Yato *chorten*.

SIGNIFICANCE

Gonpa Yokma derives it name from the fact that it is located below the *Gonpa Gongma*. It is around 300 years old and belongs to Hemis *gonpa*. A monk from Hemis is stationed here to carry out prayers and rituals in the temple. A special prayer is carried out by the monks in the ruined structure near the main temple for the prosperity of the village and all villagers participate in the occasion. The *chorten* are Changchub *chorten* symbolizing the Buddha's enlightenment and are circumambulated by villagers to accumulate merit when they visit the *gonpa*.

DESCRIPTION

The *Gonpa Yokma* is entered from the east. The entrance doorway leads onto a courtyard which is flanked by a low height gallery supported on timber columns. A flight of stairs leads to the floor below. The lower level has two rooms on the northwest side for monks which are presently not in use. A small porch with timber columns and a parapet above leads to the *dukhang*. The *dukhang* is a rectangular chamber with a stone floor and a small skylight in the centre of the chamber. To the rear of the chamber is a newly installed timber frame within which are placed images of Shakayamuni Buddha, Dolkar, Guru Rinpoche, Chanrazig, a Changchub *chorten* and the Buddhist canons of *Kangyur* on a side shelf. The walls of the *dukhang* and the side panels of the skylight are painted. The *dukhang* has a traditional roof of timber beams, joists, *taalu*, grass and compacted mud. The *gonpa* is built in random rubble and mud brick masonry with mud mortar and the walls are mud plastered and whitewashed. Near the *gonpa* are a group of *chorten*, a *mane* wall and an old stone masonry structure. The *chorten* are of different sizes and are built in stone masonry with *mane* stones placed around them. The external layer of mud plaster and whitewash appears to have completely eroded. The largest *chorten* has collapsed. Further down is a linear *mane* wall built in dry stone masonry with inscribed *mane* stones placed on the horizontal surface. To the north of the *mane* wall is a rectangular enclosure built in stone masonry which is used by the villagers for special pujas.

STATE OF PRESERVATION
Showing Signs of Deterioration

SOURCE OF INFORMATION Tundup Gombo - Zurwapa, Photoksar, Khaltse, Ladakh

Phasla Kaju Kontak

INVENTORY NO.
KHALTSE / PHOTOKSAR / 15 / 2004

Lhato | In Use | Private (Individual) | Around 200 years old

SETTING
The Phasla Kaju Kontak is oriented to the south and is located on a barren mountainside north of the village route.

SIGNIFICANCE
The Phasla Kaju Kontak is a *lhato* dedicated to the protector deity of the Changpapa and other families in the village. It is believed to be around 200 years old and is maintained and its contents renewed by the families.

DESCRIPTION
The *lhato* is a cubical structure built on a stone masonry base and has offerings of juniper branches, animal horns and *khadag* placed on the top. The *lhato* is mud plastered and painted in red on the exterior.

STATE OF PRESERVATION
Showing Signs of Deterioration

SOURCE OF INFORMATION Dorjey Angchuk, Photoksar, Khaltse, Ladakh

Gyashingpa's *Lhato*

INVENTORY NO.
KHALTSE / PHOTOKSAR / 16 / 2004

Lhato | In Use | Private (Individual) | Around 250 years old

SETTING
The Gyashingpa's *lhato* is oriented to the south and is located on a bare hill north of the village path. The Phasla Kaju Kontak lhato lies to the east.

SIGNIFICANCE
The Gyashingpa's *lhato* is dedicated to the protector deity of seven families in the village the chief of which is the Gyashingpa family. The *lhato* is believed to be 250 years old and is maintained and the contents renewed by the families.

DESCRIPTION
The Gyashingpa's *lhato* is a cubical structure built in stone masonry and is mud plastered and whitewashed on the exterior. It has a bundle of juniper branches, animal horns and *khadag* placed on the top as offerings.

STATE OF PRESERVATION
Advanced State of Decay

SOURCE OF INFORMATION Dorjey Angchuk, Photoksar, Khaltse, Ladakh

Tseb Lhamo *Lhato*

INVENTORY NO.
KHALTSE / PHOTOKSAR / 17 / 2004

Lhato | In Use | Public (Community) | Around 300 years old

SETTING
Tseb Lhamo *lhato* is located in the middle of the village. It is surrounded by village houses such as the Donstod *gongma* house to the southeast and the Kasbukharbu to its west. There is a small *lubang* to the south.

SIGNIFICANCE
The *lhato* is dedicated to the village protector deity Tseb Lhamo.

DESCRIPTION
Tseb Lhamo *lhato* is a large cubical structure with a square base which tapers upwards to form a smaller square base within which is embedded a wooden stick. The *lhato* is like a tall tower and is built in stone masonry and is devoid of any mud plaster or whitewash. It shares a common wall with Donstod *gongma* on the northeast side. There is a small cubical mud plastered, whitewashed *lubang* to the south.

STATE OF PRESERVATION
Advanced State of Decay

SOURCE OF INFORMATION Tundup Gombo - Zurwapa, Photoksar, Khaltse, Ladakh

Rigsum Gonbo

INVENTORY NO.
KHALTSE / PHOTOKSAR / 18 / 2004

Rigsum Gonbo | Abandoned | Public (Community)

SETTING
The *rigsum gonbo* is oriented to the southeast and is located on a cliff between the palace ruins and the *gonpa*. This cliff is accessed from the village via a sandy and rocky path.

SIGNIFICANCE
The *rigsum gonbo* is believed to protect the village from natural calamities and misfortune.

STATE OF PRESERVATION
Danger of Disappearance

DESCRIPTION
The *rigsum gonbo* is located on the corner of a cliff and consists of three *chorten* built on a common random rubble masonry plinth. The *chorten* are built in stone masonry and are devoid of any external plaster or colour. There are small openings at the base of each *chorten*. One *chorten* has collapsed till the base. Two of the *chorten* have a *srog-shing* embedded in the dome.

SOURCE OF INFORMATION Tundup Gombo (Sarpanch) - Zurwapa, Photoksar, Khaltse, Ladakh

NIRLAC

Khang Ltakpa House

INVENTORY NO.
KHALTSE / PHOTOKSAR / 19 / 2004

Vernacular Building | In Use | Private (Individual) | Around 200 years ago

SETTING
The Khang Ltakpa house is oriented to the south and is located in the interiors of the village. It is located opposite the Onpopa house and there are agricultural fields to the north.

SIGNIFICANCE
The Khang Ltakpa house was built around 200 years ago by ancestors of the Khang Takpa family and successive generations have resided in this house. It is built in the traditional style and is a good example of vernacular architecture in the village.

DESCRIPTION
The Khang Ltakpa house is a large three storeyed building built over an L-shaped plan. It is built along a slope and the front section of the house is three storeys while the rear is double storeyed. The front facade has a large window at the corner and smaller windows on the other sides. The ground and first floor have small window opening on the southern facade. All the window openings have timber lintels and frames. The entry to the house is from the eastern wall. The rear wall has no openings at all and it shares its west wall with the neighbouring house. The ground floor is built in random rubble masonry with mud mortar and is used for housing animals and storing fodder. The family's living quarters are housed in the first and second floors which are built in mud brick masonry. The house has a traditional roof made of timber joists, *taalu*, grass and compacted mud which is supported on timber columns and beams. There are prayer flags posted at the corners of the roof. The window openings as well as the parapet have black borders painted around them.

STATE OF PRESERVATION
Fair

Photoksar

313

SOURCE OF INFORMATION Tundup Gombo, Sarpanch, Photoksar, Khaltse, Ladakh

Gatapa House

INVENTORY NO.
KHALTSE / PHOTOKSAR / 20 / 2004

Vernacular Building | In Use | Private (Individual) | Around 200 years ago

SETTING
The Gatapa house is oriented to the south and is located in the interiors of the village. It is surrounded by other village houses and there is a cliff to the south.

SIGNIFICANCE
The Gatapa house was built around 200 years ago by the ancestors of the Gatapa family and since then successive generations have continued to reside here. It is built in the traditional style and is a good example of vernacular architecture in the village.

DESCRIPTION
The Khang Gatapa is a double storeyed building built along the slope of the hill. It is built over a long rectangular plan. The ground floor is built in random rubble masonry and has small openings for ventilation and light. It is used for housing animals. The first floor is built in mud brick masonry and comprises the family's living quarters. This level has larger windows with wooden frames and lintels.

The rooms inside are small and relatively dark as there are relatively fewer windows. The house has a traditional roof made of timber beams, joists, *taalu*, grass and compacted mud. There are prayer flags posted at the corners of the roof. The window openings as well as the parapet edging the roof are bordered in black. The foundation at one corner of the house has eroded and this section of the building is in a precarious condition.

STATE OF PRESERVATION
Advanced State of Decay

SOURCE OF INFORMATION Tundup Gombo, Sarpanch, Photoksar, Khaltse, Ladakh

Lhazhingpa House

INVENTORY NO.
KHALTSE / PHOTOKSAR / 21 / 2004

Vernacular Building | In Use | Private (Individual) | Around 120 years old

SETTING
The Lhazhingpa house is located in the interiors of the village. It lies west of the Onpopa's house.

SIGNIFICANCE
The Lhazhingpa house was built around 120 years ago by the ancestors of the Lhazhingpa family and since then successive generations have continued to reside here. It is built in the traditional style and is a good example of vernacular architecture in the village.

DESCRIPTION
The Lhazhingpa house is a large three storeyed house built along the slope of a hill. The entrance is from the main square to the northeast. Built along a slope, the house is three storeyed high to the south and a single storey to the north. The ground floor, to the south, is built in random rubble masonry and is used for storage. There are no openings in these walls. The upper floors are built in mud brick masonry with mud mortar and have small rectangular window openings. These levels house the family's living quarters. The house is mud plastered and white washed on the exterior and has a traditional roof above made of timber beams, joists, *taalu*, grass and compacted mud supported on timber columns and brackets. There is a low parapet running along the edge of the roof which is bordered in black. Prayer flags are posted at the corners of the roof.

STATE OF PRESERVATION
Advanced State of Decay

SOURCE OF INFORMATION Tundup Gombo, Sarpanch, Photoksar, Khaltse, Ladakh

Group of *Chorten* and *Mane* Wall

INVENTORY NO.
KHALTSE / PHOTOKSAR / 22 / 2004

Chorten / *Mane* Wall | In Use | Public (Community)

SETTING
The *chorten* lie along the pathway leading to Photoksar, before the village at the base of a hill. They are surrounded by agricultural fields on the south and southwest.

SIGNIFICANCE
The *chorten* are believed to date back to the time when the village was first settled. They are Changchub *chorten* which symbolize the Buddha's enlightenment. The *lubang* marks the residence of the *lu,* or underworld deities. The *chorten* and *mane* wall were built in the past along the path leading to the village and continue to be circumambulated by villagers to accumulate merit.

DESCRIPTION
The site comprises of two *chorten*, a *lubang* and a *mane* wall. The *chorten* are of different sizes. The *chorten* are built in stone masonry and are mud plastered and

whitewashed on the exterior. The external layer, however, has eroded considerably. The *mane* wall is located at the base of the larger *chorten* and is built in dry stone masonry with *mane* stones placed on its horizontal surface. The *lubang* is a small cubical structure located to the west of the chorten and is built in stone and mud brick masonry with an external layer of mud plaster and whitewash.

STATE OF PRESERVATION
Advanced State of Decay

SOURCE OF INFORMATION Tundup Gombo, Sarpanch, Photoksar, Khaltse, Ladakh

Tashi Gang *Chorten*

INVENTORY NO.
KHALTSE / PHOTOKSAR / 23 / 2004

Chorten | In Use | Public (Community)

SETTING
The *chorten* is built along the slope of a mountain above the settlement. It lies west of the Changpapa and Gyashingpa houses.

SIGNIFICANCE
The Tashi Gang *chorten* was built to protect the village from floods caused by melting snow which used to rush down the valley between the two mountains directly onto the village. There have been no floods in the village ever since. The two *lubang* located nearby mark the residence of the deities of the underworld.

DESCRIPTION
The site comprises of a small Changchub *chorten* and two *lubang*. The *chorten* is built in stone masonry and is mud plastered and whitewashed externally. The *lubang* are also

built in stone masonry and are small cubical shaped structure with a rounded roof above.

STATE OF PRESERVATION
Advanced State of Decay

SOURCE OF INFORMATION Tundup Gombo, Sarpanch, Photoksar, Khaltse, Ladakh

Onpopa House

INVENTORY NO.
KHALTSE / PHOTOKSAR / 24 / 2004

Vernacular Building | In Use | Private (Individual) | Around 120 years old

SETTING
The Onpopa house is oriented to the south and is built along the slope of a hill in the interior of the village. It is surrounded by other village houses including the Lhazingpa to the northwest. There is a cattle shed to the south of the house and a bare hill on the south.

SIGNIFICANCE
The Onpopa house was built about 120 years ago by ancestors of the Onpopa family and successive generations have continued to reside here. The house is built in the traditional style and is a good example of vernacular architecture in the village.

DESCRIPTION
Onpopa house is a triple storeyed building built along the slope of a hill on which are located other village houses as well. It is built on a long rectangular plan. The ground floor is built in stone masonry and has small openings for ventilation and light. It is used primarily for storage. The

first floor is built in mud brick masonry and houses the family's living quarters. This level has larger windows with wooden frames and lintels. The second floor is also built in mud brick masonry and is used by the family in summer whereas the first floor is used for winter habitation. The topmost floor has a terrace to the south. The second floor has large windows with decorated timber lintels. The roof is a traditional roof comprising of timber beams, joists, *taalu*, grass and compacted mud. There are prayer flags posted at the corners of the roof.

STATE OF PRESERVATION
Showing Signs of Deterioration

SOURCE OF INFORMATION Tundup Gombo, Sarpanch, Photoksar, Khaltse, Ladakh

Lhato and *Mane* Wall

INVENTORY NO.
KHALTSE / PHOTOKSAR / 25 / 2004

Lhato / *Mane* Wall | In Use | Public (Community)

SETTING
The *lhato* and *mane* wall are built along the slope of a mountain abutting the pathway which leads to the village. There is a stream flowing south of the site

SIGNIFICANCE
The *lhato* is dedicated to a protector deity and protects travellers on their journeys. The *mane* walls are circumambulated by villagers as an act of merit.

DESCRIPTION
The site consists two *mane* walls and a *lhato* along the village pathway. The *mane* walls are linear dry stone masonry walls with inscribed *mane* stones placed on the horizontal surface. To the east of the *mane* walls there is a *lhato*. The *lhato* is a dry stone masonry cubical structure with a tall pole in the centre to which are tied a bundle of juniper branches with a *khadag*.

STATE OF PRESERVATION
Showing Signs of Deterioration

SOURCE OF INFORMATION Tundup Gombo, Sarpanch, Photoksar, Khaltse, Ladakh

Thingpey Tsepa House and *Chorten*

INVENTORY NO.
KHALTSE / PHOTOKSAR / 26 / 2004

Vernacular Building / *Chorten* / *Mane* Wall | In Use | Private (Individual) |
Around 200 years old

STATE OF PRESERVATION
Advanced State of Decay

SETTING
The Thingpey Tsepa house and *chorten* are located along the pathway leading to the village. There are site is surrounded by agricultural fields to the south and bare hills to the north.

SIGNIFICANCE
The house and *chorten* are owned by the Thing pay Tsepa family and are believed to have been built by their ancestors around 200 years ago. The family continues to reside here. The house is built in the traditional style and has a number of associated structures surrounding it including *chorten*, *mane* walls, a *tarchen* and a *rigsum gonbo* to protect the family from natural calamities and misfortune.

DESCRIPTION
The site comprises of the Thingpey Tsepa house, two rectangular *mane* walls, a semi circular *mane*, two Changchub *chorten*, a *tarchen* and a *rigsum gonbo*. The house is a large double storeyed house with the rear having an additional level. The ground floor is built in stone masonry and has small window openings for ventilation and light. The first floor has a row of large windows with timber lintels and frames and a black border around the edges. This level comprises the family's living areas. The house has a traditional roof of timber beams, joists, *taalu*, grass and compacted mud. A low parapet runs along the edge of the roof and is painted in black. Near the house are three *mane* walls two linear and one semi circular which are built in dry stone masonry and have inscribed *mane* stones on the horizontal surface. Between the house and the *mane* walls are two *chorten* built in stone and mud brick masonry which are mud plastered and whitewashed on the exterior. To the west of the house is a *rigsum gonbo* comprising of three *chorten* built on a common stone masonry base.

Photoksar

317

Group of *Mane* Wall and *Rigsum Gonbo*

INVENTORY NO.
KHALTSE / PHOTOKSAR / 27 / 2004

Mane Wall / *Rigsum Gonbo* | In Use | Public (Community)

SETTING
The *mane* wall and *rigsum gonbo* are located on a elevated area along the path which leads to the village. The path lies to the northeast of the site and there is a large rock formation on the northwest.

SIGNIFICANCE
The *mane* wall lies along the path leading to the village and is circumambulated by villagers to accumulate merit. The *rigsum gonbo* is believed to protect the village from natural calamities and misfortune.

DESCRIPTION
The site comprises of a *mane* wall and a *rigsum gonbo*. The *mane* wall is a large and long rectangular wall built in dry stone masonry with inscribed *mane* stones placed on its horizontal surface. Its base to the south is at a higher elevation. To the west of the *mane* wall are three small

chorten built on a common stone masonry base which comprise the *rigsum gonbo*. The *chorten* are made of made of flat slabs piled one on top of the other. The domes of the *chorten* are missing.

STATE OF PRESERVATION
Advanced State of Decay

SOURCE OF INFORMATION Tundup Gombo, Sarpanch, Photoksar, Khaltse, Ladakh

---

Singhela Mountain and Pass

INVENTORY NO.
KHALTSE / PHOTOKSAR / 28 / 2004

Landscape (Mountain / Pass) | In Use | Public (State)

SETTING
The Singhela mountain lies en route from Photoksar to Lingshed. It is a four-hour trek from Photoksar. It is surrounded by lower mountains and the Singhela pass lies to the west.

SIGNIFICANCE / ASSOCIATED BELIEFS
The Singhela mountain is believed to represents Chanrazig riding a lion. It is a landmark in the routes of the region. The pass links Photoksar with Lingshed and is the only route linking the villages of Nyerak, Dipling, Yulchung and Lingshed with the rest of the region. It is an important trade route for the passage of goods between these villages. There is a *lhato* and *chorten* at the pass dedicated to the protector deity to protects travellers crossing these mountains.

DESCRIPTION
The Singhela mountain is covered with snow almost all the

year round and can be seen at a distance. At the pass, there is a *chorten*, *mane* wall and *lhato*. The *mane* wall and *lhato* are built in dry stone masonry. The *chorten* is built on a stone masonry platform and is whitewashed externally. Prayer flags have been tied to the *lhato*.

CULTURAL LINKAGES / CULTURAL PRACTICES
Travellers tie prayer flags at the *lhato* and seek the protection of the deity for their journey. They also circumambulate the *chorten* and *mane* wall as an act of merit.

STATE OF PRESERVATION
Fair

SOURCE OF INFORMATION Galax Paljor, Photoksar, Khaltse, Ladakh

Photoksar

318

Mane Wall

INVENTORY NO.
KHALTSE / PHOTOKSAR / 29 / 2004

Mane Wall | In Use | Public (Community)

SETTING
The *mane* wall lies along the path which leads from Photoksar to Singhela.

SIGNIFICANCE
The *mane* walls lies along the route used for centuries by traders and monks as they moved between Photoksar and Lingshed and further down to Zanskar. It is circumambulated by travellers to accumulate merit.

DESCRIPTION
The *mane* wall is a long wall made of dry stone masonry with *mane* stones placed on the horizontal surface. There is a circumambulatory pathway around the *mane*.

STATE OF PRESERVATION
Advanced State of Decay

SOURCE OF INFORMATION Galax Paljor, Photoksar, Khaltse, Ladakh

Chorten

INVENTORY NO.
KHALTSE / PHOTOKSAR / 30 / 2004

Chorten / *Mane* Wall | In Use | Public (Community)

SETTING
The *chorten* lies along the path leading to the village and near the river. The river flows to the north of the site while path lies to the west.

SIGNIFICANCE
The *chorten* is a Changchub *chorten* and symbolizes the Buddha's enlightenment. It is circumambulated by the devout as the travel to the village in order to accumulate merit.

DESCRIPTION
The site comprises of a *chorten* and a *mane* wall. The *chorten* is built in stone masonry. The outer layer of mud plaster and whitewash has eroded. Several *mane* stones are placed around the *chorten*. There is a *srog-shing* embedded in the dome of the *chorten*. The *mane* wall is a rectangular wall built in dry stone masonry and has *mane* stones placed on the horizontal surface.

STATE OF PRESERVATION
Advanced State of Decay

SOURCE OF INFORMATION Galax Paljor, Photoksar, Khaltse, Ladakh

Ridzong

The Ridzong gonpa, known as Vuma Changchupling, is situated at a distance of about 75 kms from Leh. The monastery was established by the great Lama Tsultim Nima in 1833 A.D. The monastery upholds the teachings of Tsongkhapa. Since the monastic community places particular importance to the observance of the Vinaya percepts, the traditions of the coercive rites which include sacred dances and hurling votive offerings are not especially observed. There is a nunnery called Chulichan, about 2 kms below the main monastery, where about 20 - 30 nuns reside. Ridzong is distinct from other monastic settlement in Ladakh as it is completely isolated from any village and there are no lay households residing in this valley.

Listed by: Deldan Angmo and Jassu Singh
Year: 2004

Ridzong *Gonpa*

INVENTORY NO.
KHALTSE / RIDZONG / 01 / 2004

Gonpa | In Use | Public (Ridzong *Gonpa*) | 1833 A.D.

SETTING

The *gonpa* is oriented to the southwest and is location on a hill in the village of Ridzong.

SIGNIFICANCE

Ridzong was founded in 1833 A.D. by the great religious and social reformer Lama Tsultim Nyima (1796 – 1860 A.D.). 'Ri' means mountain and 'dZong' means heaven, or the temple. The kitchen and monk cells are built according to rules laid down in Vinaya (Monastic discipline) taught by Lord Buddha. The Skudung was the first temple to be built, containing the caves where Lama Tsultim Nyima meditated for many years and which can still be seen. It now houses a *stupa* containing his relics. Tsultim Nyima, his wife, his sisters and son all renounced worldly life. His wife and sisters became nuns in the nearby Chuli Chan nunnery 'Chomoling'. His son was recognized as a Tulku (reincarnation of High Lama) and entered the monastery to became Ridzong Sras Rinpoche. He passed away in his 50's. His father, Lama Tsultim built the *dukhang,* or main assembly hall, and the statue of Lord Buddha was installed in memory of his son. Nastan Tsultim Dorjey (1833 – 1916 A.D.) built a model of the *mandala* of Shri Vajra Bhairav on top of the monastery. In 1921, the most eminent scholar Sras Rinpoche-II Lobzang Tsultim Chospel (1872 – 1926 A.D.) built the three storeyed Theckchen temple and its statues. Ridzong is a model of excellence in ethic discipline; its monks lead an exemplary monastic life, considering the Vinaya to be the treasure of Lord Buddha's teaching, which they follow in minute detail. They observe the three basic practices of Trimula i.e. the purifying ceremony (held twice a month), observance of the rainy season retreat and the celebration of the end of the retreat. It belongs to the Gelugpa order and is the only monastery where the monastic discipline is adhered to in its orthodox form. The *chomo* from the nearby nunnery are not allowed in the main monastery except for special prayers.

DESCRIPTION

The *gonpa* comprises of a number of structures. A Kagan *chorten* marks the beginning of the monastic complex after which the monastery comes into view. The *gonpa* has a stunning facade with protrusions and recesses forming an interesting composition. The lowest part of the complex comprises of classrooms which are two storeys high and with a courtyard in front. Ascending the hill, one passes through a maze of residential quarters with an interesting formation of streets, alleys and by-lanes which intersect at certain points to form small staircases, or merge at areas to form a large pathway. There is a definite hierarchy in the streets and the pathways are well lit leading to the upper levels where the *dukhang* and *lhakhang* are situated. The

dukhang complex comprises of a courtyard with the *dukhang* opening onto it. The *dukhang* Chenmo lies below the Lhamo *lhakhang*. It has a courtyard covered with a traditional roof supported on four decorated wooden columns. The walls of the portico are painted with images of the four guardian deities. An elaborate doorway leads into the *dukhang*. Twelve wooden columns and decorated tiered beams and brackets support the roof above. There are two thrones placed to the rear of the chamber for His Holiness Dalai Lama and Ven. Sras Rinpoche and seating for the monks are arranged in two rows along the aisles of the dukhang. 101 volumes of Kangyur are placed on wooden shelves located on the side walls. An image of Jigched stands in the northwest corner while on the rear wall there is a pedestal on which rest images of Shakyamuni and Chanrazig. There is a small skylight above the central space. The walls are painted with images of various guardian deities and Bodhisattvas. The *dukhang* has a wooden floor. From the courtyard doors lead to the *zimchung* and other living rooms. To the left of the *dukhang* lies the Dolma *lhakhang* which contains images of the 21 Tara's. The *zimchung* (quarter of the head Lama) lies at the back. The *gonkhang,* or the Lhamo *lhakhang,* is located towards the left of the dukhang on the first floor. It has two elaborate *rabsal* with decorated wooden lattice work frames. The Lhamo *lhakhang* is a double storeyed building and the *lhakhang* itself is located on the first floor. The facade has an elaborate *rabsal* with decorated wooden tiers and latticed frames, facing the court. The entrance is from the courtyard through a wooden doorway. From the corridor, a flight of steps leads to the Lhamo *lhakhang* which is also known as the *gonkhang*. It houses an image of the goddess Paldan Lhamo, protector of the Ridzong monastery. Lhamo *lhakhang* also contains a number of *thangka* hung from the ceiling depicting the dream sequences of the Panchen Lama. Adjacent to the Lhamo *lhakhang* is the Theckchen *dukhang*. The Thekchen *dukhang* is a three storeyed building with an elaborate timber framed *rabsal* on the front facade. The opening has decorative lattice work frames. The access to the *dukhang* is from the courtyard. A decorated wooden doorway leads through a corridor and a flight of stairs to the first floor where the *dukhang* is located. It is a large space with six ornamental columns and brackets holding the decorated tiered beams over which is laid a traditional roof made of timber beams, joists, *taalu*, grass and compacted mud. The rear section of the room is double storeyed and has a skylight through which light falls on the deities faces. There is a high pedestal to the rear which contains large images of Jo-Rinpoche and Gyawa Chamba (Maitreya). There are two silver *chorten* studded with precious stones placed on the same pedestal. There is an elaborate wooden frame and configuration around the images. Volumes of the Kangyur and Tangyur are kept towards the right. The Kilkhor *lhakhang* is a single storey building built on a square plan. The chamber has four openings on all four sides. Three of these openings are permanently locked while the fourth is opened to provide access to the Kilkhor. The model of the *mandala* is encased in a glass frame and is located in the centre of the chamber with space around for circumambulation. There is a covered corridor running around the chamber which is used for circumambulation. The building has a traditional roof comprising of timber beams, joists, *taalu*, grass and compacted mud. The walls are mud plastered and whitewashed from the exterior while the walls of the main structure are painted in ochre. The buildings are built in stone and mud brick masonry and are externally mud plastered and whitewashed. The roof of all buildings are the traditional roofs made of wooden beams, joists, *taalu*, grass and compacted mud while the floors are in timber and mud. The various *lhakhang* and *dukhang* are embellished with wall paintings.

SOURCE OF INFORMATION Resident Monks and the Information Board, Ridzong, Khaltse, Ladakh

Skudung

INVENTORY NO.
KHALTSE / RIDZONG / 02 / 2004

Temple | In Use | Public (Ridzong *Gonpa*) | Around 180 years old

SETTING
The Skudung is oriented to the southwest and is built on a lower level to the south of the main *dukhang* and *lhakhang*.

SIGNIFICANCE
The Skudung was the first temple built in Ridzong, and houses the caves where Tsultim Nyima, the founder of the *gonpa*, meditated for many years and which can still be seen. Today, it houses a *chorten* containing his relics.

DESCRIPTION
The Skudung is a simple building built on a square plan. It has a large open court to the front which is the terraced roof of the floor below. From here, a flight of steps leads to the portico of the Skudung *lhakhang*. The walls of the portico are painted with images of the four guardian deities and have two wooden columns, decorated brackets and ornamental tiers supporting the roof above. A wooden doorway leads into a square chamber containing a large Changchub *chorten*. The upper level projects out of the first level to the next and

forms a tiered structure. It has a large square base on which are placed images of Shakyamuni, Gyawa Tsongkhapa and many other Bodhisattvas. There are two *tsamskhang* - one towards the northeast and one towards the east. There are small openings that lead to the *tsamskhang* from the *lhakhang*. The *tsamskhang* is a small square space big enough for a person to sit and meditate. The walls of the Skudung are covered with paintings depicting various Bodhisattvas. The flooring is in mud and the roof comprises of wooden beams, joists, *taalu*, *yagzes* and compacted mud on the top. The exterior is mud plastered and whitewashed.

STATE OF PRESERVATION
Fair

SOURCE OF INFORMATION Information Board and Resident Monks, Ridzong, Khaltse, Ladakh

Tashi Riskyong

INVENTORY NO.
KHALTSE / RIDZONG / 03 / 2004

Lhato | In Use | Public (Ridzong *Gonpa*) | Around 180 years old

SETTING
The Tashi Riskyong *lhato* is oriented to the southwest and is built on the top of a hill above the Kilkhor *lhakhang*.

SIGNIFICANCE
The *lhato* is dedicated to the protector deity of the monastery, Tashi Riskyong. Its contents are renewed every year by the monks and prayers offered for the protection of the monastery.

STATE OF PRESERVATION
Fair

DESCRIPTION
The *lhato* is a small cubical structure built on the top of a hill. It is built in stone masonry and the exterior is mud plastered and whitewashed. The edges of the roof of the *lhato* are bordered in red. There are ritual offerings of juniper branches, *khadag* (white scarves) and prayer flags on the top of the *lhato*. There is a small structure next to the *lhato*, which is probably a *tsadkhang*.

SOURCE OF INFORMATION Resident Monks, Ridzong, Khaltse, Ladakh

324

Ridzong

Gyal Chen

INVENTORY NO.
KHALTSE / RIDZONG / 04 / 2004

Lhato | In Use | Public (Ridzong *Gonpa*) | Around 180 years old

SETTING
The Gyal Chen are oriented to the southwest and are located on the four different mountains and surround the *gonpa*.

SIGNIFICANCE
The *lhato* are dedicated to the four guardian deities of the *gonpa* and are located on each side of the *gonpa* facing, east, west, north and south. The contents of the *lhato* are renewed every year on the first day of the first month of the Tibetan calendar.

STATE OF PRESERVATION
Fair

DESCRIPTION
The *lhato* are small cubical structures built in stone masonry and are mud plastered and whitewashed externally. Some of them are painted in red color. On the top of the *lhato* are placed ritual offerings of juniper branches, *khadag*, etc.

SOURCE OF INFORMATION Resident Monks, Ridzong, Khaltse, Ladakh

Tsadkhang

INVENTORY NO.
KHALTSE / RIDZONG / 05 / 2004

Tsadkhang | In Use | Public (Ridzong *Gonpa*) | Around 180 years old

SETTING
The *tsadkhang* is oriented to the south west and is located above the vehicular road opposite the new school building.

SIGNIFICANCE
The *tsadkhang* houses ritual offerings of *tsa-tsa*.

DESCRIPTION
The *tsadkhang* comprises of two cubical stone masonry structures. The exterior surface of the *tsadkhang* is mud plastered and whitewashed. There is a small opening with a wooden frame facing the southwest. Inside are placed several *tsa-tsa*. The roof the *tsadkhang* is a traditional one made of timber joists, *taalu* and compacted mud. The edges of the roof as well as the edges of opening are bordered in red colour.

STATE OF PRESERVATION
Fair

SOURCE OF INFORMATION Information Board and Resident Monks, Ridzong, Khaltse, Ladakh

325

Tsadkhang

INVENTORY NO.
KHALTSE / RIDZONG / 06 / 2004

Tsadkhang | In Use | Pub (Ridzong *Gonpa*) | Around 180 years old

SETTING
The *tsadkhang* is oriented to the east and is located on top of a hill opposite the vehicular road.

SIGNIFICANCE
The *tsadkhang* is built to house ritual offerings or *tsa-tsa*.

DESCRIPTION
The *tsadkhang* is a small cubical structure made of stone and mud brick masonry and is mud plastered and whitewashed on the exterior. It has a small opening facing east and the *tsa-tsa* are placed inside this. The opening is bordered in red colour as is the parapet of the roof. The roof itself is made of wooden joists, *taalu*, grass and compacted mud.

STATE OF PRESERVATION
Fair

SOURCE OF INFORMATION Information Board and Resident Monks, Ridzong, Khaltse, Ladakh

Ridzong

Kagan *Chorten*

INVENTORY NO.
KHALTSE / RIDZONG / 07 / 2004

Chorten | In Use | Public (Ridzong *Gonpa*) | Around 180 years old

SETTING
The Kagan *chorten* is oriented to the southwest and is located below the monastic complex, along the vehicular road.

SIGNIFICANCE
The Kagan *chorten* is contemporary to the monastery and was built by Ven. Tsultim Nyima 180 years ago. By passing through the passage of the *chorten*, believers accrue merit seen as a first step towards enlightenment.

DESCRIPTION
The Kagan *chorten* consists of two thick parallel walls over which rests a large Changchub *chorten*. The walls are built in stone and mud brick masonry and are plastered and whitewashed on the exterior. The inner surface of the walls is painted in ochre and red. The parapet over the roof of the ceiling has a traditional motif painted around it and there are stucco relief images (*pa-tra*) on the base panels of the *chorten*. The dome of the *chorten* is surmounted by a

SOURCE OF INFORMATION Resident Monks, Ridzong, Khaltse, Ladakh

chugsum khorlo which symbolizes the 13 steps towards enlightenment. A metal crown is placed on the top. The *chorten* has been cement plastered and whitewashed recently. To the southeast of the *chorten* and adjacent to its base are several prayer wheels and small niches for butter lamps.

STATE OF PRESERVATION
Fair

Ching-Tsam

INVENTORY NO.
KHALTSE / RIDZONG / 08 / 2004

Vernacular Building | In Use | Public (Ridzong *Gonpa*) | Around 120 years old

STATE OF PRESERVATION
Showing Signs of Deterioration

SETTING
The Ching-Tsam is oriented to the east and is located below the monastic complex, at a little distance from the main complex.

SIGNIFICANCE
The Ching-Tsam was built later than the *gonpa* for the guests or pilgrims who spend the night in Ridzong. It provides basic pilgrim facilities.

DESCRIPTION
The rest house is a simple building with a plain exterior. The front is single storey with doors and windows lined in one row. The rear portion is double storeyed with a verandah at a corner supported over wooden columns and brackets. The parapet is painted with a band of red. The building is built in stone and mud brick masonry and exterior is mud plastered and whitewashed. It has a traditional roof made of wooden beams, joists, *taalu*, grass and compacted mud. The floor is laid in compacted mud.

SOURCE OF INFORMATION Resident Monks, Ridzong, Khaltse, Ladakh

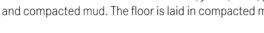

Ridzong

326

Group of *Chorten*, *Mane* Wall and *Tsadkhang*

INVENTORY NO.
KHALTSE / RIDZONG / 09 / 2004

Chorten / Mane Wall | In Use | Public (Ridzong *Gonpa*) | Around 180 years old

SETTING
Oriented to the southeast, the group of structures is located along the road as it winds up towards the *gonpa*.

SIGNIFICANCE
The structures are believed to have been built along with the *gonpa*. Located along the path leading to the *gonpa*, the *chorten* and *mane* wall are circumambulated by believers as an act of merit. The *chorten* is a Changchub *chorten* which symbolizes the Buddha's enlightenment. The *tsadkhang* houses ritual offerings of *tsa-tsa*.

DESCRIPTION
The site comprises of a *chorten*, a *tsadkhang* and a *mane* wall. The *chorten* has been recently repaired and is cement plastered and whitewashed on the exterior. It has a tall

chugsum khorlo on the top symbolizing the 13 steps towards enlightenment. The *mane* wall is a dry stone masonry wall built in a random plan with inscribed *mane* stone placed on its horizontal surface. The *tsadkhang* is a cubical structure built in stone and mud brick masonry with a traditional roof above made of timber joists, *taalu* and compacted mud. The edge of the roof has been bordered in red. Inside it houses a number of *tsa-tsa*.

STATE OF PRESERVATION
Fair

SOURCE OF INFORMATION Resident Monks, Ridzong, Khaltse, Ladakh

Ridzong

327

Mane Wall and Rock Carving

INVENTORY NO.
KHALTSE / RIDZONG / 10 / 2004

Mane Wall | In Use | Public (Ridzong *Gonpa*) | Around 180 years old

SETTING
The rock carving and *mane* wall are oriented to the east and are located west of the vehicular road amid willow trees and shrubs. The structure is well hidden in the vegetation.

SIGNIFICANCE
The rock carving and *mane* wall are believed to be as old as the *gonpa*. The site lies along the path leading to the *gonpa* and is circumambulated by the devout to accumulate merit.

DESCRIPTION
The site consists of a small rectangular enclosure adjacent to the vehicular road. The enclosure is built in stone masonry and has walls on three sides with the fourth side being open to the front. Inside the enclosure rests a rock carving depicting Shakyamuni Buddha in a seated position.

It has been engraved and then painted over. The exterior surface of the walls have been painted in red. The roof is made of slabs of stone.

STATE OF PRESERVATION
Advanced State of Decay

SOURCE OF INFORMATION Resident Monks, Ridzong, Khaltse, Ladakh

Gyes Nyan *Lhato*

INVENTORY NO.
KHALTSE / RIDZONG / 11 / 2004

Lhato | In Use | Public (Ridzong *Gonpa*) | Around 150 years old

SETTING
The *lhato* is oriented to the north and is located on the top of the hill above the vehicular road, about three kms before the main Ridzong monastery.

SIGNIFICANCE
The *lhato* is dedicated to the wrathful deity who is the protector deity of the Chulichan nunnery and is contemporary to the nunnery. The contents of the *lhato* are renewed every year and prayers are held at the time.

DESCRIPTION
The site comprises of two *lhato* built on a stone boulder on the top of a mountain. The *lhato* are cubical structures built in stone masonry which are painted in red. Ritual offering of juniper branches are tied together with *khadag* and placed on the top of the *lhato*.

STATE OF PRESERVATION
Fair

SOURCE OF INFORMATION Resident Monks, Ridzong, Khaltse, Ladakh

Rigsum Gonbo

INVENTORY NO.
KHALTSE / RIDZONG / 12 / 2004

Rigsum Gonbo | In Use | Public (Ridzong *Gonpa*) | Around 150 years old

SETTING
The *rigsum gonbo* is oriented to the south east and is located along the road leading to the *gonpa*. It is surrounded by dense vegetation and lies northwest of the main road.

SIGNIFICANCE
The *rigsum gonbo* is believed to have been built during the same period as the *gonpa*. It was built to protect the monastery from natural calamities and disease.

DESCRIPTION
The *rigsum gonbo* is a rectangular structure built in stone and mud brick masonry. It has a flat roof above comprising of wooden joists and willow twigs. It is closed on three sides while the front is open. There are three small *chorten* within representing the three Bodhisattvas. Most of the structure has crumbled and it is difficult to identify in the thick vegetative overgrowth.

STATE OF PRESERVATION
Danger of Disappearance

SOURCE OF INFORMATION Resident Nuns of Chuli Chan Nunnery, Chuli Chan, Ridzong, Khaltse, Ladakh

NIRLAC

Thardot Choling (Chuli Chan)

INVENTORY NO.
KHALTSE / RIDZONG / 13 / 2004

Gonpa | In Use | Public (Ridzong *Gonpa*) | Around 150 years old

SETTING
The Thardot Choling is oriented to the southwest and is located along the road leading to the *gonpa*, about 3 - 4 kms before the main *gonpa*. It lies northeast of the vehicular road and is surrounded by apricot orchards and willow trees.

SIGNIFICANCE
Ven. Tsultim Nyima's wife, sister and son renounced worldly life and his wife and sister became nuns establishing this nunnery a little later than the *gonpa*. Later, it became popularly known as Chuli Chan nunnery. It is considered to be the most disciplined and strict nunnery in Ladakh.

DESCRIPTION
The Chuli Chan is a large complex with the main building lying to the rear. Living quarters for the nuns are also towards the rear. The front portion of the building is double storeyed and is built on a rectangular plan. The top most floor houses images of deities and Bodhisattvas. It has an elaborate opening with a wooden frame around it. The western side of the building has been pulled down and a new structure was being constructed at the time of listing. In front of the Thardot Choling there are some *tsadkhang* housing *tsa-tsa*.

STATE OF PRESERVATION
Fair

Ridzong

329

Saspol

Saspol is situated on the right side of the River Indus, about 60 kms from Leh. Saspol is one of the biggest villages in *Sham* (lower Ladakh). It consists of four hamlets namely Yul, Madartse, Sencha and Gurphuk. The land can be cultivated twice a year and several kinds of fruits and vegetables are grown here. Saspol is also considered to be one of the oldest villages as it is said that Lhachen Takpalde built a fort in Saspol in the 11th century. At present, there are about 149 households in Saspol.

Listed by: Deldan Angmo and Jassu Singh
Year: 2004

Bawo Marpo

INVENTORY NO.
KHALTSE / SASPOL / 01 / 2004

Temple | In Use | Public (Likir *Gonpa*) | Around 14th century

SETTING

The cave temples are oriented to the south and are approached from the main Leh - Srinagar highway. A path leads through agricultural fields and to the foot of a hill from where a steep climb on a winding gravel pathway leads to the caves. The site is located below the palace ruins which lie to the west. The village is located to the north.

SIGNIFICANCE

The cave temples are associated with the legendary Lotsava Rinchen Zangpo although recent research places them to a later period of around 13th – 14th centuries. The paintings inside the cave differ stylistically from later period paintings and represent an interregnum between the early Indian influenced Buddhist art in Ladakh as seen in Alchi, Mangyu, Sumda etc. from the later Tibetan art styles. The caves are believed to have been the site of the original Likir *gonpa* which was later shifted to the Likir.

DESCRIPTION

A flight of stone steps leads to a small door which opens into the cave. The walls of the cave are adorned with beautiful painting of various Bodhisattvas. The main central image is the large of the Buddha, surrounded by various other deities. The exterior is mud plastered and whitewashed. It has been built using stone and mud brick masonry. Externally, the structure is mud plastered and whitewashed.

STATE OF PRESERVATION

Advanced State of Decay

SOURCE OF INFORMATION Nawang Norbu Gompapa, Saspol, Khaltse, Ladakh

Group of *Chorten* and *Mane* Walls

INVENTORY NO.
KHALTSE / SASPOL / 02 / 2004

Mane Wall / *Chorten* | In Use | Public (Community) | Around 250 years old

STATE OF PRESERVATION
Advanced State of Decay

SETTING
The *chorten* can be approached from the main Leh – Srinagar highway and lie along the path that leads to the Bawo Marpo. The site is surrounded by village houses to the north and fields to the south.

SIGNIFICANCE
The *chorten* and *mane* wall are believed to have been built around 250 years ago as an act of merit. The *chorten* are Changchub *chorten* symbolizing the Buddha's enlightenment. The structures are circumambulated by villagers to accumulate merit.

DESCRIPTION
The site comprises of four groups of *chorten* and *mane* walls. The first group comprises of a linear *mane* wall and four *chorten*, three of which are in complete ruins and only one survives intact. This is followed by a second group of four Changchub *chorten* and a large rectangular *mane* wall followed by another three *chorten*. The *mane* walls are built in dry stone masonry and have inscribed *mane* stones placed on the horizontal surface. The *chorten* are made of stone and mud brick masonry and are mud plastered and whitewashed externally. The third group consists of a long *mane* wall and small whitewashed *chorten*. The final cluster has a large rectangular dry stone masonry mane wall, and a high square platform on which rests large Changchub *chorten*. The largest *chorten* has a square base. A path cuts through the structure and on the other side of the path is another stone platform with three *chorten* followed by a rectangular mane and two smaller *chorten*. A little further up is a large Changchub *chorten* with stucco relief work on the base panels (*pa-tra*). Many of the *chorten* are lying in ruins and the external layer of mud plaster and whitewash has eroded over time.

Saspol

333

Group of *Chorten*

INVENTORY NO.
KHALTSE / SASPOL / 03 / 2004

Chorten | In Use | Public (Community) | Around 300 years old

SETTING
The *chorten* are oriented to the south and are approached from the main Leh - Srinagar highway. A path leads up to the Bawo Marpo and en route there is a flat stretch of land overlooking the village on which the *chorten* stand. There are fields and village houses to the south at a lower level. The caves are to the north east at a higher level.

SIGNIFICANCE
The *chorten* were built about 300 years ago as an act of merit and are largely Changchub *chorten* symbolizing the Buddha's enlightenment. The *lubang* is dedicated to the *lu,* or the deities of the underworld.

DESCRIPTION
The site comprises of a line of *chorten* and a *lubang*. The *lubang* is a cubical stone masonry structure which is mud plastered and whitewashed on the exterior. Near the *lubang* are a group of *chorten* most of which are in ruins. Only two *chorten* are intact. The *chorten* are built in stone and mud

brick masonry and are mud plastered and whitewashed externally. Most of the *chorten* have collapsed completely or have eroded and lost their original form.

STATE OF PRESERVATION
Advanced State of Decay

SOURCE OF INFORMATION Nawang Norbu, Saspol, Khaltse, Ladakh

Group of *Chorten*

INVENTORY NO.
KHALTSE / SASPOL / 04 / 2004

Chorten | In Use | Public (Community) | Around 300 years old

SETTING
The *chorten* are oriented to the northeast and can be approached from the main Leh - Srinagar highway. They are located en route to the Bawo Marpo along the path that leads to the caves. The *chorten* are scattered on a hill with the caves to the north and the village below to the east and southeast.

SIGNIFICANCE
The *chorten* were built along the route leading to the former Likir *gonpa* and are still worshipped by the villagers who circumambulate them as an act of merit while travelling along this path.

DESCRIPTION
The site comprises of five *chorten*, some of which are in ruins. The *chorten* are scattered across the hillside and lie below the caves. The *chorten* are of different sizes and are

built in stone and mud brick masonry with an external layer of mud plaster and whitewash. Most of them have eroded or collapsed and it is difficult to identify their forms.

STATE OF PRESERVATION
Danger of Disappearance

SOURCE OF INFORMATION Nawang Norbu, Saspol, Khaltse, Ladakh

Saspol *Khar*

INVENTORY NO.
KHALTSE / SASPOL / 05 / 2004

Fort / Palace | Abandoned | Public (State / Community) | Around 700 years old

SETTING

The Saspol *khar* is oriented to the south and can be approached from the main Leh - Srinagar highway. A narrow footpath winds along the stream towards the mountains where a steep climb from the foot of the hill leads up to the fort. It is located on a hill above the Bawo Marpo caves which lie to the east. Tseb Lhamo *lhato* is located to its immediate south.

SIGNIFICANCE

The fort is believed to date back to the 13th century. It possibly formed part of a defence system for lower Ladakh. A *lhato* dedicated to the protector deity still survives in the fort and its contents are renewed every year by the villages on the occasion of the Ladakhi Losar.

DESCRIPTION

The fort is a massive structure with thick walls. It was approximately three to four storeys high and only the walls stand intact today. There is a heap of debris lying to the

east of the walls. There is no defined entrance to the structure, but it can be accessed through a large arch-shaped hole on the eastern wall. There is a square space within which further leads up to a small cantilevered terrace on which is built the *lhato*. The roof no longer exists and there is another free standing wall on the northeast. It has a stone plinth on which rest thick rammed earth walls. There is another tower-like structure at a distance which has a similar construction style.

STATE OF PRESERVATION
Danger of Disappearance

SOURCE OF INFORMATION Ishey Putit, Saspol, Khaltse, Ladakh

Saspol

335

Chorten

INVENTORY NO.
KHALTSE / SASPOL / 06 / 2004

Chorten | In Use | Public (Community) | Around 180 years old

SETTING

The *chorten* is oriented to the south and can be approached from the main Leh - Srinagar highway. A footpath winds up towards the Bawo Marpo and the *chorten* is located along this path next to the caves. It is surrounded by smaller *chorten* to the south and west, and a group of ruined *chorten* to the west.

SIGNIFICANCE

The *chorten* is located along the path leading to the caves which were the site of the former Likir *gonpa* and would have been circumambulated by villagers as they visited the caves. It is a Changchub *chorten* which symbolizes the Buddha's enlightenment.

DESCRIPTION

The *chorten* is built in stone and mud brick masonry and is mud plastered and whitewashed on the exterior. The external surface of the *chorten* has eroded considerably leading to a loss in the original form of the *chorten*.

STATE OF PRESERVATION
Advanced State of Decay

SOURCE OF INFORMATION Nawang Norbu, Saspol, Khaltse, Ladakh

Group of *Chorten*

INVENTORY NO.
KHALTSE / SASPOL / 07 / 2004

Chorten | In Use | Public (Community) | Around 1000 years old

Changchub *chorten*. It is built in stone and mud brick masonry and is mud plastered and whitewashed externally.

SETTING
The *chorten* are oriented to the southeast and can be approached from the main Leh - Srinagar highway. A path winds through fields and orchards to the caves and the *chorten* are located to the west of the caves along the slope of the mountain. They are surrounded by other *chorten* to the south and west, while the caves lie to the east.

SIGNIFICANCE
The *chorten* are located along the path that leads to the caves and would have been circumambulated by villagers as an act of merit when the visited the caves. The sole surviving *chorten* is a Changchub *chorten* symbolizing the Buddha's enlightenment.

STATE OF PRESERVATION
Advanced State of Decay

DESCRIPTION
The site comprises of three *chorten* built on a stone masonry base. Two of the three *chorten* have completely collapsed. The central *chorten* still survives and is a

SOURCE OF INFORMATION Nawang Norbu, Saspol, Khaltse, Ladakh

Tseb Lhamo *Lhato*

INVENTORY NO.
KHALTSE / SASPOL / 08 / 2004

Lhato | In Use | Public (Community)

STATE OF PRESERVATION
Advanced State of Decay

SETTING
The *lhato* is oriented to the south and can be approached from the main Leh - Srinagar highway.

SIGNIFICANCE
The *lhato* is dedicated to the protector goddess of the village, Tseb Lhamo. Every year, on the occasion of Losar, the villagers gather here for rituals and prayers invoking the deity's protection for the village. The contents of the *lhato* are renewed at this time.

DESCRIPTION
The *lhato* is an irregular shaped structure built in dry stone masonry. It lies next to the fort ruins. Ritual offerings of juniper twigs and *khadag* are placed in the center of the structure.

SOURCE OF INFORMATION Nawang Norbu, Saspol, Khaltse, Ladakh

Group of *Chorten*

INVENTORY NO.
KHALTSE / SASPOL / 09 / 2004

Chorten | In Use | Public (Community) | Around 250 years old

SETTING

The *chorten* are oriented to the south and can be approached from the main Leh - Srinagar highway. Towards the end of the village, a path leads to the caves and the *chorten* are located along this path. There are apricot orchards to the east while the path lies to the west. There are poplar trees to the southeast.

SIGNIFICANCE

The *chorten* are circumambulated by villagers to accumulate merit. They are Changchub *chorten*, one of the eight traditional forms of *chorten* in Tibetan Buddhism and symbolize the Buddha's enlightenment.

DESCRIPTION

The site comprises two *chorten* of similar size. The *chorten* are built in stone masonry and are mud plastered and whitewashed externally. There is a circumambulatory path around the structure. The exterior is mud plastered and whitewashed.

SOURCE OF INFORMATION Ishey Putit, Saspol, Khaltse, Ladakh

STATE OF PRESERVATION
Showing Signs of Deterioration

Chorten and *Mane* Wall (Phikhare *Chorten*)

INVENTORY NO.
KHALTSE / SASPOL / 10 / 2004

Chorten / *Mane* Wall | In Use | Public (Community) | Around 250 years old

SETTING

The *chorten* and mane wall are oriented to the south. A narrow footpath at the end of the village leads to the school complex where these are located. The structures are located south of the school building and north of the Phigarapa house. The village *spurkhang* lies further ahead.

SIGNIFICANCE

The *chorten* and *mane* wall are circumambulated by villagers to accumulate merit. The *chorten* are Changchub *chorten* which symbolize the Buddha's enlightenment.

DESCRIPTION

The site comprises three *mane* walls and two *chorten*. The first *mane* wall is a long linear stone masonry wall with a wide horizontal surface containing numerous *mane* stones.

There other two *mane* walls are circular in shape. The *chorten* are of different sizes. Both share a common stone masonry plinth. The *chorten* are built in stone and mud brick masonry and are mud plastered and whitewashed on the exterior.

STATE OF PRESERVATION
Showing Signs of Deterioration

SOURCE OF INFORMATION Tsewing Diskit, Saspol, Khaltse, Ladakh

Tsamskhang

INVENTORY NO.
KHALTSE / SASPOL / 11 / 2004

Temple | In Use | Private (Individual) | Around 180 years old

SETTING

The *tsamskhang* is oriented to the south east and is located on a small hill above the Gompapa house. There is a small *chorten* to the south.

SIGNIFICANCE

The *tsamskhang* was built by an ancestor of the Gompapa family to serve as a meditation retreat and is still used and maintained by the family for this purpose.

DESCRIPTION

The *tsamskhang* is a small double storeyed structure built on a rectangular plan. The entrance is from the front facade. The first floor has an elaborate timber framed *rabsal* in the front. The ground floor is built in the stone masonry while the first floor is built in the mud brick masonry. The rear and the side walls have no openings. The walls are mud plastered and whitewashed. There is a small Changchub *chorten* to the south of the *tsamskhang*.

STATE OF PRESERVATION
Advanced State of Decay

SOURCE OF INFORMATION Ishey Putit, Saspol, Khaltse, Ladakh

Saspol

338

Spurkhang

INVENTORY NO.
KHALTSE / SASPOL / 12 / 2004

Cremation Ground | In Use | Public (Community)

SETTING

The *spurkhang* is oriented to the south and is located towards the end of the village and lies beyond the school complex.

SIGNIFICANCE

The *spurkhang* has been the village cremation ground for many centuries. Each family has one *spurkhang* which is reused at the time of the death of a family member.

DESCRIPTION

The *spurkhang* is a large open area located north of the school complex. It has number of square and rectangular structures built in mud brick masonry which are mud plastered and whitewashed on the exterior. Some of the units have motifs painted on the exterior. The *spurkhang* are renewed at the time of use.

STATE OF PRESERVATION
Advanced State of Decay

SOURCE OF INFORMATION Ishey Putit, Saspol, Khaltse, Ladakh

Phigarpa House

INVENTORY NO.
KHALTSE / SASPOL / 13 / 2004

Vernacular Building | In Use | Private (Individual) | Around 120 years old

SETTING
The Phigarpa house is oriented to the southwest and is located towards the end of the village. It is surrounded by fields to the south and there is a huge boulder to the northwest.

SIGNIFICANCE
The Phigarpa house was built by ancestors of the Phigarpa family around 120 years ago and the family has resided here ever since. The house is built in the traditional style and is a good example of vernacular architecture in the village.

DESCRIPTION
The Phigarpa house is built along a slope with three floors to the north and two floors to the south. The ground floor is constructed in the stone masonry and has no windows. It is used for storage. The first floor has small timber framed window openings and is constructed in mud brick masonry. The second floor houses the family temple to the north and

a large open terrace to the south. There is a *rabsal* at this level which projects out and can be accessed through a door. The house has a traditional roof made of timber beams, joists, *taalu*, grass and compacted mud which is surrounded by a low mud parapet. Prayer flags are posted at the corners of the roof. The exterior is mud plastered and whitewashed.

STATE OF PRESERVATION
Showing Signs of Deterioration

SOURCE OF INFORMATION Ishey Putit, Saspol, Khaltse, Ladakh

Saspol

339

Group of *Mane* Wall and *Chorten*

INVENTORY NO.
KHALTSE / SASPOL / 14 / 2004

Mane Wall / *Chorten* | In Use | Public (Community)

SETTING
The *chorten* and *mane* wall are oriented to the southeast and are located towards the end of the village near the school complex which lies to its north east and the Gompapa house on the south.

SIGNIFICANCE
The *chorten* and *mane* wall are located at the edge of the village and are circumambulated by villagers to accumulate merit. The *chorten* are all Changchub *chorten* which symbolize the Buddha's enlightenment.

DESCRIPTION
The site consists of a linear *mane* wall and four *chorten*. The *chorten* are placed on rectangular random rubble masonry platforms. The first three *chorten* are similar in size and share a common platform, while the fourth is larger and stand slightly apart. The *chorten* are built in stone and mud

brick masonry with mud mortar and are mud plastered and whitewashed on the exterior. The *mane* wall is a linear dry stone masonry wall with *mane* stones placed on the horizontal surface. It is whitewashed externally.

STATE OF PRESERVATION
Showing Signs of Deterioration

SOURCE OF INFORMATION Tsering Disket, Saspol, Khaltse, Ladakh

Gompapa *Khangpa*

INVENTORY NO.
KHALTSE / SASPOL / 15 / 2004

Vernacular Building | In Use | Private (Individual) | Around 180 years old

SETTING
The Gompapa *khangpa* is oriented to the southeast and is located along a footpath towards the end of the village. There is a *tsamskhang* to the northeast.

SIGNIFICANCE
The Gompapa house was built around 180 years ago by an ancestor of the Gompapa family and successive generations of the family have resided here ever since. The house is built in the traditional style and is a good example of vernacular architecture in the village.

DESCRIPTION
The Gompapa house is a large three storeyed house built on a rectangular plan. The ground floor is built in stone masonry and is used primarily for housing animals and storage while the first and second floors house the living quarters. The upper levels are built in mud brick masonry with mud mortar. Externally, the house is mud plastered and whitewashed. The entrance is from the southeast facade. There are large timber framed windows on the upper floors with tiered lintels and a black border. The house has a traditional roof above around which runs a low height parapet painted in black. There are prayer flags posted at the corners of the roof. There is a small Changchub *chorten* to the south east and a *lubang* to the northwest.

STATE OF PRESERVATION
Showing Signs of Deterioration

SOURCE OF INFORMATION Tsering Dorjey Gompapa, Saspol, Khaltse, Ladakh

Saspol

340

Hirgopa *Khangchen*

INVENTORY NO.
KHALTSE / SASPOL / 16 / 2004

Vernacular Building | In Use | Private (Individual) | Around 120 years old

SETTING
The Hirgopa house is oriented to the south and lies along the village footpath towards the end of the village. There are other villages houses to the east and west while the path lies to the south of the house.

SIGNIFICANCE
The Hirgopa house was built around 120 years ago by ancestors of the Hirgopa family and successive generations have resided here ever since. The house is built in the traditional style and is a good example of vernacular architecture in the village.

DESCRIPTION
The Hirgopa house is a large three storeyed building with an entrance directly from the village path. The ground floor is constructed in stone masonry and has small openings for ventilation and light. This level is used primarily for storage. The first and second floors are built in mud brick masonry and house the family's living quarters. The first floor has large windows while the second floor has more elaborate windows with timber frames and tiered lintels. The windows are all bordered in black. There is a large *rabsal* on the topmost floor. The house has a traditional roof made of timber beams, joists, *taalu*, grass and compacted mud. The roof is surrounded by a low height parapet painted in black. Externally, the house is mud plastered and whitewashed.

STATE OF PRESERVATION
Showing Signs of Deterioration

SOURCE OF INFORMATION Tsering Disket, Saspol, Khaltse, Ladakh

Group of *Chorten*

INVENTORY NO.
KHALTSE / SASPOL / 17 / 2004

Chorten | In Use | Public (Community) | Around 150 years old

SETTING
The group of *chorten* is oriented to the southeast and lie along a path near the Shalmarpa house. The *chorten* are surrounded by the Shalmarpa house to the southwest and Labapa house to the southeast. There is a large open space to the south and fields to the north.

SIGNIFICANCE
The *chorten* were built in the past as an act of merit. They are Changchub *chorten* which symbolize the Buddha's enlightenment.

DESCRIPTION
The site comprises three *chorten* built on a common stone masonry base. The *chorten* are built in stone and mud brick masonry and are mud plastered and whitewashed externally. There are smaller rectangular openings on the domes of the *chorten* facing southeast. The external surface has largely eroded causing a loss in the original form of the *chorten*.

SOURCE OF INFORMATION Tsering Disket, Saspol, Khaltse, Ladakh

STATE OF PRESERVATION
Advanced State of Decay

Saspol

341

Rigsum Gonbo

INVENTORY NO.
KHALTSE / SASPOL / 18 / 2004

Rigsum Gonbo | In Use | Private (Individual) | Around 150 years old

SETTING
The *rigsum gonbo* is oriented to the east and is located along the slope of a hill west of the village houses. A narrow path leads up the hill to the site.

SIGNIFICANCE
The *rigsum gonbo* was built by an ancestor of the Shalmarpa family around 120 years ago to protect the family from natural disasters and disease.

DESCRIPTION
The *rigsum gonbo* is built on a rectangular plan and has walls on three sides with the fourth side open to the east. The walls are built in stone and mud brick masonry and are mud plastered and whitewashed externally. Inside the enclosure, there is a high plinth on which rest three small *chorten* painted in orange, white and blue representing Jamyang, Chanrazig and Chagdor respectively. There are *chugsum khorlo* over the domes of the *chorten*. The *rigsum gonbo* has a traditional roof above.

SOURCE OF INFORMATION Dorjey Phuntsog, Saspol, Khaltse, Ladakh

STATE OF PRESERVATION
Fair

Kangyur *Lhakhang*

INVENTORY NO.
KHALTSE / SASPOL / 19 / 2004

Temple | In Use | Public (Community) | Around 400 years old

SETTING
The Kangyur *lhakhang* is oriented to the south and is located north of the main road. The Gyalwa Chamba *lhakhang* lies to the west.

SIGNIFICANCE
The Kangyur *lhakhang* forms a part of the Gyalwa Chamba complex and houses the Kangyur, or Buddhist canons.

DESCRIPTION
The Kangyur *lhakhang* is a simple double storeyed building with an entrance from the east. A wooden doorway leads to the main temple that houses an image of Lord Buddha, along with his disciples Maudgalyana and Shariputra on either side. The images and a large collection of Buddhists canons (Kangyur) are kept on elaborate wooden shelves. The room has four decorated wooden columns supporting a skylight and a traditional roof above. The temple is built in stone and mud brick masonry and the walls are mud plastered and whitewashed externally. The floor of the *lhakhang* is in timber.

STATE OF PRESERVATION
Advanced State of Decay

SOURCE OF INFORMATION Tsering Dorjey Larjay, Saspol, Khaltse, Ladakh

Kagan *Chorten*

INVENTORY NO.
KHALTSE / SASPOL / 20 / 2004

Chorten | In Use | Public (Community) | Around 250 years old

SETTING
The Kagan *chorten* is oriented to the south and is located along the roadside towards the west. The River Indus flows beyond.

SIGNIFICANCE
The Kagan *chorten* is a gateway *chorten* and villagers accumulate merit by passing through the passage of the *chorten*.

DESCRIPTION
The Kagan *chorten* consists of two thick parallel walls over which rests a large Changchub *chorten*. The walls are almost ten feet high and are built in stone and mud brick masonry with an external layer of mud plaster and whitewash. The ceiling of the passage is made of timber and is in the shape of a *mandala*. The *chorten* above is built in stone and mud brick masonry and is mud plastered and whitewashed externally. The dome of the *chorten* has a tall *chugsum khorlo* above symbolizing the 13 steps towards enlightenment. The base panels of the Changchub *chorten* have stucco motifs (*pa-tra*).

STATE OF PRESERVATION
Advanced State of Decay

SOURCE OF INFORMATION Nawang Norbu, Saspol, Khaltse, Ladakh

Gyalwa Chamba
Lhakhang

INVENTORY NO.
KHALTSE / SASPOL / 21 / 2004

Temple | In Use | Public (Likir *Gonpa*) | Around 400 years old

SETTING
The temple is located north of the main road opposite the State Bank of India building.

SIGNIFICANCE
The temple is believed to date back 400 years and is one of the principal places of worship in the village. Monks from Likir *gonpa* are deputed here to carry out prayers and rituals. The temple houses colossal standing clay images of Bodhisattvas in niches on either side of the main image of Chamba which are similar to those at Alchi.

DESCRIPTION
The Gyalwa Chamba *lhakhang* is accessed through a small forecourt after passing by a prayer wheel and two large Changchub *chorten*. The chorten are built in stone and mud brick masonry and are mud plastered and whitewashed externally. The base panels are painted in red with stucco motifs (*pa-tra*). The forecourt leads to a small portico with two large ornamented wooden columns. The walls of the porch are covered with images of the four guardian deities. A wooden door leads into a large hall with six ornamental columns. The front four columns support a skylight provides the light and ventilation into the hall. This hall is single storey high and the walls are adorned with painting depicting various Bodhisattvas. There is a small image of Chanrazig framed in a small wooden shelf with glass panels. In the right corner of the hall is a rock sculpture of Chamba which was obliterated when a fire broke out in the *gonpa* several years ago. There is small door in the rear wall that opens into a double storeyed chamber that houses a giant central image of Chamba in a seated position. There are two large clay images of Bodhisattvas on the either side of the Chamba, in a standing position, each placed in a niche. The walls are painted above the door and there is an opening above this. The hall has timber flooring while the enclosure housing the Chamba image has a mud floor. The temple is built in stone and mud brick masonry and is mud plastered and whitewashed on the exterior.

STATE OF PRESERVATION
Advanced State of Decay

Saspol

343

SOURCE OF INFORMATION Tsering Dorjey Phuntsog Larjay, Saspol, Khaltse, Ladakh

Rigsum Gonbo and *Chorten*

INVENTORY NO.
KHALTSE / SASPOL / 22 / 2004

Rigsum Gonbo / Chorten | In Use | Public (Community) | Around 180 years old

SETTING
The *rigsum gonbo* and *chorten* are oriented to the southeast and are located on the right side of the road with the River Indus flowing further south.

SIGNIFICANCE
The *rigsum gonbo* was built around 180 years ago to protect the village from natural disasters and disease.

DESCRIPTION
The site comprises of a *rigsum gonbo* and a group of *chorten* to the southeast. The *rigsum gonbo* consist of three *chorten* of similar size constructed on a common random rubble masonry base. Two of the three *chorten* have completely collapsed and the standing *chorten* is a Changchub *chorten*. The structure is mud plaster and whitewashed. It is built in stone and mud brick masonry.

STATE OF PRESERVATION
Danger of Disappearance

SOURCE OF INFORMATION Nawang Norbu, Saspol, Khaltse, Ladakh

Saspol

344

Group of *Chorten*

INVENTORY NO.
KHALTSE / SASPOL / 23 / 2004

Chorten | In Use | Public (Community) | Around 180 years old

SETTING
The *chorten* are oriented to the southeast and are approached from the main Leh – Srinagar highway which lies to the northwest while the river Indus flows to the southeast. There are mountains to the north and northwest beyond the road.

SIGNIFICANCE
The *chorten* were built along the main road and are circumambulated by villagers as an act of merit when passing along this path. The *chorten* are mainly Changchub *chorten* which symbolize the Buddha's enlightenment.

DESCRIPTION
The site comprises ten *chorten* placed on a U-shaped stone platform. There are four *chorten* to the northeast and one *chorten* to the northwest. This *chorten* is the largest of the group. There is a Namgyal *chorten* at the centre of the site.

The *chorten* are all built in stone and mud brick masonry with mud mortar and are mud plastered and whitewashed externally.

STATE OF PRESERVATION
Advanced State of Decay

SOURCE OF INFORMATION Nawang Norbu, Saspol, Khaltse, Ladakh

Group of *Chorten*

INVENTORY NO.
KHALTSE / SASPOL / 24 / 2004

Chorten | In Use | Public (Community) | Around 100 years old

SETTING
The *chorten* are oriented to the east and are located near the Tongyokpa house. The site is surrounded by agricultural fields to the east, a road to the north and Tongyokpa house to the west.

SIGNIFICANCE
The *chorten* are all Changchub *chorten* and symbolize the Buddha's enlightenment. The *chorten* are circumambulated by villagers to accumulate merit.

DESCRIPTION
The group consists of four *chorten* built on a common base. The *chorten* are built in stone and mud brick masonry and are mud plastered and whitewashed externally. There are small niches facing east on the domes of the *chorten*. There are red markings at the corners and centres of the base panels. The external forms of the *chorten* have eroded considerably.

STATE OF PRESERVATION
Showing Signs of Deterioration

Saspol

345

SOURCE OF INFORMATION Lobzang Richen / Tongyokpa, Saspol, Khaltse, Ladakh

Saspotse

Saspotse is located about 10 kms from Likir and is accessed from a dirt road that leads from Likir towards Hemis Shukpachan.

Listed by: Deldan Angmo and Jassu Singh
Year: 2004

Shilla

Shilla can be reached from the vehicular road that diverts from the Leh - Srinagar National Highway between Khaltse and Lamayuru, towards the village. It was also known as Shilla Kukshoma. It falls under the village head (*Goba*) of Wanla. There are about 15 households in Shilla today.

Listed by: Deldan Angmo and Jassu Singh
Year: 2004

Group of *Chorten*

INVENTORY NO.
KHALTSE / SASPOTSE / 01 / 2004

Chorten | In Use | Public (Community) | Around 100 - 150 years old

SETTING
The *chorten* are oriented to the east and are located along a path at the beginning of the village just before the residential settlement. The site is surrounded by mountains and barren land.

SIGNIFICANCE
The *chorten* were built around 100 - 150 years ago by ancestors of the Khar family as an act of merit. They are located along the old path leading to the village and are circumambulated by villagers, to accumulate merit, as they travel along this path. The *chorten* are predominantly Changchub *chorten* and symbolize the Buddha's enlightenment.

DESCRIPTION
The site consists of a group of twelve *chorten*, one Kagan *chorten* and a prayer wheel. The *chorten* are built in a row along the village pathway. The first eight *chorten* are built over a common random rubble masonry base. The rest of

the *chorten* are scattered across the site. The *chorten* are built in stone and mud brick masonry and are mud plastered and whitewashed on the exterior. The exterior surface of the *chorten* has eroded over time. The Kagan *chorten* lies to the east of the site and consist of two thick parallel walls over which rests a large Changchub *chorten*. The Kagan *chorten* is built in stone and mud brick masonry and is mud plastered and whitewashed on the exterior. The ceiling over the passage is built in timber and is in the shape of a *mandala*. There is a prayer wheel to the west of the site.

STATE OF PRESERVATION
Advanced State of Decay

SOURCE OF INFORMATION Stanzin Dolma Tsildongpa, Saspotse, Khaltse, Ladakh

Akhten Naro *Lhato*

INVENTORY NO.
KHALTSE / SASPOTSE / 02 / 2004

Lhato | In Use | Private (Individual) | Around 100 - 150 years old

SETTING
The *lhato* is oriented to the southeast and is located behind the Khar residence along the slope of the hill in the village of Saspotse.

SIGNIFICANCE
The *lhato* was built around 100 - 150 years ago by an ancestor of the Khar family and is dedicated to Akhten Naro, the protector deity of the family. The deity is believed to protect the family from evil and misfortune. The contents of the *lhato* are renewed every year on the occasion of Losar.

DESCRIPTION
The *lhato* is a small cubical structure which is mud plastered and whitewashed on the exterior. It is housed within a small square structure which is open in the front and has a traditional roof above. There are ritual offerings of juniper twigs and *khadag* placed on to the top of the *lhato*.

STATE OF PRESERVATION
Showing Signs of Deterioration

SOURCE OF INFORMATION Stanzin Dolma Tsildongpa, Saspotse, Khaltse, Ladakh

Saspotse

348

NIRLAC

Group of *Chorten*

INVENTORY NO.
KHALTSE / SASPOTSE / 03 / 2004

Chorten | In Use | Public (Community)

SETTING
The *chorten* are oriented to the south and are located near the Yulgongpa house.

SIGNIFICANCE
The *chorten* are located along a narrow village path leading to the village houses and were built in the past by a villager to accumulate merit. The *chorten* are circumambulated by villagers as an act of merit. The *chorten* are Changchub *chorten* symbolizing the Buddha's enlightenment.

DESCRIPTION
The site comprises of two *chorten* located a short distance from each other. The first *chorten* lies near the Yulgongpa house and is built in stone masonry with an external layer of mud plaster and whitewash. The second *chorten* is also built in stone masonry and has deteriorated over time with the erosion of the external surface.

STATE OF PRESERVATION
Showing Signs of Deterioration

SOURCE OF INFORMATION Stanzin Dolma Tsildongpa, Saspotse, Khaltse, Ladakh

Saspotse

349

Khar House

INVENTORY NO.
KHALTSE / SASPOTSE / 04 / 2004

Vernacular Building | In Use | Private (Individual) | Around 100 - 150 years old

SETTING
The Khar house is oriented to the southeast and is located at the foothill of a mountain on which the Akhten Naro *lhato* is located.

SIGNIFICANCE
The Khar house was built around 100 - 150 years ago by an ancestor of the Khar family and successive generations have continued to reside here. The Khar family is one of the old noble families in the village. The house is built in the traditional old and is a good example of vernacular architecture in the village.

DESCRIPTION
The house is a large three storeyed building built on a rectangular plan. The entrance is from the village footpath which leads onto a courtyard in the front. The front court is used for keeping animals and a wooden doorway leads to the ground floor of the house. The ground floor has small window openings arranged in a row and is used primarily for storage. The first floor houses the family's living rooms as well as the kitchen. The second floor has a large glass room on the southern side while the family chapel lies to the north. The first and second floors have large timber framed window openings with decorated tiered lintels. The ground floor is built in stone masonry while the upper levels are built in mud brick masonry. Externally, the house is mud plastered and whitewashed. The house has a traditional roof made of timber beams, joists, *taalu*, grass and compacted mud. There are prayer flags posted at each corner. A low height parapet surrounds the roof which is bordered in black.

STATE OF PRESERVATION
Showing Signs of Deterioration

SOURCE OF INFORMATION Tsewang Norbu-Khar, Saspotse, Khaltse, Ladakh

Chorten Shrapa

INVENTORY NO.
KHALTSE / SASPOTSE / 05 / 2004

Chorten | In Use | Public (Community)

SETTING
The *chorten* are oriented to the west and are located towards the far end of the village on the east. The site is surrounded by mountains on one side and agricultural fields on the other.

SIGNIFICANCE
The group of five *chorten* appear to be Changchub *chorten* and symbolize the Buddha's enlightenment. The *chorten* are referred to as *Chorten* Shrapa meaning five *chorten*.

DESCRIPTION
The site comprises of a group of five *chorten* (*Chorten* Shrapa) of which only one survives intact while the remaining four are in ruins. The *chorten* is built in stone masonry and has some traces of mud plaster and whitewash on the external surface. Debris from the other four *chorten* lies scattered across the site.

STATE OF PRESERVATION
Advanced State of Decay

SOURCE OF INFORMATION Stanzin Dolma Tsildongpa, Saspotse, Khaltse, Ladakh

Saspotse Rinchen Gang (Saspotse *Gonpa*)

INVENTORY NO.
KHALTSE / SASPOTSE / 06 / 2004

Gonpa | In Use | Private (Likir *Gonpa*) | Around 300 years old

SETTING
The *gonpa* is oriented to the south and is located to the north of the village, surrounded by agricultural fields and willow orchards. The site is located below the Lotsawa *lagang* hill.

SIGNIFICANCE
The *gonpa* is believed to have been built around 300 years old by Likir monastery when the Lotsawa *lagang* collapsed. Monks from Likir are deputed here to carry out prayers and rituals.

DESCRIPTION
The Saspotse Rinchen Gang is a large double storeyed building. The ground floor can be accessed from the main courtyard. A flight of stairs from the courtyard leads up to the first floor. The first floor opens directly onto a courtyard, with rooms on either side for the monks who take care of the temple as well as the store rooms. The main temple is located to the north. A wooden doorway from the court leads to the temple. The room has two wooden columns and decorated brackets holding a traditional roof above. The rear wall has an elaborate shrine that houses images of Chug-Shig-Zal, Serzang, 21 Dolma as well as shelves on either side containing the Kangyur and Bum (Buddhist canons). The walls have painting of various Bodhisattvas and there are a large number of *thangkas* hanging from the ceiling.

STATE OF PRESERVATION
Showing Signs of Deterioration

SOURCE OF INFORMATION Tsering Phuntsog (*Goba*), Saspotse, Khaltse, Ladakh

Lotsawa *Lagang Gogpo*

INVENTORY NO.
KHALTSE / SASPOTSE / 07 / 2004

Temple | In Use | Public (Community) | Around 1000 years old

STATE OF PRESERVATION
Danger of Disappearance

SETTING
The group of structures are oriented to the south and are located on a hill north of the village. A steep climb from the village below leads to the *lagang* complex located on top of a hill.

SIGNIFICANCE
The group of temples are believed to date back to the time of the great translator Lotsawa Rinchen Zangpo. The fragments of painting that survive as well as the wooden figurines appear to be very old and are similar in style to those found in Sumda Chun, Mangyu etc. The site is extremely significant as it relates to an early period of Buddhist art in the region most of which has perished over the centuries. The *lhato* is dedicated to the protector deity of the village.

DESCRIPTION
The Lotsawa *lagang* comprises of three buildings as well as a number of *chorten* and a *lhato*. The first *lagang* has a small Lhabab *chorten* placed in the centre of the room. Externally, this *chorten* is painted in different colors and there are fragments of gold relief on the exterior. The upper portion of the *chorten* has collapsed. The northern and the eastern walls appear to be original ones which still retain some fragments of the original wall paintings on them. The western and southern walls have collapsed and were rebuilt by the villagers. The temple also has 20 - 25 wooden figurines of various Bodhisattvas and *chorten*, which appear to be very old. The second shrine also houses a *chorten* but is not accessible as the entrance doorway is completely blocked with debris from the roof which has caved in. The third and fourth shrines are not accessible. It appears that the temples were built in two levels. There are several *chorten* to the west of the temples which appear to be of a later period. There is a *lhato* at the extreme southern edge of the site which is dedicated to the protector deity of the village.

SOURCE OF INFORMATION Tsering Phuntsog (*Goba*), Saspotse, Khaltse, Ladakh

Zing Gog Gay *Mane* and Changchub *Chorten*

INVENTORY NO.
KHALTSE / SASPOTSE / 08 / 2004

Chorten | In Use | Public (Community) | Around 200 years old

SETTING
The *chorten* are oriented to the south and lie near the Saspotse *gonpa*. The site is surrounded by large stone boulders and thorny bushes.

SIGNIFICANCE
The *chorten* and *mane* wall are believed to have been built around 200 years ago for the well being of all sentient beings. Located near the *gonpa*, the site is circumambulated by villagers as an act of merit as they travel along this path. The *chorten* are both Changchub *chorten* symbolizing the Buddha's enlightenment.

DESCRIPTION
The site comprises of two Changchub *chorten* and a *mane* wall. The *chorten* are built in stone masonry plinth. The external layer of mud plaster and whitewash has largely eroded over time and the *chorten* have lost their original form. The *mane* wall is located in between the two *chorten* and is a rectangular wall built in dry stone masonry. It contains a large number of *mane* stones on the top horizontal surface.

STATE OF PRESERVATION
Showing Signs of Deterioration

SOURCE OF INFORMATION Tsering Phuntsog (*Goba*), Saspotse, Khaltse, Ladakh

Saspotse

Rigsum Gonbo

INVENTORY NO.
KHALTSE / SASPOTSE / 09 / 2004

Rigsum Gonbo | In Use | Public (Community) | Around 150 years old

SETTING
The *rigsum gonbo* is oriented to the southeast and is located north of the Lotsawa *lhakhang* temples.

SIGNIFICANCE
The *rigsum gonbo* was built around 150 years ago by the villagers at the edge of the village to protect the village from natural calamities and disasters.

DESCRIPTION
The *rigsum gonbo* consists of a high stone masonry plinth over which originally rested three *chorten* of which only one survives today. The sole surviving *chorten* is built in stone masonry with traces of mud plaster on the exterior surface. It has been recently whitewashed.

STATE OF PRESERVATION
Danger of Disappearance

SOURCE OF INFORMATION Tsering Phuntsog (*Goba*), Saspotse, Khaltse, Ladakh

Dungsten *Lhato*

INVENTORY NO.
KHALTSE / SASPOTSE / 10 / 2004

Lhato | In Use | Public (Community) | Around 300 - 400 years old

SETTING
The *lhato* is oriented to the north and is located on top of a hill near the Lotsawa *lhakhang*.

SIGNIFICANCE
The *lhato* is believed to have been built around 300 - 400 years ago and is dedicated to the protector deity of the village. The contents of the *lhato* are renewed every year amid prayers and rituals.

DESCRIPTION
The lhato is a cubical structure built next to the Lotsawa *lhakhang*. It is almost 1.75 metres high and is built in stone and mud brick masonry. It is mud plastered and whitewashed on the exterior with red markings on the exterior surface. There are juniper twigs, animal horns and *khadag* embedded on the top surface of the *lhato*.

STATE OF PRESERVATION
Showing Signs of Deterioration

SOURCE OF INFORMATION Tsering Phuntsog (*Goba*), Saspotse, Khaltse, Ladakh

Lubang

INVENTORY NO.
KHALTSE / SASPOTSE / 11 / 2004

Lubang | In Use | Private (Individual) | Around 150 years old

SETTING
The *lubang* is oriented to the southeast and is located at the beginning of the village just before the village houses.

SIGNIFICANCE
The *lubang* is believed to be around 150 years old. It marks the residence of the *lu,* or serpent gods. Prayers and offerings are made at the *lubang* on a fixed date in spring known as *Lu thebs* by the monks to placate the *lu*. The prayers are offered to seek a good supply of water before the cultivation of fields begins in spring and offerings made to the *lu* are then immersed in water.

STATE OF PRESERVATION
Advanced State of Decay

DESCRIPTION
The *lubang* is a small cubical structure with a rounded roof. It is built in stone masonry and is mud plastered and whitewashed on the exterior.

SOURCE OF INFORMATION Tsering Phuntsog (*Goba*), Saspotse, Khaltse, Ladakh

Saspotse

353

Dungsten *Lhato* and *Chorten*

INVENTORY NO.
KHALTSE / SASPOTSE / 12 / 2004

Chorten / Lhato | In Use | Public (Community) | Around 150 - 200 years old

SETTING
The *lhato* is oriented to the south and is located at the beginning of the village just before the village houses. The site is surrounded by mountain peaks and barren lands. The *lhato* is located to the west of the footpath near a large boulder and tree.

SIGNIFICANCE
The *lhato* is dedicated to a village protector deity. The *chorten* are both Changchub *chorten* which symbolize the Buddha's enlightenment.

DESCRIPTION
The *lhato* is built over a square plan and is a tall structure constructed in stone masonry with mud mortar. It is mud plastered and whitewashed on the exterior. There is an opening on the eastern facade. There are two *chorten*

located opposite the *lhato*. These are built in stone and mud brick masonry and are mud plastered and whitewashed.

STATE OF PRESERVATION
Showing Signs of Deterioration

SOURCE OF INFORMATION Tsering Phuntsog (*Goba*), Saspotse, Khaltse, Ladakh

---

Skudung *Chorten*

INVENTORY NO.
KHALTSE / SASPOTSE / 13 / 2004

Chorten | In Use | Private (Individual) | Around 100 - 150 years old

SETTING
The *chorten* are oriented to the east and are surrounded by village houses notably the Khiguthing house to the north.

SIGNIFICANCE
The *chorten* were built around 100 – 150 years ago by an ancestor of the Gyamtso Malik family as an act of merit. The *chorten* are located along the village footpath and are still circumambulated by villagers to accumulate merit as they travel along this path. Both the *chorten* are Skudung *chorten* which contain relics.

DESCRIPTION
The site comprises of two large *chorten* built along the village footpath. Both *chorten* are built along a slight slope in stone and mud brick masonry and are mud plastered and whitewashed on the exterior. The exterior surface of the *chorten* has largely eroded over time. There is a tall *chugsum khorlo* over the domes of both the *chorten* made of wood over which rests a metal crown.

SOURCE OF INFORMATION Tsering Norbu Khar, Saspotse, Khaltse, Ladakh

STATE OF PRESERVATION
Advanced State of Decay

Mane Go Chorten

INVENTORY NO.
KHALTSE / SASPOTSE / 14 / 2004

Chorten / *Mane* Wall | In Use | Public (Community) | Around 150 years old

SETTING
The *mane* wall and *chorten* are located along the village road before the settlement and are surrounded by the village road on one side and mountains on the other.

SIGNIFICANCE
The *mane* wall and *chorten* were built around 150 years ago for the well being of all sentient beings. Located along the road leading to the village, the structures are circumambulated by villagers as an act of merit as they travel along this path. The *chorten* are all Changchub *chorten* which symbolize the Buddha's enlightenment.

DESCRIPTION
The site comprises a *mane* wall and four Changchub *chorten*. The *mane* wall is a very long wall built in dry stone masonry. It has inscribed *mane* stones placed on the horizontal surface. The *chorten* are all built on a common random rubble masonry base and are constructed in stone and mud brick masonry. They are mud plastered and whitewashed externally, though much of this external layer has eroded over time causing the *chorten* to lose their original form.

STATE OF PRESERVATION
Showing Signs of Deterioration

SOURCE OF INFORMATION Tsering Phuntsog (*Goba*), Saspotse, Khaltse, Ladakh

Saspotse

355

Dagang Gay *Mane*

INVENTORY NO.
KHALTSE / SASPOTSE / 15 / 2004

Chorten | In Use | Public (Community) | Around 150 years old

SETTING
The *chorten* are oriented to the east and are located before the village along the footpath leading to the settlement. There are agricultural fields to the east of the *chorten* and the village road to lies to the west.

SIGNIFICANCE
The *chorten* were built around 150 years ago along the old route to the village which was used by villagers before the road was built. The *chorten* were circumambulated by villagers as an act of merit while they travelled along this route.

DESCRIPTION
The site comprises of a large cluster of *chorten* lined up in a single row along the old village path. The *chorten* are of different sizes. They are built in both stone and mud brick masonry and have traces of the external mud plaster and whitewash. Most of the *chorten* have collapsed while others have eroded over time making them impossible to identify. The few *chorten* that survive intact are predominantly Changchub *chorten*.

STATE OF PRESERVATION
Advanced State of Decay

SOURCE OF INFORMATION Tsering Phuntsog (*Goba*), Saspotse, Khaltse, Ladakh

Dagang Gay *Mane*

INVENTORY NO.
KHALTSE / SASPOTSE / 16 / 2004

Chorten | In Use | Public (Community) | Around 150 years old

SETTING
The *chorten* are oriented to the east and are located along the old footpath leading to the village. There are agricultural fields to the east of the chorten and the village road lies to the west.

SIGNIFICANCE
The *chorten* were built around 150 years ago and are located along the old village path used by the villagers before the road was laid. The *chorten* are circumambulated by villagers as an act of merit when they travel along this path.

DESCRIPTION
The site comprises of a group of small *chorten* built over a large rectangular stone masonry base. Most of the *chorten* have completely collapsed and there is debris scattered across the site. The few *chorten* that survive are built in stone and mud brick masonry and have traces of external mud plaster and whitewash.

STATE OF PRESERVATION
Danger of Disappearance

SOURCE OF INFORMATION Tsering Phuntsog (*Goba*), Saspotse, Khaltse, Ladakh

Chorten Soma

INVENTORY NO.
KHALTSE / SASPOTSE / 17 / 2004

Chorten | In Use | Public (Community) | Around 150 years old

SETTING
The *chorten* is oriented to the south and is located before the village near the agricultural fields. It is surrounded by barren mountains on one side and by the Skildongpa field to the east.

SIGNIFICANCE
The *chorten* was built around 150 years ago as an act of merit and is a Changchub *chorten* symbolizing the Buddha's enlightenment.

DESCRIPTION
The *chorten* is built on a square random rubble masonry base. It is constructed in stone and mud brick masonry and is mud plastered and whitewashed on the exterior. There are ruins of two other *chorten* nearby of which only some debris survives.

STATE OF PRESERVATION
Advanced State of Decay

SOURCE OF INFORMATION Tsering Phuntsog (*Goba*), Saspotse, Khaltse, Ladakh

Group of *Chorten*

INVENTORY NO.
KHALTSE / SASPOTSE / 18 / 2004

Chorten | In Use | Public (Community) | Around 150 years old

SETTING
The *chorten* are oriented to the east and are located along the village road to the west of the Banzompa new house.

SIGNIFICANCE
The *chorten* were built around 150 years and lie along the village path. They are circumambulated by villagers as an act of merit when travelling along this path.

DESCRIPTION
The site consists of a group of nine *chorten* arranged in a single row along the edge of the village footpath. The *chorten* are all built in stone masonry and have traces of external mud plaster and whitewash. Most of the *chorten* have lost their original form over time. The base of the *chorten* is partially buried under mud from the neigbouring path.

STATE OF PRESERVATION
Advanced State of Decay

SOURCE OF INFORMATION Tsering Phuntsog (*Goba*), Saspotse, Khaltse, Ladakh

Saspotse

357

Oolguay *Mane*

INVENTORY NO.
KHALTSE / SASPOTSE / 19 / 2004

Chorten | In Use | Public (Community) | Around 150 years old

SETTING
The *chorten* are oriented to the east and located before the village at the turn of the footpath that leads to Saspotse.

SIGNIFICANCE
The *chorten* were built around 150 years ago by an ancestor from the village for the well being of all sentient beings. These are circumambulated by villagers as an act of merit when they travel along this path.

DESCRIPTION
The site comprises of two *chorten* built over a common rectangular stone base. One of the *chorten* has completely collapsed and only a mound of debris survives. The second *chorten* is a built in stone masonry and has largely lost its external layer of mud plaster and whitewash. There is a small square *lubang* opposite the *chorten* built in stone and mud brick masonry and is mud plastered and whitewashed externally.

STATE OF PRESERVATION
Advanced State of Decay

SOURCE OF INFORMATION Tsering Phuntsog (*Goba*), Saspotse, Khaltse, Ladakh

Rock Carvings

INVENTORY NO.
KHALTSE / SASPOTSE / 20 / 2004

Chorten | Abandoned | Public (Community)

SETTING
The rock carvings are oriented to the east and are located at before the village at the turn of the footpath that leads to Saspotse.

SIGNIFICANCE
The rock carvings depict two different types of *chorten* and appear to date to different time periods.

DESCRIPTION
The rock carvings have been executed on two surfaces of a boulder. The larger surface contains a later image of a *chorten* while the smaller surface contains an image of a earlier *chorten*.

STATE OF PRESERVATION
Danger of Disappearance

SOURCE OF INFORMATION Tsering Phuntsog (*Goba*), Saspotse, Khaltse, Ladakh

NIRLAC

Rigsum Gonbo

INVENTORY NO.
KHALTSE / SHILLA / 01 / 2004

Rigsum Gonbo | In Use | Public (Community) | Around 250 years old

SETTING
The *rigsum gonbo* is oriented to the west and is located on a large mound over a hill overlooking the agricultural fields. It is surrounded by the river to the southeast and the village road to the northwest.

SIGNIFICANCE
The *rigsum gonbo* overlooks the village and was built around 250 years ago to protect the village from the natural calamities and other misfortune.

DESCRIPTION
The *rigsum gonbo* is built over a rectangular plan. It has two parallel side walls and is open to the front and rear. There is a traditional roof above the walls enclosing the structure. The *rigsum gonbo* has a stone masonry base and the walls are constructed in the mud brick masonry. The walls are mud plastered and painted in red. Within the enclosure are three *chorten* built in stone and mud brick masonry which

are lined in a single row. The *chorten* are mud plastered and painted in red, white and blue symbolizing the Bodhisattvas Jamyang, Chanrazig and Chagdor respectively.

STATE OF PRESERVATION
Fair

Mane Wall and *Chorten* (Prinkiti *Mane*)

INVENTORY NO.
KHALTSE / SHILLA / 02 / 2004

Chorten / *Mane* Wall | In Use | Public (Community) | Around 250 years old

SETTING
The *mane* wall and chorten are located on the right side of the village road in close proximity to the *rigsum gonbo*. The *rigsum gonbo* lies to the southwest of the site.

SIGNIFICANCE
The *mane* wall and *chorten* are circumambulated by villagers, to accumulate merit, as they travel along this path. The *chorten* is a Changchub *chorten* which symbolizes the Buddha's enlightenment.

DESCRIPTION
The site consists of a group of four *mane* wall, one *chorten* and three *tarchen*. The *tarchen* have rectangular stone masonry bases with prayer flags posted in the centre. The *chorten* is built on a stone masonry plinth and is

constructed in stone and mud brick masonry with traces of mud plaster and whitewash on its external surface. A rock carving of a Buddha is placed at the base of the *chorten*. The chorten is followed by a long, linear *mane* wall of dry stone masonry. There are two more square shaped *mane* walls built in stone masonry which are mud plastered and whitewashed on the exterior. All the *mane* walls have inscribed *mane* stones placed on the top surface.

STATE OF PRESERVATION
Danger of Disappearance

SOURCE OF INFORMATION Nawang Lotus - Sherabpa, Shilla, Khaltse, Ladakh

Sherabpa House

INVENTORY NO.
KHALTSE / SHILLA / 03 / 2004

Vernacular Building | Abandoned | Private (Individual) | Around 150 years old

SETTING
The house is oriented to the southwest and is located along the slope of a hill, left of the village road. Agricultural fields lie in front of the house.

SIGNIFICANCE
The house was built by the great grand father of the present owner around 150 years ago and the family resided here till recently. The house is built in the traditional style and is a good example of vernacular architecture in the village. The family has shifted to a new house presently and this house is being used only for housing cattle and storing fodder.

DESCRIPTION
The Sherabpa house is a large double storeyed structure. The ground floor is constructed in random rubble masonry while the upper floors are built in mud brick masonry with mud mortar. The front facade has small windows on the ground floor and relatively larger windows on the first floor. The ground floor is still used by the family to house animals and store fodder. The first floor was traditionally used by the family as the living quarters and housed the kitchen, living areas and family temple. The family no longer resides here and has moved into a new house. The building has a traditional roof supported on wooden columns and beams with brackets. The external walls of the house are mud plastered and whitewashed.

STATE OF PRESERVATION
Advanced State of Decay

SOURCE OF INFORMATION Nawang Lotus - Sherabpa, Shilla, Khaltse, Ladakh

Shilla

Rigsum Gonbo and *Chorten*

INVENTORY NO.
KHALTSE / SHILLA / 04 / 2004

Rigsum Gonbo / *Chorten* / In Use | Private (Individual)

SETTING
The *rigsum gonbo* and chorten are located along a footpath, south of the Zopay house and east of the village road.

SIGNIFICANCE
The *chorten* lie along a footpath and are circumambulated by villagers as an act of merit. The *rigsum gonbo*, located on a hill above the Zopay house, was built as a protection against evil forces.

DESCRIPTION
The site comprises of a cluster of four *chorten* and a *rigsum gonbo*. Three of the *chorten* stand on a common stone masonry base, with the ruins of a boundary wall nearby. Another *chorten* stands outside the ruined boundary wall. The *chorten* are all built in stone and mud brick masonry and have traces of the external mud plaster and whitewash. The large *chorten* have red markings on the base panels.

The *rigsum gonbo* is built on a hill above the Zopay house and consists of three *chorten* standing on a common base.

STATE OF PRESERVATION
Advanced State of Decay

SOURCE OF INFORMATION Nawang Lotus - Sherabpa, Shilla, Khaltse, Ladakh

NIRLAC

Larjaypey House

INVENTORY NO.
KHALTSE / SHILLA / 05 / 2004

Vernacular Building | Abandoned | Private (Individual) | Around 200 years old

SETTING
The house is oriented to the east and is located along the base of a hill to the west of the village road.

SIGNIFICANCE
The Larjaypey house was built by an ancestor of the Larjaypey family around 200 years ago and the family resided in this house till recently. The house is built in the traditional style and is a good example of vernacular architecture in the village.

DESCRIPTION
The Larjaypey house is a double storeyed structure built in mud and random rubble masonry. The ground floor is constructed of random rubble masonry while the upper floor is built in mud brick masonry with mud mortar. The front facade of the first floor has small windows with segmental arched frames. There is an open verandah in the centre of the house. The house has a traditional roof with

prayer flags posted at the corners. The roof is supported on wooden columns and beams with brackets. The house is in a dilapidated state and has been abandoned by the owners.

STATE OF PRESERVATION
Advanced State of Decay

SOURCE OF INFORMATION Nawang Lotus - Sherabpa, Shilla, Khaltse, Ladakh

Shilla

Chorten

INVENTORY NO.
KHALTSE / SHILLA / 06 / 2004

Chorten | In Use | Public (Community) | Around 250 years old

SETTING
The *chorten* is located on a footpath along the slope of a hill, before the village. It lies to the southeast of the forest and the village road.

SIGNIFICANCE
The *chorten* is located along a village footpath and is circumambulated by villagers when they travel along this path. The *chorten* is a Changchub *chorten* which symbolizes the Buddha's enlightenment.

DESCRIPTION
The site consists of a single *chorten* located on the foothill of a mountain. The *chorten* is built on a large square random rubble masonry plinth and is constructed in stone and mud brick masonry with mud mortar. There are traces of the external mud plaster and whitewash, though most of this layer has eroded over time. One portion of the base of the *chorten* is embedded along the slope of the hill.

STATE OF PRESERVATION
Advanced State of Decay

SOURCE OF INFORMATION Nawang Lotus - Sherabpa, Shilla, Khaltse, Ladakh

Skindyang

Skindyang village is situated about 105 km from Leh, near Khaltse. The village name Skindyang has two meanings – '*wild horses*' and '*long autumn*'. Earlier, there were only 15 families residing in the village but today there are about 35 households.

{*Source: Stanzin Zangpo [Malakhapa]* }

Listed by: Dr. Sonam Wangchok, Gelong Jamyang Phuntsog and Karma Yeshi
Year: 2006

Skyumpata

Skyumpata can be reached after a three-day trek from Phanjilla. From the Leh - Srinagar highway, a road diverts between Khaltse and Lamayuru, towards Shilla. Phanjilla lies on this road. There are 8 households in Skyumpata today.

Listed by: Gelong Tsewang Jorgyes
Year: 2006

Group of *Chorten*

INVENTORY NO.
KHALTSE / SKINDYANG / 01 / 2006

Chorten | In Use | Public (Community)

SETTING
The *chorten* are oriented to the northeast and are located along the footpath that leads to the village. The site is surrounded by mountains and the village footpath.

SIGNIFICANCE
The *chorten* are located along the village path and are circumambulated by villagers as an act of merit as they travel along this route. One of the *chorten* is a Changchub *chorten* which symbolizes the Buddha's enlightenment.

DESCRIPTION
The site consists of a group of four *chorten,* one of which is a Changchub *chorten*. This *chorten* is built in stone masonry and is mud plastered and whitewashed on the exterior. It has a tall *chugsum khorlo* over the dome made of baked clay tiles with a metal crescent on the top. The external plaster of the *chorten* has eroded in several places. The other three *chorten* are embedded in mud caused by a landslide following heavy rain around five years ago. Only

the domes are visible today and the *chorten* cannot be identified. These *chorten* are also made in stone masonry and have traces of the external plaster and whitewash.

STATE OF PRESERVATION
Danger of Disappearance

SOURCE OF INFORMATION Konchok Tsering, Skindyang, Khaltse, Ladakh

Mane Wall

INVENTORY NO.
KHALTSE / SKINDYANG / 02 / 2006

Mane Wall | In Use | Public (Community)

SETTING
The *mane* wall is oriented to the northeast and is located along the footpath that leads to the village. The site is surrounded by the village footpath on one side and a grove of trees on the other.

SIGNIFICANCE
The *mane* wall was built in the past as an act of merit and is still circumambulated by villagers to accumulate merit as they travel along this path.

DESCRIPTION
The *mane* wall is a linear dry stone masonry wall built along the edge of the footpath with inscribed *mane* stones placed on the top horizontal surface. There is a small niche at one end of the *mane* wall within which is placed a finely carved image of a Buddha in stone.

STATE OF PRESERVATION
Advanced State of Decay

SOURCE OF INFORMATION Konchok Tsering, Skindyang, Khaltse, Ladakh

Group of *Chorten*

INVENTORY NO.
KHALTSE / SKINDYANG / 03 / 2006

Chorten | In Use | Public (Community)

SETTING
The *chorten* are oriented to the north and are located along the slope of a mountain near the footpath leading to the village. These are located before a small wooden bridge built over the stream.

SIGNIFICANCE
The *chorten* are located along the village path and are circumambulated by villagers as an act of merit as they travel along this route. The *chorten* are Changchub *chorten* which symbolize the Buddha's enlightenment.

DESCRIPTION
The site consists of a group of four *chorten*. One of the *chorten* is larger than the other three and stands a short distance apart, while the other *chorten* are built next to each other on a common stone masonry platform. The *chorten* are built in stone masonry and are mud plastered and whitewashed on the exterior. The outer layer of mud plaster and whitewash has eroded over the three smaller *chorten* making them difficult to identify.

STATE OF PRESERVATION
Showing Signs of Deterioration

SOURCE OF INFORMATION Konchok Tsering, Skindyang, Khaltse, Ladakh

Kagan *Chorten*

INVENTORY NO.
KHALTSE / SKINDYANG / 04 / 2006

Chorten | In Use | Public (Community) | Around 150 - 200 years old

SETTING
The Kagan *chorten* is built along the footpath leading to the village at the entrance to the village. After crossing the wooden bridge over the stream, a footpath leads to the main settlement.

SIGNIFICANCE
The Kagan *chorten* marks the entrance to the village and was built around 3 - 4 generation ago by village ancestors. The Kagan *chorten* is a gateway *chorten* and merit is believed to accrue to believers who pass through the passage of the *chorten* as well as circumambulate the *chorten*.

DESCRIPTION
The Kagan *chorten* consists of two thick parallel walls over which rests a large *chorten*. The walls as well as the *chorten* are built in stone and mud brick masonry and are mud plastered and whitewashed on the exterior. The roof over the passage has timber joists and the ceiling is also

made of timber. The dome of the *chorten* has a tall *chugsum khorlo* made of baked clay tiles topped by a metal crown.

STATE OF PRESERVATION
Showing Signs of Deterioration

SOURCE OF INFORMATION Konchok Tsering, Skindyang, Khaltse, Ladakh

Tashag

INVENTORY NO.
KHALTSE / SKINDYANG / 05 / 2006

Vernacular Building | Abandoned | Private (Individual) | Around 100 years old

SETTING
The *tashag* is oriented to the northwest and is located above the village footpath in the Chere Thang area. The house lies above the Cherethang Thurkhangbu.

SIGNIFICANCE
The *tashag* was built by a lama named Tashi Rigzen about 100 years ago. Tashi Rigzen lived as a monk in Lamayuru *gonpa* but visited the village often to perform prayers and rituals for the people. He passed away in this house and since then, it lies abandoned. The house is built in the traditional style and is a good example of vernacular architecture in the village.

DESCRIPTION
The *tashag* is a double storeyed building built in stone masonry at the ground floor level and in mud brick masonry at the first floor level. The ground floor has four rooms with narrow window openings. The first floor has three rooms and larger window opening with timber frames and

shutters. The house has a traditional roof made of timber beams joists, *taalu*, grass and compacted mud. The exterior walls are mud plastered and whitewashed. The house lies abandoned and is in a dilapidated state.

STATE OF PRESERVATION
Advanced State of Decay

SOURCE OF INFORMATION Konchok Tsering, Skindyang, Khaltse, Ladakh

Group of *Mane* Walls and *Chorten*

INVENTORY NO.
KHALTSE / SKINDYANG / 06 / 2006

Mane Wall / *Chorten* | In Use | Public (Community)

SETTING
The *mane* wall and *chorten* are located to the right of the footpath that leads to the village. The footpath also links to the village *gonpa* located above the site on a hill.

SIGNIFICANCE
The *mane* wall and *chorten* were built in the past as an act of merit and are still circumambulated by villagers, to accumulate merit, as they travel along this path.

DESCRIPTION
The site consists of a group of *mane* walls and *chorten* located along the footpath. The *chorten* are interspersed between the *mane* walls and are built in stone masonry with an external layer of mud plaster and whitewash. The *chorten* have eroded over time and have lost their original

form making them difficult to identify. The *mane* walls are built in stone masonry and are whitewashed on the exterior. Inscribed *mane* stones are placed on the top horizontal surface of the *mane* wall.

STATE OF PRESERVATION
Advanced State of Decay

SOURCE OF INFORMATION Konchok Tsering, Skindyang, Khaltse, Ladakh

Group of *Chorten* and *Rigsum Gonbo*

INVENTORY NO.
KHALTSE / SKINDYANG / 07 / 2006

Chorten / Rigsum Gonbo | In Use | Public (Community) | Around 100 - 150 years old

SETTING
The *chorten* are located along the slope of a hill near the village road which leads to the village *gonpa* and are surrounded by village houses and the footpath.

SIGNIFICANCE
The *chorten* were built in the past as an act of merit. The *rigsum gonbo* located between the *chorten* was built to protect the village from natural disasters and calamities.

DESCRIPTION
The site consists of a group of six *chorten* and a *rigsum gonbo*. The *chorten* are built in stone masonry and are mud plastered and whitewashed externally. The base panels of the *chorten* have fragments of stucco relief motifs (*pa-tra*). The external layer of the *chorten* has eroded over time and the *chorten* have lots their original form making them impossible to identify. In between the group of *chorten* is a

small *rigsum gonbo* consisting of a group of three *chorten* built on a common stone masonry platform. The *chorten* are painted in the traditional colours of ochre, white and blue symbolizing Jamyang, Chanrazig and Chagdor respectively.

STATE OF PRESERVATION
Advanced State of Decay

SOURCE OF INFORMATION Konchok Tsering, Skindyang, Khaltse, Ladakh

Skindyang

367

Group of *Chorten*

INVENTORY NO.
KHALTSE / SKINDYANG / 08 / 2006

Chorten | In Use | Public (Community) | Around 100 – 150 years old

SETTING
The *chorten* are oriented to the southeast and are located along the path leading from Skindyang to Tia on top of a mountain pass.

SIGNIFICANCE
The *chorten* were built by an ancestor of Skindyang pa as an act of merit. The *chorten* are circumambulated by villagers, as they travel along this path, to accumulate merit.

DESCRIPTION
The site consists of a group of four *chorten* built in stone masonry which are mud plastered and whitewashed externally. The external layer of mud plaster and whitewash has eroded over time and the *chorten* have lost their original form making them impossible to identify.

STATE OF PRESERVATION
Advanced State of Decay

SOURCE OF INFORMATION Konchok Tsering, Skindyang, Khaltse, Ladakh

Guru Zhabjes

INVENTORY NO.
KHALTSE / SKINDYANG / 09 / 2006

Landscape (Rock Formation) | In Use | Public (Community)

SETTING
The temple is located along a path that diverts from the village.

SIGNIFICANCE / CULTURAL BELIEFS
The temple is built around a rock that is believed to be a foot print of Guru Rinpoche. Villagers offer prayers at the site.

DESCRIPTION
The temple is a single storeyed building built in stone and mud brick masonry with mud mortar. Two windows flank the entrance door which leads to the main temple. The rock is inside this chamber. The building has a traditional roof above and is mud plastered and whitewashed on the exterior. The windows have tiered timber lintels and frames.

STATE OF PRESERVATION
Showing Signs of Deterioration

Skindyang

368

Mane Wall

INVENTORY NO.
KHALTSE / SKINDYANG / 10 / 2006

Mane Wall | In Use | Public (Community) | Around 100 - 150 years old

SETTING
A path diverts from the main village footpath towards the *gonpa*. The *mane* walls are located along this diversion. The site is surrounded by the mountain side to the rear and agricultural fields in the front.

SIGNIFICANCE
The *mane* walls were built along the path leading to the *gonpa* and are circumambulated by villagers to accumulate merit as they travel along this path.

DESCRIPTION
The site consists of two high circular *mane* walls built in stone masonry. The *mane* walls are mud plastered and whitewashed externally. Inscribed *mane* stones are placed on the top surface of the *mane* walls. There is a small niche on the outer surface of the *mane* wall.

STATE OF PRESERVATION
Showing Signs of Deterioration

SOURCE OF INFORMATION Konchok Tsering, Skindyang, Khaltse, Ladakh

NIRLAC

Group of *Chorten*

INVENTORY NO.
KHALTSE / SKINDYANG / 11 / 2006

Chorten | In Use | Public (Community) | Around 70 - 80 years old

SETTING
The *chorten* are oriented to the southeast and are located near the path leading to the *gonpa*. The site is located to the south of the *gonpa* and is near the Gongsten pa house. There are agricultural fields around the site.

SIGNIFICANCE
The *chorten* are located along a path leading to the *gonpa* and are circumambulated by villagers as an act of merit when travelling along this path. They are Changchub *chorten* which symbolize the Buddha's enlightenment.

DESCRIPTION
The site consists of two *chorten* built some distance apart. The *chorten* are built in stone masonry and are mud plastered and whitewashed externally. They stand over random rubble masonry bases.

STATE OF PRESERVATION
Showing Signs of Deterioration

SOURCE OF INFORMATION Konchok Tsering, Skindyang, Khaltse, Ladakh

Skindyang

369

Dakshospa House

INVENTORY NO.
KHALTSE / SKINDYANG / 12 / 2006

Vernacular Building | In Use | Private (Individual) | Around 200 years old

SETTING
The Dakshospa house is located along the path leading to the village *gonpa*. It lies south of the *gonpa* and near the Gongsten pa house.

SIGNIFICANCE
The Dakshospa house was built by an ancestor of the Dakshospa family named Meme Tenzin Chosphel around four generations ago and successive generations have continued to reside here. The house is built in the traditional style and is a good example of vernacular architecture in the village.

DESCRIPTION
The Dakshospa house is a large three storeyed building with an entrance from the northeast. It is built along a slight slope over a large rock. The ground floor is built in stone masonry and is used primarily for storage. It has tiny window openings for ventilation. The first floor is used for winter habitation by the family while the second floor is used during the summer. Both these levels are built in mud brick masonry. The second floor houses the old kitchen and family chapel. There is a large *rabsal* on the second floor with a small balcony in front of it. The house has few window openings. The roof is a traditional one made of timber beams, joists, *taalu*, grass and compacted mud. There is a low height parapet running along the edge of the roof and there are prayer flags posted at the edge of the roof. The external walls of the house are mud plastered and whitewashed.

STATE OF PRESERVATION
Showing Signs of Deterioration

SOURCE OF INFORMATION Stanzin Konchok Malakha, Skindyang, Khaltse, Ladakh

Chorten

INVENTORY NO.
KHALTSE / SKINDYANG / 13 / 2006

Chorten | In Use | Public (Community) | Around 100 - 150 years old

SETTING
The *chorten* is oriented to the southeast and are located along the village footpath leading to the north of the village. The *chorten* is surrounded by village houses to the east and agricultural fields to the southwest.

SIGNIFICANCE
The *chorten* is located along the village path and is circumambulated by villagers as an act of merit as they travel along this route. The chorten is a Changchub *chorten* which symbolizes the Buddha's enlightenment.

DESCRIPTION
The site consists of a large *chorten* built on a random rubble masonry base. The *chorten* is built in stone masonry with mud mortar and is mud plastered and whitewashed on the exterior. It has a tall *chugsum khorlo* over the dome made of baked clay tiles with a metal crescent on the top.

STATE OF PRESERVATION
Showing Signs of Deterioration

Mane Wall

INVENTORY NO.
KHALTSE / SKINDYANG / 14 / 2006

Mane Wall | In Use | Public (Community) | Around 100 - 150 years old

SETTING
The *mane* wall is òriented to the north and is located along the village footpath moving to the north of the village. It is surrounded by village houses to the east and agricultural fields to the southwest.

SIGNIFICANCE
The *mane* wall was built about 100 -150 years ago along the village path and is still circumambulated by villagers as an act of merit.

DESCRIPTION
The *mane* wall is a high, linear dry stone masonry wall. Inscribed *mane* stones are placed on its top horizontal surface.

STATE OF PRESERVATION
Showing Signs of Deterioration

Tsamskhang

INVENTORY NO.
KHALTSE / SKINDIYANG / 15 / 2006

Temple | In Use | Public (Lamayuru *Gonpa*) | Around 250 - 300 years old

SETTING
The *tsamskhang* is oriented to the southwest and is situated in a small valley at the end of the village. The site lies east of the village footpath and is surrounded by an old juniper tree at the entrance.

SIGNIFICANCE
The *tsamskhang* was built around 250 - 300 years ago as a meditation centre for the monks from Lamayuru *gonpa*. Monks light butter lamps in the morning and evening and come here periodically to meditate.

DESCRIPTION
The *tsamskhang* consists of a principal building and three other ancillary buildings which are not in use today. The main building is a double storeyed structure with a *yab* on the top. The first floor has rooms for meditation while the temples are on the ground floor. The main shrine contains the statue of Skyoba Jigten Gonbo. This chamber has

wooden columns supporting the roof above as well as a small skylight in the centre which acts as a source of light and ventilation. The building is built in stone masonry and is mud plastered and whitewashed externally. There are window openings on the first floor which are bordered in black paint. The structure has a traditional roof edged with a low parapet which is painted in red.

STATE OF PRESERVATION
Showing Signs of Deterioration

SOURCE OF INFORMATION Gelong Konchog Thupstan, Skindyang, Khaltse, Ladakh

Group of *Chorten*

INVENTORY NO.
KHALTSE / SKINDIYANG / 16 / 2006

Chorten | In Use | Public (Community) | Around 250 - 300 years old

SETTING
The *chorten* are located at the foot of a mountain above the agricultural fields. The site lies to the west of the *gonpa*.

SIGNIFICANCE
The *chorten* were built around 250 - 300 years ago along the village footpath and are circumambulated by villagers as the travel along this path. Villagers offer white wash on the 15th day of the 4th month of the Tibetan calendar. The *chorten* are largely Changchub *chorten* symbolizing the Buddha's enlightenment.

DESCRIPTION
The site consists of a group of nine *chorten*. All the *chorten* are built on high random rubble masonry platforms with six of them grouped together. The *chorten* are of different sizes and appear to be largely Changchub *chorten,* though several of them have lost their original form and are

difficult to identify. The *chorten* are built in stone masonry and are mud plastered and whitewashed externally. The outer layer of plaster has largely eroded in most of the *chorten*.

STATE OF PRESERVATION
Showing Signs of Deterioration

SOURCE OF INFORMATION Gelong Konchog Thupstan, Skindyang, Khaltse, Ladakh

Gonpa

INVENTORY NO.
KHALTSE / SKINDIYANG / 17 / 2006

Gonpa | In Use | Public (Lamayuru *Gonpa*)

SETTING
The *gonpa* is oriented to the southeast and is surrounded by agricultural fields and a large juniper tree.

SIGNIFICANCE
The old *gonpa* was built on a hill at the western edge of the village but later shifted to the present site. One monk from Lamayuru lives here to take care of the *gonpa* and to perform prayers. In the first month of Tibetan calendar, all villagers get together in the *gonpa* to observe fasting and to recite *mane*. Besides this, the monks perform several prayers for the protectors on different occasions. The *gonpa* and *chorten* are whitewashed by the community on the 14th day of the 4th month of the Tibetan calendar.

DESCRIPTION
The *gonpa* is a double storeyed building built in stone and mud brick masonry. The entrance to the *dukhang* on the ground floor is through a small porch. The *dukhang* has a timber floor and eight timber columns supporting the roof above. Inside the chamber are images of Guru Rinpoche, Skyoba Jigsten Gonbo, Chanrazig and Deshag Gyad. The walls of the *dukhang* have no wall paintings. The first floor houses the Kangyur *lhakhang* which also has a timber floor. The walls of the Kangyur *lhakhang* are plain without any paintings. This chamber houses a collection of volumes of the Kangyur said to have been brought from Changthang. The window openings have tiered lintels painted in red. The roof is a traditional roof made of timber beams, joists, *taalu*, grass and compacted mud. A low parapet runs along the edge of the roof and is painted in red to the rear of the gonpa. The exterior walls of the building are mud plastered and whitewashed.

STATE OF PRESERVATION
Fair

Skindyang

372

Chorten

INVENTORY NO.
KHALTSE / SKINDYANG / 18 / 2006

Chorten | In Use | Public (Community) | Around 250 - 300 years old

SETTING
The *chorten* is located to the west of the *gonpa* and lies at the foothill of a mountain. The village footpath runs near the site and there is a house and an apricot tree nearby.

SIGNIFICANCE
The *chorten* was built around 250 - 300 years ago and is still circumambulated by villagers as they travel along this path. The *chorten* is whitewashed by the villagers on the 15th day of the 4th month of the Tibetan calendar. The *chorten* is a Changchub *chorten* which symbolizes the Buddha's enlightenment.

DESCRIPTION
The *chorten* is built along a slight slope at the foothill of a mountain. It is a large *chorten* built in stone and mud brick masonry and is mud plastered and whitewashed on the exterior. There is a *srog-shing* embedded in the centre of the dome.

SOURCE OF INFORMATION Gelong Konchog Thupstan, Skindyang, Khaltse, Ladakh

STATE OF PRESERVATION
Showing Signs of Deterioration

Skindyang

373

Lhato Yanglag Chomo

INVENTORY NO.
KHALTSE / SKINDYANG / 19 / 2006

Lhato | In Use | Public (Community)

SETTING
The *lhato* is built on a rock under a large juniper tree near the *gonpa*. A small stream runs near the site.

SIGNIFICANCE
The *lhato* is dedicated to the village protector deity called Yanglag Chomo. The monk in charge of the *gonpa* offers prayers and incense to the protector on the 10th day of every month. The contents of the *lhato* are renewed on the 30th day of the 12th month and on the 15th day of the 4th month of the Tibetan calendar.

DESCRIPTION
The *lhato* is built on a rock under a juniper tree. The *lhato* is built on a square plan and rises up as a linear structure with the ritual offerings of juniper branches, animal horns and *khadag* placed on the top.

SOURCE OF INFORMATION Gelong Konchog Thupstan, Skindyang, Khaltse, Ladakh

STATE OF PRESERVATION
Fair

Group of *Chorten*

INVENTORY NO.
KHALTSE / SKINDYANG / 20 / 2006

Chorten | In Use | Public (Community) | Around 250-300 years old

SETTING
The *chorten* are located on the right side of the stream a little below the settlement. They are built on the foothills of a mountain.

SIGNIFICANCE
The *chorten* were built around 250 – 300 years ago along the village footpath. These are circumambulated by villagers as an act of merit when they travel along this path. The *chorten* are whitewashed by the villagers on the 15th day of the 4th month of the Tibetan calendar. The *chorten* are largely Changchub *chorten* which symbolize the Buddha's enlightenment.

DESCRIPTION
The *chorten* are built on a random rubble masonry base along a slight slope. They are built in stone masonry with mud mortar and are mud plastered and whitewashed externally. The outer surface of the *chorten* has eroded and they have lost their original form. There is a circumambulatory path around the *chorten*.

STATE OF PRESERVATION
Advanced State of Decay

Skindyang

374

Skyumpata Gongma *Gonpa*

INVENTORY NO.
KHALTSE / SKYUMPATA / 01 / 2006

Gonpa | In Use | Public(Lingshed *Gonpa*) | Around 150 years old

SETTING
The Skyumpata Gongma *gonpa* is situated above the village of Skyumpata.

SIGNIFICANCE
The *gonpa* is about 150 years old and it is a branch of Lingshed monastery. One monk from Lingshed lives here to take care of the *gonpa* and to perform prayers. There are several prayers performed in the year. One of the most important is called Skugar during which all the people get together at the *gonpa* and whitewash all the religious structures.

DESCRIPTION
The *gonpa* is a single storeyed structure built in random rubble and mud brick masonry. It comprises of a single *dukhang* which contains statues of Chanrazig, Jamyang etc.

and volumes of the Buddhist canons. The exterior walls are mud plastered and whitewashed. The *gonpa* has a traditional roof above.

STATE OF PRESERVATION
Showing Signs of Deterioration

Skyumpata

375

Skyapa *Khangbu*

INVENTORY NO.
KHALTSE / SKYUMPATA / 02 / 2006

Vernacular Building | In Use | Private (Individual) | Around 430 years old

STATE OF PRESERVATION
Showing Signs of Deterioration

SETTING
The Skyapa *Khangbu* is located a little below the *gonpa* on the slope of a hill.

SIGNIFICANCE
The Skyapa *Khangbu* family was separated from the Skyapa family about 430 years back. Since then, the Skyapa Khangbu family has been living in this house which was built by their ancestors. It is built in the traditional style and is an example of vernacular architecture in the village.

DESCRIPTION
The house is a double storeyed building constructed in random rubble and mud brick masonry. The ground floor has small openings for ventilation and is used primarily for storage. The first floor has larger window openings and houses the family's living quarters. The house has a traditional roof above over which is stored fodder for the winter.

SOURCE OF INFORMATION Nawang Tsering, Skyumpata, Khaltse, Ladakh

Skyapa House

INVENTORY NO.
KHALTSE / SKYUMPATA / 03 / 2006

Vernacular Building | In Use | Private (Individual) | Around 700 years old

SETTING
The house is located in the settlement of Skyumpata.

SIGNIFICANCE
The house was built by an ancestor of the Skyapa family about 700 years back. The family has been residing in the house since then and has made additions over time. It is built in the traditional style and is an example of vernacular architecture in the village.

STATE OF PRESERVATION
Showing Signs of Deterioration

DESCRIPTION
The house is a double storeyed building constructed in random rubble and mud brick masonry. There is a *rigsum gonbo* near the entrance doorway built to protect the family from evil forces. The ground floor has very small openings for ventilation and is used for storage. The first floor has larger window openings with timber lintels and frames. This level houses the family's living quarters. The house has a traditional roof made of timber beams, joists, *taalu*, grass and compacted mud.

SOURCE OF INFORMATION Tsering Morup, Skyumpata, Khaltse, Ladakh

Yokmapa *Khangbu*

INVENTORY NO.
KHALTSE / SKYUMPATA / 04 / 2006

Vernacular Building | In Use | Private (Individual) | Around 700 years old

SETTING
The house is located in the settlement of Skyumpata.

SIGNIFICANCE
The house was built by an ancestor of the Yokmapa family about 700 years ago when they separated from the Yokmapa family. The family has been residing in the house since then and has made additions over time. It is built in the traditional style and is an example of vernacular architecture in the village.

STATE OF PRESERVATION
Showing Signs of Deterioration

DESCRIPTION
The house is a double storeyed building constructed in random rubble and mud brick masonry. The ground floor has very small openings for ventilation and is used for storage. The first floor has larger window openings with timber lintels and frames. This level houses the family's living quarters. The house has a traditional roof made of timber beams, joists, *taalu*, grass and compacted mud.

SOURCE OF INFORMATION Tsering Morup, Skyumpata, Khaltse, Ladakh

Yokmapa House

INVENTORY NO.
KHALTSE / SKYUMPATA / 05 / 2006

Vernacular Building | In Use | Private (Individual) | Around 700 years old

SETTING
The house is located in the settlement of Skyumpata surrounded by fields on one side and trees on the other.

SIGNIFICANCE
The house was built by an ancestor of the Yokmapa family about 700 years ago and the family has been residing in the house since then. It is built in the traditional style and is an example of vernacular architecture in the village.

DESCRIPTION
The house is a double storeyed building constructed in random rubble and mud brick masonry. The ground floor has very small openings for ventilation and is used for storage. The first floor has larger window openings with timber lintels and frames. This level houses the family's living quarters. The house has a traditional roof made of timber beams, joists, *taalu*, grass and compacted mud.

STATE OF PRESERVATION
Showing Signs of Deterioration

SOURCE OF INFORMATION Norbu Tsering Yokmapa, Skyumpata, Khaltse, Ladakh

Skyumpata

377

Thakranpa House

INVENTORY NO.
KHALTSE / SKYUMPATA / 06 / 2006

Vernacular Building | In Use | Private (Individual) | Around 700 years old

SETTING
The house is built along the slope of a hill to the south of the village. It is surrounded by mountains.

SIGNIFICANCE
The house was built by an ancestor of the Thakranpa family about 700 years ago and the family has been residing in the house since then. It is built in the traditional style and is an example of vernacular architecture in the village.

DESCRIPTION
The house is a three storeyed building built along a slope. It is constructed in random rubble and mud brick masonry. The ground and first floor has very small openings for ventilation. The ground floor is used for storage. The second floor has larger window openings with timber lintels and frames. The first and second levels houses the family's living quarters. The house has a traditional roof made of timber beams, joists, *taalu*, grass and compacted mud.

STATE OF PRESERVATION
Showing Signs of Deterioration

SOURCE OF INFORMATION Tashi Stobgyes Thakranpa, Skyumpata, Khaltse, Ladakh

Gorgupa House

INVENTORY NO.
KHALTSE / SKYUMPATA / 07 / 2006

Vernacular Building | In Use | Private (Individual) | Around 500 years old

SETTING
The Gorgupa house is built along the slope of a hill to the north of the village on the way to Lingshed.

SIGNIFICANCE
The house was built by an ancestor of the Gorgupa family about 500 years ago and the family has been residing in the house since then. It is built in the traditional style and is an example of vernacular architecture in the village.

DESCRIPTION
The house is a double storeyed building built on a rectangular plan. It is constructed in random rubble and mud brick masonry with mud mortar. The ground and first floor has very small openings for ventilation. The ground floor is used for storage. The second floor has larger window openings with timber lintels and frames. The first and second levels house the family's living quarters. The house has a traditional roof made of timber beams, joists, *taalu*, grass and compacted mud. The external walls are mud plastered.

STATE OF PRESERVATION
Showing Signs of Deterioration

SOURCE OF INFORMATION Tsering Dorje Gorgupa, Skyumpata, Khaltse, Ladakh

Skyumpata

Chorten

INVENTORY NO.
KHALTSE / SKYUMPATA / 08 / 2006

Chorten | In Use | Public (Community) | Around 25 years old

SETTING
The *chorten* is located on the path leading to Singhela.

SIGNIFICANCE
The *chorten* was built on the path leading to Singhela pass and is circumambulated by travellers as they cross this path as an act of merit. The *chorten* is a Changchub *chorten* and symbolizes the Buddha's enlightenment.

DESCRIPTION
The *chorten* is built on a large random rubble masonry platform. It is built in stone and mud brick masonry and is mud plastered and whitewashed externally. The *chorten* has a tall *chugsum khorlo* over the dome which is painted in red.

STATE OF PRESERVATION
Showing Signs of Deterioration

SOURCE OF INFORMATION Tsering Dorje Gorgupa, Skyumpata, Khaltse, Ladakh

Skyurbuchan

Skyurbuchan is situated on the right side of the River Indus, about 125 kms from Leh. It is said that the settlement first started during the reign of the Tibetan King Srongtsan Gampo, around 638 A.D. The name Skyurbuchan means the 'place of sour fruits'. According to legend, once there was an epidemic of small pox in the village that caused the death of many children. The villagers, following the advice of the oracles and leading lamas, built many mane walls and chorten. Following this, the epidemic ended and the village became prosperous. The villagers then changed the village name to Skyidchan meaning '*happy place*'. However, the village is known as Skyurbuchan even today. There are about 113 households in the village that are scattered over the small hamlets of Olsar, Yokturma, Gongturma, Shaskam, Khangral, Lungbutse, Stambordo and Skamlungka.

Listed by: Dr. Sonam Wangchok, Gelong Jamyang Phuntsog and Karma Yeshi
Year: 2006

Mane Walls

INVENTORY NO.
KHALTSE / SKYURBUCHAN / 01 / 2006

Mane Wall | In Use | Public (Community)

SETTING
The *mane* walls are oriented to the northwest and are located to the left of the vehicular road when proceeding from the *gonpa* to the village.

SIGNIFICANCE
The *mane* walls were built along the old village footpath and were circumambulated by villager to accumulate merit.

DESCRIPTION
The *mane* walls are located along the old village path. They are circular in shape and built in random rubble masonry with inscribed *mane* stones placed on the top horizontal surface. Externally, the *mane* walls are mud plastered and whitewashed. There are *srog-shing* embedded in the centre of some of the *mane* walls.

STATE OF PRESERVATION
Showing Signs of Deterioration

Skyurbuchan

382

Group of *Chorten* and *Mane* Walls

INVENTORY NO.
KHALTSE / SKYURBUCHAN / 02 / 2006

Chorten / Mane Wall | In Use | Public (Community)

SETTING
The *mane* walls and *chorten* are located above the vehicular road which leads to the village. The structures lie along the ancient route that led from Leh to Dha-Kargil-Srinagar.

SIGNIFICANCE
The *chorten* and *mane* walls were built along the ancient route that linked Leh with Dha-Kargil-Srinagar. The structures were circumambulated as an act of merit and prayers for the well being of all sentient beings by ancient travellers as the travelled along this route. Some of the *mane* stones give details of the names in whose memory these *mane* stone were carved, for example "For the sake of grand father Tsering Zompa, 50 *mane* were carved", "For the benefit of mother Kunga Palzom, 108 *mane* were carved". The Changchub *chorten* at the site symbolize the Buddha's enlightenment.

DESCRIPTION
The site consists of *mane* walls and two Changchub *chorten*. The *chorten* are built in stone masonry and are whitewashed on the exterior. Both *chorten* have a tall *chugsum khorlo* on the dome made of baked clay tiles. The *mane* walls are made of dry stone masonry and have inscribed *mane* stones placed on the top horizontal surface.

STATE OF PRESERVATION
Showing Signs of Deterioration

SOURCE OF INFORMATION Sonam Dorjey, Skyurbuchan, Khaltse, Ladakh

NIRLAC

Group of *Chorten* and *Mane* Walls

INVENTORY NO.
KHALTSE / SKYURBUCHAN / 03 / 2006

Chorten / *Mane* Wall | In Use | Public (Community)

SETTING
The *mane* walls and *chorten* are located above the village. The structures lie along the ancient route that led from Leh to Dha-Kargil-Srinagar.

SIGNIFICANCE
The *chorten* and *mane* walls were built along the ancient route that linked Leh with Dha-Kargil-Srinagar. The structures were circumambulated as an act of merit and prayers for the well being of all sentient beings by ancient travellers and traders as the travelled along this route.

DESCRIPTION
The site consists of a Kagan *chorten*, a Changchub *chorten* and *mane* walls. The Kagan *chorten* has to thick parallel walls over which rests a large *chorten*. It is built in stone masonry and is mud plastered and whitewashed externally. The roof over the walls is a traditional made of timber

beams, joists, *taalu*, and compacted mud. The ceiling above the passage is made of timber and has traces of wall paintings below it depicting various Buddhas. The timber construction of the ceiling is in the shape of a *mandala*. There is a Changchub *chorten* near the Kagan *chorten* which is built in stone and mud brick masonry and is mud plastered and whitewashed on the exterior. Both *chorten* have tall *chugsum khorlo* over the dome made of baked clay tiles. There are *mane* walls near the *chorten* which are built in dry stone masonry and have inscribed *mane* stones placed on the top horizontal surface.

STATE OF PRESERVATION
Showing Signs of Deterioration

SOURCE OF INFORMATION Sonam Dorjey, Skyurbuchan, Khaltse, Ladakh

Skyurbuchan

383

Group of *Chorten*

INVENTORY NO.
KHALTSE / SKYURBUCHAN / 04 / 2006

Chorten | In Use | Public (Community)

SETTING
The *chorten* are oriented to the south and are located above the village on a high mountain along the ancient trade route that led from Leh to Dha-Kargil-Srinagar.

SIGNIFICANCE
The *chorten* are known as Gornya and face the four directions with one in the centre. They are said to have been built for the protection from five directions and the well being of entire Ladakh.

STATE OF PRESERVATION
Showing Signs of Deterioration

DESCRIPTION
The *chorten* are all Changchub *chorten* and are built at the edge of a cliff overlooking the valley. Each *chorten* stands on a stone masonry plinth and is built in stone masonry with an external layer of mud plaster and whitewash. The domes of the *chorten* have tall *chugsum khorlo* made of baked clay tiles.

SOURCE OF INFORMATION Sonam Gyalstan, Skyurbuchan, Khaltse, Ladakh

Group of *Chorten*

INVENTORY NO.
KHALTSE / SKYURBUCHAN / 05 / 2006

Chorten | In Use | Public (Community)

SETTING
The *chorten* are oriented to the east and are located above the five Changchub *chorten* on a high mountain along the ancient trade route that led from Leh to Dha-Kargil-Srinagar.

SIGNIFICANCE
The *chorten* are believed to have been built in the past along the old trade route and were circumambulated as an act of merit by travelers and traders as they moved from Leh to Kargil and Srinagar. Both the *chorten* are Changchub *chorten* and symbolize the Buddha's enlightenment.

DESCRIPTION
The *chorten* are built on a common dry stone masonry plinth and are constructed in stone masonry. Both the *chorten* are large *chorten* of the same size. They are mud plastered and whitewashed on the exterior and have tall *chugsum khorlo* over the domes which are made of baked clay tiles.

STATE OF PRESERVATION
Showing Signs of Deterioration

SOURCE OF INFORMATION Sonam Gyalstan, Skyurbuchan, Khaltse, Ladakh

384

Group of *Chorten* and *Mane* Walls

INVENTORY NO.
KHALTSE / SKYURBUCHAN / 06 / 2006

Chorten / *Mane* Wall | In Use | Public (Community) | Around 100-150 years old

SETTING
The *mane* walls and *chorten* are oriented to the northeast and are located above the Khache Thang hamlet, in front of the Government primary school.

SIGNIFICANCE
The *chorten* and *mane* walls were built around 2 - 3 generations ago for the well being of all sentient beings. The site is circumambulated by villagers as an act of merit. The *chorten* are Changchub *chorten* and symbolize the Buddha's enlightenment.

DESCRIPTION
The site consists of a row of *mane* walls and two *chorten*. The *chorten* are built in stone masonry and are whitewashed on the exterior. One of the *chorten* has a tall *chugsum khorlo* on the dome made of baked clay tiles. The *mane* walls are made of dry stone masonry and have

inscribed *mane* stones placed on the top horizontal surface. The *mane* walls are built along either side of the *chorten* over a large area.

STATE OF PRESERVATION
Advanced State of Decay

SOURCE OF INFORMATION Tsering Dolkar (Gochepa), Skyurbuchan, Khaltse, Ladakh

Kagan *Chorten*

INVENTORY NO.
KHALTSE / SKYURBUCHAN / 07 / 2006

Chorten | In Use | Public (Community)

SETTING
The Kagan *chorten* is oriented to the east and is located to the right of the vehicular road leading to the village. It stands in front of the old Ganchupa's house.

SIGNIFICANCE
The Kagan *chorten* is located across the old path leading to the village. It is a gateway *chorten* and merit is believed to accrue to believers who pass through the passage of the chorten as well as circumambulate the *chorten*.

DESCRIPTION
The Kagan *chorten* consists of thick parallel walls over which rests a large *chorten*. The entire structure is made of stone masonry and has a timber roof above the passage. The exterior surface is mud plastered and whitewashed and the dome of the *chorten* has a tall *chugsum khorlo* made of wood. The ceiling above the passage is made of timber and is in the form of a *mandala* with paintings in the centre. Most of the paintings have faded over time. However, a

SOURCE OF INFORMATION Sonam Dorjey, Skyurbuchan, Khaltse, Ladakh

depiction of a *mandala* can still be seen. There is another large Changchub *chorten* near the Kagan *chorten* which is built in stone and mud brick masonry and is mud plastered and whitewashed on the exterior. Both the *chorten* have flat inscribed stones placed on them.

STATE OF PRESERVATION
Advanced State of Decay

Mane Wall

INVENTORY NO.
KHALTSE / SKYURBUCHAN / 08 / 2006

Mane Wall | In Use | Public (Community)

SETTING
The *mane* wall is oriented to the northeast and is located to the right of the vehicular road leading to the village. It stands in front of the Stagopa house and can be seen from the Kagan *chorten*.

SIGNIFICANCE
The *mane* wall and the Kagan *chorten* are built in front of the Stagopa house. An ancestor of the Stagopa family served as a royal guard in the past and it is possible that the structures were built during this time. However, no details are available today. The *mane* wall contains numerous *mane* stones inscribed with *mantras* and religious texts placed there by the devout as an act of merit.

DESCRIPTION
The *mane* wall is built in dry stone masonry and contains numerous stones inscribed with sacred *mantras* and

religious texts piled across the horizontal surface as well as placed against the sides of the rectangular wall.

STATE OF PRESERVATION
Showing Signs of Deterioration

Kagan *Chorten*

INVENTORY NO.
KHALTSE / SKYURBUCHAN / 09 / 2006

Chorten | In Use | Public (Community) | Around 300 years old

SETTING
The Kagan *chorten* are oriented to the east and are located near the vehicular road leading to the village. The site is surrounded by village houses and agricultural fields. A small stream flows near the site.

SIGNIFICANCE
The Kagan *chorten* appear to be around 300 years old and are unusual as both the *chorten* are joined together to form a long covered passageway. The Kagan *chorten* are gateway *chorten* and merit is believed to accrue to believers who pass through the passage of the *chorten* and circumambulate them.

DESCRIPTION
The site consist of two Kagan *chorten* joined together at the top such that both the passages are linked to each other. The *chorten* have thick parallel walls over which rests two separate *chorten*. The structures are built in stone and mud brick masonry and are mud plastered and whitewashed on the exterior. The external surface layer of the *chorten* has largely eroded over time and one of the domes has collapsed. The *chorten* have no paintings inside as is often found in Kagan *chorten*.

STATE OF PRESERVATION
Advanced State of Decay

386

Group of *Chorten* and *Mane* Walls

INVENTORY NO.
KHALTSE / SKYURBUCHAN / 10 / 2006

Chorten / *Mane* Wall | In Use | Public (Community)

SETTING
The *mane* walls and *chorten* are oriented to the east and lie to the right of the vehicular road in front of a row of village houses.

SIGNIFICANCE
The *chorten* and *mane* walls were built in the past for the well being of all sentient beings. The site is circumambulated by villagers as an act of merit.

DESCRIPTION
The site consists of a row of *mane* walls and *chorten* built in dry stone masonry. The *chorten* and *mane* walls are interspersed and have collapsed in many areas making them difficult to distinguish and identify.

STATE OF PRESERVATION
Danger of Disappearance

Group of *Chorten* and *Mane* Wall

INVENTORY NO.
KHALTSE / SKYURBUCHAN / 11 / 2006

Chorten / *Mane* Wall | In Use | Private (Individual)

SETTING
The *mane* walls and *chorten* are oriented to the south and lie along the village cemented path in front of Togoche Rigzin Dorjey house.

SIGNIFICANCE
The *chorten* and *mane* walls were built in the past by an ancestor of Togoche Rigzin Dorjey's family for the well being of all sentient beings. The site is circumambulated by villagers as an act of merit. The *chorten* are Changchub *chorten* which symbolize the Buddha's enlightenment.

DESCRIPTION
The site consists of two *chorten* and a *mane* wall located in front of Togoche Rigzen Dorjey house. The *chorten* are built on high dry stone masonry plinths and are constructed in stone and mud brick masonry. The *chorten* are mud plastered and whitewashed on the exterior and have tall

chugsum khorlo on the domes made of baked clay tiles. The *mane* wall is built in stone masonry and has flat inscribed *mane* stones placed on the horizontal surface.

STATE OF PRESERVATION
Showing Signs of Deterioration

SOURCE OF INFORMATION Rigzin Dorjey, Skyurbuchan, Khaltse, Ladakh

Group of *Chorten*

INVENTORY NO.
KHALTSE / SKYURBUCHAN / 12 / 2006

Chorten | In Use | Private (Individual)

SETTING
The *chorten* are oriented to the south east and are located along the village footpath in front of the Migchepa house.

SIGNIFICANCE
The *chorten* are believed to have been built in the past by an ancestor of the Migchepa family as an act of merit. Both the *chorten* are Changchub *chorten* and symbolize the Buddha's enlightenment. The *chorten* are circumambulated by villagers to accumulate merit.

DESCRIPTION
The *chorten* are built on a common dry stone masonry plinth and are constructed in stone masonry. Both the *chorten* are large *chorten* of the same size. They are mud plastered and whitewashed on the exterior and have tall *chugsum khorlo* over the domes made of baked clay tiles. There are inscribed stones placed over the plinth of the *chorten*. The outer surface of the *chorten* has largely eroded and a section of one of the *chorten* has collapsed.

STATE OF PRESERVATION
Advanced State of Decay

SOURCE OF INFORMATION Sonam Stobdan, Migchepa, Skyurbuchan, Khaltse, Ladakh

Skyurbuchan

387

Group of *Chorten*

INVENTORY NO.
KHALTSE / SKYURBUCHAN / 13 / 2006

Chorten | In Use | Public (Community)

STATE OF PRESERVATION
Advanced State of Decay

SETTING

The *chorten* are located along a small village footpath next to the Mon Tsang Yamo house.

SIGNIFICANCE

The *chorten* are believed to have been built in the past by a village ancestor as an act of merit for the well being of all sentient beings. The *chorten* are circumambulated by villagers to accumulate merit.

DESCRIPTION

The *chorten* are built on dry stone masonry plinths and are constructed in stone masonry. Some of the *chorten* still retain the outer surface layer of mud plaster and whitewash although in most *chorten* this layer has eroded. The *chorten* can no longer be identified as they have completely lost their original form and are collapsing in some cases.

SOURCE OF INFORMATION Tsetan Wangchuck (Togochey), Skyurbuchan, Khaltse, Ladakh

Chorten

INVENTORY NO.
KHALTSE / SKYURBUCHAN / 14 / 2006

Chorten | In Use | Public (Community) | Around 200 - 250 years old

STATE OF PRESERVATION
Advanced State of Decay

SETTING

The *chorten* is oriented to the east and is located along a small village footpath surrounded by fields. It can be approached from the main village intersection. There is an old willow tree growing next to the *chorten*.

SIGNIFICANCE

The *chorten* is believed to have been built in the past by a village ancestor as an act of merit for the well being of all sentient beings. The *chorten* is circumambulated by villagers to accumulate merit. The *chorten* is a Changchub *chorten* which symbolizes the Buddha's enlightenment.

DESCRIPTION

The *chorten* is built on a slight mound and is constructed in stone and mud brick masonry with mud mortar. It is mud plastered and whitewashed on the exterior.

Kagan *Chorten*

INVENTORY NO.
KHALTSE / SKYURBUCHAN / 15 / 2006

Chorten | In Use | Public (Community) | Around 300 years old

SETTING
The Kagan *chorten* is located on old foot path of the village that leads to the Mithang area and is surrounded by fields.

SIGNIFICANCE
The Kagan *chorten* was built around 300 years ago for the protection of the fields. The Kagan *chorten* is a gateway *chorten* and merit is believed to accrue to believers who pass through the passage of the *chorten* and circumambulate it.

DESCRIPTION
The Kagan *chorten* consists of thick parallel walls over which rests a *chorten*. The structure is built in stone and mud brick masonry and is mud plastered and whitewashed on the exterior. Over the walls is a traditional roof made of timber joists, stones and compacted mud on which rests the large *chorten*. There are four tall columns at the four corners of the roof. The ceiling of the passage is built in timber and is in the shape of a *mandala*. It is devoid of any

paintings. There is a small prayer wheel near the entrance to the *chorten*. The *chorten* was restored by the villagers two years ago.

STATE OF PRESERVATION
Fair

SOURCE OF INFORMATION Sonam Ladol, Skyurbuchan,Khalste, Ladakh

Rigsum Gonbo

INVENTORY NO.
KHALTSE / SKYURBUCHAN / 16 / 2006

Rigsum Gonbo | In Use | Public (Community) | Around 300 years old

SETTING
The *rigsum gonbo* are located above the hamlet of Mithang to the right of the link Road.

SIGNIFICANCE
The *rigsum gonbo* were built by the Mithang village community to protect the village from natural disasters such as floods. The old *rigsum gonbo* was built around 300 years ago while the new one was built in 1996.

DESCRIPTION
The site consists of two *rigsum gonbo*. The older structure is larger than the new one and comprises of three large *chorten* built in stone masonry with traces of the external mud plaster and whitewash still evident. The new *rigsum gonbo* is built in front of the older structure and consists of three small *chorten* built on a plinth. The *chorten* of the new *rigsum gonbo* are cement plastered and painted in ochre, white and blue symbolizing the three Bodhisattvas Jamyang, Chanrazig and Chagdor respectively. These *chorten* have a small niche in the domes facing the front

which are enclosed within a gilded frame. The domes have *chugsum khorlo* on the top symbolizing the 13 steps towards enlightenment.

STATE OF PRESERVATION
Advanced State of Decay

Skyurbuchan

389

Group of *Chorten* and *Mane* Walls

INVENTORY NO.
KHALTSE / SKYÜRBUCHAN / 17 / 2006

Chorten / Mane Wall | In Use | Public (Community) | Around 18th century

SETTING

The group of *mane* walls and *chorten* are oriented to the south and lie along the ancient trade route from Leh to Kargil, at the beginning of the hamlet of Mithang.

SIGNIFICANCE

The *chorten* and *mane* walls were built along the old route in a single row and are believed to have been built during the period of King Nyima Namgyal (1705 – 1734 A.D.). Inscriptions on a *mane* wall state that these *mane* walls and *chorten* were built for the well beings of all Ladakhi kings and well beings of the entire country. It also records the fact that 1235 *mane* had been erected all over at this time all around the country. The *chorten* and *mane* walls are still circumambulated by villagers as they travel along this path.

DESCRIPTION

The site consists of a large group of *chorten* and *mane* walls built in a row along the village path. The *chorten* are of various sizes and appear to be predominantly Changchub *chorten*. The *chorten* are built in stone masonry and have traces of mud plaster and whitewash on the external surface. Some of the *chorten* have been restored by the villagers. The *mane* walls are long linear stone masonry walls running along the edge of the road. They contain numerous inscribed stones on the top horizontal surface of the walls.

STATE OF PRESERVATION

Advanced State of Decay

SOURCE OF INFORMATION Sonam Gyaltsan, Skyurbuchan, Khaltse, Ladakh

390

Group of *Chorten* and *Mane* Walls

INVENTORY NO.
KHALTSE / SKYURBUCHAN / 18 / 2006

Chorten / Mane Wall | In Use | Public (Community) | Around 18th century

Photograph Not Available

SETTING

The *mane* walls and *chorten* are oriented to the south and lie along the ancient trade route from Leh to Kargil. The site begins at the Government Higher Secondary school and ends at the Mithang hamlet.

SIGNIFICANCE

The *chorten* and *mane* walls were built along the old route in a single row and are believed to have been built during the period of King Nyima Namgyal (1705 – 1734 A.D.). Inscriptions on a *mane* wall state that these *mane* walls and *chorten* were built for the well beings of all Ladakhi kings and well beings of the entire country. It also records the fact that 1235 *mane* had been erected all over at this time all around the country. The *chorten* and *mane* walls are still circumambulated by villagers as they travel along this path.

DESCRIPTION

The site consists of a large group of *chorten* and *mane* walls built in a row along the village path. The *chorten* are of various sizes and appear to be predominantly Changchub *chorten*. The *chorten* are built in stone and mud brick masonry and have traces of mud plaster and whitewash on the external surface. The *mane* walls are long linear dry stone masonry walls running along the edge of the road. Inscribed *mane* stones are placed on the top horizontal surface.

STATE OF PRESERVATION

Advanced State of Decay

SOURCE OF INFORMATION Inscriptions on *mane* wall, Skyurbuchan, Khaltse, Ladakh

Skyurbuchan *Khar*

INVENTORY NO.
KHALTSE / SKYURBUCHAN / 19 / 2006

Fort / Palace | In Use | Public (Community) | Around 500 years old

SETTING
The *khar* is oriented to the north east and is located on a hill overlooking the village. A narrow footpath from the village leads up to the site.

SIGNIFICANCE
The *khar* was built in the beginning of the 15th century and it is said that earlier all the houses were located inside the boundary of the fort. One family used to be the gate keeper who is still known as Stago pa. There is chapel of Chanrazig inside the fort. A monk from the main Skyurbuchan *gonpa* is posted here to take care of the chapel.

DESCRIPTION
The *khar* is built along the slope of a hill. A staircase leads to the main entrance which is oriented to the northeast and overlooks the village. There are two rooms on the first floor one of which has a large *rabsal* on the northeast facade. This room has wall paintings as well and is said to have been a meditation room for the King. The temple also has paintings depicting Chanrazig and other deities. Both the meditation room and temple have a traditional *arga* floor. The palace is built in random rubble and mud brick masonry with mud mortar and the walls have traces of external mud plaster and whitewash. Timber beams are placed at intervals in the walls which gives the building seismic stability. The fort has a traditional roof made of timber beams, joists, beams, *taalu*, grass and compacted mud. The roof has a low parapet all around and prayer flags are posted at the corners.

STATE OF PRESERVATION
Advanced State of Decay

Skyurbuchan

391

SOURCE OF INFORMATION Gelong Naughdup of Chathpa pa, Skyurbuchan, Khaltse, Ladakh

Lharjey Pa House

INVENTORY NO.
KHALTSE / SKYURBUCHAN / 20 / 2006

Vernacular Building | In Use | Private (Individual) | Around 250 - 300 years old

SETTING

The Lharjey pa house is located in the Pharkha hamlet of the village. From the bridge, after around 200 metres, a village path leads to the site.

SIGNIFICANCE

The house was built around 250 - 300 years ago by an ancestor of the Lharjey pa family and the family continues to reside here. The family were the traditional *amchi*. The house is built in the traditional style and is a good example of vernacular architecture in the village.

DESCRIPTION

The Lharjey pa house is a large three storeyed building built on a rectangular plan. The ground floor is built in random rubble masonry with mud mortar and has very few window openings for ventilation and light. It is used primarily for housing cattle. The entrance leads directly to the first floor which is connected with the second floor through a flight of stairs. Both these levels are built in mud brick masonry.

The first floor is used for winter habitation while the second floor is used during the summer. The second floor houses the family chapel. The house has a traditional roof made of timber beams, joists, *taalu*, grass and compacted mud supported on timber columns and brackets beneath. There is a low height parapet all around the edge of the roof on the corners of which are posted prayer flags. The exterior walls are mud plastered and whitewashed.

STATE OF PRESERVATION
Showing Signs of Deterioration

SOURCE OF INFORMATION Cholden Sangmo, Lharjey pa, Skyurbuchan, Khaltse, Ladakh

Shugu Ting pa House

INVENTORY NO.
KHALTSE / SKYURBUCHAN / 21 / 2006

Vernacular Building | In Use | Private (Individual) | Around 150 - 200 years old

SETTING

The Shugu Ting pa house is located in the Pharkha hamlet of the village. From the bridge, after around 200 metres, a village path leads to the site. It is surrounded by other village houses and trees.

SIGNIFICANCE

The house was built around four generations ago by an ancestor, Apo Rinchen, of the Shugu Ting pa family and the family continues to reside here. The house is built in the traditional style and is a good example of vernacular architecture in the village.

DESCRIPTION

The Shugu Ting pa house is a large three storeyed building built on a rectangular plan. The ground floor is built in stone masonry and has very few window openings for ventilation and light. The first and second floors are built in mud brick

masonry and have larger window openings. There are two large *rabsal* on the eastern facade of the second floor. The *rabsal* have elaborately carved timber frames and shutters. The first floor is used for winter habitation while the second floor is used during the summer. The house has a traditional roof made of timber beams, joists, *taalu*, grass and compacted mud supported on timber columns and brackets beneath. There is a low height parapet all around the edge of the roof on the corners of which are posted prayer flags. The exterior walls are mud plastered and whitewashed.

STATE OF PRESERVATION
Showing Signs of Deterioration

SOURCE OF INFORMATION Naugtup Dorjey, Shugu Tingpa, Skyurbuchan, Khaltse, Ladakh

Skyurbuchan

392

Bhutith pa House

INVENTORY NO.
KHALTSE / SKYURBUCHAN / 22 / 2006

Vernacular Building | In Use | Private (Individual) | Around 150 - 200 years old

SETTING
The Bhutith pa house is located in the Pharkha hamlet of the village. From the bridge, after around 200 metres, a village path leads to the site.

SIGNIFICANCE
The house was built around four generations ago by an ancestor, Apo Phuntsog Stanzin, of the Bhutith pa family and the family continues to reside here. The house is built in the traditional style and is a good example of vernacular architecture in the village.

DESCRIPTION
The Bhutith pa house is a large double storeyed building built on a rectangular plan. It has a small entrance from the eastern facade. The ground floor is built in stone masonry while the first floor is built in mud brick masonry. The house has a traditional roof made of timber beams, joists, *taalu*, grass and compacted mud supported on timber columns and brackets beneath. There is a low height parapet all around the edge of the roof on the corners of which are posted prayer flags. The exterior walls are mud plastered and whitewashed.

STATE OF PRESERVATION
Showing Signs of Deterioration

SOURCE OF INFORMATION Tsering Wangdus Bhutith pa, Skyurbuchan, Khaltse, Ladakh

Group of *Chorten*

INVENTORY NO.
KHALTSE / SKYURBUCHAN / 23 / 2006

Chorten | In Use | Public (Community)

SETTING
The *chorten* are oriented to the south east and are built along a hill below the *khar*.

SIGNIFICANCE
The *chorten* were built in the past by a village ancestor as an act of merit for the well being of all sentient beings. They are still circumambulated by villagers as they travel along this path. The *chorten* is a Changchub *chorten* and symbolizes the Buddha's enlightenment.

DESCRIPTION
The site consists of three *chorten* built in stone masonry which are mud plastered and whitewashed on the exterior. The exterior surface of the *chorten* has largely eroded. The *chorten* have a tall *chugsum khorlo* on the dome made of baked clay tiles.

STATE OF PRESERVATION
Advanced State of Decay

Skyurbuchan

393

Stago pa House

INVENTORY NO.
KHALTSE / SKYURBUCHAN / 24 / 2006

Vernacular Building | In Use | Private (Individual)

SETTING
The Stago pa house is located near the *khar*.

SIGNIFICANCE
The house was built around in the past by an ancestor of the Stago pa family and the family continues to reside here. The family are believed to have been in charge of the King's stables and hence, the name Stago pa. The house is built in the traditional style and is a good example of vernacular architecture in the village.

DESCRIPTION
The Stago pa house is a large double storeyed building built on a rectangular plan. The ground floor is built in stone masonry and has narrow slit like window openings for ventilation and light. The first floor is built in mud brick masonry and has a large *rabsal* with an elaborate timber frame as lintel as well as finely carved timber shutters. There are narrow slit-like openings on the side of the *rabsal*. The first floor constitutes the family's living

quarters. The house has a traditional roof above made of timber beams, joists, *taalu*, grass and compacted mud supported on timber columns and brackets. The exterior walls of the house are mud plastered and whitewashed.

STATE OF PRESERVATION
Showing Signs of Deterioration

SOURCE OF INFORMATION Tashi Phuntsok, Stago pa, Skyurbuchan, Khaltse, Ladakh

Dakshos pa House

INVENTORY NO.
KHALTSE / SKYURBUCHAN / 25 / 2006

Vernacular Building | In Use | Private (Individual) | Around 500 years old

SETTING
The Dakshos pa house is oriented to the southwest and is built against a mountainside near the village *gonpa*. There is a large *chorten* in front of the house.

SIGNIFICANCE
The house was built around in the past by an ancestor of the Dakshos pa family and the family continues to reside here. The family is believed to have been an influential family who looked after the King's affairs in his absence. The house is built in the traditional style and is a good example of vernacular architecture in the village.

DESCRIPTION
The Dakshos pa house is a large four storeyed building built on a rectangular plan. The rear of the house is built against the mountainside. The ground and first floors are built in stone masonry and have narrow slit-like window openings for ventilation and light. The second and third floors are built in mud brick masonry and have larger window

openings. There is a large *rabsal* on the third floor facing southwest with an elaborate timber frame and lintel. The second and third floors constitute the family's living areas while the lower levels are used primarily for storage. The chapel as well as the main kitchen are located on the top most floor. The house has a traditional roof above made of timber beams, joists, *taalu*, grass and compacted mud supported on timber columns and brackets. The exterior walls of the house are mud plastered and whitewashed.

STATE OF PRESERVATION
Showing Signs of Deterioration

SOURCE OF INFORMATION Dorjey Rinchen, Non pa, Skyurbuchan, Khaltse, Ladakh

Kagan *Chorten*

INVENTORY NO.
KHALTSE / SKYURBUCHAN / 26 / 2006

Chorten | In Use | Private (Individual) | Around 500 years old

SETTING
The Kagan *chorten* is oriented to the southeast and is located on the way to the Dakshos pa house near the village *gonpa*.

SIGNIFICANCE
The Kagan *chorten* was built around 500 years ago during the time of the royal family's residence in the palace. It is owned by the Dakshos pa family. The Kagan *chorten* is a gateway *chorten* and merit is believed to accrue to believers who pass through the passage of the *chorten* and circumambulate it.

DESCRIPTION
The Kagan *chorten* consists of thick parallel walls over which rests a *chorten*. The structure is built in stone and mud brick masonry and is mud plastered and whitewashed on the exterior. Over the walls is a traditional roof made of timber beams, joists, stones and compacted mud on which rests the large *chorten*. The ceiling of the passage is built in timber and is in the shape of a *mandala*. The ceiling as well as the side walls above the gateway have elaborate paintings depicting a central *mandala* surrounded by figures of various Buddhist deities.

STATE OF PRESERVATION
Showing Signs of Deterioration

Group of *Chorten* and *Mane* Walls

INVENTORY NO.
KHALTSE / SKYURBUCHAN / 27 / 2006

Chorten / *Mane* Wall | In Use | Public (Community) | Around 450 - 500 years old

SETTING
The *mane* walls and chorten are oriented to the east and lie about 300 metres from the village *gonpa* along the path leading to the gonpa.

SIGNIFICANCE
The *chorten* and *mane* walls are built along the route leading to the *gonpa* and are circumambulated by villagers as they travel along this path in order to accumulate merit. The structures are believed to have been built at the time of the *khar*.

DESCRIPTION
The site consists of a large group of *chorten* and *mane* walls built in a row along the path. The *chorten* are of various sizes and appear to be predominantly Changchub *chorten* built on a stone masonry plinth. The *chorten* are built in stone and have traces of mud plaster and whitewash on the external surface. Some of the *chorten* have fragments of stucco relief motifs (*pa-tra*) on the base panels. The *mane* wall is a high, circular shaped wall made of stone masonry with inscribed *mane* stones placed on the horizontal surface. The *mane* wall is not plastered on the exterior but has some traces of whitewash towards the south.

STATE OF PRESERVATION
Advanced State of Decay

Group of *Chorten*

INVENTORY NO.
KHALTSE / SKYURBUCHAN / 28 / 2006

Chorten | In Use | Public (Community) | Around 450 - 500 years old

SETTING
The *chorten* are oriented to the south east and are built along the path leading to the *gonpa*.

SIGNIFICANCE
The *chorten* were built in the past by a village ancestor as an act of merit for the well being of all sentient beings. These are still circumambulated by villagers as they travel along this path.

DESCRIPTION
The site consists of four *chorten*, three of which are similar in size while the fourth is smaller. The *chorten* are built on a leveled stretch of land near the village path but are partially embedded along the path. The *chorten* are built in stone masonry and are mud plastered and whitewashed on the exterior. The exterior surface of the *chorten* has largely eroded making them difficult to identify.

STATE OF PRESERVATION
Advanced State of Decay

Group of *Chorten*

INVENTORY NO.
KHALTSE / SKYURBUCHAN / 29 / 2006

Chorten | In Use | Public (Community) | Around 450 - 500 years old

SETTING
The *chorten* are oriented to the southeast and are built along the path leading to the *gonpa*. The site is surrounded by the village path and agricultural fields.

SIGNIFICANCE
The *chorten* were built in the past by a village ancestor as an act of merit for the well being of all sentient beings. The *chorten* are both Changchub *chorten* and symbolize the Buddha's enlightenment.

DESCRIPTION
The site consists of two *chorten* built on a high stone masonry platform adjacent to the path. The *chorten* are built in stone masonry and are mud plastered and whitewashed on the exterior. There are *chugsum khorlo* over the domes of the *chorten* which appear to be made of timber.

STATE OF PRESERVATION
Showing Signs of Deterioration

Skyurbuchan

396

Thegchen Dargyas Ling (Skyurbuchan *Gonpa*)

INVENTORY NO.
KHALTSE / SKYURBUCHAN / 30 / 2006

Gonpa | In Use | Public (Lamayuru *Gonpa*) | Around 500 years old

SETTING
The *gonpa* is built on a hill overlooking the village. A path from the village leads up to the *gonpa*.

SIGNIFICANCE
The *gonpa* originated from a small cave located at the site. During the reign of King Tashi Namgyal (1500 - 1535 A.D.), Chosje Danma Kunga visited Ladakh at which time only the cave existed and was known as Tashi Choszong. The *dukhang* and *gonkhang* were built later by a villager, Duwang Konchog Wangpo, popularly known as Meme Samphel in around 1710 A.D. In 1720, another resident of the village, Tsamspa Jorldan, built the *dukhang* dedicated to Chug-Shig-Zhal.

DESCRIPTION
The Thegchen Dargyas Ling *gonpa* is built on a hill overlooking the village. It is a large three storeyed structure built in stone and mud brick masonry. On the second floor there are two temples called Chanrazig *lhakhang*, facing west, and the *gonkhang*, facing southwest. The Chanrazig *lhakhang* contains a principal image of Charanzig and has no wall paintings. The *gonkhang* contains statues of the protector deities including Apchi, Gonbo, Namsras, Chagmen as well as photographs of teachers of the Drigung Kargyud lineage. The cave is also at this level and is a low height and dark chamber containing images of Skyoba Jigten Gonbo, Atisha etc. The *dukhang* is located on the first floor and houses images of Chanrazig, Gyalwa Chamba, Jo Rinpoche, Tsepakmed and *chorten* made of gold, silver and other precious stones. The ground floor is used primarily for storage as well as houses some monks' cells. Other monks' quarters are built around the main building some of which are single storeyed while others are double storeyed structures.

STATE OF PRESERVATION
Showing Signs of Deterioration

Skyurbuchan

397

SOURCE OF INFORMATION Konyer of *Gonpa*, and 'History of Ladakh Monasteries', published by All Ladakh *Gonpa* Association, 1995

Group of *Chorten*

INVENTORY NO.
KHALTSE / SKYURBUCHAN / 31 / 2006

Chorten | In Use | Public (Community) | Around 300 years old

SETTING
The *chorten* are oriented to the northeast and are built along the path leading to the *gonpa*. The site is surrounded by barren land and the village path.

SIGNIFICANCE
The *chorten* were built in the past by a village ancestor as an act of merit for the well being of all sentient beings. The *chorten* appear to be predominantly Changchub *chorten* and symbolize the Buddha's enlightenment. The *chorten* are circumambulated by villagers to accumulate merit as they travel along this path.

DESCRIPTION
The site consists of ten *chorten* built on a common stone masonry platform adjacent to the path. The *chorten* are built in stone masonry and are mud plastered and whitewashed externally. The external surface of the *chorten*

has eroded over time and one of the *chorten* has already collapsed while several others appear to be endangered. There is a tall *tarchen* located near the group of *chorten*.

STATE OF PRESERVATION
Advanced State of Decay

Mane Chuskor Gonpa

INVENTORY NO.
KHALTSE / SKYURBUCHAN / 32 / 2006

Temple | In Use | Public (Community) | Around 150 years old

SETTING
The *gonpa* is oriented to the southwest and is located in the upper part of the valley between two small hamlets of Pachak on the west and Kumba on the east. A small spring flows near the site.

SIGNIFICANCE
The Mane Chuskor *gonpa* was built about 150 years ago and since then villagers offer prayers at the site. Villagers gather here on the 15th day of the 5th month of the Tibetan calendar Tibetan to observe fasting. The *gonpa* contains many small prayer wheels, rotated by the flow of the spring water, for the benefit of all sentient beings.

DESCRIPTION
The *gonpa* consists of a single shrine containing many small prayer wheels, which are rotated by the flow of spring water below. Several old *thangka* also hang in the chamber. The

building is constructed in stone masonry with traces of external mud plaster and whitewash still evident. It has large timber framed window openings and a traditional roof above. The structure is in an advanced state of decay and a new temple is being constructed in front of the old temple.

STATE OF PRESERVATION
Danger of Disappearance

SOURCE OF INFORMATION Tashi Nurboo, Skyurbuchan, Khaltse, Ladakh

Dosku

INVENTORY NO.
KHALTSE / SKYURBUCHAN / 33 / 2006

Rock Carving | In Use | Public (Community) | Around 60 years old

SETTING
The rock carving is oriented to the southeast and is located in the upper part of the valley. It is carved on a large rock on a hill which lies a little before the Mane Chuskor *gonpa*.

SIGNIFICANCE
The rock carving was carved by Spon Rigzin and commissioned by Apo Chungmalik (Mukpa). The community had planned to build a shrine around the site which was later abandoned.

DESCRIPTION
The rock carving consists of two figures of Chanrazig and Jamyang carved on a flat rock surface. There is an unfinished figure of Chanrazig on the left.

STATE OF PRESERVATION
Fair

SOURCE OF INFORMATION Tashi Norboo, Skyurbuchan, Khaltse, Ladakh

399

S k y u r b u c h a n

Skangke Kagan

INVENTORY NO.
KHALTSE / SKYURBUCHAN / 34 / 2006

Chorten | In Use | Private (Individual) | Around 55 years old

SETTING
The Kagan *chorten* is located in the upper part of the valley about one km before the Mane Chuskor *gonpa* at Siksik. Bushes of wild rose grow around the *chorten*.

SIGNIFICANCE
The Skangke Kagan was sponsored by the villagers and built by Bagpa Tashi Nurboo around 55 years ago to protect the village from evil and misfortune. The Kagan *chorten* is a gateway *chorten* and merit is believed to accrue to believers who pass through the passage of the *chorten* and circumambulate it.

DESCRIPTION
The Kagan *chorten* consists of thick parallel walls over which rests a *chorten*. The structure is built in stone masonry and has traces of mud plaster and whitewash on the *chorten* above the passage. Over the walls is a traditional roof made of timber joists, stones and compacted mud on which rests the large *chorten*. The

chorten has a tall *chugsum khorlo* over the dome made of wood and painted red. The ceiling of the passage is built in timber and is in the shape of a *mandala*. The ceiling has elaborate paintings depicting a central *mandala* surrounded by figures of various Buddhist deities.

STATE OF PRESERVATION
Showing Signs of Deterioration

SOURCE OF INFORMATION Tashi Norboo, Skyurbuchan, Khaltse, Ladakh

Group of *Chorten*

INVENTORY NO.
KHALTSE / SKYURBUCHAN / 35 / 2006

Chorten | In Use | Public (Community) | Around 200 - 300 years old

SETTING

The *chorten* are located at the entrance to the village when approached from the Leh-Dha-Hanu route. The site is located to the left of the River Indus and is surrounded by mountains and barren land on all sides.

SIGNIFICANCE

The *chorten* mark the entrance to the village when approaching the village from Leh. The *chorten* are circumambulated by villagers to accumulate merit as they travel along this path. The *chorten* appear to be predominantly Changchub *chorten* and symbolize the Buddha's enlightenment. The Kagan *chorten* is a gateway *chorten* and merit is believed to accrue to believers who pass through the passage of the *chorten* and circumambulate it.

DESCRIPTION

The site consists of a group of six Changchub *chorten* and a Kagan *chorten* all built along the village path. The Changhub *chorten* are arranged in a single row and are all of the same size. They are built in stone masonry and have traces of external mud plaster and whitewash, most of which has eroded over time. The *chorten* are built on a common stone masonry platform. The Kagan *chorten* consists of two thick parallel walls over which rests a large *chorten*. The walls are built in stone masonry with timber beams at intervals. The roof of the structure is made of timber joists, stones and compacted mud over which rests the *chorten* made of stone and mud brick masonry. The *chorten* above is mud plastered and whitewashed and has a tall *chugsum khorlo* over the dome. The ceiling over the passage is made in timber and is in the shape of a *mandala* with paintings of various Buddhist deities and a *mandala*.

STATE OF PRESERVATION
Advanced State of Decay

Skyurbuchan

400

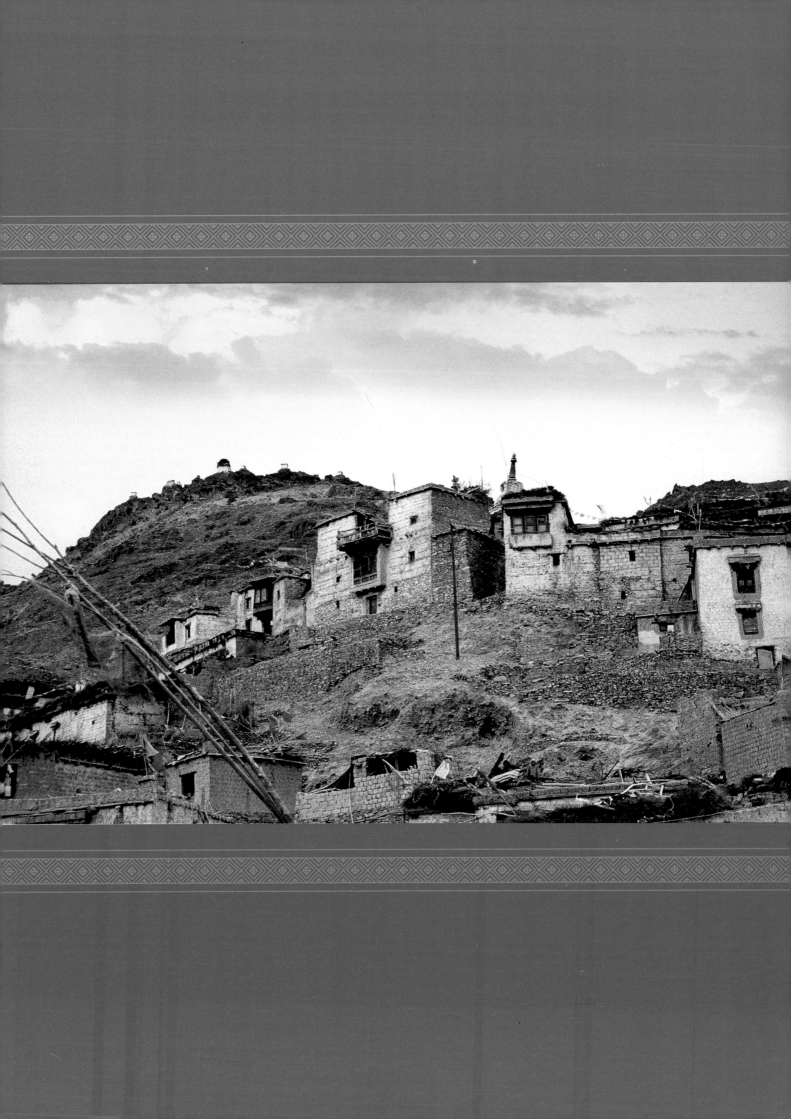

Tagmachig

The village of Tagmachig is situated at the left bank of the
River Indus, about 105 kms from Leh. According to legend, a
wandering monk from Shang came across a beautiful place
and decided to settle here. While he was thinking of a suitable
name for the place, an old tigress walked by. He tied the
tigress to a log of wood (which can still be seen today in the
Shagudpa house) and named the place as Stagmo Ching ('*tied
tigress*'). This later changed to Tagmachig. The descendents of
this monk are the Devapa family who still reside here. Today,
there are about 63 households in the village.

{*Source: Sonam Angchuk [Togopa]*}

Listed by: Deldan Angmo, Jassu Singh and Dr. Sonam Wangchok
Year: 2004, 2006

Mane Wall

INVENTORY NO.
KHALTSE / TAGMACHIG / 01 / 2004

Mane Wall | In Use | Public (Community) | Around 500 years old

SETTING
The *mane* wall is oriented towards the south and is located on the right of the vehicular road approximately one km before the village of Tagmachig. It lies between the main road and the River Indus.

SIGNIFICANCE
The *mane* wall is located on the approach to the village and is circumambulated by villagers as an act of merit as they travel along this route.

STATE OF PRESERVATION
Advanced State of Decay

DESCRIPTION
The *mane* wall is a long linear wall. It is around about 900 feet in length. It is constructed in dry stone masonry and has flat *mane* stones on the horizontal surface.

SOURCE OF INFORMATION Tsetan Namgyal, Tagmachig, Khaltse, Ladakh

Group of *Chorten* and *Mane* Walls (*Chorten Gongma*)

INVENTORY NO.
KHALTSE / TAGMACHIG / 02 / 2004

Chorten / *Mane* Wall | In Use | Public (Community) | Around 500 years old

SETTING
Oriented towards the northeast, the site is located along the River Indus to the left of the main vehicular road on a barren stretch of land. It is surrounded by trees and fields to the southwest and the river and highway lie to its north.

SIGNIFICANCE
The *chorten* and *mane* walls lie near the approach to the village and are circumambulated by villagers as an act of merit. The chorten are largely Changchub chorten and symbolize the Buddha's enlightenment.

DESCRIPTION
The site comprises of a group of sixteen *chorten* and six *mane* walls placed one after the other in a single row and ending with a cluster of *chorten*. There are two circular and four rectangular *mane* walls built in dry stone masonry. The *chorten* are of different sizes and are constructed in stone and brick masonry with mud mortar. The external surfaces of the *chorten* are mud plastered and whitewashed. Some of the larger *chorten* are built over a random rubble masonry platform.

STATE OF PRESERVATION
Advanced State of Decay

SOURCE OF INFORMATION Tsetan Namgyal, Tagmachig, Khaltse, Ladakh

Tagmachig

404

Group of Chorten and *Mane* Walls

INVENTORY NO.
KHALTSE / TAGMACHIG / 03 / 2004

Chorten / Mane Wall | In Use | Public (Community) | Around 500 years old

SETTING
The structures are oriented towards the south and are located on the left of the main vehicular road leading to the village. Beyond the site, the River Indus flows parallel to the road.

SIGNIFICANCE
The *chorten* and *mane* walls are located near the road leading to the village and are circumambulated by the villagers as an act of merit. The *chorten* is a Changchub *chorten* and symbolizes the Buddha's enlightenment.

DESCRIPTION
The site consists of a *chorten* and two *mane* walls on either side of the *chorten*. The *chorten* is built in stone masonry at the lower level and in mud brick masonry at the upper level. The external surface of the *chorten* is mud plastered and whitewashed. The *mane* walls on either side of the

SOURCE OF INFORMATION Tsetan Namgyal, Tagmachig, Khaltse, Ladakh

chorten are linear walls of low height built in dry stone masonry. The flat surface of the walls is covered with inscribed *mane* stones.

STATE OF PRESERVATION
Advanced State of Decay

Tongspon pa House

INVENTORY NO.
KHALTSE / TAGMACHIG / 04 / 2004

Vernacular Building | Abandoned | Private (Individual) | Around 200 years old

SETTING
The house is oriented towards the east and is located along a path en route to the *gonpa*. It is surrounded by other residential buildings and the village pathway runs along its north and east sides.

SIGNIFICANCE
The Tongspon pa house is a good example of vernacular architecture in the village. It was built by the great grand father of the present owner over 200 years ago.

DESCRIPTION
The Tongspon pa house is a three storeyed whitewashed structure built over a random plan with an entrance from the east. The ground floor is constructed in random rubble masonry with very small openings which have timber lintels. The upper floor is built in mud brick masonry with mud mortar. It has larger openings and ornamented timber

lintels. The house has a flat traditional roof with timber beams, joists, *taalu*, dry grass and a layer of compacted mud. A low parapet runs along the edge of the roof. The house is no longer used by the family, who have moved to a new house, and is, therefore, not regularly maintained.

STATE OF PRESERVATION
Advanced State of Decay

SOURCE OF INFORMATION Tsering Angchuk (Goba), Tagmachig, Khaltse, Ladakh

Group of *Chorten*, *Mane* Wall and *Rigsum Gonbo*

INVENTORY NO.
KHALTSE / TAGMACHIG / 05 / 2004

Chorten / *Mane* Wall / *Rigsum Gonbo* | In Use | Public (Community)
| Around 200 years old

SETTING
The site is oriented towards the east and is located along the village footpath near the Chugunpa house.

SIGNIFICANCE
The Kagan *chorten* is believed to be one of the oldest religious structures in the village and provides access to the village through the passage below. Passing through the Kagan *chorten* is seen as an act of merit. The *rigsum gonbo* was built to protect the village from evil forces.

DESCRIPTION
The site consists of a group of structures including a Kagan *chorten*, Kumbum *mane* wall and a *rigsum gonbo* located at the entrance to the settlement. The Kagan *chorten* consists of two parallel random rubble and mud brick masonry side walls over which rests a Changchub *chorten* built in mud brick masonry. The ceiling over the passage is built in timber and is in the shape of a *mandala*. The ceiling and the wall panels inside the *chorten* are painted with images of various Bodhisattvas and Buddhas. The Changchub *chorten* on top has a *chugsum khorlo* over the dome over which rests a metal crown. The Kagan *chorten* is mud plastered and whitewashed externally. To the front and rear of the *chorten* are two *mane* walls built in stone masonry. The Kumbum *mane* to the rear of the Kagan *chorten* is cylindrical in shape with *mane* stones placed on the top. Between the *chorten* and the Kumbum *mane* is a small *rigsum gonbo*, rectangular in plan and housing three small *chorten*. The structure is open towards the front and is covered with a sheet of polythene.

STATE OF PRESERVATION
Showing Signs of Deterioration

SOURCE OF INFORMATION Tsetan Namgyal - Chugunpa, Tagmachig, Khaltse, Ladakh

Tagmachig

NIRLAC

Nyerpa *Khangpa*

INVENTORY NO.
KHALTSE / TAGMACHIG / 06 / 2004

Vernacular Building | Abandoned | Private (Individual) | Around 500 years old

SETTING
The house is oriented towards the east and is situated along the path leading to the *gonpa*. It is surrounded by Tongspon pa house towards the north and Sheshapa house towards the south.

SIGNIFICANCE
The house is one of the oldest houses in the village and is a fine example of vernacular architecture. It was built by an ancestor of the Nyerpa family around 500 years ago. The family no longer resides here.

DESCRIPTION
The Nyerpa house lies abandoned as the family has moved into a new house. It is built in the traditional style over three levels. The ground floor is used primarily for storing fodder and stabling animals. The first floor consists of three rooms with elaborate timber opening embellished with wooden lattice work. The central room has an elaborately decorated timber *rabsal* with painted frames and tiered

lintels. It is built in random rubble masonry at the lower level and mud brick masonry has been used in the upper level. The house has a flat traditional roof comprising of wooden beams, joists, *taalu*, dried grass and mud.

STATE OF PRESERVATION
Advanced State of Decay

SOURCE OF INFORMATION Norbu Zangpo - Nyerpa Pa, Tagmachig, Khaltse, Ladakh

---

Churupa *Khangpa*

INVENTORY NO.
KHALTSE / TAGMACHIG / 07 / 2004

Vernacular Building| Abandoned | Private (Individual) | Around 200 years old

SETTING
The house is oriented towards the east and is located on a hill surrounded by residential buildings on all sides.

SIGNIFICANCE
The house is built in the traditional style and is believed to be about 200 years old. It was built by an ancestor of the Churupa family as a *tashag* or monk's cell.

DESCRIPTION
The Churupa *Khangpa* is a large three storeyed structure built over a rectangular plan. The ground floor is constructed in random rubble masonry without any openings and is used as a storage space. The first and second floors are built in rammed earth. The entrance to the house is from the front at the ground floor level. The first and second floors constituted the living areas. The first floor has an elaborate wooden opening with wooden lattice work shutters. The frame is painted in blue and green. The

second floor has a cantilevered open verandah at the centre. The structure is covered with a flat traditional roof with prayer flags posted on it.

STATE OF PRESERVATION
Advanced State of Decay

SOURCE OF INFORMATION Tsering Angchuk (Goba), Tagmachig, Khaltse, Ladakh

Tagmachig

407

Nyenas *Lhakhang* (Tagmachig *Gonpa*)

INVENTORY NO.
KHALTSE / TAGMACHIG / 08 / 2004

Gonpa | In Use | Public (Lamayuru *Gonpa*)

STATE OF PRESERVATION
Advanced State of Decay

SETTING
Oriented towards the northeast, the *gonpa* is located on a hillock and is surrounded by *chorten* and *mane* walls towards the north and west. It is located near the Rongpapa Khangbu house (*tashag*).

SIGNIFICANCE
The *gonpa* is believed to have been built a little later than the Lamayuru *gonpa*. The *gonpa* is the principal religious building in the village and is thus of prime importance to the villagers. The *gonpa* is a branch monastery of Lamayuru *gonpa*. The *gonpa* houses the main assembly hall or *dukhang* as well as residential quarters for the monks who are deputed here from the main monastery at Lamayuru to carry out prayers and rituals for the village.

DESCRIPTION
The *gonpa* is a two storeyed structure built along the slope of a hill. There is a forecourt at the lower level and a porch along the northeast accessed through a flight of stone steps. The roof over the porch is supported on wooden columns and beams. There are three doors opening onto the porch. The first one leads towards the *dukhang* which houses the images of Chanrazig and other Bodhisattvas. The central door leads to the store while the third one leads to the kitchen which is on the first floor. There are two living quarters for the lamas on the first floor. At the rear of the building, towards the southeast, there is a large courtyard flanked by a gallery supported on wooden columns. In the centre of the courtyard is a large Indoom *chorten*. The *chorten* is housed in a square enclosure with a flat traditional roof supported on four columns at each corner. The *chorten* is built in stone and mud brick masonry and is mud plastered and whitewashed on the exterior. The *chorten* has a *chugsum khorlo* over the dome which projects out of the roof. The same courtyard also leads to the *dukhang* owned and managed by the local community. It has decorated wooden openings with painted lintels.

SOURCE OF INFORMATION Sonam Gyaltsan - *Mane*pa, Tagmachig, Khaltse, Ladakh

NIRLAC

Shimi *Chorten*

INVENTORY NO.
KHALTSE / TAGMACHIG / 09 / 2004

Chorten | In Use | Public (Community) | Around 200 years old

SETTING
The site is oriented towards the northeast and is located on the way to the *gonpa*. It is surrounded by Tongspon pa house to the wèst and Tunpa house towards the east.

SIGNIFICANCE
The *chorten* is around 200 years old. On the death anniversary of a family member, the family takes offerings to the *chorten* and a feast is held in its vicinity. The offerings are made at the *lubang*, near the base of the *chorten*.

DESCRIPTION
The site consists of two Changchub *chorten*, a *mane* wall and a *lubang* near the base of one of the *chorten*. The *chorten* are of different sizes. The *chorten* near the *lubang* is slightly larger. The *chorten* are built in stone and mud brick masonry with mud mortar. The dome is surmounted by a tall *chugsum khorlo* which is topped with a crescent shaped crown. Externally, the *chorten* are mud plastered

and whitewashed. There is a small *lubang*, to the northwest, near one of the larger *chorten*. The *mane* wall is rectangular in plan and built in dry stone masonry.

STATE OF PRESERVATION
Advanced State of Decay

SOURCE OF INFORMATION Tsering Angchuk, Tagmachig, Khaltse, Ladakh

Tagmachig

409

Chugunpa House (*Tashag*)

INVENTORY NO.
KHALTSE / TAGMACHIG / 10 / 2004

Vernacular Building | In Use | Private (Individual)

SETTING
The Chugunpa house is oriented towards the east and is located along the slope of a hill surrounded by other residential buildings namely the Tunpa house towards the north and the Yultakpa Khangbu house towards the south.

SIGNIFICANCE
The house is a large structure built in the traditional style and forms part of the vernacular architecture of the village. Today, it is used as a *tashag*.

DESCRIPTION
The house is a three storeyed structure built on a rectangular plan. It is entered through a wooden doorway on the eastern facade. The ground floor is constructed in random rubble masonry without any openings except the doorway. The upper floors are built in mud brick masonry with mud mortar and have large openings with elaborate

timber lintels. The house has a traditional roof surrounded by a low mud parapet with prayer flags posted on the corners.

STATE OF PRESERVATION
Showing Signs of Deterioration

SOURCE OF INFORMATION Tsering Angchuk-Goba, Tagmachig, Khaltse, Ladakh

Chorten and Deshag Gyadpa

INVENTORY NO.
KHALTSE / TAGMACHIG / 11 / 2004

Chorten | In Use | Public (Community)

STATE OF PRESERVATION
Showing Signs of Deterioration

SETTING
Oriented towards the north, the *chorten* are located near the *gonpa* on an elevated area south of the main village. It is surrounded to the south by Tunpa house and in the southwest by the *gonpa*.

SIGNIFICANCE
The *chorten* were built in the past as an act of merit. These form part of the sacred geography of the *gonpa* and are circumambulated by pilgrims. The Changchub *chorten* is one of the 8 traditional types of Tibetan *chorten* and symbolizes the Buddha's enlightenment. The Deshag Gyadpa comprises of all eight types of *chorten* each symbolizing an event in the Buddha's life.

DESCRIPTION
The site consists of a Changchub *chorten*, housed in an enclosure, and a Deshag Gyad. The enclosure of the Changchub *chorten* is built in random rubble masonry at the base. There are walls on two sides and it is open on two sides with columns at the corners. The walls and columns are built in mud brick masonry with mud mortar. The *chorten* is located within the enclosure and is constructed in stone and mud brick masonry with mud mortar. The enclosure has a traditional roof and like the *chorten* within is mud plastered and whitewashed externally. Towards the west of the *chorten* is a Deshag Gyad comprising of the eight types of chorten – Changchub, Namgyal, Padspung, Choskor, Lhabab, Chotul, Indoom and Nyangdas. These are enclosed in a structure with a traditional flat roof and opening towards the north. The internal walls contain paintings depicting the thousand Buddhas. The *chorten* are mud plastered and whitewashed externally. The roof of the enclosure is supported on timber columns and capitals. The two side walls of the enclosure have small window openings to the front which have timber frames and lintels.

SOURCE OF INFORMATION Tsering Angchuk, Tagmachig, Khaltse, Ladakh

NIRLAC

Group of *Chorten* and *Mane* Wall

INVENTORY NO.
KHALTSE / TAGMACHIG / 12 / 2004

Chorten / *Mane* Wall | In Use | Public (Community)

SETTING
Oriented towards the southeast, this cluster of structures is located en route to the *gonpa* and are surrounded by residential buildings such as the Churupa house to the north.

SIGNIFICANCE
The group of structures lies along the route leading to the *gonpa* and is circumambulated by villagers as they travel along this route. These were built in the past for the well being of the village and are still worshipped today. The Kagan *chorten* is built over the pathway and passage through the *chorten* is believed to gather merit for the believers.

DESCRIPTION
The site consists of a cluster of Kagan *chorten*, a *mane* wall, a small white washed *lubang* and three Changchub *chorten*.

SOURCE OF INFORMATION Tsering Angchuk, Tagmachig, Khaltse, Ladakh

The *mane* wall does not have a definite shape but is quite large in size. It is built of loosely piled stone with inscribed *mane* stones on the horizontal surface. The Kagan *chorten* has two thick side walls in random rubble and mud brick masonry supporting the Changchub *chorten* on top. The ceiling over the passage is built in timber and is in the shape of a *mandala*. The ceiling is embellished with paintings. There is a group of three Changchub *chorten* nearby which are built in stone and mud brick masonry and are mud plastered and whitewashed on the exterior. These *chorten* have tall *chugsum khorlo* over the dome.

STATE OF PRESERVATION
Showing Signs of Deterioration

Zappa House (*Tashag*)

INVENTORY NO.
KHALTSE / TAGMACHIG / 13 / 2004

Vernacular Building | In Use | Private (Individual) | Around 300 years old

SETTING
The house is oriented towards the east and is located on a hill along with several other buildings. To the north lies the Tashi Kunpa house.

SIGNIFICANCE
The house is believed to have been built three centuries ago by the monk Gelong Konchok Tsultim. It is still used as a *tashag*. It is a good example of vernacular architecture in the village.

DESCRIPTION
The Zappa house is a double storeyed structure built over a rectangular plan. The ground floor is constructed in random rubble masonry while the upper floor is built in mud brick masonry with mud mortar. Externally, the house is mud plastered and white washed. It is entered through a small wooden doorway on the front facade. Above the main door

SOURCE OF INFORMATION Tsering Angchuk -Goba, Tagmachig, Khaltse, Ladakh

way, on the first floor, is a *rabsal* with a timber frame. On its either side there are smaller openings with lattice work shutters. The house has a traditional roof and a string of prayer flags are tied on the roof.

STATE OF PRESERVATION
Showing Signs of Deterioration

Tagmachig

411

Tashi Kunpa *Khangpa (Tashag)*

INVENTORY NO.
KHALTSE / TAGMACHIG / 14 / 2004

Vernacular Building | In Use | Private (Individual) | Around 300 years old

SETTING
The house is oriented towards the east and is located north of the Zappa house on a hill.

SIGNIFICANCE
The house was built by ancestors of the Tashi Kunpa family 300 years ago to serve as a *tashag*, a function it continues to serve today. Along with the Zappa house, this structure is representative of the traditional architecture of the region.

DESCRIPTION
The house is a double storeyed structure built over a rectangular plan. Built in random rubble masonry at the lower level and mud brick masonry at the upper level, the house is mud plastered and whitewashed externally. It is entered through a small wooden doorway from the front facade. Just above the door way, there is an elaborate

rabsal on the first floor with a timber frame. There are small window openings on both levels. The house has a traditional roof with a prayer flag posted on the roof.

STATE OF PRESERVATION
Advanced State of Decay

SOURCE OF INFORMATION Tsering Angchuk (Goba), Tagmachig, Khaltse, Ladakh

Tagmachig

Tagmachig Castle *(Gyamkhar)*

INVENTORY NO.
KHALTSE / TAGMACHIG / 15 / 2004

Fort / Palace | Abandoned | Public (Community) | Around 400 - 500 years old

SETTING
The ruins of the castle are oriented towards the south and are located on a bare hill to the left of the main settlement.

SIGNIFICANCE
The castle is believed to be around 400 years old and served as a shelter for the villagers when the village was under attack. The construction technique is similar to that employed in the construction of other forts in the region primarily in rammed earth.

STATE OF PRESERVATION
Danger of Disappearance

DESCRIPTION
The castle is in complete ruins and little survives apart from the ruined walls and watch towers. These are built in rammed earth and the walls stand at right angles to each other. The walls are thicker at the base and taper as they rise up.

SOURCE OF INFORMATION Sonam Gyaltsan-Manepa, Tagmachig, Khaltse, Ladakh

Mane Wall

INVENTORY NO.
KHALTSE / TAGMACHIG / 16 / 2004

Mane Wall | In Use | Public (Community)

SETTING
The *mane* wall is oriented towards the northwest and is located on a hill en route to the *gonpa*. It is surrounded by Nyerpa pa house to the northwest and a group of *chorten* and *mane* walls on the northeast.

SIGNIFICANCE
The *mane* wall is located along the route leading to the *gonpa* and is circumambulated by villagers as an act of merit while travelling along this route.

DESCRIPTION
The *mane* wall is built of loosely piled stones placed in a linear manner to form a low wall. The horizontal surface of the wall contains numerous *mane* stone. The wall no longer retains its original shape and the stones are scattered in the vicinity.

STATE OF PRESERVATION
Danger of Disappearance

SOURCE OF INFORMATION Tsering Angchuk, Tagmachig, Khaltse, Ladakh

Urbis Chomo *Lhato*

INVENTORY NO.
KHALTSE / TAGMACHIG / 17 / 2004

Lhato | In Use | Public (Community) | Around 400 years old

SETTING
The *lhato* is oriented to the south and is located on a hill behind the *gonpa*. A pathway runs along the southern edge.

SIGNIFICANCE
According to legend, the protector deity Urbis Chomo has seven sisters (*spundun*). One of them is in Tagmachig village, another in Urbis and one in Lehdo. They are all known by same name. The *lhato* is dedicated to the village protector deity and is believed to be around 400 years old. The juniper plants, *khadag* etc. in the *lhato* are changed every year on the occasion of Losar. Rituals are carried out at the site on this occasion.

STATE OF PRESERVATION
Advanced State of Decay

DESCRIPTION
The site consists of a cluster of seven *lhato*. Built in stone masonry, the *lhato* are cubical in shape with offerings of juniper branches, animal horns and *khadag* placed on the top. Externally, the *lhato* are mud plastered and whitewashed.

SOURCE OF INFORMATION Tsering Angchuk, Tagmachig, Khaltse, Ladakh

Tagmachig

413

Mane Wall

INVENTORY NO.
KHALTSE / TAGMACHIG / 18 / 2004

Mane Wall | In Use | Public (Community)

STATE OF PRESERVATION
Advanced State of Decay

SETTING
The *mane* wall is oriented towards the northwest and is located on a hill behind the *gonpa*. The site is linear with a cliff to its south, the village and *gonpa* to the north, Tashi Kunpa and Zappa to the northeast and Nyerpa pa to the north.

SIGNIFICANCE
The *mane* walls were built in the past as an act of merit and are still circumambulated by villagers.

DESCRIPTION
The site consists of a linear arrangement of rectangular and circular *mane* walls. At the beginning of the site is a small whitewashed and mud plastered *mane* wall. This is followed by a much larger, mud plastered, whitewashed *mane* wall and two more linear *mane* walls. All the *mane* walls are built in dry stone masonry and have inscribed *mane* stones on the horizontal surface.

SOURCE OF INFORMATION Tsering Angchuk, Tagmachig, Khaltse, Ladakh

Shime *Chorten*

INVENTORY NO.
KHALTSE / TAGMACHIG / 19 / 2004

Chorten / Rigsum Gonbo | In Use | Public (Community) | Around 200 years old

SETTING
The site is located along a path en route from the *gonpa* to the village pond. It is surrounded by residential buildings such as the Shaudpa and Dakshospa.

SIGNIFICANCE
The site comprises of *chorten*, *rigsum gonbo* and a *lubang*. The *rigsum gonbo* was built to protect the village from evil forces. The *chorten* were also built as an act of merit and are still circumambulated by villagers in order to accumulate merit. The *lubang* marks the residence of the *lu,* or serpent gods of the underworld.

DESCRIPTION
The site consists of a cluster of three *chorten*, a *rigsum gonbo* and a *lubang*. The *rigsum gonbo* shares a common wall with the Dakshospa house. It is built in stone and mud brick masonry and the external surface is mud plastered and whitewashed. Enclosed on three sides, the fourth side is open and contains three *chorten* within. The *rigsum*

gonbo has a traditional roof. Of the group of *chorten*, two are in ruins while the third appears to be a Changchub *chorten*. It is built in stone and mud brick masonry with mud mortar and has traces of mud plaster and whitewash on the exterior surface. There is a small rectangular white washed *lubang* near the base of the *rigsum gonbo*.

STATE OF PRESERVATION
Danger of Disappearance

SOURCE OF INFORMATION Tsering Angchuk, Tagmachig, Khaltse, Ladakh

Tagmachig

414

Group of *Mane* Walls and *Chorten*

INVENTORY NO.
KHALTSE / TAGMACHIG / 20 / 2004

Chorten / Mane Wall | In Use | Public (Community)

STATE OF PRESERVATION
Showing Signs of Deterioration

SETTING

The site is oriented towards the northeast and is located on a hill along northwestern side of the *gonpa*. The village lies further north of the site.

SIGNIFICANCE

The *mane* walls form a part of the sacred geography of the *gonpa*. A circumambulatory path around both the *gonpa* and the *mane* walls is used by the villagers as an act of merit. Every year for two days, the villagers come to the *gonpa* to inscribe mane stones with the sacred Buddhist *mantra 'Om Mani Padme Hung'*. The newly inscribed stones are placed over existing *mane* walls and new *mane* walls are also constructed at this time. Most of the inscribed stones at this site were inscribed by Phuntsog Angchuk, grand father of the present village head, Tsering Angchuk. These were inscribed in Pali script known as Lantsa. The Changchub *chorten* symbolize the enlightenment of the Buddha and are circumambulated by villagers as an act of merit.

DESCRIPTION

The site comprises of a number of *mane* walls and five Changchub *chorten* of different sizes. The first cluster consists of three *chorten* and are located near the *gonpa* wall. The *chorten* are built in stone and mud brick masonry with mud mortar. Externally, the *chorten* are mud plastered and whitewashed and are surmounted by a tapering red *chugsum khorlo* on the top. The *mane* walls are linear rectangular structures in close proximity to each other forming a large cluster. The *chorten* are placed randomly near this structure. The *mane* walls have been constructed using flat stone slabs brought in from the neighbouring hill. The horizontal surface of the *mane* walls are covered with hundreds of *mane* stones.

Tagmachig

415

SOURCE OF INFORMATION Tsering Angchuk, Tagmachig, Khaltse, Ladakh, 194106, J&K

Group of *Chorten* and *Mane* Wall

INVENTORY NO.
KHALTSE / TAGMACHIG / 21 / 2004

Chorten / Mane Wall | In Use | Community | Around 250 years old

SETTING
The structures are located en route to the village near the main vehicular road. The road itself lies to the north while the river flows to the south of the site.

SIGNIFICANCE
The *chorten* and *mane* wall lie on the path leading to the village and are circumambulated by villagers as an act of merit when they travel along this path. The *chorten* are Changchub *chorten* and symbolize the Buddha's enlightenment.

DESCRIPTION
The site comprises of a group of two *chorten* and a long *mane* wall. The *mane* wall is built in dry stone masonry and the horizontal surface is lined up with inscribed *mane* stones. The *chorten* are located at either end of the *mane*

wall and are of similar size. These are built in stone and mud brick masonry with mud mortar and are mud plastered and whitewashed externally.

STATE OF PRESERVATION
Showing Signs of Deterioration

SOURCE OF INFORMATION Tsering Angchuk, Tagmachig, Khaltse, Ladakh

Tagmachig

416

Shagutpa House

INVENTORY NO.
KHALTSE / TAGMACHIG / 22 / 2006

Vernacular Building | In Use | Private (Individual) | Around 250 years old

SETTING
The Shagutpa house is oriented towards the north and is located in the middle of the old settlement. The house is surrounded by other village houses on all side.

SIGNIFICANCE
The house is believed to be one of the oldest in the village. According to legend, the first religious being who came to the site of the present day village found an old tigress in the area. He bound the tigress to the trunk of a tree thereby giving the village its name of Tagmachig ('a bound tigress'). The trunk of this tree is said to be inside the old section of the house. The house itself is more than 200 years old and was built by an ancestor of the Shagutpa family. The family continues to reside here.

DESCRIPTION
The Shagutpa house has been added on to over a period of time. The oldest part is a double storeyed structure. The ground floor is constructed in stone masonry and the upper

floor is in mud brick masonry with mud mortar. Some supporting timber members can be seen in the wall. The house has small wooden windows and has a flat traditional roof on top. The roof is enclosed within a low height mud parapet.

STATE OF PRESERVATION
Advanced State of Decay

SOURCE OF INFORMATION Sonam Angchuk (Togopa), Tagmachig, Khaltse, Ladakh

Hemar *Gonpa*

INVENTORY NO.
KHALTSE / TAGMACHIG / 23 / 2006

Gonpa | In Use | Public (Community) | Around 300 years old

SETTING

The Hemar *gonpa* is oriented to the south and is located on a hill above the fields and groves of apricot trees. It is located about three kms from the village.

SIGNIFICANCE

The *gonpa* is contemporary to the Nyenas *lhakhang* built by Lama Konchok Chosphel Togopa around 300 years ago. It is said that the Lama himself created the wood carving and paintings. Villagers get together and perform prayer (*Tseschu*) for Guru Rinpoche on the tenth day of every month.

DESCRIPTION

The *gonpa* is a small complex dedicated to Chamba, Guru Rinpoche and other protectors. There is a place for storing grain to the right of the courtyard and the kitchen is to the left. The courtyard has seven pillars all around and a door way leads into the main prayer hall. The shrine has a low wooden door with wooden windows on either side. The main statue is that of Chamba and the walls are painted with images of the protectors and lamas. The shrine has two wooden pillars with brackets supporting the roof above. It has a wooden floor.

STATE OF PRESERVATION
Showing Sign of Deterioration

Tagmachig

417

SOURCE OF INFORMATION Sonam Angchuk, Tagmachig, Khaltse, Ladakh

Tsamskhang

INVENTORY NO.
KHALTSE / TAGMACHIG / 24 / 2006

Temple | In Use | Public (Community) | Around 200 years old

SETTING
On crossing the Tagmachig bridge, a link road diverts near the *chorten* and *mane* walls towards the left which leads on to the *tsamskhang*. The *tsamskhang* is surrounded by apricot and willow trees in the front and mountains to the rear. There is a spring near the temple.

SIGNIFICANCE
The old part of the *tsamskhang* is said to be very old though an exact date could not be discovered. However, the new part was built about 80 years ago by the villagers. Today, one monk meditates there and villagers offer prayers to the protectors every month. Villagers come to worship at the temple before the start of the Losar festival. The main shrine is dedicated to Jo Rinpoche.

DESCRIPTION
The *tsamskhang* is a double storeyed structure with an old and a new section. The ground floor is constructed in random rubble masonry and the first floor is in mud brick masonry with mud mortar. The building has small windows on the ground floor and a large window on the first floor. A staircase in the centre leads to the main shrine. The shrine has two columns in the centre. The main image is that of Jo Rinpoche and there is a small mask of a protector which is said to have been brought from Tibet by a monk called Meme Chosje. The exterior walls are painted in yellow and red colours. There are no wall paintings in the shrine. The structure is covered with a flat traditional roof.

STATE OF PRESERVATION
Showing Signs of Deterioration

SOURCE OF INFORMATION Sonam Angchuk (Togopa), Tagmachig, Khaltse, Ladakh

Dewapa House

INVENTORY NO.
KHALTSE / TAGMACHIG / 25 / 2006

Vernacular Building | In Use | Private (Individual) | Around 250 years old

SETTING
The Dewapa house is oriented to the north and is located next to the Shagutpa house in the middle of the old settlement. It is surrounded by village houses on all side.

SIGNIFICANCE
A wandering monk is believed to have been the first settler in the village and his descendents, the Dewapa family, continue to reside in the village. The house was built by more than 200 years ago and is one of the oldest houses in the village. It is built in the traditional style.

DESCRIPTION
The house is a three storeyed structure. The ground and first floors are constructed in random rubble masonry while the second floor is built in mud brick masonry with mud mortar. The second floor has a *rabsal* in the middle and small wooden windows on either side. The lower floors do not have any openings. The structure is covered with a flat traditional roof comprising of wooden beams, joists, *taalu*, grass and a layer of compacted mud on top. There is a low parapet surrounding the roof. The exterior walls of the house are mud plastered and white washed.

STATE OF PRESERVATION
Showing Signs of Deterioration

SOURCE OF INFORMATION Sonam Angchuk (Togopa), Tagmachig, Khaltse, Ladakh

Tar

Tar village can be reached from a bridge over the river Indus that diverts from the main Leh - Srinagar highway just before Nyurla and leads to the left bank of the Indus. After crossing the bridge, a footpath diverts to the left through a narrow valley towards the village.

Listed by: Deldan Angmo and Jassu Singh
Year: 2004

Tarchid

The village of Tarchid is located near Wanla, about 114 kms from Leh. The village was also known as Tarchid Padmachan. Today, there are about 23 households in the village.

Listed by: Deldan Angmo and Jassu Singh
Year: 2004

Azhangpe *Mane Chorten*

INVENTORY NO.
KHALTSE / TAR / 01 / 2004

Chorten | In Use | Private (Individual) | Around 200 years old

SETTING
The *chorten* are oriented to the southwest and are located near agricultural field and apricot trees in front of the Azangpe house.

SIGNIFICANCE
The *chorten* were built as an act of merit by the grand parents of the present generation of the Azhangpe family when he returned from Tibet.

DESCRIPTION
The site consists of a cluster of four small *chorten* built in stone and mud brick masonry. The chorten are completely eroded and it is difficult to identify their original form.

STATE OF PRESERVATION
Danger of Disappearance

SOURCE OF INFORMATION Tsering Angchuk, Azangpe, Tar, Khaltse, Ladakh

Deshag Gyad

INVENTORY NO.
KHALTSE / TAR / 02 / 2004

Chorten | In Use | Private (Individual) | Around 200 years old

SETTING
The *chorten* are oriented to the east and are located east of the group of *chorten* and the *mane* walls located below the hill on which stands the Tar *gonpa*.

SIGNIFICANCE
The Deshag Gyad was built by an ancestor of the Azhangpe family named Konchok Tundup, as an act of merit on his return from the Tibet. It forms part of a group of structures including the chorten, mane walls and *rigsum gonbo*. The Deshag Gyad consists of the 8 traditional forms of *chorten* In Tibetan Buddhism representing significant events in the life of the Buddha.

DESCRIPTION
The Deshag Gyad consists of an enclosure built in random rubble and mud brick masonry with walls on three sides and a small wooden framed opening in the eastern facade. The *chorten* are visible from these openings. The *chorten* are of the 8 different styles and are built in mud brick

masonry with mud mortar. The external layer of mud plaster and whitewash has eroded over time. The structure has a traditional roof above.

STATE OF PRESERVATION
Advanced State of Decay

SOURCE OF INFORMATION Tsering Angchuk, Azangpe, Tar, Khaltse, Ladakh

Group of *Chorten* and *Mane* Walls

INVENTORY NO.
KHALTSE / TAR / 03 / 2004

Chorten / *Mane* Wall | In Use | Private (Individual) | Around 200 years old

SETTING
The *chorten* are oriented to the east and are located west of the Deshag Gyad, below the hill on which stands the Tar *gonpa*.

SIGNIFICANCE
The group of *chorten* and *mane* walls are part of a group of structures built by an ancestor of the Azhangpe family following his return from Tibet. It is said that he commissioned a thousand *mantras* engraved on stones and installed them in the *mane* wall as an act of merit. The *chorten* are all Changchub *chorten* and symbolize the Buddha's enlightenment. The group of structures are circumambulated by villagers as an act of merit while travelling along this path.

DESCRIPTION
The sit consists of a cluster of four *mane* walls and four Changchub *chorten* all placed in a row. Behind the Deshag Gyad structure is a large *chorten* with a smaller *chorten* located behind it. This is followed by alternate *mane* walls and *chorten*. The first two *mane* walls are linear in shape while the last two are cylindrical in shape. The surface of the *mane* walls contains numerous *mane* stones including one with the name of the builder and the year in which it was built. The Changchub *chorten* are built in random rubble and mud brick masonry with mud mortar and are mud plastered and whitewashed on the exterior. The domes of the *chorten* have small niches with wooden frames. On the top of the dome is a tall *chugsum khorlo*, symbolizing the 13 steps towards enlightenment. Each *chorten* has a crescent shaped crown at the top. The base panels of the plinth are decorated with stucco relief motifs (*pa-tra*).

STATE OF PRESERVATION
Advanced State of Decay

Tar

423

SOURCE OF INFORMATION Tsering Angchuk, Azangpe, Tar, Khaltse, Ladakh

Tar *Gonpa*

INVENTORY NO.
KHALTSE / TAR / 04 / 2004

Gonpa | In Use | Public (Lamayuru *Gonpa*) | Around 30 years old

SETTING
The *gonpa* is oriented to the south and is located on a hill above the village. The Azangpe group of *chorten* and Deshag Gyad lie at the base of the hill. A narrow gravel footpath leads from the village, passing the group of *chorten* and *mane* walls, to the *gonpa*.

SIGNIFICANCE
The *gonpa* was built relatively recently and houses the images and ritual objects of the old *gonpa*. It falls under the purview of Lamayuru *gonpa* and a monk is deputed here to carry out prayers and rituals in the temple. It is the principal place of worship in the village.

DESCRIPTION
The *gonpa* is a small single storeyed building built in stone and mud brick masonry with mud mortar. There is a small courtyard with a *tarchen* in the front. From here, steps lead to the portico which has low height walls in the front and two wooden columns supporting the roof above. A wooden

doorway leads into a square chamber. The walls have wall paintings all over and the rear wall has some wooden pedestals on which the images are kept. On the west wall are images of Chanrazig, the central one is Skyoba Jigsten Gonbo and on the east is Guru Rinpoche. The east wall has two wooden window openings with glass panes. The roof is a traditional one made of timber beams, joists, *taalu*, grass and a layer of compacted mud. Externally, the walls are mud plastered and whitewashed.

STATE OF PRESERVATION
Showing Signs of Deterioration

SOURCE OF INFORMATION Tsering Angchuk, Azangpe, Tar, Khaltse, Ladakh

Azhangpe *Tashag*

INVENTORY NO.
KHALTSE / TAR / 05 / 2004

Vernacular Building | Abandoned | Private (Individual) | Around 200 years old

SETTING
The *tashag* is oriented to the south and is located below the *gonpa* to the south near the Azhangpe *chorten* and the mane walls.

SIGNIFICANCE
The *tashag* was built around 200 years ago by an ancestor of the Azhangpe family for the monks who looked after the *gonpa* and performed prayers and rituals there. The *tashag* is built in the traditional style and is a good example of vernacular architecture in the village.

DESCRIPTION
The *tashag* is a double storeyed house built on an L-shaped plan. The entrance leads to an open court from where a small wooden door leads to the ground floor which is used for storing fodder. The upper floor formerly housed the monks' living quarters. The building is abandoned at present and is used only for storage. The window openings are on the southern facade and have timber frames and

lintels. The roof is a traditional one made of timber beams, joists, *taalu*, grass and compacted mud. The building itself is constructed in random rubble and mud brick masonry with mud mortar and is mud plastered and whitewashed externally.

STATE OF PRESERVATION
Advanced State of Decay

SOURCE OF INFORMATION Tsering Angchuk, Azangpe, Tar, Khaltse, Ladakh

Rigsum Gonbo and *Tsadkhang*

INVENTORY NO.
KHALTSE / TAR / 06 / 2004

Rigsum Gonbo / Tsadkhang / *Mane* Wall | In Use | Private (Individual) |
Around 200 years old

SETTING
The *rigsum gonbo* is oriented to the west and is located
south of the Tar *gonpa* and east of the Azhangpe's *tashag*.

SIGNIFICANCE
The *rigsum gonbo* forms part of the group of structures built
by an ancestor of the Azhangpe family on his return from
Tibet. It was built to protect the village from natural
calamities and disease. The site also contains a *tsadkhang*
which houses offerings of *tsa-tsa*. The *mane* walls are
circumambulated by villagers to gather merit.

DESCRIPTION
The *rigsum gonbo* is located on the same hill on which the
gonpa stands. It is a rectangular structure with walls on
three sides and an opening to the front facing the village. It
is built in stone and mud brick masonry with mud mortar
and has three small *chorten* inside. There are two *mane*
walls to the north of the *rigsum gonbo*. One is circular and
the other is rectangular in shape. The *mane* walls are both
constructed in random rubble masonry and have inscribed
mane stones placed on the horizontal surface. To the
northwest is a small *tsadkhang* which is a tall structure
built on a square plan in mud brick masonry. It has an
opening on one side and inside the *tsadkhang* are placed
several *tsa-tsa*. The *tsadkhang* has a traditional roof above
and is mud plastered and whitewashed externally. Near this
group are some *lubang* made in stone and mud brick
masonry with a mud roof above.

STATE OF PRESERVATION
Advanced State of Decay

Tar

425

SOURCE OF INFORMATION Tsering Angchuk, Azangpe, Tar, Khaltse, Ladakh, 194106, J&K

Chotar *Lhato*

INVENTORY NO.
KHALTSE / TAR / 07 / 2004

Lhato | In Use | Public (Community) | Around 300-350 years old

SETTING
The *lhato* is oriented to the south and is built on top of a large boulder surrounded by a stream to the northwest, a forest to the northeast and the Kutipa house to the south.

SIGNIFICANCE
The *lhato* is dedicated to the protector deity of the village named 'Chotar'. The ritual offerings of juniper twigs and *khadag* in the *lhato* are renewed every year amid prayers and rituals when the protection of the deity is sought.

STATE OF PRESERVATION
Fair

DESCRIPTION
The *lhato* is a tall linear structure built on a square plan. The walls taper towards the top and are covered by a mud roof. On the top are placed the ritual offerings of juniper branches, animal horns and *khadag*. The *lhato* is built in stone and mud brick masonry and is mud plastered and whitewashed on the exterior.

SOURCE OF INFORMATION Tsering Angchuk, Azangpe, Tar, Khaltse, Ladakh

---

Abagon Ne House

INVENTORY NO.
KHALTSE / TAR / 08 / 2004

Vernacular Building | In Use | Private (Individual) | Around 100 years old

SETTING
The Abagon Ne house is oriented to the west and is located to the east of the village, surrounded by mountains on one side and fields on the other.

SIGNIFICANCE
The house was built by an ancestor of the Abagon Ne family around 100 years ago. It is built in the traditional style and is a good example of vernacular architecture in the village.

DESCRIPTION
The Abagon Ne house is built at the foot of the mountains. A narrow pathway leads to the courtyard of the house. The courtyard has a small cylindrical *mane* wall with *mane* stones placed on the surface. A long flight of staircase from the courtyard leads to the new section of the house which has been recently built. It opens into a large living room. A small doorway leads to the kitchen which is the oldest part of the building. A part of the mountainside forms one of the walls of the kitchen and is an uneven rock surface. A small door from the kitchen leads to an open verandah and a small stone staircase leads to the ground floor. There is a small store and a traditional toilet on the other side of the kitchen. The ground floor is reserved for animals and has no window opening while on the first floor there are small window openings on either side of the verandah. The ground floor is built in stone masonry while the upper floors are built in mud blocks. The exterior walls of the house are mud plastered and whitewashed.

STATE OF PRESERVATION
Advanced State of Decay

SOURCE OF INFORMATION Yontan Zangmo Abagon, Tar, Khaltse, Ladakh

Mane Wall and Rock Inscription

INVENTORY NO.
KHALTSE / TAR / 09 / 2004

Mane Wall | In Use | Public (Community)

SETTING
The *mane* wall is oriented to the south and is located along the path leading to the village. It is surrounded on two sides by mountains.

SIGNIFICANCE
The *mane* wall is located along the path leading to the village and is circumambulated by villagers to accumulate merit as they travel along this path.

DESCRIPTION
The *mane* wall is a long linear structure built in dry stone masonry with inscribed *mane* stones placed on the top horizontal surface. The wall has collapsed at many places. The rock inscription is in a small cave at the foot of the mountain. It cannot be clearly identified.

STATE OF PRESERVATION
Danger of Disappearance

SOURCE OF INFORMATION Tsering Angchuk, Azangpe, Tar, Khaltse, Ladakh

Tar

427

21 Dolma *Rangjon* (*Rangjon* Nyishu-Tsag-chig)

INVENTORY NO.
KHALTSE / TAR / 10 / 2004

Landscape (Sacred Rock Formation) | In Use | Public (Community)

SETTING
The Dolma *Rangjon* is oriented to the east and is located in Tar Yokma on the opposite side of the pathway. It is located before the village to the right while moving towards the village.

SIGNIFICANCE / ASSOCIATED BELIEFS
It is believed that the surface of the mountain represents naturally formed images of the 21 Dolma (Tara). The base of the rock surface represents scenes of hell. It was discovered by Ven. Togdan Rinpoche.

DESCRIPTION
The mountain side has several *tarchen* and prayer flags tied across. The rock surface of the mountain has indentations.

SOURCE OF INFORMATION Tsering Angchuk, Azangpe, Tar, Khaltse, Ladakh

CULTURAL LINKAGES / CULTURAL PRACTICES
The site is associated with the *Rangjon Gonbo*, another naturally formed image of a deity, which is located a little away from the *Rangjon* Dolma 21. Prayer flags are offered by the villagers on all auspicious days of the Tibetan calendar.

STATE OF PRESERVATION
Showing Signs of Deterioration

Gonbo Rangjon

INVENTORY NO.
KHALTSE / TAR / 11 / 2004

Landscape (Rock Formation) | In Use | Public (Community)

SETTING

The *Gonbo Rangjon* is oriented to the west and is located near the *Rangjon* Dolma 21 on the left hand side of the path while moving towards the village.

SIGNIFICANCE / ASSOCIATED BELIEFS

The rock formation is believed to be in the shape of the face of the *Gonbo* or protector deity. It was discovered by the Ven. Togdan Rinpoche during one of his visits to the village and is believed to be naturally formed.

DESCRIPTION

The rock formation is on a large plain surface of the mounatin. It is towards the top right side of the mountain and appears like a part of a face wearing a hat looking north.

CULTURAL LINKAGES / CULTURAL PRACTICES

It is associated with the *Rangjon* Dolma 21, which is located a little ahead of it and the villagers offers prayers here.

STATE OF PRESERVATION

Fair

SOURCE OF INFORMATION Tsering Angchuk, Azangpe, Tar, Khaltse, Ladakh

Tar

428

Mane Wall

INVENTORY NO.
KHALTSE / TAR / 12 / 2004

Mane Wall | In Use | Public (Community) | Around 250 years old

SETTING

The *mane* wall is oriented to the south and is located on the route leading to the village. It is surrounded on two sides by mountains.

SIGNIFICANCE

The *mane* wall is located in the summer habitation, or Dok, which consists of a few houses. Villagers move down to the Dok during summer to tend to their fields and graze cattle. The *mane* walls are circumambulated by villagers to accumulate merit as the travel along this path.

DESCRIPTION

The site consists of two *mane* walls - one circular and the other rectangular in shape. The circular one in located on the footpath that leads to the village. The *mane* walls are built in dry stone masonry and have *mane* stones placed on the top horizontal surface.

STATE OF PRESERVATION

Showing Signs of Deterioration

SOURCE OF INFORMATION Tsering Angchuk, Azangpe, Tar, Khaltse, Ladakh

NIRLAC

Shugpa Tree

INVENTORY NO.
KHALTSE / TAR / 13 / 2004

Landscape (Sacred Tree) | In Use | Private (Individual)

SETTING
The *Shugpa* tree is located north of the Dagshanpa house and is surrounded by boulders and shrubs

SIGNIFICANCE / ASSOCIATED BELIEFS
It is one of the oldest trees in the village. *Shugpa* is known for its purification qualities. Its branches are used while performing *puja* as well in the *lhato* as offering to the protector deity.

DESCRIPTION
The *Shugpa,* or juniper tree, is an old tree with a large trunk and dense foliage. Juniper is an endangered species in Ladakh today and there are very few juniper trees surviving.

STATE OF PRESERVATION
Advanced State of Decay

SOURCE OF INFORMATION Sonam Rinchen Dangshanpa, Tar, Khaltse, Ladakh

Tar

429

Yul Lha Lhato

INVENTORY NO.
KHALTSE / TAR / 14 / 2004

Lhato | In Use | Public (Community) | Around 300 years old

SETTING
The *lhato* is oriented to the southwest and is located along the slope of the hill, northeast of the footpath. There is a *mane* wall and a poplar tree nearby.

SIGNIFICANCE
The *lhato* is dedicated to the *yul lha,* or protector deity, of the village and is believed to date back to the time when the village was first settled. The juniper twigs, *khadag* etc., placed as ritual offerings in the *lhato*, are renewed every year amid prayers and rituals.

DESCRIPTION
The *lhato* is located above the footpath along the slope of a hill. It is a small square structure built in stone and is mud plastered and whitewashed on the exterior. Ritual offerings of juniper branches, *khadag* and animal horns are placed on the top at the center of the structure. There is a

rectangular *mane* wall to the southwest of the *lhato* which is built in stone masonry and has inscribed *mane* stones placed on the horizontal surface.

STATE OF PRESERVATION
Advanced State of Decay

SOURCE OF INFORMATION Sonam Rinchen Dangshanpa, Tar, Khaltse, Ladakh

Chorten and *Mane* Walls

INVENTORY NO.
KHALTSE / TAR / 15 / 2004

Chorten / Mane Wall | Abandoned | Private (Individual) | Around 200 years old

SETTING
The *chorten* and *mane* wall are oriented to the southwest and are located in Tar Yokma next to Dagshanpa house.

SIGNIFICANCE
The *chorten* and *mane* wall were built at the time when the old settlement was inhabited and before villagers moved higher up the valley in search of better water supply for their fields. The ruins of the old settlement can still be seen nearby.

DESCRIPTION
The site consists of a *chorten* and a *mane* wall located along a footpath that leads to the village. The *chorten* is built in random rubble and mud brick masonry with an outer layer of mud plaster and whitewash which has completely eroded. The *chorten* has lost its original form and is difficult to identify. The *mane* wall is half embedded in the pathway. It is built in stone masonry and has inscribed *mane* stones placed on the horizontal surface.

STATE OF PRESERVATION
Danger of Disappearance

SOURCE OF INFORMATION Sonam Rinchen Dangshanpa, Tar, Khaltse, Ladakh

Tar *Brog*

INVENTORY NO.
KHALTSE / TAR / 16 / 2004

Precinct | Abandoned | Public (Community) | Around 200 years old

SETTING
The *brog* is oriented to the south west and is located in Tar Yokma on the opposite side of the pathway. It is located along the slope of a hill at the foot of a mountain.

SIGNIFICANCE
The *brog* is the original settlement of Tar which was abandoned when the villagers migrated to the upper reaches of the valley in search of a better water supply for their fields.

STATE OF PRESERVATION
Danger of Disappearance

DESCRIPTION
The *brog* consists of a cluster of many houses built in random rubble masonry at the foot of a mountain. The houses are small and modest structures of which only the ground floors survive. The timber has been taken by the villagers to construct their new houses. Some traces of the exterior mud plaster and whitewash still survive.

SOURCE OF INFORMATION Sonam Rinchen Dangshanpa, Tar, Khaltse, Ladakh

Shugpa Tree (*Shuk-tsher*)

INVENTORY NO.
KHALTSE / TARCHID / 01 / 2004

Landscape (Sacred Tree) | In Use | Public (Community)

SETTING
The *Shugpa* tree is located across the village river and marks the entry to the village of Tarchid. The tree grows beside the river to the left of the village bridge.

SIGNIFICANCE / ASSOCIATED BELIEFS
Juniper is an endangered specie in the region. It is used for purification and ritual ceremonies in Ladakh and is placed as a ritual offering in *lhato*. Branches from the tree are used by the villagers in their *puja* and performing the necessary rituals.

DESCRIPTION
It is a very old tree and has a large trunk, with the roots spread over a large area. The tree has been adversely affected with the construction of the nearby road which has increased pollution around this area. The branches appear to be withering at a rapid rate.

CULTURAL PRACTICES / LINKAGE
There is a *lhato* under the tree, the contents of which are changed every year on the eve of Losar.

STATE OF PRESERVATION
Advanced State of Decay

SOURCE OF INFORMATION Rinchen Palmo, Tarchid, Khaltse, Ladakh

Tarchid

431

Chorten

INVENTORY NO.
KHALTSE / TARCHID / 02 / 2004

Chorten | In Use | Public (Community)

SETTING
The *chorten* marks the beginning of the village and is located along the main road near the bridge.

SIGNIFICANCE
The *chorten* marks the beginning of the village and is circumambulated by villagers to accumulate merit. The *chorten* is a Changchub *chorten*, symbolizing the Buddha's enlightenment.

DESCRIPTION
The *chorten* is built along the main road and has a circumambulatory path around it. It is built on a square base made of random rubble masonry and is constructed in stone and mud brick masonry with mud mortar. It is mud plastered and whitewashed externally. There is a *srog-shing* embedded in the dome of the *chorten*.

STATE OF PRESERVATION
Fair

SOURCE OF INFORMATION Rinchen Palmo, Tarchid, Khaltse, Ladakh

Mane Wall

INVENTORY NO.
KHALTSE / TARCHID / 03 / 2004

Mane Wall | In Use | Public (Community)

SETTING
The *mane* wall is built along the slope of a barren hill and is surrounded by the village stream, trees and agricultural fields.

SIGNIFICANCE
The *mane* wall was built in the past by a village ancestor and is circumambulated by villagers as an act of merit.

DESCRIPTION
The *mane* wall is rectangular in plan and is built in random rubble masonry with inscribed *mane* stones placed on the horizontal surface above. The *mane* wall is mud plastered and whitewashed, although much of this external layer has eroded over time.

STATE OF PRESERVATION
Showing Signs of Deterioration

SOURCE OF INFORMATION Rinchen Palmo, Tarchid, Khaltse, Ladakh

Skyapa House

INVENTORY NO.
KHALTSE / TARCHID / 04 / 2004

Vernacular Building | In Use | Private (Individual) | Around 120 years old

SETTING
The house is located amid other village houses and is oriented to the south. It has apricot orchards to the north while the Shinipa house lies to the southwest.

SIGNIFICANCE
The Skyapa house was built around 120 years ago by ancestors of the Skyapa family and successive generations have continued to reside here. The house is built in the traditional style and is a good example of vernacular architecture in the village.

DESCRIPTION
The Skyapa house is a small building located towards the rear of the new Skyapa house. The ground floor is built in random rubble masonry while the first floor is built in mud brick masonry with mud mortar. The ground floor is used for housing cattle as well as for storage while the first floor houses the family's living quarters. The house has a traditional flat roof made of timber beams, joists, *taalu*, grass and compacted mud. Externally, the walls are mud plastered and whitewashed.

STATE OF PRESERVATION
Showing Signs of Deterioration

SOURCE OF INFORMATION Rinchen Palmo, Tarchid, Khaltse, Ladakh

Mane Wall

INVENTORY NO.
KHALTSE / TARCHID / 05 / 2004

Mane Wall | In Use | Public (Community)

SETTING
The *mane* wall is located in the middle of the agricultural fields.

SIGNIFICANCE
The *mane* wall is circumambulated by villagers to accumulate merit and possibly was built to protect the fields from natural calamities.

DESCRIPTION
The *mane* wall is rectangular in plan and is built in dry stone masonry with inscribed *mane* stones placed on its horizontal surface. There is a smaller semi-circular *mane* wall attached to it which has a *tarchen* next to it.

STATE OF PRESERVATION
Advanced State of Decay

SOURCE OF INFORMATION Rinchen Palmo, Tarchid, Khaltse, Ladakh

Chorten

INVENTORY NO.
KHALTSE / TARCHID / 06 / 2004

Chorten | In Use | Public (Community)

SETTING
The *chorten* are located on top of a hill on the left of the village road before the village.

SIGNIFICANCE
The *chorten* are located before the entrance to the village and were built in the past as an act of merit. The *chorten* are all Changchub *chorten* and symbolize the Buddha's enlightenment.

STATE OF PRESERVATION
Advanced State of Decay

DESCRIPTION
The site comprises of a group of four *chorten* of similar size. The *chorten* are built in stone and mud brick masonry with mud mortar and are mud plastered and whitewashed externally. However, the outer surface of the chorten has eroded over time and the *chorten* have lost their original form.

SOURCE OF INFORMATION Rinchen Palmo, Tarchid, Khaltse, Ladakh

Group of *Mane* Walls and *Chorten*

INVENTORY NO.
KHALTSE / TARCHID / 07 / 2004

Chorten / Mane Wall | In Use | Public (Community)

STATE OF PRESERVATION
Showing Signs of Deterioration

SETTING
The *mane* walls are located on the right side of the village road after crossing the settlement. The river flows to the south of the site while the village settlement lies to the southwest.

SIGNIFICANCE
The *chorten* and *mane* wall are located beyond the village and are circumambulated by villagers to accumulate merit as they travel along this path. The *chorten* are Changchub *chorten and* symbolize the Buddha's enlightenment. The *tsadkhang*, which forms part of this group of structures, contains *tsa-tsa*.

DESCRIPTION
The site comprises of a group of *chorten* and *mane* walls. There is a large whitewashed *tsadkhang* with an opening towards the south which houses the *tsa-tsa*. The *tsadkhang* is built in mud brick masonry. This is followed by a circular shaped *mane* wall built in random rubble masonry which is mud plastered and whitewashed externally. *Mane* stones are placed on the horizontal surface above. Next to this are two smaller *mane* walls built on a common rectangular plinth. Behind this is another group of a *mane* wall and *chorten*. The *mane* wall and *chorten* are alternatively placed in a single row. The *chorten* are built in stone and mud brick masonry with mud mortar and are mud plastered and whitewashed on the exterior. The *chorten* have a tall *chugsum khorlo* on the dome which symbolizes the 13 steps towards enlightenment. The *mane* wall is a long wall and is built in random rubble masonry with inscribed *mane* stones placed on the horizontal surface.

SOURCE OF INFORMATION Rinchen Palmo, Tarchid, Khaltse, Ladakh

Temisgang

Temisgang is situated at a distance of about 92 kms from Leh. The historical name was derived from two words Teng ('*deep bottom*') and Gang ('*hill-spur*'). It was called Teng as the fields and plantations were located in the bottom of the valley. It was called Gang as the palace, temple and settlement were on a hill-spur. Hence, the village was named as Tengang and later changed to Temisgang or Tengmogang. Temisgang served as one of the capitals of Dagspa Bum, the brother of Dagspa Bum-Ide, in the 15th century. At present, there are about 149 households living in this village.

Listed by: Deldan Angmo and Jassu Singh
Year: 2004

Group of *Chorten and Mane* Walls

INVENTORY NO.
KHALTSE / TEMISGANG / 01 / 2004

Chorten / Mane Wall | In Use | Public (Community) | Around 530 years old

SETTING
The *chorten* and *mane* wall are oriented to the south and are located in between two hills. The village settlement lies to the north and the fort lies lower down on another hill.

SIGNIFICANCE
The *chorten* and *mane* walls are believed to have been built during the same period as the neighboring temples located within the fort (around 530 years ago). The structures are still circumambulated by villagers as an act of merit.

DESCRIPTION
The site is a large precinct comprising of a large number of *chorten* and *mane* walls. Predominant among the group are three large Changchub *chorten* built in random rubble and mud brick masonry with mud mortar which have stucco relief motifs (*pa-tra*) on the base panels. The other *chorten* are smaller in size. Some *chorten* have a niche in the dome on the northwestern side. The *mane* wall is a long linear random rubble masonry wall running parallel to the village road. The horizontal surface of the *mane* wall contains numerous *mane* stones. Some of the *chorten* are located on the other side of the *mane* wall.

STATE OF PRESERVATION
Showing Signs of Deterioration

SOURCE OF INFORMATION Ven. Nawang Tsondus, Resident Monk, Temisgang, Khaltse, Ladakh

Singhe Osrung

INVENTORY NO.
KHALTSE / TEMISGANG / 02 / 2004

Chorten | In Use | Public (Community) | Around 200 - 250 years old

SETTING
The *chorten* is oriented to the south and is located on a hill a little above the larger precinct of *chorten*. The *chorten* lies to the north of the village and below the fort and temples.

SIGNIFICANCE
The *chorten* is believed to have been built around 200 – 250 years ago and contains the relics of a great lama. The *chorten* is located along the path which leads onto the fort and temples and is circumambulated by villagers to accumulate merit. It is a Changchub *chorten* and symbolizes the Buddha's enlightenment.

DESCRIPTION
The *chorten* is built on a high random rubble masonry plinth and is constructed in stone and mud brick masonry with mud mortar. There are *mane* stones placed on the plinth of the *chorten*. The *chorten* is mud plastered and whitewashed externally although much of this outer layer has eroded over time.

STATE OF PRESERVATION
Advanced State of Decay

SOURCE OF INFORMATION Ven. Nawang Tsondus, Resident Monk, Temisgang, Khaltse, Ladakh

Group of *Chorten*

INVENTORY NO.
KHALTSE / TEMISGANG / 03 / 2004

Chorten | In Use | Public (Community) | Around 550 years old

SETTING

The *chorten* are oriented to the east and are located on the edge of a hill over which stand the fort and temples.

SIGNIFICANCE

The *chorten* are believed to have been built during the same period as the temples inside the fort i.e. around 530 years old. The *chorten* are circumambulated by villagers to accumulate merit as the travel along the path leading to the temples. Both the *chorten* are Changchub *chorten* and symbolize the Buddha's enlightenment.

DESCRIPTION

The site consists of two Changchub *chorten* built on the edge of a hill above the village. The *chorten* are built on a random rubble masonry base and are built in stone and mud brick masonry. Externally, the *chorten* are mud plastered and whitewashed. The base panels of the *chorten* are embellished with red markings and there are tall

chugsum khorlo on the domes of the *chorten*. A small niche is recessed into the domes of the *chorten* which house images of deities.

STATE OF PRESERVATION
Fair

SOURCE OF INFORMATION Ven. Nawang Tsondus, Resident Monk, Temisgang, Khaltse

439

Chanrazig *Lhakhang*

INVENTORY NO.
KHALTSE / TEMISGANG / 04 / 2004

Gonpa | In Use | Public (Chemday *Gonpa*) | Around 530 years old

SETTING

The Chanrazig *lhakhang* is oriented to the south and is located on a hill above the settlement. To the north of the Chanrazig *lhakhang* is the Chamba *lhakhang*.

SIGNIFICANCE

The Chanrazig *lhakhang* forms a part of the main *gonpa* complex and was built during the reign of King Dagspa Bum, in the 15th century. The temple has a unique self manifested image of Chanrazig brought from Kamrup (ancient Assam). The temple today falls under the purview of Chemday *gonpa* and a monk from Chemday is deputed here to carry out prayers and rituals within the temple.

DESCRIPTION

The temple has been recently rebuilt and lies on the second floor of the *gonpa* building. A flight of steps leads through a corridor to the second floor that further leads to Chanrazig

and Guru *lhakhang*. A large wooden door next to the landing leads to a small chamber which has an elaborate wooden doorway on the south. The doorway leads into a room with large window opening on the east and west as well as a skylight above the central space. There is an elaborate wooden frame placed against the rear wall housing the main image of Chanrazig in marble along with various other deities. The walls are freshly painted and several *thangka* are hung from the walls.

STATE OF PRESERVATION
Fair

SOURCE OF INFORMATION Ven. Nawang Tsondus, Resident Monk, Temisgang, Khaltse, Ladakh

Temisgang

Chamba *Lhakhang* (Tsuglakhang Marpo)

INVENTORY NO.
KHALTSE / TEMISGANG / 05 / 2004

Temple | In Use | Public (Likir *Gonpa*) | Around 530 years old

SETTING
The Chamba *lhakhang* is oriented to the south and is located on a hill above the village which lies to the south.

SIGNIFICANCE
The Chamba *lhakhang* was built during the reign of King Dagspa Bum in the 15th century when Temisgang served as the capital of his kingdom. The temple is dedicated to Chamba and is also called Chamba *lhakhang*.

DESCRIPTION
The temple is built over a rectangular plan and is effectively three storeys high. It is entered through an open space in the front, from where a flight of steps leads to the portico. The front portion of the building is double storeyed while the rear is three storeyed high. The entrance wall of the portico has paintings of four guardian deities and has wooden columns with decorated brackets. A large wooden doorway leads inside a square chamber which has a colossal three storey high gilded Chamba image placed to the rear of the room. The image is placed on a square pedestal and the head of the image extends up to the second and third floor levels. Along with the Chamba, there are images of Chanrazig, Tsongkhapa, Jigched and Chagdor. Four wooden columns support the traditional roof above. On the eastern side of the chamber, there is are wooden shelves on which are placed the Kangyur. It has a small skylight above from where light falls directly on the Buddha's face. The third storey has several window openings with decorated tiered lintels. The walls of the chapel are decorated with the images of various guardians' deities which are newly painted. The temple is built in stone and mud brick masonry which tapers from the base towards the roof. It is mud plastered and the external walls are painted in red. There are prayer flag posted at each corner of the parapet.

STATE OF PRESERVATION
Showing Signs of Deterioration

SOURCE OF INFORMATION Ven. Nawang Tsondus, Resident Monk, Temisgang, Khaltse, Ladakh

NIRLAC

Temisgang

440

Guru *Lhakhang*

INVENTORY NO.
KHALTSE / TEMISGANG / 06 / 2004

Temple | In Use | Public (Chemday *Gonpa*) | Around 530 years old

SETTING
The Guru *lhakhang* is oriented to the south and is located on a hill above the village.

SIGNIFICANCE
The Guru *lhakhang* forms a part of the main *gonpa* complex and was built in the 15th century during the reign of King Dagspa Bum, younger brother of Dagspa Bum-lde. The temple is dedicated to Guru Rinpoche and hence called Guru *lhakhang*. The temple, today, is under the purview of Chemday *gonpa* and a monk from Chemday is deputed here to carry out prayers and rituals in the temple.

DESCRIPTION
The temple is a part of the main *gonpa* complex and is located on the first floor. A staircase to the north leads to the first floor onto a large courtyard. The courtyard has a low height gallery all around. To the north, there is a portico which provides access to the Guru *lhakhang*. The entrance walls are painted with images of the four guardian deities and small prayer wheels are lined up against the exterior walls of the lhakhang. An elaborate wooden doorway leads into a small rectangular chamber which has four columns in the centre. There are several images of guardian deities placed on a pedestal against the rear wall to the north. There is a skylight above this space. Adjacent to this shrine is another shrine which lies between two rooms. The partition is an intricately carved wooden latticed partition. The main deity here is Guru Rinpoche, seated in the centre, against the rear wall and other deities, including an image of Chanrazig. There is a small silver coated wooden *chorten* next to this. The walls are covered with paintings of various deities. The rooms also house the Buddhist canons – Kangyur and Bum written in gold and numerous *thangka* hang from the wooden ceiling.

STATE OF PRESERVATION
Advanced State of Decay

Temisgang

441

Temisgang *Khar*

INVENTORY NO.
KHALTSE / TEMISGANG / 07 / 2004

Fort / Palace | Abandoned | Public (State / Community) | Around 530 years old

SETTING
The fort is oriented to the south and is located all around the *gonpa* hill above the settlement.

SIGNIFICANCE
The fort was built by Dagspa Bum, brother of King Dagspa Bum-Ide (1410 - 1440 A.D.), who held a small principality with its capital at Temisgang in the 15th century.

DESCRIPTION
The fort consists of only fragments of walls and watchtowers scattered along the mountainside. The thickness of the walls varies from around 1.50 meters near the base to around 0.80 meters towards the upper level. The foundations of these wall are built using random rubble while the upper section of the wall comprises of mud brick masonry and rammed earth construction. In between the walls, there are tall linear structures which were the watchtowers.

STATE OF PRESERVATION
Danger of Disappearance

SOURCE OF INFORMATION Ven. Nawang Tsondus, Resident Monk, Temisgang, Khaltse, Ladakh

Shugpa Tree

INVENTORY NO.
KHALTSE / TEMISGANG / 08 / 2004

Landscape (Sacred Tree) | In Use | Public (Lamayuru *Gonpa*) | Around 500 years old

SETTING
The *Shugpa* tree is located in the interior of the village. It is located on the right of the pathway leading to Tses Karmo *gonpa*.

SIGNIFICANCE / ASSOCIATED BELIEFS
The juniper tree is the oldest tree in the village and is believed to be around 500 years old. The branches or leaves of the tree cannot be cut as it is said that a curse would befall on anyone damaging the tree. Juniper is a relatively rare species in Ladakh today.

DESCRIPTION
The tree is a juniper tree and appears to be very old with a large trunk and branches.

CULTURAL LINKAGE / CULTURAL PRACTICES
The tree is considered sacred and villagers offer prayers near it.

STATE OF PRESERVATION
Advanced State of Decay

SOURCE OF INFORMATION Ven. Nawang Tsondus, Resident Monk, Temisgang, Khaltse, Ladakh

Tses Karmo *Gonpa*

INVENTORY NO.
KHALTSE / TEMISGANG / 09 / 2004

Gonpa | In Use | Public (Lamayuru *Gonpa*) | Around 200 - 250 years old

SETTING

The Tses Karmo *gonpa* is oriented to the east and is located some distance away from the main settlement on a hill. It is located north of the village settlement.

SIGNIFICANCE

The Tses Karmo *gonpa* was built around 200 - 250 years ago and falls under the purview of the Lamayuru *gonpa* from where a monk is deputed here to carry out prayers and rituals. The temple within the *gonpa* is one of the principal places of worship in the village.

DESCRIPTION

The *gonpa* consists of two *lhakhang*. A flight of steps leads to the first floor from where a corridor leads onto a courtyard. From the courtyard, there is an entrance to the first *lhakhang* which is a small chamber housing an image of Chanrazig. This chamber has a small window and the walls are not painted. The image has been recently shifted to this room. From the courtyard, another door leads to the main *lhakhang*. Both the *lhakhang* have large elaborate openings facing the larger courtyard. It has intricate wooden lattice work shutters with decorated and painted wooden lintels and frame. The main *lhakhang* is dark as the only source of light and ventilation is through the entrance doorway. This chamber has wooden columns supporting the roof above and wooden shelves stacked with images of Guru Rinpoche, Apchi and Shakyamuni Buddha as well as the Buddhist canons (Kangyur) and *thangka*. The flooring is in mud while the roof is made of wooden beams, joists, *taalu* and compacted mud. Externally, the walls are mud plastered and whitewashed. The window openings are highlighted in black while the parapets is coloured in red. The roof top has prayer flags posted at each corner. There is a *tsamskhang* right above the temple higher up the hill.

STATE OF PRESERVATION
Showing Signs of Deterioration

SOURCE OF INFORMATION Tsering Dorjey-Dogapa, Temisgang, Khaltse, Ladakh

Group of *Chorten* and *Mane* Walls

INVENTORY NO.
KHALTSE / TEMISGANG / 10 / 2004

Chorten / *Mane* Wall | In Use | Public (Community)

SETTING
The *chorten* and *mane* wall are located along the path leading to the Tses Karmo *gonpa*.

SIGNIFICANCE
The *chorten* and *mane* wall are built along the path leading to the *gonpa* and are circumambulated by villagers to accumulate merit, as they travel along this path. The *chorten* is a Changchub *chorten* and symbolizes the Buddha's enlightenment.

DESCRIPTION
The site consists of a *chorten* and some *mane* walls. The *chorten* is built in stone and mud brick masonry and is mud plastered and whitewashed on the exterior. It has a tall *chugsum khorlo* on the dome made of baked clay tiles. The *mane* walls are built in dry stone masonry and are rectangular in shape with inscribed *mane* stones placed on the top horizontal surface. Part of the base of the *chorten* and the *mane* wall are embedded in the path.

STATE OF PRESERVATION
Advanced State of Decay

SOURCE OF INFORMATION Ven. Nawang Tsondus, Resident Monk, Temisgang, Khaltse, Ladakh

Temisgang

Group of *Chorten*

INVENTORY NO.
KHALTSE / TEMISGANG / 11 / 2004

Chorten | In Use | Private (Individual) / Public (Community)

SETTING
The *chorten* are oriented to the southeast and are located along the road leading to the village. The structures are located west of the vehicular road. There are some thorny bushes and fields surrounding the *chorten*.

SIGNIFICANCE
The *chorten* were built in the past as an act of merit and are Changchub *chorten* symbolizing the Buddha's enlightenment. They are still circumambulated by villagers. The prayer wheel is rotated by villagers, as they pass along this route, to accumulate merit.

DESCRIPTION
The site consists of a group of three *chorten* and a prayer wheel. The *chorten* stands on a base along the roadside. The *chorten* are built in random rubble and mud brick masonry and are mud plastered and whitewashed on the exterior. The external surface of the *chorten* has largely eroded and the *chorten* have lost their original form. The prayer wheel is placed within a square enclosure built in mud brick masonry. The larger wheel is placed in the centre with a smaller one fixed at the window. There is a tall *tarchen* posted on a stone masonry base next to the prayer wheel.

STATE OF PRESERVATION
Showing Signs of Deterioration

SOURCE OF INFORMATION Kunzes Dolma, Temisgang, Khaltse, Ladakh

Chorten Makpape

INVENTORY NO.
KHALTSE / TEMISGANG / 12 / 2004

Chorten | In Use | Private (Individual) | Around 150 - 180 years old

SETTING
The *chorten* is oriented to the east and is located along the village road, southeast of the Makpapa house.

SIGNIFICANCE
The *chorten* is believed to be around 150 - 180 years old and was possibly built in the past as an act of merit. It has, however, lost its original form and is difficult to identify.

DESCRIPTION
The site consists of a single *chorten* built on a large stone boulder. It is built over a square random rubble base in stone masonry and has traces of mud plaster and whitewash on the exterior surface most of which has eroded.

STATE OF PRESERVATION
Advanced State of Decay

SOURCE OF INFORMATION Kunzes Dolma, Temisgang, Khaltse, Ladakh

Saman Ne House

INVENTORY NO.
KHALTSE / TEMISGANG / 13 / 2004

Vernacular Building | In Use | Private (Individual) | Around 150 - 180 years old

SETTING
The Saman Ne house is oriented to the south and is located along the path leading to the village. It is located to the north of the village road.

SIGNIFICANCE
The Saman Ne house was built around 150 - 180 years ago by an ancestor of the Saman Ne family and the family has continued to reside here ever since. The house is built in the traditional and is a good example of vernacular architecture in the village.

DESCRIPTION
The Saman Ne house is a large four storeyed building built on a rectangular plan and entered from the village road to the north. Several steps from the road lead to the courtyard which has a large *tarchen* in the centre. The ground floor is built in random rubble masonry and is used for housing animals. The ground floor does not have any window openings. From the court, a flight of steps leads to the first floor which has small slit-like windows with no frames or shutters. The second floor houses the kitchen and living room while the top most floor has the temple and guest rooms. The room adjacent to the court has an elaborate timber framed *rabsal*. The lintels of all the openings have decorated wooden tiers carved with intricate detail. The house has a traditional roof above made of timber beams, joists, *taalu*, grass and compacted mud. There are prayer flags posted on the roof.

STATE OF PRESERVATION
Fair

SOURCE OF INFORMATION Kunzes Dolma-Makpapay, Temisgang, Khaltse, Ladakh

Sbulipa House

INVENTORY NO.
KHALTSE / TEMISGANG / 14 / 2004

Vernacular Building | In Use | Private (Individual) | Around 150 - 200 years old

SETTING
The Sbulipa house is oriented to the south and is located along the path leading to the village. It is located north of the village road. There is a large apricot tree in front of the house.

SIGNIFICANCE
The Sbulipa house was built around 150 - 200 years ago by an ancestor of the Sbulipa family and the family continues to reside here. It is built in the traditional style and is a good example of vernacular architecture in the village.

DESCRIPTION
The Sbulipa house is built on a square plan over a raised platform above the road level. The ground floor is built in random rubble masonry and has small slit-like openings. It is used for housing animals. The first and second floors constitute the living areas and are built in mud brick masonry with mud mortar. There is a large *rabsal* at the

centre of the second floor which has elaborate wood work. The first and second floors have larger window openings with tiered timber lintels and timber frames. There are timber members introduced at intervals as earthquake resistant members. The house has a traditional roof above and there are prayer flags posted at the corners of the roof.

STATE OF PRESERVATION
Fair

SOURCE OF INFORMATION Kunzes Dolma-Makpape, Temisgang, Khaltse, Ladakh

Temisgang

446

Padepa House

INVENTORY NO.
KHALTSE / TEMISGANG / 15 / 2004

Vernacular Building | In Use | Private (Individual) | Around 150 - 200 years old

SETTING
The Padepa house is oriented to the south and is located at the foot of the hill among other village houses.

SIGNIFICANCE
The Padepa house was built around 150 - 200 ago by ancestors of the Padepa family, initially as a *tashag* for monks. It is built in the traditional style and is a good example of vernacular architecture in the village.

DESCRIPTION
The Padepa House is a double storeyed building built along the slope of a hill. The ground floor is built in random rubble masonry and is used primarily for storage. The house is entered from the ground floor. There is a large *rabsal* on the front (south) facade. It has a wooden frame with intricate lattice work. There are smaller window openings on either side of the *rabsal*. The first floor is built in mud brick masonry with mud mortar. The house has a traditional roof

bordered by a low height parapet painted in red. The window openings are bordered in black. The exterior walls of the house are mud plastered and whitewashed.

STATE OF PRESERVATION
Showing Signs of Deterioration

SOURCE OF INFORMATION Kunzes Dolma-Makpapay, Temisgang, Khaltse, Ladakh

Manego House

INVENTORY NO.
KHALTSE / TEMISGANG / 16 / 2004

Vernacular Building | Abandoned | Private (Individual) | Around 150 - 200 years old

SETTING
The Manego house is oriented to the southeast and is located at the edge of the hill, right above the village road. It is surrounded by other village houses.

SIGNIFICANCE
The Manego house was built around 150 - 200 years ago by ancestors of the Manego family as a *tashag* for resident monks. Presently, it is lying abandoned. The house is built in the traditional style and is a good example of vernacular architecture in the village.

DESCRIPTION
The Manego house is a double storeyed building built along the slope of a hill. The ground floor is built in random rubble masonry while the first floor is built in mud brick masonry with mud mortar. Access to the house is from the village road at the first floor level. The house has few window openings. However, the front facade has a large *rabsal* which has been partially blocked with mud bricks while the

other half has a wooden shutter. There are some walls still standing on the second floor level without a roof above. The exterior walls have traces of external mud plaster and whitewash.

STATE OF PRESERVATION
Advanced State of Decay

SOURCE OF INFORMATION Kunzes Dolma-Makpapay, Temisgang, Khaltse, Ladakh

Rudpa House

INVENTORY NO.
KHALTSE / TEMISGANG / 17 / 2004

Vernacular Building | Abandoned | Private (Individual)

SETTING
The Rudpa house is oriented to the east and is located at the edge of a hill, above the village road. It is surrounded by other village houses to the rear and there are some trees in the front.

SIGNIFICANCE
The Rudpa house was built by an ancestor of the Rudpa family. The family no longer resides here. The house is built in the traditional style and is a good example of vernacular architecture in the village.

DESCRIPTION
The Rudpa house is a double storeyed building built along the slope of a hill. The ground floor is built in stone masonry and has small window openings. The first floor is built in mud brick masonry and comprised the family's living quarters. At the centre of the first floor there is a large *rabsal* with an elaborately carved timber frame, shutters

and lintels. The house has a traditional roof bordered by a low height parapet which is painted in black. The exterior walls of the house are mud plastered and whitewashed.

STATE OF PRESERVATION
Advanced State of Decay

SOURCE OF INFORMATION Kunzes Dolma-Makpape, Temisgang, Khaltse, Ladakh

Group of *Chorten* and *Mane* Wall

INVENTORY NO.
KHALTSE / TEMISGANG / 18 / 2004

Chorten / *Mane* Wall | In Use | Public (Community)

SETTING

The *chorten* and *mane* wall are oriented to the southeast and are located at the foot of a hill along the path leading to the village. The structures are located northwest of the village road.

SIGNIFICANCE

The *chorten* and *mane* wall are located along the path leading to the village and are circumambulated by villagers as they travel along this path in order to accumulate merit. The *chorten* are of two types – the first is a Namgyal *chorten* which symbolizes the Buddha's victory over illness and the second is a Changchub *chorten* symbolizing the Buddha's enlightenment.

DESCRIPTION

The site consists of two *chorten* and a *mane* wall. The first *chorten* is a Namgyal *chorten* while the second is a

Changchub *chorten*. Both *chorten* are built on square random rubble masonry plinths and are built in stone and mud brick masonry with mud mortar. Externally, the *chorten* are mud plastered and whitewashed. The base panels of the *chorten* have stucco relief motifs (*pa-tra*). There are tall *chugsum khorlo* on the domes of the two made of baked clay tiles. The *mane* wall is a linear rectangular random rubble masonry wall with inscribed *mane* stones on its top horizontal surface.

STATE OF PRESERVATION
Showing Signs of Deterioration

SOURCE OF INFORMATION Kunzes Dolma-Makpapay, Temisgang, Khaltse, Ladakh

---

Rigsum Gonbo

INVENTORY NO.
KHALTSE / TEMISGANG / 19 / 2004

Rigsum Gonbo / *Mane* Wall | In Use | Public (Community) | Around 200 - 225 years old

SETTING

The *rigsum gonbo* is oriented to the southeast and is located along the path leading to the village. The structures lie to the northwest of the village road opposite a Kagan *chorten*. There are village houses and willow trees behind the *rigsum gonbo*.

SIGNIFICANCE

The *rigsum gonbo* was built around 200 - 225 years old to protect the village from natural calamities and disasters.

DESCRIPTION

The site consists of three *chorten* built over a rectangular random rubble masonry base. The *chorten* are of types, namely Namgyal, Changchub and Indoom built on a common platform. These are built in stone and mud brick masonry with an external layer of mud plaster and whitewash. There is a single brick wall to the rear of the *chorten* with a few timber members of what appears to be remains of a roof that once covered the *chorten*. The

timber frame in the front has segmental arches and decorated tiered lintels which are decaying. All the *chorten* have tall *chugsum khorlo* on the dome made of baked clay tiles. There is a *mane* wall near the *rigsum gonbo* made in dry stone masonry which has inscribed *mane* stones placed on its horizontal surface.

STATE OF PRESERVATION
Showing Signs of Deterioration

SOURCE OF INFORMATION Kunzes Dolma-Makpapay, Temisgang, Khaltse, Ladakh

Kagan *Chorten*

INVENTORY NO.
KHALTSE / TEMISGANG / 20 / 2004

Chorten | In Use | Public (Community)

SETTING

The *chorten* is oriented to the northeast and is located along the path leading to the village. There is a *rigsum gonbo* to the north of the site and some trees nearby.

SIGNIFICANCE

The Kagan *chorten* is a gateway chorten built over the path leading to the village. Merit is believed to accrue to believers who pass through the passage of the *chorten* as well as circumambulate it. The Kagan *chorten* has been used by the villagers since early times before the village road was built.

DESCRIPTION

The Kagan *chorten* consist of two thick parallel walls over which rests a large Changchub *chorten*. The walls are built in random rubble and mud brick masonry with mud mortar while the *chorten* above is made in stone and mud brick masonry. The ceiling of the passageway is made in wood and has paintings of a *mandala*. Externally, the *chorten* is

mud plastered and whitewashed. There is a *chugsum khorlo* made of baked clay tiles over the dome of the *chorten*.

STATE OF SIGNIFICANCE

Showing Signs of Deterioration

SOURCE OF INFORMATION Kunzes Dolma-Makpape, Temisgang, Khaltse, Ladakh

Stagopa House

INVENTORY NO.
KHALTSE / TEMISGANG / 21 / 2004

Vernacular Building | In Use | Private (Individual) | Around 200 - 250 years old

SETTING

The Stagopa house is oriented to the south and is located along the slope of a hill surrounded by other village houses. The house faces the rest of the village.

SIGNIFICANCE

The Stagopa house was built by an ancestor of the Stagopa family around 200 - 250 years ago and successive generations have continued to reside here. The location and size of the house indicate that the family held an important position in the village. The house is built in the traditional style and is a good example of vernacular architecture in the village.

DESCRIPTION

The Stagopa house is large three storeyed house built along the slope of a hill. The ground floor is built in random rubble masonry and is used primarily for storage. The house is entered from the ground floor. The first and second floors constitute the living areas and are built in mud brick

masonry with mud mortar. There are two large *rabsal* with wooden frames and shutters on the second floor with an open verandah in between and a large terrace on one side. The first floor level has small window openings lined up in one single row. The house has a traditional roof with prayer flags posted at the corners. The exterior is mud plastered and whitewashed.

STATE OF PRESERVATION

Showing Signs of Deterioration

SOURCE OF INFORMATION Tsewang Dolma, Temisgang, Khaltse, Ladakh

Chopa House

INVENTORY NO.
KHALTSE / TEMISGANG / 22 / 2004

Vernacular Building | In Use | Private (Individual) | Around 200 - 250 years old

SETTING
The Chopa house is oriented to the southeast and is located along the slope of a hill surrounded by other village houses. The Chotar *lhato* and Stagopa house are located nearby.

SIGNIFICANCE
The Chopa house was built by an ancestor of the Chopa family around 200 - 250 years ago and successive generations have continued to reside here. The location and size of the house indicate that the family held an important position in the village. The house is built in the traditional style and is a good example of vernacular architecture in the village.

DESCRIPTION
The Chopa house is a double storeyed building built along the slope of a hill on a horizontal plan. The ground floor is built in random rubble masonry and is used primarily for storage. The house is entered from the ground floor. The first floor is built in mud brick masonry with mud mortar and constitutes the family's living quarters. This level has larger window openings with tiered timber lintels. The exterior walls are mud plastered and whitewashed. The house has a traditional roof above and there are prayer flags posted on the roof.

STATE OF PRESERVATION
Showing Signs of Deterioration

SOURCE OF INFORMATION Tsewang Dolma, Temisgang, Khaltse, Ladakh

Chotar *Lhato*

INVENTORY NO.
KHALTSE / TEMISGANG / 23 / 2004

Lhato | In Use | Public (Community) | Around 200 - 250 years old

SETTING
The *lhato* is oriented to the southwest and is located in front of the Stagopa house on a hill and is adjacent to the Chopa house.

SIGNIFICANCE
The *lhato* is believed to be around 200 - 250 years old and is dedicated to the guardian deity of the village, Chotar. The villagers offer prayers at the *lhato* during Losar.

DESCRIPTION
The *lhato* is a large single storey building built on a square plan. There is a small door on the southwest side and a small window on the northwest facade. The *lhato* is built in stone and mud brick masonry with mud mortar and is mud plastered and whitewashed. It has a traditional roof above.

STATE OF PRESERVATION
Showing Signs of Deterioration

SOURCE OF INFORMATION Tsewang Dolma, Temisgang, Khaltse, Ladakh

Kagan *Chorten*

INVENTORY NO.
KHALTSE / TEMISGANG / 24 / 2004

Chorten | In Use | Public (Community)

SETTING
The *chorten* is oriented to the south east and is located in front of the Stagopa house and adjacent to the Chopa house. It is located southwest of the village road and there is a grove of poplar trees to the west.

SIGNIFICANCE
The Kagan *chorten* is a gateway *chorten* and merit is believed to accrue to believers who walk through the passage of the *chorten*. The site, including the *mane* wall, the Kagan *chorten* and the Namgyal *chorten* are circumambulated by villagers to accumulate merit.

DESCRIPTION
The site consists of a Kagan *chorten*, *mane* wall and a Namgyal *chorten*. The Kagan *chorten* has two thick parallel side walls over which rest a large Changchub *chorten*. The walls are built in random rubble masonry and the *chorten* above is in stone and mud brick masonry. The base panels of the Changchub *chorten* have stucco relief motifs (*pa-tra*). The dome of the *chorten* has a tall *chugsum khorlo* made of baked clay tiles. The *mane* wall is built alongside the *chorten* wall in dry stone masonry with inscribed *mane* stones placed on the horizontal surface. To the extreme north of the site, there is a Namgyal *chorten* built in stone and mud brick masonry. Both the *chorten* are mud plastered and whitewashed on the exterior. There is a pathway around the structure for circumambulation.

STATE OF PRESERVATION
Showing Signs of Deterioration

Temisgang

451

SOURCE OF INFORMATION Tsewang Lhamo, Temisgang, Khaltse, Ladakh

Kagan *Chorten*

INVENTORY NO.
KHALTSE / TEMISGANG / 25 / 2004

Chorten | In Use | Public (Community) | Around 150 - 200 years old

SETTING
The Kagan *chorten* is oriented to the southeast and is located along the road that leads to the village. There is a *tarchen* and a large apricot tree next to it.

SIGNIFICANCE
The Kagan *chorten* is a gateway chorten built over the path leading to the village. Merit is believed to accrue to believers who walk through the passage of the *chorten*.

DESCRIPTION
The Kagan *chorten* consists of two thick side walls over which rests a large Changchub *chorten*. The walls are built in random rubble masonry while the *chorten* is built in stone and mud brick masonry with mud mortar. The entire structure is mud plastered and whitewashed on the exterior. There is a passage below the *chorten* which has a ceiling in the shape of a *mandala*. The *chorten* has a tall

chugsum khorlo over the dome made of baked clay tiles. This is topped by a metal crown. There is a tall *tarchen* next to the *chorten*.

STATE OF PRESERVATION
Showing Signs of Deterioration

SOURCE OF INFORMATION Tsewang Lhamo, Temisgang, Khaltse, Ladakh

Group of *Chorten* and *Mane* Wall

INVENTORY NO.
KHALTSE / TEMISGANG / 26 / 2004

Chorten / *Mane* Wall | In Use | Public (Community)

SETTING
The *chorten* is oriented to the east and is located near a house amid willow and poplar trees. The village road lies to the north of the site.

SIGNIFICANCE
The *chorten* and *mane* wall were built in the past as an act of merit. The *chorten* is a Changchub *chorten* and symbolizes the Buddha's enlightenment. The *chorten* and *mane* wall are circumambulated by villagers as an act of merit.

DESCRIPTION
The site comprises of a large *chorten* and a *mane* wall. The *chorten* is built in stone and mud brick masonry and is mud plastered and whitewashed on the exterior. There is a small

niche on the east side of the dome. The mane wall is a rectangular shaped dry stone masonry wall with inscribed *mane* stones placed on its top horizontal surface.

STATE OF PRESERVATION
Showing Signs of Deterioration

SOURCE OF INFORMATION Tsewang Lhamo, Temisgang, Khaltse, Ladakh

Group of *Chorten*

INVENTORY NO.
KHALTSE / TEMISGANG / 27 / 2004

Chorten | In Use | Public (Community)

SETTING
The *chorten* is oriented to the south and is located on a hill near the village road that leads to Ang, north of Temisgang. The site overlooks agricultural fields.

SIGNIFICANCE
The *chorten* are located along the road leading from Temisgang to Ang and are circumambulated by villagers as they travel along this road as an act of merit.

DESCRIPTION
The site comprises of a group of two *chorten* located on a mound. One of the *chorten* is larger than the other. The *chorten* are both built on random rubble masonry bases in stone and mud brick masonry with mud mortar. The external layer of mud plaster and whitewash has eroded over time and the *chorten* have lost their original form making them difficult to identify.

STATE OF PRESERVATION
Advanced State of Decay

SOURCE OF INFORMATION Nawang Chotak, Kunepa, Temisgang, Khaltse, Ladakh

Temisgang

453

Chorten

INVENTORY NO.
KHALTSE / TEMISGANG / 28 / 2004

Chorten | In Use | Public (Community)

SETTING
The *chorten* is oriented to the south and is located on a rocky mound along the road that leads to Ang.

SIGNIFICANCE
The *chorten* is located along the road leading from Temisgang to Ang and is circumambulated by villagers as an act of merit when travelling on this route. The *chorten* is a Changchub *chorten* and symbolizes the Buddha's enlightenment.

STATE OF PRESERVATION
Advanced State of Decay

DESCRIPTION
The *chorten* is built on a rocky mound and is surrounded by poplar trees. It is built on a square random rubble masonry base in stone and mud brick masonry with mud mortar. Fragments of stucco relief motifs (*pa-tra*) can be seen on the base panels of the *chorten*. The exterior surface is mud plastered and whitewashed, though much of this layer has eroded over time. There is a small ruined cubical structure which looks like a *lubang* near the *chorten*.

SOURCE OF INFORMATION Nawang Chotak, Kunepa, Temisgang, Khaltse, Ladakh

Group of *Chorten*

INVENTORY NO.
KHALTSE / TEMISGANG / 29 / 2004

Chorten | In Use | Public (Community) | Around 150 - 200 years old

SETTING
The *chorten* are oriented to the south and is built on a hill surrounded by apricot orchard on three sides while the Lartsa *lhakhang* is located on a hill to the south east of the site.

SIGNIFICANCE
The *chorten* were built around 150 - 200 years ago as an act of merit. One of the *chorten* appears to be a Namgyal *chorten* symbolizing the Buddha's victory while the second *chorten* cannot be identified as it is badly eroded. The *chorten* are still circumambulated by villagers to accumulate merit.

DESCRIPTION
The site consists of two *chorten* – one is located on the pathway while the other is located on a boundary wall near the agricultural fields. The first *chorten* is built on a high stone plinth and appears to be a Namgyal *chorten*. There are several inscribed stones placed at the base of the *chorten* as well as over the plinth. The *chorten* is built in stone and mud brick masonry with mud mortar and is mud plastered and whitewashed on the exterior. There are red markings on the base panel of the *chorten*. The dome of the *chorten* has a *chugsum khorlo* made of baked clay tiles which is topped with a metal crown. The second *chorten* is also built over a square stone base but it is badly eroded and difficult to identify.

STATE OF PRESERVATION
Showing Signs of Deterioration

Temisgang

454

Phurongpa House, *Rigsum Gonbo* and Kagan *Chorten*

INVENTORY NO.
KHALTSE / TEMISGANG / 30 / 2004

Vernacular Building / *Rigsum Gonbo* / Chorten | In Use |
Private (Individual) | Around 200 - 250 years old

SETTING

The structures are oriented to the southwest and are located on a hill adjacent to the Chopa house. The site lies along the road leading to Ang.

SIGNIFICANCE

The Phurongpa house was built by an ancestor of the Phurongpa family around 4 - 5 generations ago and the family has continued to reside here. The house is one of the oldest in the village and is built in the traditional style. The Kagan *chorten* and *rigsum gonbo* located nearby, date to the same period. The Kagan *chorten* is a gateway *chorten* and merit is believed to accrue to believers who walk through the passage of the *chorten*. The *rigsum gonbo* was built to protect the family from natural calamities and misfortune.

DESCRIPTION

The site comprises of the Phurongpa house, a *rigsum gonbo* and a Kagan *chorten*. The house is a three storeyed building built in random rubble and mud brick masonry with mud mortar. There is a small *rigsum gonbo* above the entrance gate. There is a second larger *rigsum gonbo* near the house which consists of a small enclosure with a wall to the rear and open on three sides with columns at the corners. Inside the enclosure are three *chorten* painted in orange, white and blue symbolizing the Bodhisattvas Jamyang, Chanrazig and Chagdor respectively. The *rigsum gonbo* is also constructed in stone and mud brick masonry and has a traditional roof above. There is a tall tarchen beyond the *rigsum gonbo*. The Kagan *chorten* is located near the *rigsum gonbo* and consists of two thick parallel walls over which rests a large *chorten*. The walls are built in random rubble and mud brick masonry and the Kagan *chorten* is mud plastered and whitewashed on the exterior.

STATE OF PRESERVATION
Advanced State of Decay

Temisgang

455

SOURCE OF INFORMATION Nawang Chotak, Kunepa, Temisgang, Khaltse, Ladakh

Lartse *Lhakhang*

INVENTORY NO.
KHALTSE / TEMISGANG / 31 / 2004

Temple | In Use | Public (Community) | Around 250 years old

SETTING
The *lhakhang* is oriented to the east and is located on a hill to the Nyerpapa house. The village road lies to the south of the *lhakhang*.

SIGNIFICANCE
The *lhakhang* is a small village temple dedicated to the Jo Rinpoche and is maintained by the Lartse Junu Tsogspa.

DESCRIPTION
The Lartse *lhakhang* is a rectangular structure built on an elevated area some distance away from the main village. From the village road and the Nyeragspa house, a narrow passage leads to the forecourt of the *lhakhang*. The entrance to the *lhakhang* is preceded by a small portico with three wooden columns and a side wall on the north supporting a traditional roof above. There are traces of paintings on the walls of the portico which are eroded. A single wooden doorway leads into the main hall which has two wooden columns in the centre. There is an

antechamber to the rear separated from the main hall by a wooden frame. The images of various deities including the principal image of Jo Rinpoche are kept in this room, which has a skylight above. There are no other openings except for the skylight and the entrance door. The walls are plain without any paintings. The *lhakhang* is built in random rubble and mud brick masonry with mud mortar and the walls are mud plastered and whitewashed. There are red markings at the corners of the building as well as along the portico symbolizing the colour of the guardian deity. The building has a traditional roof made of timber beams, joists, *taalu*, grass and compacted mud which has a low parapet all around it.

STATE OF PRESERVATION
Showing Signs Deterioration

SOURCE OF INFORMATION Nawang Chotak, Kunepa, Temisgang, Khaltse, Ladakh

Temisgang

Nyerpapa House

INVENTORY NO.
KHALTSE / TEMISGANG / 32 / 2004

Vernacular Building | Abandoned | Private (Individual) | Around 150 - 200 years old

SETTING
The house is oriented to the south and is built along the slope of a small hill on which the Lartse *lhakhang* is built. It is located to the south of the *lhakhang* and north of the Phurongpa house.

SIGNIFICANCE
The Nyerpapa house was built by ancestors of the Nyerpapa family around 150 – 200 years ago. It is built in the traditional style and is a good example of vernacular architecture in the village.

DESCRIPTION
The Nyerpapa house is built over a large rock and has a high random rubble masonry foundation. The structure is single storeyed with a high plinth. The superstructure is built in mud brick masonry with mud mortar. From the village road, a steep climb leads to the entrance of the house. The house is presently abandoned. There are rows of window on the southern facade while the northern facade is

embedded against the slope of the hill. The roof of the house opens onto the forecourt of the *lhakhang*. The roof is a traditional flat roof with square posts at the corners for prayer flags. The exterior walls are mud plastered and whitewashed.

STATE OF SIGNIFICANCE
Showing Signs Deterioration

SOURCE OF INFORMATION Nawang Chotak, Kunepa, Temisgang, Khaltse, Ladakh

Lhakhang and *Chorten*

INVENTORY NO.
KHALTSE / TEMISGANG / 33 / 2004

Chorten / Temple | In Use | Public (Community) | Around 200 - 250 years old

SETTING
The *lhakhang* and *chorten* are oriented to the southeast and are located to the north of the village, surrounded by the agriculture fields and willow trees.

SIGNIFICANCE
The *lhakhang* and *chorten* were built around 200 - 250 years ago. The *chorten* are circumambulated as an act of merit.

DESCRIPTION
The precinct comprises of a small *lhakhang* and a group of five *chorten*. The *lhakhang* has a simple exterior without any window openings. The only source of light and ventilation is through the main entrance door and a skylight above. It has been the locked for many months and access was not possible at the time of the visit. The external walls are built in random rubble and mud brick masonry and are mud

plastered and whitewashed. The parapet is painted in red. The *chorten* are scattered across an open space southeast of the *lhakhang* and are of various sizes. The *chorten* are built in stone and mud brick masonry and are mud plastered and whitewashed on the exterior. Some of the *chorten* have stucco motifs (*pa-tra*) on the base panels as well as red markings.

STATE OF PRESERVATION
Showing Signs Deterioration

SOURCE OF INFORMATION Nawang Chotak, Kunepa, Temisgang, Khaltse, Ladakh

457

Temisgang

Kagan *Chorten*

INVENTORY NO.
KHALTSE / TEMISGANG / 34 / 2004

Chorten | In Use | Public (Community)

SETTING
The Kagan *chorten* is oriented to the southwest and is built along the slope of a small hill. It is located to the north of the village road. A stream flows nearby and there are boulders and willow tree around the site.

SIGNIFICANCE
The Kagan *chorten* is located near the entrance to the village along what was possibly the old road to the village before the current road was laid. It is a gateway *chorten* and merit is believed to accrue to believers who walk through the passage of the *chorten*.

DESCRIPTION
The Kagan *chorten* consists of two thick parallel walls over which rests a large Namgyal *chorten*. The walls are built in random rubble and mud brick masonry with mud mortar and are mud plastered and whitewashed on the exterior. There is a passage below the main *chorten*. The *chorten* has red markings on the corners of the base panels and there is

a *chugsum khorlo* over the dome. There are three smaller *chorten* nearby. These *chorten* are built on a common random rubble masonry platform. The *chorten* are built in stone and mud brick masonry with mud mortar and are mud plastered and whitewashed on the exterior. There are red markings on the base panels of the *chorten*. The top sections of the *chorten* have largely eroded making it difficult to identify them.

STATE OF PRESERVATION
Showing Signs Deterioration

SOURCE OF INFORMATION Nawang Chotak, Kunepa, Temisgang, Khaltse, Ladakh

Group of *Chorten* and *Mane* Walls

INVENTORY NO.
KHALTSE / TEMISGANG / 35 / 2004

Chorten / *Mane* Wall | In Use | Public (Community) | Around 200 years old

SETTING
The *chorten* and *mane* wall are oriented to the southwest and are located along the vehicular road leading to the village.

SIGNIFICANCE
The *chorten* and *mane* wall are located along the road leading to the village and are circumambulated by villagers when the travel along this route as an act of merit. The *chorten* are predominantly Changchub *chorten* and symbolize the Buddha's enlightenment.

DESCRIPTION
The site comprises of a large cluster of *chorten* and *mane* wall. The largest of the *chorten* is a Changchub *chorten* which is built in stone and mud brick masonry with a tall *chugsum khorlo* on the dome made of baked clay tiles. The *chorten* are all mud plastered and whitewashed. The *mane*

walls are linear dry stone masonry walls with *mane* stones placed on the top horizontal surface. There is a small cylindrical shaped *mane* in between the group.

STATE OF PRESERVATION
Advanced State of Decay

SOURCE OF INFORMATION Nawang Chotak, Kunepa, Temisgang, Khaltse, Ladakh

Group of *Chorten* and *Mane* Walls

INVENTORY NO.
KHALTSE / TEMISGANG / 36 / 2004

Chorten / *Mane* Wall | In Use | Public (Community) | Around 200 years old

SETTING
The *chorten* and *mane* wall are oriented to the west and are built to the east of the main vehicular road about two kms from the village.

SIGNIFICANCE
The *chorten* and *mane* wall are located along the road leading to the village and are circumambulated by villagers as an act of merit as they travel along this route. The *chorten* are both Changchub *chorten* symbolizing the Buddha's enlightenment.

DESCRIPTION
The site comprises of a group of two *chorten* and two *mane* walls. The *chorten* are built on a square random rubble masonry base and are built in stone and mud brick masonry with an external layer of mud plaster and whitewash. The

mane walls lie on either side of the *chorten* and are long linear random rubble masonry walls with *mane* stones placed on the top horizontal surface.

STATE OF PRESERVATION
Showing Signs of Deterioration

SOURCE OF INFORMATION Nawang Chotak, Kunepa, Temisgang, Khaltse, Ladakh

Group of *Chorten*

INVENTORY NO.
KHALTSE / TEMISGANG / 37 / 2004

Chorten | In Use | Public (Community) | Around 200 years old

SETTING
The *chorten* are oriented to the southeast and are built on the top of a hill northwest of the TV tower.

SIGNIFICANCE
The *chorten* were built in the past as an act of merit and are still maintained by the villagers. The site is circumambulated by villagers to accumulate merit. The *chorten* are all Changchub *chorten* and symbolize the Buddha's enlightenment.

DESCRIPTION
The precinct consists of three large *chorten* with several smaller ones scattered nearby. The *chorten* are built in stone and mud brick masonry and are mud plastered and whitewashed externally. The base panels of the *chorten* have large stucco relief motifs (*pa-tra*). The domes of the *chorten* are surmounted by tall *chugsum khorlo* made of baked clay tiles over which rests a metal crown.

SOURCE OF INFORMATION Stobdan Namra, Temisgang, Khaltse, Ladakh

STATE OF PRESERVATION
Showing Signs of Deterioration

Temisgang

459

Chamba *Lhakhang*

INVENTORY NO.
KHALTSE / TEMISGANG / 38 / 2004

Temple | In Use | Public (Likir *Gonpa*) | Around 80 years old

SETTING
Oriented towards the south, the temple is located in Ang hamlet along a pathway which diverts from the vehicular road towards the village. The *lhakhang* is surrounded by agricultural fields on the north and east and residential buildings such as the Kagapay house towards the south.

SIGNIFICANCE
The *lhakhang* is the principal place of worship in the village where villagers gather to pray. The temple belongs to the Gelugpa sect and is under the ownership of the Likir *gonpa*. Chamba *lhakhang* is dedicated to the Shakyamuni Buddha and also houses images of Tsongkhapa.

DESCRIPTION
The *lhakhang* is a single storeyed structure, constructed in random rubble and mud brick masonry. Externally, it is mud plastered and whitewashed in white and red. Entrance to the *lhakhang* is through a flight of stairs which lead onto a small courtyard from where a doorway provides access into

the main hall. The *lhakhang* has a traditional mud floor and the walls bear paintings from the Buddhist pantheon among which the principal images are those of Shakyamuni Buddha and Gyalwa Tsongkhapa located on the northern end of the temple. The temple roof is supported on timber beams and four timber columns located at the centre of the *lhakhang*.

STATE OF PRESERVATION
Showing Signs of Deterioration

SOURCE OF INFORMATION Tundup Namgyal- Changpa, Temisgang, Khaltse, Ladakh

Chore *Mane*

INVENTORY NO.
KHALTSE / TEMISGANG / 39 / 2004

Mane Wall / Rock Inscription / *Chorten* | In Use | Public (Community)

SETTING
The Chore *mane* is oriented towards the north west and is located in Ang hamlet along a pathway, which diverts from the vehicular road towards the village. The *mane* wall is surrounded by agricultural fields towards the south and east and the Palchin pa house towards the west.

SIGNIFICANCE
The *mane* wall and *chorten* are located along a path leading to the village and are circumambulated by villagers as an act of merit when travelling along this path. The *chorten* is a Changchub *chorten* and symbolizes the Buddha's enlightenment.

DESCRIPTION
The site comprise of a *mane* wall and a *chorten*. The *mane* is circular in plan. It is constructed in dry stone masonry. At the base of the *mane*, there is a rock inscription painted in red which is embedded along the northern face of the *mane* wall. The Changchub *chorten* is built in stone and mud

brick masonry and is mud plastered and whitewashed externally. There is a tall *chugsum khorlo* over the dome of the *chorten* made of baked clay tiles.

STATE OF PRESERVATION
Showing Signs of Deterioration

SOURCE OF INFORMATION Tundup Namgyal-Changpa, Ang, Temisgang, Khaltse, Ladakh

---

Rigsum Gonbo

INVENTORY NO.
KHALTSE / TEMISGANG / 40 / 2004

Rigsum Gonbo / *Chorten* | In Use | Public (Community) | Around 120 years old

SETTING
The *chorten* and *rigsum gonbo* are located on a bare hill facing the Ang hamlet. The village road runs to the southwest.

SIGNIFICANCE
The *rigsum gonbo* is believed to have been built around 120 years ago to protect the village from natural calamities. The *chorten* near the *rigsum gonbo* are Changchub *chorten* and symbolize the Buddha's enlightenment.

DESCRIPTION
The site consists of a *rigsum gonbo* and two Changchub *chorten*. The *rigsum gonbo* stands on a whitewashed random rubble masonry platform and is enclosed on three sides. The fourth side, which is open to the front, contains three Changchub *chorten* within it. The two *chorten* near the *rigsum gonbo* are of similar size and are built in stone and mud brick masonry. Externally, the *chorten* are mud

plastered and whitewashed. The cubical base of the *chorten* are decorated with stucco relief and are painted in red. The *chorten* are surmounted with a prayer flag.

STATE OF PRESERVATION
Advanced State of Decay

SOURCE OF INFORMATION Tundup Namgyal-Changpa, Ang, Temisgang, Khaltse, Ladakh

Group of *Chorten and Mane* Walls

INVENTORY NO.
KHALTSE / TEMISGANG / 41 / 2004

Chorten / Mane Wall | In Use | Public (Community) | Around 180 years old

SETTING
The structures are oriented towards the northeast and are located along the road leading to Ang hamlet. The vehicular road lies towards the northwest of the site while agricultural fields lie along the south and east of the site.

SIGNIFICANCE
Located before the village, the *chorten* and *mane* walls are circumambulated by villagers as an act of merit as they travel along this route. The *chorten* are Changchub *chorten* and symbolize the Buddha's enlightenment.

DESCRIPTION
The site comprises of eight *chorten*, two *mane* walls and a small, whitewashed *lubang*. The *chorten* are all Changchub *chorten* and are located between the *mane* walls. The *chorten* are all built in stone and mud brick masonry with mud mortar and are mud plastered and whitewashed

externally. Between the *chorten* are two groups of *mane* walls which are built in random rubble masonry. The *lubang*, to the south, is built on a common platform in between the *chorten*.

STATE OF PRESERVATION
Advanced State of Decay

SOURCE OF INFORMATION Tundup Namgyal-Changpa, Ang, Temisgang, Khaltse, Ladakh

Temisgang

461

Group of *Chorten*

INVENTORY NO.
KHALTSE / TEMISGANG / 42 / 2004

Chorten | In Use | Public (Community)

SETTING
The structures are oriented towards the northeast and are located along the road leading to Ang hamlet. The vehicular road lies towards the north of the site while agricultural fields lie along the south of the site.

SIGNIFICANCE
The *chorten* are located along the road that leads to the village and are circumambulated by villagers as the travel along the path.

STATE OF PRESERVATION
Advanced State of Decay

DESCRIPTION
The site comprises of two *chorten* of similar size erected over square random rubble masonry bases. The *chorten* are built in stone and mud brick masonry with mud mortar. Externally, the *chorten* have traces of mud plaster and whitewash, most of which has eroded over time. The *chorten* have lost their original form and are difficult to identify.

SOURCE OF INFORMATION Tundup Namgyal-Changpa, Ang, Temisgang, Khaltse, Ladakh

Spurkhang

INVENTORY NO.
KHALTSE / TEMISGANG / 43 / 2004

Cremation Ground / *Chorten* | In Use | Public (Community) | Around 250 years old

SETTING
The *spurkhang* and *chorten* are oriented towards the southeast and are located along the road leading to Ang hamlet on an elevated barren stretch of land . The road runs on the southeastern side and there are houses further east and southeast of the site.

SIGNIFICANCE
The site consists of two *spurkhang* and a Changchub *chorten*. Most families in the village have a *spurkhang* which is reused by them on the death of a family member. The *chorten* appears to have been built in memory of a deceased family member.

DESCRIPTION
The site contains two *spurkhang* and a *chorten*. The *spurkhang* are constructed in mud brick masonry and are mud plastered externally. The base of the *chorten* is built in stone and mud brick masonry with mud mortar. Externally, the *chorten* is mud plastered and whitewashed.

SOURCE OF INFORMATION Tashi Rigzen, Ang, Temisgang, Khaltse, Ladakh

STATE OF PRESERVATION
Advanced State of Decay

Group of *Chorten* and *Lubang*

INVENTORY NO.
KHALTSE / TEMISGANG / 44 / 2004

Chorten / *Lubang* | In Use | Public (Community)

SETTING
The *chorten* and *lubang* are oriented towards the east and are located along the road leading to the village. They are surrounded by the road towards the west, a community open space and residential structures towards the south and the east.

SIGNIFICANCE
The shape of the *chorten* can no longer be discerned as it has collapsed. However, the *lubang* still survives. The *lubang* marks the residence of the *lu,* or serpent gods.

DESCRIPTION
The site comprises of a *chorten* and a *lubang*. The *chorten* has collapsed and it is not possible to identify its form. It is built in stone masonry and is mud plastered and

whitewashed externally. The *lubang* is constructed in mud brick masonry and is a small cubical structure which is whitewashed externally.

STATE OF PRESERVATION
Advanced State of Decay

SOURCE OF INFORMATION Tashi Rigzen, Ang, Temisgang, Khaltse, Ladakh

Group of *Chorten*

INVENTORY NO.
KHALTSE / TEMISGANG / 45 / 2004

Chorten | In Use | Public (Community) | Around 225 years old

SETTING
The *chorten* are oriented towards the north and are located along the road leading to Ang. The road lies towards the east of the site while the Khangsarpa house is towards the west.

SIGNIFICANCE
The *chorten* are located before the entrance to the village and are circumambulated by villagers as an act of merit as they travel along this path. All the *chorten* are Changchub *chorten* and symbolize the Buddha's enlightenment.

DESCRIPTION
The site consists of a cluster of eleven *chorten*. The first group, consisting of six *chorten* of similar size, is built on a common random rubble masonry platform. The next group consists of five *chorten* sharing a common base. All the *chorten* are built in stone and mud brick masonry with mud

mortar. Externally, the *chorten* are mud plastered and whitewashed. Some of the *chorten* have *srog-shing* embedded in their domes.

STATE OF PRESERVATION
Showing Signs of Deterioration

SOURCE OF INFORMATION Tashi Rigzen, Ang , Temisgang, Khaltse, Ladakh

Mane Chorten

INVENTORY NO.
KHALTSE / TEMISGANG / 46 / 2004

Chorten | In Use | Public (Community) | Around 220 years old

SETTING
The *chorten* are oriented to the south and are approached by a narrow pathway diverting from the main village road. There is a camping site towards the west. The agricultural fields and the pathway lie towards the south and the north respectively.

SIGNIFICANCE
The group of *chorten* is built along the pathway which connects the village to Hemis Shukpachan. This path is used by villagers travelling between Ang and Hemis Shukpachan and the *chorten* are circumambulated by them as an act of merit. All the *chorten* are Changchub *chorten* that symbolize the Buddha's enlightenment.

DESCRIPTION
The site consists of a group of nine *chorten*. Eight of these are similar in size and are placed in two rows of four each adjacent to one other. To the north of the rows is the ninth and the largest *chorten*. All the *chorten* are built in stone

and mud brick masonry and are mud plastered and whitewashed externally. In addition, the larger chorten has decorative stucco relief (*pa-tra*) and symbolic red markings.

STATE OF PRESERVATION
Advanced State of Decay

SOURCE OF INFORMATION Tashi Rigzen, Ang, Temisgang, Khaltse, Ladakh

Temisgang

463

Gashukpa House

INVENTORY NO.
KHALTSE / TEMISGANG / 47 / 2004

Vernacular Building | Abandoned | Private (Individual) | Around 150 years old

SETTING
The house is approached from a narrow footpath which diverts from the main Ang village road running to its south east while the other village houses are located to the northeast.

SIGNIFICANCE
The Gashukpa house was built by the ancestors of the Gashukpa family and forms part of the traditional vernacular architecture of the village.

DESCRIPTION
The house is a three storeyed structure with a ground floor used largely for storage purposes and the upper floors as the family's living areas. The ground floor is constructed in random rubble masonry without any openings. The upper floors are constructed in mud brick masonry with mud mortar. These first and second floors have small rectangular window openings with timber frames and decorative lintels. The uppermost floor houses the family temple. Externally, the front facade of the house has a *rabsal* on the left side of the front facade and a L-shaped, cantilevered projection on the right corner. There is a large terrace in the centre of the upper most floor. Externally, the house would have been mud plastered and white washed, though most of this is eroded now. The floors within the house are traditional mud floors while the roof is a traditional one of timber beams, joists, *taalu*, dried grass and a layer of mud.

STATE OF PRESERVATION
Advanced State of Decay

SOURCE OF INFORMATION Tashi Rigzen, Ang, Temisgang, Khaltse, Ladakh

Group of *Chorten*

INVENTORY NO.
KHALTSE / TEMISGANG / 48 / 2004

Chorten | In Use | Public (Community)

SETTING
The *chorten* are oriented towards the east and are located in Ang hamlet along a narrow pathway which diverts from the main village road. The village road runs east of the *chorten* while the Gashukpa house is located to its west.

SIGNIFICANCE
Although difficult to discern the form of the first *chorten*, the second *chorten* appears to be a Changchub *chorten*, which represents the Buddha's enlightenment. The *chorten* were built in the past for the well being of the village.

DESCRIPTION
The site consists of two *chorten* placed on a high random rubble masonry platform. One of the *chorten* has completely collapsed while the other *chorten* appears to be a Changchub *chorten* built over a square base. The *chorten* is constructed in stone masonry and is mud plastered and whitewashed externally. The mud plaster has eroded over time.

STATE OF PRESERVATION
Advanced State of Decay

SOURCE OF INFORMATION Tashi Rigzen, Ang, Temisgang, Khaltse, Ladakh

Group of *Chorten* and *Mane* Walls

INVENTORY NO.
KHALTSE / TEMISGANG / 49 / 2004

Chorten / Mane Wall | In Use | Public (Community) | Around 220 years old

SETTING
Located in Ang hamlet, the site is oriented towards the east and can be approached directly from the main village road which runs along the northeast side. The Angdopa house is located towards the southwest.

SIGNIFICANCE
The *chorten* and *mane* walls are located near the main village road and are circumambulated by villagers as an act of merit. The *chorten* are all Changchub *chorten* symbolic of the Buddha's enlightenment.

DESCRIPTION
The site comprises of six *chorten*, a circular *mane* wall and a long *mane* wall. The circular *mane* wall is adjacent to the village road and has a stone masonry base. This is followed by a long *mane* wall with a random rubble masonry base. Inscribed *mane* stones are placed on the horizontal surface

of the *mane* wall. To the south of the circular *mane* wall is a row of *chorten* which are parallel to the long *mane* wall. At the end of the long *mane* wall is another group of two *chorten*. All the *chorten* are built in stone and mud brick masonry with mud mortar. Externally, the *chorten* are mud plastered and whitewashed.

STATE OF PRESERVATION
Danger of Disappearance

SOURCE OF INFORMATION Tashi Rigzen, Ang, Temisgang, Khaltse, Ladakh

Temisgang

465

Mane Walls

INVENTORY NO.
KHALTSE / TEMISGANG / 50 / 2004

Mane Wall | In Use | Public (Community) | Around 100 years old

SETTING
The *mane* walls are accessed directly from the Ang village road (going on to Temisgang) which runs southeast of the site. There are willow plantations to the west and northwest of the *mane* walls.

SIGNIFICANCE
The *mane* walls were constructed by a resident of the village, Rinchen Spalchinpa as an act of merit. Located along the main village road, the villagers circumambulate the *mane* walls to accumulate merit.

DESCRIPTION
The site consists of three *mane* walls. The first is a linear *mane* wall with a rectangular base along the vehicular road from Temisgang to Ang. To its west is the second *mane* wall built over a random plan. To its southwest is the third linear *mane* wall. All the *mane* walls are built of dry stone masonry with *mane* stones placed on the top.

STATE OF PRESERVATION
Showing Signs of Deterioration

SOURCE OF INFORMATION Tashi Rigzen, Ang, Temisgang, Khaltse, Ladakh

Mane Ringmo

INVENTORY NO.
KHALTSE / TEMISGANG / 51 / 2004

Mane Wall / *Chorten* | In Use | Public (Community) | Around 100 years old

SETTING
Oriented towards the south, the *mane* walls and *chorten* can be directly approached from the village road. The road runs along the southern edge of the site and there is a grove of willow trees to the north of the site.

SIGNIFICANCE
The *mane* walls and *chorten* lie along the main village road and are circumambulated by villagers as an act of merit when travelling along this route.

DESCRIPTION
The site consists of three long *mane* walls and a *chorten*. The first two *mane* walls are at a higher level than the road which abuts the site. The third *mane* wall is located further away next to a *chorten* that has lost much of its original form. The *mane* walls are all constructed in dry stone masonry. The *chorten* appears to be a Changchub *chorten* and is built in stone masonry. There are traces of mud plaster and whitewash on the external surface.

STATE OF PRESERVATION
Showing Signs of Deterioration

Temisgang

466

SOURCE OF INFORMATION Tashi Rigzen, Ang, Temisgang, Khaltse, Ladakh

NIRLAC

Tia

The village of Tia village is situated next to Temisgang, about 95 kms from Leh. It was originally called ITewa meaning '*centre*' or '*middle*' as the settlement is located between two streams. Later, it was changed to Tia. At present, there are about 179 households in the village. The village comes under the *Goba* of Temisgang.

Listed by: Deldan Angmo and Jassu Singh
Year: 2004

Mane Wall

INVENTORY NO.
KHALTSE / TIA / 01 / 2004

Mane Wall | In Use | Public (Community) | Around 150 - 200 years old

SETTING
The *mane* wall is oriented to the east and is located along the village road amid agricultural fields. It is located between two boundary walls.

SIGNIFICANCE
The *mane* wall is located along the village road and is circumambulated by villagers as an act of merit when travelling along this path.

DESCRIPTION
The *mane* wall is a linear dry stone masonry wall built along the village pathway. It has a mud infill in the centre and the top surface of the wall is covered with numerous *mane* stones. There is a *tarchen* embedded in one end of the wall.

STATE OF PRESERVATION
Showings Signs of Deterioration

SOURCE OF INFORMATION Tashi Dolma Yokmapa, Tia, Khaltse, Ladakh,

Tia

470

Appi Changshar *Chomo Lhato*

INVENTORY NO.
KHALTSE / TIA / 02 / 2004

Lhato | In Use | Private (Individual) | Around 300 - 350 years old

SETTING
The *lhato* is oriented to the southeast and is located on top of a boulder surrounded by agricultural fields. The Cha Charpey house is located nearby.

SIGNIFICANCE
The *lhato* is located at the entrance to the village and is dedicated to Appi Changshar *Chomo*, the guardian goddess, of the families. Prayers are held every year on the occasion of Losar and the contents of the *lhato* are renewed at the time.

DESCRIPTION
The *lhato* is a small cubical structure built in dry stone masonry which rests on a large boulder. There are juniper branches, *khadag*, and animal horns placed at the centre.

STATE OF PRESERVATION
Showing Signs of Deterioration

SOURCE OF INFORMATION Tashi Dolma Yokmapa, Tia, Khaltse, Ladakh

Chorten

INVENTORY NO.
KHALTSE / TIA / 03 / 2004

Chorten | Abandoned | Public (Community) | Around 200 - 250 years old

SETTING
The *chorten* is oriented to the east and is located along the village road surrounded by fields. The Charcharpa and Serapey houses are located a short distance away.

SIGNIFICANCE
The *chorten* was built in the past by an ancestor from the village as an act of merit for the well being of all sentient beings.

DESCRIPTION
The *chorten* has almost completely collapsed with only a part of the base still standing. It was built in stone masonry and debris from the *chorten* lies all around the site.

STATE OF PRESERVATION
Danger of Disappearance

SOURCE OF INFORMATION Tsering Pazom Churponpa, Tia, Khaltse, Ladakh

Tia

471

Serapey House

INVENTORY NO.
KHALTSE / TIA / 04 / 2004

Vernacular Building | In Use | Private (Individual) | Around 150 - 200 years old

SETTING
The house is oriented to the southwest and is situated along the village road with a ruined *chorten* nearby. The Charcharpa house is located in the front.

SIGNIFICANCE
The Serapey house was built around 150 - 200 years ago by ancestors of the Serapey family and successive generations continue to reside here. The house is built in the traditional style and is a good example of vernacular architecture in the village.

DESCRIPTION
The Serapey house is a small double storeyed building built on a rectangular plan. The ground floor is built in random rubble masonry and is very low in height. There are no windows on this floor. The first floor is built in mud brick masonry and has small windows with traditional wooden frames and decorated lintels.

STATE OF PRESERVATION
Advanced State of Decay

SOURCE OF INFORMATION Tsering Pazom Churponpa, Tia, Khaltse, Ladakh

Group of *Chorten* and *Mane* Wall

INVENTORY NO.
KHALTSE / TIA / 05 / 2004

Chorten / Mane Wall | Abandoned | Public (Community)

STATE OF PRESERVATION
Danger of Disappearance

SETTING
The site is oriented to the northwest and is located on an elevated stretch of land at the foot of the mountains. It lies above the agricultural fields and the settlement.

SIGNIFICANCE
The *chorten* and *mane* wall were built in the past as an act of merit.

DESCRIPTION
The site comprises of a long *mane* wall and a group of five *chorten*. The *mane* wall and one *chorten* are located to the southeast of the other four *chorten*. The group of four *chorten* are in almost complete ruins and appear to have been built in stone and mud brick masonry. Each *chorten* has a small niche towards the northeast. The *mane* wall is built in dry stone masonry and has inscribed *mane* stones on its horizontal surface.

SOURCE OF INFORMATION Tsering Palzom Churponpa, Tia, Khaltse, Ladakh

Tia

472

Rigsum Gonbo

INVENTORY NO.
KHALTSE / TIA / 06 / 2004

Rigsum Gonbo | In Use | Public (Community) | Around 150 - 200 year old

STATE OF PRESERVATION
Showing Signs of Deterioration

SETTING
The *rigsum gonbo* is oriented to the south and is surrounded by agricultural fields and willow trees.

SIGNIFICANCE
The *rigsum gonbo* was built to protect the village from natural calamities and other evil forces . The *chorten* themselves are older and were built to protect the village from diseases and evil forces.

DESCRIPTION
The *rigsum gonbo* is oriented towards the south and is a rectangular structure housing three small *chorten* within. The structure has a traditional roof with a large opening in the front. The *chorten* are painted in orange, white and blue symbolizing wisdom, compassion and strength. The structure is whitewashed with prayer flags on top. There is a *tarchen* in the front and a *mane* wall towards the west. Inscribed stones have been placed on the horizontal surface of the *mane* wall.

SOURCE OF INFORMATION Tashi Dolma, Yokmapa, Temisgang, Khaltse, Ladakh

Chorten Travo

INVENTORY NO.
KHALTSE / TIA / 07 / 2004

Chorten | In Use | Public (Community) | Around 150 years old

SETTING
The *chorten* is oriented to the southeast and is located northeast of the primary school in the Charcharpa area. It is surrounded by agricultural fields and willow trees.

SIGNIFICANCE
The *chorten* was built in the past as an act of merit for the welfare of all sentient beings and is still circumambulated by villagers. It is a Changchub *chorten* and symbolizes the Buddha's enlightenment.

DESCRIPTION
The *chorten* is built on a square stone masonry base and is constructed in stone and mud brick masonry. It is mud plastered and whitewashed externally. Stone slabs engraved with religious inscriptions are placed on the plinth of the *chorten*.

STATE OF PRESERVATION
Showing Signs of Deterioration

SOURCE OF INFORMATION Sonam Stanzin Horchopa, Tia, Khaltse, Ladakh

Tia

473

Charcharpa House

INVENTORY NO.
KHALTSE / TIA / 08 / 2004

Vernacular Building | In Use | Private (Individual) | Around 250 years old

SETTING
The house is oriented to the south and is located near the Changshar *lhato* and is surrounded by agricultural fields.

SIGNIFICANCE
The Charcharpa house was built around 250 years ago by an ancestor of the Charcharpa family and successive generations have continued to reside in the house. It is the oldest house in the hamlet and the hamlet is named after the family name Charcharpa. The house is built in the traditional style and is a good example of vernacular architecture in the village.

DESCRIPTION
The house is built on an elevated site and is surrounded by fields. It is a double storeyed building with very few window openings. There is an open yard adjacent to the house where cattle are kept. The ground floor is also used as cattle stable while the first floor houses the family's living areas. The walls are built in stone and mud brick masonry and the floors are laid in mud. The house has a traditional roof above supported on timber columns and beams below. The roof is used for storing fodder and firewood.

STATE OF PRESERVATION
Advanced State of Decay

SOURCE OF INFORMATION Tsering Palzom Churponpa, Tia, Khaltse, Ladakh

Yokmapa House

INVENTORY NO.
KHALTSE / TIA / 09 / 2004

Vernacular Building | In Use | Private (Individual) | Around 200 - 250 years old

SETTING
The Yokmapa house is oriented to the south east and is located near the *Chorten* Travo. It is surrounded by agricultural fields and willow trees.

SIGNIFICANCE
The Yokmapa house was built around 200 - 250 years ago by an ancestor of the Yokmapa family and continues to be used as the ancestral family residence. It is built in the traditional style and is a good example of vernacular architecture in the village.

DESCRIPTION
The house is a double storeyed structure built in stone and mud brick masonry. The ground floor is used for stabling animals and has no window openings. The first floor houses the living areas of the family and is accessed through a flight of wooden stairs. A portion of the house has been demolished and a new section has been constructed there.

The roof is a traditional one made of timber beams, joists, *taalu*, dried grass and a layer of compacted mud. The rooftop is used to stack firewood and willow twigs.

STATE OF PRESERVATION
Showing Signs of Deterioration

SOURCE OF INFORMATION Sonam Stanzin Horchopa, Tia, Khaltse, Ladakh

Kagan *Chorten*

INVENTORY NO.
KHALTSE / TIA / 10 / 2004

Chorten | In Use | Public (Community) | Around 150 - 180 years old

SETTING
The *chorten* is oriented to the east and is located on the way to the Charchar hamlet. There is a small stream flowing to the east.

SIGNIFICANCE
The Kagan *chorten* is a gateway chorten located en route to the Charchar hamlet. Merit is believed to accrue to believers who pass through the passage of the *chorten* and circumambulate it.

DESCRIPTION
The Kagan *chorten* has two thick parallel walls over which rest a Changchub *chorten*. There is a passage beneath the *chorten*. The *chorten* is built in stone and mud brick masonry and is mud plastered and whitewashed externally. The ceiling over the passage has wooden members and is painted with a *mandala*. There is a small niche facing the east on the dome of the *chorten*. The dome is surmounted

by a tall *chugsum khorlo* made of baked clay tiles over which rests a metal crown.

STATE OF PRESERVATION
Showing Signs of Deterioration

SOURCE OF INFORMATION Sonam Stanzin Horchopa, Temisgang, Khaltse, Ladakh

Khatsa *Gonpa*

INVENTORY NO.
KHALTSE / TIA / 11 / 2004

Gonpa | In Use | Public (Hemis *Gonpa*) | Around 300 - 400 years old

STATE OF PRESERVATION
Fair

SETTING

The *gonpa* is oriented to the southeast and is built on a an elevated stretch of land along the road from Temisgang to Charchar. It is located northwest of the village road.

SIGNIFICANCE

The *gonpa* was built around 300 - 400 years ago and is under the purview of Hemis monastery. Monks from Hemis are deputed here to carry out prayers and rituals at the temples. According to legend, an image of Chagdor while flying from Tibet landed at this spot and the temples were subsequently built here, hence the name 'Khatsa'.

DESCRIPTION

The *gonpa* is a large double storeyed building with a forecourt in front. There is a *tarchen* at the centre of the forecourt. The *gonpa* is built in stone and mud brick masonry. The *zimchung*, kitchen and stores for the resident lamas are adjacent to the main *gonpa* building. A steep staircase from the forecourt leads to a corridor on the first floor and to the portico of the *gonpa*. The walls of the portico are elaborately painted with images of the guardian deities. An elaborate doorway leads into a large hall which has four wooden columns supporting the roof above. There are two rows of seating and a throne for the head lama. There are images of Chanrazig, Chagdor, 21 Dolma, and Guru Rinpoche to the rear of the chamber. There is a niche in the rear wall which has a wooden segmental arched frame. The walls are lined with images of various Bodhisattvas. There are a row of *mane* wheels on the ground floor level. The exterior walls of the *gonpa* are mud plastered and whitewashed. The *gonpa* has undergone many alterations and additions over time. The original entrance is blocked and a new one has been provided in its place. A new structure is being constructed in front of the old *gonpa*.

Tia

475

SOURCE OF INFORMATION Sonam Stanzin Horchopa, Temisgang, Khaltse, Ladakh

Mane Chuskor

INVENTORY NO.
KHALTSE / TIA / 12 / 2004

Prayer Wheel | In Use | Public (Community) | Around 100 - 150 years old

SETTING
The *mane chuskor* are oriented to the northwest and are located southeast of the Khatsa *gonpa*, across the village stream and village road. There is a solitary house to the southwest of the site.

SIGNIFICANCE
The *mane chuskor* were built around 2 - 3 generations ago by village ancestors. The mane wheels rotate with the flow of water.

DESCRIPTION
The site comprises of two *mane chuskor*, square in plan and double storeyed in height. The *mane chuskor* at the upper level is the older structure built in stone masonry. The prayer wheel is fixed on an axis around which the wheel rotates. The lower *mane chuskor* is a new one built in concrete with a new wheel inside. The prayer wheel rotates with the current of the water running beneath.

STATE OF PRESERVATION
Showing Signs of Deterioration

SOURCE OF INFORMATION Sonam Stanzin Horchopa, Temisgam, Khaltse, Ladakh

Chorten and Mane Wall

INVENTORY NO.
KHALTSE / TIA / 13 / 2004

Chorten / *Mane* Wall | In Use | Public (Community) | Around 15th century

SETTING
The *chorten* and *mane* walls are oriented to the south and are located along the village road. The site is surrounded by agricultural fields.

SIGNIFICANCE
The site is located north of the *Khar* Nonpa, the summer palace of King Dagspa Bum, when he ruled lower Ladakh from his headquarters at Temisgang. The *chorten* and *mane* wall are also believed to date back to this period. Located along the village road these chorten and mane wall are circumambulated by villagers as an act of merit when traveling along this path.

DESCRIPTION
The site comprises of a large *mane* wall and three *chorten*. The *mane* wall is a large irregular shaped stone masonry wall with a large surface area on top over which are placed numerous inscribed *mane* stones and inscriptions. The *chorten* are located to the northeast of the mane wall. The *chorten* are of three kinds i.e. Changchub, Namgyal and Indoom *chorten* built on a common stone masonry base. The *chorten* are built in stone and mud brick masonry and are mud plastered and whitewashed on the exterior. There is a narrow circumambulatory path around the site.

STATE OF PRESERVATION
Showing Signs of Deterioraion

SOURCE OF INFORMATION Ishey Zangpo Stagopa, Tia, Temisgang, Khaltse, Ladakh

NIRLAC

Chorten Mermer

INVENTORY NO.
KHALTSE / TIA / 14 / 2004

Chorten | In Use | Public (Community) | Around 200 - 250 years old

SETTING
The *chorten* is oriented to the south and is located on an elevated stretch of land above the settlement and is surrounded by fields on one side and barren mountains on the other.

SIGNIFICANCE
The *chorten* was built in the past by an ancestor from the village, as an act of merit, for the well being of all sentient beings. The shape of the *chorten* is unique and does not conform to the traditional eight forms of *chorten* in Tibetan Buddhism.

DESCRIPTION
The *chorten* is built on an elevated stretch of barren land. It has a unique shape with a high square base over which rests another smaller cubical structure and a semi circular dome-like structure over this. It is built in stone masonry and is mud plastered and whitewashed on the exterior.

STATE OF PRESERVATION
Showing Signs of Deterioration

SOURCE OF INFORMATION Tashi Norbu Kharnonpa, Temisgang, Khaltse, Ladakh

Tia

477

Khangsarmo *Chorten*

INVENTORY NO.
KHALTSE / TIA / 15 / 2004

Chorten | In Use | Public (Community) | Around 250 - 300 years old

SETTING
The *chorten* are oriented to the northeast and is located on a hill below the main mountain range. A steep narrow pathway leads up to the *chorten* from the village below.

SIGNIFICANCE
The *chorten* are believed to be very old and are of significance to the community as rituals are carried out near the *chorten*. The *chorten* are also circumambulated by villagers to accumulate merit seen as the first step towards attaining enlightenment.

STATE OF PRESERVATION
Showing Signs of Deterioration

DESCRIPTION
The site comprises of four *chorten* built randomly along the slope of a hill. The *chorten* are of different forms and are built in stone and mud brick masonry with an external layer of mud plaster and whitewash.

SOURCE OF INFORMATION Tashi Norbu Kharnonpa, Temisgang, Khaltse, Ladakh

Khar Nonpa

INVENTORY NO.
KHALTSE / TIA / 16 / 2004

Fort / Palace | In Use | Private (Individual) | Around 500 years old

SETTING
The palace is oriented to the south and can be approached either directly from the main road or from the village below. The village road and agricultural fields lie to the north while the village of Tia is lies to the south. The building is located at the highest level of the village and has a commanding view of the settlement below.

SIGNIFICANCE
The palace is believed to have been the summer palace of King Dagspa Bum who ruled the lower Ladakh region from his capital at Temisgang. A portion of the structure still remains and is used by the Kharnonpa family. It is the oldest building in Tia and is built in the traditional style contributing to the village's vernacular architecture.

DESCRIPTION
The palace is a large building built on a random plan. The rear of the building is effectively double storeyed high with two or three small openings. It is built largely in exposed stone masonry with some of the upper levels built in mud brick masonry. A narrow winding path passing via residential buildings leads to the entrance of the house. The front as well as the sides are three storeys high. Most of the building has been abandoned. However, some sections have been repaired and altered and are still in use. The ground floor is used to house animals and store fodder while the upper floors constitute the living areas for the family. The roof is a traditional one made of timber joists, *taalu*, grass and compacted mud. The roof has collapsed towards the rear of the house while new additions have been made to the front of the house.

STATE OF PRESERVATION
Advanced State of Decay

Tia

478

Rigsum Gonbo and Kagan Chorten

INVENTORY NO.
KHALTSE / TIA / 17 / 2004

Rigsum Gonbo / Chorten | In Use | Public (Community) |
Around 250 - 300 years old

SETTING

The *rigsum gonbo* and Kagan *chorten* are oriented to the east and are surrounded by the village. These are located on a footpath which connects the village to the main road and lie below the hill on which the Kharnonpa stands.

SIGNIFICANCE

Both the *rigsum gonbo* and the Kagan *chorten* are built over the path linking the village to the main road. The Kagan *chorten* is a gateway *chorten* and merit is believed to accrue to believers who pass through its passage and circumambulate it. The *rigsum gonbo* protects the village from calamities and misfortune.

DESCRIPTION

The site comprises of a *rigsum gonbo* and a Kagan *Chorten* which have a common passage running beneath them. The Kagan *Chorten* has two thick parallel walls built in stone masonry over which rests a large Changchub *chorten*. The *chorten* has a tall *chugsum khorlo* over the dome with a metal crown on top. The *rigsum gonbo* also has two thick parallel side walls over which rests a small enclosure housing three small *chorten* painted in orange, blue and white representing the three Bodhisattvas. The enclosure has two parallel mud brick masonry walls and is open to the front and rear. It has a traditional mud roof above supported on wooden columns.

STATE OF PRESERVATION
Showing Signs of Deterioration

Tia

479

Nyeringpa House

INVENTORY NO.
KHALTSE / TIA / 18 / 2004

Vernacular Building | In Use | Private (Individual) | Around 200 - 250 years old

SETTING
The house is oriented to the south and is approached from a narrow pathway that leads from the main village road to the group of houses. It is adjacent to the Bangkapa house and is surrounded by other houses.

SIGNIFICANCE
The Nyeringpa house was built around 200 - 250 years ago by an ancestor of the Nyeringpa family and is one of the oldest houses in the village. Successive generations of the Nyeringpa family continued to reside here and only recently has the family shifted to a new houses built near the old family house. The house is built in the traditional style and is a good example of vernacular architecture in the village.

DESCRIPTION
The house is a double storeyed building built over a rectangular plan. It has a large gateway passage on the ground floor that leads to the neighbor's house. The ground floor is built in stone masonry and has no window openings.

SOURCE OF INFORMATION Stanzin Angchuk Nyeringpa, Tia, Khaltse, Ladakh

It is used for housing animals and storing fodder. The first floor is built in mud brick masonry and has a wooden gallery all around which is decorated with lattice work and segmental arches. The roof is a traditional one made of timber joists, beams, willow twigs, dried grass and compacted mud on top. The flooring in the house is in mud.

STATE OF PRESERVATION
Fair

Tia

480

Rigsum Gonbo

INVENTORY NO.
KHALTSE / TIA / 19 / 2004

Rigsum Gonbo | In Use | Public (Community) | Around 150 - 200 years old

SETTING
The *rigsum gonbo* is oriented to the north and is located south of the Nyeringpa house. A narrow path from the main village road leads to the *rigsum gonbo*. It is surrounded by houses on three sides and agricultural fields on the fourth. A group of *chorten* and *mane* are located to the southwest.

SIGNIFICANCE
The *rigsum gonbo* was built in the past to protect the village from natural calamities and misfortune.

DESCRIPTION
The *rigsum gonbo* is a linear structure built on a rectangular plan. It has a high plinth built in stone masonry over which rest two parallel side walls. The front and rear of the enclosure are open. Three small *chorten* are housed within the structure and are painted in white, orange and blue. The enclosure has a traditional roof above of timber beams, joists, grass and compacted mud supported over two wooden columns and brackets on either side.

SOURCE OF INFORMATION Stanzin Angchuk Nyeringpa, Tia, Khaltse, Ladakh

STATE OF PRESERVATION
Showing Signs of Deterioration

Chorten Mangpo (Sarig Ge Zug)

INVENTORY NO.
KHALTSE / TIA / 20 / 2004

Chorten / Mane Wall | In Use | Public (Community) | Around 150 - 200 years old

SETTING
The *chorten* is oriented to the south and is located south of the Nyeringpa house. It is surrounded by houses on three sides and a *rigsum gonbo* on the fourth.

SIGNIFICANCE
The group of *chorten*, *mane* wall and prayer wheel are located on the village road leading to the village houses nearby. The *chorten* and *mane* wall are circumambulated and the prayer wheel rotated by villagers as acts of merit. The *chorten* are both Changchub *chorten* and symbolize the Buddha's enlightenment.

DESCRIPTION
The site comprises of two Changchub *chorten*, a prayer wheel and a *mane* wall. The *chorten* are built on a common dry stone masonry plinth. One of the *chorten* is enclosed within a square structure with a traditional mud roof supported over two stone and mud brick masonry walls and two wooden posts. The interior wall surface has panels with inscriptions on them. The second *chorten* is sandwiched between the enclosed chorten and the prayer wheel and is larger in size. Both the *chorten* are built in stone and mud brick masonry and are mud plastered and whitewashed on the exterior. The *mane* wall is an irregular shaped dry stone masonry wall with inscribed *mane* stones placed on the horizontal surface. The prayer wheel is enclosed within a square building.

STATE OF PRESERVATION
Showing Signs of Deterioration

SOURCE OF INFORMATION Stanzin Angchuk Nyeringpa, Tia, Khaltse, Ladakh

481

Bang Kapa House

INVENTORY NO.
KHALTSE / TIA / 21 / 2004

Vernacular Building | In Use | Public (Hemis *Gonpa*) | Around 200 - 250 years old

SETTING
The house is oriented to the south and is located east of the Nyeringpa house with which it shares a wall.

SIGNIFICANCE
The house was built around 200 – 250 years ago by an ancestor of the Bang Kapa family to whom it belonged. The ancestors of the Bang Kapa family served in ancient times as the warriors for the King. The house has recently been handed over to Hemis monastery and monks from Hemis currently reside here. The house is built in the traditional style and is a good example of vernacular architecture in the village.

DESCRIPTION
The Bang Kapa house is built along a slope with an imposing front facade almost three storeys high. There are almost no window openings till the third floor. The fourth floor has a row of openings and an open verandah on the eastern side. This level is used as residences by the monks. The building is built in stone masonry till the third floor and the fourth floor is built in mud brick masonry. There are wooden beams inserted in the masonry between the second and third floor levels. This provides resistance during earthquakes. The first and second floors are essentially the plinth over which the upper floors rest. The roof is a traditional one made of timber beams, joists, willow twigs, grass and compacted mud. There are prayer flags posted at the four corners of the roof. The building has been altered over time with new repairs being carried out on the fourth floor currently used as monks' dwellings.

STATE OF PRESERVATION
Showing Signs of Deterioration

SOURCE OF INFORMATION Stanzin Angchuk Nyeringpa, Tia, Khaltse, Ladakh

Group of *Chorten* and *Mane* Walls

INVENTORY NO.
KHALTSE / TIA / 26 / 2004

Chorten / Mane Wall | In Use | Public (Community) | Around 200 years old

SETTING
The *chorten* and *mane* walls are oriented to the east and are located east of the hill on which the houses stand. The site is surrounded by willow trees and fields.

SIGNIFICANCE
The *chorten* and *mane* wall were built around 200 years ago by a village ancestor as an act of merit for the well being of all sentient beings. The structures are circumambulated by villagers when the travel along this path. The *chorten* is a Changchub *chorten* and symbolizes the Buddha's enlightenment.

DESCRIPTION
The site comprises of two small *mane* walls and one *chorten*. The *chorten* is built on a high dry stone masonry plinth and is constructed in stone and mud brick masonry. It is mud plastered and whitewashed externally. The *mane*

walls are cylindrical in shape and are built in dry stone masonry. Inscribed *mane* stones are placed on the top horizontal surface.

STATE OF PRESERVATION
Showing Signs of Deterioration

SOURCE OF INFORMATION Jigmet Yangskit Nyeringpa, Tia, Khaltse, Ladakh

Group of *Chorten* and *Mane* Walls

INVENTORY NO.
KHALTSE / TIA / 27 / 2004

Chorten / Mane Wall | In Use | Public (Community) | Around 250 - 300 years old

SETTING
The *chorten* are oriented to the northeast and are located at the foot of a mountain with the village and fields to the northeast. A narrow pathway runs along its side.

SIGNIFICANCE
The *chorten* appear to be very old and are located on an ancient route that led from Tia to Khaltse. Villagers would circumambulate these *chorten*, as an act of merit, while travelling along this route.

DESCRIPTION
The site comprises of a group of *chorten* and *mane* walls built along a single row. The *chorten* are of different sizes. The second and third *chorten* are the largest in the group which are followed by a small group of five *chorten* of similar size arranged next to each other. Some distance away from the group is the last *chorten* built on a higher

level. The *chorten* are built in stone and mud brick masonry and are mud plastered and whitewashed externally. There is a small circular *mane* wall at the beginning of the site built in stone masonry with inscribed *mane* stones placed on the horizontal surface.

STATE OF PRESERVATION
Showing Signs of Deterioration

SOURCE OF INFORMATION Stanzin Angchuk, Tia, Khaltse, Ladakh

Uletokpo

Uletokpo is located along the Leh - Srinagar highway.

Listed by: Deldan Angmo and Jassu Singh
Year: 2004

Urbis

The village of Urbis is situated in a hidden valley on the left bank of the River Indus. The village can be reached after trekking for about 3 hours from the main road and crossing the river near Domkhar. The exact meaning of the name is not known but it is believed that originally it was Ur-babs meaning '*valley of rolling stone*'. There are about 20 households in the village today.

{*Source: Tsering Phuntsog*}

Listed by: Deldan Angmo and Jassu Singh
Year: 2004

Mane Wall

INVENTORY NO.
KHALTSE / ULETOKPO / 01 / 2004

Mane Wall | In Use | Public (Community)

SETTING
The *mane* wall is oriented to the south and is located along the main road. It stands to the north of the road near a boundary wall and orchards.

SIGNIFICANCE
The *mane* wall lies near the main village road and is circumambulated by villagers as an act of merit.

DESCRIPTION
The *mane* wall is a rectangular dry stone masonry wall which has larger stones placed near the base and smaller stones towards the top of the wall. Inscribed *mane* stones are placed on the top of the wall.

STATE OF PRESERVATION
Showing Signs of Deterioration

SOURCE OF INFORMATION Lamchung Tsering, Uleytokpo, Khaltse, Ladakh

Chorten

INVENTORY NO.
KHALTSE / ULETOKPO / 02 / 2004

Chorten | In Use | Public (Community)

SETTING
The *chorten* is located along the main road near an apricot tree. There is a mustard field to the north and ruins of a structure towards the south. A narrow stream flows on the southwestern side.

SIGNIFICANCE
The *chorten* was built in the past for the well being of the village and is still circumambulated by villagers as an act of merit. It is a Changchub *chorten* and symbolizes the Buddha's enlightenment.

DESCRIPTION
The *chorten* is built on a high stone masonry plinth. The *chorten* is built in stone and mud brick masonry with mud mortar and is mud plastered and whitewashed on the exterior.

STATE OF PRESERVATION
Advanced State of Decay

SOURCE OF INFORMATION Lamchung Tsering, Uletokpo, Khaltse, Ladakh

Mane Wall

INVENTORY NO.
KHALTSE / ULETOKPO / 03 / 2004

Mane Wall | In Use | Public (Community)

SETTING
The *mane* wall is located to the east of the main road, near the Uletokpo house.

SIGNIFICANCE
The *mane* wall was built in the past for the well being of the village. It is circumambulated by villagers as an act of merit.

DESCRIPTION
The *mane* wall is a cylindrical dry stone masonry wall, with an infill of mud. Inscribed *mane* stones are placed on the top of the *mane* wall which is rounded with a slope towards the edge. There is a circumambulatory path around the *mane* wall.

STATE OF PRESERVATION
Showing Signs of Deterioration

SOURCE OF INFORMATION Lamchung Tsering, Uletokpo, Khaltse, Ladakh

Uletokpo

489

Uletokpo Pa House

INVENTORY NO.
KHALTSE / ULETOKPO / 04 / 2004

Vernacular Building | In Use | Private (Individual)

SETTING
The Uletokpo Pa house is located along the main road and is surrounded by agricultural fields and apricot trees with the resort to the west. It is oriented to the southeast.

SIGNIFICANCE
The house belongs the Uletokpo family and is built in the traditional style.

DESCRIPTION
The house is built on a rectangular plan and is accessed directly from the main road. A large wooden doorway leads into the forecourt of the house and a narrow cemented pathway leads into the house. The house is a double storeyed structure with storage space on the ground floor and the living areas, kitchen and temple on the first floor. The front facade has window openings arranged in rows. The rear side of the structure has a single room for keeping animals. The forecourt of the house has a large *tarchen* in the centre. The house is built in stone and mud brick

masonry and is mud plastered and whitewashed on the exterior.

STATE OF PRESERVATION
Showing Signs of Deterioration

SOURCE OF INFORMATION Tsering Angmo, Uletokpo, Khaltse, Ladakh

Petroglyph

INVENTORY NO.
KHALTSE / URBIS / 01 / 2004

Rock Carving | Abandoned | Public (State)

SETTING
The petroglyph is located on the path leading to the village and is surrounded by the path to the east and a stream to the west.

SIGNIFICANCE
The petroglyph is one of several thousand petroglyphs scattered across Ladakh and indicate some of the earliest evidence of human habitation in the region.

DESCRIPTION
It is a large piece of rock with a even surface dark in color. The surface has images of both human and animal figures pecked on the rock. A later inscription of the word '*Om*' appears on the top of the rock. The petroglyph is threatened as it lies along the path leading to the village and, in the event of the path being constructed or widened, could be damaged or destroyed.

STATE OF PRESERVATION
Danger of Disappearance

SOURCE OF INFORMATION Padma Yangchen, Urbis, Khaltse, Ladakh

Kushupa *Khangpa*

INVENTORY NO.
KHALTSE / URBIS / 02 / 2004

Vernacular Building | In Use | Private (Individual) | Around 150 years old

SETTING
The house is oriented to the east and is located along the path leading to the village. There is a small stream and a willow tree to the south of the house.

SIGNIFICANCE
The house was built by the great grand father of the present owner from the Kushupa family about 150 years ago. The family continues to reside in the house. The house is built in the traditional style and is a good example of vernacular architecture in the village.

DESCRIPTION
The house is a double storeyed building built on a random plan. The ground floor is constructed in stone masonry and does not have any window openings. It is used for housing animals and storing fodder. The first floor has small cubic units placed randomly and these are used as living areas. Each room has a different entrance. This level is constructed in mud brick masonry. The house has a flat

traditional roof above made of timber joists, *taalu*, *yagzes* and a layer of compacted mud. Externally the house is mud plastered and whitewashed.

STATE OF PRESERVATION
Advanced State of Decay

SOURCE OF INFORMATION Padma Yangchen-Karpa Kangbu and Sonam Wangdan-Kushupa, Urbis, Khaltse, Ladakh

Group of *Chorten* and *Mane* Walls

INVENTORY NO.
KHALTSE / URBIS / 03 / 2004

Chorten / *Mane* Wall | In Use | Public (Community) | Around 300 years old

SETTING

The *chorten* and *mane* walls are oriented to the northeast and are located to the left of the pathway which leads to the village. This path leads on from Urbis to Tagmachig. The structures are built along the mountainside and there is a stream flowing below.

SIGNIFICANCE

The group of *chorten* and mane walls is believed to have been built around 300 years ago and lie along the pathway which leads from Tagmachig to Urbis *gonpa*. The *chorten* and *mane* wall are circumambulated by villagers, to accumulate merit, as they travel along this path. The *chorten* are largely Changchub *chorten* and symbolize the Buddha's enlightenment.

DESCRIPTION

The site consists of a group of about twenty five *chorten* and three *mane* walls. The *chorten* are predominantly Changchub *chorten* and are built in stone and mud brick masonry with an external layer of mud plaster and whitewash. Some of the *chorten* have tall *chugsum khorlo* over the dome which symbolizes the 13 steps towards enlightenment. The *mane* walls are built in dry stone masonry and have inscribed *mane* stones placed on the horizontal surface.

STATE OF PRESERVATION
Advanced State of Decay

SOURCE OF INFORMATION Padma Yangchen, Urbis, Khaltse, Ladakh

Urbis

491

Mane Wall

INVENTORY NO.
KHALTSE / URBIS / 04 / 2004

Mane Wall | In Use | Public (Community) | Around 250 years old

SETTING

The *mane* wall is oriented to the east and is located along the pathway leading to the village. It is surrounded by agricultural fields.

SIGNIFICANCE

The *mane* wall was constructed about 250 years ago. It is located along the pathway leading to the village and is circumambulated by villagers, as they travel along this path, to accumulate merit.

DESCRIPTION

The *mane* wall is a circular dry stone masonry wall with an infill of mud. There are inscribed *mane* stones placed on the top horizontal surface. There is a *tarchen* posted in the centre of the *mane*.

STATE OF PRESERVATION
Showing Signs of Deterioration

SOURCE OF F INFORMATION Padma Yangchen, Urbis, Khaltse, Ladakh

Pharkapa *Khangpa*

INVENTORY NO.
KHALTSE / URBIS / 05 / 2004

Vernacular Building | In Use | Private (Individual) | Around 150 years old

SETTING
The Khangpa is oriented to the south and is located along a footpath. It is surrounded by the Kharpa house to the north and the footpath to the south.

SIGNIFICANCE
The house was built around 150 years ago by an ancestor of the Pharkapa family and the family continues to reside in the house. The house is built in the traditional style and is a good example of vernacular architecture in the village

DESCRIPTION
The Pharkapa house is a double storeyed building built on a random plan along the slope of a hill. The entry to the main house is from the eastern facade. There is a *tarchen* next to the door with openings on the rear side. The ground floor is built in stone masonry and is used primarily for housing animals and storing fodder. The first floor is built in mud brick masonry and is dominated by an elaborate wooden *rabsal* placed in the centre of the first floor. There are small window openings on either side of the *rabsal*. The exterior walls are mud plastered and whitewashed. The house is covered by a flat traditional roof made of timber beams, joists, *taalu*, *yagzes* and compacted mud.

STATE OF PRESERVATION
Showing Signs of Deterioration

SOURCE OF INFORMATION Konchok Dolma- Karpa, Urbis, Khaltse, Ladakh

---

Thupstan Tharpalling *Gonpa* (Urbis *Gonpa*)

INVENTORY NO.
KHALTSE / URBIS / 06 / 2004

Gonpa | In Use | Public (Community)

SETTING
The *gonpa* is oriented to the east and is located on the slope of a hill. It is surrounded by a *rigsum gonbo* to the south, Deshag Gyad to the north and by agricultural fields to the east.

SIGNIFICANCE
The *gonpa* was rebuilt after it collapsed and the images and ritual objects were shifted from the old *gonpa* here. It is the principal place of worship in the village.

DESCRIPTION
The *gonpa* is built on a rectangular plan over a high stone masonry plinth. It is accessed through a flight of stone steps which leads onto a porch. The porch has two wooden columns in front which support the roof above. A large decorated wooden doorway from the porch leads to the *dukhang* which houses a colossal image of Chanrazig along with images of other Bodhisattvas. There is a skylight above the main deity supported on columns. The *gonpa* is built in stone and mud brick masonry and is mud plastered and whitewashed on the exterior. It has a traditional roof above made of timber beams, joists, *taalu*, grass and compacted mud. There is a *tarchen* near the entrance to the *gonpa*.

STATE OF PRESERVATION
Showing Signs of Deterioration

SOURCE OF INFORMATION Konchok Dolma- Karpa, Urbis, Khaltse, Ladakh

Rigsum Gonbo

INVENTORY NO.
KHALTSE / URBIS / 07 / 2004

Rigsum Gonbo | In Use | Public (Community) | Around 300 years old

SETTING
The *rigsum gonbo* is oriented to the east and is located on the slope of a hill south of the Urbis *gonpa*.

SIGNIFICANCE
The *rigsum gonbo* was built by the community around 300 years ago to protect the village from natural calamities and other disasters.

DESCRIPTION
The *rigsum gonbo* is a small rectangular structure built in random rubble masonry on a slope of a hillock. It stands on a high plinth and has walls on three sides with an opening to the east. The walls are built in stone and mud brick masonry and are mud plastered and whitewashed externally. Inside the enclosure on a high plinth stand three *chorten* of different forms namely, Changchub, Namgyal and Indoom. The *rigsum gonbo* has a traditional roof above supported on timber columns and beams.

STATE OF PRESERVATION
Showing Signs of Deterioration

SOURCE OF INFORMATION Ishey Dolma, Urbis, Khaltse, Ladakh

Urbis

493

Deshag Gyad

INVENTORY NO.
KHALTSE / URBIS / 08 / 2004

Chorten | In Use | Public (Community) | Around 300 years old

SETTING
The Deshag Gyad is oriented to the east and is located along the slope of a hill west of the Urbis *gonpa*.

SIGNIFICANCE
The Deshag Gyad was built by the community around 300 years ago to protect the village from disasters and to bring prosperity to the village. The Deshag Gyad consist of the 8 traditional forms of *chorten* in Tibetan Buddhism namely Padspung, Changchub, Tashi Gomang, Chotul, Lhabab, Indoom, Namgyal and Nyangdas which symbolize events in the life of the Buddha.

plastered and whitewashed externally. There are two small openings on either side of front facade. The structure houses eight different type of chorten placed on a high platform.

STATE OF PRESERVATION
Showing Signs of Deterioration

DESCRIPTION
The Deshag Gyad is a single storeyed rectangular enclosure. It stands on a high random rubble masonry plinth with a large opening to the east. The roof is supported on timber columns and brackets. The walls are built in stone and mud brick masonry and are mud

SOURCE OF INFORMATION Ishey Dolma-Stanpa, Urbis, Khaltse, Ladakh

Kagan *Chorten*

INVENTORY NO.
KHALTSE / URBIS / 09 / 2004

Chorten | In Use | Public (Community) | Around 150 years old

SETTING
The Kagan *chorten* is oriented to the south east and is located near the base of the *gonpa* hill. It is surrounded by agricultural fields with the village stream flowing next to it.

SIGNIFICANCE
The *chorten* was built around 150 years ago. It is a Kagan or gateway *chorten* and merit is believed to accrue to believers who pass through the *chorten* as well as circumambulate the *chorten*.

DESCRIPTION
The Kagan *chorten* consists of two thick stone masonry walls supporting a Changchub *chorten* above. The walls of the base of are constructed in dry stone masonry. The *chorten* above is built in stone masonry and is mud plastered and whitewashed externally. There is a tall *chugsum khorlo* over the dome of the *chorten* which is made of baked clay tiles. The passage beneath the *chorten* has a timber ceiling with elaborate paintings of a *mandala* and Buddhas and Bodhisattvas.

STATE OF PRESERVATION
Danger of Disappearance

SOURCE OF INFORMATION Ishey Dolma-Stanpey, Urbis, Khaltse, Ladakh

Urbis

494

Changrhug *Chorten*

INVENTORY NO.
KHALTSE / URBIS / 10 / 2004

Chorten / Tarchen | In Use | Public (Community) | Around 80 years old

SETTING
The Changrhug *chorten* is located ahead of the Kagan *chorten* on the foothills of the *gonpa* hill. It is surrounded by a community open space to the north and agricultural fields to the south. The Stanpey house lies to the southeast while the village stream flows nearby to the west.

SIGNIFICANCE
The *chorten* was built around 80 years ago and is a Changchub *chorten* symbolizing the Buddha's enlightenment. It is circumambulated by villagers to accumulate merit.

DESCRIPTION
The *chorten* is built on a high random rubble masonry platform. It is built in stone and mud brick masonry with mud mortar and is mud plastered and whitewashed externally. There is a small niche in the dome of the *chorten* where in the past an image of a Buddhist deity would have been placed. The *chorten* has a tall *chugsum khorlo* over the dome. There are several inscribed *mane* stones placed over the plinth of the *chorten*. There is a tarchen to the east of the *chorten*.

STATE OF PRESERVATION
Showing Signs of Deterioration

SOURCE OF INFORMATION Ishey Dolma-Stanpey, Urbis, Khaltse, Ladakh

Baltipey *Tashag*

INVENTORY NO.
KHALTSE / URBIS / 11 / 2004

Vernacular Building | Abandoned | Private (Individual)

SETTING
The *tashag* is oriented to the east and is located on the top of a hill next to the old *gonpa*. The old *gonpa* lies to the west of the Baltipey *tashag* while the village lies to the south and southeast.

SIGNIFICANCE
The *tashag* was used as a residence for the monks when the old village *gonpa* was in use. It is built in the traditional style and is a fine example of vernacular architecture in the village.

DESCRIPTION
The *tashag* is a three storeyed high building built on a random plan along the slope of a hill. The two lower floors are constructed in random rubble masonry and have small window openings for ventilation. The entrance is from the ground floor. There is a finely carved timber *rabsal* on the first floor. The second floor has an open terrace in between right above the *rabsal* with rooms on either sides. The top

most floors have large openings on either side. The house has a flat traditional roof made of timber beams, joists, taalu, grass and compacted mud. The roof is supported on timber beams and columns with timber brackets. The external walls are mud plastered and white washed. Part of the house has already collapsed.

STATE OF PRESERVATION
Advanced State of Decay

SOURCE OF INFORMATION Ishey Dolma, Urbis, Khaltse, Ladakh

Urbis

495

Group of *Chorten*

INVENTORY NO.
KHALTSE / URBIS / 12 / 2004

Chorten | In Use | Public (Community)

SETTING
The *chorten* are oriented to the east and are located on the top of the *gonpa* hill. The chorten is surrounded by Kharmapa house to the west and a bare hill to the east. There are trees to the south.

SIGNIFICANCE
The *chorten* are all Changchub *chorten* which symbolize the Buddha's enlightenment. The chorten are circumambulated by villagers as an act of merit.

DESCRIPTION
The site consists of a group of three *chorten* built on a common random rubble masonry platform. The *chorten* are built in stone and mud brick masonry and have traces of external mud plaster and whitewash.

STATE OF PRESERVATION
Advanced State of Decay

SOURCE OF INFORMATION Ishey Dolma-Stanpa, Urbis, Khaltse, Ladakh

Prayer Wheel and *Mane* Wall (*Mane* Tungchur)

INVENTORY NO.
KHALTSE / URBIS / 13 / 2004

Prayer Wheel / *Mane* Wall | In Use | Public (Community) | Around 200 years old

SETTING
The *mane* wall and prayer wheel are oriented to the east and are located in the middle of the village. The site is surrounded by village houses with a huge rock to the south west and the Baltipey house to the west.

SIGNIFICANCE
The *mane* wall and prayer wheel are believed to have been built around 200 years ago as an act of merit. The prayer wheel is rotated by the devout and the *mane* wall circumambulated as acts of merit.

DESCRIPTION
The site consists of a prayer wheel, a *tarchen* and a *mane* wall. The *mane* wall is circular in shape and is built in random rubble masonry. It is mud plastered and

whitewashed externally and has inscribed *mane* stones placed on the horizontal surface. The prayer wheel is housed in a circular structure with an opening to the east. Externally, the structure is plastered and whitewashed. There is a *tarchen* near the *mane* wall.

STATE OF PRESERVATION
Showing Signs of Deterioration

SOURCE OF INFORMATION Ishey Dolma-Stanpa, Urbis, Khaltse, Ladakh

Urbis

496

Chorten and *Mane* Wall

INVENTORY NO.
KHALTSE / URBIS / 14 / 2004

Chorten / *Mane* Wall | In Use | Public (Community) | Around 200 years old

SETTING
The *chorten* and *mane* wall are oriented to the south and are located along the path which leads to the village. The site is surrounded by village houses to the north while the village lies to the south.

SIGNIFICANCE
The *chorten* and *mane* wall were built around 200 years ago, along the path leading to the village. The site is circumambulated by the villagers, to accumulate merit, as they travel along this path.

DESCRIPTION
The site consists of two *chorten* and a *mane* wall. The *mane* wall has a dry stone masonry base which is divided into two levels. The horizontal surface of the *mane* wall has

numerous *mane* stones. The *chorten* are built on a square base but have completely collapsed and it is difficult to identify their original form.

STATE OF PRESERVATION
Danger of Disappearance

SOURCE OF INFORMATION Ishey Dolma- Stanpa, Urbis, Khaltse, Ladakh

Rigsum Gonbo, *Chorten* and *Mane* Wall

INVENTORY NO.
KHALTSE / URBIS / 15 / 2004

Rigsum Gonbo / *Chorten* / *Mane* Wall | In Use | Public (Community) |
Around 120 years old

SETTING
The structures are oriented to the south east and are located on a hill overlooking the path which leads to the village. The site lies above the village settlement in front of the new school complex.

SIGNIFICANCE
The *chorten*, mane wall and *rigsum gonbo* were built around 120 years ago at the beginning of the village, along the path leading to the village. The structures are circumambulated by villagers, to accumulate merit, as they travel along this path. The *rigsum gonbo* is believed to protect the village from natural calamities and other disasters.

DESCRIPTION
The site consists of a Changchub *chorten*, a mane wall, a *rigsum gonbo* and a *tarchen*. The *chorten* is built on a square random rubble masonry base. It is built in stone and mud brick masonry with mud mortar and is mud plastered and whitewashed externally. The *chorten* has lost its original form due to the erosion of the external surface over a period of time. The *mane* wall has a dry stone masonry rectangular base and is filled with mud at the centre. The horizontal surface of the *mane* wall has inscribed *mane* stones. The *rigsum gonbo* is next to the *mane* wall. It consists of an enclosure with walls on two sides and openings to the front and rear. Inside the enclosure, on a high plinth stand three *chorten*. The walls of the *rigsum gonbo* are built in random rubble and mud brick masonry and are mud plastered and whitewashed externally. The structure has a traditional roof above.

STATE OF PRESERVATION
Showing Signs of Deterioration

Urbis

497

SOURCE OF INFORMATION Padma Yangchen, Urbis, Khaltse, Ladakh

Baltipey House

INVENTORY NO.
KHALTSE / URBIS / 16 / 2004

Vernacular Building | In Use | Private (Individual) | Around 180 years old

SETTING

The house is oriented to the south and is located below the village *gonpa*. It is surrounded by other village houses and streets on all sides.

SIGNIFICANCE

The Baltipey house was built around 180 years ago by an ancestor of the Baltipey family and the family continues to reside here. The house is built in the traditional style and is a good example of vernacular architecture in the village.

DESCRIPTION

The Baltipey house is three storeys high and built on a random plan along the slope of a hill. The ground floor is constructed in random rubble masonry while the first and second floors are built in mud brick masonry with mud mortar. The ground floor has small square window openings for ventilation and is used primarily for storage. The first floor has larger timber framed window openings and there is a large *rabsal* on the second floor which has a decorated

timber lintel and frame. The entrance to the house is from the east which leads directly onto the first floor. The first and second floors constitute the family's living areas. The house has a flat traditional roof made of timber beams, joists, *taalu*, grass and compacted mud. Externally, the walls are mud plastered and whitewashed.

STATE OF PRESERVATION
Showing Signs of Deterioration

SOURCE OF INFORMATION Ishey Dolma, Urbis, Khaltse, Ladakh

Mane Wall and *Tarchen*

INVENTORY NO.
KHALTSE / URBIS / 17 / 2004

Mane Wall | In Use | Public (Community) | Around 200 years old

SETTING

The *mane* wall and *tarchen* are oriented to the south and located along the vehicular road leading to the village. The road runs to the south of the site.

SIGNIFICANCE

The *mane* wall and *tarchen* were built around 200 years ago and mark the entrance to the village. They are circumambulated by villagers as they travel along this route.

DESCRIPTION

The site comprises of a *tarchen* and a *mane* wall. The *mane* wall is a rectangular dry stone masonry wall with *mane* stones placed on the top horizontal surface. There is a tall *tarchen* with a prayer flag on top located next to the *mane* wall.

STATE OF PRESERVATION
Showing Signs of Deterioration

SOURCE OF INFORMATION Padma Yangchen-Karpa, Urbis, Khaltse, Ladakh

Ursi

The village of Ursi can be reached from the link road that diverts from the Leh - Srinagar highway towards Shilla. The road ends at Phanjilla from where a path leads to Ursi *Dho*. A further one-hour trek leads to Ursi. Formerly, it came under the village head of Wanla, but today it has an independent village head. The village was sometimes known as Ursi Skyityul meaning '*the prosperous valley of Ursi village*'.

Listed by: Deldan Angmo and Jassu Singh
Year: 2004

Wanla

Wanla is situated about 112 kms from Leh. Originally, the village was known as Wada as it was situated in a valley that was shaped like a bow and arrow. It was also known Gya shing Wada. It was called Gya shing because there used to be hundred varieties of trees in the valley. Earlier, there used be only18 families in the village but today there are about 100 households. The village is divided into several small hamlets namely - Shilla, Zomal, Namtsas, Tarchid and Bhukbhuk.

{Source: Stanzin Dadul [Solponpa] }

Listed by: Deldan Angmo and Jassu Singh
Year: 2004

Bale *Mane*

INVENTORY NO.
KHALTSE / URSI / 01 / 2004

Mane Wall / *Tsadkhang* | In Use | Public (Community) | Around 150 years old

SETTING
The Bale *mane* is oriented to the east and is located along a pathway leading to the village The *mane* is surrounded by the path to the south and willow trees and agricultural fields to the north.

SIGNIFICANCE
The Bale *mane* was constructed about 150 years ago by a local village monk named Gelong Sonam Phuntsog. The *mane* wall was constructed as an act of merit. The *tsadkhang* contains small *tsa-tsa*.

DESCRIPTION
The site comprises of a *mane* wall, a *tsadkhang* and a *tarchen*. The *mane* wall is a linear dry stone masonry wall. Inscribed *mane* stones are placed on its horizontal surface. Near to the *mane* wall is a *tsadkhang* built in stone and mud brick masonry which is mud plastered and whitewashed externally. It has a small opening to the south and the *tsa-tsa* are placed inside this. The *tarchen* lies to the east of the *tsadkhang*.

STATE OF PRESERVATION
Advanced State of Decay

SOURCE OF INFORMATION Tsewang Dolma - Tokpo Khangbu, Ursi, Khaltse, Ladakh

Ursi

502

Mane Wall

INVENTORY NO.
KHALTSE / URSI / 02 / 2004

Mane Wall | In Use | Public (Community) | Around 200 years old

SETTING
The *mane* wall is oriented to the south and is built along the slope of a hill near the path leading to the village.

SIGNIFICANCE
The *mane* wall was built around 200 years ago as an act of merit and is still circumambulated by villagers, to accumulate merit, as they travel along the path leading to the village.

DESCRIPTION
The *mane* wall is a linear dry stone masonry wall. Inscribed *mane* stones are placed on the horizontal surface. There is a large carved stone placed vertically in the middle of the structure.

STATE OF PRESERVATION
Showing Signs of Deterioration

SOURCE OF INFORMATION Tsewang Dolma - Tokpo Khangbu, Ursi, Khaltse, Ladakh

Ursi Chomo *Lhato*

INVENTORY NO.
KHALTSE / URSI / 03 / 2004

Lhato | In Use | Public (Community) | Around 300 years old

SETTING
The *lhato* is oriented to the north and is built on a hill located in a valley on the farther side of the settlement.

SIGNIFICANCE
The *lhato* is dedicated to the protector deity of the village, Ursi Chomo and was built by the villagers around 300 years ago. The *lhato* protects both the villagers as well as cattle from attacks by wild animals, coming down from the hills into the nearby forest. The juniper plants, *khadag* etc. in the *lhato* are renewed every year amid rituals and prayers.

DESCRIPTION
The *lhato* is a cubical shaped structure built in stone masonry and is mud plastered and whitewashed on the exterior. It tapers towards the top to smaller square within which are placed the ritual offerings of animal horns, *khadag* and juniper plants.

STATE OF PRESERVATION
Advanced State of Decay

SOURCE OF INFORMATION Tundup Paljor, Ursi, Khaltse, Ladakh

Ursi

503

Group of *Chorten* (Bale *Chorten*)

INVENTORY NO.
KHALTSE / URSI / 04 / 2004

Chorten | In Use | Public (Community) | Around 250 years old

SETTING
The *chorten* are oriented to the east and are built on a cliff at the beginning of the village. The Bale Pa house lies to the west.

SIGNIFICANCE
The *chorten* are located at the beginning of the village and are circumambulated by villagers to accumulate merit as the travel to the village.

DESCRIPTION
The site consists of a group of three *chorten*. Two of these are built on a cliff while the third is built on a huge stone boulder, next to the Bale Pa house. The two *chorten* on the cliff have collapsed and are difficult to identify. The third *chorten* is a Changchub *chorten* and is built in stone and mud brick masonry and is mud plastered and whitewashed on the exterior.

STATE OF PRESERVATION
Danger of Disappearance

SOURCE OF INFORMATION Phuntsog Angmo - Gongmapa, Ursi, Khaltse, Ladakh

Lhaten *Chorten*

INVENTORY NO.
KHALTSE / URSI / 05 / 2004

Chorten | In Use | Public (Community) | Around 200 years old

SETTING
The *chorten* is oriented to the north and is built on a bare hill with agricultural fields to the north and the Ursi Chomo *lhato* to the west.

SIGNIFICANCE
The *chorten* was built around 200 years ago. The village monks perform prayers here every year to protect the villagers and their cattle from attacks by wild animals which come down from the mountains.

DESCRIPTION
The *chorten* is a Changchub *chorten* built on a large random rubble masonry platform. It is constructed in stone and mud brick masonry with mud mortar and is mud plastered and whitewashed externally.

STATE OF PRESERVATION
Advanced State of Decay

SOURCE OF INFORMATION Tsewang Dolma-Tokpo Khangbu, Ursi, Khaltse, Ladakh

Ursi

504

Chorten

INVENTORY NO.
KHALTSE / URSI / 06 / 2004

Chorten | In Use | Private (Individual) | Around 150 years old

SETTING
The *chorten* is oriented to the southwest and is located at the end of the village next to the village *gonpa*. There are village houses such as Bale Khangbu to the southeast and the Ursi *gonpa* lies to the northwest.

SIGNIFICANCE
The *chorten* was built by ancestors of the Bale Khangbu family around 150 years ago for the health and long life of children born in the family. It is a Changchub *chorten* and symbolizes the Buddha's enlightenment.

DESCRIPTION
The Changchub *chorten* stands on a random rubble masonry base. It is built in stone and mud brick masonry with mud mortar and is mud plastered and whitewashed on the exterior. There is a tall *chugsum khorlo* on the dome of the *chorten* symbolizing the 13 steps towards enlightenment.

STATE OF PRESERVATION
Showing Signs of Deterioration

SOURCE OF INFORMATION Tundup Namgyal-Baley Khaun, Ursi, Khaltse, Ladakh

Ursi *Gonpa*

INVENTORY NO.
KHALTSE / URSI / 07 / 2004

Gonpa | In Use | Public (Lamayuru *Gonpa*) | Around 100 years old

SETTING
The *gonpa* is oriented to the east and is built on the top of a hill towards the end of the settlement. It is surrounded by the Balepa house and a *chorten* to the northeast and a new school building to the west. There is a large open space to the east.

SIGNIFICANCE
The *gonpa* was built around 100 years ago and is a branch of the Lamayuru *gonpa* following the Drigung Kagyud sect. A monk from Lamayuru *gonpa* is deputed here to carry out prayers and rituals within the temple as well as in the village. Villagers gather here for prayers as it is the principal place of worship in the village.

DESCRIPTION
The *gonpa* is a single storeyed structure built in random rubble and mud brick masonry with a large forecourt. There is a small portico which leads into the main temple. There is a circumambulatory path around the *gonpa* and two circular and linear *mane* walls to the north. The roof of the structure is flat and comprises of timber beams, joists, dried grass, willow twigs and mud. It is supported by timber columns and beams. Externally, the structure is mud plastered and whitewashed. The temple was closed during the visit and it was not possible to examine the interior.

STATE OF PRESERVATION
Advanced State of Decay

SOURCE OF INFORMATION Tundup Namgyal-Baley Khaun, Ursi, Khaltse, Ladakh

Ursi

505

Lhato Gogpo

INVENTORY NO.
KHALTSE / URSI / 08 / 2004

Lhato | Abandoned | Public (Community) | Around 500 years old

SETTING
The *lhato* is oriented to the south and is built on a bare hill, north of the village. The remains of the old *gonpa* lie to the east.

SIGNIFICANCE
The old *lhato* is believed to have been built 500 years ago and is dedicated to the protector deity.

DESCRIPTION
The *lhato* is a small cubical structure built in stone and mud brick masonry. The external layer of mud plaster and whitewash have eroded and the structure is almost in ruins today. The juniper branches have not been renewed as the *lhato* is no longer used by the villagers.

STATE OF PRESERVATION
Danger of Disappearance

SOURCE OF INFORMATION Tundup Paljor – Tokpo Khaun, Ursi, Khaltse, Ladakh

Laguzur *Chorten*

INVENTORY NO.
KHALTSE / URSI / 09 / 2004

Chorten | In Use | Public (Community) | Around 200 years old

SETTING
The *chorten* are oriented to the east and are located at the base of the hill on which the lhato gogpo is built. The village lies to the west while the *lhato gogpo* lies to the northwest.

SIGNIFICANCE
The *chorten* were built around 200 years by the villagers to protect the village from floods.

DESCRIPTION
The site consists of a cluster of whitewashed *chorten* in different sizes. They are placed on a common platform and constructed in stone masonry with mud mortar. The *chorten* are mud plastered and whitewashed externally. Most of the *chorten* have eroded over time and lost their original form making them difficult to identify.

STATE OF PRESERVATION
Advanced State of Decay

SOURCE OF INFORMATION Phuntsog Angmo - Gongmapa, Ursi, Khaltse, Ladakh

Ursi

506

Gongmapa *Chorten*

INVENTORY NO.
KHALTSE / URSI / 10 / 2004

Chorten | In Use | Private (Individual) | Around 200 years old

SETTING
The *chorten* is oriented to the south and is located on the way down from the village *gonpa*. The *chorten* is surrounded by village houses on three sides and the pathway on the fourth.

SIGNIFICANCE
The *chorten* was built about 200 years ago by an ancestor of the Gongmapa family to ensure a good harvest for the family. The *chorten* are Changchub chorten, which symbolize the Buddha's enlightenment. The *tsadkhang* houses the *tsa-tsa*.

DESCRIPTION
The site consists of a group of two *chorten* with a *tsadkhang* in the centre. The *chorten* are placed on a random rubble masonry platform and are built in stone and mud brick masonry with an external layer of mud plaster and whitewash. The *chorten* have largely eroded and have lost their original form. One *chorten* has stucco relief motifs

(*pa-tra*) on the base panels. The *tsadkhang* is a cubical structure built in mud brick masonry and mud plastered and whitewashed externally. It has a traditional roof above and a opening to the south through which are placed the *tsa-tsa*.

STATE OF PRESERVATION
Advanced State of Decay

SOURCE OF INFORMATION Jigmet Dorjey - Gongmapa, Ursi, Khaltse, Ladakh

Zampe *Chorten*

INVENTORY NO.
KHALTSE / WANLA / 01 / 2004

Chorten / *Mane* Wall | In Use | Public (Community) | Around 250 years old

SETTING
The *chorten* are located at the junction where the link road leading to Shilla meets the Wanla village road.

SIGNIFICANCE
The *chorten* were built around 250 years ago and are among the oldest *chorten* in the village. The *chorten* and *mane* walls are built at the junction of the road leading from Shilla to Wanla and are circumambulated by villagers as an act of merit when travelling along this path. One of the *chorten* is a Changchub chorten symbolizing the Buddha's enlightenment while the second is a Lhabab *chorten* which symbolizes the Buddha's return from heaven at Vaishali.

DESCRIPTION
The site comprises of two *chorten* and two *mane* walls. The *mane* walls are linear stone masonry walls with *mane* stones placed on the horizontal surface. The Changchub *chorten* stands on a large square base and is built in mud

SOURCE OF INFORMATION Stanzin Dorjey, Wanla, Khaltse, Ladakh

brick and stone masonry. The Lhabab *chorten* is also built on a large square base in mud brick and stone masonry. Both *chorten* have been recently repaired by the community and have been cement plastered and whitewashed on the exterior. There are tall *chugsum khorlo*, symbolizing the 13 steps towards enlightenment, on the domes of both *chorten*.

STATE OF PRESERVATION
Showing Signs of Deterioration

Wanla

507

Goa-Chumik Ge *Chorten*

INVENTORY NO.
KHALTSE / WANLA / 02 / 2004

Chorten | In Use | Public (Community) | Around 200 years old

SETTING
The *chorten* are built on top of a hill near the junction where the link road from Shilla meets the Wanla village road. There are some trees near the *chorten* and the Zampe *chorten* lies across the road.

SIGNIFICANCE
The *chorten* are believed to have been built around 200 years ago as an act of merit. Both are Changchub *chorten* and symbolize the Buddha's enlightenment. The *chorten* are circumambulated by villagers as they travel along this route.

DESCRIPTION
There are two *chorten* on the site both of which are Changchub *chorten* built on a common random rubble masonry base. The *chorten* are built in stone and mud brick

masonry and are mud plastered and whitewashed on the exterior.

STATE OF PRESERVATION
Showing Signs of Deterioration

SOURCE OF INFORMATION Stanzin Dorjey, Wanla, Khaltse, Ladakh

Mane Ringmo

INVENTORY NO.
KHALTSE / WANLA / 03 / 2004

Mane Wall | In Use | Public (Community) | Around 250 years old

STATE OF PRESERVATION
Showing Signs of Deterioration

SETTING
The *mane* wall is oriented to the southeast and is built along the edge of the road leading to the village. The village road runs to the north of the site while the site lies southwest to the Yurkhangpa house.

SIGNIFICANCE
The *mane* wall was built around 150 years ago along the road leading to the village. It is circumambulated by villagers to accumulate merit as they travel along this road.

DESCRIPTION
The *mane* wall is a long dry stone masonry wall with *mane* stones placed on the horizontal surface.

SOURCE OF INFORMATION Stanzin Dorjey, Wanla, Khaltse, Ladakh

Rigsum Gonbo

INVENTORY NO.
KHALTSE / WANLA / 04 / 2004

Rigsum Gonbo | In Use | Private (Individual) | Around 150 years old

STATE OF PRESERVATION
Showing Signs of Deterioration

SETTING
The *rigsum gonbo* is located near the agricultural fields owned by the Yurkhangpa family. It lies south of the road leading to the settlement.

SIGNIFICANCE
The *rigsum gonbo* was constructed around 150 years ago by ancestors of the Yurkhangpa family to protect their crops from natural calamities and disease. There is a small square shaped *spurkhang* south of the *rigsum gonbo* which is used by the family for cremation.

DESCRIPTION
The site comprises of three *chorten* built on a common random rubble masonry base. The *chorten* are all Changchub *chorten* and are built in stone and mud brick masonry. The exterior surfaces of the *chorten* are mud plastered and whitewashed. The *spurkhang* is built in mud brick masonry and is mud plastered and whitewashed on the exterior.

SOURCE OF INFORMATION Stanzin Dorjey -Yurkhangpa, Wanla, Khaltse, Ladakh

Mane Wall

INVENTORY NO.
KHALTSE / WANLA / 05 / 2004

Mane Wall | In Use | Public (Community)

SETTING
The *mane* wall is built on the right side of the road after crossing the main village. The road leading to the settlement is to its north and there are agricultural fields to the south. There is group of *chorten* to the west of the site.

SIGNIFICANCE
The *mane* wall lies along the road leading to the village and is circumambulated by villagers to accumulate merit. There was an older *mane* wall further down the road and at the time of constructing this *mane*, *mane* stones from the older *mane* were removed and placed here.

DESCRIPTION
The *mane* wall is a long dry stone masonry wall. It has inscribed *mane* stones placed on the horizontal surface.

STATE OF PRESERVATION
Showing Signs of Deterioration

SOURCE OF INFORMATION Stanzin Dorjey, Wanla, Khaltse, Ladakh

Sharchog *Lhato*

INVENTORY NO.
KHALTSE / WANLA / 06 / 2004

Lhato | In Use | Public (Community)

SETTING
The *lhato* are oriented to the southwest and are built on a hill, left side of the village road and beyond the village. The site is surrounded by the river and the road on the southwest.

SIGNIFICANCE
The main *lhato* is dedicated to the deity 'Sharchog'. The ritual offering of juniper twigs, *khadag* etc. are renewed every year amid prayers and rituals when the protection of the deity is sought.

DESCRIPTION
The site consists of a group of four *lhato*, the main being the Sharchog *lhato*. They are cubical structures made of stone masonry which are mud plastered and whitewashed on the exterior. Ritual offerings of juniper branches and *khadag* are placed on the top of the *lhato*.

STATE OF PRESERVATION
Advanced State of Decay

SOURCE OF INFORMATION Sonam Tundup, Wanla, Khaltse, Ladakh

Group of *Chorten*

INVENTORY NO.
KHALTSE / WANLA / 07 / 2004

Chorten | In Use | Public (Community) | Around 400 years old

SETTING
The group of *chorten* is oriented to the south and is located along the village road on a gravel path leading to the village *gonpa*.

SIGNIFICANCE
The *chorten* are believed to have been built around the same time as the Wanla palace, around 400 years ago. Located along the path leading to the *gonpa*, the *chorten* are circumambulated by villagers to accumulate merit as they travel along this path. The *chorten* are all Changchub chorten and symbolize the Buddha's enlightenment.

DESCRIPTION
The site comprises of a group of around fifty eight *chorten* built at intervals in a line along the pathway leading towards the village *gonpa*. The *chorten* are in different sizes. They are built in stone and mud brick masonry with mud

mortar and are mud plastered and whitewashed on the exterior. Many of them have stucco relief motifs (*pa-tra*) on the base panels which are highlighted in red colour.

STATE OF PRESERVATION
Advanced State of Decay

SOURCE OF INFORMATION Stanzin Dorjey-Yurkhangpa, Wanla , Khaltse, Ladakh

Yograpa House

INVENTORY NO.
KHALTSE / WANLA / 08 / 2004

Vernacular Building | Abandoned | Private (Individual) | Around 200 years old

SETTING
The house is oriented to the south and built on an elevated area above the main village settlement. A zigzag path leads up the house. It is located south of the Wanla *gonpa* and above the village settlement.

SIGNIFICANCE
The Yograpa house is one of the oldest houses in the village built by an ancestor of the Yograpa family. The family has moved out of this house into a new house in the village and it currently lies abandoned. The house is built in the traditional style and contributes to the vernacular architecture of the village.

DESCRIPTION
The Yogra pa house is a double storeyed building, built along the slope of a hill. The ground floor is built in random rubble masonry and has no window openings. The first floor is built in mud brick masonry with mud mortar and has

small windows facing south. The structure is covered with a flat traditional roof made of timber beams, joists, *taalu*, *yagzes* and compacted mud and has prayer flags posted at the corners.

STATE OF PRESERVATION
Showing Signs of Deterioration

SOURCE OF INFORMATION Tashi Rabgyas-Chubipa, Wanla, Khaltse, Ladakh

Nyenas *Khang*

INVENTORY NO.
KHALTSE / WANLA / 09 / 2004

Temple | In Use | Public (Community) | Around 250 years old

SETTING
The Nyenas *Khang* is oriented to the south and is built along the slope of a hill on which the gonpa and the Castle are also located. The Yograpa house lies to the south east.

SIGNIFICANCE
The Nyenas *Khang* is one of the oldest temples in the village and is used by the community on the occasion of Nyenas i.e. fasting during the first month of Tibetan calendar.

DESCRIPTION
The Nyenas *Khang* is a small square building which is single storeyed in height. The entrance to the building is from the south which leads directly into the main meditation hall. Two small windows on the southern facade provide light and ventilation into the hall. It is built in random rubble masonry and has traces of the external mud plaster and whitewash. The building has a traditional roof above.

SOURCE OF INFORMATION Tashi Rabgyas-Chubipa, Wanla, Khaltse, Ladakh

STATE OF PRESERVATION
Showing Signs of Deterioration

Wanla

511

Zalkin House

INVENTORY NO.
KHALTSE / WANLA / 10 / 2004

Vernacular Building | In Use | Private (Individual) | Around 120 years old

SETTING
The Zalkin house is oriented to the south and is located left of the road leading to the village. The road runs to the south and there are other village houses to the north and northeast.

SIGNIFICANCE
The house was built by the grandparents of the present owners about 120 years ago and successive generations have continued to reside here. The house is built in the traditional style and is a good example of vernacular architecture in the village.

DESCRIPTION
The Zalkin house is a double storeyed building with the ground floor built in random rubble masonry and the upper floors in mud brick masonry with mud mortar. The ground floor has small window openings while the first floor has larger windows with segmental arches and tiered wooden lintels. The upper floor is flanked by a terrace in the centre of the structure. Fodder is stored on the ground floor while the first floor houses the family's living quarters. The house has a flat traditional roof made of timber beams, joists, *taalu*, grass and compacted mud which is supported on timber beams and columns with brackets.

STATE OF PRESERVATION
Fair

SOURCE OF INFORMATION Sonam Tundup, Wanla, Khaltse, Ladakh

Kagan *Chorten*

INVENTORY NO.
KHALTSE / WANLA / 11 / 2004

Chorten / Rock Inscription | In Use | Public (Community) | Around 200 years old

SETTING

The Kagan *chorten* lies in the middle of the village east of the Khangsar house and southwest of Lamyodpa house.

SIGNIFICANCE

The Kagan *chorten* was built around 200 years ago. It is a gateway *chorten* and merit is accrued to believers who pass through the passage of the *chorten* and circumambulate it.

DESCRIPTION

The Kagan *chorten* has two thick parallel walls made in random rubble and mud brick masonry supporting a Changchub *chorten* on the top. The wooden ceiling over the passage is in the shape of a *mandala*. The ceiling and the wall panels inside the *chorten* are painted with images of Buddhas and Bodhisattvas. The paintings on the ceiling have been done on canvas which has then been pasted onto the wooden base. The Changchub *chorten* on top has been recently plastered and whitewashed. The dome of the *chorten* has a tall *chugsum khorlo* with a crescent shaped crown on the top. At the entrance of the *chorten*, there are a few rock inscriptions and carvings.

STATE OF PRESERVATION

Fair

Wanla

512

Khangsar House

INVENTORY NO.
KHALTSE / WANLA / 12 / 2004

Vernacular Building | In Use | Private (Individual) | Around 150 years old

SETTING
The Khangsar house is oriented to the south and is located on the left side of the road leading to the village. The house is surrounded by other village houses and a Kagan *chorten* lies to the east.

SIGNIFICANCE
The Khangsar house was built by the grandparents of the present owner about 150 years ago and the family continues to reside in the house. It is built in the traditional style and is a good example of vernacular architecture in the village.

DESCRIPTION
The Khangsar house is a double storeyed building with an entrance from the east. The ground floor is built in random rubble masonry while the first floor is in mud brick masonry. The window openings on both floors are large with tiered wooden lintels. The first floor has a large glazed corner window on the southwestern side. The ground floor has a traditional mud floor while the first floor has a timber floor. The house has a traditional roof made of timber beams, joists, *taalu*, grass and compacted mud. The parapet of the roof is painted in black and the windows are also bordered in black. There are prayer flags posted at the corners of the roof.

STATE OF PRESERVATION
Fair

SOURCE OF INFORMATION Mingyur Chospel - Khangsar, Wanla, Khaltse, Ladakh

Lamyodpa House

INVENTORY NO.
KHALTSE / WANLA / 13 / 2004

Vernacular Building | In Use | Private (Individual) | Around 120 years old

SETTING
The house is located to the left of the vehicular road leading to the village. It is surrounded by other village houses and a shop to the south. There is a Kagan *chorten* to the west.

SIGNIFICANCE
The house was constructed around 120 years ago by ancestors of the Lamyodpa family and the family continues to reside here. It is built in the traditional style and is a good example of vernacular architecture in the village. There is a *rigsum gonbo*, above the entrance door built to protect the family from evil forces.

DESCRIPTION
The Lamyodpa house is a double storeyed building and is accessed through an exterior flight of steps. The ground floor is built in random rubble masonry while the first floor is built in mud brick masonry. Externally, the house is mud plastered and whitewashed. There is a *rigsum gonbo* above the entrance door. The house has large window openings with decorated tiered lintels. There is a terrace in the middle of the first floor. The flooring is in timber on all the floors. The house has a flat traditional roof made of timber beams, joists, *taalu*, grass and compacted mud. A low height parapet borders the terrace and is painted in black. There are prayer flags posted at the corners of the roof.

STATE OF PRESERVATION
Fair

SOURCE OF INFORMATION Tsewang Namgyal - Lamyodpa, Wanla, Khaltse, Ladakh

Wanla

513

Chug-Shig-Zhal
Gonpa

INVENTORY NO.
KHALTSE / WANLA / 14 / 2004

Temple | In Use | Public (Lamayuru *Gonpa*) | Late 13th - Early 14th century

SETTING

The *gonpa* is oriented to the north and is located on a mountain cliff near the Wanla palace. It lies to the east of the palace and is accessed through a zigzag path.

SIGNIFICANCE

According to an inscription, the Chug-shig-zhal *gonpa* was built in the castle founded by the Ladakhi king Lhachen-Naglug. The temple itself was erected by Bhag-dar-skyab, the eldest son of a minister in an unnamed government. The wall paintings inside the temple derive from a local and Central Tibetan derived style which is distinct from earlier temples of the 12th century such as those at Alchi, Mangyu and Sumda Chun. Today, the temple is today under the purview of the Lamayuru *gonpa*. It is one of the principal places of worship in the village. Monks from Lamayuru are deputed here to carry out prayers and rituals for the village.

DESCRIPTION

The temple is a small square structure with a simple but interesting exterior painted in red and white. The roof of the temple is staggered over three levels stepping up towards a central clerestory space. The roof is a traditional one with a wooden ceiling which still has traces of fabric painting intact. There is a small courtyard in front of the temple in which rests a rectangular structure with a galvanized iron sheet roof used for burning butter lamps. The front facade of the temple is elaborate with decorative carved wooden columns and beams flanked with lion shaped brackets. A small low height wooden doorway leads into the temple through a porch with three niches on the north, east and west walls housing colossal images of Chanrazig, Buddha and Chamba. The central image is that of an eleven headed and eight armed Chanrazig. Above the first floor roof, there is a kind of gallery which houses a number of small stucco images of Bodhisattvas flanked by two large wooden decorated columns and bracket. The walls are embellished with wall paintings depicting *mandalas* and images of a thousand miniature Buddhas. All around the structure, there are a group of small prayer wheels embedded in the exterior walls.

STATE OF PRESERVATION
Advanced State of Decay

SOURCE OF INFORMATION Stanzin Dorjey-Yurkhangpa, Wanla, Khaltse, Ladakh; and, 'Buddhist Sculpture in Clay – Early Western Himalayan Art, Late 10th to Early 13th Centuries' by Christian Luczanits

Rabo *Chorten*

INVENTORY NO.
KHALTSE / WANLA / 15 / 2004

Chorten | In Use | Public (Community) | Around 250 years old

SETTING
The *chorten* are oriented to the northeast and are located below the *gonpa*. The *gonpa* lies to the southwest and there is a Kagan *chorten* to the east.

SIGNIFICANCE
The *chorten* and *mane* wall were built around 250 years ago. They lie en route to the *gonpa* and are circumambulated by villagers to accumulate merit. The *chorten* are Changchub *chorten* and symbolize the Buddha's enlightenment.

DESCRIPTION
The site comprises of a cluster of six *chorten* and a *mane* wall. The *chorten* are placed in two rows. They are built in stone and mud brick masonry with mud mortar and are mud plastered and whitewashed on the exterior. However, most of the *chorten* have eroded over time and have lost their original form. The *mane* wall is a rectangular shaped dry stone masonry wall with inscribed *mane* stones placed

SOURCE OF INFORMATION Caretaker Monk, Wanla Gompa, Wanla, Khaltse, Ladakh

on the horizontal surface. There is a tall *tarchen* posted near the *mane* wall.

STATE OF PRESERVATION
Danger of Disappearance

Kagan *Chorten*

INVENTORY NO.
KHALTSE / WANLA / 16 / 2004

Chorten | In Use | Public (Community)

SETTING
The *chorten* are located on the foothills of the hill over which are built the *gonpa* and the fort. The site is surrounded by the Rabo *chorten* to the northwest and the *gonpa* to the southwest. The river flows to the north of the site.

SIGNIFICANCE
The *chorten* circumambulated by villagers to accumulate merit. The Kagan *chorten* is a gateway chorten and merit is believed to accrue to believers who pass through the passage of the *chorten*. The *chorten* are all Changchub *chorten* and symbolize the Buddha's enlightenment.

DESCRIPTION
The site consists of a group of four Changchub *chorten*, a Kagan *chorten* and a *tarchen*. The *chorten* are built in stone and mud brick masonry and are mud plastered and whitewashed externally. The Kagan *chorten* has thick parallel walls built in stone and mud brick masonry over

SOURCE OF INFORMATION Migyur Chosphel-Khangsar, Wanla village, Khaltse Ladakh

Photograph Not Available

which rests a large Changchub *chorten*. The wooden ceiling over the passage is in the shape of a *mandala*. The ceiling and the wall panels inside the *chorten* are painted with images of various Bodhisattvas. The Changchub *chorten* on top has a square base with square tiers tapering to towards the cylindrical dome above. The dome is surmounted by a linear tall structure with bands painted in red. It also has a crescent shaped crown on top.

STATE OF PRESERVATION
Showing Sign of Deterioration

Phishun House

INVENTORY NO.
KHALTSE / WANLA / 17 / 2004

Vernacular Building | In Use | Private (Individual)

SETTING

The Phishun house is oriented to the south west and is built on a hill behind the new *gonpa*. The house is surrounded by other village houses to the northeast and northwest and a group of chorten to the southwest. There is a large tree to the south of the house.

SIGNIFICANCE

The house was built by ancestors of the Phishun family who continue to reside here. It is built in the traditional style and is a good example of vernacular architecture in the village.

DESCRIPTION

The Phishun house is a large double storeyed building. The ground floor is constructed in random rubble masonry while the first floor is built in mud brick masonry with mud mortar. The ground floor has no openings and is used primarily for storage. The first floor houses the family's living quarters and has windows which are bordered in black. There is a large *rabsal* on the first floor. The house has a flat traditional roof made of timber beams, joists, *taalu*, grass and compacted mud. There is a small *lhato* on the roof of the house dedicated to the family's protector deity.

STATE OF PRESERVATION
Advanced State of Decay

Wanla

516

Wanla Castle

INVENTORY NO.
KHALTSE / WANLA / 18 / 2004

Fort / Palace | Abandoned | Public (State / Community) | 12th century

SETTING
The castle is oriented to the south and is located on top of a hill facing the village. It lies to the west of the Chug-shig-zhal temple facing the village settlement.

SIGNIFICANCE
According to an inscription, the castle was founded by the King Lhachen Ngaglug in a tiger year in the 12th century. The castle lies largely in ruins but for some towers and remains of rammed earth walls. The castle lies abandoned today but for a *lhato* built near the palace which is still in use. The *lhato* is dedicated to the protector deity Tseb Lhamo and its contents are renewed every year with prayers and rituals on the 12th month of Tibetan calendar.

DESCRIPTION
The castle is largely in ruins except for some watch towers built on a square plan which rise up to a considerable height towering over the *gonpa* and the monk cells. It is located on top of a hill. Most of the structure has collapsed except for two walls on either side. The first tower has a *lhato* on top of it. There is a wooden frame around the top of the tower. The other tower is to the east of the *gonpa*. This structure has some portion of its roof still intact over the three walls. The walls are a meter thick and built in rammed earth.

STATE OF PRESERVATION
Danger of Disappearance

Wanla

517

SOURCE OF INFORMATION Mingyur Chospel-Khangsar, Wanla, Khaltse, Ladakh

Dzong Phug *Gonpa*

INVENTORY NO.
KHALTSE / WANLA / 19 / 2004

Gonpa | In Use | Public (Lamayuru *Gonpa*) | Around 350 years old

SETTING
The *gonpa* is located on top of a hill, facing the valley and settlement below. It is accessed via a zigzag pathway which leads from the village to the *gonpa*.

SIGNIFICANCE
The *gonpa* is believed to have been constructed 350 years ago and falls under the purview of Lamayuru *gonpa*. A monk from the *gonpa* is deputed here to carry out prayers and rituals within the temple.

DESCRIPTION
The *gonpa* is built along the slope of a hill and is a single storeyed building built on a rectangular plan. There is a small courtyard in front with a large *tarchen* posted at the centre. From the courtyard, steps lead onto the porch of the main temple. The porch has a traditional roof supported on four wooden columns. There is a small chorten to the left of the porch. From the porch, a wooden doorway leads into the small room that housing an image of Tundup Chorgyal and smaller images of other Bodhisattvas. Volumes of the Kangyur are placed on the shelves. Timber columns support the traditional roof above. The *gonpa* is built in stone and mud brick masonry and is mud plastered and whitewashed on the exterior.

STATE OF PRESERVATION
Showing Signs of Deterioration

SOURCE OF INFORMATION Stanzin Dorjey-Yurkhangpa, Wanla, Khaltse, Ladakh

Yurkhangpa *Mane*

INVENTORY NO.
KHALTSE / WANLA / 20 / 2004

Mane Wall | In Use | Private (Individual) | Around 200 years old

SETTING
The *mane* walls are built near the Yurkhangpa house. It lies southeast of the Yurkhangpa house.

SIGNIFICANCE
The *mane* walls were built around 200 years ago by ancestors of the Yurkhangpa family as an act of merit. They are circumambulated by family members to accumulate merit.

DESCRIPTION
The site consists of a long *mane* wall with two circular *mane* walls at either ends. The mane walls are of different heights and are built in dry stone masonry with inscribed *mane* stones placed on the horizontal surface.

STATE OF PRESERVATION
Showing Signs of Deterioration

SOURCE OF INFORMATION Stanzin Dorjey, Wanla, Khaltse, Ladakh

Yangthang

The village of Yangthang is situated at a distance of about 25 kms from the diversion near Likir. According to legend, at the beginning no one lived here as there was no water for cultivation or to drink. Three brothers from Basgo came here for the first time and they began to live here. As there was an acute shortage of water, many lamas were invited to bless the land for more water. The name Yangthang derives from the words Yang meaning '*again*' and thang meaning '*plains*' or '*another stretch of plains*'. The old house of one of the three brothers can still be seen today. One of the houses was that of Skildong pa. Today, there are around 30 houses in this village.

Listed by: Deldan Angmo and Jassu Singh
Year: 2004

Yulchung

Yulchung lies about an 8-hour trek from Photoksar after crossing the Singhela. From the Leh - Srinagar highway a road diverts between Khaltse and Lamayuru, towards Shilla. Phanjilla lies at the end of this road from where a trekking route starts which leads via Shishila, Hanupatta and Photoksar to Yulchung. The name Yulchung means '*small village*'. There are 13 households in the village.

Listed by: Deldan Angmo and Jassu Singh
Year: 2004

Yangthang
Lagchung

INVENTORY NO.
KHALTSE / YANGTHANG / 01 / 2004

Gonpa | In Use | Public (Ridzong *Gonpa*) | Around 300 - 350 years old

STATE OF PRESERVATION
Advance State of Decay

SETTING
The *lagchung* is oriented to the west and is located in the middle of the village, surrounded by residential buildings. To the west is a *labrang* and there is a *tarchen* to the north.

SIGNIFICANCE
It is believed that the *lagchung* was built by the lama Tsultim Nyima, the founder of Ridzong *gonpa*, who first settled in this village. Unlike other villages, none of the houses have a family temple within the house. Instead, all families perform their prayers in the *lagchung* and therefore, have just one temple amongst themselves. The temple falls under the purview of the Ridzong *gonpa* and a monk is deputed from Ridzong *gonpa* to perform prayers and rituals inside the temple. According to legend, a previous incarnation of the Ven Sras Rinpoche's mother was from this village and on her death miniature sculptures were made of her ashes and pinned inside the temple. A reincarnation of the Ven Sras Rinpoche is believed to have been a great scholar and artist and he painted the temple using organic colours extracted from flowers.

DESCRIPTION
The *lagchung* is a double storeyed building which is entered through a courtyard. From the courtyard, a small wooden door leads into the *lagchung*. It has a small porch in the front. The *lagchung* itself is a square chamber with six decorated wooden columns supporting timber beams which in turn support the traditional roof above. The first four columns support the skylight above, which has walls on three sides and a glass opening on the front side. The panels of the skylight are covered with paintings and the lower portion has small miniature sculptures pinned against the walls. The temple houses an elaborate image of Chug-Shig-Zhal as well as a Changchub *chorten*, the Buddhist canons - Kangyur, Bum and a large number of *thangka* hung from the walls and ceiling. The temple has wooden flooring while the outer court has mud flooring. To the right of the court is a flight of stairs that leads to the roof of the temple. The parapet is bordered in red color and prayer flags are posted at every corner.

SOURCE OF INFORMATION Tsering Padma Skildongpa (Panch), Yangthang, Khaltse, Ladakh

Labrang

INVENTORY NO.
KHALTSE / YANGTHANG / 02 / 2004

Vernacular Building | In Use | Public (Ridzing *Gonpa*) | Around 200 years old

SETTING
The *labrang* is oriented to the south east and is located in the *gonpa* square and is surrounded by other village houses such as the Skildongpa to the northeast and Korponpa to the southeast. The Yangthang *lagchung* lies to the east.

SIGNIFICANCE
The building is built in the traditional style and is a good example of vernacular architecture in the village. The *labrang* was originally built to serve as the residence for monks deputed by the *gonpa* to the village to administer the lands owned by the *gonpa* in the village. Grain would be collected and distributed to farmers who had leased lands from the gonpa.

DESCRIPTION
The *labrang* is a triple storeyed building with an entrance from the south eastern facade which leads onto the first floor. The ground floor is constructed in random rubble masonry while the upper floors are built in mud brick

masonry. The ground floor has very small window openings for ventilation and light and is used primarily for storage. The first and second floors have larger window openings with timber frames and tiered lintels. There is a large timber framed *rabsal* on the second floor facing the southeast. These two levels comprise the living areas. There is an open to sky courtyard on the top floor, in the centre of the building. The house has a traditional timber roof made of timber beams, joists, *taalu*, grass and compacted mud which is supported on timber columns and brackets below. The roof has a low mud parapet all around. The exterior walls are mud plastered and whitewashed.

STATE OF PRESERVATION
Showing Signs of Deterioration

SOURCE OF INFORMATION Tsering Padma, Yangthang, Khaltse, Ladakh

Skildongpa House

INVENTORY NO.
KHALTSE / YANGTHANG / 03 / 2004

Vernacular Building | Abandoned | Private (Individual) | Around 250 - 300 years old

SETTING
The Skildongpa house is oriented to the south and is located south of the *lagchung* with the Tongsponpa house towards the west.

SIGNIFICANCE
The house belongs to the Skildongpa family who were one of the earliest settlers in the village. It was built around 250 - 300 years ago by an ancestor of the Skildongpa family in the traditional style and contributes to the vernacular architecture of the village. The family has moved out of this house into a new house in the village and the building currently lies abandoned.

DESCRIPTION
The Skildongpa house is a double storeyed building built on an L-shaped plan. The entrance is from a courtyard. The ground floor is built in random rubble masonry while the first floor is in mud brick masonry with mud mortar. The ground floor was used for housing animals and the facade is

free of any openings. The first floor housed the family's living area. It has a large verandah in front of the court. The verandah has a thin roof projection supported on timber columns and beams. It is an interesting feature of the house and was possibly the most commonly used space. The house has a traditional roof made of timber beams, joists, *taalu*, grass and compacted mud supported on timber columns below. The external walls are mud plastered and whitewashed.

STATE OF PRESERVATION
Showing Signs of Deterioration

SOURCE OF INFORMATION Tsering Padma Skildongpa, Yangthang, Khaltse, Ladakh

Korponpa House

INVENTORY NO.
KHALTSE / YANGTHANG / 04 / 2004

Vernacular Building | In Use | Private (Individual) | Around 200 years old

SETTING

The Korponpa house is oriented to the north east and is located in the middle of the village. A path from the road leads to the *lagchung* and the Korpanpa house. The house is surrounded by other residential buildings such as the *labrang* to the northwest, Skildongpa house is to the north and the Yangthang *lagchung* to the northeast. The Markhang house lies to the southeast of the site.

SIGNIFICANCE

The Korponpa house was built around 200 years ago by an ancestor of the Korponpa family and successive generations have continued to reside in the house. It is built in the traditional style and contributes, along with the other village houses, to the overall vernacular architecture of the village.

DESCRIPTION

The house is a double storeyed building built on a rectangular plan. The entrance is from the northwest

facade directly from the street. The ground floor is constructed in random rubble masonry and the first floor is built in mud brick masonry with mud mortar. The house has small rectangular timber framed window openings. The exterior walls of the house are mud plastered and whitewashed. The roof is a traditional one made of timber beams, joists, *taalu*, grass and a layer of compacted mud supported on timber columns and brackets below.

STATE OF PRESERVATION
Showing Signs of Deterioration

SOURCE OF INFORMATION Tsering Padma, Yangthang, Khaltse, Ladakh

Yangthang

524

Rigsum Gonbo

INVENTORY NO.
KHALTSE / YANGTHANG / 05 / 2004

Rigsum Gonbo | In Use | Public (Community) | Around 200 years old

SETTING

The *rigsum gonbo* is oriented to the north and is located along the path from the *lagchung* to the fields. It is surrounded by fields to the northeast and village houses to the southeast and southwest. The path runs along the north of the site.

SIGNIFICANCE

The *rigsum gonbo* was built about 200 years ago to protect the village from natural calamities and other disasters.

DESCRIPTION

The *rigsum gonbo* consists of three Changchub *chorten* built on a high platform within an enclosure which is open to the front and rear. The walls of the enclosure are built in stone and mud brick masonry and have been recently plastered and whitewashed. The roof is a traditional one made of timber beams, joists, *taalu*, grass and compacted mud. The *chorten* within are painted in the traditional colours of ochre, white and blue representing Jamyang,

Chanrazig and Chagdor respectively. Each of the *chorten* has a small niche enclosed within a glass and metal frame within which are images of the deities. There are *chugsum khorlo* on the domes of the *chorten* symbolizing the 13 steps towards enlightenment.

STATE OF PRESERVATION
Showing Signs of Deterioration

SOURCE OF INFORMATION Tsering Padma, Yangthang, Khaltse, Ladakh

Larjepa House

INVENTORY NO.
KHALTSE / YANGTHANG / 06 / 2004

Vernacular Building | In Use | Private (Individual) | Around 150 years old

SETTING
The Larjepa house is oriented to the north and is located along the path which leads from the Lagchung to the fields. The house is surrounded by fields to the north, a *rigsum gonbo* to the northeast and the Korpanpa house to the east.

SIGNIFICANCE
The Larjepa house was built by an ancestor of the Larjepa family around 150 years ago and the family continues to reside here. It is built in the traditional style and is a good example of vernacular architecture in the village.

DESCRIPTION
The Larjepa house is a double storeyed structure with an entrance from the ground floor. The ground floor is built in random rubble masonry while the first floor is constructed in mud brick masonry with mud mortar. There is a huge open to sky courtyard on the ground floor and all the rooms look out into the courtyard. The house has a traditional roof with timber beams, joists, *taalu*, grass and a layer of

compacted mud. The window openings are timber framed and tiered lintels and timber shutters. The exterior walls are mud plastered and whitewashed.

STATE OF PRESERVATION
Showing Signs of Deterioration

SOURCE OF INFORMATION Tsering Padma, Yangthang, Khaltse, Ladakh

Yangthang

525

Lubang (Pharkape) and *Tsadkhang*

INVENTORY NO.
KHALTSE / YANGTHANG / 07 / 2004

Lubang / Tsadkhang | In Use | Private (Individual)

SETTING
The *lubang* and *tsadkhang* are oriented to the east and are located at the beginning of the village over a small rocky mound, west of the Pharkape new house.

SIGNIFICANCE
The *lubang* marks the residence of the *lu*. Prayers are offered here in the spring at the time of the *Lu Thebs*. The *tsadkhang* contains ritual offerings of the *tsa-tsa*.

DESCRIPTION
The *lubang* is a small cubical shaped structure built in stone and mud brick masonry. The top is covered by a mud roof. The exterior is mud plastered and the whitewashed. The *tsadkhang* is also a cubical shaped structure which is larger than the *lubang*. It has a small opening on one side and houses a number of *tsa-tsa* within. It is built in stone

and mud brick masonry and is mud plastered and whitewashed on the exterior. It has a traditional roof above.

STATE OF PRESERVATION
Showing Signs of Deterioration

SOURCE OF INFORMATION Tsering Padma Shildongpa (Sarpanch), Yangthang, Khaltse, Ladakh

Tsadkhang

INVENTORY NO.
KHALTSE / YANGTHANG / 08 / 2004

Tsadkhang | In Use | Public (Community) | Around 250 years old

SETTING
The *tsadkhang* is located on the top of a hill to the left of the village road.

SIGNIFICANCE
The *tsadkhang* is believed to have been built around 250 years ago to house *tsa-tsa*.

DESCRIPTION
The *tsadkhang* is a tall structure built on a square plan. It has a small opening on one side through which numerous *tsa-tsa* are placed inside. The *tsadkhang* is built in stone and mud brick masonry and is mud plastered externally. It has a traditional roof above.

STATE OF PRESERVATION
Showing Signs of Deterioration

SOURCE OF INFORMATION Tsering Padma, Yangthang, Khaltse, Ladakh

Yangthang

526

Yultsa *Lhato* (Tashi Stanskyong)

INVENTORY NO.
KHALTSE / YANGTHANG / 09 / 2004

Lhato | In Use | Public (Community) | Around 300 years old

SETTING
The *lhato* is oriented to the south and is located north of the road leading to Hemis Shukpachan. A small *choskhor mane* is located below the *lhato*.

SIGNIFICANCE
The *lhato* is dedicated to the guardian deity of the village, Tashi Stanskyong, who came from Tibet centuries ago when the village was first settled. Images of the deity can also be seen on the walls of the *lagchung*. The deity is believed to protect the village and the contents of the *lhato* are renewed every year amid prayers and rituals.

DESCRIPTION
The *lhato* is a small structure built on a square plan on top of a hill facing the village. It is built in stone and mud brick masonry and is mud plastered and whitewashed externally. It has red markings on the exterior symbolizing the deity.

Ritual offerings of juniper branches, animal horns and *khadag* are placed on the top of the *lhato*. There is a small whitewashed *choskhor* below the *lhato* which is rotated with the water that flows down from the mountains.

STATE OF PRESERVATION
Showing Signs of Deterioration

SOURCE OF INFORMATION Tsering Padma Skildongpa, Yangthang, Khaltse, Ladakh

Chorten and *Mane* Wall

INVENTORY NO.
KHALTSE / YANGTHANG / 10 / 2004

Chorten / Mane Wall | In Use | Public (Ridzong *Gonpa*)

SETTING
The *chorten* and *mane* wall are oriented to the northeast and are located along the main road after crossing the village. The site is surrounded by fields to the south and southeast and mountains to the north. The vehicular road lies to the north.

SIGNIFICANCE
The *chorten* and *mane* wall lie along the road leading from the village and are circumambulated by villagers, as they travel along this route, to accumulate merit. The *chorten* is a Changchub *chorten*, one of the eight traditional forms of *chorten* in Tibetan Buddhism, symbolizing the Buddha's enlightenment. The *tsadkhang* was built in the past to house ritual offerings of *tsa-tsa*.

DESCRIPTION
The site comprises a *mane* wall, a Changchub *chorten* and a *tsadkhang*. The *mane* wall is a long wall and has a linear dry stone masonry base. Inscribed *mane* stones are placed on the horizontal surface. To the northeast of the *mane* wall there is a large *chorten* built over a square base. The *chorten* has been cement plastered and whitewashed recently. The base panels of the *chorten* are embellished with painted relief motifs (*pa-tra*). The dome of the *chorten* has a tall *chugsum khorlo* symbolizing the 13 steps towards enlightenment. To the northeast is a small *tsadkhang* which is a cubical structure built over a square base. It has an opening on one side and there are *tsa-tsa* placed inside. The *tsadkhang* has also been recently repaired and has been cement plastered and whitewashed.

STATE OF PRESERVATION
Advanced State of Decay

Yangthang

527

Khagsta *Chorten*

INVENTORY NO.
KHALTSE / YULCHUNG / 01 / 2004

Chorten | In Use | Public (Community) | Around 200 years old

SETTING
The Khagsta *chorten* is oriented to the south and is built on a small hill. A footpath leads to the site and it is surrounded by the Yulpapa house to the west and *chorten* Chenmo and a *mane* wall to the north.

SIGNIFICANCE
The *chorten* was built by an ancestor of the Yulpapa family, as an act of merit, on the land on which their old house formerly stood. The ruins of the house can still be seen all around the *chorten*. The *chorten* is a Changchub *chorten* and symbolizes the Buddha's enlightenment. It is circumambulated by villagers to accumulate merit.

DESCRIPTION
The Khagsta *chorten* is a Changchub chorten built in stone and mud brick masonry. It is mud plastered and whitewashed externally and has a small circumambulatory

path around the base. The *chorten* has a tall *chorten khorlo* on the dome on which rests a metal crown. The *chorten* was repaired by the village community in the recent past.

STATE OF PRESERVATION
Showing Signs of Deterioration

SOURCE OF INFORMATION Tsering Angchuk Yulpapa (Goba), Yulchung, Khaltse, Ladakh

528

Yulchung

Chorten Chenmo and *Mane* Wall

INVENTORY NO.
KHALTSE / YULCHUNG / 02 / 2004

Chorten | In Use | Public (Community) | Around 200 years old

SETTING
The *chorten* and *mane* wall are oriented to the south and are located on a small hill along a footpath. The *chorten* and *mane* wall are surrounded by the Yulpapa house and Khagsta house to the south and the Baltipe *chorten* to the north.

SIGNIFICANCE
The *chorten* is the largest in the village and was built approximately 200 years ago. The *chorten* is a Changchub *chorten* and symbolizes the Buddha's enlightenment. The *chorten* and *mane* wall are circumambulated by the villagers to gather merit seen as the first step towards enlightenment.

DESCRIPTION
The Changchub *chorten* is built on a large stone masonry square base. The *chorten* is built in stone masonry and is

mud plastered and whitewashed on the exterior. There is a small opening on the dome of the *chorten* facing the south. There is a prayer flag posted on the top of the *chorten*. To the south of the *chorten* is a small rectangular *mane* wall built in dry stone masonry with *mane* stones placed on the top horizontal surface.

STATE OF PRESERVATION
Showing Signs of Deterioration

SOURCE OF INFORMATION Tsering Angchuk Yulpapa (Village Head), Yulchung, Khaltse, Ladakh

Yulma do *Chorten*

INVENTORY NO.
KHALTSE / YULCHUNG / 03 / 2004

Chorten | In Use | Public (Community)

SETTING
The *chorten* are oriented to the southeast and are built on a small hill. The site can be accessed along a footpath. The *chorten* are located near agricultural fields, below the village settlement.

SIGNIFICANCE
The *chorten* appear to form a *rigsum gonbo* and were built for the well being of the village and it from natural calamities.

DESCRIPTION
The Yulma do *chorten* are a group of four *chorten* placed in one row. The first three *chorten* are placed on a common plinth and appear to form a *rigsum gonbo* but cannot be clearly identified because of their dilapidated state. The remains of some walls can be seen around the *chorten*. The *chorten* are built in stone masonry and have traced of mud plaster and whitewash on the exterior.

STATE OF PRESERVATION
Danger of Disappearance

SOURCE OF INFORMATION Tsering Angchuk Yulpapa (Goba), Yulchung, Khaltse, Ladakh

Baltipe *Chorten*

INVENTORY NO.
KHALTSE / YULCHUNG / 04 / 2004

Chorten | In Use | Public (Community)

SETTING
The *chorten* are located on a rocky hill and can be approached along a muddy pathway. The *chorten* lie to the north of *chorten* Chenmo and Yulpapa house. There are large boulders all around the *chorten*.

SIGNIFICANCE
The *chorten* were built in the past as an act of merit. They appear to be Changchub *chorten* although it is difficult to identify them as they have lost their original form.

DESCRIPTION
The Baltipe *chorten* are a group of two *chorten* of almost the same size, located next to each other. Both *chorten* appear to be Changchub *chorten* and are built in stone masonry with traces of the external mud plaster and whitewash visible in some areas. The *chorten* have lost their original form with the erosion of the external surface.

STATE OF PRESERVATION
Advanced State of Decay

SOURCE OF INFORMATION Tsering Angchuk Yulpapa (Goba), Yulchung, Khaltse, Ladakh

Khalang pa House

INVENTORY NO.
KHALTSE / YULCHUNG / 05 / 2004

Vernacular Building | In Use | Private (Individual) | Around 200 years old

SETTING
The Khalang pa house is oriented to the west and is located on the way from Yulchung to Nyerak village. It is located near a group of *chorten* and *mane* walls. The Tashi Thong Gyas *gonpa* lies to the north.

SIGNIFICANCE
It is one of the oldest houses in the village and is a landmark on the way from Yulchung to Nyerak. The house was built approximately 200 years ago by an ancestor of the Khalang pa family and successive generations have continued to reside here. It is built in the traditional style and is a good example of vernacular architecture in the village.

DESCRIPTION
The Khalang pa house is a large double storeyed structure located along the slope of a mountain. The walls are built in random rubble masonry on the ground floor and mud brick masonry with mud mortar on the upper levels. The ground floor is used primarily for storage and for housing animals while the upper level houses the family's living quarters. There are small square window openings on the ground floor for ventilation and light while the first floor has a row of large windows with timber frames and lintels. The house has a traditional roof of timber beams, joists, *taalu*, grass and compacted mud. The roof has a low parapet with prayer flags at the corners. The exterior walls are mud plastered and whitewashed.

STATE OF PRESERVATION
Showing Signs of Deterioration

SOURCE OF INFORMATION Tashi Darjey Gompapa, Yulchung, Khaltse, Ladakh

Kong Ge La *Chorten*

INVENTORY NO.
KHALTSE / YULCHUNG / 06 / 2004

Chorten / *Rigsum Gonbo* / *Mane* Wall | In Use | Public (Community)

SETTING
The *chorten* are located on a bare hill on the way to Nyerak. These lie beyond the village. There is a *rigsum gonbo* towards the northeast and a *mane* wall to the southwest.

SIGNIFICANCE
The *chorten* lie along the way to Nyerak from Yulchung. Kong Ge la stands for 'their pass', where 'their' refers to Nyerak by the Yulchung community. The *rigsum gonbo* protects the village from natural calamities. The *chorten* and *mane* wall may be circumambulated by villagers as they travel to and from Nyerak.

DESCRIPTION
The site consists of *chorten*, *rigsum gonbo* and a *mane* wall. Three of the *chorten* appear to form a *rigsum gonbo* while the fourth stands apart. The *chorten* share a common random rubble masonry base. The fourth *chorten* has collapsed partially and is difficult to identify. The *chorten* are all built in stone and mud brick masonry with mud mortar and are mud plastered and whitewashed on the exterior. There is a *mane* wall to the southwest of the *chorten* which is built in dry stone masonry. It is linear in form and has inscribed *mane* stones placed on the top horizontal surface.

STATE OF PRESERVATION
Danger of Disappearance

SOURCE OF INFORMATION Tsering Angchuk Yulpapa (Goba), Yulchung, Khaltse, Ladakh

Tashi Thong Gyas *Gonpa*

INVENTORY NO.
KHALTSE / YULCHUNG / 07 / 2004

Gonpa / *Chorten* / Fort / *Mane* Wall | In Use | Public (Lingshed *Gonpa* / Community) | Around 300 years old

STATE OF PRESERVATION
Danger of Disappearance

SETTING
The *gonpa* is located on the top of a mountain opposite the main settlement along the footpath that leads to Nyerak. It is surrounded by *chorten* and mountains.

SIGNIFICANCE
The *gonpa* is believed to date back to the time when the village was first settled around 300 years ago. The palace ruins near the *gonpa* also date back to this period. The *gonpa* is a branch of the Lingshed *gonpa* and monks are deputed here to carry out prayers and rituals for the village. It is the principal place of worship in the village. The nearby *chorten*, which form a part of this group, do not conform to the eight Tibetan forms of *chorten.*

DESCRIPTION
The site consists of a small *gonpa*, ruins of a palace, a new structure and a group of seven *chorten* along the way to *gonpa*. The *chorten* have a square base and some of them are stylistically similar to *chorten* seen in Alchi and Sumda Chun. The *gonpa* is built on a rectangular plan with an entrance from the south east. The building is constructed in random rubble masonry and the walls are mud plastered and whitewashed on the exterior. The *dukhang* is a small chamber housing images of Chanrazig, Jamyang, Standin and Shakyamuni Buddha. The floor is in mud and the window openings have timber frames and lintels. The *gonpa* has a traditional roof above. There is another *dukhang* below the main one which is entered from the courtyard itself. Only fragments of the walls survive. To the left of *gonpa* are the ruins of the palace of which only two walls still remain.

Yulchung

531

SOURCE OF INFORMATION Tsering Angchuk Yulpapa (Goba), Yulchung, Khaltse, Ladakh

Gya Ste *Mane*

INVENTORY NO.
KHALTSE / YULCHUNG / 08 / 2004

Mane Wall | In Use | Public (Community)

SETTING
The *mane* wall is oriented to the southwest and is located on a bare hillside along the path leading to Nyerak.

SIGNIFICANCE
The *mane* wall is located along the path from Yulchung to Nyerak and is circumambulated by villagers as they travel along this path to accumulate merit.

DESCRIPTION
The *mane* wall is a stone masonry wall built on a rectangular plan with inscribed *mane* stones placed on the top horizontal surface.

STATE OF PRESERVATION
Advanced State of Decay

SOURCE OF INFORMATION Tashi Dorjey - Gompapa, Yulchung, Khaltse, Ladakh

Thongros Se *Rigsum Gonbo*

INVENTORY NO.
KHALTSE / YULCHUNG / 09 / 2004

Rigsum Gonbo | In Use | Public (Community)

SETTING
The *rigsum gonbo* is oriented to the east and located along the slope of a barren mountainside on the path which leads from Yulchung to Nyerak.

SIGNIFICANCE
The *rigsum gonbo* was built to protect the village from natural calamities and other evil forces striking from this end of the village.

DESCRIPTION
The *rigsum gonbo* consists of three chorten built on a common random rubble masonry base. The *chorten* are built in stone masonry with mud mortar and are mud plastered and whitewashed on the exterior.

STATE OF PRESERVATION
Advanced State of Decay

SOURCE OF INFORMATION Tashi Dorjey - Gompapa, Yulchung, Khaltse, Ladakh

Yulchung

532

Yulpapa *Khangbu*

INVENTORY NO.
KHALTSE / YULCHUNG / 10 / 2004

Vernacular Building | In Use | Private (Individual) | Around 160 years old

SETTING
The Yulpapa house is one of the first houses at the entrance to the village. The house is located to the south of *chorten* Chenmo.

SIGNIFICANCE
The Yulpapa *khangbu* is among the oldest houses in the village and was built by an ancestor of the Yulpapa family around 160 years ago. The older section of the house is presently in ruins and the new house was built nearby. The house is built in the traditional style and is a good example of vernacular architecture in the village.

DESCRIPTION
The house is built along the slope of the hill and faces the valley with maximum window openings on the southern facade. The entrance is from the front as well as from the rear and leads directly to the first floor. The ground floor is built in random rubble masonry and is used for housing animals while the first floor houses the family's living areas and is built in mud brick masonry. There is a large glass framed opening in the centre of the house and an open verandah on the first floor. The roof is a traditional roof and has prayer flags at the corners of the parapet. Fodder for animals and firewood have been stacked on the roof for the winter months. The ruined walls of the old house can be seen to the north and south of the house.

STATE OF PRESERVATION
Advanced State of Decay

SOURCE OF INFORMATION Tsering Angchuk - Yulpapa, Yulchung, Khaltse, Ladakh

Mashen Chepa House

INVENTORY NO.
KHALTSE / YULCHUNG / 11 / 2004

Vernacular Building | In Use | Private (Individual) | Around 250 years old

SETTING
The house marks the beginning of Yulchung village. The house is built along a slope of a hill, a little lower than the village. There are cattle sheds towards the southwest and a *rigsum gonbo* towards the north east.

SIGNIFICANCE
The Mashen Chepa house is one of the oldest houses in the village and was built by ancestors of the present owner 5 - 6 generations ago. The family has resided here ever since. The house is built in the traditional style and is a good example of vernacular architecture in the village.

DESCRIPTION
Owing to the natural terrain of the site, the front portion of the house is at a lower height than the rear. The house is built on a rectangular plan and is three storeys high. The ground floor is constructed in random rubble masonry while the upper levels are in mud brick masonry with mud mortar. The ground floor has a few small rectangular openings for ventilation while the upper floors have large timber framed windows. The ground floor is used for storage and for housing animals while the upper levels form the family's living quarters. The family temple is in the northwestern end of the house. The roof is a traditional one and is made of wooden beams, joists, *taalu*, grass and compacted mud. There is a terrace on third floor. Externally, the house is mud plastered and whitewashed.

STATE OF PRESERVATION
Showing Signs of Deterioration

SOURCE OF INFORMATION Tashi Dorjey – Gonpapa, Yulchung, Khaltse, Ladakh

Gonpapa House

INVENTORY NO.
KHALTSE / YULCHUNG / 12 / 2004

Vernacular Building | In Use | Private (Individual) | Around 250 - 300 years old

SETTING
The Gonpapa house is oriented to the southeast and is built at the foothills of a hill. It is surrounded by the fields to the south and east and two Changchub *chorten* to the west. The mountainside lies to the north of the house.

SIGNIFICANCE
The Gonpapa house was been built around 250 - 300 years ago by an ancestor of the Gonpapa family and successive generations have continued to reside here. The house is built in the traditional style and it is a good example of vernacular architecture in the village.

DESCRIPTION
The house does not have a definite plan and is somewhat organically built. The house is a large four storeyed structure. Due to the natural terrain of the area, it is entered from the first floor. The house is constructed in both random rubble and mud brick masonry with mud mortar. There are very few openings in the ground floor

which is used primarily for storage. The upper levels have large rectangular window openings with timber frames and lintels and these levels form the family's living areas. The roof is a traditional one made of timber beams, joists, *taalu*, grass and compacted mud. The house rises to four storeys at the four corners and there is an open terrace in the middle .

STATE OF PRESERVATION
Showing Signs of Deterioration

SOURCE OF INFORMATION Tashi Dorjey - Gonpapa, Yulchung, Khaltse, Ladakh

Gonpapa *Chorten*

INVENTORY NO.
KHALTSE / YULCHUNG / 13 / 2004

Chorten / *Mane* Wall | In Use | Private (Individual) | Around 250 - 300 years old

SETTING
The Gonpapa *chorten* are located on a flat piece of land near the Gonpapa house. The house lies to the northeast and there is a school to the north. It is surrounded by agricultural fields towards the south and southeast.

SIGNIFICANCE
The Gonpapa *chorten* are believed to have been built at the same period as the Gonpapa house around 250 - 300 years ago by an ancestor of the family as an act of merit. The *chorten* are Changchub *chorten* and symbolize the Buddha's enlightenment. Both the *chorten* and *mane* wall are circumambulated by members of the Gonpapa family to accumulate merit.

DESCRIPTION
The site consists of two *chorten* and a *mane* wall. The *mane* wall is a square dry stone masonry wall and contains numerous *mane* stones on the top horizontal surface. The *chorten* are similar in size. They are built on separate

random rubble masonry bases and mud brick masonry with mud mortar. The *chorten* are mud plastered and whitewashed on the exterior. The domes of the *chorten* have tall *chugsum khorlo* made of baked clay tiles.

STATE OF PRESERVATION
Showing Signs of Deterioration

SOURCE OF INFORMATION Tashi Dorjey - Gompapa, Yulchung, Khaltse, Ladakh

Domang *Mane*

INVENTORY NO.
KHALTSE / YULCHUNG / 14 / 2004

Mane Wall | In Use | Public (Community) | Around 300 years old

SETTING
The *mane* wall is located on a stretch of land south east of the village school. Willow trees surround the site to the north and northeast.

SIGNIFICANCE
The *mane* wall was built around 300 years ago for the well being of the village and is still circumambulated by villagers to accumulate merit.

DESCRIPTION
The *mane* wall is a randomly arranged dry stone masonry wall without a definite shape. Inscribed *mane* stones are placed on the horizontal surface. There is a circumambulatory path around the site.

STATE OF PRESERVATION
Advanced State of Decay

SOURCE OF INFORMATION Tashi Dorjey - Gonpapa, Yulchung, Khaltse, Ladakh

Yulpape House

INVENTORY NO.
KHALTSE / YULCHUNG / 15 / 2004

Vernacular Building | In Use | Private (Individual) | Around 200 years old

SETTING
The Yulpape house is oriented to the southeast and is located southeast of the Tashi Domang *gonpa*. There is a Changchub *chorten* and a Kagan *chorten* to the east of the house.

SIGNIFICANCE
The Yulpape house was built around 200 years ago by an ancestor of the Yulpape family and successive generations have continued to reside here. The house is built in the traditional style and is a good example of vernacular architecture in the village.

DESCRIPTION
The Yulpape house is a three storeyed building built on a rectangular plan. The house stands on a high random rubble masonry foundation. The ground floor is built in random rubble masonry while the upper floors are in mud brick masonry with mud mortar. The ground floor has small window openings for ventilation and is used primarily for storage while the upper levels have larger windows and house the family's living quarters. The house has a traditional roof made of timber beams, joists, *taalu*, grass and compacted mud which is edged by a low height parapet. The walls are plastered in mud both internally as well externally.

STATE OF PRESERVATION
Fair

SOURCE OF INFORMATION Tashi Dorjey- Gompapa, Yulchung, Khaltse, Ladakh

Tashi Domang
Gonpa

INVENTORY NO.
KHALTSE / YULCHUNG / 16 / 2004

Gonpa / Chorten / Prayer Wheel | In Use | Public (Lingshed *Gonpa*) |
Around 1000 years old

SETTING
The *gonpa* is built near the ruins of old palace above
Yulchung village. The Yulpapa house lies to the south and
there is a small school building to the north.

SIGNIFICANCE
According to legend, Lotsawa Rinchen Zangpo after
building the *gonpa* at Wanla, headed towards Lingshed and
stopped near Yulchung village at the present site of *gonpa*
to meditate in the serene mountains. He spent around
three years of his life here writing the religious canons with
gold and silver. It is also said that when he got tired of
writing with his hand, he used his feet to write. This is the
reason that the script is large and not written in a uniform
manner. The script has a long circular ring in between and
hence is called Kangyur Aalongpa. Out of all the volumes
(Putis), four are in Changthang, four are in Zanskar and
forty one are in this *gonpa*. The *gonpa* today is under the
purview of the Lingshed *gonpa* and a monk is deputed from
Lingshed here to offer prayers and carry out rituals in the
temple. The *gonpa* houses several images of which the
most significant is that of the Buddha which, according to
popular belief, is believed to have spoken. The *chorten* are
circumambulated by villagers as they visit the temple.

DESCRIPTION
The *gonpa* complex is built on an elevated area in the
village. A steep climb from the fields leads to the entrance
of the *gonpa*. The *gonpa* complex includes a Kagan *chorten*,
a large *chorten* and a relatively smaller *chorten*. All the
gonpa are Changchub *chorten*. The larger *chorten* shares a
wall with the *gonpa*. A small wooden doorway leads into a
courtyard which has a large *tarchen* in the centre. The
courtyard has a single height gallery on all three sides with
small openings on the southern wall. The gallery has a
traditional roof above. A flight of wooden staircase carved
out of a large tree trunk leads to the porch of the *dukhang*.
One side of the wall has been repainted. A wooden doorway
leads into the *dukhang* which is a small clear space. The
left wall is covered with paintings of Buddha whereas the
right wall has paintings of 21 Dolma. The rear wall has a
large image of Buddha and 16 *arhat*. There are many
thangka hung from the wall and columns. The rear wall has
an elaborate wooden frame housing the images of
Chanrazig, Buddha, Tsepakmed, and Standin. The right side
of the shelf comprises of the Kangyur Aalongpa which is
handwritten in both gold and silver by Lotsava Rinchen
Zangpo himself. Externally, the *gonpa* is simple mud
plastered and whitewashed. Decorative motifs on the
parapet and wooden members have been done in red color.

STATE OF PRESERVATION
Advanced State of Decay

SOURCE OF INFORMATION Tashi Dorjey - Gonpapa, Yulchung, Khaltse, Ladakh

Yulchung

536

Yultsa *Lhato*

INVENTORY NO.
KHALTSE / YULCHUNG / 17 / 2004

Lhato | In Use | Public (Community) | Around 400 years old

SETTING
The Yultsa *lhato* is oriented to the south and is built on a rocky outcrop which marks the beginning of the village. The village lies further to the south and southwest.

SIGNIFICANCE
The *lhato* is believed to be around 400 years old and is dedicated to the protector deity of the village. It marks the beginning of the village. Juniper plants and *khadag* etc. in the *lhato* are renewed every year and the deity's protection sought for the welfare of the village.

DESCRIPTION
The *lhato* is built on a rocky outcrop in random rubble masonry. It is a cubical shaped structure which tapers a little towards the top. Ritual offerings of juniper branches and *khadag* are placed on the top.

STATE OF PRESERVATION
Advanced State of Decay

SOURCE OF INFORMATION Tashi Dorjey - Gonpapa, Yulchung, Khaltse, Ladakh

Yulchung

537

Chanrazig Rock Formation (Kha-Tsar Pani)

INVENTORY NO.
KHALTSE / YULCHUNG / 18 / 2004

Landscape (Sacred Mountain) | In Use | Public (State)

SETTING
The mountain is located southeast of the village.

SIGNIFICANCE / ASSOCIATED BELIEFS
According to popular belief, the tall rock formation on the mountain top above the settlement represents Chanrazig and it faces the Karja Phagspa in Himachal Pradesh.

DESCRIPTION
The rock formation is oriented to the west and faces the village. It forms part of the mountain range.

CULTURAL LINKAGES / CULTURAL PRACTICES
The mountain site is part of a pilgrimage route and falls on the way from Phanjilla to Yulchung and further towards Lingshed.

STATE OF PRESERVATION
Fair

SOURCE OF INFORMATION Tashi Dorjey - Gompapa, Yulchung, Khaltse, Ladakh

Pake *Chorten* (Yulma do *Chorten*)

INVENTORY NO.
KHALTSE / YULCHUNG / 19 / 2004

Chorten / *Mane* Wall | In Use | Public (Community)

SETTING
The *chorten* are oriented to the north and marks the beginning of the village when coming in from Lingshed. A footpath leads to the site. It is surrounded by agricultural fields to the north and northeast.

SIGNIFICANCE
The group of *chorten* lie along the path leading to the village and mark the beginning of the village. The *chorten* and *mane* wall are circumambulated by villagers as an act of merit. The *chorten* are all Changchub *chorten* and symbolize the Buddha's enlightenment.

DESCRIPTION
The site consists of a group of *chorten* and a *mane* wall. The *mane* wall is a L-shaped dry stone masonry wall with *mane* stones places on the top horizontal surface. The *chorten* are located to the west of the *mane* wall and are built on

random rubble masonry bases in stone masonry with an external layer of mud plaster and whitewash. There is a tall *chugsum khorlo* on the dome of the *chorten* which symbolize the 13 steps towards enlightenment.

STATE OF PRESERVATION
Showing Signs of Deterioration

SOURCE OF INFORMATION Tsering Angchuk Yulpapa (Goba), Yulchung, Khaltse, Ladakh

Chorten and *Mane* Wall

INVENTORY NO.
KHALTSE / YULCHUNG / 20 / 2004

Chorten / *Mane* Wall | In Use | Public (Community) | Around 250 years old

SETTING
The *chorten* and *mane* wall are oriented to the northeast and are located at one of the highest points in the village. The Yanam Khangbu residence lies to the northeast while there agricultural fields further below towards the south of the site.

SIGNIFICANCE
The *chorten* and *mane* wall were built in the past for the well being of the village. The *chorten* is a Changchub *chorten* that symbolizes the Buddha's enlightenment.

DESCRIPTION
The site consists of a *chorten* and a *mane* wall. The *chorten* stands on a square random rubble masonry base. The *chorten* is built in stone and mud brick masonry with mud mortar and is mud plastered and whitewashed on the exterior. There is a tall *chugsum khorlo* on the top of the

dome made of baked clay tiles. The *mane* wall is a long rectangular dry stone masonry wall with inscribed *mane* stones placed on the top horizontal surface.

STATE OF PRESERVATION
Advanced State of Decay

SOURCE OF INFORMATION Tashi Dorjey - Gompapa, Yulchung, Khaltse, Ladakh

Mane Wall

INVENTORY NO.
KHALTSE / YULCHUNG / 21 / 2004

Mane Wall | In Use | Public (Community)

SETTING
The *mane* wall is oriented to the northeast and is located on a stretch of barren land along the path leading from Lingshed to Yulchung. There is a cliff to the north of the *mane* wall and a rough pathway leading to Yulchung on the south.

SIGNIFICANCE
The *mane* wall is located along the route linking Lingshed with Yulchung and is circumambulated by villagers as they travel along this path.

DESCRIPTION
The *mane* wall is a long rectangular dry stone masonry wall. There are inscribed *mane* stones placed on the top horizontal surface.

STATE OF PRESERVATION
Advanced State of Decay

SOURCE OF INFORMATION Tashi Dorjey - Gompapa, Yulchung, Khaltse, Ladakh

Index

Khaltse

542

S.No.	NAME	CATEGORY	INVENTORY NO.	PAGE NO.
43.	Alchi *Lonpo* House	Vernacular Building	Khaltse / Alchi / 20 / 2004	**32**
44.	Group of *Chorten*	*Chorten*	Khaltse / Alchi / 21 / 2004	**32**
45.	Skumbum *Chorten*	*Chorten*	Khaltse / Alchi / 22 / 2004	**33**
46.	Group of *Chorten* and *Lhakhang*	Temple / *Chorten*	Khaltse / Alchi / 23 / 2004	**33**
47.	*Chorten* Marpo	*Chorten*	Khaltse / Alchi / 24 / 2004	**34**
48.	Chotarpa *Lhato*	*Lhato*	Khaltse / Alchi / 25 / 2004	**34**
49.	Skudung *Chorten* and *Mane* Wall	*Chorten* / *Mane* Wall / *Tarchen*	Khaltse / Alchi / 26 / 2004	**35**
50.	Druggyasling *Gonpa*	*Gonpa*	Khaltse / Alchi / 27 / 2004	**36**
51.	*Labrang*	Vernacular Building	Khaltse / Alchi / 28 / 2004	**37**
52.	Bongrapa House	Vernacular Building	Khaltse / Alchi / 29 / 2004	**37**
53.	*Chorten* and Old *Lhakhang*	*Chorten* / Temple	Khaltse / Alchi / 30 / 2004	**38**
54.	Orkorpa *Chorten*	*Chorten*	Khaltse / Alchi / 31 / 2004	**38**
55.	*Chorten* and *Lubang* (Skubar *Chorten*)	*Chorten* / *Lubang*	Khaltse / Alchi / 32 / 2004	**39**
56.	Group of *Chorten*	*Chorten*	Khaltse / Alchi / 33 / 2004	**39**
57.	*Chorten* and *Lubang*	*Chorten* / *Lubang*	Khaltse / Alchi / 34 / 2004	**40**
58.	*Rigsum Gonbo* (Zimskhang) and *Lhato*	*Rigsum Gonbo* / *Lhato*	Khaltse / Alchi / 35 / 2004	**40**
59.	Banka *Chorten* Area	*Chorten* / Rock Carving / Precinct	Khaltse / Alchi / 36 / 2004	**41**
60.	Tseblhamo *Lhato* and *Lubang*	*Lhato* / *Lubang*	Khaltse / Alchi / 37 / 2004	**42**
61.	Kharmadpa Old House	Vernacular Building	Khaltse / Alchi / 38 / 2004	**42**
62.	Alchi Lonpo Zimskhang	Vernacular Building	Khaltse / Alchi / 39 / 2004	**43**
63.	Group of *Chorten* and *Mane* Walls	*Chorten* / *Mane* Wall	Khaltse / Alchi / 40 / 2004	**44**
64.	*Spurkhang*	Cremation Ground	Khaltse / Alchi / 41 / 2004	**44**
65.	*Group of Chorten* and *Mane* Walls	*Chorten* / *Mane* Wall / *Rigsum Gonbo*	Khaltse / Alchi / 42 / 2004	**45**
66.	Thangpa Khangbu *Chorten*	*Chorten*	Khaltse / Alchi / 43 / 2004	**46**
67.	*Chorten*	*Chorten*	Khaltse / Alchi / 44 / 2004	**46**
68.	Group of *Chorten* and *Mane* Walls	*Chorten* / *Mane* Wall	Khaltse / Alchi / 45 / 2004	**47**
69.	Petroglyphs	Rock Carvings	Khaltse / Alchi / 46 / 2004	**47**

Atitse

S.No.	NAME	CATEGORY	INVENTORY NO.	PAGE NO.
70.	*Chorten* and *Mane* Wall	*Chorten* / *Mane* Wall / *Lubang*	Khaltse / Atitse / 01 / 2004	**48**
71.	*Gonpa*	*Gonpa*	Khaltse / Atitse / 02 / 2004	**49**
72.	*Chorten* and *Mane* Wall	*Chorten* / *Mane* Wall	Khaltse / Atitse / 03 / 2004	**50**

Baima

S.No.	NAME	CATEGORY	INVENTORY NO.	PAGE NO.
73.	Chamakpa House	Vernacular Building	Khaltse / Baima / 01 / 2004	**54**
74.	Malchang Tree	Landscape (Sacred Tree)	Khaltse / Baima / 02 / 2004	**54**
75.	*Sharstepa*	Vernacular Building	Khaltse / Baima / 03 / 2004	**55**
76.	Logbupa House	Vernacular Building	Khaltse / Baima / 04 / 2004	**55**
77.	Migsugpa House	Vernacular Building	Khaltse / Baima / 05 / 2004	**56**
78.	*Mane* Wall	*Mane* Wall	Khaltse / Baima / 06 / 2004	**56**
79.	Phrogpa House	Vernacular Building	Khaltse / Baima / 07 / 2004	**57**
80.	Street (Next to Serkyangpa)	Precinct	Khaltse / Baima / 08 / 2004	**57**
81.	Community Space	Community Space	Khaltse / Baima / 09 / 2004	**58**
82.	Gesar's Drum (Gesar-re-Daman)	Landscape (Rock Formation)	Khaltse / Baima / 10 / 2004	**58**
83.	Gesar's Ear (Gesar *Namchog*)	Landscape (Rock Formation)	Khaltse / Baima / 11 / 2004	**59**
84.	Petroglyphs	Rock Carvings	Khaltse / Baima / 12 / 2007	**59**

543

S.No.	NAME	CATEGORY	INVENTORY NO.	PAGE NO.
Baldesh				
85.	*Mane* Wall	*Mane* Wall	Khaltse / Baldesh / 01 / 2004	60
86.	*Mane* Wall	*Mane* Wall	Khaltse / Baldesh / 02 / 2004	60
87.	*Rigsum Gonbo*	*Rigsum Gonbo*	Khaltse / Baldesh / 03 / 2004	61
88.	*Changra*	Landscape (Community Space)	Khaltse / Baldesh / 04/ 2004	61
89.	*Rigsum Gonbo*	*Rigsum Gonbo*	Khaltse / Baldesh / 05 / 2004	62
90.	*Mane* Wall	*Mane* Wall	Khaltse / Baldesh / 06 / 2004	62
91.	Tsangyapa House	Vernacular Building	Khaltse / Baldesh / 07 / 2004	63
Bhuk-Bhuktse				
92.	*Mane* Wall	*Mane* Wall	Khaltse / Bhuk-Bhuktse / 01 / 2004	66
93.	*Rigsum Gonbo*	*Rigsum Gonbo*	Khaltse / Bhuk-Bhuktse / 02 / 2004	66
94.	*Mane* Wall	*Mane* Wall	Khaltse / Bhuk-Bhuktse / 03 / 2004	67
Dha				
95.	Michungpa House	Vernacular Building	Khaltse / Dha / 01 / 2004	68
96.	*Lagskor*	Prayer Wheel	Khaltse / Dha / 02 / 2004	68
97.	Dha *Gonpa*	*Gonpa*	Khaltse / Dha / 03 / 2004	69
98.	*Mane* Wall	*Mane* Wall	Khaltse / Dha / 04 / 2004	70
99.	*Chorten*	*Chorten*	Khaltse / Dha / 05 / 2004	70
100.	*Mane* Wall	*Mane* Wall	Khaltse / Dha / 06 / 2004	71
101.	Skyabapa House	Vernacular Building	Khaltse / Dha / 07 / 2004	71
102.	Walnut Tree (*Starga*)	Landscape (Sacred Tree)	Khaltse / Dha / 08 / 2004	72
103.	Old Settlement	Precinct	Khaltse / Dha / 09 / 2004	72
104.	Kagan *Chorten*	*Chorten*	Khaltse / Dha / 10 / 2004	73
105.	Dha *Changra* (*Attande*)	Landscape (Community Space)	Khaltse / Dha / 11 / 2004	73
106.	Gyalchupi House	Vernacular Building	Khaltse / Dha / 12 / 2004	74
107.	Dha *Khar*	Fort	Khaltse / Dha / 13 / 2006	74
108.	Dagopa House	Vernacular Building	Khaltse / Dha / 14 / 2006	75
109.	Petroglyphs	Rock Carvings	Khaltse / Dha / 15 / 2006	75
110.	*Munal*	Cremation Ground	Khaltse / Dha / 16 / 2006	76
111.	*Chumig*	Landscape (Water Body)	Khaltse / Dha / 17 / 2006	76
112.	Dha *Brog*	Landscape (Mountains, Sacred Water Body)	Khaltse / Dha / 18 / 2007	77
Dipling				
113.	*Gonchung*	*Gonpa*	Khaltse / Dipling / 01 / 2006	80
114.	Phuntsog Lingpa House	Vernacular Building	Khaltse / Dipling / 02 / 2006	80
115.	*Mane* Ringmo	*Chorten* / *Mane* Wall	Khaltse / Dipling / 03 / 2006	81
116.	Doktha *Yokma*	Vernacular Building	Khaltse / Dipling / 04 / 2006	81
117.	Doktha *Gongma*	Vernacular Building	Khaltse / Dipling / 05 / 2006	82
118.	Khyunge *Lhato*	*Lhato*	Khaltse / Dipling / 06 / 2006	82
119.	Phuntsog Tundup pa House	Vernacular Building	Khaltse / Dipling / 07 / 2006	83
120.	Yokmapa House	Vernacular Building	Khaltse / Dipling / 08 / 2006	83
121.	Tseringpa House	Vernacular Building	Khaltse / Dipling / 09 / 2006	84
122.	Lungse Zhung *Chorten*	*Chorten* / *Mane* Wall	Khaltse / Dipling / 10 / 2006	84
123.	Tashi Gangpa House	Vernacular Building	Khaltse / Dipling / 11 / 2006	85
124.	Lingshed *Labrang*	Vernacular Building	Khaltse / Dipling / 12 / 2006	85
125.	Srangzhung	Landscape (Community Space)	Khaltse / Dipling / 13 / 2006	86
126.	Group of *Chorten* and *Mane* Wall	*Chorten* / *Mane* Wall	Khaltse / Dipling / 14 / 2006	86
127.	Dipling *Gonpa*	*Gonpa*	Khaltse / Dipling / 15 / 2006	87
128.	Zhukthipa House	Vernacular Building	Khaltse / Dipling / 16 / 2006	88

544

S.No.	NAME	CATEGORY	INVENTORY NO.	PAGE NO.
129.	Phuntsog Ling *Khangbu*	Vernacular Building	Khaltse / Dipling / 17 / 2006	**88**
130.	Barmela	Landscape (Pass)	Khaltse / Dipling / 18 / 2006	**89**

Domkhar

S.No.	NAME	CATEGORY	INVENTORY NO.	PAGE NO.
131.	Kagan *Chorten*	*Chorten*	Khaltse / Domkhar Barma / 01 / 2004	**92**
132.	Group of *Chorten*	*Chorten*	Khaltse / Domkhar Barma / 02 / 2004	**92**
133.	Onpunpa House	Vernacular Building	Khaltse / Domkhar Barma / 03 / 2004	**93**
134.	*Mane* Wall	*Mane* Wall	Khaltse / Domkhar Barma / 04 / 2004	**93**
135.	Old *Gonpa*	*Gonpa*	Khaltse / Domkhar Barma / 05 / 2004	**94**
136.	Village Street	Precinct	Khaltse / Domkhar Dho / 01 / 2004	**95**
137.	Pugapa's House	Vernacular Building	Khaltse / Domkhar Dho / 02 / 2004	**95**
138.	Standup pa House	Vernacular Building	Khaltse / Domkhar Dho / 03 / 2004	**96**
139.	Standup pa House	Vernacular Building	Khaltse / Domkhar Dho / 04 / 2004	**96**
140.	Balupa *Khangpa*	Vernacular Building	Khaltse / Domkhar Dho / 05 / 2004	**97**
141.	*Chorten*	*Chorten*	Khaltse / Domkhar Dho / 06 / 2004	**97**
142.	*Rigsum Gonbo*	*Rigsum Gonbo*	Khaltse / Domkhar Dho / 07 / 2004	**98**
143.	*Tashag*	Vernacular Building	Khaltse / Domkhar Dho / 08 / 2004	**98**
144.	*Gonpa*	*Gonpa* / *Chorten* / *Mane* Wall	Khaltse / Domkhar Dho / 09 / 2004	**99**
145.	*Chorten*	*Chorten*	Khaltse / Domkhar Dho / 10 / 2004	**100**
146.	Group of *Mane* Wall and Deshag Gyad	*Chorten* / *Mane* Wall	Khaltse / Domkhar Dho / 11 / 2004	**100**
147.	Group of *Chorten* and *Mane* Walls	*Chorten*	Khaltse / Domkhar Dho / 12 / 2004	**101**
148.	Group of *Chorten* and *Mane* Walls	*Chorten* / *Mane* Wall	Khaltse / Domkhar Dho / 13 / 2004	**101**
149.	Group of *Chorten*	*Chorten*	Khaltse / Domkhar Dho / 14 / 2004	**102**
150.	Group of *Chorten* and *Mane* Wall	*Chorten* / *Mane* Wall	Khaltse / Domkhar Dho / 15 / 2004	**102**
151.	Group of *Chorten*	*Chorten*	Khaltse / Domkhar Dho / 16 / 2004	**103**
152.	Group of *Chorten* and *Mane* Walls	*Chorten* / *Mane* Wall	Khaltse / Domkhar Dho / 17 / 2004	**103**
153.	Group of *Chorten* and *Mane* Wall	*Chorten* / *Mane* Wall	Khaltse / Domkhar Gongma / 01 / 2006	**104**
154.	Zurkhang pa House	Vernacular Building	Khaltse / Domkhar Gongma / 02 / 2006	**104**
155.	*Lubang*	*Lubang*	Khaltse / Domkhar Gongma / 03 / 2006	**105**
156.	Group of *Chorten*	*Chorten*	Khaltse / Domkhar Gongma / 04 / 2006	**105**
157.	Group of *Chorten*	*Chorten*	Khaltse / Domkhar Gongma / 05 / 2006	**106**
158.	*Mane* Wall	*Mane* Wall	Khaltse / Domkhar Gongma / 06 / 2006	**106**
159.	Group of *Chorten*	*Chorten*	Khaltse / Domkhar Gongma / 07 / 2006	**107**
160.	*Lhakhang* Nyingpa	Temple	Khaltse / Domkhar Gongma / 08 / 2006	**107**
161.	Group of *Chorten*	*Chorten*	Khaltse / Domkhar Gongma / 09 / 2006	**108**
162.	Domkhar *Gonpa*	*Gonpa*	Khaltse / Domkhar Gongma / 10 / 2006	**108**
163.	*Lhakhang*	Temple	Khaltse / Domkhar Gongma / 11 / 2006	**109**
164.	Group of *Chorten* and *Mane* Wall	*Chorten* / *Mane* Wall	Khaltse / Domkhar Gongma / 12 / 2006	**109**
165.	Group of *Chorten*	*Chorten*	Khaltse / Domkhar Gongma / 13 / 2006	**110**
166.	*Chorten*	*Chorten*	Khaltse / Domkhar Gongma / 14 / 2006	**110**
167.	Group of *Chorten*	*Chorten*	Khaltse / Domkhar Gongma / 15 / 2006	**111**
168.	Sharchog Spundun *Lhato*	*Lhato*	Khaltse / Domkhar Gongma / 16 / 2006	**111**
169.	Stambu Lharten *Lhato*	*Lhato*	Khaltse / Domkhar Gongma / 17 / 2006	**112**

Gongma

S.No.	NAME	CATEGORY	INVENTORY NO.	PAGE NO.
170.	*Chorten*	*Chorten*	Khaltse / Gongma / 01 / 2006	**116**
171.	Lingshed *Labrang Gongma* (Thango)	Vernacular Building	Khaltse / Gongma / 02 / 2006	**116**
172.	*Lhakhang Gogpo*	Temple	Khaltse / Gongma / 03 / 2006	**117**
173.	*Chorten*	*Chorten*	Khaltse / Gongma / 04 / 2006	**117**
174.	*Tsamphuk* (Joshila Kangshan)	Cave	Khaltse / Gongma / 05 / 2006	**118**
175.	Thangopa House	Vernacular Building	Khaltse / Gongma / 06 / 2006	**118**

S.No.	NAME	CATEGORY	INVENTORY NO.	PAGE NO.
176.	*Rigsum Gonbo*	*Rigsum Gonbo*	Khaltse / Gongma / 07 / 2006	119
177.	Srangyokpa House	Vernacular Building	Khaltse / Gongma / 08 / 2006	119
178.	Gongmapa House	Vernacular Building	Khaltse / Gongma / 09 / 2006	120
179.	*Chorten*	*Chorten*	Khaltse / Gongma / 10 / 2006	120

Gyera

S.No.	NAME	CATEGORY	INVENTORY NO.	PAGE NO.
180.	Gongmapa *Chorten*	*Chorten*	Khaltse / Gyera / 01 / 2004	121
181.	Gongmapa House	Vernacular Building	Khaltse / Gyera / 02 / 2004	121
182.	Gongmapa *Mane* Wall and *Chorten*	*Chorten / Mane* Wall	Khaltse / Gyera / 03 / 2004	122
183.	Group of *Chorten*	*Chorten*	Khaltse / Gyera / 04 / 2004	122
184.	Chotar *Lhato*	*Lhato*	Khaltse / Gyera / 05 / 2004	123
185.	*Spurkhang*	Cemetery / Cremation Ground / Tomb	Khaltse / Gyera / 06 / 2004	123
186.	Khang gyab-pe *Chorten*	*Chorten*	Khaltse / Gyera / 07 / 2004	124
187.	*Chorten* Chan	*Chorten*	Khaltse / Gyera / 08 / 2004	124
188.	*Chorten Gogpo*	*Chorten*	Khaltse / Gyera / 09 / 2004	125
189.	Gyera *Lhakhang*	Temple	Khaltse / Gyera / 10 / 2004	125
190.	Dagchanpa's *Rigsum Gonbo*	*Rigsum Gonbo*	Khaltse / Gyera / 11 / 2004	126
191.	Tongspon (Gyerapa) House and *Rigsum Gonbo*	Vernacular Building / *Rigsum Gonbo*	Khaltse / Gyera / 12 / 2004	127
192.	Tongspon (Kagan *Chorten*)	*Chorten*	Khaltse / Gyera / 13 / 2004	128
193.	*Mane* Wall and Rock Inscription	*Mane* Wall	Khaltse / Gyera / 14 / 2004	129
194.	*Chorten* and *Mane* Wall	*Chorten / Mane* Wall	Khaltse / Gyera / 15 / 2004	129

Hanu

S.No.	NAME	CATEGORY	INVENTORY NO.	PAGE NO.
195.	Kagan *Chorten* (Pharka)	*Chorten*	Khaltse / Hanu Gongma / 01 / 2004	132
196.	Kagan *Chorten*	*Chorten*	Khaltse / Hanu Gongma / 02 / 2004	132
197.	*Mane* Wall	*Mane* Wall	Khaltse / Hanu Gongma / 03 / 2004	133
198.	Nas Mal *Mane*	Landscape (Community Space)	Khaltse / Hanu Gongma / 04 / 2006	133
199.	Gangapa House	Vernacular Building	Khaltse / Hanu Gongma / 05 / 2006	134
200.	Skyi Sonampa House	Vernacular Building	Khaltse / Hanu Gongma / 06 / 2006	134
201.	Gangu Lhundup pa *Khangchen*	Vernacular Building	Khaltse / Hanu Gongma / 07 / 2006	135
202.	*Gonpa Gogpo*	*Gonpa*	Khaltse / Hanu Gongma / 08 / 2006	135
203.	*Chorten*	*Chorten*	Khaltse / Hanu Gongma / 09 / 2006	136
204.	*Rigsum Gonbo*	*Rigsum Gonbo*	Khaltse / Hanu Gongma / 10 / 2006	136
205.	*Gonpa*	*Gonpa*	Khaltse / Hanu Gongma / 11 / 2006	137
206.	Garwapa House	Vernacular Building	Khaltse / Hanu Gongma / 12 / 2006	137
207.	Ganchungpa House	Vernacular Building	Khaltse / Hanu Gongma / 13 / 2006	138
208.	Doangpa *Khangpa*	Vernacular Building	Khaltse / Hanu Yokma / 01 / 2004	139
209.	*Mane* Wall	*Mane* Wall	Khaltse / Hanu Yokma / 02 / 2004	139
210.	Nas Mal *Mane*	Community Space / *Mane* Wall	Khaltse / Hanu Yokma / 03 / 2004	140
211.	Dompa House	Vernacular Building	Khaltse / Hanu Yokma / 04 / 2004	140
212.	Sotopa House	Vernacular Building	Khaltse / Hanu Yokma / 05 / 2004	141
213.	Khachaype House	Vernacular Building	Khaltse / Hanu Yokma / 06 / 2004	141
214.	Lokhil Dorjey *Lhakhang* (*Lhakhang* Nyingpa)	*Gonpa*	Khaltse / Hanu Yokma / 07 / 2004	142
215.	Hanu *Yokma Gonpa*	*Gonpa*	Khaltse / Hanu Yokma / 08 / 2004	142
216.	Zangldan *Lhato*	*Lhato*	Khaltse / Hanu Yokma / 09 / 2004	143
217.	Precinct of Old Houses	Precinct	Khaltse / Hanu Yokma / 10 / 2004	143
218.	Gonjongpa House	Vernacular Building	Khaltse / Hanu Yokma / 11 / 2006	144
219.	Kagan *Chorten*	*Chorten*	Khaltse / Hanu Yokma / 12 / 2006	144

546

S.No.	NAME	CATEGORY	INVENTORY NO.	PAGE NO.

Hanupatta

S.No.	NAME	CATEGORY	INVENTORY NO.	PAGE NO.
220.	Dungsten *Chorten*	*Chorten* / *Mane* Wall	Khaltse / Hanupatta / 01 / 2004	**148**
221.	*Mane* Wall	*Mane* Wall	Khaltse / Hanupatta / 02 / 2004	**148**
222.	*Chorten* and *Mane* Wall (Manego)	*Chorten* / *Mane* Wall	Khaltse / Hanupatta / 03 / 2004	**149**
223.	*Mane* Wall	*Mane* Wall	Khaltse / Hanupatta / 04 / 2004	**149**
224.	*Mane* Walls	*Mane* Wall	Khaltse / Hanupatta / 05 / 2004	**150**
225.	Larten *Chorten*	*Chorten* / *Mane* Wall	Khaltse / Hanupatta / 06 / 2004	**150**
226.	*Lhashug* and Kaju Konra *Lhato*	Landscape (Tree) / *Lhato*	Khaltse / Hanupatta / 07 / 2004	**151**
227.	Yokmapa House	Vernacular Building	Khaltse / Hanupatta / 08 / 2004	**152**
228.	Hanupatta *Gonpa*	*Gonpa*	Khaltse / Hanupatta / 09 / 2004	**152**
229.	*Chorten Yogma*	*Chorten* / *Mane* Wall	Khaltse / Hanupatta / 10 / 2004	**153**
230.	*Chorten Yogma*	*Chorten*	Khaltse / Hanupatta / 11 / 2004	**153**
231.	Manego *Chorten*	*Chorten*	Khaltse / Hanupatta / 12 / 2004	**154**
232.	*Chorten*	*Chorten*	Khaltse / Hanupatta / 13 / 2004	**154**

Hanuthang

S.No.	NAME	CATEGORY	INVENTORY NO.	PAGE NO.
233.	*Mane* Wall	*Mane* Wall	Khaltse / Hanuthang / 01 / 2004	**155**
234.	*Mane* Wall	*Mane* Wall	Khaltse / Hanuthang / 02 / 2004	**155**
235.	*Mane* Wall	*Mane* Wall	Khaltse / Hanuthang / 03 / 2004	**156**
236.	*Kabristan*	Cemetery	Khaltse / Hanuthang / 04 / 2007	**156**
237.	Jamia *Masjid*	Mosque	Khaltse / Hanuthang / 05 / 2007	**157**
238.	Banpa House	Vernacular Building	Khaltse / Hanuthang / 06 / 2007	**157**
239.	Ehsarpa House	Vernacular Building	Khaltse / Hanuthang / 07 / 2007	**158**

Hemis Shukpachan

S.No.	NAME	CATEGORY	INVENTORY NO.	PAGE NO.
240.	Toropa House and *Chorten*	Vernacular Building	Khaltse / Hemis Shukpachan / 01 / 2004	**162**
241.	Phikarpe *Tsadkhang*	*Tsadkhang*	Khaltse / Hemis Shukpachan / 02 / 2004	**163**
242.	Group of *Chorten* and *Tsadkhang*	*Chorten* / *Tsadkhang*	Khaltse / Hemis Shukpachan / 03 / 2004	**163**
243.	Phikare Kagan	*Chorten*	Khaltse / Hemis Shukpachan / 04 / 2004	**164**
244.	Chug shig-zhal *Gonpa*	*Gonpa*	Khaltse / Hemis Shukpachan / 05 / 2004	**164**
245.	Phikarpa *Khangpa*	Vernacular Building	Khaltse / Hemis Shukpachan / 06 / 2004	**165**
246.	Phuntsog Ling *Chomoling*	*Gonpa*	Khaltse / Hemis Shukpachan / 07 / 2004	**165**
247.	Padma Tsering House	Vernacular Building	Khaltse / Hemis Shukpachan / 08 / 2004	**166**
248.	Tseb-Lhamo (Tseb-lha-gyal-mo) *Lhato* and *Chorten*	*Lhato* / *Chorten* / *Tsadkhang*	Khaltse / Hemis Shukpachan / 09 / 2004	**167**
249.	Dungsten *Chorten*	*Chorten* / *Mane* Wall	Khaltse / Hemis Shukpachan / 10 / 2004	**168**
250.	Paldan Dzomba *Lhato*	*Lhato*	Khaltse / Hemis Shukpachan / 11 / 2004	**168**
251.	Surichana *Mane*	*Mane* Wall	Khaltse / Hemis Shukpachan / 12 / 2004	**169**
252.	Samba Tsering *Chorten*	*Chorten* / *Mane* Wall	Khaltse / Hemis Shukpachan / 13 / 2004	**169**
253.	Aba Gune *Mane*	*Mane* Wall / *Chorten*	Khaltse / Hemis Shukpachan / 14 / 2004	**170**
254.	Tsesemo dzing	Landscape (Community Space)	Khaltse / Hemis Shukpachan / 15 / 2004	**170**
255.	Shalipa *Spurkhang*	*Chorten* / *Mane* Wall / Cremation Ground	Khaltse / Hemis Shukpachan / 16 / 2004	**171**
256.	Changpa pa House	Vernacular Building	Khaltse / Hemis Shukpachan / 17 / 2004	**171**
257.	Yurogpa *Mane* and Yurogpa *Khangpa*	Vernacular Building / *Mane* Wall / *Chorten*	Khaltse / Hemis Shukpachan / 18 / 2004	**172**
258.	Lung Thed de *Chorten*	*Chorten*	Khaltse / Hemis Shukpachan / 19 / 2004	**172**
259.	Stamgo Kagan	*Chorten*	Khaltse / Hemis Shukpachan / 20 / 2004	**173**
260.	Aba Gune *Chorten*	*Chorten*	Khaltse / Hemis Shukpachan / 21 / 2004	**173**
261.	Lha chang Tree	Landscape (Sacred Tree)	Khaltse / Hemis Shukpachan / 22 / 2004	**174**
262.	Lagekhore *Mane*	*Mane* Wall	Khaltse / Hemis Shukpachan / 23 / 2004	**174**

547

S.No.	NAME	CATEGORY	INVENTORY NO.	PAGE NO.
263.	Kali Kagan	Chorten / Mane Wall / Prayer Wheel	Khaltse / Hemis Shukpachan / 24 / 2004	175
264.	Khaltag Kangar	Chorten / Tsadkhang	Khaltse / Hemis Shukpachan / 25 / 2004	175
265.	Methog Khar	Fort / Palace	Khaltse / Hemis Shukpachan / 26 / 2004	176
266.	Tomba House	Vernacular Building	Khaltse / Hemis Shukpachan / 27 / 2004	176
267.	Chorten Kurkur	Chorten	Khaltse / Hemis Shukpachan / 28 / 2004	177
268.	Rigsum Gonbo	Rigsum Gonbo	Khaltse / Hemis Shukpachan / 29 / 2004	177
269.	Pastures	Landscape (Pastures / Waterbody)	Khaltse / Hemis Shukpachan / 30 / 2004	178
270.	Sasa Kongkar	Chorten / Mane Wall	Khaltse / Hemis Shukpachan / 31 / 2004	178
271.	Serpay Lhakhang	Gonpa	Khaltse / Hemis Shukpachan / 32 / 2004	179
272.	Shugpa Forest	Landscape (Sacred Grove)	Khaltse / Hemis Shukpachan / 33 / 2004	179

Hinju

S.No.	NAME	CATEGORY	INVENTORY NO.	PAGE NO.
273.	Lame Mane	Mane Wall	Khaltse / Hinju / 01 / 2004	182
274.	Shistipa House	Vernacular Building	Khaltse / Hinju / 02 / 2004	182
275.	Lhachang Tree	Landscape (Sacred Tree)	Khaltse / Hinju / 03 / 2004	183
276.	Tsabgyat Mane and Lhato	Chorten / Lhato	Khaltse / Hinju / 04 / 2004	183
277.	Rhoungi Mane	Chorten / Mane Wall	Khaltse / Hinju / 05 / 2004	184
278.	Mathang Mane	Chorten / Lhato	Khaltse / Hinju / 06 / 2004	184
279.	Chorten	Chorten	Khaltse / Hinju / 07 / 2004	185
280.	Kagan Chorten	Chorten	Khaltse / Hinju / 08 / 2004	185

Kanji

S.No.	NAME	CATEGORY	INVENTORY NO.	PAGE NO.
281.	Lotsava Lhakhang	Temple	Khaltse / Kanji / 01 / 2004	186
282.	Rigsum Gonbo	Rigsum Gonbo	Khaltse / Kanji / 02 / 2004	186
283.	Dzum-me Rigsum Gonbo	Rigsum Gonbo / Chorten	Khaltse / Kanji / 03 / 2004	187
284.	Nyerbak Chorten	Chorten	Khaltse / Kanji / 04 / 2004	187
285.	Zurkhangpa House	Vernacular Building	Khaltse / Kanji / 05 / 2004	188
286.	Kakapey Khangpa	Vernacular Building	Khaltse / Kanji / 06 / 2004	188
287.	Lugupey House	Vernacular Building	Khaltse / Kanji / 07 / 2004	189

Khaltse

S.No.	NAME	CATEGORY	INVENTORY NO.	PAGE NO.
288.	Goche Chorten	Chorten	Khaltse / Khaltse / 01 / 2004	192
289.	Group of Chorten and Mane Wall	Chorten / Mane Wall	Khaltse / Khaltse / 02 / 2004	192
290.	Ralupey Khangpa	Vernacular Building	Khaltse / Khaltse / 03 / 2004	193
291.	Sgang Ge Mane	Mane Wall	Khaltse / Khaltse / 04 / 2004	193
292.	Khaltse Gonpa	Gonpa / Chorten / Mane Wall	Khaltse / Khaltse / 05 / 2004	194
293.	Tashag (Khangchakpe)	Vernacular Building	Khaltse / Khaltse / 06 / 2004	195
294.	Group of Chorten	Chorten	Khaltse / Khaltse / 07 / 2004	195
295.	Petroglyph	Petroglyph	Khaltse / Khaltse / 08 / 2004	196
296.	Snumpa House	Vernacular Building	Khaltse / Khaltse / 09 / 2004	196
297.	Saipa House	Vernacular Building	Khaltse / Khaltse / 10 / 2004	197
298.	Chorten and Rigsum Gonbo	Chorten / Rigsum Gonbo	Khaltse / Khaltse / 11 / 2004	197
299.	Group of Chorten	Chorten	Khaltse / Khaltse / 12 / 2004	198
300.	Dakschanpa Tashag	Vernacular Building	Khaltse / Khaltse / 13 / 2004	199
301.	Gongmapa Khangchen House	Vernacular Building	Khaltse / Khaltse / 14 / 2004	199
302.	Zhabzes	Landscape (Rock Formation)	Khaltse / Khaltse / 15 / 2004	200
303.	Rigsum Gonbo	Rigsum Gonbo	Khaltse / Khaltse / 16 / 2004	200
304.	Mane Wall	Mane Wall	Khaltse / Khaltse / 17 / 2004	201
305.	Zangsthar Starga	Landscape (Tree)	Khaltse / Khaltse / 18 / 2004	201
306.	Api Daknak Chomo Lhato	Lhato	Khaltse / Khaltse / 19 / 2004	202

549

S.No.	NAME	CATEGORY	INVENTORY NO.	PAGE NO.
351.	Chosangpa House	Vernacular Building	Khaltse / Lehdo / 13 / 2006	232
352.	*Mane* Wall	*Mane* Wall	Khaltse / Lehdo / 14 / 2006	233
353.	Tashispa House	Vernacular Building	Khaltse / Lehdo / 15 / 2006	233
354.	Lobdhepa House	Vernacular Building	Khaltse / Lehdo / 16 / 2006	234
355.	*Mane* Wall	*Mane* Wall	Khaltse / Lehdo / 17 / 2006	234
356.	Gambupa House	Vernacular Building	Khaltse / Lehdo / 18 / 2006	235
357.	Singey Thangpa	Vernacular Building	Khaltse / Lehdo / 19 / 2006	236
358.	Group of *Chorten*	*Chorten*	Khaltse / Lehdo / 20 / 2006	236
359.	Guntsar Thangpa	Vernacular Building	Khaltse / Lehdo / 21 / 2006	237
360.	Kabto *Gonpa*	*Gonpa*	Khaltse / Lehdo / 22 / 2006	237
361.	Group of *Chorten* and *Mane* Walls	*Chorten* / *Mane* Wall	Khaltse / Lehdo / 23 / 2006	238
362.	Urbis Chomo *Lhato*	*Lhato*	Khaltse / Lehdo / 24 / 2006	238
363.	*Mane* Wall	*Mane* Wall	Khaltse / Lehdo / 25 / 2006	239
364.	*Chorten*	*Chorten*	Khaltse / Lehdo / 26 / 2006	239
365.	Lehdo *Gonpa*	*Gonpa*	Khaltse / Lehdo / 27 / 2006	240
366.	Kagan *Chorten*	*Chorten*	Khaltse / Lehdo / 28 / 2006	241
367.	Chomaksang *Lhato*	*Lhato*	Khaltse / Lehdo / 29 / 2006	241
368.	Group of *Chorten*	*Chorten*	Khaltse / Lehdo / 30 / 2006	242
369.	Group of *Chorten* and *Mane* Wall	*Chorten* / *Mane* Wall	Khaltse / Lehdo / 31 / 2006	242
370.	Group of *Chorten* and *Mane* Wall	*Chorten* / *Mane* Wall	Khaltse / Lehdo / 32 / 2006	243
371.	Group of *Chorten* and *Mane* Wall	*Chorten* / *Mane* Wall	Khaltse / Lehdo / 33 / 2006	243
372.	Gonbopa House	Vernacular Building	Khaltse / Lehdo / 34 / 2006	244

Lingshed

S.No.	NAME	CATEGORY	INVENTORY NO.	PAGE NO.
373.	Group of *Chorten* and *Rigsum Gonbo* (Pagthabe *Chorten*)	*Chorten* / *Rigsum Gonbo*	Khaltse / Lingshed / 01 / 2004	248
374.	Pagthabe *Chorten*	*Chorten*	Khaltse / Lingshed / 02 / 2004	249
375.	*Mane* Ringmo *Chorten*	*Chorten* / *Mane* Wall	Khaltse / Lingshed / 03 / 2004	249
376.	*Chorten* Nyis-tsag	*Chorten* / *Mane* Wall	Khaltse / Lingshed / 04 / 2004	250
377.	Bandoma *Lhato* and Bandopa House	*Lhato* / Vernacular Building	Khaltse / Lingshed / 05 / 2004	250
378.	Group of *Chorten* and *Mane* Walls	*Chorten* / *Mane* Wall	Khaltse / Lingshed / 06 / 2004	251
379.	Bothepa House and *Chorten*	Vernacular Building / *Chorten*	Khaltse / Lingshed / 07 / 2004	251
380.	Sharchog *Chorten*, *Lhato* and *Rigsum Gonbo*	*Chorten* / *Rigsum Gonbo*	Khaltse / Lingshed / 08 / 2004	252
381.	*Chorten*	*Chorten*	Khaltse / Lingshed / 09 / 2004	253
382.	Gyapo Dungsten *Chorten*	*Chorten*	Khaltse / Lingshed / 10 / 2004	253
383.	Goypa House	Vernacular Building	Khaltse / Lingshed / 11 / 2004	254
384.	Garbi *Mane*	*Mane* Wall	Khaltse / Lingshed / 12 / 2004	254
385.	Pangong *Lhato* and Shalangpa House	Vernacular Building / *Lhato*	Khaltse / Lingshed / 13 / 2004	255
386.	Lung Ze *Mane*	*Chorten* / *Mane* Wall	Khaltse / Lingshed / 14 / 2004	256
387.	*Chorten* Chugpe *Mane*	*Chorten*	Khaltse / Lingshed / 15 / 2004	256
388.	Lingshed Palace (Ringsten *Khar* / Sumur *Khar*)	Fort / Palace	Khaltse / Lingshed / 16 / 2004	257
389.	Phunis Gang *Lhato*	*Lhato*	Khaltse / Lingshed / 17 / 2004	257
390.	Tashi Odbar *Gonpa* (Lingshed *Gonpa*)	*Chorten*	Khaltse / Lingshed / 18 / 2004	258
391.	Pharkapa House	Vernacular Building	Khaltse / Lingshed / 19 / 2004	259
392.	*Chorten*	*Chorten* / Prayer Wheel	Khaltse / Lingshed / 20 / 2004	260
393.	Zong-ge Bawo (*Tsamskhang*)	Landscape (Sacred Cave)	Khaltse / Lingshed / 21 / 2004	261

S.No.	NAME	CATEGORY	INVENTORY NO.	PAGE NO.
Mangyu				
394.	Tsa-Tsa Puri *Chorten*	*Chorten*	Khaltse / Mangyu / 01 / 2004	**264**
395.	Likir *Tashag*	Vernacular Building	Khaltse / Mangyu / 02 / 2004	**265**
396.	Mangyu *Chorten*	*Chorten*	Khaltse / Mangyu / 03 / 2004	**265**
397.	Dugyal *Gonpa*	*Gonpa*	Khaltse / Mangyu / 04 / 2004	**266**
398.	Cholgog *Chorten*	*Chorten*	Khaltse / Mangyu / 05 / 2004	**266**
399.	Group of *Chorten*	*Chorten*	Khaltse / Mangyu / 06 / 2004	**267**
400.	Chemday *Tashag*	Vernacular Building	Khaltse / Mangyu / 07 / 2004	**267**
401.	Nang-Bar-Nang Dzad	*Gonpa*	Khaltse / Mangyu / 08 / 2004	**268**
402.	Nag-Ldan *Chorten*	*Chorten*	Khaltse / Mangyu / 09 / 2004	**269**
403.	*Chorten* Thugu (Cholgog)	*Chorten* / *Mane* Wall	Khaltse / Mangyu / 10 / 2004	**270**
404.	*Lhato*	*Lhato*	Khaltse / Mangyu / 11 / 2004	**270**
405.	*Chorten* and *Mane* Wall	*Chorten* / *Mane* Wall	Khaltse / Mangyu / 12 / 2004	**271**
406.	*Spurkhang*	Cemetery / Cremation Ground / Tomb	Khaltse / Mangyu / 13 / 2004	**271**
407.	*Chorten*	*Chorten*	Khaltse / Mangyu / 14 / 2004	**272**
408.	*Chorten* and *Spurkhang*	*Chorten* / Cremation Ground	Khaltse / Mangyu / 15 / 2004	**272**
409.	*Rigsum Gonbo*	*Rigsum Gonbo*	Khaltse / Mangyu / 16 / 2004	**273**
410.	*Chorten*	*Chorten*	Khaltse / Mangyu / 17 / 2004	**273**
411.	Rongpa *Chorten*	*Chorten*	Khaltse / Mangyu / 18 / 2004	**274**
412.	Meme Sku	Rock Carving / Rock Inscription	Khaltse / Mangyu / 19 / 2004	**274**
Nyerak				
413.	Bridge	Bridge	Khaltse / Nyerak / 01 / 2006	**278**
414.	Nyerak *Khar*	Vernacular Building	Khaltse / Nyerak / 02 / 2006	**278**
415.	Sharchok *Lhato*	*Lhato*	Khaltse / Nyerak / 03 / 2006	**279**
416.	*Chorten*	*Chorten*	Khaltse / Nyerak / 04 / 2006	**279**
417.	*Lhato* Sharchok	*Lhato*	Khaltse / Nyerak / 05 / 2006	**280**
418.	Phelepa House	Vernacular Building	Khaltse / Nyerak / 06 / 2006	**280**
419.	Tsuksapa House	Vernacular Building	Khaltse / Nyerak / 07 / 2006	**281**
420.	Onpopa House	Vernacular Building	Khaltse / Nyerak / 08 / 2006	**281**
421.	Onpo *Khangbu*	Vernacular Building	Khaltse / Nyerak / 09 / 2006	**282**
422.	Tashi Samstanling (Nyerak *Gonpa*)	*Gonpa*	Khaltse / Nyerak / 10 / 2006	**282**
423.	*Mane* Wall and Ruila *Chorten*	*Mane* Wall / *Chorten*	Khaltse / Nyerak / 11 / 2006	**283**
424.	Shugtser Spundun	Landscape (Grove)	Khaltse / Nyerak / 12 / 2006	**283**
425.	*Chorten* Sumpo	*Chorten* / *Mane* Wall	Khaltse / Nyerak / 13 / 2006	**284**
426.	Khumbupa House	Vernacular Building	Khaltse / Nyerak / 14 / 2006	**284**
427.	Katpe *Chorten*	*Chorten*	Khaltse / Nyerak / 15 / 2006	**285**
428.	Chocho Kuru la	Landscape (Mountain Pass)	Khaltse / Nyerak / 16 / 2006	**285**
429.	Katpe *Rigsum Gonbo*	*Rigsum Gonbo*	Khaltse / Nyerak / 17 / 2006	**286**
Nyurla				
430.	Group of *Chorten*	*Chorten* / *Mane* Wall	Khaltse / Nyurla / 01 / 2004	**290**
431.	Khargogpa House	Vernacular Building	Khaltse / Nyurla / 02 / 2004	**291**
432.	Khargogpa *Chorten*	*Chorten*	Khaltse / Nyurla / 03 / 2004	**291**
433.	Chug-Shig-Zhal *Gonpa*	*Gonpa*	Khaltse / Nyurla / 04 / 2004	**292**
434.	Kirkirope House	Vernacular Building	Khaltse / Nyurla / 05 / 2004	**292**
435.	Petugpa House	Vernacular Building	Khaltse / Nyurla / 06 / 2004	**293**
436.	Thangpe *Chorten*	*Chorten*	Khaltse / Nyurla / 07 / 2004	**293**
437.	*Spurkhang*	Cremation Ground	Khaltse / Nyurla / 08 / 2004	**294**
438.	Petroglyphs	Rock Carving	Khaltse / Nyurla / 09 / 2004	**294**
439.	Group of *Chorten* and *Mane* Wall	*Chorten* / *Mane* Wall	Khaltse / Nyurla / 10 / 2004	**295**

551

S.No.	NAME	CATEGORY	INVENTORY NO.	PAGE NO.
Phanjilla				
440.	Group of *Chorten* and *Mane* Walls	*Chorten* / *Mane* Wall	Khaltse / Phanjilla / 01 / 2004	**296**
441.	*Chorten*	*Chorten*	Khaltse / Phanjilla / 02 / 2004	**296**
442.	*Rigsum Gonbo*	*Rigsum Gonbo*	Khaltse / Phanjilla / 03 / 2004	**297**
443.	Group of *Chorten* and *Mane* Wall	*Chorten* / *Mane* Wall	Khaltse / Phanjilla / 04 / 2004	**297**
444.	*Rigsum Gonbo*	*Rigsum Gonbo*	Khaltse / Phanjilla / 05 / 2004	**298**
445.	Monpa House	Vernacular Building	Khaltse / Phanjilla / 06 / 2004	**298**
446.	Group of *Mane* Wall and *Chorten*	*Chorten* / *Mane* Wall	Khaltse / Phanjilla / 07 / 2004	**299**
447.	*Mane* Walls	*Mane* Wall	Khaltse / Phanjilla / 08 / 2004	**299**
Photoksar				
448.	Shishila Pass	Landscape (Pass)	Khaltse / Photoksar / 01 / 2004	**302**
449.	Kagan *Chorten*	*Chorten* / *Mane* Wall / *Lhato*	Khaltse / Photoksar / 02 / 2004	**302**
450.	*Mane* Wall	*Mane* Wall	Khaltse / Photoksar / 03 / 2004	**303**
451.	Group of *Chorten*	*Chorten*	Khaltse / Photoksar / 04 / 2004	**303**
452.	Konchok *Mane*	*Mane* Wall	Khaltse / Photoksar / 05 / 2004	**304**
453.	Zurwa *Khangpa*	Vernacular Building	Khaltse / Photoksar / 06 / 2004	**304**
454.	*Lagang Mane*	Temple / *Chorten*	Khaltse / Photoksar / 07 / 2004	**305**
455.	Rchachan, Tiruma, Spumsal *Lhato* (Yurla)	*Lhato*	Khaltse / Photoksar / 08 / 2004	**306**
456.	Yato *Chorten*	*Mane* Wall / *Chorten* / *Tsadkhang*	Khaltse / Photoksar / 09 / 2004	**306**
457.	*Gonpa Gongma*	*Gonpa*	Khaltse / Photoksar / 10 / 2004	**307**
458.	*Rigsum Gonbo*	*Rigsum Gonbo*	Khaltse / Photoksar / 11 / 2004	**308**
459.	Ldal Thong Ge *Khar* (*Khargog*)	Fort / Palace	Khaltse / Photoksar / 12 / 2004	**308**
460.	Photoksar *Gonpa Gongma*	*Gonpa* / *Mane* Wall / *Chorten* / *Rigsum Gonbo*	Khaltse / Photoksar / 13 / 2004	**309**
461.	*Gonpa Yokma*	*Gonpa* / *Chorten* / *Mane* Wall	Khaltse / Photoksar / 14 / 2004	**310**
462.	Phasla Kaju Kontak	*Lhato*	Khaltse / Photoksar / 15 / 2004	**311**
463.	Gyashingpa's *Lhato*	*Lhato*	Khaltse / Photoksar / 16 / 2004	**311**
464.	Tseb Lhamo *Lhato*	*Lhato*	Khaltse / Photoksar / 17 / 2004	**312**
465.	*Rigsum Gonbo*	*Rigsum Gonbo*	Khaltse / Photoksar / 18 / 2004	**312**
466.	Khang Ltakpa House	Vernacular Building	Khaltse / Photoksar / 19 / 2004	**313**
467.	Gatapa House	Vernacular Building	Khaltse / Photoksar / 20 / 2004	**314**
468.	Lhazhingpa House	Vernacular Building	Khaltse / Photoksar / 21 / 2004	**314**
469.	Group of *Chorten* and *Mane* Wall	*Chorten* / *Mane* Wall	Khaltse / Photoksar / 22 / 2004	**315**
470.	Tashi Gang *Chorten*	*Chorten*	Khaltse / Photoksar / 23 / 2004	**315**
471.	Onpopa House	Vernacular Building	Khaltse / Photoksar / 24 / 2004	**316**
472.	*Lhato* and *Mane* Wall	*Lhato*	Khaltse / Photoksar / 25 / 2004	**316**
473.	Thingpey Tsepa House and *Chorten*	Vernacular Building / *Chorten* / *Mane* Wall	Khaltse / Photoksar / 26 / 2004	**317**
474.	Group of *Mane* Wall and *Rigsum Gonbo*	*Mane* Wall / *Rigsum Gonbo*	Khaltse / Photoksar / 27 / 2004	**318**
475.	Singhela Mountain and Pass	Landscape (Mountain / Pass)	Khaltse / Photoksar / 28 / 2004	**318**
476.	*Mane* Wall	*Mane* Wall	Khaltse / Photoksar / 29 / 2004	**319**
477.	*Chorten*	*Chorten*	Khaltse / Photoksar / 30 / 2004	**319**
Ridzong				
478.	Ridzong *Gonpa*	*Gonpa*	Khaltse / Ridzong / 01 / 2004	**322**
479.	Skudung	Temple	Khaltse / Ridzong / 02 / 2004	**323**
480.	Tashi Riskyong	*Lhato*	Khaltse / Ridzong / 03 / 2004	**324**
481.	Gyal Chen	*Lhato*	Khaltse / Ridzong / 04 / 2004	**324**
482.	*Tsadkhang*	*Tsadkhang*	Khaltse / Ridzong / 05 / 2004	**325**

S.No.	NAME	CATEGORY	INVENTORY NO.	PAGE NO.
483.	*Tsadkhang*	*Tsadkhang*	Khaltse / Ridzong / 06 / 2004	**325**
484.	Kagan *Chorten*	*Chorten*	Khaltse / Ridzong / 07 / 2004	**326**
485.	Ching-Tsam	*Chorten / Mane* Wall	Khaltse / Ridzong / 08 / 2004	**326**
486.	Group of *Chorten, Mane* Wall and *Tsadkhang*	*Chorten / Mane* Wall	Khaltse / Ridzong / 09 / 2004	**327**
487.	*Mane* Wall and Rock Carving	*Mane* Wall	Khaltse / Ridzong / 10 / 2004	**327**
488.	Gyes Nyan *Lhato*	*Lhato*	Khaltse / Ridzong / 11 / 2004	**328**
489.	*Rigsum Gonbo*	*Rigsum Gonbo*	Khaltse / Ridzong / 12 / 2004	**328**
490.	Thardot Choling (Chuli Chan)	*Gonpa*	Khaltse / Ridzong / 13 / 2004	**329**

Saspol

S.No.	NAME	CATEGORY	INVENTORY NO.	PAGE NO.
491.	Bawo Marpo	Temple	Khaltse / Saspol / 01 / 2004	**332**
492.	Group of *Chorten* and *Mane* Walls	*Mane* Wall / *Chorten*	Khaltse / Saspol / 02 / 2004	**333**
493.	Group of *Chorten*	*Chorten*	Khaltse / Saspol / 03 / 2004	**334**
494.	Group of *Chorten*	*Chorten*	Khaltse / Saspol / 04 / 2004	**334**
495.	Saspol *Khar*	Fort / Palace	Khaltse / Saspol / 05 / 2004	**335**
496.	*Chorten*	*Chorten*	Khaltse / Saspol / 06 / 2004	**335**
497.	Group of *Chorten*	*Chorten*	Khaltse / Saspol / 07 / 2004	**336**
498.	Tseb Lhamo *Lhato*	*Lhato*	Khaltse / Saspol / 08 / 2004	**336**
499.	Group of *Chorten*	*Chorten*	Khaltse / Saspol / 09 / 2004	**337**
500.	*Chorten* and *Mane* Wall (Phikhare *Chorten*)	*Mane* Wall	Khaltse / Saspol / 10 / 2004	**337**
501.	*Tsamskhang*	Temple	Khaltse / Saspol / 11 / 2004	**338**
502.	*Spurkhang*	Cremation Ground	Khaltse / Saspol / 12 / 2004	**338**
503.	Phigarpa House	Vernacular Building	Khaltse / Saspol / 13 / 2004	**339**
504.	Group of *Mane* Wall and *Chorten*	*Mane* Wall / *Chorten*	Khaltse / Saspol / 14 / 2004	**339**
505.	Gompapa *Khangpa*	Vernacular Building	Khaltse / Saspol / 15 / 2004	**340**
506.	Hirgopa *Khangchen*	Vernacular Building	Khaltse / Saspol / 16 / 2004	**340**
507.	Group of *Chorten*	*Chorten*	Khaltse / Saspol / 17 / 2004	**341**
508.	*Rigsum Gonbo*	*Rigsum Gonbo*	Khaltse / Saspol / 18 / 2004	**341**
509.	Kangyur *Lhakhang*	Temple	Khaltse / Saspol / 19 / 2004	**342**
510.	Kagan *Chorten*	*Chorten*	Khaltse / Saspol / 20 / 2004	**342**
511.	Gyalwa Chamba *Lhakhang*	Temple	Khaltse / Saspol / 21 / 2004	**343**
512.	*Rigsum Gonbo* and *Chorten*	*Rigsum Gonbo / Chorten*	Khaltse / Saspol / 22 / 2004	**344**
513.	Group of *Chorten*	*Chorten*	Khaltse / Saspol / 23 / 2004	**344**
514.	Group of *Chorten*	*Chorten*	Khaltse / Saspol / 24 / 2004	**345**

Saspotse

S.No.	NAME	CATEGORY	INVENTORY NO.	PAGE NO.
515.	Group of *Chorten*	*Chorten*	Khaltse / Saspotse / 01 / 2004	**348**
516.	Akhten Naro *Lhato*	*Lhato*	Khaltse / Saspotse / 02 / 2004	**348**
517.	Group of *Chorten*	*Chorten*	Khaltse / Saspotse / 03 / 2004	**349**
518.	Khar House	Vernacular Building	Khaltse / Saspotse / 04 / 2004	**349**
519.	*Chorten* Shrapa	*Chorten*	Khaltse / Saspotse / 05 / 2004	**350**
520.	Saspotse Rinchen Gang (Saspotse *Gonpa*)	*Gonpa*	Khaltse / Saspotse / 06 / 2004	**350**
521.	Lotsawa *Lagang Gogpo*	Temple	Khaltse / Saspotse / 07 / 2004	**351**
522.	Zing Gog Gay *Mane* and Changchub *Chorten*	*Mane* Wall / *Chorten*	Khaltse / Saspotse / 08 / 2004	**352**
523.	*Rigsum Gonbo*	*Rigsum Gonbo*	Khaltse / Saspotse / 09 / 2004	**352**
524.	Dungsten *Lhato*	*Lhato*	Khaltse / Saspotse / 10 / 2004	**353**
525.	*Lubang*	*Lubang*	Khaltse / Saspotse / 11 / 2004	**353**
526.	Dungsten *Lhato* and *Chorten*	*Chorten / Lhato*	Khaltse / Saspotse / 12 / 2004	**354**

553

S.No.	NAME	CATEGORY	INVENTORY NO.	PAGE NO.
527.	Skudung *Chorten*	*Chorten*	Khaltse / Saspotse / 13 / 2004	354
528.	*Mane* Go *Chorten*	*Chorten* / *Mane* Wall	Khaltse / Saspotse / 14 / 2004	355
529.	Dagang Gay *Mane*	*Chorten*	Khaltse / Saspotse / 15 / 2004	355
530.	Dagang Gay *Mane*	*Chorten*	Khaltse / Saspotse / 16 / 2004	356
531.	*Chorten* Soma	*Chorten*	Khaltse / Saspotse / 17 / 2004	356
532.	Group of *Chorten*	*Chorten*	Khaltse / Saspotse / 18 / 2004	357
533.	Oolguay *Mane*	*Chorten*	Khaltse / Saspotse / 19 / 2004	357
534.	Rock Carvings	*Chorten*	Khaltse / Saspotse / 20 / 2004	358

Shilla

S.No.	NAME	CATEGORY	INVENTORY NO.	PAGE NO.
535.	*Rigsum Gonbo*	*Rigsum Gonbo*	Khaltse / Shilla / 01 / 2004	359
536.	*Mane* Wall and *Chorten* (Prinkiti *Mane*)	*Chorten* / *Mane* Wall	Khaltse / Shilla / 02 / 2004	359
537.	Sherabpa House	Vernacular Building	Khaltse / Shilla / 03 / 2004	360
538.	*Rigsum Gonbo* and *Chorten*	*Rigsum Gonbo* / *Chorten*	Khaltse / Shilla / 04 / 2004	360
539.	Larjaypey House	Vernacular Building	Khaltse / Shilla / 05 / 2004	361
540.	*Chorten*	*Chorten*	Khaltse / Shilla / 06 / 2004	361

Skindyang

S.No.	NAME	CATEGORY	INVENTORY NO.	PAGE NO.
541.	Group of *Chorten*	*Chorten*	Khaltse / Skindyang / 01 / 2006	364
542.	*Mane* Wall	*Mane* Wall	Khaltse / Skindyang / 02 / 2006	364
543.	Group of *Chorten*	*Chorten*	Khaltse / Skindyang / 03 / 2006	365
544.	Kagan *Chorten*	*Chorten*	Khaltse / Skindyang / 04 / 2006	365
545.	*Tashag*	Vernacular Building	Khaltse / Skindyang / 05 / 2006	366
546.	Group of *Mane* Walls and *Chorten*	*Mane* Wall / *Chorten*	Khaltse / Skindyang / 06 / 2006	366
547.	Group of *Chorten* and *Rigsum Gonbo*	*Chorten* / *Rigsum Gonbo*	Khaltse / Skindyang / 07 / 2006	367
548.	Group of *Chorten*	*Chorten*	Khaltse / Skindyang / 08 / 2006	367
549.	Guru Zhabjes	Landscape (Rock Formation)	Khaltse / Skindyang / 09 / 2006	368
550.	*Mane* Wall	*Mane* Wall	Khaltse / Skindyang / 10 / 2006	368
551.	Group of *Chorten*	*Chorten*	Khaltse / Skindyang / 11 / 2006	369
552.	Dakshospa House	Vernacular Building	Khaltse / Skindyang / 12 / 2006	369
553.	*Chorten*	*Chorten*	Khaltse / Skindyang / 13 / 2006	370
554.	*Mane* Wall	*Mane* Wall	Khaltse / Skindyang / 14 / 2006	370
555.	*Tsamskhang*	Temple	Khaltse / Skindyang / 15 / 2006	371
556.	Group of *Chorten*	*Chorten*	Khaltse / Skindyang / 16 / 2006	371
557.	*Gonpa*	*Gonpa*	Khaltse / Skindyang / 17 / 2006	372
558.	*Chorten*	*Chorten*	Khaltse / Skindyang / 18 / 2006	373
559.	*Lhato* Yanglag Chomo	*Lhato*	Khaltse / Skindyang / 19 / 2006	373
560.	Group of *Chorten*	*Chorten*	Khaltse / Skindyang / 20 / 2006	374

Skyumpata

S.No.	NAME	CATEGORY	INVENTORY NO.	PAGE NO.
561.	Skyumpata Gongma *Gonpa*	*Gonpa*	Khaltse / Skyumpata / 01 / 2006	375
562.	Skyapa *Khangbu*	Vernacular Building	Khaltse / Skyumpata / 02 / 2006	375
563.	Skyapa House	Vernacular Building	Khaltse / Skyumpata / 03 / 2006	376
564.	Yokmapa *Khangbu*	Vernacular Building	Khaltse / Skyumpata / 04 / 2006	376
565.	Yokmapa House	Vernacular Building	Khaltse / Skyumpata / 05 / 2006	377
566.	Thakranpa House	Vernacular Building	Khaltse / Skyumpata / 06 / 2006	377
567.	Gorgupa House	Vernacular Building	Khaltse / Skyumpata / 07 / 2006	378
568.	*Chorten*	*Chorten*	Khaltse / Skyumpata / 08 / 2006	378

S.No.	NAME	CATEGORY	INVENTORY NO.	PAGE NO.
	Skyurbuchan			
569.	*Mane* Walls	*Mane* Wall	Khaltse / Skyurbuchan / 01 / 2006	**382**
570.	Group of *Chorten* and *Mane* Walls	*Chorten* / *Mane* Wall	Khaltse / Skyurbuchan / 02 / 2006	**382**
571.	Group of *Chorten* and *Mane* Walls	*Chorten* / *Mane* Wall	Khaltse / Skyurbuchan / 03 / 2006	**383**
572.	Group of *Chorten*	*Chorten*	Khaltse / Skyurbuchan / 04 / 2006	**383**
573.	Group of *Chorten*	*Chorten*	Khaltse / Skyurbuchan / 05 / 2006	**384**
574.	Group of *Chorten* and *Mane* Walls	*Chorten* / *Mane* Wall	Khaltse / Skyurbuchan / 06 / 2006	**384**
575.	Kagan *Chorten*	*Chorten*	Khaltse / Skyurbuchan / 07 / 2006	**385**
576.	*Mane* Wall	*Mane* Wall	Khaltse / Skyurbuchan / 08 / 2006	**385**
577.	Kagan *Chorten*	*Chorten*	Khaltse / Skyurbuchan / 09 / 2006	**386**
578.	Group of *Chorten* and *Mane* Walls	*Chorten* / *Mane* Wall	Khaltse / Skyurbuchan / 10 / 2006	**386**
579.	Group of *Chorten* and *Mane* Wall	*Chorten* / *Mane* Wall	Khaltse / Skyurbuchan / 11 / 2006	**387**
580.	Group of *Chorten*	*Chorten*	Khaltse / Skyurbuchan / 12 / 2006	**387**
581.	Group of *Chorten*	*Chorten*	Khaltse / Skyurbuchan / 13 / 2006	**388**
582.	*Chorten*	*Chorten*	Khaltse / Skyurbuchan / 14 / 2006	**388**
583.	Kagan *Chorten*	*Chorten*	Khaltse / Skyurbuchan / 15 / 2006	**389**
584.	*Rigsum Gonbo*	*Rigsum Gonbo*	Khaltse / Skyurbuchan / 16 / 2006	**389**
585.	Group of *Chorten* and *Mane* Walls	*Chorten* / *Mane* Wall	Khaltse / Skyurbuchan / 17 / 2006	**390**
586.	Group of *Chorten* and *Mane* Walls	*Chorten* / *Mane* Wall	Khaltse / Skyurbuchan / 18 / 2006	**390**
587.	Skyurbuchan *Khar*	Fort / Palace	Khaltse / Skyurbuchan / 19 / 2006	**391**
588.	Lharjey Pa House	Vernacular Building	Khaltse / Skyurbuchan / 20 / 2006	**392**
589.	Shugu Ting pa House	Vernacular Building	Khaltse / Skyurbuchan / 21 / 2006	**392**
590.	Bhutith pa House	Vernacular Building	Khaltse / Skyurbuchan / 22 / 2006	**393**
591.	Group of *Chorten*	*Chorten*	Khaltse / Skyurbuchan / 23 / 2006	**393**
592.	Stago pa House	Vernacular Building	Khaltse / Skyurbuchan / 24 / 2006	**394**
593.	Dakshos pa House	Vernacular Building	Khaltse / Skyurbuchan / 25 / 2006	**394**
594.	Kagan *Chorten*	*Chorten*	Khaltse / Skyurbuchan / 26 / 2006	**395**
595.	Group of *Chorten* and *Mane* Walls	*Chorten* / *Mane* Wall	Khaltse / Skyurbuchan / 27 / 2006	**395**
596.	Group of *Chorten*	*Chorten*	Khaltse / Skyurbuchan / 28 / 2006	**396**
597.	Group of *Chorten*	*Chorten*	Khaltse / Skyurbuchan / 29 / 2006	**396**
598.	Thegchen Dargyas Ling (Skyurbuchan *Gonpa*)	*Gonpa*	Khaltse / Skyurbuchan / 30 / 2006	**397**
599.	Group of *Chorten*	*Chorten*	Khaltse / Skyurbuchan / 31 / 2006	**398**
600.	*Mane* Chuskor Gonpa	Temple	Khaltse / Skyurbuchan / 32 / 2006	**398**
601.	*Dosku*	Rock Carving	Khaltse / Skyurbuchan / 33 / 2006	**399**
602.	Skangke Kagan	*Chorten*	Khaltse / Skyurbuchan / 34 / 2006	**399**
603.	Group of *Chorten*	*Chorten*	Khaltse / Skyurbuchan / 35 / 2006	**400**
	Tagmachig			
604.	*Mane* Wall	*Chorten* / *Mane* Wall /	Khaltse / Tagmachig / 01 / 2004	**404**
605.	Group of *Chorten*, and *Mane* Walls (Chorten Gongma)	*Chorten* / *Mane* Wall	Khaltse / Tagmachig / 02 / 2004	**404**
606.	Group of *Chorten* and *Mane* Walls	*Chorten* / *Mane* Wall	Khaltse / Tagmachig / 03 / 2004	**405**
607.	Tongspon pa House	Vernacular Building	Khaltse / Tagmachig / 04 / 2004	**405**
608.	Group of *Chorten*, *Mane* Wall and *Rigsum Gonbo*	*Chorten* / *Mane* Wall / *Rigsum Gonbo*	Khaltse / Tagmachig / 05 / 2004	**406**
609.	Nyerpa *Khangpa*	Vernacular Building	Khaltse / Tagmachig / 06 / 2004	**407**
610.	Churupa *Khangpa*	Vernacular Building	Khaltse / Tagmachig / 07 / 2004	**407**
611.	Nyenas *Lhakhang* (Tagmachig *Gonpa*)	*Gonpa*	Khaltse / Tagmachig / 08 / 2004	**408**
612.	Shimi *Chorten*	*Chorten*	Khaltse / Tagmachig / 09 / 2004	**409**
613.	Chugunpa House *(Tashag)*	Vernacular Building	Khaltse / Tagmachig / 10 / 2004	**409**

S.No.	NAME	CATEGORY	INVENTORY NO.	PAGE NO.
614.	*Chorten* and Deshag Gyadpa	*Chorten*	Khaltse / Tagmachig / 11 / 2004	**410**
615.	Group of *Chorten* and *Mane* Wall	*Chorten* / *Mane* Wall	Khaltse / Tagmachig / 12 / 2004	**411**
616.	Zappa House (*Tashag*)	Vernacular Building	Khaltse / Tagmachig / 13 / 2004	**411**
617.	Tashi Kunpa *Khangpa (Tashag)*	Vernacular Building	Khaltse / Tagmachig / 14 / 2004	**412**
618.	Tagmachig Castle *(Gyamkhar)*	Fort / Palace	Khaltse / Tagmachig / 15 / 2004	**412**
619.	*Mane* Wall	*Mane* Wall	Khaltse / Tagmachig / 16 / 2004	**413**
620.	Urbis Chomo *Lhato*	*Lhato*	Khaltse / Tagmachig / 17 / 2004	**413**
621.	*Mane* Wall	*Mane* Wall	Khaltse / Tagmachig / 18 / 2004	**414**
622.	Shime *Chorten*	*Chorten* / *Rigsum Gonbo*	Khaltse / Tagmachig / 19 / 2004	**414**
623.	Group of *Mane* Walls and *Chorten*	*Chorten* / *Mane* Wall	Khaltse / Tagmachig / 20 / 2004	**415**
624.	Group of *Chorten* and *Mane* Wall	*Chorten* / *Mane* Wall	Khaltse / Tagmachig / 21 / 2004	**416**
625.	Shagutpa House	Vernacular Building	Khaltse / Tagmachig / 22 / 2006	**416**
626.	Hemar *Gonpa*	*Gonpa*	Khaltse / Tagmachig / 23 / 2006	**417**
627.	*Tsamskhang*	Temple	Khaltse / Tagmachig / 24 / 2006	**418**
628.	Dewapa House	Vernacular Building	Khaltse / Tagmachig / 25 / 2006	**418**

Tar

S.No.	NAME	CATEGORY	INVENTORY NO.	PAGE NO.
629.	Azhangpe *Mane Chorten*	*Chorten*	Khaltse / Tar / 01 / 2004	**422**
630.	Deshag Gyad	*Chorten*	Khaltse / Tar / 02 / 2004	**422**
631.	Group of *Chorten* and *Mane* Walls	*Chorten* / *Mane* Wall	Khaltse / Tar / 03 / 2004	**423**
632.	Tar *Gonpa*	*Gonpa*	Khaltse / Tar / 04 / 2004	**424**
633.	Azhangpe *Tashag*	Vernacular Building	Khaltse / Tar / 05 / 2004	**424**
634.	*Rigsum Gonbo* and *Tsadkhang*	*Rigsum Gonbo* / *Tsadkhang* / *Mane* Wall	Khaltse / Tar / 06 / 2004	**425**
635.	Chotar *Lhato*	*Lhato*	Khaltse / Tar / 07 / 2004	**426**
636.	Abagon Ne House	Vernacular Building	Khaltse / Tar / 08 / 2004	**426**
637.	*Mane* Wall and Rock Inscription	*Mane* Wall	Khaltse / Tar / 09 / 2004	**427**
638.	21 Dolma *Rangjon* (*Rangjon* Nyishu-Tsag-chig)	Landscape (Sacred Rock Formation)	Khaltse / Tar / 10 / 2004	**427**
639.	*Gonbo Rangjon*	Landscape (Rock Formation)	Khaltse / Tar / 11 / 2004	**428**
640.	*Mane* Wall	*Mane* Wall	Khaltse / Tar / 12 / 2004	**428**
641.	*Shugpa* Tree	Landscape (Sacred Tree)	Khaltse / Tar / 13 / 2004	**429**
642.	*Yul Lha Lhato*	*Lhato*	Khaltse / Tar / 14 / 2004	**429**
643.	*Chorten* and *Mane* Walls	*Chorten* / *Mane* Wall	Khaltse / Tar / 15 / 2004	**430**
644.	Tar *Brog*	Precinct	Khaltse / Tar / 16 / 2004	**430**

Tarchid

S.No.	NAME	CATEGORY	INVENTORY NO.	PAGE NO.
645.	*Shugpa* Tree (*Shuk-tsher*)	Landscape (Sacred Tree)	Khaltse / Tarchid / 01 / 2004	**431**
646.	*Chorten*	*Chorten*	Khaltse / Tarchid / 02 / 2004	**431**
647.	*Mane* Wall	*Mane* Wall	Khaltse / Tarchid / 03 / 2004	**432**
648.	Skyapa House	Vernacular Building	Khaltse / Tarchid / 04 / 2004	**432**
649.	*Mane* Wall	*Mane* Wall	Khaltse / Tarchid / 05 / 2004	**433**
650.	*Chorten*	*Chorten*	Khaltse / Tarchid / 06 / 2004	**433**
651.	Group of *Mane* Walls and *Chorten*	*Chorten* / *Mane* Wall	Khaltse / Tarchid / 07 / 2004	**434**

Temisgang

S.No.	NAME	CATEGORY	INVENTORY NO.	PAGE NO.
652.	Group of *Chorten* and *Mane* Walls	*Chorten* / *Mane* Wall	Khaltse / Temisgang / 01 / 2004	**438**
653.	Singhe Osrung	*Chorten*	Khaltse / Temisgang / 02 / 2004	**438**
654.	Group of *Chorten*	*Chorten*	Khaltse / Temisgang / 03 / 2004	**439**
655.	Chanrazig *Lhakhang*	*Gonpa*	Khaltse / Temisgang / 04 / 2004	**439**
656.	Chamba *Lhakhang* (Tsuglakhang Marpo)	Temple	Khaltse / Temisgang / 05 / 2004	**440**

556

S.No.	NAME	CATEGORY	INVENTORY NO.	PAGE NO.
657.	Guru *Lhakhang*	Temple	Khaltse / Temisgang / 06 / 2004	**441**
658.	Temisgang *Khar*	Fort / Palace	Khaltse / Temisgang / 07 / 2004	**442**
659.	*Shugpa* Tree	Landscape (Sacred Tree)	Khaltse / Temisgang / 08 / 2004	**442**
660.	Tses Karmo *Gonpa*	*Gonpa*	Khaltse / Temisgang / 09 / 2004	**443**
661.	Group of *Chorten* and *Mane* Walls	*Chorten* / *Mane* Wall	Khaltse / Temisgang / 10 / 2004	**444**
662.	Group of *Chorten*	*Chorten*	Khaltse / Temisgang / 11 / 2004	**444**
663.	*Chorten* Makpape	*Chorten*	Khaltse / Temisgang / 12 / 2004	**445**
664.	Saman Ne House	Vernacular Building	Khaltse / Temisgang / 13 / 2004	**445**
665.	Sbulipa House	Vernacular Building	Khaltse / Temisgang / 14 / 2004	**446**
666.	Padepa House	Vernacular Building	Khaltse / Temisgang / 15 / 2004	**446**
667.	Manego House	Vernacular Building	Khaltse / Temisgang / 16 / 2004	**447**
668.	Rudpa House	Vernacular Building	Khaltse / Temisgang / 17 / 2004	**447**
669.	Group of *Chorten* and *Mane* Wall	*Chorten* / *Mane* Wall	Khaltse / Temisgang / 18 / 2004	**448**
670.	*Rigsum Gonbo*	*Rigsum Gonbo* / *Mane* Wall	Khaltse / Temisgang / 19 / 2004	**448**
671.	Kagan *Chorten*	*Chorten*	Khaltse / Temisgang / 20 / 2004	**449**
672.	Stagopa *House*	Vernacular Building	Khaltse / Temisgang / 21 / 2004	**449**
673.	Chopa House	Vernacular Building	Khaltse / Temisgang / 22 / 2004	**450**
674.	Chotar *Lhato*	*Lhato*	Khaltse / Temisgang / 23 / 2004	**450**
675.	Kagan *Chorten*	*Chorten*	Khaltse / Temisgang / 24 / 2004	**451**
676.	Kagan *Chorten*	*Chorten*	Khaltse / Temisgang / 25 / 2004	**452**
677.	Group of *Chorten* and *Mane* Wall	*Chorten* / *Mane* Wall	Khaltse / Temisgang / 26 / 2004	**452**
678.	Group of *Chorten*	*Chorten*	Khaltse / Temisgang / 27 / 2004	**453**
679.	*Chorten*	*Chorten*	Khaltse / Temisgang / 28 / 2004	**453**
680.	Group of *Chorten*	*Chorten*	Khaltse / Temisgang / 29 / 2004	**454**
681.	Phurongpa House, *Rigsum Gonbo* and Kagan *Chorten*	Vernacular Building / *Rigsum Gonbo* / *Chorten*	Khaltse / Temisgang / 30 / 2004	**455**
682.	Lartse *Lhakhang*	Temple	Khaltse / Temisgang / 31 / 2004	**456**
683.	Nyerpapa House	Vernacular Building	Khaltse / Temisgang / 32 / 2004	**456**
684.	*Lhakhang* and *Chorten*	*Chorten* / Temple	Khaltse / Temisgang / 33 / 2004	**457**
685.	Kagan *Chorten*	*Chorten*	Khaltse / Temisgang / 34 / 2004	**457**
686.	Group of *Chorten* and *Mane* Walls	*Chorten* / *Mane* Wall	Khaltse / Temisgang / 35 / 2004	**458**
687.	Group of *Chorten* and *Mane* Walls	*Chorten* / *Mane* Wall	Khaltse / Temisgang / 36 / 2004	**458**
688.	Group of *Chorten*	*Chorten*	Khaltse / Temisgang / 37 / 2004	**459**
689.	Chamba *Lhakhang*	Temple	Khaltse / Temisgang / 38 / 2004	**459**
690.	Chore *Mane*	*Mane* Wall / Rock Inscription / *Chorten*	Khaltse / Temisgang / 39 / 2004	**460**
691.	*Rigsum Gonbo*	*Rigsum Gonbo* / *Chorten*	Khaltse / Temisgang / 40 / 2004	**460**
692.	Group of *Chorten* and *Mane* Walls	*Chorten* / *Mane* Wall	Khaltse / Temisgang / 41 / 2004	**461**
693.	Group of *Chorten*	*Chorten*	Khaltse / Temisgang / 42 / 2004	**461**
694.	*Spurkhang*	Cremation Ground / *Chorten*	Khaltse / Temisgang / 43 / 2004	**462**
695.	Group of *Chorten* and *Lubang*	*Chorten* / *Lubang*	Khaltse / Temisgang / 44 / 2004	**462**
696.	Group of *Chorten*	*Chorten*	Khaltse / Temisgang / 45 / 2004	**463**
697.	*Mane Chorten*	*Chorten*	Khaltse / Temisgang / 46 / 2004	**463**
698.	Gashukpa House	Vernacular Building	Khaltse / Temisgang / 47 / 2004	**464**
699.	Group of *Chorten*	*Chorten*	Khaltse / Temisgang / 48 / 2004	**464**
700.	Group of *Chorten* and *Mane* Walls	*Chorten* / *Mane* Wall	Khaltse / Temisgang / 49 / 2004	**465**
701.	*Mane* Walls	*Mane* Wall	Khaltse / Temisgang / 50 / 2004	**465**
702.	*Mane* Ringmo	*Mane* Wall / *Chorten*	Khaltse / Temisgang / 51 / 2004	**466**

S.No.	NAME	CATEGORY	INVENTORY NO.	PAGE NO.
Tia				
703.	*Mane* Wall	*Mane* Wall	Khaltse / Tia / 01 / 2004	**470**
704.	Appi Changshar *Chomo Lhato*	Lhato	Khaltse / Tia / 02 / 2004	**470**
705.	*Chorten*	*Chorten*	Khaltse / Tia / 03 / 2004	**471**
706.	Serapey House	Vernacular Building	Khaltse / Tia / 04 / 2004	**471**
707.	Group of *Chorten* and *Mane* Wall	*Chorten* / *Mane* Wall	Khaltse / Tia / 05 / 2004	**472**
708.	*Rigsum Gonbo*	*Rigsum Gonbo*	Khaltse / Tia / 06 / 2004	**472**
709.	*Chorten* Travo	*Chorten*	Khaltse / Tia / 07 / 2004	**473**
710.	Charcharpa House	Vernacular Building	Khaltse / Tia / 08 / 2004	**473**
711.	Yokmapa House	Vernacular Building	Khaltse / Tia / 09 / 2004	**474**
712.	Kagan *Chorten*	*Chorten*	Khaltse / Tia / 10 / 2004	**474**
713.	Khatsa *Gonpa*	*Gonpa*	Khaltse / Tia / 11 / 2004	**475**
714.	*Mane Chuskor*	Prayer Wheel	Khaltse / Tia / 12 / 2004	**476**
715.	*Chorten* and *Mane* Wall	*Chorten* / *Mane* Wall	Khaltse / Tia / 13 / 2004	**476**
716.	*Chorten* Mermer	*Chorten*	Khaltse / Tia / 14 / 2004	**477**
717.	Khangsarmo *Chorten*	*Chorten*	Khaltse / Tia / 15 / 2004	**477**
718.	*Khar* Nonpa	Fort / Palace	Khaltse / Tia / 16 / 2004	**478**
719.	*Rigsum Gonbo* and Kagan *Chorten*	*Rigsum Gonbo* / *Chorten*	Khaltse / Tia / 17 / 2004	**479**
720.	Nyeringpa House	Vernacular Building	Khaltse / Tia / 18 / 2004	**480**
721.	*Rigsum Gonbo*	*Rigsum Gonbo*	Khaltse / Tia / 19 / 2004	**480**
722.	*Chorten* Mangpo (Sarig Ge Zug)	*Chorten* / *Mane* Wall	Khaltse / Tia / 20 / 2004	**481**
723.	Bang Kapa House	Vernacular Building	Khaltse / Tia / 21 / 2004	**481**
724.	Chus-skyab-pa House	Vernacular Building	Khaltse / Tia / 22 / 2004	**482**
725.	*Khar-chud-de Mane*	*Mane* Wall	Khaltse / Tia / 23 / 2004	**482**
726.	Group of *Chorten*	*Chorten*	Khaltse / Tia / 24 / 2004	**483**
727.	Group of *Chorten*	*Chorten*	Khaltse / Tia / 25 / 2004	**483**
728.	Group of *Chorten* and *Mane* Walls	*Chorten* / *Mane* Wall	Khaltse / Tia / 26 / 2004	**484**
729.	Group of *Chorten* and *Mane* Walls	*Chorten* / *Mane* Wall	Khaltse / Tia / 27 / 2004	**484**
Uletokpo				
730.	*Mane* Wall	*Mane* Wall	Khaltse / Uletokpo / 01 / 2004	**488**
731.	*Chorten*	*Chorten*	Khaltse / Uletokpo / 02 / 2004	**488**
732.	*Mane* Wall	*Mane* Wall	Khaltse / Uletokpo / 03 / 2004	**489**
733.	Uletokpo Pa House	Vernacular Building	Khaltse / Uletokpo / 04 / 2004	**489**
Urbis				
734.	Petroglyph	Rock Carving	Khaltse / Urbis / 01 / 2004	**490**
735.	Kushupa *Khangpa*	Vernacular Building	Khaltse / Urbis / 02 / 2004	**490**
736.	Group of *Chorten* and *Mane* Walls	*Chorten* / *Mane* Wall	Khaltse / Urbis / 03 / 2004	**491**
737.	*Mane* Wall	*Mane* Wall	Khaltse / Urbis / 04 / 2004	**491**
738.	Pharkapa *Khangpa*	Vernacular Building	Khaltse / Urbis / 05 / 2004	**492**
739.	Thupstan Tharpalling *Gonpa* (Urbis *Gonpa*)	*Gonpa*	Khaltse / Urbis / 06 / 2004	**492**
740.	*Rigsum Gonbo*	*Rigsum Gonbo*	Khaltse / Urbis / 07 / 2004	**493**
741.	Deshag Gyad	*Chorten*	Khaltse / Urbis / 08 / 2004	**493**
742.	Kagan *Chorten*	*Chorten*	Khaltse / Urbis / 09 / 2004	**494**
743.	Changrhug *Chorten*	*Chorten* / *Tarchen*	Khaltse / Urbis / 10 / 2004	**494**
744.	Baltipey *Tashag*	Vernacular Building	Khaltse / Urbis / 11 / 2004	**495**
745.	Group of *Chorten*	*Chorten*	Khaltse / Urbis / 12 / 2004	**495**
746.	Prayer Wheel and *Mane* Wall (*Mane* Tungchur)	Prayer Wheel / *Mane* Wall	Khaltse / Urbis / 13 / 2004	**496**
747.	*Chorten* and *Mane* Wall	*Chorten* / *Mane* Wall	Khaltse / Urbis / 14 / 2004	**496**

S.No.	NAME	CATEGORY	INVENTORY NO.	PAGE NO.
	Yulchung			
791.	Khagsta *Chorten*	*Chorten*	Khaltse / Yulchung / 01 / 2004	**528**
792.	*Chorten* Chenmo and *Mane* Wall	*Chorten*	Khaltse / Yulchung / 02 / 2004	**528**
793.	Yulma do *Chorten*	*Chorten*	Khaltse / Yulchung / 03 / 2004	**529**
794.	Baltipe *Chorten*	*Chorten*	Khaltse / Yulchung / 04 / 2004	**529**
795.	Khalang pa House	Vernacular Building	Khaltse / Yulchung / 05 / 2004	**530**
796.	Kong Ge La *Chorten*	*Chorten* / *Rigsum Gonbo* / *Mane* Wall	Khaltse / Yulchung / 06 / 2004	**530**
797.	Tashi Thong Gyas *Gonpa*	*Gonpa* / *Chorten* / Fort / *Mane* Wall	Khaltse / Yulchung / 07 / 2004	**531**
798.	Gya Ste *Mane*	*Mane* Wall	Khaltse / Yulchung / 08 / 2004	**532**
799.	Thongros Se *Rigsum Gonbo*	*Rigsum Gonbo*	Khaltse / Yulchung / 09 / 2004	**532**
800.	Yulpapa *Khangbu*	Vernacular Building	Khaltse / Yulchung / 10 / 2004	**533**
801.	Mashen Chepa House	Vernacular Building	Khaltse / Yulchung / 11 / 2004	**533**
802.	Gonpapa House	Vernacular Building	Khaltse / Yulchung / 12 / 2004	**534**
803.	Gonpapa *Chorten*	*Chorten* / *Mane* Wall	Khaltse / Yulchung / 13 / 2004	**534**
804.	Domang *Mane*	*Mane* Wall	Khaltse / Yulchung / 14 / 2004	**535**
805.	Yulpape House	Vernacular Building	Khaltse / Yulchung / 15 / 2004	**535**
806.	Tashi Domang *Gonpa*	*Gonpa* / *Chorten* / Prayer Wheel	Khaltse / Yulchung / 16 / 2004	**536**
807.	Yultsa *Lhato*	*Lhato*	Khaltse / Yulchung / 17 / 2004	**537**
808.	Chanrazig Rock Formation (Kha-Tsar Pani)	Landscape (Sacred Mountain)	Khaltse / Yulchung / 18 / 2004	**537**
809.	Pake *Chorten* (Yulma do *Chorten*)	*Chorten* / *Mane* Wall	Khaltse / Yulchung / 19 / 2004	**538**
810.	*Chorten* and *Mane* Wall	*Chorten* / *Mane* Wall	Khaltse / Yulchung / 20 / 2004	**538**
811.	*Mane* Wall	*Mane* Wall	Khaltse / Yulchung / 21 / 2004	**539**

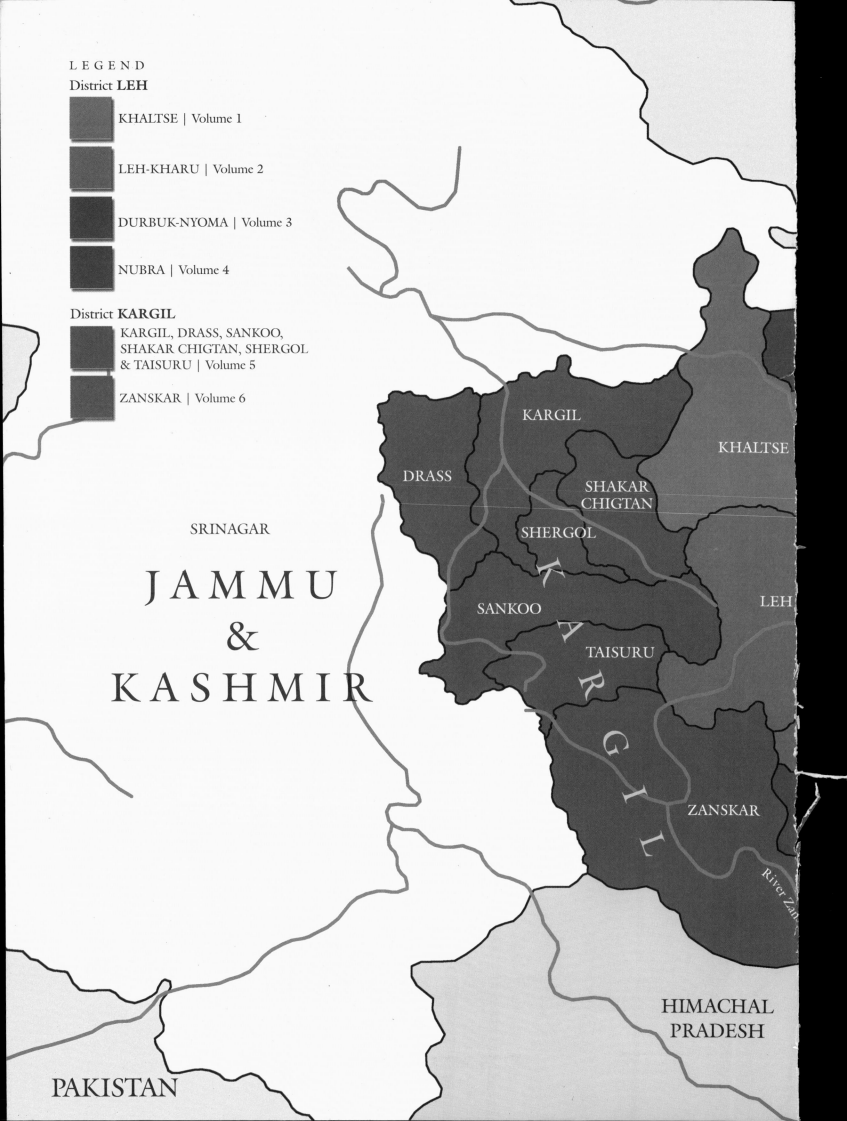

LEGEND

District **LEH**

KHALTSE | Volume 1

LEH-KHARU | Volume 2

DURBUK-NYOMA | Volume 3

NUBRA | Volume 4

District **KARGIL**

KARGIL, DRASS, SANKOO,
SHAKAR CHIGTAN, SHERGOL
& TAISURU | Volume 5

ZANSKAR | Volume 6

SRINAGAR

JAMMU
&
KASHMIR

PAKISTAN

KARGIL

DRASS

KHALTSE

SHAKAR
CHIGTAN

SHERGOL

LEH

SANKOO

K A R G I L

TAISURU

ZANSKAR

River Zan

HIMACHAL
PRADESH